Developing Games in Java™

David Brackeen
with Bret Barker
and Laurence Vanhelsuwé

New
Riders

800 E. 96th Street, Suite 200, Indianapolis, Indiana 46240
An Imprint of Pearson Education
Boston • Indianapolis • London • Munich • New York • San Francisco

Developing Games in Java™

International Standard Book Number: 1-5927-3005-1

Library of Congress Catalog Card Number: 2003107019

Printed in the United States of America

First printing: August, 2003

08 07 06 05 04   7 6 5 4 3

Interpretation of the printing code: The rightmost double-digit number is the year of the book's printing; the rightmost single-digit number is the number of the book's printing. For example, the printing code 03-1 shows that the first printing of the book occurred in 2003.

Trademarks

Warning and Disclaimer

Publisher
Stephanie Wall

Production Manager
Gina Kanouse

Executive Development Editor
Lisa Thibault

Project Editor
Michael Thurston

Copy Editor
Krista Hansing

Indexer
Joy Dean Lee

Proofreader
Beth Trudell

Composition
Gloria Schurick

Manufacturing Coordinator
Dan Uhrig

Interior Designer
Kim Scott

Cover Designer
Aren Howell

Marketing
Scott Cowlin
Tammy Detrich
Hannah Onstad Latham

Publicity Manager
Susan Nixon

To Mom and Dad.

Table of Contents

Part II   3D Graphics and Advanced Techniques

Part III   Tuning and Finishing Your Game

About the Author

David Brackeen grew up in Texas and has a B.S. in Computer Science from the University of North Texas. He has created many games, level editors, and multimedia products in Java, including *Scared* (a 3D shooter game) and Race3d (a 3D racing engine used in several games). He will neither confirm nor deny allegations that he ever drank rainwater from a shoe. He currently resides in Los Angeles, but you can find him at www.brackeen.com.

About the Contributing Authors

Bret Barker grew up in upstate New York and studied Electrical Engineering and Computer Science at Worcester Polytechnic Institute in Massachusetts. A refugee of the San Francisco dot-com implosion, he currently lives in Portland, Maine, working as a free-lance software developer. He specializes in Java games, mobile application development, and 3D graphics programming. He can be reached at bret@hypefiend.com.

Laurence Vanhelsuwé is a self-taught, independent software engineer. He has worked on such diverse technologies as X.25 WAN routers, virtual reality flight simulation, Postscript, real-time digitized video-based traffic analysis, and interactive map-based multimedia CD-ROMs. When not being stuck behind a screen all day, Laurence likes rock climbing and windsurfing to get the blood circulation going again.

About the Technical Reviewers

These reviewers contributed their considerable hands-on expertise to the entire development process for *Developing Games in Java*. As the book was being written, these dedicated professionals reviewed all the material for technical content, organization, and flow. Their feedback was critical to ensuring that *Developing Games in Java* fits our readers' needs for the highest-quality technical information.

David Fox has designed and developed numerous CD-ROM, web, and wireless games for companies such as Fox Interactive, Byron Preiss Multimedia, and PlayLink. Currently he is one of the principals of Next Game, Inc., working on a system that allows people to wager on games of skill. David is also the author of several best-selling books about Internet technologies. His writing has appeared in publications such as *Gamasutra*, Salon.com, and Developer.com, and he has presented topics on Java gaming at the JavaOne Conference for the past few years.

Tom Jacobson received his undergraduate degree at St. John's College in Santa Fe, New Mexico. Upon graduation, he began helping create interactive computer games aimed at rehabilitating dyslexic children as part of a joint research project between UCSF and Rutgers University. Tom is co-founder of Gamelet.com, an online web game company that has created numerous Java games for companies such as Snapple, Sony, and Subaru. He is currently the Chief Gaming Officer for `www.superdudes.net`.

Acknowledgments

First of all, I'd like to thank the development editor for this book, Lisa Thibault, for being determined, patient, enthusiastic, and encouraging. Also, thanks to tech editors Tom Jacobson and David Fox for providing valuable feedback and suggestions along the way.

Thanks to Charles Alderton, whose creation has kept me motivated throughout the years.

Thanks to my parents, who had the intuition to make sure I had access to computers as I was growing up, whether it was a PC in high school, those incredibly fast 286 machines in my Dad's office, or the Epson QX-10 in 1985.

And of course, thanks to my friends and the rest of my family, who never stopped asking, "Is the book done yet?" or demanding, "Finish the book!"

Naturally, though, the real gratitude goes to the countless programmers and computer scientists who were intelligent enough to come up with all these game programming ideas in the first place, and who were wise enough to share their ideas.

Tell Us What You Think

As the reader of this book, you are the most important critic and commentator. We value your opinion and want to know what we're doing right, what we could do better, what areas you'd like to see us publish in, and any other words of wisdom you're willing to pass our way.

As the Executive Development Editor for New Riders Publishing, I welcome your comments. You can fax, email, or write me directly to let me know what you did or didn't like about this book—as well as what we can do to make our books stronger. When you write, please be sure to include this book's title, ISBN, and author, as well as your name and phone or fax number. I will carefully review your comments and share them with the author and editors who worked on the book.

Please note that I cannot help you with technical problems related to the topic of this book, and that due to the high volume of email I receive, I might not be able to reply to every message.

Fax: 317-581-4663

Email: lisa.thibault@newriders.com

Mail: Lisa Thibault
        Executive Development Editor
        New Riders Publishing
        800 E. 96th Street, Suite 200
        Indianapolis, IN 46240 USA

Introduction

If you've picked up this book, you want to get serious about making Java games.

A lot of modern games look, sound, and behave so well that it can be hard to imagine how you'd even begin to program something like that. But even the biggest, most detailed games start with some basic game-programming concepts. This book aims to cover those concepts so you can create your own impressive games.

Many previous Java game-programming books focused on making simple web-based game applets, such as card or puzzle games. But you know Java can do much more than that. In this Java game-programming book, you'll make fast, full-screen action games such as side scrollers and 3D shooters that take full advantages of the capabilities of Java.

But this book really isn't about making Java games—it's about making games that happen to be written in Java. We'll cover a lot of Java game-programming topics, such as using certain APIs to get desired results, but we'll also cover a lot of generic game-programming topics such as collision detection, path finding, artificial intelligence, and BSP trees.

Why Java?

Well, why not? With Java 1.4, you can make fast, full-screen, hardware-accelerated games while having the benefits of developing for the Java platform. Developing for the Java platform means you get a simple, modern, safe, object-oriented language with a comprehensive API, simple multithreading, automatic garbage collection, and, of course, portability. Also, an abundance of tools is available for Java development, including lots of open-source libraries and some fantastic IDEs.

The main complaint about Java is speed, but with the HotSpot VM and hardware-accelerated graphics, speed isn't much of a factor anymore. HotSpot compiles the "hot" parts of your game to native code at runtime, and with hardware-accelerated graphics, you can take advantage of a powerful video card.

What You Need

Having previous game-programming experience isn't necessary for understanding the concepts in this book. However, you will need a few things:

➤ You should already know how to program in Java. If you're still learning Java or you are more familiar with other object-oriented languages such as C++, then a book like *Learning Java*, by Patrick Niemeyer and Jonathan Knudsen (O'Reilly and Associates, 2002), will help.

➤ You'll need Java 2 Standard Edition SDK version 1.4.1 or newer. You can get this from `http://java.sun.com`.

➤ It's a good idea to get your hands on the J2SE documentation as well. Having quick access to the J2SE API documentation can greatly speed up the coding process. You can either download it from `http://java.sun.com` or view it directly on that site.

➤ Most of the code in this book is compiled using Ant, a Java-based build tool. You'll need to get your hands on Ant if you want to use the build files in this book. We'll talk about Ant later in the "Using Ant" section.

➤ Finally, you'll almost certainly want to download all the code for this book, which is available at `www.brackeen.com/javagamebook`.

But the biggest thing you need is the actual *desire* to make games. It's often hard work, and there will be days when you get stuck on something and can't move on. But if you have a strong desire to accomplish something, you'll also have the will to do so.

What Is in This Book

Overall, this book covers topics for creating both 2D and 3D games. Here's a quick overview:

Chapter 1, "Java Threads," is a quick primer on threads. Threads are one of those concepts many people have trouble with, and this chapter clears up a lot of issues and points out situations when to use threads and when not to use them in games.

Chapters 2, "2D Graphics and Animation," through 5, "Creating a 2D Platform Game," thrash out the basics of any game: graphics, input, and sound. Some of the topics include full-screen hardware-accelerated graphics, animation, and sprites, how to create a system for customizing keyboard and mouse controls, how to integrate Swing within a full-screen game, how to play multiple sounds simultaneously, and how to apply sound effects such as an echo or a pseudo-3D sound filter. Chapter 5 uses these concepts to create a cool 2D side-scrolling game.

Chapter 6, "Multi-Player Games," covers creating multi-player games using NIO, starting with a multi-user chat server and then creating a multi-player game framework. Along the way, plenty of advanced issues and "gotchas" are discussed.

Chapters 7, "3D Graphics," through 9, "3D Objects," focus on 3D graphics, from the basics of 3D to texture mapping, lighting, 3D objects, and Z-buffering. In Chapter 10, "3D Scene Management Using BSP Trees," you create a 3D engine using BSP trees.

Chapters 11, "Collision Detection," through 14, "Game Scripting," talk about various game-programming techniques and apply them to the 3D engine. We'll discuss various collision-detection techniques, path finding (using the A* algorithm), artificial intelligence (including mimicked evolution), and game events and scripting. We apply these techniques in a 3D world, but they can easily be used in 2D games, as well.

Chapters 15, "Persistence—Saving the Game," through 18, "Game Design and the Last 10%," discuss everything else a game is going to need, including persistence (saving the game state), optimization, ways to create art and sounds, game design, and the last 10% of your game (including debugging tips and game distribution).

The final chapter is an overview of the future of Java: what is coming to the Java platform and what needs to happen to make Java even better for games.

Throughout the book, there is a focus on reusing code and building frameworks. The code you make in the first few chapters will be used all throughout the book, and you'll add on to exiting classes to extend their functionality.

What's Not in This Book

This book is about concepts, not APIs. We won't go over every API in the Java 1.4 SDK. The Java API documentation is all you need for learning how to draw a circle or a rectangle, or to just get more in-depth with the API. Also, this book is not an introduction to Java—we assume the reader already knows how to program in Java.

This book is focused on the Java 1.4 standard edition, not Java 1.1 or applets. Microsoft's Java 1.1 VM is still the most common VM used for applets because it's included with Internet Explorer. However, this book's focus is on Java 1.4 and later, so we won't get into common applet issues or workarounds. If you're interested in Java 1.1 or applets, this book will still help with a lot of game-programming concepts, but other books you might want to look into are *Black Art of Java Game Programming*, by Joel Fan (Waite Group, 1996), and *Java Game Programming for Dummies*, by Wayne Holder (IDG Books Worldwide, 1998).

Also, this book isn't about J2ME (Java for cell phones and other types of devices). You'll want to check out *Micro Java Game Development*, by David Fox (Addison Wesley Professional, 2002), for information on this subject.

We get into a massive discussion on 3D graphics, including things such as texture mapping, lighting, collision detection, and BSP trees, but you should note that there's no discussion of any hardware-accelerated 3D graphics in this book. At the moment, no hardware-accelerated 3D APIs are included with the Java 1.4 SDK. However, several APIs are available, notably Java3D and gl4java. A Java3D or OpenGL book makes a great complement to this book. This book aims to give you a thorough knowledge of 3D graphics programming, and with this knowledge, it will be easier to move to the hardware-accelerated 3D API of your choice.

Finally, this book isn't meant to be the last discussion on game programming you'll ever need. This book is designed to give you a solid foundation on where to start, but game programming is a huge subject and there is a seemingly endless amount of game-programming concepts. Many of the concepts you can figure out on your own, but other articles or books can always help.

About the Code in This Book

In this book, almost all the code will go into packages. This means you won't end up with hundreds of Java files in the same directory, and the layout of the packages will make the entire code library easier to understand. The only code that won't go in packages is simple Java files designed specifically for a chapter demo, which are usually named with the word *Test*, as in CollisionTest.

The code is divided into segregated directories for each chapter so that code from one chapter doesn't interfere with another. With all of the code reuse in this book, this means the code for one chapter usually contains all the code from the previous chapter, possibly with a few add-ons as the code progresses forward.

Also, most of the code for each chapter includes Ant build files so you can easy compile and build the code.

Using Ant

Apache Ant is a free Java-based build tool and can be downloaded from http://ant.apache.org. Because Ant is Java-based, Ant build files can be compiled on any platform. Also, Ant is integrated into many Java IDEs, so you can get up and running quickly.

Ant build files are XML files, usually named build.xml. Listing I.1 contains an example build file.

Listing I.1 Sample Ant Build File

```xml
<?xml version="1.0"?>
<project name="myBuild" default="build" basedir=".">

  <property name="srcdir" value="src"/>
  <property name="destdir" value="build"/>


  <target name="clean" description="Deletes the class files">
    <delete>
```

continues

Listing I.1   Sample Ant Build File   *continued*

```
            <fileset dir="${destdir}" includes="**/*.class"/>
        </delete>
    </target>


    <target name="compile" description="Compiles the source code">
        <javac srcdir="${srcdir}"
               destdir="${destdir}"
               debug="on">
        </javac>
    </target>


    <target name="build" depends="compile"
        description="Compiles the source code and creates a jar file">

        <jar jarfile="${basedir}/myjar.jar">
            <fileset dir="${destdir}" includes="**/*.class"/>
        </jar>
    </target>


    <target name="rebuild" depends="clean, build"
        description="Performs a clean build"/>

</project>
```

The sample Ant file almost describes itself. First, two properties are created to specify the srcdir and destdir directories. Properties can be referred to using the ${varName} syntax.

The build file contains four targets: clean, compile, build, and rebuild.

The `compile` target compiles all Java files in the source directory, putting the compiled class files in the destination directory. The `clean` target deletes all of these classes.

The `build` target depends on the `compile` target, so running the `build` target automatically runs the `compile` target first. The `build` target packs all the compiled class files into a .jar file.

Finally, the `rebuild` target does nothing by itself, but depends on the `clean` and `build` targets to perform a clean build.

After you've got Ant installed, just open a command prompt in the directory of the build file and type in the target you want to execute, like this:

```
ant compile
```

This command loads the build.xml file in the current directory and executes the `compile` target. If you were to name no target, as in the following, the `build` target is executed because it's defined to be the default target in the build file:

```
ant
```

Besides running Ant from the command line, Ant is also tightly integrated into many IDEs and text editors, such as JBuilder, jEdit, Eclipse, IDEA, and NetBeans. For example, in jEdit (see Figure I.1), the AntFarm plug-in enables you to browse Ant files, execute targets with the click of the mouse, and even send compile errors to jEdit's ErrorList plug-in so you can click on errors to go directly to the source of the compile error.

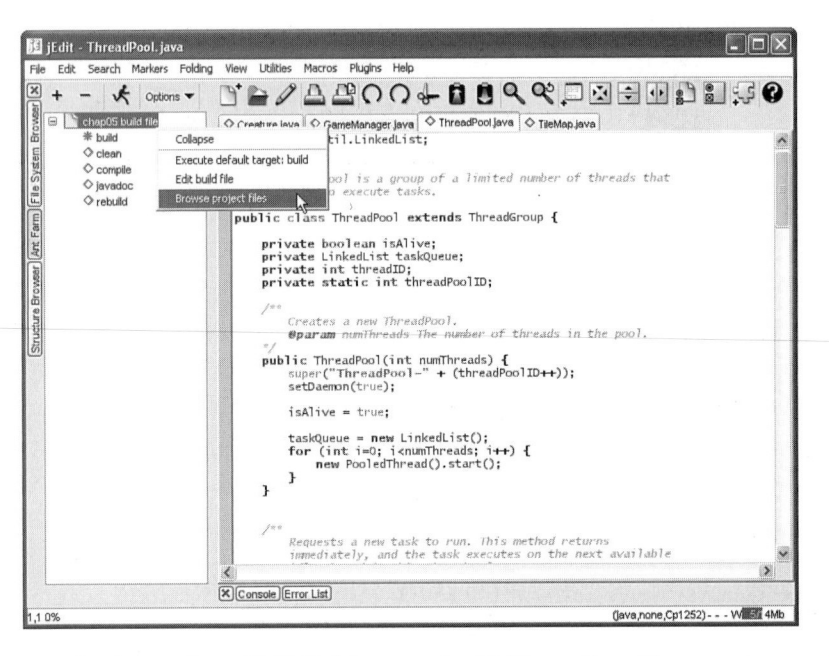

Figure I.1   Ant integration with jEdit 4.1: a popular, highly configurable open-source editor.

This Ant build file example really just scratches the surface for what Ant can do. There are lots of built-in Ant tasks and many more optional tasks, and you can even write your own tasks. You can see what all the available tasks are and get more information on using Ant at http://ant.apache.org/manual/.

Summary

I hope you enjoy and learn a lot from this book. If you need to contact me with any questions regarding this book, go to the game's site: www.brackeen.com/javagamebook. Remember, you can get all of the source code for the book at that site as well.

Okay, let's get started making some games!

Part I

Java Game Fundamentals

Chapter 1

Java Threads

It's lunchtime, and you decide to treat yourself to a meal at your favorite restaurant. You take a seat and look around—the place is pretty empty. There's one waiter, one customer eating, and you.

The waiter is helping the other customer, but oddly, you're being ignored. Even when you ask for a menu, the waiter acts as if you're not there and just refills the other customer's beverage. Finally, after the other customer leaves, the waiter acknowledges your existence and helps you.

So what is the problem? The waiter hasn't been fired, that's the problem.

Actually, the problem is that the waiter didn't *multitask*. A multitasking waiter could serve two or more customers at once instead of waiting for one customer to finish before serving a new customer.

The multitasking waiter is a rough analogy to how *threads* work in computer science. In this chapter, we go over all about how Java threads work and how to synchronize them, and we teach you the tips and tricks along the way.

What Is a Thread?

Imagine the multitasking waiter is your computer's processor and the customers are *tasks*. Each task runs in its own thread, and a processor with a modern operating system can run many threads concurrently. For example, you've probably downloaded a file from the Internet while writing a paper at the same time.

Modern operating systems run threads concurrently by splitting a thread's task into smaller chunks. This is called *concurrency*. One thread is executed for a small amount of time (*time slices*). Then the thread is *pre-empted*, enabling another thread to run, and so on, as shown in Figure 1.1. The time slices are small enough so that it seems as if several things are happening at once.

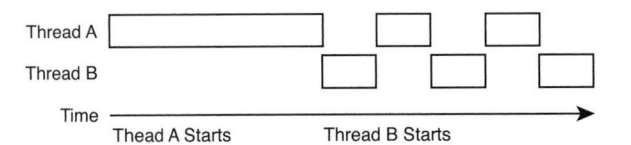

Figure 1.1   Concurrency means running multiple threads on one processor.

On machines with more than one processor, threads might actually run simultaneously, depending on the JVM implementation.

Creating and Running Threads in Java

Java was designed with threads in mind, so you'll find it easier to work with threads in Java than in many other languages. To create and start a new thread, just create an instance of the Thread object and call the start() method:

```
Thread myThread = new Thread();
myThread.start();
```

Of course, this code won't do anything useful because the thread isn't assigned a task. The JVM creates a new system thread, starts it, and calls the Thread object's run() method. By default, the run() method doesn't do anything, so the thread dies.

If you want to give a thread a task, and I'm sure you do, give the run() method something to do. You can do this in three basic ways:

➤ Extend the Thread class

➤ Implement the Runnable interface

➤ Use anonymous inner classes

Extending the *Thread* Class

A quick way to give a thread a task is simply to extend the Thread class and override the run() method:

```
public class MyThread extends Thread {

    public void run() {
        System.out.println("Do something cool here.");
    }
}
```

Then create and start the thread the same way as before:

```
Thread myThread = new MyThread();
myThread.start();
```

Now you've got two threads running: the main thread and the thread you just started.

Implementing the *Runnable* Interface

Extending the Thread class is easy, but most of the time you probably don't want to write a new class just to start a thread. For example, you might want a class that extends another class and can also be run as a thread. In this case, implement the Runnable interface:

```
public class MyClass extends SomeOtherClass implements Runnable {

    public MyClass() {
        Thread thread = new Thread(this);
        thread.start();
    }
```

```
    public void run() {
        System.out.println("Do something cool here.");
    }
}
```

In this example, the `MyClass` object starts a new thread on construction. The `Thread` class takes a `Runnable` object as a parameter in its constructor, and that `Runnable` is executed when the thread is started.

Using Anonymous Inner Classes

Sometimes you want to spawn a new thread without the bother of creating a new class, or perhaps it's not convenient to implement the `Runnable` interface. In this case, you can use an anonymous inner class to start a new thread:

```
new Thread() {
    public void run() {
        System.out.println("Do something cool here.");
    }
}.start();
```

This example is simple enough, but it can quickly become unreadable if the code in the `run()` method is too long. Use this one sparingly.

Waiting for a Thread to Finish

If you want your current thread to wait until a thread is finished, use the `join()` method:

```
myThread.join();
```

This could be useful when a player exits your game, when you want to make sure all threads are finished before you do any cleanup.

Sleepy Threads

Sometimes your threads might get tired, and you'll be nice enough to give them a break. Now you're thinking, "What? My threads get tired? This is too complicated!"

No, your threads don't really get tired. But sometimes you might need a thread to pause for a bit, so use the static `sleep()` method:

```
Thread.sleep(1000);
```

This causes the currently running thread to sleep for 1000 milliseconds, or any amount of time you choose. A sleeping thread doesn't consume any CPU time—so it doesn't even dream.

Synchronization

Great, now you've got some threads running and they're doing all sorts of cool things at once. It's not all sunshine and lollipops, though—if you've got multiple threads trying to access the same objects or variables, you can run into synchronization problems.

Why Synchronize?

Let's say you're creating a maze game. Any thread can set the position of the player, and any thread can check to see if the player is at the exit. For simplicity, let's say the exit is at position x = 0, y = 0.

```java
public class Maze {

    private int playerX;
    private int playerY;

    public boolean isAtExit() {
        return (playerX == 0 && playerY == 0);
    }

    public void setPosition(int x, int y) {
        playerX = x;
        playerY = y;
    }
}
```

Most of the time, this code works fine. But keep in mind that threads can be pre-empted at any time. Imagine this scenario, in which the player moves from (1,0) to (0,1):

1. Starting off, the object's variables are `playerX = 1` and `playerY = 0`.

2. Thread A calls `setPosition(0,1)`.

3. The line `playerX = x;` is executed. Now `playerX = 0`.

4. Thread A is pre-empted by Thread B.

5. Thread B calls `isAtExit()`.

6. Currently, `playerX = 0` and `playerY = 0`, so `isAtExit()` returns `true`!

In this scenario, the player is reported as solving the maze when it's not the case. To fix this, you need to make sure the `setPosition()` and `isAtExit()` methods can't execute at the same time.

How to Synchronize

Enter the synchronized keyword. In the maze example, if you make the methods synchronized, only one method can run at a time.

Here's the updated, thread-safe code:

```
public class Maze {

    private int playerX;
    private int playerY;

    public synchronized boolean isAtExit() {
        return (playerX == 0 && playerY == 0);
    }

    public synchronized void setPosition(int x, int y) {
        playerX = x;
        playerY = y;
    }
}
```

When the JVM executes a synchronized method, it acquires a *lock* on that object. Only one lock can be acquired on an object at a time. The lock is released when the method is finished executing either by returning normally or by throwing an exception.

So, if one synchronized method owns a lock, no other synchronized method can run until the lock is released.

You can think of locks as a lock on a restroom door. Only one person is in the restroom at a time. The door is unlocked when the person leaves or, in the case of an exception, when the person jumps out the window.

Besides method synchronization, there's also object synchronization. Object synchronization enables you to treat any object as the lock—with method synchronization, the current instance (`this`) is the lock. Method synchronization is essentially shorthand for object synchronization with `this`. For example, from the previous maze code, the method

```
public synchronized void setPosition(int x, int y) {
    playerX = x;
    playerY = y;
}
```

is essentially the same as this:

```
public void setPosition(int x, int y) {
    synchronized(this) {
        playerX = x;
        playerY = y;
    }
}
```

The only exception is that the second example has some extra bytecode instructions.

Object synchronization is useful when you need more than one lock, when you need to acquire a lock on something other than `this`, or when you don't need to synchronize an entire method.

A lock can be any object, even arrays—basically, anything except primitive types. If you need to roll your own lock, just create a plain Object:

```
Object myLock = new Object();
...
synchronized (myLock) {
    ...
}
```

What to Synchronize

But what should you synchronize? The answer is any time two or more threads will access the same object or field.

What Not to Synchronize

When synchronizing your code, the general rule is not to *oversynchronize*—don't synchronize more code than you have to. Doing so creates unnecessary delays when two or more threads try to execute the same synchronized block of code.

For example, don't synchronize an entire method if only parts of the method need to be synchronized. Instead, just put a synchronized block around the critical parts of code:

```
public void myMethod() {
    synchronized(this) {
        // code that needs to be synchronized
    }
    // code that is already thread-safe
}
```

Also, you don't have to synchronize a method that uses only local variables. Local variables are stored on the stack, and each thread has its own separate stack, so there isn't a chance of running into synchronization problems. For example, this method doesn't need to be synchronized because it uses only local variables:

```
public int square(int n) {
    int s = n * n;
    return s;
}
```

Finally, don't worry about synchronizing code that isn't accessed by multiple threads. However, if you know that some code is accessed by only one thread and you don't synchronize, be sure to mention in your JavaDoc comments that the code isn't thread-safe. By doing this, you'll know you have to change it if multiple threads in a future version access that code.

If you're not sure what threads are accessing your code, just print the name of the currently running thread to the console:

```
System.out.println(Thread.currentThread().getName());
```

Avoiding Deadlock

Deadlock is the result of two threads that stall because they are waiting on each other to do something. Consider this example:

1. Thread A acquires lock 1.

2. Thread B acquires lock 2.

3. Thread B waits for lock 1 to be released.

4. Thread A waits for lock 2 to be released.

As you can see, both threads are waiting on the lock that the other has, so they both stall indefinitely.

Deadlock can occur as soon as you have multiple threads trying to acquire multiple locks out of order.

How do you avoid deadlock? The best way is to simply write your synchronization code in such a way that it cannot occur. Think about which threads acquire which locks and in what order. Carefully try to consider every possibility.

If you think your game might be stalling because of deadlock, there are ways to detect it. As of version 1.4.1 of the HotSpot VM, Sun has provided a deadlock detector. Run your game from a console, and when it stalls, press Ctrl+\ (or Ctrl+break, in Windows). The VM displays information on the state of threads, whether they are waiting on anything, and whether deadlock is detected.

Using *wait()* and *notify()*

Let's say you have two threads and they need to talk to each other. For example, let's say Thread A is waiting on Thread B to send a message:

```
// Thread A
public void waitForMessage() {
    while (hasMessage == false) {
        Thread.sleep(100);
    }
}

// Thread B
public void setMessage(String message) {
    ...
    hasMessage = true;
}
```

Although this works, it's a clunky solution. Thread A has to constantly check whether Thread B has sent the message every 100 milliseconds, or 10 times a second. Thread A could *oversleep* and be late in getting the message. Also, what would happen if several threads were waiting for a message? Wouldn't it be nice if Thread A could just stay idle and be notified when Thread B sends the message?

Lucky for us, the wait() and notify() methods provide this capability.

The wait() method is used in synchronized blocks of code. When the wait() method executes, the lock is released and the thread waits to be notified.

The `notify()` method is also used in a synchronized block of code. The `notify()` method notifies one thread waiting on the same lock. If several threads are waiting on the lock, one of them is notified randomly.

Here's the updated message code:

```
// Thread A
public synchronized void waitForMessage() {
    try {
        wait();
    }
    catch (InterruptedException ex) { }
}

// Thread B
public synchronized void setMessage(String message) {
    ...
    notify();
}
```

After Thread B calls `notify()` and leaves its synchronized method (releasing the lock on `this`), Thread A reacquires the lock and finishes its synchronized block of code. In this case, it just returns.

You can also choose to wait for a maximum amount of time. The `wait()` method can take a maximum amount of time to wait as a parameter:

```
wait(100);
```

If the thread is never notified, this is equivalent to putting the thread to sleep for the specified amount of time. Unfortunately, there's no way to tell whether the `wait()` method returned because of a timeout or because the thread was notified.

A second notify method, `notifyAll()`, notifies all threads waiting on the lock, instead of just one.

The `wait()`, `notify()`, and `notifyAll()` methods are methods of the Object class, so any Java object has these methods—just like any Java object can be used as a lock.

The Java Event Model

You might think your game has only one thread and you don't have to worry about synchronization, but that's not the case. All graphical applications have at least two threads that can run your code: the main thread and the AWT event dispatch thread.

The main thread is (surprise!) the main thread of your program. It starts execution with the `main()` method of your main class.

The AWT event dispatch thread handles user-input events: mouse clicks, keyboard presses, and other events such as window resizing. We'll talk about these input events later in Chapter 3, "Interactivity and User Interfaces," but for now, just know that these input events can access your code through the AWT event dispatch thread.

When to Use Threads

Use threads whenever it will provide a more enjoyable experience for the user. This means any time some code can stall or take a long time, run the code in another thread so the user doesn't think your game has stalled.

For example, use threads in these situations:

➤ When loading lots of files from the local file system

➤ When doing any network communication, such as sending high scores to a server

➤ When doing any massive calculations, such as terrain generation

When Not to Use Threads

When you look at any game, you'll notice a lot of things going on at once—enemies running around, doors opening, bullets flying, and so on. This leads some people to think, "I know, every enemy runs in its own thread," but this is not the case. Not only is this a waste of resources—running too many threads at once can drain the system—but this creates problems such as these:

➤ An enemy could move in the middle of a draw operation, temporarily showing the enemy in two different places at once.

➤ The time slices of each thread could be unbalanced, leading to jerky or inconsistent movement.

➤ Synchronized code could lead to unneeded delays.

There are more efficient ways to have lots of things happening at the same time, which we'll get into in the next chapter, "2D Graphics and Animation."

Sum It Up: Thread Pools

Now with all this Java thread information, let's create something useful: a thread pool. A *thread pool* is a group of threads designed to execute arbitrary tasks. Perhaps you want to limit the number of threads used for simultaneous network or I/O connections, or you just want to control the maximum number of threads on the system for processor-intensive tasks.

The ThreadPool class in Listing 1.1 enables you to choose the number of threads in the pool and to run tasks defined as *Runnables*. Here's an example of how to use ThreadPool—creating a pool of eight threads, running a simple task, and then waiting for the task to finish:

```
ThreadPool myThreadPool = new ThreadPool(8);
myThreadPool.runTask(new Runnable() {
    public void run() {
        System.out.println("Do something cool here.");
    }
});
myThreadPool.join();
```

The runTask() method returns immediately. If all the threads in the pool are busy executing tasks, calls to runTask() will store new tasks in a queue until a thread is available to run it.

Listing 1.1   ThreadPool.java

```java
import java.util.LinkedList;

/**
    A thread pool is a group of a limited number of threads that
    are used to execute tasks.
*/
public class ThreadPool extends ThreadGroup {

    private boolean isAlive;
    private LinkedList taskQueue;
    private int threadID;
    private static int threadPoolID;

    /**
        Creates a new ThreadPool.
        @param numThreads The number of threads in the pool.
    */
    public ThreadPool(int numThreads) {
        super("ThreadPool-" + (threadPoolID++));
        setDaemon(true);

        isAlive = true;

        taskQueue = new LinkedList();
        for (int i=0; i<numThreads; i++) {
            new PooledThread().start();
        }
    }


    /**
        Requests a new task to run. This method returns
        immediately, and the task executes on the next available
        idle thread in this ThreadPool.
        <p>Tasks start execution in the order they are received.
        @param task The task to run. If null, no action is taken.
        @throws IllegalStateException if this ThreadPool is
        already closed.
```

```
*/
public synchronized void runTask(Runnable task) {
    if (!isAlive) {
        throw new IllegalStateException();
    }
    if (task != null) {
        taskQueue.add(task);
        notify();
    }

}


protected synchronized Runnable getTask()
    throws InterruptedException
{
    while (taskQueue.size() == 0) {
        if (!isAlive) {
            return null;
        }
        wait();
    }
    return (Runnable)taskQueue.removeFirst();
}


/**
    Closes this ThreadPool and returns immediately. All
    threads are stopped, and any waiting tasks are not
    executed. Once a ThreadPool is closed, no more tasks can
    be run on this ThreadPool.
*/
public synchronized void close() {
    if (isAlive) {
        isAlive = false;
        taskQueue.clear();
        interrupt();
    }
```

continues

Listing 1.1   ThreadPool.java   *continued*

```
    }


    /**
        Closes this ThreadPool and waits for all running threads
        to finish. Any waiting tasks are executed.
    */
    public void join() {
        // notify all waiting threads that this ThreadPool is no
        // longer alive
        synchronized (this) {
            isAlive = false;
            notifyAll();
        }

        // wait for all threads to finish
        Thread[] threads = new Thread[activeCount()];
        int count = enumerate(threads);
        for (int i=0; i<count; i++) {
            try {
                threads[i].join();
            }
            catch (InterruptedException ex) { }
        }
    }


    /**
        A PooledThread is a Thread in a ThreadPool group,
        designed to run tasks (Runnables).
    */
    private class PooledThread extends Thread {


        public PooledThread() {
```

```java
            super(ThreadPool.this,
                "PooledThread-" + (threadID++));
        }


    public void run() {
        while (!isInterrupted()) {

            // get a task to run
            Runnable task = null;
            try {
                task = getTask();
            }
            catch (InterruptedException ex) { }

            // if getTask() returned null or was interrupted,
            // close this thread by returning.
            if (task == null) {
                return;
            }

            // run the task, and eat any exceptions it throws
            try {
                task.run();
            }
            catch (Throwable t) {
                uncaughtException(this, t);
            }
        }
    }
  }
}
```

The only concept the ThreadPool class uses that we haven't mentioned yet is use of
the ThreadGroup class. A ThreadGroup is what you'd expect it to be—a group of
threads and some functions to modify the threads. For example, in this code,

ThreadGroup's interrupt() method is used to stop all waiting threads when the ThreadPool is closed.

Now let's test the ThreadPool with the ThreadPoolTest class, shown in Listing 1.2. ThreadPoolTest starts a few threads in a ThreadPool and also gives the ThreadPool several tasks to run. In this case, each task simply prints a message to the console.

The program takes the number of tasks and the number of threads as arguments. To run the test, at the command line, enter something like this:

```
java ThreadPoolTest 8 4
```

This runs the test with eight tasks and four threads in the thread pool. Of course, you can try any other combination of tasks and threads you want!

Listing 1.2   ThreadPoolTest.java

```java
public class ThreadPoolTest {

    public static void main(String[] args) {
        if (args.length != 2) {
            System.out.println("Tests the ThreadPool task.");
            System.out.println(
                "Usage: java ThreadPoolTest numTasks numThreads");
            System.out.println(
                "    numTasks - integer: number of task to run.");
            System.out.println(
                "    numThreads - integer: number of threads " +
                "in the thread pool.");
            return;
        }
        int numTasks = Integer.parseInt(args[0]);
        int numThreads = Integer.parseInt(args[1]);

        // create the thread pool
        ThreadPool threadPool = new ThreadPool(numThreads);

        // run example tasks
```

```java
        for (int i=0; i<numTasks; i++) {
            threadPool.runTask(createTask(i));
        }

        // close the pool and wait for all tasks to finish.
        threadPool.join();
    }


    /**
        Creates a simple Runnable that prints an ID, waits 500
        milliseconds, then prints the ID again.
    */
    private static Runnable createTask(final int taskID) {
        return new Runnable() {
            public void run() {
                System.out.println("Task " + taskID + ": start");

                // simulate a long-running task
                try {
                    Thread.sleep(500);
                }
                catch (InterruptedException ex) { }

                System.out.println("Task " + taskID + ": end");
            }
        };
    }
}
```

Because printing a message to the console takes virtually no time, `ThreadPoolTest` simulates a longer-running task by sleeping for 500 milliseconds.

Summary

That's it for threads! In this chapter, you've learned the basics of how threads work and how to work with them. Now you can make sure your games don't have thread-synchronization problems or cause deadlock. You've also learned that you can't avoid dealing with threads in Java games because all graphical Java applications have at least two threads. Finally, you've created a generic `ThreadPool` class that can be useful in many situations.

Chapter 2

2D Graphics and Animation

First off, you can create three types of graphical games in Java: an applet game, a windowed game, and a full-screen game.

> **Applet games**. Java applet games are applications that run in a web browser. The benefit here is that the user doesn't have to install anything. But players have to be online and running a web browser to play, and, unfortunately, applets have a few security restrictions to keep malicious code from causing harm. For example, applets can't save information such as preferences or saved games to the user's hard drive. Also, an applet can make a network connection only to the server that it came from.

> **Windowed games**. Windowed Java games don't have the security restrictions that applets do. In fact, they look and behave like a normal application, with a title bar, a close button, and so on. However, these user interface elements can be distracting to the player, especially when you want players to become immersed in your game.

> **Full-screen games**. Full-screen Java games give you total control over the visual presentation on your game, with no desktop user interface elements such as title bars, task bars, or docks. The player can become completely immersed in your game.

For these reasons, full-screen games are the focus of this book. In this chapter, we cover full-screen graphics, animation, and sprites. Because we haven't talked about keyboard or mouse input yet (that's in the next chapter, "Interactivity and User Interfaces"), in this chapter you create short graphical demos.

Full-Screen Graphics

Let's take a quick look at how the hardware works before you start programming it. There are two parts to display hardware: the video card and the monitor.

The video card stores what's on the screen in its memory and has several functions for modifying what's displayed. Also, the video card works behind the scenes to push what's in its memory to the monitor.

The monitor simply displays the information that the video card tells it to.

Screen Layout

The monitor's screen is divided into tiny little color pixels that are all the same size. A pixel, derived from the term *picture element*, is a single point of light displayed by the monitor. The number of horizontal and vertical pixels that make up a screen is called the screen's resolution.

The screen's origin is in the upper-left corner of the screen, as shown in Figure 2.1. The pixels are stored in video memory like you read a book, starting from the upper-left corner and reading left to right, top to bottom. A location on the screen can be expressed as (x,y), where x is the number of horizontal pixels from the origin, and y is the number of vertical pixels from the origin.

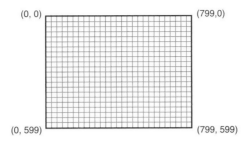

(0, 0)   (799,0)

(0, 599)   (799, 599)

Figure 2.1   The screen is divided into tiny pixels, and the origin is in the upper-left corner. This figure depicts a 800×600 screen.

What resolutions you can pick depends on the capabilities of the video card and monitor. Typical resolutions are 640×480, 800×600, 1024×768, and 1280×1024.

Typical monitors and televisions have a display size ratio of 4:3. That means the height of the display is three quarters of the size of the width. Some newer monitors have a wider screen with a display size ratio of 3:2 or 16:10. To compare, wide-screen movies typically have a display size ratio of 16:9.

Big old CRT (cathode ray tube) monitors are capable of showing all sorts of resolutions cleanly because CRTs draw pixels with an electron beam. Leaner LCD (liquid crystal display) monitors found on laptops and newer computer systems are a different story, however. Because each pixel on a LCD is lit with a physical transistor, LCDs have one native resolution, which is the resolution that the LCD was designed to display. Non-native resolutions might appear blocky or fuzzy on LCDs. Because of this, it's a good idea to make sure your game can run in two or three different resolutions so players can pick the one that looks best on their system.

Pixel Color and Bit Depth

As a child, you were probably taught the three primary colors of red, yellow, and blue. You also probably heard the phrase, "yellow plus blue is green." The idea is that when you are painting or using another physical medium, you can combine these three colors to create any color you want. This is known as a subtractive color model, in which the absence of all color is white. (Actually, it's not an exact color model—modern printers use a more sophisticated color model using cyan, magenta, yellow, and black instead.)

This is similar to how computer monitors and televisions work. Monitors combine red, blue, and green to create any color. Instead of a physical medium such as paint or inks, monitors emit light, so the RGB color model is an additive color model, in which adding all the colors together creates white.

The number of colors a monitor can display depends on the bit depth of the display mode. Common bit depths are 8, 15, 16, 24, and 32 bits.

> ➤ 8-bit color has 2^8 = 256 colors. Only 256 colors can be displayed at a time, based on a palette of colors. Unfortunately, there is currently no way in Java to change the palette, and the specification doesn't say what those colors are. The Java runtime can use a web-safe palette, which has 216 possible colors: 6 possible values each for red, green, and blue (6×6×6=216).

> ➤ 15-bit color has 5 bits for red, green, and blue, for a total of 2^{15} = 32,768 colors.

> ➤ 16-bit color has 5 bits for red and blue, and 6 bits for green, for a total of 2^{16} = 65,536 colors.

> ➤ 24-bit color has 8 bits for red, green, and blue, or 2^{24} = 16,777,216 colors.

> ➤ 32-bit color is the same as 24-bit color, but with an extra 8 bits of padding to keep pixel data aligned on 32-bit boundaries.

Most modern video cards support 8-, 16-, and 32-bit modes. Because the human eye can see about 10 million colors, 24-bit color is ideal. 16-bit color is a little faster than 24-bit color because there is less data to transfer, but the color quality isn't as accurate.

Refresh Rate

Even though your monitor looks like it's displaying a solid image, each pixel actually fades away after a few milliseconds. To make up for this, the monitor continuously refreshes the display to keep it from fading. How fast it refreshes the display is known as the *refresh rate*. The refresh rate is measured in Hertz (Hz), which means cycles per second. A refresh rate between 75Hz and 85Hz is usually suitable for the human eye.

Switching the Display to Full-Screen Mode

Now that you know all about resolutions, bit depths, and refresh rates, let's write some code. You'll need a few objects to switch the display to full-screen mode:

➤ A **Window** object. The Window object is an abstraction of what is displayed on the screen—think of it as a canvas to draw on. The examples here actually use a JFrame, which is a subclass of the Window class and can also be used for making windowed applications.

➤ A **DisplayMode** object. The DisplayMode object specifies the resolution, bit depth, and refresh rate to switch the display to.

➤ A **GraphicsDevice** object. The GraphicsDevice object enables you to change the display mode and inspect display properties. Think of it as an interface to your video card. The GraphicsDevice object is acquired from the GraphicsEnvironment object.

Here's an example of how to switch the display to full-screen mode:

```
JFrame window = new JFrame();
DisplayMode displayMode = new DisplayMode(800, 600, 16, 75);

// get the GraphicsDevice
GraphicsEnvironment environment =
    GraphicsEnvironment.getLocalGraphicsEnvironment();
GraphicsDevice device = environment.getDefaultScreenDevice();

// use the JFrame as the full screen window
device.setFullScreenWindow(window);

// change the display mode
device.setDisplayMode(displayMode);
```

Afterward, to switch back to the previous display mode, set the full-screen Window to null:

```
device.setFullScreenWindow(null);
```

Note that this code isn't complete. Some systems won't allow you to change the display mode, and `setDisplayMode()` throws an `IllegalArgumentException` on those systems.

Also, by default, `JFrame`s still show their borders and title bars, even in full-screen mode. We'll deal with these issues and simplify the functions by creating a wrapper class called `SimpleScreenManager`.

The `SimpleScreenManager` class shown in Listing 2.1 is a simple interface to change the display to full-screen mode. Behind the scenes, `SimpleScreenManager` catches Exceptions and removes the `JFrame`'s border and title bar with a call to `setUndecorated(true)`. Also, the `JFrame` is disposed when the screen is restored.

Listing 2.1 SimpleScreenManager.java

```java
import java.awt.*;
import javax.swing.JFrame;

/**
    The SimpleScreenManager class manages initializing and
    displaying full screen graphics modes.
*/
public class SimpleScreenManager {

    private GraphicsDevice device;

    /**
        Creates a new SimpleScreenManager object.
    */
    public SimpleScreenManager() {
        GraphicsEnvironment environment =
            GraphicsEnvironment.getLocalGraphicsEnvironment();
        device = environment.getDefaultScreenDevice();
    }


    /**
        Enters full screen mode and changes the display mode.
    */
    public void setFullScreen(DisplayMode displayMode,
```

```java
        JFrame window)
    {
        window.setUndecorated(true);
        window.setResizable(false);

        device.setFullScreenWindow(window);
        if (displayMode != null &&
            device.isDisplayChangeSupported())
        {
            try {
                device.setDisplayMode(displayMode);
            }
            catch (IllegalArgumentException ex) {
                // ignore - illegal mode for this device
            }
        }
    }


    /**
        Returns the window currently used in full screen mode.
    */
    public Window getFullScreenWindow() {
        return device.getFullScreenWindow();
    }


    /**
        Restores the screen's display mode.
    */
    public void restoreScreen() {
        Window window = device.getFullScreenWindow();
        if (window != null) {
            window.dispose();
        }
        device.setFullScreenWindow(null);
    }

}
```

Now let's put the `SimpleScreenManager` to use. The `FullScreenTest` class in Listing 2.2 tests the methods of the `SimpleScreenManager` class. It changes the display to full-screen mode, displays a "Hello World!" message, waits five seconds, and exits.

`FullScreenTest` runs in a resolution of 800×600 and a bit depth of 16. If you want to run at a different resolution, just specify the different display mode at the command line. The program treats the first, second, and third arguments passed to it as the width, height, and bit depth of the display mode. For example, entering this at the console runs the program at resolution of 1024×768 and a bit depth of 32:

```
java FullScreenTest 1024 768 32
```

Note that the code doesn't allow you to set an "illegal" mode that will do something crazy like set the monitor on fire. If the display mode you request isn't available or the system doesn't have full-screen support, an `IllegalArgumentException` is thrown and the demo mimics full-screen mode using the current display mode.

Listing 2.2   FullScreenTest.java

```
import java.awt.*;
import javax.swing.JFrame;

public class FullScreenTest extends JFrame {

    public static void main(String[] args) {

        DisplayMode displayMode;

        if (args.length == 3) {
            displayMode = new DisplayMode(
                Integer.parseInt(args[0]),
                Integer.parseInt(args[1]),
                Integer.parseInt(args[2]),
                DisplayMode.REFRESH_RATE_UNKNOWN);
        }
        else {
            displayMode = new DisplayMode(800, 600, 16,
```

```
                    DisplayMode.REFRESH_RATE_UNKNOWN);
        }

        FullScreenTest test = new FullScreenTest();
        test.run(displayMode);
    }

    private static final long DEMO_TIME = 5000;


    public void run(DisplayMode displayMode) {
        setBackground(Color.blue);
        setForeground(Color.white);
        setFont(new Font("Dialog", Font.PLAIN, 24));

        SimpleScreenManager screen = new SimpleScreenManager();
        try {
            screen.setFullScreen(displayMode, this);
            try {
                Thread.sleep(DEMO_TIME);
            }
            catch (InterruptedException ex) { }
        }
        finally {
            screen.restoreScreen();
        }
    }


    public void paint(Graphics g) {
        g.drawString("Hello World!", 20, 50);
    }
}
```

One thing to note in FullScreenTest is the use of the try/finally block in the run() method. Restoring the screen in the finally block guarantees that the screen will always be restored, even if an Exception is thrown in the try block.

Besides that, the first thing you might notice in `FullScreenTest` is the `Graphics` object used in the `paint()` method. The `Graphics` object provides all sorts of functions for drawing text, lines, rectangles, ovals, polygons, images, and so on. Most of the methods are self-explanatory, so check out the Java API specification for all the juicy details.

If you're asking yourself, "Hey, how does that `paint()` method get called, anyway?" the answer is, well, magic. Actually, you'll notice that `FullScreenTest` is a `JFrame`. When a `JFrame` (or any other component, for that matter) is displayed, Java's Abstract Window Toolkit, or AWT, calls the component's `paint()` method.

If you want to force the AWT to call the `paint()` method, call `repaint()`. This signals to the AWT to call the `paint()` method when it gets around to it. The AWT send `paint` events in a separate thread, so if you want to send a `repaint` event and then wait for the painting to complete, use something like this:

```
public class MyComponent extends SomeComponent {
    . . .
    public synchronized void repaintAndWait() {
        repaint();
        try {
            wait();
        }
        catch (InterruptedException ex) { }
    }

    public synchronized void paint(Graphics g) {
        // do painting here
        . . .
        // notify that we're done painting
        notifyAll();
    }
}
```

Anti-Aliasing

You might notice that the "Hello World" text from `FullScreenTest` looks a little jagged around the edges. This is because the text isn't anti-aliased. It might sound strange, but anti-aliasing makes the text look sharper by blurring the edges so that the text's color blends with the background color, making the staircase of pixels appear to be smoother. See Figures 2.2 and 2.3 for a comparison.

Hello World!

Figure 2.2   Normal text appears jagged around the edges.

Hello World!

Figure 2.3   Anti-aliased text blurs the edges a bit for a cleaner look.

To make text anti-aliased, set the appropriate rendering hint before drawing any text. The rendering hint functionality is present only in the `Graphics2D` class, which is a subclass of `Graphics`.

For backward compatibility, the `paint()` method takes a `Graphics` object as a parameter. However, starting with Java SDK 1.2, it's actually a `Graphics2D` object that is passed to the method. Here's the code for a `paint()` method with text anti-aliasing:

```
public void paint(Graphics g) {

    if (g instanceof Graphics2D) {
        Graphics2D g2 = (Graphics2D)g;
        g2.setRenderingHint(
            RenderingHints.KEY_TEXT_ANTIALIASING,
            RenderingHints.VALUE_TEXT_ANTIALIAS_ON);
    }
    g.drawString("Hello World!", 20, 50);
}
```

Other rendering hints exist, including making all geometric lines and shapes anti-aliased, setting rendering quality, and so on. See the documentation for the `RenderingHints` class for details.

Which Display Mode to Use

A lot of display modes are available, but which one should your game run at?

Well, make sure your game runs in at least two resolutions. The general rule is to allow players to change display modes so they can pick the one they like best on their display.

If possible, initially run your game at the same resolution as the current resolution. On LCDs, the current resolution is most likely the LCD's native resolution, so the game will look nicer if you use the current one.

As for bit depth, using 16-, 24-, or 32-bit color is a good idea for modern games. 16-bit color is usually a little faster, but use a higher bit depth if you need more accurate color representation.

Also, a refresh rate between 75Hz and 85Hz is suitable for the human eye.

Images

Drawing text on the screen is fun and all, but you probably want to have some images in your game, right? Right. Before you draw images on the screen, let's learn about some image fundamentals: transparency types and file formats.

Transparency

Imagine you have a simple image you want to display, as shown in Figure 2.4.

Figure 2.4   The image of the hero shows that he's really just a big sphere.

The image in Figure 2.4 is a character on a white background, but is the background part of the image, and does it get drawn, too? That depends on the image's transparency. You can use three types of image transparency: opaque, transparent, and translucent.

> ➤ **Opaque**. Every pixel in the image is visible.

> ➤ **Transparent**. Every pixel in the image is either completely visible or completely see-through. In the image, the white background could be transparent so that what's "underneath" the image shows through when it is drawn.

> ➤ **Translucent**. Pixels can be partially transparent, to create a ghostlike, partially see-through effect. Also, translucency can be used just on the edges of an image, to create an anti-aliased image.

In the character image, you probably want to make the white background transparent so that when the image is drawn, what's behind the character is shown rather than having the character surrounded by a white box. Optionally, you can make the edges translucent so the image would be anti-aliased.

File Formats

Two basic types of image formats exist: raster and vector. A raster image format describes images just like your display does, in terms of pixels with a specified bit depth. A vector image format describes an image geometrically and can be resized without degrading the quality.

The Java API doesn't have any vector formats built in, so we focus on raster images. If you're interested in vector images, check out Apache's Scalable Vector Graphics (SVG) implementation, called Batik, at `http://xml.apache.org/batik/`.

The Java runtime has three different raster formats built in, and you can read them with hardly any effort. These three formats are GIF, PNG, and JPEG:

> ➤ **GIF**. GIF images can be either opaque or transparent, and can have 8-bit color or less. Although GIF has high compression for graphics images without a lot of color variation, PNG supercedes GIF's functionality, so there's no reason to use GIF anymore.

➤ **PNG**. PNG images can have any type of transparency: opaque, transparent, or translucent. Also, PNG images can have any bit depth, all the way up to 24-bit color. The compression ratio for 8-bit PNG images is about the same as for GIF images.

➤ **JPEG**. JPEG images can be opaque, 24-bit images only. JPEG has high compression for photographic images, but it is a lossy compression, so the image isn't an exact replica of its source.

These image file formats can be created in common paint programs such as Adobe Photoshop (www.adobe.com), Jasc Paint Shop Pro (www.jasc.com), and the GIMP (www.gimp.org).

Reading Images

So how do you translate a GIF, PNG, or JPEG file into something you can display? This is done via Toolkit's getImage() method: It parses the image file and returns an Image object. Here's an example:

```
Toolkit toolkit = Toolkit.getDefaultToolkit();
Image image = toolkit.getImage(fileName);
```

This code looks innocent enough, but it doesn't actually load the image. The image begins loading in another thread. If you display the image before it is finished loading, only part (or none) of the image actually gets displayed.

You can use a MediaTracker object to watch the image and wait for it to finish loading, but there is an easier solution. The ImageIcon class loads an image using MediaTracker for you. The ImageIcon class in the javax.swing package loads an image using the Toolkit and waits for it to finish loading before it returns. For example:

```
ImageIcon icon = new ImageIcon(fileName);
Image image = icon.getImage();
```

Okay, now that you can load images, you can try it. The ImageTest class in Listing 2.3 works similarly to the FullScreenTest class, also using SimpleScreenManager. ImageTest draws one JPEG background image and four PNG foreground images, waits 10 seconds, and then exits.

The background is a JPEG file because it is photographic quality, so the JPEG format compresses it better than a PNG would.

The PNG images it displays are opaque, transparent, and translucent. One translucent image is entirely translucent, while the other is translucent only around the edges, to make the image anti-aliased. See Figure 2.5 for a screen capture of ImageTest.

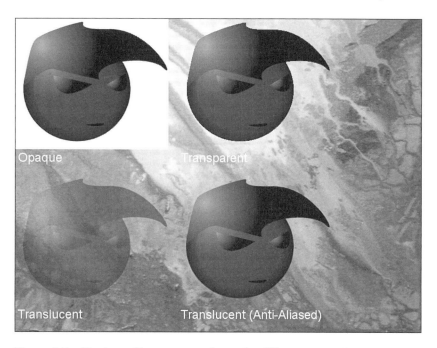

Figure 2.5   The ImageTest program shows the different types of transparency.

Again, if you'd like to run ImageTest at a different display mode, specify the mode at the command line, just like in `FullScreenTest`.

Listing 2.3   ImageTest.java

```
import java.awt.*;
import javax.swing.ImageIcon;
import javax.swing.JFrame;

public class ImageTest extends JFrame {

    public static void main(String[] args) {
```

continues

Listing 2.3   ImageTest.java   *continued*

```java
        DisplayMode displayMode;

        if (args.length == 3) {
            displayMode = new DisplayMode(
                Integer.parseInt(args[0]),
                Integer.parseInt(args[1]),
                Integer.parseInt(args[2]),
                DisplayMode.REFRESH_RATE_UNKNOWN);
        }
        else {
            displayMode = new DisplayMode(800, 600, 16,
                DisplayMode.REFRESH_RATE_UNKNOWN);
        }

        ImageTest test = new ImageTest();
        test.run(displayMode);
    }

    private static final int FONT_SIZE = 24;
    private static final long DEMO_TIME = 10000;

    private SimpleScreenManager screen;
    private Image bgImage;
    private Image opaqueImage;
    private Image transparentImage;
    private Image translucentImage;
    private Image antiAliasedImage;
    private boolean imagesLoaded;

    public void run(DisplayMode displayMode) {
        setBackground(Color.blue);
        setForeground(Color.white);
        setFont(new Font("Dialog", Font.PLAIN, FONT_SIZE));
        imagesLoaded = false;

        screen = new SimpleScreenManager();
        try {
            screen.setFullScreen(displayMode, this);
```

```
            loadImages();
            try {
                Thread.sleep(DEMO_TIME);
            }
            catch (InterruptedException ex) { }
        }
        finally {
            screen.restoreScreen();
        }
    }


    public void loadImages() {
        bgImage = loadImage("images/background.jpg");
        opaqueImage = loadImage("images/opaque.png");
        transparentImage = loadImage("images/transparent.png");
        translucentImage = loadImage("images/translucent.png");
        antiAliasedImage = loadImage("images/antialiased.png");
        imagesLoaded = true;
        // signal to AWT to repaint this window
        repaint();
    }


    private Image loadImage(String fileName) {
        return new ImageIcon(fileName).getImage();
    }


    public void paint(Graphics g) {
        // set text anti-aliasing
        if (g instanceof Graphics2D) {
            Graphics2D g2 = (Graphics2D)g;
            g2.setRenderingHint(
                RenderingHints.KEY_TEXT_ANTIALIASING,
                RenderingHints.VALUE_TEXT_ANTIALIAS_ON);
        }
```

continues

Listing 2.3   ImageTest.java   *continued*

```java
        // draw images
        if (imagesLoaded) {
            g.drawImage(bgImage, 0, 0, null);
            drawImage(g, opaqueImage, 0, 0, "Opaque");
            drawImage(g, transparentImage, 320, 0, "Transparent");
            drawImage(g, translucentImage, 0, 300, "Translucent");
            drawImage(g, antiAliasedImage, 320, 300,
                "Translucent (Anti-Aliased)");
        }
        else {
            g.drawString("Loading Images...", 5, FONT_SIZE);
        }
    }


    public void drawImage(Graphics g, Image image, int x, int y,
        String caption)
    {
        g.drawImage(image, x, y, null);
        g.drawString(caption, x + 5, y + FONT_SIZE +
            image.getHeight(null));
    }

}
```

Before the images are loaded, the ImageTest class shows a "Loading images" message. After the images are loaded, repaint() is called to signal the AWT to repaint the screen. At that point, the background and four PNGs are drawn.

Hardware-Accelerated Images

Hardware-accelerated images are images that are stored in video memory rather than system memory. Images that are hardware-accelerated can be copied to the screen faster than images that aren't.

Java tries to hardware-accelerate any image you load by using Toolkit's `getImage()` method. Because Java makes it automatic, you usually don't have to take any extra effort to make an image hardware-accelerated.

However, a few issues will keep your images from being accelerated:

➤ If you constantly change the contents of the image (for example, drawing graphics primitives onto the image), the image won't be accelerated.

➤ As of Java SDK 1.4.1, translucent images aren't accelerated. Only opaque and transparent images are accelerated. Because of this, translucent images are used sparingly in this book.

➤ Not every system has accelerated image capability.

If you want to force an image to be hardware-accelerated on systems that support it, you can create a VolatileImage. *VolatileImages* are images that are stored in video memory.

VolatileImages are created using Component's `createVolatileImage(int w, int h)` method or GraphicsConfiguration's `createCompatibleVolatileImage(int w, int h)` method. Unfortunately, VolatileImages can be only opaque.

VolatileImages can lose their contents at any time, hence the word "volatile." For example, if a screen saver starts up or the display mode changes, the VolatileImage might be wiped out of video memory, forcing you to redraw whatever is supposed to be there.

You can check whether a VolatileImage has lost its contents by using the `validate()` and `contentsLost()` methods. The `validate()` method makes sure the image is compatible with the current display mode, and the `contentsLost()` method returns information about whether the contents of the image have been lost since the last `validate()` call. Here's an example of how to check and restore a VolatileImage:

```
// create the image
VolatileImage image = createVolatileImage(w, h);
...
// draw the image
do {
```

```
    int valid = image.validate(getGraphicsConfiguration());
    if (valid == VolatileImage.IMAGE_INCOMPATIBLE) {
        // image isn't compatible with this display; re-create it
        image = createVolatileImage(w, h);
    }
    else if (valid == VolatileImage.IMAGE_RESTORED) {
        // restore the image
        Graphics2D g = image.createGraphics();
        myDrawMethod(g);
        g.dispose();
    }
    else {
        // draw the image on the screen
        Graphics g = screen.getDrawGraphics();
        g.drawImage(image, 0, 0, null);
        g.dispose();
    }
}
while (image.contentsLost());
```

This code simply loops until the image is successfully drawn on the screen.

Image-Drawing Benchmarks

Well, opaque and transparent images are accelerated, but just how fast are they?

To find out, let's modify the ImageTest class to create an ImageSpeedTest class, shown in Listing 2.4. ImageSpeedTest draws the four images used in ImageTest repeatedly for a specified time period and then prints how many images were drawn per second to the console.

> **CAUTION**
>
> You should never spend this much time in the paint() method. In this simple example, no damage is done, but in a real game, this wouldn't work. The AWT event dispatch thread calls the paint() method, but the AWT event dispatch thread also handles keyboard, mouse, and lots of other events (which we'll get into in the next chapter), so doing this is essentially "choking" the AWT thread. We'll get into a better way to do something like this in the next section.

Listing 2.4   ImageSpeedTest.java

```java
import java.awt.*;
import javax.swing.ImageIcon;
import javax.swing.JFrame;

public class ImageSpeedTest extends JFrame {

    public static void main(String args[]) {

        DisplayMode displayMode;

        if (args.length == 3) {
            displayMode = new DisplayMode(
                Integer.parseInt(args[0]),
                Integer.parseInt(args[1]),
                Integer.parseInt(args[2]),
                DisplayMode.REFRESH_RATE_UNKNOWN);
        }
        else {
            displayMode = new DisplayMode(800, 600, 16,
                DisplayMode.REFRESH_RATE_UNKNOWN);
        }

        ImageSpeedTest test = new ImageSpeedTest();
        test.run(displayMode);
    }

    private static final int FONT_SIZE = 24;
    private static final long TIME_PER_IMAGE = 1500;

    private SimpleScreenManager screen;
    private Image bgImage;
    private Image opaqueImage;
    private Image transparentImage;
    private Image translucentImage;
    private Image antiAliasedImage;
    private boolean imagesLoaded;
```

continues

Listing 2.4 ImageSpeedTest.java *continued*

```java
    public void run(DisplayMode displayMode) {
        setBackground(Color.blue);
        setForeground(Color.white);
        setFont(new Font("Dialog", Font.PLAIN, FONT_SIZE));
        imagesLoaded = false;

        screen = new SimpleScreenManager();
        try {
            screen.setFullScreen(displayMode, this);
            synchronized (this) {
                loadImages();
                // wait for test to complete
                try {
                    wait();
                }
                catch (InterruptedException ex) { }
            }
        }
        finally {
            screen.restoreScreen();
        }
    }


    public void loadImages() {
        bgImage = loadImage("images/background.jpg");
        opaqueImage = loadImage("images/opaque.png");
        transparentImage = loadImage("images/transparent.png");
        translucentImage = loadImage("images/translucent.png");
        antiAliasedImage = loadImage("images/antialiased.png");
        imagesLoaded = true;
        // signal to AWT to repaint this window
        repaint();
    }


    private final Image loadImage(String fileName) {
        return new ImageIcon(fileName).getImage();
```

```
    }


public void paint(Graphics g) {
    // set text anti-aliasing
    if (g instanceof Graphics2D) {
        Graphics2D g2 = (Graphics2D)g;
        g2.setRenderingHint(
            RenderingHints.KEY_TEXT_ANTIALIASING,
            RenderingHints.VALUE_TEXT_ANTIALIAS_ON);
    }

    // draw images
    if (imagesLoaded) {
        drawImage(g, opaqueImage, "Opaque");
        drawImage(g, transparentImage, "Transparent");
        drawImage(g, translucentImage, "Translucent");
        drawImage(g, antiAliasedImage,
            "Translucent (Anti-Aliased)");

        // notify that the test is complete
        synchronized (this) {
            notify();
        }
    }
    else {
        g.drawString("Loading Images...", 5, FONT_SIZE);
    }
}


public void drawImage(Graphics g, Image image, String name) {
    int width = screen.getFullScreenWindow().getWidth() -
        image.getWidth(null);
    int height = screen.getFullScreenWindow().getHeight() -
        image.getHeight(null);
    int numImages = 0;
```

continues

Listing 2.4   ImageSpeedTest.java   *continued*

```
        g.drawImage(bgImage, 0, 0, null);

        long startTime = System.currentTimeMillis();
        while (System.currentTimeMillis() - startTime
            < TIME_PER_IMAGE)
        {
            int x = Math.round((float)Math.random() * width);
            int y = Math.round((float)Math.random() * height);
            g.drawImage(image, x, y, null);
            numImages++;
        }
        long time = System.currentTimeMillis() - startTime;
        float speed = numImages * 1000f / time;
        System.out.println(name + ": " + speed + " images/sec");

    }

}
```

Don't think of this as the ultimate image-drawing benchmark. Remember, you're test-ing only four images on one machine. The results will vary depending on the comput-er's video card, processor speed, display mode, and whether your computer really feels like drawing quickly.

To give you an idea, here are the results of this test on a 600MHz Athlon with a GeForce-256 video card, a display resolution of 800×600, and a bit depth of 16—and in a good mood at the time:

```
Opaque: 5550.599 images/sec
Transparent: 5478.6953 images/sec
Translucent: 85.2197 images/sec
Translucent (Anti-Aliased): 113.18243 images/sec
```

As you can see, on this machine, translucent images are much slower than the hard-ware-accelerated opaque and transparent images. The reason the anti-aliased image is slightly faster than the fully translucent image is probably because there are more solid pixels in the image, so less blending is done when the image is drawn.

In this case, transparent images are almost as fast as opaque ones. Note that some older video cards might not have the capability to draw hardware-accelerated transparent images and will have to resort to the same slow method used by translucent images.

Okay, enough about hardware-accelerated images and drawing benchmarks! Let's move on to something you can use in a game: animation.

Animation

The first type of animation we'll go over is cartoon-style animation. This type of animation is displayed as a sequence of images, one after another. This is how animated cartoons work.

For an example, let's use a more dynamic version of our hero. What if our hero's hair moved and eyes blinked, as shown in Figure 2.6?

Figure 2.6   The three animated frames of our hero show that he looks quite innocent with his eyes closed.

The images in an animation can be referred to as frames. Each frame displays for a certain amount of time, but frames don't all have to display for the same amount of time. For example, the first frame might display for 200 milliseconds, the second for 75 milliseconds, and so on, as in Figure 2.7.

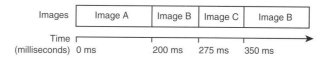

Figure 2.7   An animation is made of several images, and each image displays for a certain amount of time. The same image can be used more than once.

Now we'll take the concept of an animation and turn it into code. We'll make it so our animations can use the same image more than once. Also, the animations will loop indefinitely instead of just playing through once.

The `Animation` class in Listing 2.5 has three important methods: `addFrame()`, `update()`, and `getImage()`. The `addFrame()` method adds an image to the animation with a specified time (in milliseconds) to display. The `update()` method tells the animation that a specified amount of time has passed. Finally, the `getImage()` method gets the image that should be displayed based on the amount of time that has passed.

Listing 2.5   Animation.java

```
import java.awt.Image;
import java.util.ArrayList;

/**
    The Animation class manages a series of images (frames) and
    the amount of time to display each frame.
*/
public class Animation {

    private ArrayList frames;
    private int currFrameIndex;
    private long animTime;
    private long totalDuration;


    /**
        Creates a new, empty Animation.
    */
    public Animation() {
        frames = new ArrayList();
        totalDuration = 0;
        start();
    }


    /**
        Adds an image to the animation with the specified
```

```java
        duration (time to display the image).
*/
public synchronized void addFrame(Image image,
    long duration)
{
    totalDuration += duration;
    frames.add(new AnimFrame(image, totalDuration));
}



/**
    Starts this animation over from the beginning.
*/
public synchronized void start() {
    animTime = 0;
    currFrameIndex = 0;
}



/**
    Updates this animation's current image (frame), if
    necessary.
*/
public synchronized void update(long elapsedTime) {
    if (frames.size() > 1) {
        animTime += elapsedTime;

        if (animTime >= totalDuration) {
            animTime = animTime % totalDuration;
            currFrameIndex = 0;
        }

        while (animTime > getFrame(currFrameIndex).endTime) {
            currFrameIndex++;
        }
    }
}
```

continues

Listing 2.5 Animation.java   *continued*

```java
    /**
        Gets this Animation's current image. Returns null if this
        animation has no images.
    */
    public synchronized Image getImage() {
        if (frames.size() == 0) {
            return null;
        }
        else {
            return getFrame(currFrameIndex).image;
        }
    }


    private AnimFrame getFrame(int i) {
        return (AnimFrame)frames.get(i);
    }


    private class AnimFrame {

        Image image;
        long endTime;

        public AnimFrame(Image image, long endTime) {
            this.image = image;
            this.endTime = endTime;
        }
    }
}
```

In the Animation class, you might notice the odd % character in the following line:

```java
animTime = animTime % totalDuration;
```

In case you are unfamiliar with this, the % character is the remainder operator, returning the remainder from an integer division. For example, (10 % 3) equals 1—the integer result of 10 divided by 3 is 3, with 1 left over. It's used here to make sure the animation time starts over when the animation is done so that the animation loops.

The Animation code is fairly straightforward. The inner class AnimFrame contains an image and the amount of time to display it. Most of the work is done in Animation's update() method, which selects the correct AnimFrame to use based on how much time has elapsed.

Active Rendering

To implement animation, you need a way to continuously update the screen in an efficient way. Before, you relied on the paint() method to do any rendering. You could call repaint() to signal the AWT event dispatch thread to repaint the screen, but this can cause delays because the AWT thread might be busy doing other things.

Another option is to use active rendering. *Active rendering* is a term to describe drawing directly to the screen in the main thread. This way, you have control over when the screen actually gets drawn, and it simplifies the code a bit.

To use the active rendering technique, use Component's getGraphics() method to get the graphics context for the screen:

```
Graphics g = screen.getFullScreenWindow().getGraphics();
draw(g);
g.dispose();
```

Pretty simple, isn't it? As in this example, don't forget to dispose of the Graphics object when you're done drawing. This cleans up some resources that the garbage collector might not get around to for a while.

The Animation Loop

Now you'll use active rendering to continuously draw in a loop. This loop is known as the animation loop. An animation loop follows these steps:

1. Updates any animations

2. Draws to the screen

3. Optionally sleeps for a short period

4. Starts over with step 1

In code, the animation loop might look something like this:

```
while (true) {

    // update any animations
    updateAnimations();

    // draw to screen
    Graphics g = screen.getFullScreenWindow().getGraphics();
    draw(g);
    g.dispose();

    // take a nap
    try {
        Thread.sleep(20);
    }
    catch (InterruptedException ex) { }
}
```

Obviously, in a real-world example, the animation loop shouldn't loop forever. In our examples, we'll make the animation loop stop after a few seconds.

Now you have everything you need to try out some animation! `AnimationTest1` in Listing 2.6 is a simple example that makes our hero blink.

In `AnimationTest1`, you will update the entire screen every time you draw. Alternatively, you could update only the parts of the screen that have changed since the last draw. This method works great for games in which the background is static, such as the maze in Pac-Man. But most modern games have a dynamic background or have several things happening at once. Also, redrawing only what has changed since the last draw doesn't work when you're using page flipping, which we discuss later. In short, you'll just go ahead and update the entire screen in these examples.

Listing 2.6   AnimationTest1.java

```java
import java.awt.*;
import javax.swing.ImageIcon;
import javax.swing.JFrame;

public class AnimationTest1 {

    public static void main(String args[]) {

        DisplayMode displayMode;

        if (args.length == 3) {
            displayMode = new DisplayMode(
                Integer.parseInt(args[0]),
                Integer.parseInt(args[1]),
                Integer.parseInt(args[2]),
                DisplayMode.REFRESH_RATE_UNKNOWN);
        }
        else {
            displayMode = new DisplayMode(800, 600, 16,
                DisplayMode.REFRESH_RATE_UNKNOWN);
        }

        AnimationTest1 test = new AnimationTest1();
        test.run(displayMode);
    }

    private static final long DEMO_TIME = 5000;

    private SimpleScreenManager screen;
    private Image bgImage;
    private Animation anim;

    public void loadImages() {
        // load images
        bgImage = loadImage("images/background.jpg");
        Image player1 = loadImage("images/player1.png");
```

continues

Listing 2.6   AnimationTest1.java   *continued*

```
        Image player2 = loadImage("images/player2.png");
        Image player3 = loadImage("images/player3.png");

        // create animation
        anim = new Animation();
        anim.addFrame(player1, 250);
        anim.addFrame(player2, 150);
        anim.addFrame(player1, 150);
        anim.addFrame(player2, 150);
        anim.addFrame(player3, 200);
        anim.addFrame(player2, 150);
    }


    private Image loadImage(String fileName) {
        return new ImageIcon(fileName).getImage();
    }


    public void run(DisplayMode displayMode) {
        screen = new SimpleScreenManager();
        try {
            screen.setFullScreen(displayMode, new JFrame());
            loadImages();
            animationLoop();
        }
        finally {
            screen.restoreScreen();
        }
    }


    public void animationLoop() {
        long startTime = System.currentTimeMillis();
        long currTime = startTime;
```

```java
        while (currTime - startTime < DEMO_TIME) {
            long elapsedTime =
                System.currentTimeMillis() - currTime;
            currTime += elapsedTime;

            // update animation
            anim.update(elapsedTime);

            // draw to screen
            Graphics g =
                screen.getFullScreenWindow().getGraphics();
            draw(g);
            g.dispose();

            // take a nap
            try {
                Thread.sleep(20);
            }
            catch (InterruptedException ex) { }
        }

    }


    public void draw(Graphics g) {
        // draw background
        g.drawImage(bgImage, 0, 0, null);

        // draw image
        g.drawImage(anim.getImage(), 0, 0, null);
    }

}
```

Getting Rid of Flicker and Tearing

When you run `AnimationTest1`, you probably notice a big problem: The animated character flickers. And it's annoying. Why does this happen, and how can you get rid of it?

This is happening because you're constantly drawing directly to the screen, like in Figure 2.8. That means you erase the character with the background and then redraw the character, so there are sometimes brief moments that you see the background where the character should be. Because it's happening so fast, it appears as flicker.

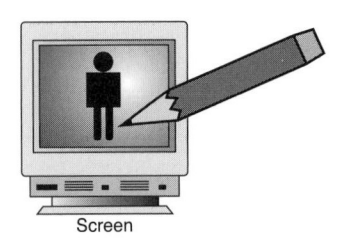

Screen

Figure 2.8   When you draw directly to the screen, the user sees what you're drawing as it is being drawn.

How can you get rid of the flicker? The answer is to use double buffering.

Double Buffering

A *buffer* is simply an off-screen area of memory used for drawing. When you use *double buffering*, instead of drawing directly to the screen, you draw to a back buffer and then copy the entire buffer to the screen, as shown in Figure 2.9. That way the whole screen is updated at once and players see only what they're supposed to see.

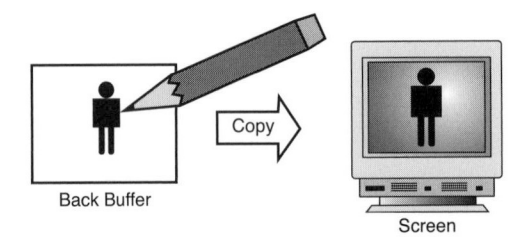

Back Buffer   Copy   Screen

Figure 2.9   Double buffering works by first drawing to a buffer and then copying the buffer to the screen.

The back buffer can be just a normal Java image. You can use Component's createImage(int w, int h) method to create a back buffer. For example, if you want to double buffer an applet that isn't using active rendering, you could override the update() method to use a double buffer and call the paint() method with the double buffer's graphics context:

```
private Image doubleBuffer;
...
public void update(Graphics g) {
    Dimension size = getSize();
    if (doubleBuffer == null ||
        doubleBuffer.getWidth(this) != size.width ||
        doubleBuffer.getHeight(this) != size.height)
    {
        doubleBuffer = createImage(size.width, size.height);
    }


    if (doubleBuffer != null) {
        // paint to double buffer
        Graphics g2 = doubleBuffer.getGraphics();
        paint(g2);
        g2.dispose();

        // copy double buffer to screen
        g.drawImage(doubleBuffer, 0, 0, null);
    }
    else {
        // couldn't create double buffer, just paint to screen
        paint(g);
    }
}

public void paint(Graphics g) {
    // do drawing here
    ...
}
```

Page Flipping

One drawback to using double buffering is the amount of time it takes to copy the back buffer to the screen. A display resolution of 800×600 at a bit depth of 16 takes 800×600×2 bytes, or 938KB. That's nearly a megabyte of memory that has to get shuffled around at 30 frames per second. Although copying that amount of memory is fast enough for many games, what if you didn't have to copy a buffer at all and could instantly make the back buffer the display buffer?

You can: This technique is called *page flipping*. With page flipping, you use two buffers, one as a back buffer and the other as a display buffer, as in Figure 2.10.

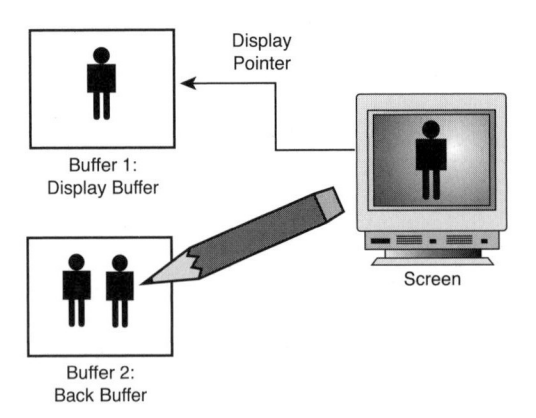

Figure 2.10   The display pointer points to buffer 1, and buffer 2 is used as the back buffer.

The display pointer points to buffer being displayed. This display pointer can be changed on most modern systems. When you are finished drawing to the back buffer, the display pointer can be switched from the current display buffer to the back buffer, as in Figure 2.11. When the display pointer is changed, the display buffer instantly becomes the back buffer, and vice versa.

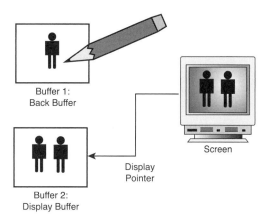

Figure 2.11   After flipping the page, the display pointer points to buffer 2, and buffer 1 is used as the back buffer.

Of course, changing a pointer is a lot faster than copying a huge block of memory, so this gives you a performance boost over double buffering.

Monitor Refresh and Tearing

Remember that your monitor has a refresh rate. This refresh rate is usually around 75Hz or so, which means the monitor is refreshed 75 times a second. But what happens when page flipping occurs or a buffer is copied in the middle of a monitor refresh? Yes, you guessed it: Part of the old buffer can display at the same time as part of the new buffer. This effect, similar to flickering, is called *tearing* (see Figure 2.12). It happens so fast it might barely be noticeable, but when it is noticeable, it appears as tears somewhere in the screen.

Figure 2.12   When tearing occurs, the old buffer (top) is still displayed when the new buffer (bottom) first appears. The imaginary dotted line represents the location of a tear.

To get around this, it's possible to perform the page flip at just the right moment, right before the monitor is about to be refreshed. This might sound like a complicated task, but don't worry—the Java runtime does it all for you, using the `BufferStrategy` class.

The *BufferStrategy* Class

Double buffering, page flipping, and waiting for the monitor refresh all are handled by the `BufferStrategy` class. `BufferStrategy` chooses the best buffering method based on the capabilities of the system. First, it tries page flipping. If that's not possible, it tries double buffering. Also, it waits on the monitor refresh to finish before performing any page flip. In short, it does all the work for you, without you having to think about it.

One drawback to waiting for the monitor refresh is that the game is limited in the number of frames per second it can display. If the monitor is set at a 75Hz refresh rate, the game displays a maximum of 75 frames per second. This means you can't use the game's frame rate as a "benchmark" for how fast a system runs.

Of course, it really doesn't matter whether your game runs at 200 frames per second— you'll still see only what your monitor is capable of. No matter how fast your game runs, you'll still see 75 frames per second on a monitor with a 75Hz refresh rate.

Both the `Canvas` and `Window` objects can have a `BufferStrategy`. Use the `createBufferStrategy()` method to create a `BufferStrategy` based on the number of buffers you want. You'll want at least two buffers for double buffering and page flipping to work. For example:

```
frame.createBufferStrategy(2);
```

After you've created the `BufferStrategy`, get a reference to it by calling the `getBufferStrategy()` method and use the `getDrawGraphics()` method to get the graphics context for the draw buffer. After you finish drawing, call the `show()` method to show the draw buffer, either by using a page flip or by copying the draw buffer to the display buffer. Here's an example:

```
BufferStrategy strategy = frame.getBufferStrategy();
Graphics g = strategy.getDrawGraphics();
draw(g);
g.dispose();
strategy.show();
```

Creating a Screen Manager

Now let's update the `SimpleScreenManager` with these new features. Here are some of the things you'll add:

➤ Double buffering and page flipping by creating a `BufferStrategy`

➤ `getGraphics()`, which gets the graphics context for the display

➤ `update()`, which updates the display

➤ `getCompatibleDisplayModes()`, which gets a list of the compatible display modes

➤ `getCurrentDisplayMode()`, which gets the current display mode

➤ `findFirstCompatibleMode()`, which gets the first compatible mode from a list of modes

Also, now that you're doing active rendering, there's no need for the `JFrame` used as the full-screen window to receive `paint` events from the operating system, so you can turn them off:

```
frame.ignoreRepaint(true);
```

This doesn't turn off normal `repaint` events, however. Calling `repaint()` on the `JFrame` stills send a `paint` event.

The `SimpleScreenManager` is updated in the `ScreenManager` class, shown here in Listing 2.7.

Listing 2.7   ScreenManager.java

```
import java.awt.*;
import java.awt.image.BufferStrategy;
```

continues

Listing 2.7 ScreenManager.java *continued*

```java
import javax.swing.JFrame;

/**
    The ScreenManager class manages initializing and displaying
    full screen graphics modes.
*/
public class ScreenManager {

    private GraphicsDevice device;

    /**
        Creates a new ScreenManager object.
    */
    public ScreenManager() {
        GraphicsEnvironment environment =
            GraphicsEnvironment.getLocalGraphicsEnvironment();
        device = environment.getDefaultScreenDevice();
    }


    /**
        Returns a list of compatible display modes for the
        default device on the system.
    */
    public DisplayMode[] getCompatibleDisplayModes() {
        return device.getDisplayModes();
    }


    /**
        Returns the first compatible mode in a list of modes.
        Returns null if no modes are compatible.
    */
    public DisplayMode findFirstCompatibleMode(
        DisplayMode modes[])
    {
        DisplayMode goodModes[] = device.getDisplayModes();
```

```java
    for (int i = 0; i < modes.length; i++) {
        for (int j = 0; j < goodModes.length; j++) {
            if (displayModesMatch(modes[i], goodModes[j])) {
                return modes[i];
            }
        }

    }

    return null;
}


/**
    Returns the current display mode.
*/
public DisplayMode getCurrentDisplayMode() {
    return device.getDisplayMode();
}


/**
    Determines if two display modes "match". Two display
    modes match if they have the same resolution, bit depth,
    and refresh rate. The bit depth is ignored if one of the
    modes has a bit depth of DisplayMode.BIT_DEPTH_MULTI.
    Likewise, the refresh rate is ignored if one of the
    modes has a refresh rate of
    DisplayMode.REFRESH_RATE_UNKNOWN.
*/
public boolean displayModesMatch(DisplayMode mode1,
    DisplayMode mode2)
{
    if (mode1.getWidth() != mode2.getWidth() ||
        mode1.getHeight() != mode2.getHeight())
    {
        return false;
    }
```

continues

Listing 2.7   ScreenManager.java   *continued*

```java
        if (mode1.getBitDepth() != DisplayMode.BIT_DEPTH_MULTI &&
            mode2.getBitDepth() != DisplayMode.BIT_DEPTH_MULTI &&
            mode1.getBitDepth() != mode2.getBitDepth())
        {
            return false;
        }

        if (mode1.getRefreshRate() !=
            DisplayMode.REFRESH_RATE_UNKNOWN &&
            mode2.getRefreshRate() !=
            DisplayMode.REFRESH_RATE_UNKNOWN &&
            mode1.getRefreshRate() != mode2.getRefreshRate())
        {
            return false;
        }

        return true;
    }


    /**
        Enters full screen mode and changes the display mode.
        If the specified display mode is null or not compatible
        with this device, or if the display mode cannot be
        changed on this system, the current display mode is used.
        <p>
        The display uses a BufferStrategy with 2 buffers.
    */
    public void setFullScreen(DisplayMode displayMode) {
        JFrame frame = new JFrame();
        frame.setUndecorated(true);
        frame.setIgnoreRepaint(true);
        frame.setResizable(false);

        device.setFullScreenWindow(frame);
        if (displayMode != null &&
            device.isDisplayChangeSupported())
        {
```

```java
        try {
            device.setDisplayMode(displayMode);
        }
        catch (IllegalArgumentException ex) { }
    }
    frame.createBufferStrategy(2);
}


/**
    Gets the graphics context for the display. The
    ScreenManager uses double buffering, so applications must
    call update() to show any graphics drawn.
    <p>
    The application must dispose of the graphics object.
*/
public Graphics2D getGraphics() {
    Window window = device.getFullScreenWindow();
    if (window != null) {
        BufferStrategy strategy = window.getBufferStrategy();
        return (Graphics2D)strategy.getDrawGraphics();
    }
    else {
        return null;
    }
}


/**
    Updates the display.
*/
public void update() {
    Window window = device.getFullScreenWindow();
    if (window != null) {
        BufferStrategy strategy = window.getBufferStrategy();
        if (!strategy.contentsLost()) {
            strategy.show();
        }
```

continues

Listing 2.7 ScreenManager.java *continued*

```
        }
        // Sync the display on some systems.
        // (on Linux, this fixes event queue problems)
        Toolkit.getDefaultToolkit().sync();
    }


    /**
        Returns the window currently used in full screen mode.
        Returns null if the device is not in full screen mode.
    */
    public Window getFullScreenWindow() {
        return device.getFullScreenWindow();
    }


    /**
        Returns the width of the window currently used in full
        screen mode. Returns 0 if the device is not in full
        screen mode.
    */
    public int getWidth() {
        Window window = device.getFullScreenWindow();
        if (window != null) {
            return window.getWidth();
        }
        else {
            return 0;
        }
    }


    /**
        Returns the height of the window currently used in full
        screen mode. Returns 0 if the device is not in full
        screen mode.
    */
```

```java
public int getHeight() {
    Window window = device.getFullScreenWindow();
    if (window != null) {
        return window.getHeight();
    }
    else {
        return 0;
    }
}


/**
    Restores the screen's display mode.
*/
public void restoreScreen() {
    Window window = device.getFullScreenWindow();
    if (window != null) {
        window.dispose();
    }
    device.setFullScreenWindow(null);
}


/**
    Creates an image compatible with the current display.
*/
public BufferedImage createCompatibleImage(int w, int h,
    int transparency)
{
    Window window = device.getFullScreenWindow();
    if (window != null) {
        GraphicsConfiguration gc =
            window.getGraphicsConfiguration();
        return gc.createCompatibleImage(w, h, transparency);
    }
    return null;
}
}
```

In `ScreenManager`, you'll notice the following line in the `update()` method:

`Toolkit.getDefaultToolkit().sync();`

This method makes sure the display is synchronized with the window system. On many systems, this method does nothing, but on Linux, calling this method fixes problems with the AWT event queue. Without calling this method, some Linux systems might experience delayed mouse and keyboard input events.

Two new `ScreenManager` methods to note are `displayModesMatch()` and `createCompatibleImage()`.

The `displayModesMatch()` method checks whether two `DisplayMode` objects "match." They match if the resolution, bit depth, and refresh rate are equal. The bit depth and the refresh rate are ignored if they aren't specified in one of the `DisplayMode` objects.

`createCompatibleImage()` creates an image that is compatible with the display—that is, the image would have the same bit depth and color model as the display. The image class created is a `BufferedImage`, which is a nonaccelerated image stored in system memory. This method is useful for creating transparent or translucent images because the normal `createImage()` method creates only opaque images.

Now you'll update `AnimationTest1` to use the new and improved `ScreenManager`, creating the `AnimationTest2` class in Listing 2.8. Hooray, no more flickering!

Listing 2.8   AnimationTest2.java

```java
import java.awt.*;
import javax.swing.ImageIcon;

public class AnimationTest2 {

    public static void main(String args[]) {
        AnimationTest2 test = new AnimationTest2();
        test.run();
    }
```

```
private static final DisplayMode POSSIBLE_MODES[] = {
    new DisplayMode(800, 600, 32, 0),
    new DisplayMode(800, 600, 24, 0),
    new DisplayMode(800, 600, 16, 0),
    new DisplayMode(640, 480, 32, 0),
    new DisplayMode(640, 480, 24, 0),
    new DisplayMode(640, 480, 16, 0)
};

private static final long DEMO_TIME = 10000;

private ScreenManager screen;
private Image bgImage;
private Animation anim;


public void loadImages() {
    // load images
    bgImage = loadImage("images/background.jpg");
    Image player1 = loadImage("images/player1.png");
    Image player2 = loadImage("images/player2.png");
    Image player3 = loadImage("images/player3.png");

    // create animation
    anim = new Animation();
    anim.addFrame(player1, 250);
    anim.addFrame(player2, 150);
    anim.addFrame(player1, 150);
    anim.addFrame(player2, 150);
    anim.addFrame(player3, 200);
    anim.addFrame(player2, 150);
}


private Image loadImage(String fileName) {
    return new ImageIcon(fileName).getImage();
}
```

continues

Listing 2.8   AnimationTest2.java   *continued*

```java
public void run() {
    screen = new ScreenManager();
    try {
        DisplayMode displayMode =
            screen.findFirstCompatibleMode(POSSIBLE_MODES);
        screen.setFullScreen(displayMode);
        loadImages();
        animationLoop();
    }
    finally {
        screen.restoreScreen();
    }
}


public void animationLoop() {
    long startTime = System.currentTimeMillis();
    long currTime = startTime;

    while (currTime - startTime < DEMO_TIME) {
        long elapsedTime =
            System.currentTimeMillis() - currTime;
        currTime += elapsedTime;

        // update animation
        anim.update(elapsedTime);

        // draw and update screen
        Graphics2D g = screen.getGraphics();
        draw(g);
        g.dispose();
        screen.update();

        // take a nap
        try {
            Thread.sleep(20);
        }
```

```
            catch (InterruptedException ex) { }
        }

    }


    public void draw(Graphics g) {
        // draw background
        g.drawImage(bgImage, 0, 0, null);

        // draw image
        g.drawImage(anim.getImage(), 0, 0, null);
    }

}
```

Not much has changed in the move from `AnimationTest1` to `AnimationTest2`. One thing that has changed is how `AnimationTest2` selects a display mode. Instead of using a default display mode or getting the display mode from the command line, `AnimationTest2` provides the `ScreenManager` with a list of possible modes to use, and the `ScreenManager` selects the first compatible mode in the list.

Also, the `ScreenManager` creates its own `JFrame` object, so `AnimationTest2` doesn't have to deal with creating the `JFrame` used as the full-screen window.

Sprites

The animation is now running smoothly, but it's not that exciting to see something animate in one place on the screen. Let's make it move by creating a sprite.

A *sprite* is a graphic that moves independently around the screen. In this case, the sprite is also animated, so it can animate and move at the same time.

Besides an animation, the sprites will be composed of two things: a position and a velocity. If you were sleeping the day they told you about velocity in school, a velocity is both a speed (such as 55mph) and a direction (such as north). In this case, we'll break down velocity into horizontal and vertical components. Instead of miles per hour or meters per second, we'll use pixels per millisecond.

You might be asking, "Why use velocity? Why not just update the sprite's position a certain amount each frame?" Well, if you did that, the sprite would move at different speeds depending on the speed of the machine. A faster frame rate would mean a faster-moving sprite. Tying the sprite's movement to real time causes the sprite to move at a consistent pace, whether the time between frames is short or long.

As with the animation, the sprite updates based on the number of milliseconds that have passed since the last time the sprite was drawn. You'll say, "Hey, sprite, 50 milliseconds have passed," and the sprite will update its position (based on its velocity) and its animation.

The Sprite class, in Listing 2.9, has an animation, a position, and a velocity.

You could make the sprite's position an integer, but what if a sprite is moving slowly? For example, imagine a sprite moving a tenth of a pixel every time the update() method is called. That means the sprite would have nonvisible movement on 9 out of 10 calls to update(). If the sprite's position were an integer, the sprite would never move because the result would be rounded each time.

If the sprite's position is a floating-point value, the sprite position could increment these nonvisible movements, and the sprite would move 1 pixel on every tenth call to update(), as expected. For this reason, you'll make the sprites' position a floating-point value. To get its exact pixel position, use Math.round().

Listing 2.9   Sprite.java

```
import java.awt.Image;

public class Sprite {

    private Animation anim;
    // position (pixels)
    private float x;
    private float y;
    // velocity (pixels per millisecond)
    private float dx;
    private float dy;
```

```
/**
    Creates a new Sprite object with the specified Animation.
*/
public Sprite(Animation anim) {
    this.anim = anim;
}

/**
    Updates this Sprite's Animation and its position based
    on the velocity.
*/
public void update(long elapsedTime) {
    x += dx * elapsedTime;
    y += dy * elapsedTime;
    anim.update(elapsedTime);
}

/**
    Gets this Sprite's current x position.
*/
public float getX() {
    return x;
}

/**
    Gets this Sprite's current y position.
*/
public float getY() {
    return y;
}

/**
    Sets this Sprite's current x position.
*/
public void setX(float x) {
    this.x = x;
}
```

continues

Listing 2.9 Sprite.java *continued*

```java
/**
    Sets this Sprite's current y position.
*/
public void setY(float y) {
    this.y = y;
}


/**
    Gets this Sprite's width, based on the size of the
    current image.
*/
public int getWidth() {
    return anim.getImage().getWidth(null);
}


/**
    Gets this Sprite's height, based on the size of the
    current image.
*/
public int getHeight() {
    return anim.getImage().getHeight(null);
}


/**
    Gets the horizontal velocity of this Sprite in pixels
    per millisecond.
*/
public float getVelocityX() {
    return dx;
}


/**
    Gets the vertical velocity of this Sprite in pixels
    per millisecond.
*/
public float getVelocityY() {
    return dy;
}
```

```
/**
    Sets the horizontal velocity of this Sprite in pixels
    per millisecond.
*/
public void setVelocityX(float dx) {
    this.dx = dx;
}


/**
    Sets the vertical velocity of this Sprite in pixels
    per millisecond.
*/
public void setVelocityY(float dy) {
    this.dy = dy;
}


/**
    Gets this Sprite's current image.
*/
public Image getImage() {
    return anim.getImage();
}
}
```

The `Sprite` class is fairly simple. Mostly it's a just bunch of `get` and `set` methods. All the work is done in the `update()` method, which updates the sprite's position based on its velocity and the amount of time elapsed.

Now let's have some fun. Let's use the `Sprite` class to make the character animate and bounce around the screen. `SpriteTest1`, in Listing 2.10, does just that. Every time the sprite hits the edge of the screen, its velocity is changed to reflect the bounce.

Listing 2.10 SpriteTest1.java

```
import java.awt.*;
import javax.swing.ImageIcon;

public class SpriteTest1 {
```

continues

Listing 2.10   SpriteTest1.java   *continued*

```java
public static void main(String args[]) {
    SpriteTest1 test = new SpriteTest1();
    test.run();
}

private static final DisplayMode POSSIBLE_MODES[] = {
    new DisplayMode(800, 600, 32, 0),
    new DisplayMode(800, 600, 24, 0),
    new DisplayMode(800, 600, 16, 0),
    new DisplayMode(640, 480, 32, 0),
    new DisplayMode(640, 480, 24, 0),
    new DisplayMode(640, 480, 16, 0)
};

private static final long DEMO_TIME = 10000;

private ScreenManager screen;
private Image bgImage;
private Sprite sprite;

public void loadImages() {
    // load images
    bgImage = loadImage("images/background.jpg");
    Image player1 = loadImage("images/player1.png");
    Image player2 = loadImage("images/player2.png");
    Image player3 = loadImage("images/player3.png");

    // create sprite
    Animation anim = new Animation();
    anim.addFrame(player1, 250);
    anim.addFrame(player2, 150);
    anim.addFrame(player1, 150);
    anim.addFrame(player2, 150);
    anim.addFrame(player3, 200);
    anim.addFrame(player2, 150);
    sprite = new Sprite(anim);
```

```java
        // start the sprite off moving down and to the right
        sprite.setVelocityX(0.2f);
        sprite.setVelocityY(0.2f);
    }


    private Image loadImage(String fileName) {
        return new ImageIcon(fileName).getImage();
    }


    public void run() {
        screen = new ScreenManager();
        try {
            DisplayMode displayMode =
                screen.findFirstCompatibleMode(POSSIBLE_MODES);
            screen.setFullScreen(displayMode);
            loadImages();
            animationLoop();
        }
        finally {
            screen.restoreScreen();
        }
    }


    public void animationLoop() {
        long startTime = System.currentTimeMillis();
        long currTime = startTime;

        while (currTime - startTime < DEMO_TIME) {
            long elapsedTime =
                System.currentTimeMillis() - currTime;
            currTime += elapsedTime;

            // update the sprites
            update(elapsedTime);
```

continues

Listing 2.10 SpriteTest1.java *continued*

```java
            // draw and update the screen
            Graphics2D g = screen.getGraphics();
            draw(g);
            g.dispose();
            screen.update();

            // take a nap
            try {
                Thread.sleep(20);
            }
            catch (InterruptedException ex) { }
        }
    }


    public void update(long elapsedTime) {
        // check sprite bounds
        if (sprite.getX() < 0) {
            sprite.setVelocityX(Math.abs(sprite.getVelocityX()));
        }
        else if (sprite.getX() + sprite.getWidth() >=
            screen.getWidth())
        {
            sprite.setVelocityX(-Math.abs(sprite.getVelocityX()));
        }
        if (sprite.getY() < 0) {
            sprite.setVelocityY(Math.abs(sprite.getVelocityY()));
        }
        else if (sprite.getY() + sprite.getHeight() >=
            screen.getHeight())
        {
            sprite.setVelocityY(-Math.abs(sprite.getVelocityY()));
        }

        // update sprite
        sprite.update(elapsedTime);
```

```
    }


    public void draw(Graphics g) {
        // draw background
        g.drawImage(bgImage, 0, 0, null);

        // draw sprite
        g.drawImage(sprite.getImage(),
            Math.round(sprite.getX()),
            Math.round(sprite.getY()),
            null);
    }

}
```

Because the Sprite object handles its own movement, there's not much new happening in the SpriteTest1 class. The newest thing is the update() method, which causes the sprite to "bounce" when it hits the edge of the screen. If the sprite hits the left or right edge of the screen, the horizontal velocity is reversed. If the sprite hits the top or bottom edge of the screen, the vertical velocity is reversed.

Simple Effects

As you can imagine, it's pretty easy to add more sprites at this point. Just create more Sprite objects, and be sure to update and draw each one—for example:

```
for (int i=0; i<sprites.length; i++) {
    sprites[i].update(elapsedTime);
    g.drawImage(sprites[i].getImage(),
        Math.round(sprite[i].getX()),
        Math.round(sprite[i].getY()),
        null);
}
```

One thing to note is that sprites update their own animations, so sprites can't share the same `Animation` object; the `Animation` object would get updated too many times. If you're using a lot of animations that are the same, you might want to add a `clone()` method to the animation to make them easier to duplicate.

Image Transforms

One cool effect is rotating or scaling an image. This is called an *image transform*. Image transforms enable you to translate, flip, scale, shear, and rotate images, even on the fly.

An `AffineTransform` object describes a transform. The `AffineTransform` class stores its transform data in a 2D 3×3 matrix, but it's not necessary to understand how matrices work with graphics. Instead, the class provides several easy methods such as `rotate()`, `scale()`, and `translate()` that do the calculations for you.

The `Graphics2D` class is where the transform actually takes place. There's a special `drawImage()` method in `Graphics2D` that takes an `AffineTransform` as a parameter. Here's an example of drawing an image scaled twice as large:

```
AffineTransform transform = new AffineTransform();
transform.scale(2,2);
transform.translate(100,100);
g.drawImage(image, transform, null);
```

Note that transform operations are based on an origin, which is the upper-left corner of the image. That means you might have to translate the image to get the results you expect.

Now, let's add a couple more sprites and some image transforms to `SpriteTest1`.

The character normally always faces right, but let's make the character face left when it's moving left. Instead of loading separate images for facing left, let's use transforms to create a mirror of the image on the fly. To do this, scale the width of the image by –1, and then translate the result so it is positioned correctly.

```
transform.scale(-1, 1);
transform.translate(-sprite.getWidth(), 0);
```

Just for fun, SpriteTest2, in Listing 2.11, also has a fade effect. When the program first starts, the graphics fade from black like you are opening horizontal blinds. The same effect happens in reverse as the program exits. This effect is created by using the fillRect() method of the Graphics object to create solid black "blinds" that have a size based on the amount of time the demo has run.

See Figure 2.13 for a screen capture of SpriteTest2.

Figure 2.13   SpriteTest2 animates several sprites at once and uses transforms to create mirror images.

Listing 2.11   SpriteTest2.java

```
import java.awt.*;
import java.awt.geom.AffineTransform;
import javax.swing.ImageIcon;

public class SpriteTest2 {

    public static void main(String args[]) {
        SpriteTest2 test = new SpriteTest2();
        test.run();
    }

    private static final DisplayMode POSSIBLE_MODES[] = {
        new DisplayMode(800, 600, 32, 0),
        new DisplayMode(800, 600, 24, 0),
        new DisplayMode(800, 600, 16, 0),
        new DisplayMode(640, 480, 32, 0),
        new DisplayMode(640, 480, 24, 0),
```

continues

Listing 2.11   SpriteTest2.java   *continued*

```java
        new DisplayMode(640, 480, 16, 0)
    };

    private static final long DEMO_TIME = 10000;
    private static final long FADE_TIME = 1000;
    private static final int NUM_SPRITES = 3;

    private ScreenManager screen;
    private Image bgImage;
    private Sprite sprites[];

    public void loadImages() {
        // load images
        bgImage = loadImage("images/background.jpg");
        Image player1 = loadImage("images/player1.png");
        Image player2 = loadImage("images/player2.png");
        Image player3 = loadImage("images/player3.png");

        // create and init sprites
        sprites = new Sprite[NUM_SPRITES];
        for (int i = 0; i < NUM_SPRITES; i++) {
            Animation anim = new Animation();
            anim.addFrame(player1, 250);
            anim.addFrame(player2, 150);
            anim.addFrame(player1, 150);
            anim.addFrame(player2, 150);
            anim.addFrame(player3, 200);
            anim.addFrame(player2, 150);
            sprites[i] = new Sprite(anim);

            // select random starting location
            sprites[i].setX((float)Math.random() *
                (screen.getWidth() - sprites[i].getWidth()));
            sprites[i].setY((float)Math.random() *
                (screen.getHeight() - sprites[i].getHeight()));

            // select random velocity
```

```
        sprites[i].setVelocityX((float)Math.random() - 0.5f);
        sprites[i].setVelocityY((float)Math.random() - 0.5f);
    }

}


private Image loadImage(String fileName) {
    return new ImageIcon(fileName).getImage();
}


public void run() {
    screen = new ScreenManager();
    try {
        DisplayMode displayMode =
            screen.findFirstCompatibleMode(POSSIBLE_MODES);
        screen.setFullScreen(displayMode);
        loadImages();
        animationLoop();
    }
    finally {
        screen.restoreScreen();
    }
}


public void animationLoop() {
    long startTime = System.currentTimeMillis();
    long currTime = startTime;

    while (currTime - startTime < DEMO_TIME) {
        long elapsedTime =
            System.currentTimeMillis() - currTime;
        currTime += elapsedTime;

        // update the sprites
        update(elapsedTime);
```

continues

Listing 2.11 SpriteTest2.java *continued*

```java
            // draw and update screen
            Graphics2D g = screen.getGraphics();
            draw(g);
            drawFade(g, currTime - startTime);
            g.dispose();
            screen.update();

            // take a nap
            try {
                Thread.sleep(20);
            }
            catch (InterruptedException ex) { }
        }

    }


    public void drawFade(Graphics2D g, long currTime) {
        long time = 0;
        if (currTime <= FADE_TIME) {
            time = FADE_TIME - currTime;
        }
        else if (currTime > DEMO_TIME - FADE_TIME) {
            time = FADE_TIME - DEMO_TIME + currTime;
        }
        else {
            return;
        }

        byte numBars = 8;
        int barHeight = screen.getHeight() / numBars;
        int blackHeight = (int)(time * barHeight / FADE_TIME);

        g.setColor(Color.black);
        for (int i = 0; i < numBars; i++) {
            int y = i * barHeight + (barHeight - blackHeight) / 2;
```

```
            g.fillRect(0, y, screen.getWidth(), blackHeight);
        }

}


public void update(long elapsedTime) {

    for (int i = 0; i < NUM_SPRITES; i++) {

        Sprite s = sprites[i];

        // check sprite bounds
        if (s.getX() < 0.) {
            s.setVelocityX(Math.abs(s.getVelocityX()));
        }
        else if (s.getX() + s.getWidth() >=
            screen.getWidth())
        {
            s.setVelocityX(-Math.abs(s.getVelocityX()));
        }
        if (s.getY() < 0) {
            s.setVelocityY(Math.abs(s.getVelocityY()));
        }
        else if (s.getY() + s.getHeight() >=
            screen.getHeight())
        {
            s.setVelocityY(-Math.abs(s.getVelocityY()));
        }

        // update sprite
        s.update(elapsedTime);
    }

}


public void draw(Graphics2D g) {
```

continues

Listing 2.11   SpriteTest2.java   *continued*

```
                // draw background
                g.drawImage(bgImage, 0, 0, null);

                AffineTransform transform = new AffineTransform();
                for (int i = 0; i < NUM_SPRITES; i++) {
                    Sprite sprite = sprites[i];

                    // translate the sprite
                    transform.setToTranslation(sprite.getX(),
                        sprite.getY());

                    // if the sprite is moving left, flip the image
                    if (sprite.getVelocityX() < 0) {
                        transform.scale(-1, 1);
                        transform.translate(-sprite.getWidth(), 0);
                    }

                    // draw it
                    g.drawImage(sprite.getImage(), transform, null);
                }

            }

        }
```

In `SpriteTest2`, the sprites' images are flipped on the fly. There's just one problem with this: Transforming images does not take advantage of hardware acceleration. Even if only a simple transform such as translation is done, the image isn't accelerated. So, normally, it might be a good idea to use transforms sparingly.

You should note a couple things about these sprite demos. First, although we kept all sprites on the screen, it's okay to draw sprites partially off-screen or completely off-screen—Java2D takes care of clipping for you.

Second, we're tying our animation to the system clock, which isn't very granularity on Windows platforms. We create a workaround for this problem later in Chapter 16, "Optimization Techniques."

Summary

Whew! That was a lot of information in this chapter. You've done a lot and come out with some useful, reusable code: `ScreenManager`, `Animation`, and `Sprite`. These classes will be used in later chapters.

Remember that these classes might not necessarily be the "best" way to do things. You might want to come up with your own code to suit your needs better. There is no "right" way to do things, so feel free to experiment to find what works best for you and your game.

Chapter 3

Interactivity and User Interfaces

If you've ever played a chess game by yourself in which the chess pieces were glued to the board, you know what it's like to play a game without any interactivity. It's boring.

Interactivity is essentially taking input from the user and changing what's displayed on the screen based on that input. Without interactivity, there would be no games—or, at least, the games would be really boring.

In this chapter, you'll learn how to receive input—namely, keyboard and mouse events—from the user. You'll also integrate this input into your games and learn about how to implement user interfaces with Swing.

As of Java SDK 1.4, there is no way to receive input from a joystick. Although this is a shortcoming, it won't affect too many people because most people don't have joysticks for their computers. Also, many prefer to use the mouse or keyboard anyway.

Before we get started, let's note what code we will use. For the remainder of the book, we'll be organizing the reusable code into subpackages of com.brackeen.javagamebook. This will keep the code organized and easier to find.

The ScreenManager, Animation, and Sprite classes created in Chapter 2, "2D Graphics and Animation," are in the com.brackeen.javagamebook.graphics package. Reusable code created in this chapter belongs to the com.brackeen.javagamebook.input package. Also, any code that's just a quick test will be in the default, unnamed package.

Finally, we'll need a simple class to make the quick test programs easier to implement. The GameCore class in Listing 3.1 does just that, implementing some of the common techniques from the previous chapter, such as setting the display mode and running an animation loop. All we have to do is extend this abstract class and implement the draw() and update() methods.

Listing 3.1   GameCore.java

```java
package com.brackeen.javagamebook.test;

import java.awt.*;
import javax.swing.ImageIcon;

import com.brackeen.javagamebook.graphics.ScreenManager;

/**
    Simple abstract class used for testing. Subclasses should
    implement the draw() method.
*/
public abstract class GameCore {

    protected static final int FONT_SIZE = 24;

    private static final DisplayMode POSSIBLE_MODES[] = {
        new DisplayMode(800, 600, 32, 0),
        new DisplayMode(800, 600, 24, 0),
        new DisplayMode(800, 600, 16, 0),
        new DisplayMode(640, 480, 32, 0),
        new DisplayMode(640, 480, 24, 0),
        new DisplayMode(640, 480, 16, 0)
    };

    private boolean isRunning;
    protected ScreenManager screen;
```

```java
/**
    Signals the game loop that it's time to quit
*/
public void stop() {
    isRunning = false;
}


/**
    Calls init() and gameLoop()
*/
public void run() {
    try {
        init();
        gameLoop();
    }
    finally {
        screen.restoreScreen();
    }
}


/**
    Sets full screen mode and initiates and objects.
*/
public void init() {
    screen = new ScreenManager();
    DisplayMode displayMode =
        screen.findFirstCompatibleMode(POSSIBLE_MODES);
    screen.setFullScreen(displayMode);

    Window window = screen.getFullScreenWindow();
    window.setFont(new Font("Dialog", Font.PLAIN, FONT_SIZE));
    window.setBackground(Color.blue);
    window.setForeground(Color.white);

    isRunning = true;
```

continues

Listing 3.1   GameCore.java   *continued*

```java
    }


    public Image loadImage(String fileName) {
        return new ImageIcon(fileName).getImage();
    }



    /**
        Runs through the game loop until stop() is called.
    */
    public void gameLoop() {
        long startTime = System.currentTimeMillis();
        long currTime = startTime;

        while (isRunning) {
            long elapsedTime =
                System.currentTimeMillis() - currTime;
            currTime += elapsedTime;

            // update
            update(elapsedTime);

            // draw the screen
            Graphics2D g = screen.getGraphics();
            draw(g);
            g.dispose();
            screen.update();

            // take a nap
            try {
                Thread.sleep(20);
            }
            catch (InterruptedException ex) { }
        }
    }
```

```
/**
    Updates the state of the game/animation based on the
    amount of elapsed time that has passed.
*/
public void update(long elapsedTime) {
    // do nothing
}


/**
    Draws to the screen. Subclasses must override this
    method.
*/
public abstract void draw(Graphics2D g);
}
```

By default, the update() method doesn't do anything, but in subclasses, you'll use it for updating sprites and such. Also, you'll probably extend the init() method to do things such as load images or initialize any variables.

One last thing to note is that, from now on, the code can be compiled with Apache Ant. In the source code for this book, the source lives in the src folder and Ant compiles the classes in a build folder. If you are unfamiliar with Ant, skip on back to the Introduction or check out http://ant.apache.org. Don't worry, I'll still be here when you get back.

Okay, now let's move on to what you're here for: interactivity.

The AWT Event Model

As mentioned before, the AWT has its own event dispatch thread. This thread dispatches all sorts of events, such as mouse clicks and key presses coming in from the operating system.

Where does the AWT dispatch these events? When an event occurs on a particular component, the AWT checks to see if there are any *listeners* for that event. A listener is an object that receives events from another object. In this case, events come from the AWT event dispatch thread.

There is a different type of listener for every type of event. For example, for key input events, there is a KeyListener interface.

Here's an example of how the event model works for a key press:

1. The user presses a key.

2. The operating system sends the key event to the Java runtime.

3. The Java runtime posts the event to the AWT's event queue.

4. The AWT event dispatch thread dispatches the event to any KeyListeners.

5. The KeyListener receives the key event and does whatever it wants with it.

All listeners are interfaces, so any object can be a listener by implementing a listener interface. Also note that there can be several listeners for the same event type. For example, several objects could be listening for mouse events. This can be a useful feature, but you won't need to deal with multiple listeners for the same type of event in your code.

There is a way to capture all AWT events. Although doing this isn't useful for a real game, it can be helpful for debugging your code or seeing what events get dispatched. The following code captures all the events by creating an AWTEventListener and prints the events to the console:

```
Toolkit.getDefaultToolkit().addAWTEventListener(
    new AWTEventListener() {
        public void eventDispatched(AWTEvent event) {
            System.out.println(event);
        }
    }, -1);
```

Remember, don't use something like this in a real game; use it only for debugging.

Keyboard Input

For a game, you want to use lots of keys, such as the arrow keys for movement and maybe the Control key for firing a weapon. We really aren't going to deal with things like text input—we can leave that for Swing components discussed later in this chapter.

To capture key events, you need to do two things: create a `KeyListener` and register the listener to receive events. To register a listener, just call the `addKeyListener()` method on the component that you want to receive key events on. For games here, that component is the full-screen window:

```
Window window = screen.getFullScreenWindow();
window.addKeyListener(keyListener);
```

To create a `KeyListener`, you just need to create an object that implements the `KeyListener` interface. The `KeyListener` interface has three methods: `keyPressed()`, `keyReleased()`, and `keyTyped()`. The "typed" event occurs when a key is first pressed and then repeatedly based on the key repeat rate. Receiving events when a key is "typed" is pretty useless for a game, so we just focus on the key presses and releases.

Each of these three methods takes a `KeyEvent` as a parameter. The `KeyEvent` object enables you to inspect what key was actually pressed or released, in the form of a *virtual key code*. A virtual key code is the Java-defined code to a particular keyboard key, but it is not the same as the character. For example, although Q and q are different characters, they have the same key code.

All the virtual key codes are defined in `KeyEvent` in the form VK_xxx. For example, the Q key has the key code `KeyEvent.VK_Q`. Most of the time, you can guess the name of a key code (such as VK_ENTER or VK_1), but be sure to look up the `KeyEvent` class in the Java API documentation for the full list of virtual key codes.

Now let's try it out. The `KeyTest` class in Listing 3.2 is an implementation of the `KeyListener` interface. It simply displays key press and release events to the screen. Press Escape to exit the program.

Listing 3.2   KeyTest.java

```java
import java.awt.event.KeyListener;
import java.awt.event.KeyEvent;
import java.util.LinkedList;

import com.brackeen.javagamebook.graphics.*;
import com.brackeen.javagamebook.test.GameCore;


/**
    A simple keyboard test. Displays keys pressed and released to
    the screen. Useful for debugging key input, too.
*/
public class KeyTest extends GameCore implements KeyListener {

    public static void main(String[] args) {
        new KeyTest().run();
    }

    private LinkedList messages = new LinkedList();

    public void init() {
        super.init();

        Window window = screen.getFullScreenWindow();

        // allow input of the TAB key and other keys normally
        // used for focus traversal
        window.setFocusTraversalKeysEnabled(false);

        // register this object as a key listener for the window
        window.addKeyListener(this);

        addMessage("KeyInputTest. Press Escape to exit");
    }


    // a method from the KeyListener interface
    public void keyPressed(KeyEvent e) {
```

```java
        int keyCode = e.getKeyCode();

        // exit the program
        if (keyCode == KeyEvent.VK_ESCAPE) {
            stop();
        }
        else {
            addMessage("Pressed: " +
                KeyEvent.getKeyText(keyCode));

            // make sure the key isn't processed for anything else
            e.consume();
        }
    }


    // a method from the KeyListener interface
    public void keyReleased(KeyEvent e) {
        int keyCode = e.getKeyCode();
        addMessage("Released: " + KeyEvent.getKeyText(keyCode));

        // make sure the key isn't processed for anything else
        e.consume();
    }


    // a method from the KeyListener interface
    public void keyTyped(KeyEvent e) {
        // this is called after the key is released - ignore it
        // make sure the key isn't processed for anything else
        e.consume();
    }


    /**
        Add a message to the list of messages.
    */
```

continues

Listing 3.2 KeyTest.java *continued*

```java
    public synchronized void addMessage(String message) {
        messages.add(message);
        if (messages.size() >= screen.getHeight() / FONT_SIZE) {
            messages.remove(0);
        }
    }


    /**
        Draw the list of messages
    */
    public synchronized void draw(Graphics2D g) {

        Window window = screen.getFullScreenWindow();

        g.setRenderingHint(
            RenderingHints.KEY_TEXT_ANTIALIASING,
            RenderingHints.VALUE_TEXT_ANTIALIAS_ON);

        // draw background
        g.setColor(window.getBackground());
        g.fillRect(0, 0, screen.getWidth(), screen.getHeight());

        // draw messages
        g.setColor(window.getForeground());
        int y = FONT_SIZE;
        for (int i=0; i<messages.size(); i++) {
            g.drawString((String)messages.get(i), 5, y);
            y+=FONT_SIZE;
        }
    }
}
```

You should note a couple things about this code. First, the init() method uses this line:

```java
window.setFocusTraversalKeysEnabled(false);
```

This, of course, disables focus traversal keys. Focus traversal keys are the keys pressed to change the keyboard focus from one component to another. For example, on a web page, you've probably pressed Tab to move from field to field in a form. Normally, the Tab key event is swallowed up by the AWT's focus traversal code, but in this case we want to receive the Tab key event. Calling this method allows us to do so.

If you're curious what the various focus traversal keys are, call the `getFocusTraversalKeys()` method.

The Tab key isn't the only key that can cause some strange behavior. The Alt key can also cause a problem. On most systems, the Alt key is used to activate a *mnemonic*. A mnemonic is a shortcut or accelerator key for a particular user interface element. For example, pressing Alt+F activates the File menu on most applications that have a menu bar. The AWT thinks the next key pressed after Alt is a mnemonic and ignores the key. To disable this, in `KeyTest` you stop every `KeyEvent` in each `KeyListener` from being processed in the default manner by calling this:

```
e.consume();
```

This makes sure no other object processes the Alt key (or whatever modifier key activates a mnemonic), so the Alt key is treated like a normal key.

A side effect to `KeyTest` is that it's a useful program for testing how keys behave on different systems. "Gasp! You mean key input isn't the same on all systems?" Unfortunately, no, it's not.

Let's take key repetition for an example. When the user holds down a key, the operating system sends multiple events for that key. In a text editor, for example, when you hold down the Q key, several Qs appear. On some systems (such as Linux), both the key press and the key release event are sent for each key repeat. On other systems (such as Windows), only the key press event is sent for each repetition, and the key release event isn't sent until the user actually releases the key.

Also, there could be other subtle differences, such as the Windows Start key behaving differently depending on what version of Windows is running. Or, the key behavior could be different depending on what Java VM is running.

Luckily, these differences aren't drastic; most of the time, you won't have to deal with them.

Mouse Input

The keyboard is fundamentally just a board with a bunch of buttons on it, but the mouse is a more complicated device. Not only does it have buttons (depending on the mouse, it could have one, two, three, or more buttons), but it also has movement and possibly a scroll wheel.

That said, you can receive three different types of mouse events:

> ➤ Mouse button clicks

> ➤ Mouse motion

> ➤ Mouse wheel scrolls

Mouse buttons behave like keyboard buttons, but without the key repetition. Mouse motion is broken down into x and y screen coordinates. Finally, mouse wheel events tell how far the wheel was scrolled.

Each mouse event type has its own listener: MouseListener, MouseMotionListener, and MouseWheelListener. Each listener takes a MouseEvent as a parameter.

Like KeyListener, the MouseListener interface has methods for detecting mouse presses, releases, and clicks (pressing and then releasing). We'll ignore clicks in our games just as we ignore KeyTyped events and deal with just presses and releases. You can tell which button was pressed or released by calling the getButton() method of MouseEvent.

Also, the MouseListener interface has methods to signal when the mouse has entered and exited the component. Because the component we use covers the entire screen, we can ignore these methods as well.

For mouse movement, you can detect two types of motion with the MouseMotionListener interface: regular motion and drag motion. Drag motion events occur when the user moves the mouse while holding down a button. For either type of motion, you can get the current position of the mouse by calling the getX() and getY() methods of MouseEvent.

The `MouseWheelListener` uses a subclass of `MouseEvent` called `MouseWheelEvent`. It has the method `getWheelRotation()` to inspect how much the mouse wheel was moved. Negative values mean scrolling up, and positive values mean scrolling down.

Okay, that's enough about mouse input basics. Let's create a program to try it out.

The `MouseTest` program in Listing 3.3 draws a "Hello World!" message at the location of the mouse. When you click, it changes to "trail mode" by drawing the last 10 mouse locations to make a "trail." Scrolling with the mouse wheel causes the text color to change. As before, press Escape to exit.

Listing 3.3   MouseTest.java

```
import java.awt.*;
import java.awt.event.*;
import java.util.LinkedList;

import com.brackeen.javagamebook.graphics.*;
import com.brackeen.javagamebook.test.GameCore;

/**
    A simple mouse test. Draws a "Hello World!" message at
    the location of the cursor. Click to change to "trail mode"
    to draw several messages. Use the mouse wheel (if available)
    to change colors.
*/
public class MouseTest extends GameCore implements KeyListener,
    MouseMotionListener, MouseListener, MouseWheelListener

{

    public static void main(String[] args) {
        new MouseTest().run();
    }

    private static final int TRAIL_SIZE = 10;
    private static final Color[] COLORS = {
        Color.white, Color.black, Color.yellow, Color.magenta
```

continues

Listing 3.3 MouseTest.java *continued*

```java
    };

    private LinkedList trailList;
    private boolean trailMode;
    private int colorIndex;


    public void init() {
        super.init();
        trailList = new LinkedList();

        Window window = screen.getFullScreenWindow();
        window.addMouseListener(this);
        window.addMouseMotionListener(this);
        window.addMouseWheelListener(this);
        window.addKeyListener(this);
    }


    public synchronized void draw(Graphics2D g) {
        int count = trailList.size();

        if (count > 1 && !trailMode) {
            count = 1;
        }

        Window window = screen.getFullScreenWindow();

        // draw background
        g.setColor(window.getBackground());
        g.fillRect(0, 0, screen.getWidth(), screen.getHeight());

        // draw instructions
        g.setRenderingHint(
                RenderingHints.KEY_TEXT_ANTIALIASING,
                RenderingHints.VALUE_TEXT_ANTIALIAS_ON);
        g.setColor(window.getForeground());
```

```
        g.drawString("MouseTest. Press Escape to exit.", 5,
            FONT_SIZE);

        // draw mouse trail
        for (int i=0; i<count; i++) {
            Point p = (Point)trailList.get(i);
            g.drawString("Hello World!", p.x, p.y);
        }
    }
}


// from the MouseListener interface
public void mousePressed(MouseEvent e) {
    trailMode = !trailMode;
}


// from the MouseListener interface
public void mouseReleased(MouseEvent e) {
    // do nothing
}


// from the MouseListener interface
public void mouseClicked(MouseEvent e) {
    // called after mouse is released - ignore it
}


// from the MouseListener interface
public void mouseEntered(MouseEvent e) {
    mouseMoved(e);
}


// from the MouseListener interface
public void mouseExited(MouseEvent e) {
    mouseMoved(e);
```

continues

Listing 3.3 MouseTest.java *continued*

```java
    }


    // from the MouseMotionListener interface
    public void mouseDragged(MouseEvent e) {
        mouseMoved(e);
    }


    // from the MouseMotionListener interface
    public synchronized void mouseMoved(MouseEvent e) {
        Point p = new Point(e.getX(), e.getY());
        trailList.addFirst(p);
        while (trailList.size() > TRAIL_SIZE) {
            trailList.removeLast();
        }
    }


    // from the MouseWheelListener interface
    public void mouseWheelMoved(MouseWheelEvent e) {
        colorIndex = (colorIndex + e.getWheelRotation()) %
            COLORS.length;

        if (colorIndex < 0) {
            colorIndex+=COLORS.length;
        }
        Window window = screen.getFullScreenWindow();
        window.setForeground(COLORS[colorIndex]);
    }


    // from the KeyListener interface
    public void keyPressed(KeyEvent e) {
        if (e.getKeyCode() == KeyEvent.VK_ESCAPE) {
            // exit the program
            stop();
```

```
        }
    }


    // from the KeyListener interface
    public void keyReleased(KeyEvent e) {
        // do nothing
    }


    // from the KeyListener interface
    public void keyTyped(KeyEvent e) {
        // do nothing
    }
}
```

The code in MouseTest is pretty straightforward, and there really isn't any weird behavior to work around. Whenever the mouse is moved, a new Point object is added to trailList. The Point object contains an x and y value. At most, 10 Points exist in the list. If the trail mode is on, the draw() method simply draws "Hello World" at every Point in the list. Otherwise, "Hello World" is drawn only at the first Point. Clicking the mouse toggles trail mode on and off.

Mouselook-Style Mouse Movement

If you've ever played a first-person shooter such as *Quake III*, you've probably used the *mouselook* feature. The mouselook feature allows your player to look around by moving the mouse. For example, if you move the mouse left, your player looks left. The cool thing about this feature is that you can keep moving the mouse as much as you want because the mouse isn't constrained to the screen. You can move the mouse until you get dizzy or run out of mousepad.

In the previous example, you could detect the location of the mouse on the screen, but when you moved the mouse too far left, the mouse would stop because it hits the edge of the screen. This obviously wouldn't work in a first-person shooter because you don't want to limit how much the player can look. Instead of detecting the absolute location of the mouse, you need to detect the relative motion, but how can you do this?

The Java API doesn't directly provide methods to detect the relative motion of the mouse, but there are ways to trick the mouse to do what you want.

To do this, you just need to make sure the mouse never hits the edge of the screen. Every time the mouse moves, you'll just reposition the mouse to the center of the screen. That way, the mouse will never be stopped by the edge of the screen, and you can always calculate how much the mouse has moved based on its previous location.

Here's a breakdown of how it works:

1. The mouse starts at the center of the screen.

2. The user moves the mouse, and you calculate how much it moved.

3. You send an event to reposition the mouse to the center of the screen.

4. When you detect that that the mouse was recentered, you ignore the event.

You can reposition the mouse using the `Robot` class. No, the `Robot` class doesn't cause a real robot to come to your desk and move the mouse for you. The `Robot` class was designed to automate testing of graphical applications. Besides being capable of programmatically moving the mouse, it has all sorts of functions for doing things such as emulating key presses and making screen captures. Moving the mouse is as simple as you'd like it to be:

```
robot.mouseMove(x, y);
```

One note of caution: The `Robot` class might not work on some rare systems. Some systems don't allow you to programmatically move the mouse or emulate key presses. However, it will work just fine on modern Windows and Linux systems.

For the `Robot` privileged, let's try it out. You're not ready to create a first-person shooter just yet, so you'll create a simple background pattern that can be scrolled indefinitely using mouselook. The `MouselookTest` class in Listing 3.4 does just that. For the curious, you can turn off mouselook by pressing the spacebar. As usual, press Escape to exit.

Listing 3.4 MouselookTest.java

```java
import java.awt.*;
import java.awt.event.*;
import javax.swing.SwingUtilities;

import com.brackeen.javagamebook.graphics.*;
import com.brackeen.javagamebook.test.GameCore;

/**
    A simple mouselook test. Using mouselook, the user can
    virtually move the mouse in any direction indefinitely.
    Without mouselook, the mouse stops when it hits the edge of
    the screen.
    <p>Mouselook works by recentering the mouse whenever it is
    moved, so it can always measure the relative mouse movement,
    and the mouse never hits the edge of the screen.
*/
public class MouselookTest extends GameCore
    implements MouseMotionListener, KeyListener
{

    public static void main(String[] args) {
        new MouselookTest().run();
    }

    private Image bgImage;
    private Robot robot;
    private Point mouseLocation;
    private Point centerLocation;
    private Point imageLocation;
    private boolean relativeMouseMode;
    private boolean isRecentering;

    public void init() {
        super.init();
        mouseLocation = new Point();
        centerLocation = new Point();
        imageLocation = new Point();
```

continues

Listing 3.4 MouselookTest.java *continued*

```
        relativeMouseMode = true;
        isRecentering = false;

        try {
            robot = new Robot();
            recenterMouse();
            mouseLocation.x = centerLocation.x;
            mouseLocation.y = centerLocation.y;
        }
        catch (AWTException ex) {
            System.out.println("Couldn't create Robot!");
        }
        Window window = screen.getFullScreenWindow();
        window.addMouseMotionListener(this);
        window.addKeyListener(this);
        bgImage = loadImage("../images/background.jpg");
    }


    public synchronized void draw(Graphics2D g) {

        int w = screen.getWidth();
        int h = screen.getHeight();

        // make sure position is correct
        imageLocation.x %= w;
        imageLocation.y %= screen.getHeight();
        if (imageLocation.x < 0) {
            imageLocation.x += w;
        }
        if (imageLocation.y < 0) {
            imageLocation.y += screen.getHeight();
        }

        // draw the image in four places to cover the screen
        int x = imageLocation.x;
        int y = imageLocation.y;
        g.drawImage(bgImage, x, y, null);
```

```
        g.drawImage(bgImage, x-w, y, null);
        g.drawImage(bgImage, x, y-h, null);
        g.drawImage(bgImage, x-w, y-h, null);

        // draw instructions
        g.setRenderingHint(
                RenderingHints.KEY_TEXT_ANTIALIASING,
                RenderingHints.VALUE_TEXT_ANTIALIAS_ON);
        g.drawString("Press Space to change mouse modes.", 5,
            FONT_SIZE);
        g.drawString("Press Escape to exit.", 5, FONT_SIZE*2);
    }


    /**
        Uses the Robot class to try to position the mouse in the
        center of the screen.
        <p>Note that use of the Robot class may not be available
        on all platforms.
    */
    private synchronized void recenterMouse() {
        Window window = screen.getFullScreenWindow();
        if (robot != null && window.isShowing()) {
            centerLocation.x = window.getWidth() / 2;
            centerLocation.y = window.getHeight() / 2;
            SwingUtilities.convertPointToScreen(centerLocation,
                    window);
            isRecentering = true;
            robot.mouseMove(centerLocation.x, centerLocation.y);
        }
    }


    // from the MouseMotionListener interface
    public void mouseDragged(MouseEvent e) {
        mouseMoved(e);
    }
```

continues

Listing 3.4 MouselookTest.java   *continued*

```java
// from the MouseMotionListener interface
public synchronized void mouseMoved(MouseEvent e) {
    // this event is from re-centering the mouse - ignore it
    if (isRecentering &&
        centerLocation.x == e.getX() &&
        centerLocation.y == e.getY())
    {
        isRecentering = false;
    }
    else {
        int dx = e.getX() - mouseLocation.x;
        int dy = e.getY() - mouseLocation.y;
        imageLocation.x += dx;
        imageLocation.y += dy;
        // recenter the mouse
        if (relativeMouseMode) {
            recenterMouse();
        }

    }

    mouseLocation.x = e.getX();
    mouseLocation.y = e.getY();

}


// from the KeyListener interface
public void keyPressed(KeyEvent e) {
    if (e.getKeyCode() == KeyEvent.VK_ESCAPE) {
        // exit the program
        stop();
    }
    else if (e.getKeyCode() == KeyEvent.VK_SPACE) {
        // change relative mouse mode
        relativeMouseMode = !relativeMouseMode;
    }
```

```
    }


    // from the KeyListener interface
    public void keyReleased(KeyEvent e) {
        // do nothing
    }


    // from the KeyListener interface
    public void keyTyped(KeyEvent e) {
        // do nothing
    }

}
```

In the code, if a `Robot` object can't be created, it throws an `AWTException`. Here, you just ignore the exception and print a message to the console.

When you tell the `Robot` class to move the mouse, the mouse move event might not immediately occur. Some normal mouse move events could be sent before the recentering event. Therefore, the code checks whether the mouse move event results in the mouse being located in the center of the screen. If it is, it's treated as a recentering event, and the event is ignored. Otherwise, the event is treated as a normal mouse move event.

Hiding the Cursor

In the `MouselookTest` example, you might notice that the mouse cursor in the middle of the screen doesn't look too attractive. When it's recentered, it might flicker or you might see the mouse move for a brief moment. What you need to do next is just hide the mouse cursor.

Luckily, the Java API has methods to change the mouse cursor. Unluckily, the Java API doesn't define an invisible cursor.

Some of the cursors it does define are listed here:

➤ CROSSHAIR_CURSOR   A cursor in the shape of a plus sign

➤ DEFAULT_CURSOR   The normal arrow cursor

➤ HAND_CURSOR   The hand cursor that you normally see when you mouse over hyperlinks on web pages

➤ TEXT_CURSOR   The text cursor, normally I-shaped

➤ WAIT_CURSOR   The wait cursor, normally an hourglass

All is not lost, however. The Java API enables you to create your own cursors using custom images, so you'll just create a cursor that has a blank image. You do this by calling the createCustomCursor() method of the Toolkit class:

```
Cursor invisibleCursor =
    Toolkit.getDefaultToolkit().createCustomCursor(
    Toolkit.getDefaultToolkit().getImage(""),
    new Point(0,0),
    "invisible");
```

Here you just create an "invalid" image, which the Toolkit interprets as being an invisible cursor. You can change the cursor for your games by calling the setCursor() method:

```
Window window = screen.getFullScreenWindow();
window.setCursor(invisibleCursor);
```

Later, you can get the default cursor by calling Cursor's getPredefinedCursor() method:

```
Cursor normalCursor =
    Cursor.getPredefinedCursor(Cursor.DEFAULT_CURSOR);
```

That's it! Now you can use this code so you don't have to look at that annoying cursor anymore.

Creating an Input Manager

Now that you've mastered key and mouse input, you'll put it all together and create an Input Manager. But first, let's point out some of the pitfalls of the previous code examples that you need to address in your Input Manager.

One thing you might have noticed about the previous examples is all of the synchronized methods. Remember that all events are sent in from the AWT event dispatch thread, which is a different thread than the main thread. Obviously, you don't want to modify the game state (change sprite locations, for example) in the middle of a draw operation, so the methods are synchronized to make sure this doesn't happen.

For future games, however, you will want to handle all input at a specific point in the game loop. You can do this easily by setting Boolean variables when a key is pressed. For example, a `jumpIsPressed` Boolean can be set in the `keyPressed()` method when the spacebar is pressed, and later in the game loop, you can check whether the `jumpIsPressed` variable is set. If it is, the code can make the player jump.

Also, for some actions, such as jumping, you want to perform an action only on the initial key press. For other actions, such as moving, you want to move as long as the key is down. For jumping, if you want to detect initial key presses for jumping, whenever we see that `jumpIsPressed` is `true` in the game loop, you can just set it to `false`. That way, the player won't jump again until he or she presses the key again.

But what if the user doesn't like pressing the spacebar to jump and instead wants to press Control? Simple: In that case, you just say, "Sorry, you can't do that."

Okay, maybe you'll be nice and let the user configure the keyboard. To do this, you need to be able to map a generic action to a key and let the action be mapped to different keys on the fly. For now, put this on the wish list for your `InputManager` class.

To sum it up, here's everything you want `InputManager` to do:

➤ Handle all key and mouse events, including relative mouse movement.

➤ Save the events so you can query them precisely when you want to, instead of changing game state in the AWT event dispatch thread.

➤ Detect the initial press for some keys and detect whether the key is held down for others.

➤ Map keys to generic game actions, such as mapping the spacebar to a jump action.

➤ Change the key mapping on the fly so the user can configure the keyboard.

First, let's focus on the generic game actions. The GameAction class in Listing 3.5 is easy to use, with methods such as isPressed() for keys and getAmount() to see how much the mouse has moved. It handles both initial press and normal key behavior, too. Finally, it has methods for the Input Manager to call, such as press() and release().

Listing 3.5   GameAction.java

```
package com.brackeen.javagamebook.input;

/**
    The GameAction class is an abstract to a user-initiated
    action, like jumping or moving. GameActions can be mapped
    to keys or the mouse with the InputManager.
*/
public class GameAction {

    /**
        Normal behavior. The isPressed() method returns true
        as long as the key is held down.
    */
    public static final int NORMAL = 0;

    /**
        Initial press behavior. The isPressed() method returns
        true only after the key is first pressed, and not again
        until the key is released and pressed again.
    */
    public static final int DETECT_INITAL_PRESS_ONLY = 1;

    private static final int STATE_RELEASED = 0;
    private static final int STATE_PRESSED = 1;
```

```
private static final int STATE_WAITING_FOR_RELEASE = 2;

private String name;
private int behavior;
private int amount;
private int state;

/**
    Create a new GameAction with the NORMAL behavior.
*/
public GameAction(String name) {
    this(name, NORMAL);
}



/**
    Create a new GameAction with the specified behavior.
*/
public GameAction(String name, int behavior) {
    this.name = name;
    this.behavior = behavior;
    reset();
}



/**
    Gets the name of this GameAction.
*/
public String getName() {
    return name;
}



/**
    Resets this GameAction so that it appears like it hasn't
    been pressed.
*/
public void reset() {
```

continues

Listing 3.5   GameAction.java   *continued*

```
        state = STATE_RELEASED;
        amount = 0;
    }



    /**
        Taps this GameAction. Same as calling press() followed
        by release().
    */
    public synchronized void tap() {
        press();
        release();
    }



    /**
        Signals that the key was pressed.
    */
    public synchronized void press() {
        press(1);
    }



    /**
        Signals that the key was pressed a specified number of
        times, or that the mouse moved a specified distance.
    */
    public synchronized void press(int amount) {
        if (state != STATE_WAITING_FOR_RELEASE) {
            this.amount+=amount;
            state = STATE_PRESSED;
        }

    }



    /**
```

```
        Signals that the key was released
    */
    public synchronized void release() {
        state = STATE_RELEASED;
    }


    /**
        Returns whether the key was pressed or not since last
        checked.
    */
    public synchronized boolean isPressed() {
        return (getAmount() != 0);
    }


    /**
        For keys, this is the number of times the key was
        pressed since it was last checked.
        For mouse movement, this is the distance moved.
    */
    public synchronized int getAmount() {
        int retVal = amount;
        if (retVal != 0) {
            if (state == STATE_RELEASED) {
                amount = 0;
            }
            else if (behavior == DETECT_INITAL_PRESS_ONLY) {
                state = STATE_WAITING_FOR_RELEASE;
                amount = 0;
            }
        }
        return retVal;
    }
}
```

Finally, you'll create the `InputManager` class in Listing 3.6. The `InputManager` class has all the code from the previous input examples, including invisible cursors and relative mouse motion.

Also, it has code for mapping keys and mouse events to `GameActions`. When a key is pressed, the code checks to see whether a `GameAction` is mapped to that key and, if so, calls the `GameAction`'s `press()` method.

How does the mapping work? An array of `GameActions` is created. Each index in the array corresponds to a virtual key code. Most of the virtual key codes have a value that is less than 600, so the array of `GameActions` has a length of 600.

The mapping works similarly for mouse events. Because mouse events don't have codes, fake mouse codes are made up in `InputManager`. There are mouse codes for mouse movement (left, right, up, and down), mouse wheel scrolling, and mouse buttons.

Listing 3.6   InputManager.java

```
package com.brackeen.javagamebook.input;

import java.awt.*;
import java.awt.event.*;
import java.util.List;
import java.util.ArrayList;
import javax.swing.SwingUtilities;

/**
    The InputManager manages input of key and mouse events.
    Events are mapped to GameActions.
*/
public class InputManager implements KeyListener, MouseListener,
    MouseMotionListener, MouseWheelListener
{
    /**
        An invisible cursor.
    */
    public static final Cursor INVISIBLE_CURSOR =
```

```
        Toolkit.getDefaultToolkit().createCustomCursor(
            Toolkit.getDefaultToolkit().getImage(""),
            new Point(0,0),
            "invisible");

// mouse codes
public static final int MOUSE_MOVE_LEFT = 0;
public static final int MOUSE_MOVE_RIGHT = 1;
public static final int MOUSE_MOVE_UP = 2;
public static final int MOUSE_MOVE_DOWN = 3;
public static final int MOUSE_WHEEL_UP = 4;
public static final int MOUSE_WHEEL_DOWN = 5;
public static final int MOUSE_BUTTON_1 = 6;
public static final int MOUSE_BUTTON_2 = 7;
public static final int MOUSE_BUTTON_3 = 8;

private static final int NUM_MOUSE_CODES = 9;

// key codes are defined in java.awt.KeyEvent.
// most of the codes (except for some rare ones like
// "alt graph") are less than 600.
private static final int NUM_KEY_CODES = 600;

private GameAction[] keyActions =
    new GameAction[NUM_KEY_CODES];
private GameAction[] mouseActions =
    new GameAction[NUM_MOUSE_CODES];

private Point mouseLocation;
private Point centerLocation;
private Component comp;
private Robot robot;
private boolean isRecentering;

/**
    Creates a new InputManager that listens to input from the
    specified component.
*/
```

continues

Listing 3.6 InputManager.java *continued*

```java
public InputManager(Component comp) {
    this.comp = comp;
    mouseLocation = new Point();
    centerLocation = new Point();

    // register key and mouse listeners
    comp.addKeyListener(this);
    comp.addMouseListener(this);
    comp.addMouseMotionListener(this);
    comp.addMouseWheelListener(this);

    // allow input of the TAB key and other keys normally
    // used for focus traversal
    comp.setFocusTraversalKeysEnabled(false);
}


/**
    Sets the cursor on this InputManager's input component.
*/
public void setCursor(Cursor cursor) {
    comp.setCursor(cursor);
}


/**
    Sets whether relative mouse mode is on or not. For
    relative mouse mode, the mouse is "locked" in the center
    of the screen, and only the changed in mouse movement
    is measured. In normal mode, the mouse is free to move
    about the screen.
*/
public void setRelativeMouseMode(boolean mode) {
    if (mode == isRelativeMouseMode()) {
        return;
    }
```

```
        if (mode) {
            try {
                robot = new Robot();
                recenterMouse();
            }
            catch (AWTException ex) {
                // couldn't create robot!
                robot = null;
            }
        }
        else {
            robot = null;
        }
}


/**
    Returns whether or not relative mouse mode is on.
*/
public boolean isRelativeMouseMode() {
    return (robot != null);
}


/**
    Maps a GameAction to a specific key. The key codes are
    defined in java.awt.KeyEvent. If the key already has
    a GameAction mapped to it, the new GameAction overwrites
    it.
*/
public void mapToKey(GameAction gameAction, int keyCode) {
    keyActions[keyCode] = gameAction;
}


/**
    Maps a GameAction to a specific mouse action. The mouse
    codes are defined here in InputManager (MOUSE_MOVE_LEFT,
```

continues

Listing 3.6 InputManager.java *continued*

```
        MOUSE_BUTTON_1, etc). If the mouse action already has
        a GameAction mapped to it, the new GameAction overwrites
        it.
    */
    public void mapToMouse(GameAction gameAction,
        int mouseCode)
    {
        mouseActions[mouseCode] = gameAction;
    }



    /**
        Clears all mapped keys and mouse actions to this
        GameAction.
    */
    public void clearMap(GameAction gameAction) {
        for (int i=0; i<keyActions.length; i++) {
            if (keyActions[i] == gameAction) {
                keyActions[i] = null;
            }
        }

        for (int i=0; i<mouseActions.length; i++) {
            if (mouseActions[i] == gameAction) {
                mouseActions[i] = null;
            }
        }

        gameAction.reset();
    }



    /**
        Gets a List of names of the keys and mouse actions mapped
        to this GameAction. Each entry in the List is a String.
    */
    public List getMaps(GameAction gameCode) {
```

```
        ArrayList list = new ArrayList();

        for (int i=0; i<keyActions.length; i++) {
            if (keyActions[i] == gameCode) {
                list.add(getKeyName(i));
            }
        }

        for (int i=0; i<mouseActions.length; i++) {
            if (mouseActions[i] == gameCode) {
                list.add(getMouseName(i));
            }
        }
        return list;
}


/**
    Resets all GameActions so they appear like they haven't
    been pressed.
*/
public void resetAllGameActions() {
    for (int i=0; i<keyActions.length; i++) {
        if (keyActions[i] != null) {
            keyActions[i].reset();
        }
    }

    for (int i=0; i<mouseActions.length; i++) {
        if (mouseActions[i] != null) {
            mouseActions[i].reset();
        }
    }
}


/**
    Gets the name of a key code.
```

continues

Listing 3.6 InputManager.java *continued*

```java
*/
public static String getKeyName(int keyCode) {
    return KeyEvent.getKeyText(keyCode);
}


/**
    Gets the name of a mouse code.
*/
public static String getMouseName(int mouseCode) {
    switch (mouseCode) {
        case MOUSE_MOVE_LEFT: return "Mouse Left";
        case MOUSE_MOVE_RIGHT: return "Mouse Right";
        case MOUSE_MOVE_UP: return "Mouse Up";
        case MOUSE_MOVE_DOWN: return "Mouse Down";
        case MOUSE_WHEEL_UP: return "Mouse Wheel Up";
        case MOUSE_WHEEL_DOWN: return "Mouse Wheel Down";
        case MOUSE_BUTTON_1: return "Mouse Button 1";
        case MOUSE_BUTTON_2: return "Mouse Button 2";
        case MOUSE_BUTTON_3: return "Mouse Button 3";
        default: return "Unknown mouse code " + mouseCode;
    }
}


/**
    Gets the x position of the mouse.
*/
public int getMouseX() {
    return mouseLocation.x;
}


/**
    Gets the y position of the mouse.
*/
public int getMouseY() {
```

```java
        return mouseLocation.y;
}


/**
    Uses the Robot class to try to position the mouse in the
    center of the screen.
    <p>Note that use of the Robot class may not be available
    on all platforms.
*/
private synchronized void recenterMouse() {
    if (robot != null && comp.isShowing()) {
        centerLocation.x = comp.getWidth() / 2;
        centerLocation.y = comp.getHeight() / 2;
        SwingUtilities.convertPointToScreen(centerLocation,
            comp);
        isRecentering = true;
        robot.mouseMove(centerLocation.x, centerLocation.y);
    }
}


private GameAction getKeyAction(KeyEvent e) {
    int keyCode = e.getKeyCode();
    if (keyCode < keyActions.length) {
        return keyActions[keyCode];
    }
    else {
        return null;
    }
}

/**
    Gets the mouse code for the button specified in this
    MouseEvent.
*/
public static int getMouseButtonCode(MouseEvent e) {
      switch (e.getButton()) {
```

continues

Listing 3.6 InputManager.java   *continued*

```java
            case MouseEvent.BUTTON1:
                return MOUSE_BUTTON_1;
            case MouseEvent.BUTTON2:
                return MOUSE_BUTTON_2;
            case MouseEvent.BUTTON3:
                return MOUSE_BUTTON_3;
            default:
                return -1;
        }
    }


    private GameAction getMouseButtonAction(MouseEvent e) {
        int mouseCode = getMouseButtonCode(e);
        if (mouseCode != -1) {
            return mouseActions[mouseCode];
        }
        else {
            return null;
        }
    }


    // from the KeyListener interface
    public void keyPressed(KeyEvent e) {
        GameAction gameAction = getKeyAction(e);
        if (gameAction != null) {
            gameAction.press();
        }
        // make sure the key isn't processed for anything else
        e.consume();
    }


    // from the KeyListener interface
    public void keyReleased(KeyEvent e) {
        GameAction gameAction = getKeyAction(e);
```

```java
        if (gameAction != null) {
            gameAction.release();
        }
        // make sure the key isn't processed for anything else
        e.consume();
    }


    // from the KeyListener interface
    public void keyTyped(KeyEvent e) {
        // make sure the key isn't processed for anything else
        e.consume();
    }


    // from the MouseListener interface
    public void mousePressed(MouseEvent e) {
        GameAction gameAction = getMouseButtonAction(e);
        if (gameAction != null) {
            gameAction.press();
        }
    }


    // from the MouseListener interface
    public void mouseReleased(MouseEvent e) {
        GameAction gameAction = getMouseButtonAction(e);
        if (gameAction != null) {
            gameAction.release();
        }
    }


    // from the MouseListener interface
    public void mouseClicked(MouseEvent e) {
        // do nothing
    }
```

continues

Listing 3.6 InputManager.java *continued*

```java
// from the MouseListener interface
public void mouseEntered(MouseEvent e) {
    mouseMoved(e);
}


// from the MouseListener interface
public void mouseExited(MouseEvent e) {
    mouseMoved(e);
}


// from the MouseMotionListener interface
public void mouseDragged(MouseEvent e) {
    mouseMoved(e);
}


// from the MouseMotionListener interface
public synchronized void mouseMoved(MouseEvent e) {
    // this event is from re-centering the mouse - ignore it
    if (isRecentering &&
        centerLocation.x == e.getX() &&
        centerLocation.y == e.getY())
    {
        isRecentering = false;
    }
    else {
        int dx = e.getX() - mouseLocation.x;
        int dy = e.getY() - mouseLocation.y;
        mouseHelper(MOUSE_MOVE_LEFT, MOUSE_MOVE_RIGHT, dx);
        mouseHelper(MOUSE_MOVE_UP, MOUSE_MOVE_DOWN, dy);

        if (isRelativeMouseMode()) {
            recenterMouse();
        }
    }
}
```

```
        mouseLocation.x = e.getX();
        mouseLocation.y = e.getY();


    }



    // from the MouseWheelListener interface
    public void mouseWheelMoved(MouseWheelEvent e) {
        mouseHelper(MOUSE_WHEEL_UP, MOUSE_WHEEL_DOWN,
            e.getWheelRotation());
    }

    private void mouseHelper(int codeNeg, int codePos,
        int amount)
    {
        GameAction gameAction;
        if (amount < 0) {
            gameAction = mouseActions[codeNeg];
        }
        else {
            gameAction = mouseActions[codePos];
        }
        if (gameAction != null) {
            gameAction.press(Math.abs(amount));
            gameAction.release();
        }
    }

}
```

Whew! That's a lot of code. One additional feature that InputManager has is functionality to get the name of the key or mouse event. The KeyEvent class already has this functionality for keys, but you implement your own for mouse events. This feature, used in the getKeyName() and getMouseName() methods, is useful for telling the user which keys do what, and you'll use it later for letting the user configure the keyboard.

Also, the InputManager has the resetAllGameActions() method, which resets any GameActions that are currently "pressed." This can be useful for situations such as switching from the main menu to the game. Without clearing the GameActions, pressing the spacebar in a menu could cause the player to jump later, as soon as the game starts.

Using the Input Manager

To try out the InputManager, first you'll create a simple game. Later, you'll add functionality to allow the player to configure the keyboard.

The first game you create will have the hero be able to move left and right and to jump. Also, you'll add the capability to pause the game. It's not really a game yet—there are no bad guys or even goals—but it's a step closer.

Pausing the Game

Believe it or not, the user occasionally might want to temporarily stop playing a game to get a soda or run to the restroom. And to top it off, the user will want to—gasp!—return to the game later, expecting to play it right where he or she left off. Can you believe it?

Also, you'll probably want to pause the game when switching the game to the main menu, unless you want the game to continue running while the menu is displayed.

So, let's add the ability to pause the game. But what really happens when a game is paused? Basically two things: The game object and animations aren't updated, and input is ignored (except for the key to unpause the game, of course). To do this, you'll modify the animation loop a bit and check for input and update game objects only if the game isn't paused. For example:

```
if (!paused) {
    checkInput();
    updateGameObjects();
}
```

Of course, you'll continue drawing the screen even if the game is paused. You could do extra drawing as well, such as having an animated "paused" message. Also, you'll be sure to update the paused state when the user presses the P key, for example.

Adding Gravity

The other thing you want to add is the capability for the player to jump. If this were outer space, the player would jump and keep moving forever (or, at least, until the player hits a comet or something). But this isn't outer space. This is the real world, and in the real world there's gravity. (The real world also has spherical blue people, right?) Adding gravity makes the player "fall" back down to the ground after jumping into the air.

To implement gravity in your game, you need to understand what gravity really is. The effect of gravity is essentially a downward acceleration. Whereas speed is the measurement of distance over time, such as miles per hour, acceleration is the measurement of change in speed, such as when a car can accelerate from 0 to 60 miles per hour in 7 seconds.

In the `Sprite` class from the last chapter, the sprite's position is updated based on its velocity. Likewise, for a sprite with gravity, the sprite's velocity is updated based on its acceleration. For example:

```
velocityY = velocityY + GRAVITY * elapsedTime;
```

The gravity of the Earth is about 9.8 meters per second, but that's not important for your game. You're using pixels and milliseconds as your measurements, so you'll just use whatever value "feels" right. Here, the value of `GRAVITY` is `0.002`. This allows the player to jump but prevents the player from jumping past the top of the screen.

We'll sum up the gravity feature in the `Player` class in Listing 3.7. The `Player` class extends the `Sprite` class, adding gravity along with the capability to jump.

Listing 3.7   Player.java

```
import com.brackeen.javagamebook.graphics.*;

/**
```

continues

Listing 3.7 Player.java *continued*

```
    The Player class extends the Sprite class to add states
    (STATE_NORMAL or STATE_JUMPING) and gravity.
*/
public class Player extends Sprite {

    public static final int STATE_NORMAL = 0;
    public static final int STATE_JUMPING = 1;

    public static final float SPEED = .3f;
    public static final float GRAVITY = .002f;

    private int floorY;
    private int state;

    public Player(Animation anim) {
        super(anim);
        state = STATE_NORMAL;
    }


    /**
        Gets the state of the Player (either STATE_NORMAL or
        STATE_JUMPING);
    */
    public int getState() {
        return state;
    }


    /**
        Sets the state of the Player (either STATE_NORMAL or
        STATE_JUMPING);
    */
    public void setState(int state) {
        this.state = state;
    }
```

```
/**
    Sets the location of "floor", where the Player starts
    and lands after jumping.
*/
public void setFloorY(int floorY) {
    this.floorY = floorY;
    setY(floorY);
}



/**
    Causes the Player to jump
*/
public void jump() {
    setVelocityY(-1);
    state = STATE_JUMPING;
}



/**
    Updates the player's position and animation. Also, sets the
    Player's state to NORMAL if a jumping Player landed on
    the floor.
*/
public void update(long elapsedTime) {
    // set vertical velocity (gravity effect)
    if (getState() == STATE_JUMPING) {
        setVelocityY(getVelocityY() + GRAVITY * elapsedTime);
    }

    // move player
    super.update(elapsedTime);

    // check if player landed on floor
    if (getState() == STATE_JUMPING && getY() >= floorY) {
        setVelocityY(0);
        setY(floorY);
```

continues

Listing 3.7   Player.java   *continued*

```
                setState(STATE_NORMAL);
        }


    }
}
```

The `Player` class is state-based. It has two states: NORMAL and JUMPING. Because the `Player` keeps track of its state, it can make checks to make sure to jump only if the player is in the normal state and also to apply gravity only if the player is jumping.

The `Player` also must be told where the "floor" is. This is set with the `setFloorY()` method.

Now you have everything you need to create a simple game to try out the `InputManager`. The `InputManagerTest` class in Listing 3.8 enables the user to move the player and make the player jump. It creates several `GameActions` to provide this functionality. Each `GameAction` is mapped to at least one key or mouse event. Finally, it even allows you to pause the game!

Move the player by using the arrow keys, and press the spacebar to jump. The P key pauses the game, and, as always, pressing Escape exits the game.

Listing 3.8   InputManagerTest.java

```
import java.awt.*;
import java.awt.event.KeyEvent;
import javax.swing.ImageIcon;

import com.brackeen.javagamebook.graphics.*;
import com.brackeen.javagamebook.input.*;
import com.brackeen.javagamebook.test.GameCore;

/**
    InputManagerTest tests the InputManager with a simple
    run-and-jump mechanism. The player moves and jumps using
    the arrow keys and the spacebar.
    <p>Also, InputManagerTest demonstrates pausing a game
```

```
        by not updating the game elements if the game is paused.
*/
public class InputManagerTest extends GameCore {

    public static void main(String[] args) {
        new InputManagerTest().run();
    }

    protected GameAction jump;
    protected GameAction exit;
    protected GameAction moveLeft;
    protected GameAction moveRight;
    protected GameAction pause;
    protected InputManager inputManager;
    private Player player;
    private Image bgImage;
    private boolean paused;

    public void init() {
        super.init();
        Window window = screen.getFullScreenWindow();
        inputManager = new InputManager(window);

        // use these lines for relative mouse mode
        //inputManager.setRelativeMouseMode(true);
        //inputManager.setCursor(InputManager.INVISIBLE_CURSOR);

        createGameActions();
        createSprite();
        paused = false;
    }


    /**
        Tests whether the game is paused or not.
    */
    public boolean isPaused() {
        return paused;
```

continues

Listing 3.8 InputManagerTest.java *continued*

```java
    }


    /**
        Sets the paused state.
    */
    public void setPaused(boolean p) {
        if (paused != p) {
            this.paused = p;
            inputManager.resetAllGameActions();
        }
    }


    public void update(long elapsedTime) {
        // check input that can happen whether paused or not
        checkSystemInput();

        if (!isPaused()) {
            // check game input
            checkGameInput();

            // update sprite
            player.update(elapsedTime);
        }
    }


    /**
        Checks input from GameActions that can be pressed
        regardless of whether the game is paused or not.
    */
    public void checkSystemInput() {
        if (pause.isPressed()) {
            setPaused(!isPaused());
        }
        if (exit.isPressed()) {
```

```
            stop();
        }
    }



/**
    Checks input from GameActions that can be pressed
    only when the game is not paused.
*/
public void checkGameInput() {
    float velocityX = 0;
    if (moveLeft.isPressed()) {
        velocityX-=Player.SPEED;
    }
    if (moveRight.isPressed()) {
        velocityX+=Player.SPEED;
    }
    player.setVelocityX(velocityX);

    if (jump.isPressed() &&
        player.getState() != Player.STATE_JUMPING)
    {
        player.jump();
    }
}


public void draw(Graphics2D g) {
    // draw background
    g.drawImage(bgImage, 0, 0, null);

    // draw sprite
    g.drawImage(player.getImage(),
        Math.round(player.getX()),
        Math.round(player.getY()),
        null);
}
```

continues

Listing 3.8 InputManagerTest.java *continued*

```java
/**
    Creates GameActions and maps them to keys.
*/
public void createGameActions() {
    jump = new GameAction("jump",
        GameAction.DETECT_INITAL_PRESS_ONLY);
    exit = new GameAction("exit",
        GameAction.DETECT_INITAL_PRESS_ONLY);
    moveLeft = new GameAction("moveLeft");
    moveRight = new GameAction("moveRight");
    pause = new GameAction("pause",
        GameAction.DETECT_INITAL_PRESS_ONLY);

    inputManager.mapToKey(exit, KeyEvent.VK_ESCAPE);
    inputManager.mapToKey(pause, KeyEvent.VK_P);

    // jump with spacebar or mouse button
    inputManager.mapToKey(jump, KeyEvent.VK_SPACE);
    inputManager.mapToMouse(jump,
        InputManager.MOUSE_BUTTON_1);

    // move with the arrow keys...
    inputManager.mapToKey(moveLeft, KeyEvent.VK_LEFT);
    inputManager.mapToKey(moveRight, KeyEvent.VK_RIGHT);

    // ... or with A and D.
    inputManager.mapToKey(moveLeft, KeyEvent.VK_A);
    inputManager.mapToKey(moveRight, KeyEvent.VK_D);

    // use these lines to map player movement to the mouse
    //inputManager.mapToMouse(moveLeft,
    //   InputManager.MOUSE_MOVE_LEFT);
    //inputManager.mapToMouse(moveRight,
    //   InputManager.MOUSE_MOVE_RIGHT);
```

```
    }


    /**
        Load images and creates the Player sprite.
    */
    private void createSprite() {
        // load images
        bgImage = loadImage("../images/background.jpg");
        Image player1 = loadImage("../images/player1.png");
        Image player2 = loadImage("../images/player2.png");
        Image player3 = loadImage("../images/player3.png");

        // create animation
        Animation anim = new Animation();
        anim.addFrame(player1, 250);
        anim.addFrame(player2, 150);
        anim.addFrame(player1, 150);
        anim.addFrame(player2, 150);
        anim.addFrame(player3, 200);
        anim.addFrame(player2, 150);

        player = new Player(anim);
        player.setFloorY(screen.getHeight() -
player.getHeight());
    }

}
```

In InputManagerTest, whenever the user pauses or unpauses the game, the GameActions are reset. This makes sure that any keys pressed while the game is paused don't take effect when the game is unpaused.

Another thing to note is that there are a few lines of code commented out. These lines turn on relative mouse mode and map the mouse movement to the player's movement. Uncomment these lines if you want to use the mouse to move the player. Either way, the mouse button causes the player to jump.

Designing Intuitive User Interfaces

Now we're going to move on to something that you'll find in all games: the user interface. The user interface isn't just what keys to press to get the player to move; it's also the opening menu, the configuration screens, and the in-game, onscreen buttons.

Designing a useful, intuitive, and attractive user interface is one of the most important aspects of creating a game. Lacking a useful interface can make a game no fun to play.

User Interface Design Tips

When you are creating the user interface for your game, the basic rule is to keep it simple, descriptive, and fast. Here are a few tips:

➤ Keep your user interfaces simple and uncluttered. Not every option has to be presented to the user at once. Instead, you can keep the most common or most useful options on the main screen and provide an easy way to view the less common options.

➤ Make sure every option or button is easy to get to. If it takes too many clicks to find certain functionality, it will frustrate the users.

➤ Use Tooltips. Tooltips are pop-up descriptions that appear when your mouse lingers over a particular object. They can tell you what a button does or give status on other user interface elements. Tooltips are a quick way to answer the question "What's this?" Swing has Tooltips built in, so it's easy to implement.

➤ Give the user a response to every action. This can be as simple as playing a sound or displaying the wait cursor. Also avoid pauses between the time a user clicks something and when the action occurs.

➤ Test your user interfaces on someone you know. What a button does might be obvious to you, but to someone else it could be confusing. When you test to see how someone else might use your interface, don't say anything—just watch to see what the person does and take notes. Remember, in the real world, when users play your game, you're not going to be right next to them telling them what to do!

➤ After some people test your user interfaces, ask them what they think would be easier or more useful. Also ask them whether the icons make sense. Don't hold them back or say things like, "But the code won't work that way." Just listen and take everything into consideration. Who knows, later you might find a way to make the code "work that way" after all.

➤ Be prepared to overhaul your user interface if it just doesn't work. You might have spent days coding and creating icons for what you thought was the perfect interface, but don't fret if you have to throw it all away. If it's to create a better game, it's worth it.

Finding friends or relatives to help you test your user interface shouldn't be too much a problem, but if it is, you can always lure people with goodies such as free pizza.

Using Swing Components

You've heard Swing mentioned here and there so far in this book, but what exactly is it? Swing, in a nutshell, is a set of classes used to create user interface elements. It includes all sorts of common components such as windows, buttons, pop-up menus, drop-down lists, text-input boxes, check boxes, and labels.

You'll use Swing components to implement your user interfaces. You've already seen Swing's `JFrame` used as the full-screen window in the `ScreenManager` class. Actually, you used a `JFrame` object instead of just a `Window` or `Frame` just so you can integrate with Swing.

Because Swing renders its own components, you can draw Swing components in your own rendering loop. This is great news because it means that you can integrate all of Swing's functionality into your full-screen games. You don't have to reinvent the wheel by creating your own user interface architecture! Plus, Swing can be customized with your own look-and-feels, so you can create an individual look for your user interface.

Swing has a pretty large API, and this is a game book, not a Swing book, so not everything about Swing is discussed here. If you're looking for the nitty-gritty details on Swing, plenty of books and web tutorials are available on the subject. What we will talk about is getting Swing to work with your games and creating some basic user interface components. So let's get started!

Swing Basics

Creating most Swing components is straightforward. Most user interface elements are a class, so you just have to create an instance of that class. For example, to create an OK button, simply create a new JButton object:

```
JButton okButton = new JButton("OK");
```

This creates a JButton with all the default parameters and with a text label of OK. Swing components start with J, as in JLabel, JTextField, and so on, and they're all derived from the JComponent class.

Next, you need to actually add it to the screen so it can be clicked on. The components are added to a top-level container, which, in this case, is the JFrame. Components are added to the JFrame's content pane. When a component is added to the content pane, Swing handles all the mouse clicks for it, so you don't have to. Here's an example of adding a button to the content pane:

```
JFrame frame = screen.getFullScreenWindow();
frame.getContentPane().add(okButton);
```

This adds the button to the content pane, but by default the button is not positioned anywhere and will probably just end up in the upper-left corner of the screen. You can do two things to fix this. The first is to lay out all components explicitly by calling the setLocation() method:

```
okButton.setLocation(200, 100);
```

Explicit layout is easy to implement, but it's not perfect. Imagine you lay out two buttons next to each other. On your system, it could look fine, but on a different system, the default Swing look and feel could create larger buttons that end up overlapping each other or otherwise just look unattractive.

The second way to lay out components is to use a LayoutManager. LayoutManagers take each component's size into consideration and position the components according to certain rules. Several different LayoutManagers exist, and each positions components in different ways. FlowLayout, for example, lays out components on the screen in a left-to-right, top-to-bottom fashion.

To use a `LayoutManager`, call the `setLayout()` method of the content pane. Here's an example of using a `FlowLayout`:

```
frame.getContentPane().setLayout(new FlowLayout());
```

This makes sure all components added to the content pane are repositioned according to `FlowLayout`'s rules.

Tricking Swing to Work in Full-Screen Mode

As mentioned before, all components are added to `JFrame`'s content pane. The content pane is actually a component in another container—namely, `JFrame`'s layered pane. The layered pane contains many different "layers" of components so that certain components can appear on top of others. For example, Tooltips and pop-up menus should appear above components in the content pane, so they are positioned above the content pane in the layered pane.

To draw all the Swing components, just draw what's in the layered pane by calling the `paintComponents()` method. This is done in the animation loop:

```
// draw our graphics
draw(g);
// draw Swing components
JFrame frame = screen.getFullScreenWindow();
frame.getLayeredPane().paintComponents(g);
```

Two problems arise here. The first problem is that the content pane actually draws its background, which hides everything underneath it. You want your Swing components to appear above your own graphics. This problem is easy to fix—you just need to make the content pane transparent:

```
if (contentPane instanceof JComponent) {
    ((JComponent)contentPane).setOpaque(false);
}
```

This code makes sure the content pane draws only its components, not its background.

The second problem has to do with how Swing renders its components. In a normal Swing application, you don't have to call `paintComponents()`—Swing does all its rendering automatically in the AWT event dispatch thread. However, you haven't turned off this functionality. Whenever a component changes its appearance, such as when you hold down a button and it appears to be pressed, the component requests that it be repainted by calling the `repaint()` method.

Obviously, you don't want any rendering to occur in the AWT event dispatch thread because this can conflict with your own rendering and cause flicker or other conflicts. In your code, you could potentially ignore the repaint request because if a button is pressed, its appearance will change in the next draw in the animation loop.

To fix this, how do you capture the repaint requests and ignore them? Well, all repaint requests go to a `RepaintManager`, which basically manages the requests and forwards the requests to actually paint the components. You can simply override this functionality by creating a `NullRepaintManager`, shown in Listing 3.9. `NullRepaintManager` simply causes repaint requests to disappear.

Listing 3.9   NullRepaintManager.java

```java
package com.brackeen.javagamebook.graphics;

import javax.swing.RepaintManager;
import javax.swing.JComponent;

/**
    The NullRepaintManager is a RepaintManager that doesn't
    do any repainting. Useful when all the rendering is done
    manually by the application.
*/
public class NullRepaintManager extends RepaintManager {

    /**
        Installs the NullRepaintManager.
    */
    public static void install() {
        RepaintManager repaintManager = new NullRepaintManager();
        repaintManager.setDoubleBufferingEnabled(false);
```

```
        RepaintManager.setCurrentManager(repaintManager);
    }

    public void addInvalidComponent(JComponent c) {
        // do nothing
    }

    public void addDirtyRegion(JComponent c, int x, int y,
        int w, int h)
    {
        // do nothing
    }

    public void markCompletelyDirty(JComponent c) {
        // do nothing
    }

    public void paintDirtyRegions() {
        // do nothing
    }

}
```

Easy enough right? `NullRepaintManager` extends the default `RepaintManager` class and overrides key methods to simply do nothing. That way, repaint events aren't sent to the AWT, and you won't see flickering components.

That's it! To install the `NullRepaintManager`, just call `NullRepaintManager.install()`.

> **NOTE**
> Keep in mind that Swing components aren't thread-safe. When a Swing component is visible, you don't want to modify its state at the same time the AWT event dispatch thread modifies its state. If you need to modify a Swing component after it is visible, do so in the event dispatch thread, like this:

```
EventQueue.invokeAndWait(new Runnable() {
    public void run() {
        doSomething();
    }
});
```

This invokes the code in the Runnable in the AWT event dispatch thread and waits for it to finish. Alternatively, you can use `invokeLater()` if you don't need to wait for it to finish.

Creating a Simple Menu

Now you can extend your game from `InputManagerTest` to add a simple user interface with pause, configuration, and exit buttons. For now, the configuration button won't do anything, but you'll go ahead and put it on the screen.

First, when you click a button, what exactly happens? Swing sees the click and checks to see whether the button has any `ActionListeners`. If it does, those `ActionListeners` are notified that the button was clicked in the AWT event dispatch thread.

Like `KeyListener` or `MouseListener`, `ActionListener` is an interface that any object can implement. It has one method named `actionPerformed()` that takes an `ActionEvent` as a parameter. You can check to see what component generated the event by calling `ActionEvent`'s `getSource()` method. For example:

```
public void actionPerformed(ActionEvent e) {
    Object src = e.getSource();
    if (src == okButton) {
        // do something
    }
}
```

Finally, in the user interface, you can do a few things to your buttons to make them more usable:

> ► Add Tooltips. Just call something like `setToolTip("Hello World")`, and Swing handles the rest.

➤ Use icons. Instead of having text in your buttons, you can use icons. There can be different icons for the default, rollover, and pressed states.

➤ Hide the default look. You want your icons to appear by themselves, so turn off the button's border and call `setContentAreaFilled(false)` to make sure the button background isn't drawn.

➤ Change the cursor. Make the cursor appear as a hand when you roll over a button by calling the `setCursor()` method.

➤ Turn off key focus. If the button is focusable, the button can "steal" keyboard focus away from the game when it is clicked. To fix this, just call `setFocusable(false)`. The only drawback to this is that only the mouse can activate a button.

All of these changes are done in the `createButton()` method of the `MenuTest` class. The `MenuTest` class, in Listing 3.10, extends the `InputManagerTest` and adds the buttons on top of it. For a screen capture of `MenuTest`, see Figure 3.1.

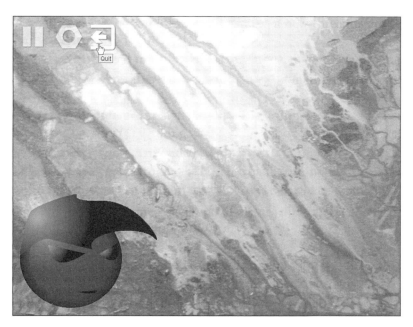

Figure 3.1 The `MenuTest` class creates a simple user interface on top of your game.

Listing 3.10 MenuTest.java

```java
import java.awt.*;
import java.awt.event.*;
import javax.swing.*;

import com.brackeen.javagamebook.graphics.*;
import com.brackeen.javagamebook.input.GameAction;

/**
    Extends the InputManagerTest demo and adds Swing buttons
    for pause, config and quit.
*/
public class MenuTest extends InputManagerTest
    implements ActionListener
{

    public static void main(String[] args) {
        new MenuTest().run();
    }

    protected GameAction configAction;

    private JButton playButton;
    private JButton configButton;
    private JButton quitButton;
    private JButton pauseButton;
    private JPanel playButtonSpace;

    public void init() {
        super.init();
        // make sure Swing components don't paint themselves
        NullRepaintManager.install();

        // create an additional GameAction for "config"
        configAction = new GameAction("config");

        // create buttons
        quitButton = createButton("quit", "Quit");
```

```
        playButton = createButton("play", "Continue");
        pauseButton = createButton("pause", "Pause");
        configButton = createButton("config", "Change Settings");

        // create the space where the play/pause buttons go.
        playButtonSpace = new JPanel();
        playButtonSpace.setOpaque(false);
        playButtonSpace.add(pauseButton);

        JFrame frame = super.screen.getFullScreenWindow();
        Container contentPane = frame.getContentPane();

        // make sure the content pane is transparent
        if (contentPane instanceof JComponent) {
            ((JComponent)contentPane).setOpaque(false);
        }

        // add components to the screen's content pane
        contentPane.setLayout(new FlowLayout(FlowLayout.LEFT));
        contentPane.add(playButtonSpace);
        contentPane.add(configButton);
        contentPane.add(quitButton);

        // explicitly lay out components (needed on some systems)
        frame.validate();
    }


    /**
        Extends InputManagerTest's functionality to draw all
        Swing components.
    */
    public void draw(Graphics2D g) {
        super.draw(g);
        JFrame frame = super.screen.getFullScreenWindow();

        // the layered pane contains things like popups (tooltips,
```

continues

Listing 3.10   MenuTest.java   *continued*

```java
            // popup menus) and the content pane.
            frame.getLayeredPane().paintComponents(g);
        }


    /**
        Changes the pause/play button whenever the pause state
        changes.
    */
    public void setPaused(boolean p) {
        super.setPaused(p);
        playButtonSpace.removeAll();
        if (isPaused()) {
            playButtonSpace.add(playButton);
        }
        else {
            playButtonSpace.add(pauseButton);
        }
    }


    /**
        Called by the AWT event dispatch thread when a button is
        pressed.
    */
    public void actionPerformed(ActionEvent e) {
        Object src = e.getSource();
        if (src == quitButton) {
            // fire the "exit" gameAction
            super.exit.tap();
        }
        else if (src == configButton) {
            // doesn't do anything (for now)
            configAction.tap();
        }
        else if (src == playButton || src == pauseButton) {
            // fire the "pause" gameAction
```

```
            super.pause.tap();
        }
    }



    /**
        Creates a Swing JButton. The image used for the button is
        located at "../images/menu/" + name + ".png". The image is
        modified to create a "default" look (translucent) and a
        "pressed" look (moved down and to the right).
        <p>The button doesn't use Swing's look-and-feel and
        instead just uses the image.
    */
    public JButton createButton(String name, String toolTip) {

        // load the image
        String imagePath = "../images/menu/" + name + ".png";
        ImageIcon iconRollover = new ImageIcon(imagePath);
        int w = iconRollover.getIconWidth();
        int h = iconRollover.getIconHeight();

        // get the cursor for this button
        Cursor cursor =
            Cursor.getPredefinedCursor(Cursor.HAND_CURSOR);

        // make translucent default image
        Image image = screen.createCompatibleImage(w, h,
            Transparency.TRANSLUCENT);
        Graphics2D g = (Graphics2D)image.getGraphics();
        Composite alpha = AlphaComposite.getInstance(
            AlphaComposite.SRC_OVER, .5f);
        g.setComposite(alpha);
        g.drawImage(iconRollover.getImage(), 0, 0, null);
        g.dispose();
        ImageIcon iconDefault = new ImageIcon(image);

        // make a pressed image
```

continues

Listing 3.10 MenuTest.java *continued*

```
        image = screen.createCompatibleImage(w, h,
            Transparency.TRANSLUCENT);
        g = (Graphics2D)image.getGraphics();
        g.drawImage(iconRollover.getImage(), 2, 2, null);
        g.dispose();
        ImageIcon iconPressed = new ImageIcon(image);

        // create the button
        JButton button = new JButton();
        button.addActionListener(this);
        button.setIgnoreRepaint(true);
        button.setFocusable(false);
        button.setToolTipText(toolTip);
        button.setBorder(null);
        button.setContentAreaFilled(false);
        button.setCursor(cursor);
        button.setIcon(iconDefault);
        button.setRolloverIcon(iconRollover);
        button.setPressedIcon(iconPressed);

        return button;
    }

}
```

In MenuTest, only one PNG image exists for each button. The other images are generated in code when the program starts.

The loaded image is treated as the rollover image, shown when the mouse is over the button. The default image is a slightly faded image that is created by copying the rollover image with an AlphaComposite of 0.5. The AlphaComposite class simply signifies to the Graphics2D class to blend the source image with its destination, creating a translucent effect. Finally, offsetting the rollover image by a few pixels creates the pressed image. This makes the pressed image look like the user is pressing the button down.

Another note about `MenuTest` is how pausing works in the interface. When the game is paused, the pause button becomes a play button. To achieve this functionality, the pause button is placed in a `JPanel`, which is a container for other components. When the user pauses or unpauses the game, the `JPanel`'s contents are changed to display the correct button.

Of course, the configuration button in `MenuTest` doesn't do anything—yet.

Letting the Player Configure the Keyboard

Finally, you'll add a feature we've been planning for a while: the ability to let the user configure the keyboard, as shown in Figure 3.2.

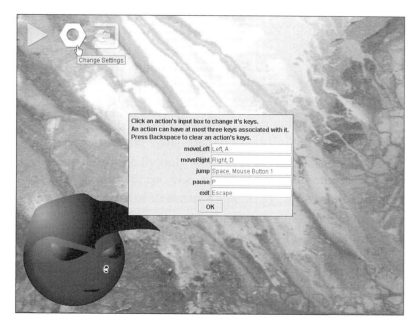

Figure 3.2   The Configure dialog box enables the user to customize the game controls.

This feature enables the user to map any key or mouse event to any game action. All the user has to do is select a game action and press a key or click the mouse, and that key is assigned to the game action.

The keyboard configuration feature can be broken into two parts:

1. First, you need to actually create the configuration dialog box.

2. Second, you need to create a special component that enables the user to enter a key or mouse click.

Creating the Configuration dialog box is not a difficult task. The dialog box lists all the possible game actions for a game and also contains instructions and an OK button. The dialog box itself is a JPanel, and everything within the dialog box can be created using a series of components, panels, and layouts.

Creating the special input component is a little more difficult. You need this component to display what key is currently mapped to a game action, and also to enable the user to press a key or a mouse button to change its setting. When input is done, you'll also have to make sure that the input component gives the keyboard focus back to the game's main window.

The component that you create is called InputComponent, and it's an inner class of the KeyConfigTest class in Listing 3.11.

InputComponent is a subclass of JTextField. Although a normal JTextField component enables the user to type in any amount of plain text, you want the user to type only one key or mouse click, so you need to override JTextField's input methods. Normally, you would create a KeyListener and MouseListener to listen for the input events, but this time you're going to get keys in a different way. That's right, there's more than one way to get input events.

Every Swing component is an instance of the Component class. The Component class has methods such as processKeyEvent() and processMouseEvent(). The methods work just like the KeyListener or MouseListener methods. All you have to do is override these methods and enable input events by calling the enableEvents() method.

The result is pretty much the same as if you had used listeners. This is just to show you an alternative.

Listing 3.11   KeyConfigTest.java

```java
import java.awt.event.*;
import java.awt.*;
import java.util.List;
import java.util.ArrayList;
import javax.swing.*;
import javax.swing.border.Border;

import com.brackeen.javagamebook.graphics.*;
import com.brackeen.javagamebook.input.*;

/**
    The KeyConfigTest class extends the MenuTest demo to add
    a dialog box to configure the keyboard keys.
*/
public class KeyConfigTest extends MenuTest {

    public static void main(String[] args) {
        new KeyConfigTest().run();
    }

    private static final String INSTRUCTIONS =
        "<html>Click an action's input box to change its keys." +
        "<br>An action can have at most three keys associated " +
        "with it.<br>Press Backspace to clear an action's keys.";

    private JPanel dialog;
    private JButton okButton;
    private List inputs;

    public void init() {
        super.init();

        inputs = new ArrayList();

        // create the list of GameActions and mapped keys
        JPanel configPanel = new JPanel(new GridLayout(5,2,2,2));
        addActionConfig(configPanel, moveLeft);
```

continues

Listing 3.11 KeyConfigTest.java *continued*

```java
        addActionConfig(configPanel, moveRight);
        addActionConfig(configPanel, jump);
        addActionConfig(configPanel, pause);
        addActionConfig(configPanel, exit);

        // create the panel containing the OK button
        JPanel bottomPanel = new JPanel(new FlowLayout());
        okButton = new JButton("OK");
        okButton.setFocusable(false);
        okButton.addActionListener(this);
        bottomPanel.add(okButton);

        // create the panel containing the instructions.
        JPanel topPanel = new JPanel(new FlowLayout());
        topPanel.add(new JLabel(INSTRUCTIONS));

        // create the dialog border
        Border border =
            BorderFactory.createLineBorder(Color.black);

        // create the config dialog.
        dialog = new JPanel(new BorderLayout());
        dialog.add(topPanel, BorderLayout.NORTH);
        dialog.add(configPanel, BorderLayout.CENTER);
        dialog.add(bottomPanel, BorderLayout.SOUTH);
        dialog.setBorder(border);
        dialog.setVisible(false);
        dialog.setSize(dialog.getPreferredSize());

        // center the dialog
        dialog.setLocation(
            (screen.getWidth() - dialog.getWidth()) / 2,
            (screen.getHeight() - dialog.getHeight()) / 2);

        // add the dialog to the "modal dialog" layer of the
        // screen's layered pane.
        screen.getFullScreenWindow().getLayeredPane().add(dialog,
```

```
                JLayeredPane.MODAL_LAYER);
}



/**
    Adds a label containing the name of the GameAction and an
    InputComponent used for changing the mapped keys.
*/
private void addActionConfig(JPanel configPanel,
    GameAction action)
{
    JLabel label = new JLabel(action.getName(), JLabel.RIGHT);
    InputComponent input = new InputComponent(action);
    configPanel.add(label);
    configPanel.add(input);
    inputs.add(input);
}



public void actionPerformed(ActionEvent e) {
    super.actionPerformed(e);
    if (e.getSource() == okButton) {
        // hides the config dialog
        configAction.tap();
    }
}



public void checkSystemInput() {
    super.checkSystemInput();
    if (configAction.isPressed()) {
        // hide or show the config dialog
        boolean show = !dialog.isVisible();
        dialog.setVisible(show);
        setPaused(show);
    }
}
```

continues

Listing 3.11 KeyConfigTest.java *continued*

```java
/**
    Resets the text displayed in each InputComponent, which
    is the names of the mapped keys.
*/
private void resetInputs() {
    for (int i=0; i<inputs.size(); i++) {
        ((InputComponent)inputs.get(i)).setText();
    }
}


/**
    The InputComponent class displays the keys mapped to a
    particular action and allows the user to change the mapped
    keys. The user selects an InputComponent by clicking it,
    then can press any key or mouse button (including the
    mouse wheel) to change the mapped value.
*/
class InputComponent extends JTextField  {

    private GameAction action;

    /**
        Creates a new InputComponent for the specified
        GameAction.
    */
    public InputComponent(GameAction action) {
        this.action = action;
        setText();
        enableEvents(KeyEvent.KEY_EVENT_MASK |
            MouseEvent.MOUSE_EVENT_MASK |
            MouseEvent.MOUSE_MOTION_EVENT_MASK |
            MouseEvent.MOUSE_WHEEL_EVENT_MASK);
    }
```

```
/**
    Sets the displayed text of this InputComponent to the
    names of the mapped keys.
*/
private void setText() {
    String text = "";
    List list = inputManager.getMaps(action);
    if (list.size() > 0) {
        for (int i=0; i<list.size(); i++) {
            text+=(String)list.get(i) + ", ";
        }
        // remove the last comma
        text = text.substring(0, text.length() - 2);
    }

    // make sure we don't get deadlock
    synchronized (getTreeLock()) {
        setText(text);
    }

}


/**
    Maps the GameAction for this InputComponent to the
    specified key or mouse action.
*/
private void mapGameAction(int code, boolean isMouseMap) {
    if (inputManager.getMaps(action).size() >= 3) {
        inputManager.clearMap(action);
    }
    if (isMouseMap) {
        inputManager.mapToMouse(action, code);
    }
    else {
        inputManager.mapToKey(action, code);
    }
```

continues

Listing 3.11   KeyConfigTest.java   *continued*

```java
            resetInputs();
            screen.getFullScreenWindow().requestFocus();
    }


    // alternative way to intercept key events
    protected void processKeyEvent(KeyEvent e) {
        if (e.getID() == e.KEY_PRESSED) {
            // if backspace is pressed, clear the map
            if (e.getKeyCode() == KeyEvent.VK_BACK_SPACE &&
                inputManager.getMaps(action).size() > 0)
            {
                inputManager.clearMap(action);
                setText("");
                screen.getFullScreenWindow().requestFocus();
            }
            else {
                mapGameAction(e.getKeyCode(), false);
            }
        }
        e.consume();
    }


    // alternative way to intercept mouse events
    protected void processMouseEvent(MouseEvent e) {
        if (e.getID() == e.MOUSE_PRESSED) {
            if (hasFocus()) {
                int code = InputManager.getMouseButtonCode(e);
                mapGameAction(code, true);
            }
            else {
                requestFocus();
            }
        }
        e.consume();
```

```
        }


        // alternative way to intercept mouse events
        protected void processMouseMotionEvent(MouseEvent e) {
            e.consume();
        }


        // alternative way to intercept mouse events
        protected void processMouseWheelEvent(MouseWheelEvent e)
{
            if (hasFocus()) {
                int code = InputManager.MOUSE_WHEEL_DOWN;
                if (e.getWheelRotation() < 0) {
                    code = InputManager.MOUSE_WHEEL_UP;
                }
                mapGameAction(code, true);
            }
            e.consume();
        }
    }
}
```

The KeyConfigTest class extends the MenuTest class. The init() method creates the configuration dialog box and adds it to the layered pane. The checkSystemInput() method is overridden to check to see whether the configuration button is pressed (the bolt icon); if it is, the configuration dialog box is shown.

InputComponent has several methods to get input and also maps keys and mouse events to game actions by using InputManager's methods. Also, InputComponent limits the number of keys that can be mapped to a game action to three. This is just an artificial limit; in reality, there isn't a limit to the number of mapped keys the InputManager can have per game action.

Also, `InputComponent` treats the Backspace key as special. If the Backspace key is pressed, it clears all the mapped keys for a game action. However, if an action has no mapped keys, the Backspace key is mapped to it.

One cool thing not mentioned before is that `JLabels` can contain HTML, the language of the web. Here, you use HTML to make the `JLabel` that contains the instructions to be broken up into multiple lines by using HTML's line break tag, `<br>`.

Summary

In this chapter, you learned how to receive keyboard and mouse input, and you created an Input Manager to handle it all. You also learned how to implement mouselook and hide the cursor, two small but critical features when designing a first-person game. Also, you got some tips on how to create intuitive user interfaces and how to use Swing to create those interfaces, even in full-screen mode.

Chapter 4

Sound Effects and Music

Unless you've never managed to figure out how to hook up speakers to your computer, you've noticed that games have sound effects—cool sound effects—and sometimes music, too.

When you're playing a game (with the speakers on, of course), you might hear the sound effects but not really notice them. That's because you expect to hear them—sometimes sound effects are something you notice only when they're missing. They're sort of like electricity. To sum it up, sound effects are an important part of a game. People expect to hear them, and they shouldn't be left out.

In this chapter, you'll learn the basics of playing sound and then move on to real-time sound-effect filters (such as echoes). You'll also create a sound manager to handle it all. In addition, you'll learn to play music (such as CD audio, MP3, Ogg Vorbis, and MIDI) and to make the music dynamically change to adapt to the state of the game.

Sound Basics

Sound is created when something vibrates through a medium. In this case, this medium is air and the vibration comes from the computer's speakers. Your eardrums pick up the vibration and signal your brain, which interprets it as sound.

This vibration through the air creates pressure fluctuations. Faster fluctuations create a higher sound wave frequency, leading you to hear a higher pitch. The amount of pressure in each fluctuation is known as its *amplitude*. Higher amplitude causes you to hear louder sound. In short, sound waves are just changing amplitudes over time, as shown in Figure 4.1.

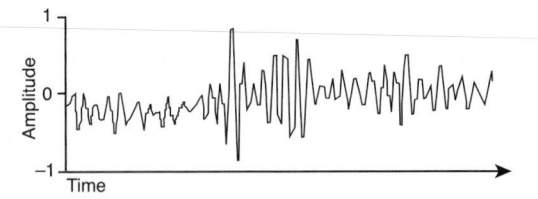

Figure 4.1   Sound waves are composed of changing amplitudes over time.

Digital sound, such as that in CD audio and many computer sound formats, contains sound as a series of discrete samples of the sound's amplitudes. The amount of samples stored per second is called the sample rate. CD audio, for example, has a sample rate of 44,100Hz. Of course, higher sample rates result in a more accurate audio representation, and lower sample rates mean poorer quality but a smaller file size. The samples themselves are typically 16 bits, giving 65,536 amplitude possibilities.

Many sound formats allow for multichannel sound. CD audio has two channels, one for a left speaker and one for a right speaker.

The Java Sound API

To play sampled sound in your Java game, you use the Java Sound API, in the package, `javax.sound.sampled`.

Java Sound can play sound formats with 8- or 16-bit samples with sample rates from 8000Hz to 48,000Hz. Also, it can play either mono or stereo sound. What sound format you use for your game depends on what you want. For these examples, we use 16-bit, mono, 44,100Hz sound.

If you are feeling brave, you could generate all these samples yourself in code, but typically you'll want to get sound samples from a sound file. Java Sound provides support for reading three sampled sound file formats: AIFF, AU, and WAV. All formats are very flexible, and it doesn't make much of a difference which one you use. We use the WAV format in our examples.

Some sound programs that you can use to create, record, and edit sounds are Pro Tools FREE (`www.digidesign.com/ptfree`), Cool Edit (`www.syntrillium.com/cooledit`), GoldWave (`www.goldwave.com`), and Audacity (`audacity.sourceforge.net`). Be sure to check out Chapter 17, "Creating Game Art and Sounds," to get some ideas on creating sounds.

Opening a Sound File

You can load a sound file with Java Sound using the `AudioSystem` class. The `AudioSystem` class contains several static functions, most of which you won't use. But it provides several `getAudioInputStream()` methods to open an audio file from the file system or other source, such as the Internet. These methods return an `AudioInputStream` object.

With an `AudioInputStream` object, you can read the samples of a sound without having to mess with the sound file header or other extra information in the file. Also, you can query the format of the sound by calling the `getFormat()` method:

```
File file = new File("sound.wav");
AudioInputStream stream = AudioSystem.getAudioInputStream(file);
AudioFormat format = stream.getFormat();
```

The `AudioFormat` class provides a way to get information about the format of the sound, such as the sample rate and number of channels. Also, it provides a way to get the frame size, which is the number of bytes required for every sample for every channel. For 16-bit stereo sound, the frame size is four, or 2 bytes for each sample (left and right). This can be useful if you want to find out how many bytes it takes to store a sound in memory. For example, a three-second-long sound with an audio format of 16-bit samples, stereo, 44,100Hz would be 44,100×3×4 bytes, or about 517KB. Using mono instead of stereo would cut the size in half.

Using a Line

Okay, now that you have a way to get the sound samples and the format they are in, what do you do with them? The answer is to feed them through a Line.

A *Line* is an interface to send or receive audio from the sound system. You can use Lines to send sound samples to the sound system to play or to receive sound from, say, a microphone.

The Line interface has several subinterfaces. The main Line subinterface used here is a SourceDataLine, which enables you to write audio data to the sound system.

Lines are created by using AudioSystem's getLine() method. You pass this method a Line.Info object, which specifies the type of Line you want to create. Line.Info has a DataLine.Info subclass, which you'll use to create your Lines because it contains information on the line's audio format.

Besides SourceDataLine, we'll touch on another Line called a Clip. A Clip does a lot of work for you, loading samples into memory from an AudioInputStream and feeding them to the audio system automatically. Here is how you would extend the AudioInputStream to play it using a Clip:

```
// specify what kind of line we want to create
DataLine.Info info = new DataLine.Info(Clip.class, format);
// create the line
Clip clip = (Clip)AudioSystem.getLine(info);
// load the samples from the stream
clip.open(stream);
// begin playback of the sound clip
clip.start();
```

Clips are convenient and easy to use, and are similar to AudioClips introduced in Java SDK 1.0. But Clips have some drawbacks. Java Sound has a limit to the number of Lines you can have open at the same time, which is usually a maximum of 32 Lines. Because Clips are Lines, this means you can open only a limited number of sounds, even before you play any one of them.

Also, although several Clips can play simultaneously, each Clip can play only one sound at a time. For example, if you want two or three explosions to play simultaneously, you'll need a Clip for each one.

Because of these drawbacks, in the next section you'll create a solution that will enable you to load any number of sounds and play several copies of each sound simultaneously.

Playing a Sound

To get started, you'll create a `SimpleSoundPlayer` to play sound. This class loads samples from an `AudioInputStream` into a byte array. It also plays sound from any `InputStream` by copying data from it to a Line.

In the `SimpleSoundPlayer` example in Listing 4.1, the samples loaded are converted to an `InputStream` by using a `ByteArrayInputStream`. This enables you to read samples from memory instead of from disk. You could just write the byte array directly to the Line, but you'll need to read from `InputStream`s to add some more advanced functionality later.

Because you're using a `ByteArrayInputStream` wrapped around a byte array, you can create as many `ByteArrayInputStream`s for the same sound as you want, so you can play multiple copies of the same sound simultaneously.

Listing 4.1   SimpleSoundPlayer.java

```
import java.io.*;
import javax.sound.sampled.*;

/**
    The SimpleSoundPlayer encapsulates a sound that can be opened
    from the file system and later played.
*/
public class SimpleSoundPlayer  {

    public static void main(String[] args) {
        // load a sound
```

continues

Listing 4.1 SimpleSoundPlayer.java *continued*

```java
        SimpleSoundPlayer sound =
            new SimpleSoundPlayer("../sounds/voice.wav");

        // create the stream to play
        InputStream stream =
            new ByteArrayInputStream(sound.getSamples());

        // play the sound
        sound.play(stream);

        // exit
        System.exit(0);
    }

    private AudioFormat format;
    private byte[] samples;

    /**
        Opens a sound from a file.
    */
    public SimpleSoundPlayer(String filename) {
        try {
            // open the audio input stream
            AudioInputStream stream =
                AudioSystem.getAudioInputStream(
                    new File(filename));

            format = stream.getFormat();

            // get the audio samples
            samples = getSamples(stream);
        }
        catch (UnsupportedAudioFileException ex) {
            ex.printStackTrace();
        }
        catch (IOException ex) {
            ex.printStackTrace();
        }
```

```
}


/**
    Gets the samples of this sound as a byte array.
*/
public byte[] getSamples() {
    return samples;
}


/**
    Gets the samples from an AudioInputStream as an array
    of bytes.
*/
private byte[] getSamples(AudioInputStream audioStream) {
    // get the number of bytes to read
    int length = (int)(audioStream.getFrameLength() *
        format.getFrameSize());

    // read the entire stream
    byte[] samples = new byte[length];
    DataInputStream is = new DataInputStream(audioStream);
    try {
        is.readFully(samples);
    }
    catch (IOException ex) {
        ex.printStackTrace();
    }

    // return the samples
    return samples;
}


/**
    Plays a stream. This method blocks (doesn't return) until
    the sound is finished playing.
```

continues

Listing 4.1 SimpleSoundPlayer.java *continued*

```java
*/
public void play(InputStream source) {

    // use a short, 100ms (1/10th sec) buffer for real-time
    // change to the sound stream
    int bufferSize = format.getFrameSize() *
        Math.round(format.getSampleRate() / 10);
    byte[] buffer = new byte[bufferSize];

    // create a line to play to
    SourceDataLine line;
    try {
        DataLine.Info info =
            new DataLine.Info(SourceDataLine.class, format);
        line = (SourceDataLine)AudioSystem.getLine(info);
        line.open(format, bufferSize);
    }
    catch (LineUnavailableException ex) {
        ex.printStackTrace();
        return;
    }

    // start the line
    line.start();

    // copy data to the line
    try {
        int numBytesRead = 0;
        while (numBytesRead != -1) {
            numBytesRead =
                source.read(buffer, 0, buffer.length);
            if (numBytesRead != -1) {
                line.write(buffer, 0, numBytesRead);
            }
        }
    }
    catch (IOException ex) {
        ex.printStackTrace();
```

```
    }

    // wait until all data is played
    line.drain();

    // close the line
    line.close();

    }

}
```

In SimpleSoundPlayer, the getSamples(AudioInputStream) method reads from an AudioInputStream and stores the data in the samples byte array. The play() method reads data from an InputStream to a buffer and then writes the buffer to a SourceDataLine, which plays the sound. Also, the main() method in SimpleSoundPlayer tests the class by playing the voice.wav sound.

Note that because of a bug in Java Sound, Java programs won't exit by themselves. Usually, the Java VM exits when there are only daemon threads running, but when you use Java Sound, a nondaemon thread always runs in the background. So, to exit your Java programs that use Java Sound, be sure to call System.exit(0).

Well, you can play sounds yourself, but what if you want to play a sound repeatedly in a loop? This could be really useful for background ambient sounds or, say, for a buzzing fly.

To loop sound, you don't even need to make any changes to the SimpleSoundPlayer. Instead of using a ByteArrayInputStream, you'll create a LoopingByteInputStream in Listing 4.2, which works similarly to ByteArrayInputStream. The only difference is that LoopingByteInputStream indefinitely reads the byte array in a loop until its close() method is called.

Listing 4.2   LoopingByteInputStream.java

```
package com.brackeen.javagamebook.util;

import java.io.ByteArrayInputStream;
import java.io.IOException;
```

continues

Listing 4.2   LoopingByteInputStream.java   *continued*

```java
/**
    The LoopingByteInputStream is a ByteArrayInputStream that
    loops indefinitely. The looping stops when the close() method
    is called.
    <p>Possible ideas to extend this class:<ul>
    <li>Add an option to only loop a certain number of times.
    </ul>
*/
public class LoopingByteInputStream extends ByteArrayInputStream {

    private boolean closed;

    /**
        Creates a new LoopingByteInputStream with the specified
        byte array. The array is not copied.
    */
    public LoopingByteInputStream(byte[] buffer) {
        super(buffer);
        closed = false;
    }


    /**
        Reads <code>length</code> bytes from the array. If the
        end of the array is reached, the reading starts over from
        the beginning of the array. Returns -1 if the array has
        been closed.
    */
    public int read(byte[] buffer, int offset, int length) {
        if (closed) {
            return -1;
        }
        int totalBytesRead = 0;
```

```
        while (totalBytesRead < length) {
            int numBytesRead = super.read(buffer,
                offset + totalBytesRead,
                length - totalBytesRead);

            if (numBytesRead > 0) {
                totalBytesRead += numBytesRead;
            }
            else {
                reset();
            }
        }
        return totalBytesRead;
    }


    /**
        Closes the stream. Future calls to the read() methods
        will return 1.
    */
    public void close() throws IOException {
        super.close();
        closed = true;
    }

}
```

There's nothing special about LoopingByteInputStream. It extends
ByteArrayInputStream, and whenever the end of the stream is reached, it calls the
reset() method to start reading from the beginning of the array again.

Now you can easily play and loop sound stored in a byte array. Also, because you have
access to all the sound samples, you can manipulate the samples to create different
effects, or filters.

Creating a Real-Time Sound Filter Architecture

Sound filters are simple audio processors that can modify existing sound samples, usually in real time. Sound filters, also known as *digital signal processors*, are used in audio production all the time—for example, to add distortion to a guitar or an echo to a voice.

Sound filters can make your game more dynamic. You might have a level in your game in which the player is wandering around a cave. In that case, you could add an echo to any sounds played. Or, if a rocket is whizzing past the player, you could make the sound shift from the left to right speaker.

In this section, you'll create a real-time sound filter architecture and create two filters: an echo filter and a simulated 3D sound filter.

First, you'll create the architecture. It is fairly straightforward—all you need is a simple class that can modify sound samples in a buffer. The `SoundFilter` class, in Listing 4.3, accomplishes this task. It's an abstract class that you can extend to create sound filters and has three important methods:

- `filter(byte[] buffer, int offset, int length)`   Filters an array of samples.

- `getRemainingSize()`   Gets the remaining size, in bytes, that this filter can play after the sound is finished. For example, an echo would play longer than the original sound.

- `reset()`   Resets the filter so that it can be used again on a different sound.

Because `SoundFilter` is an abstract class, it won't actually filter anything. Subclasses do the filtering work.

Listing 4.3   SoundFilter.java

```
package com.brackeen.javagamebook.sound;

/**
    An abstract class designed to filter sound samples.
    Since SoundFilters may use internal buffering of samples,
    a new SoundFilter object should be created for every sound
    played. However, SoundFilters can be reused after they are
```

```
        finished by calling the reset() method.
        Assumes all samples are 16-bit, signed, little-endian.
        format.
        @see FilteredSoundStream
*/
public abstract class SoundFilter{

    /**
        Resets this SoundFilter. Does nothing by default.
    */
    public void reset() {
        // do nothing
    }


    /**
        Gets the remaining size, in bytes, that this filter
        plays after the sound is finished. An example would
        be an echo that plays longer than its original sound.
        This method returns 0 by default.
    */
    public int getRemainingSize() {
        return 0;
    }


    /**
        Filters an array of samples. Samples should be in
        16-bit, signed, little-endian format.
    */
    public void filter(byte[] samples) {
        filter(samples, 0, samples.length);
    }


    /**
        Filters an array of samples. Samples should be in
        16-bit, signed, little-endian format. This method
        should be implemented by subclasses. Note that the
```

continues

Listing 4.3 SoundFilter.java *continued*

```
        offset and length are number of bytes, not samples.
    */
    public abstract void filter(
        byte[] samples, int offset, int length);


    /**
        Convenience method for getting a 16-bit sample from a
        byte array. Samples should be in 16-bit, signed,
        little-endian format.
    */
    public static short getSample(byte[] buffer, int position) {
        return (short)(
            ((buffer[position+1] & 0xff) << 8) |
            (buffer[position] & 0xff));
    }


    /**
        Convenience method for setting a 16-bit sample in a
        byte array. Samples should be in 16-bit, signed,
        little-endian format.
    */
    public static void setSample(byte[] buffer, int position,
        short sample)
    {
        buffer[position] = (byte)(sample & 0xff);
        buffer[position+1] = (byte)((sample >> 8) & 0xff);
    }

}
```

SoundFilter objects may contain state data, so a different SoundFilter object
should be used for every sound played.

To make it simple, allow the SoundFilter class to assume all sound is 16-bit, signed,
little-endian format. The term *little-endian* refers to the byte order of the data. Little-
endian means the least significant byte is stored first in the 16-bit sample; *big-endian*

means the most significant byte is stored first. Signed data means the samples have a signed bit, so they range from -32768 to 32767 instead of from 0 to 65536. Signed little-endian samples are the default for the WAV format.

Java Sound likes its data in bytes, so you must convert those bytes to 16-bit signed shorts to work with them. The `SoundFilter` class provides this with some static methods for getting and setting samples from a byte array: `getSample()` and `setSample()`.

Now you need an easy way to apply a `SoundFilter` to your sounds. You could apply the filter directly to your array of samples, but this would be a good idea only if you want the filter to be permanent because it would modify the original samples. Some filters, such as a 3D sound filter, rely on specific game elements that change in real time, so you need to apply your filters in real time, keeping the original sound intact.

Because the `SimpleSoundPlayer` class plays sounds from an `InputStream`, you can create a new `InputStream` subclass that applies a `SoundFilter`. The `FilteredSoundStream` class in Listing 4.4 does just that. Besides a `SoundFilter`, it takes an `InputStream` as a source (you'll use a `ByteArrayInputStream` or a `LoopingByteInputStream`, as before). This means that every byte read from the input source is passed through the `SoundFilter` to the sound player, resulting in a real-time filter that doesn't modify the original sound.

Listing 4.4   FilteredSoundStream.java

```
package com.brackeen.javagamebook.sound;

import java.io.FilterInputStream;
import java.io.InputStream;
import java.io.IOException;

/**
    The FilteredSoundStream class is a FilterInputStream that
    applies a SoundFilter to the underlying input stream.
    @see SoundFilter
*/
public class FilteredSoundStream extends FilterInputStream {
```

continues

Listing 4.4 FilteredSoundStream.java *continued*

```java
private static final int REMAINING_SIZE_UNKNOWN = -1;

private SoundFilter soundFilter;
private int remainingSize;

/**
    Creates a new FilteredSoundStream object with the
    specified InputStream and SoundFilter.
*/
public FilteredSoundStream(InputStream in,
    SoundFilter soundFilter)
{
    super(in);
    this.soundFilter = soundFilter;
    remainingSize = REMAINING_SIZE_UNKNOWN;
}


/**
    Overrides the FilterInputStream method to apply this
    filter whenever bytes are read
*/
public int read(byte[] samples, int offset, int length)
    throws IOException
{
    // read and filter the sound samples in the stream
    int bytesRead = super.read(samples, offset, length);
    if (bytesRead > 0) {
        soundFilter.filter(samples, offset, bytesRead);
        return bytesRead;
    }

    // if there are no remaining bytes in the sound stream,
    // check if the filter has any remaining bytes ("echoes").
    if (remainingSize == REMAINING_SIZE_UNKNOWN) {
        remainingSize = soundFilter.getRemainingSize();
        // round down to nearest multiple of 4
        // (typical frame size)
```

```
            remainingSize = remainingSize / 4 * 4;
        }
        if (remainingSize > 0) {
            length = Math.min(length, remainingSize);

            // clear the buffer
            for (int i=offset; i<offset+length; i++) {
                samples[i] = 0;
            }

            // filter the remaining bytes
            soundFilter.filter(samples, offset, length);
            remainingSize-=length;

            // return
            return length;
        }
        else {
            // end of stream
            return -1;
        }
    }

}
```

The `FilteredSoundStream` class extends the `FilterInputStream` class, which is an abstract class designed to filter an `InputStream`. It needs only one method, `read()`, to do its work.

As mentioned before, when a filter such as an echo is played, the echoes are often played back long after the original sound has finished playing. In `FilteredSoundStream`, if the `SoundFilter` still has some sound remaining in it, the `read()` method takes care of this by clearing the source buffer to all zeroes (making it silent) and then filtering that silent buffer. Finally, after everything is done, it returns -1 to signify the end of the stream.

We've talked a lot about an echo filter. Now you will actually create one.

Creating a Real-Time Echo Filter

You've just bought an SUV, and you decide to do what they do in those SUV commercials on TV: drive to the top of a mountain. Everyone who owns an SUV does that, right?

When you get to the top of the mountain, you step outside of your vehicle, absorb the beautiful scenery, and shout, "Hello!"

A second later, your echo replies in a quieter voice: "Hello!" Another second later, you might hear a second reply, even quieter than the first.

You've just discovered the two elements of an echo: delay and decay, as shown in Figure 4.2. The *delay* is how long it takes for the echo to occur. The *decay* is how much quieter the echo was compared to the original sound. In the case of you shouting on top of the mountain, the delay was about one second, and the decay was probably less than 50%. A decay value of 100% means the echo never dies out.

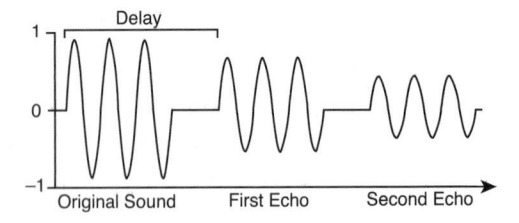

Figure 4.2   An echo repeats the original sound after a delay. The echoes are quieter than the original sound, at about a 60% decay.

Because your SoundFilter class is format-agnostic, it doesn't matter whether the sound you are filtering has a 44,100Hz sample rate or an 8,000Hz sample rate. So, you can't simply tell the echo filter the amount of time to delay. Instead, you tell it how many samples to delay. For a 44,100Hz sample rate and a one-second delay, tell the filter to delay by 44,100 samples. Remember, the delay counts from the beginning of the sound, not the end. So, if you want to delay one second after a 44,100Hz sound is finished, set the delay to the number of samples in the sound plus 44,100. Usually, though, you'll want the same echo delay across all sounds, which means that with longer sounds, the first echo might kick into action while the original sound is still playing.

The decay itself is simple enough. Use a value from 0 to 1, where a decay of 0 means no echo and a decay of 1 means the echo is the same volume as the original sound. Be careful with values close to 1, though. The "Hello!" example is innocent enough because the echo takes place after the sound is finished, but for many sounds, the echo occurs while the sound is still playing. For decay values close to 1, this will mostly likely lead to distortion because the parts of the original sound added to the echo could be larger that the 16-bit range of the sample.

When you're done exploring the mountain with your SUV, let's create the EchoFilter class. The EchoFilter class, in Listing 4.5, is a subclass of SoundFilter. To implement the echo, it keeps a delay buffer, which is a buffer of the same length as the amount of samples to delay. Whenever a sample is processed, the sample is copied to the delay buffer. This makes creating an echo effect easy. The echo is created by adding a decayed sample from the delay buffer to the original sample:

```
short newSample = (short)(oldSample + decay *
    delayBuffer[delayBufferPos]);
```

Because the delay buffer starts off as all zeroes, or silent, the first bit of sound heard is the original sound with no filter. Also, after the original sound is done playing, the FilteredSoundStream makes sure to keep filtering, using a silent original sound. That way, just the echoes are still heard. That's right, everything is happening according to plan.

Finally, getRemainingSize() is implemented to calculate the number of bytes that could be filtered after the original sound is done. Here, you use a calculation to make sure the final echo has 1% of the original sound's volume, which is close enough to being silent.

Listing 4.5   EchoFilter.java

```
package com.brackeen.javagamebook.sound;

/**
    The EchoFilter class is a SoundFilter that emulates an echo.
    @see FilteredSoundStream
*/
public class EchoFilter extends SoundFilter {
```

continues

Listing 4.5 EchoFilter.java *continued*

```java
private short[] delayBuffer;
private int delayBufferPos;
private float decay;

/**
    Creates an EchoFilter with the specified number of delay
    samples and the specified decay rate.
    <p>The number of delay samples specifies how long before
    the echo is initially heard. For a 1 second echo with
    mono, 44100Hz sound, use 44100 delay samples.
    <p>The decay value is how much the echo has decayed from
    the source. A decay value of .5 means the echo heard is
    half as loud as the source.
*/
public EchoFilter(int numDelaySamples, float decay) {
    delayBuffer = new short[numDelaySamples];
    this.decay = decay;
}


/**
    Gets the remaining size, in bytes, of samples that this
    filter can echo after the sound is done playing.
    Ensures that the sound will have decayed to below 1%
    of maximum volume (amplitude).
*/
public int getRemainingSize() {
    float finalDecay = 0.01f;
    // derived from Math.pow(decay,x) <= finalDecay
    int numRemainingBuffers = (int)Math.ceil(
        Math.log(finalDecay) / Math.log(decay));
    int bufferSize = delayBuffer.length * 2;

    return bufferSize * numRemainingBuffers;
}
```

```
/**
    Clears this EchoFilter's internal delay buffer.
*/
public void reset() {
    for (int i=0; i<delayBuffer.length; i++) {
        delayBuffer[i] = 0;
    }
    delayBufferPos = 0;
}



/**
    Filters the sound samples to add an echo. The samples
    played are added to the sound in the delay buffer
    multiplied by the decay rate. The result is then stored in
    the delay buffer, so multiple echoes are heard.
*/
public void filter(byte[] samples, int offset, int length) {

    for (int i=offset; i<offset+length; i+=2) {
        // update the sample
        short oldSample = getSample(samples, i);
        short newSample = (short)(oldSample + decay *
            delayBuffer[delayBufferPos]);
        setSample(samples, i, newSample);

        // update the delay buffer
        delayBuffer[delayBufferPos] = newSample;
        delayBufferPos++;
        if (delayBufferPos == delayBuffer.length) {
            delayBufferPos = 0;
        }
    }
}
```

}

As mentioned before, a new `SoundFilter` should be created for every sound played. Several sounds using the same `EchoFilter` could cause some weird things to happen because each sound would be copied to its delay buffer. If you need to reuse `SoundFilters` after they are done, call the `reset()` method.

For an example of how to use the `EchoFilter`, see `EchoFilterTest` in Listing 4.6. This example adds only a couple steps to `SimpleSoundPlayer`'s example: namely, creating an `EchoFilter` and a `FilteredSoundStream`.

Listing 4.6   EchoFilterTest.java

```
import java.io.*;

import com.brackeen.javagamebook.sound.*;

/**
    An example of playing a sound with an echo filter.
    @see EchoFilter
    @see SimpleSoundPlayer
*/
public class EchoFilterTest {

    public static void main(String[] args) {

        // load the sound
        SimpleSoundPlayer sound =
            new SimpleSoundPlayer("../sounds/voice.wav");

        // create the sound stream
        InputStream is =
            new ByteArrayInputStream(sound.getSamples());

        // create an echo with a 11025-sample buffer
        // (1/4 sec for 44100Hz sound) and a 60% decay
        EchoFilter filter = new EchoFilter(11025, .6f);

        // create the filtered sound stream
        is = new FilteredSoundStream(is, filter);
```

```
        // play the sound
        sound.play(is);

        // due to bug in Java Sound, explicitly exit the VM.
        System.exit(0);
    }

}
```

This example uses a 1/4th second delay and a 60% decay to give the playing voice a space-age echo.

The echo filter is finished and working great, so now you'll create another filter—one to emulate 3D sound.

Emulating 3D Sound

3D sound, also called *directional hearing*, creates a richer audio experience for players by positioning virtual sound sources in 3D space. Sounds are more realistic and give the game an extra dimension—you might be able to hear a bad guy sneaking up on you from behind, or hear a door opening far off in the distance.

Many different effects are used to create 3D sound. Here are some of the most common ones:

➤ Make sound diminish with distance so the farther away a sound source is, the quieter it is.

➤ Pan sounds to the appropriate speaker so a sound source on the left of the player is played in the left speaker, and a sound source on the right of the player is played in the right speaker. This can also be extended to four-speaker surround sound.

➤ Apply room effects so sound waves bounce off walls, creating echoes and reverberation.

➤ Apply the Doppler effect so a sound source's movement affects its pitch. For instance, a sound source quickly moving toward the player has a higher pitch than a stationary one. If you've ever heard a fire engine or train whiz past you, you've experienced this effect.

"3D sound? But we haven't even discussed 3D graphics yet!" Don't worry; 3D sound doesn't apply only to 3D space. All of the effects used to create 3D sound can also be applied to a 2D game.

The Idea Behind Creating a 3D Filter

So now we move on to creating a 3D filter. We already discussed a way to create echoes, so we won't focus on room effects. Instead, we focus on creating a sound that diminishes with distance. But first, how can we change the volume of a sound?

Using Java Sound's Controls, you can dynamically change the volume and pan of a sound. Unfortunately, the Controls don't have the best quality for real-time use, and using them for such can create clicks or "wobbly" sounds. Therefore, you'll do the volume change yourself instead of using Controls. This means it is your task to avoid clicks and pops.

"How do clicks and pops occur?" you ask. Good question! Clicks and pops can happen when the volume of a sound abruptly changes, as in Figure 4.3.

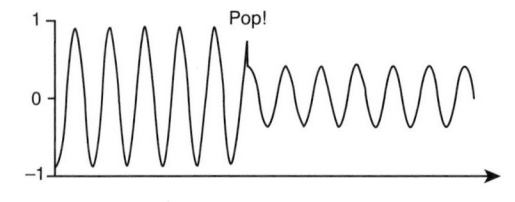

Figure 4.3   Abruptly changing the volume of a sound can result in "pops."

To avoid this in your 3D filter, whenever you need to change the volume of a sound, be sure to gradually change the volume over time, as in Figure 4.4.

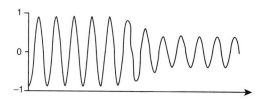

Figure 4.4   Gradually changing the volume of a sound creates a more natural listening experience.

Because your samples are stored in 16-bit signed format, to change the volume, just multiply each sample by a factor. For example:

```
sample = (short)(sample * volume);
```

If you want to play the sound at half the volume, multiply each sample by 0.5.

Implementing a 3D Filter

The `Filter3d` class, in Listing 4.7, modifies the volume of a sound to make it get quieter with distance. It keeps track of two `Sprite` objects: one as a sound source and one as a listener. The farther away the source `Sprite` is from the listener `Sprite`, the quieter the sound is. Distance is measured using the Pythagorean Theorem:

$$A^2 + B^2 = C^2$$

Also, the `Filter3d` class has a maximum distance that sound can be heard. If the listener is more than the maximum distance from the sound source, the sound isn't heard at all. The sound's volume is scaled linearly from 0 to the maximum distance.

The `Filter3d` class is designed so that the sound is changed whenever the sprites' positions change. However, the change in the sound might fall a split second behind the sprites' change in position. Internally, Lines use a buffer to store sound samples before they're actually sent to the native sound system. Then the native sound system might have its own buffer. After that, the sound card might have its own internal buffer. All these buffers create a small delay.

To minimize the delay, we set up a short 100ms buffer in the `SimpleSoundPlayer` class. Although this minimizes the effect, it doesn't eliminate it.

Listing 4.7 Filter3d.java

```java
package com.brackeen.javagamebook.sound;

import com.brackeen.javagamebook.graphics.Sprite;

/**
    The Filter3d class is a SoundFilter that creates a 3D sound
    effect. The sound is filtered so that it is quieter the farther
    away the sound source is from the listener.
    <p>Possible ideas to extend this class:
    <ul><li>pan the sound to the left and right speakers
    </ul>
    @see FilteredSoundStream
*/
public class Filter3d extends SoundFilter {

    // number of samples to shift when changing the volume.
    private static final int NUM_SHIFTING_SAMPLES = 500;

    private Sprite source;
    private Sprite listener;
    private int maxDistance;
    private float lastVolume;

    /**
        Creates a new Filter3d object with the specified source
        and listener Sprites. The Sprite's position can be
        changed while this filter is running.
        <p> The maxDistance parameter is the maximum distance
        that the sound can be heard.
    */
    public Filter3d(Sprite source, Sprite listener,
        int maxDistance)
    {
        this.source = source;
        this.listener = listener;
        this.maxDistance = maxDistance;
        this.lastVolume = 0.0f;
```

```
}


/**
    Filters the sound so that it gets more quiet with
    distance.
*/
public void filter(byte[] samples, int offset, int length) {

    if (source == null || listener == null) {
        // nothing to filter - return
        return;
    }

    // calculate the listener's distance from the sound source
    float dx = (source.getX() - listener.getX());
    float dy = (source.getY() - listener.getY());
    float distance = (float)Math.sqrt(dx * dx + dy * dy);

    // set volume from 0 (no sound) to 1
    float newVolume = (maxDistance - distance) / maxDistance;
    if (newVolume <= 0) {
        newVolume = 0;
    }

    // set the volume of the sample
    int shift = 0;
    for (int i=offset; i<offset+length; i+=2) {

        float volume = newVolume;

        // shift from the last volume to the new volume
        if (shift < NUM_SHIFTING_SAMPLES) {
            volume = lastVolume + (newVolume - lastVolume) *
                shift / NUM_SHIFTING_SAMPLES;
            shift++;
        }
```

continues

Listing 4.7   Filter3d.java   *continued*

```
                // change the volume of the sample
                short oldSample = getSample(samples, i);
                short newSample = (short)(oldSample * volume);
                setSample(samples, i, newSample);
            }

        lastVolume = newVolume;
    }

}
```

In `Filter3d` you create a diminishing-with-distance effect—the minimum amount necessary for a 3D effect.

If you wanted to add panning, you would need to update the `SoundFilter` architecture to enable you to turn a mono sound into a stereo sound. Then you could calculate the pan you wanted from `-1` to `1`, where `-1` is the left speaker, `1` is the right speaker, and `0` is in the middle. Finally, the samples for each speaker could be calculated as follows:

```
short sampleLeft = (short)(sample * (1-pan));
short sampleRight = (short)(sample * (1+pan));
```

For a 2D game, the pan could be determined by the position where a sound source is on the screen. A sound source on the left side of the screen would play in the left speaker, and so on.

Trying Out the 3D Filter

Although you don't have panning in the `Filter3d` class, the diminishing-with-distance effect is cool enough for many games; you can try it out by creating the `Filter3dTest` class, in Listing 4.8.

The `Filter3dTest` class is a graphical demo that enables you to move a fly around on the screen using the mouse, as shown in the screenshot in Figure 4.5. Along with the fly is a virtual "ear" in the middle of the screen. The fly makes a buzzing sound, and the closer the fly is to the ear, the louder the buzzing sound is.

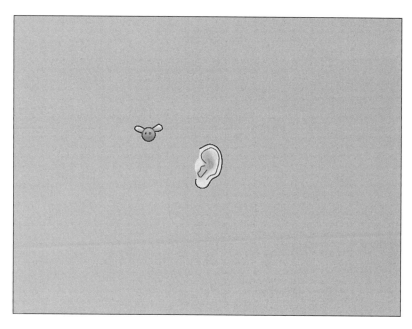

Figure 4.5 The `Filter3dTest` class plays the fly's buzzing
sound louder the closer it is to the ear.

The fly is a simple three-frame animation that is drawn wherever the mouse is located.
As usual, press Escape to exit the demo.

Listing 4.8 Filter3dTest.java

```
import java.awt.*;
import java.awt.event.KeyEvent;
import java.io.InputStream;
import java.io.IOException;
import javax.sound.sampled.*;

import com.brackeen.javagamebook.graphics.*;
import com.brackeen.javagamebook.input.*;
import com.brackeen.javagamebook.sound.*;
import com.brackeen.javagamebook.test.GameCore;
import com.brackeen.javagamebook.util.LoopingByteInputStream;

/**
```

continues

Listing 4.8   Filter3dTest.java   *continued*

```
       The Filter3dTest class demonstrates the Filter3d
       functionality. A fly buzzes around the listener, and the
       closer the fly is, the louder it's heard.
       @see Filter3d
       @see SimpleSoundPlayer
*/
public class Filter3dTest extends GameCore {

    public static void main(String[] args) {
        new Filter3dTest().run();
    }

    private Sprite fly;
    private Sprite listener;
    private InputManager inputManager;
    private GameAction exit;

    private SimpleSoundPlayer bzzSound;
    private InputStream bzzSoundStream;

    public void init() {
        super.init();

        // set up input manager
        exit = new GameAction("exit",
            GameAction.DETECT_INITAL_PRESS_ONLY);
        inputManager = new InputManager(
            screen.getFullScreenWindow());
        inputManager.mapToKey(exit, KeyEvent.VK_ESCAPE);
        inputManager.setCursor(InputManager.INVISIBLE_CURSOR);

        createSprites();

        // load the sound
        bzzSound = new SimpleSoundPlayer("../sounds/fly-bzz.wav");

        // create the 3D filter
```

```
        Filter3d filter =
            new Filter3d(fly, listener, screen.getHeight());

        // create the filtered sound stream
        bzzSoundStream = new FilteredSoundStream(
            new LoopingByteInputStream(bzzSound.getSamples()),
            filter);

        // play the sound in a separate thread
        new Thread() {
            public void run() {
                bzzSound.play(bzzSoundStream);
            }
        }.start();
    }


    /**
        Loads images and creates sprites.
    */
    private void createSprites() {
        // load images
        Image fly1 = loadImage("../images/fly1.png");
        Image fly2 = loadImage("../images/fly2.png");
        Image fly3 = loadImage("../images/fly3.png");
        Image ear = loadImage("../images/ear.png");

        // create "fly" sprite
        Animation anim = new Animation();
        anim.addFrame(fly1, 50);
        anim.addFrame(fly2, 50);
        anim.addFrame(fly3, 50);
        anim.addFrame(fly2, 50);

        fly = new Sprite(anim);

        // create the listener sprite
        anim = new Animation();
```

continues

Listing 4.8 Filter3dTest.java *continued*

```
            anim.addFrame(ear, 0);
            listener = new Sprite(anim);
            listener.setX(
                (screen.getWidth() - listener.getWidth()) / 2);
            listener.setY(
                (screen.getHeight() - listener.getHeight()) / 2);
        }


        public void update(long elapsedTime) {
            if (exit.isPressed()) {
                stop();
            }
            else {
                listener.update(elapsedTime);
                fly.update(elapsedTime);
                fly.setX(inputManager.getMouseX());
                fly.setY(inputManager.getMouseY());
            }
        }


        public void stop() {
            super.stop();
            // stop the bzz sound
            try {
                bzzSoundStream.close();
            }
            catch (IOException ex) { }
        }


        public void draw(Graphics2D g) {

            // draw background
            g.setColor(new Color(0x33cc33));
            g.fillRect(0, 0, screen.getWidth(), screen.getHeight());
```

```
        // draw listener
        g.drawImage(listener.getImage(),
            Math.round(listener.getX()),
            Math.round(listener.getY()),
            null);

        // draw fly
        g.drawImage(fly.getImage(),
            Math.round(fly.getX()),
            Math.round(fly.getY()),
            null);
    }

}
```

One thing to note about `Filter3dTest` is that a separate thread is created to play the sound. The `play()` method of `SimpleSoundPlayer` blocks until the sound is done playing, and because you're using a looping sound, this method could theoretically block forever. To keep the program from getting stuck, a new thread is created.

Also, don't forget that you need to call `System.exit(0)` to exit Java programs that use Java Sound. To take care of this, you can add an extra method, `lazilyExit()`, to the `GameCore` class that `Filter3dTest` extends:

```
public void lazilyExit() {
    Thread thread = new Thread() {
        public void run() {
            // first, wait for the VM exit on its own.
            try {
                Thread.sleep(2000);
            }
            catch (InterruptedException ex) { }
            // system is still running, so force an exit
            System.exit(0);
        }
    };
    thread.setDaemon(true);
    thread.start();
}
```

This method creates a new daemon thread that waits two seconds and then exits the VM. Because the VM normally exits when all nondaemon threads are finished, if this thread is running only with other daemon threads, the VM exits cleanly on its own. Otherwise, after two seconds, the System.exit(0) method is called. The lazilyExit() method is called in the GameCore class right after restoring the screen.

Now you might notice a problem: Creating a new thread every time you play a sound isn't the cleanest solution. You'll fix this by creating a more advanced sound manager.

Creating a Sound Manager

Whenever you play a new sound with the SimpleSoundPlayer, the following steps occur:

1. Create a new thread.

2. Create a new byte buffer.

3. Create, open, and start a new Line.

That's a lot of object creation. Plus, a new thread must start and native resources that operate the Line must be allocated. All this adds up to one thing: lag. It takes too long from the time you request to play a sound to the time when the sound is actually played.

Although the lag might not matter in some instances, such as when you play a startup sound, other times the lag is very noticeable, such as when you're blasting a gun several times a second. You want to eliminate the lag as much as possible.

To reduce the lag, rework the sound-playing architecture. Instead of starting a new thread for every sound played, you'll use the ThreadPool class from Chapter 1, "Java Threads." This keeps several threads ready and waiting to be assigned a sound to play.

Second, each thread in the thread pool can contain its own buffer and Line object, so you don't have to allocate those every time a sound is played.

The drawback to this technique is that every line must be assigned an `AudioFormat` beforehand, so you can play only one type of audio format. This shouldn't be a problem—just pick an audio format that you want to use for your game, and make sure all your sounds have that same format.

The *Sound* Class

Now let's implement this architecture. First you'll create a simple class that contains a sound sample, called `Sound`, in Listing 4.9.

Listing 4.9   Sound.java

```
package com.brackeen.javagamebook.sound;

/**
    The Sound class is a container for sound samples. The sound
    samples are format-agnostic and are stored as a byte array.
*/
public class Sound {

    private byte[] samples;

    /**
        Create a new Sound object with the specified byte array.
        The array is not copied.
    */
    public Sound(byte[] samples) {
        this.samples = samples;
    }


    /**
        Returns this Sound's objects samples as a byte array.
    */
    public byte[] getSamples() {
        return samples;
    }

}
```

The Sound class is a wrapper class for a byte buffer that contains sound samples. It doesn't serve much of a purpose other than making the code more understandable and hiding the contents of a sound, in case you want to change it later.

The *SoundManager* Class

Next create the SoundManager class in Listing 4.10. Along with implementing similar functions to SimpleSoundPlayer, such as loading a sound from a file, SoundManager reduces the lag and gives you the capability to pause playing sounds.

Listing 4.10   SoundManager.java

```java
package com.brackeen.javagamebook.sound;

import java.io.*;
import javax.sound.sampled.*;
import javax.sound.midi.*;
import com.brackeen.javagamebook.util.ThreadPool;
import com.brackeen.javagamebook.util.LoopingByteInputStream;


/**
    The SoundManager class manages sound playback. The
    SoundManager is a ThreadPool, with each thread playing back
    one sound at a time. This allows the SoundManager to
    easily limit the number of simultaneous sounds being played.
    <p>Possible ideas to extend this class:<ul>
    <li>add a setMasterVolume() method, which uses Controls to
        set the volume for each line.
    <li>don't play a sound if more than, say, 500ms have passed
        since the request to play
    </ul>
*/
public class SoundManager extends ThreadPool {

    private AudioFormat playbackFormat;
    private ThreadLocal localLine;
    private ThreadLocal localBuffer;
```

```
private Object pausedLock;
private boolean paused;

/**
    Creates a new SoundManager using the maximum number of
    simultaneous sounds.
*/
public SoundManager(AudioFormat playbackFormat) {
    this(playbackFormat,
        getMaxSimultaneousSounds(playbackFormat));
}


/**
    Creates a new SoundManager with the specified maximum
    number of simultaneous sounds.
*/
public SoundManager(AudioFormat playbackFormat,
    int maxSimultaneousSounds)
{
    super(maxSimultaneousSounds);
    this.playbackFormat = playbackFormat;
    localLine = new ThreadLocal();
    localBuffer = new ThreadLocal();
    pausedLock = new Object();
    // notify threads in pool it's okay to start
    synchronized (this) {
        notifyAll();
    }
}


/**
    Gets the maximum number of simultaneous sounds with the
    specified AudioFormat that the default mixer can play.
*/
public static int getMaxSimultaneousSounds(
    AudioFormat playbackFormat)
```

continues

Listing 4.10 SoundManager.java *continued*

```java
    {
        DataLine.Info lineInfo = new DataLine.Info(
            SourceDataLine.class, playbackFormat);
        Mixer mixer = AudioSystem.getMixer(null);
        return mixer.getMaxLines(lineInfo);
    }


    /**
        Does any clean up before closing.
    */
    protected void cleanUp() {
        // signal to unpause
        setPaused(false);

        // close the mixer (stops any running sounds)
        Mixer mixer = AudioSystem.getMixer(null);
        if (mixer.isOpen()) {
            mixer.close();
        }
    }


    public void close() {
        cleanUp();
        super.close();
    }


    public void join() {
        cleanUp();
        super.join();
    }


    /**
        Sets the paused state. Sounds may not pause immediately.
```

```
*/
public void setPaused(boolean paused) {
    if (this.paused != paused) {
        synchronized (pausedLock) {
            this.paused = paused;
            if (!paused) {
                // restart sounds
                pausedLock.notifyAll();
            }
        }
    }
}



/**
    Returns the paused state.
*/
public boolean isPaused() {
    return paused;
}



/**
    Loads a Sound from the file system. Returns null if an
    error occurs.
*/
public Sound getSound(String filename) {
    return getSound(getAudioInputStream(filename));
}



/**
    Loads a Sound from an AudioInputStream.
*/
public Sound getSound(AudioInputStream audioStream) {
    if (audioStream == null) {
        return null;
    }
```

continues

Listing 4.10   SoundManager.java   *continued*

```
            // get the number of bytes to read
            int length = (int)(audioStream.getFrameLength() *
                audioStream.getFormat().getFrameSize());

            // read the entire stream
            byte[] samples = new byte[length];
            DataInputStream is = new DataInputStream(audioStream);
            try {
                is.readFully(samples);
            }
            catch (IOException ex) {
                ex.printStackTrace();
            }

            // return the samples
            return new Sound(samples);
        }


        /**
            Creates an AudioInputStream from a sound from the file
            system.
        */
        public AudioInputStream getAudioInputStream(String filename) {

            try {
                // open the source file
                AudioInputStream source =
                AudioSystem.getAudioInputStream(new File(filename));

                // convert to playback format
                return AudioSystem.getAudioInputStream(
                    playbackFormat, source);
            }
            catch (UnsupportedAudioFileException ex) {
                ex.printStackTrace();
            }
```

```java
        catch (IOException ex) {
            ex.printStackTrace();
        }
        catch (IllegalArgumentException ex) {
            ex.printStackTrace();
        }

        return null;
    }


    /**
        Plays a sound. This method returns immediately.
    */
    public InputStream play(Sound sound) {
        return play(sound, null, false);
    }


    /**
        Plays a sound with an optional SoundFilter, and optionally
        looping. This method returns immediately.
    */
    public InputStream play(Sound sound, SoundFilter filter,
        boolean loop)
    {
        InputStream is;
        if (sound != null) {
            if (loop) {
                is = new LoopingByteInputStream(
                    sound.getSamples());
            }
            else {
                is = new ByteArrayInputStream(sound.getSamples());
            }

            return play(is, filter);
        }
```

continues

Listing 4.10 SoundManager.java *continued*

```java
            return null;
        }


        /**
            Plays a sound from an InputStream. This method
            returns immediately.
        */
        public InputStream play(InputStream is) {
            return play(is, null);
        }


        /**
            Plays a sound from an InputStream with an optional
            sound filter. This method returns immediately.
        */
        public InputStream play(InputStream is, SoundFilter filter) {
            if (is != null) {
                if (filter != null) {
                    is = new FilteredSoundStream(is, filter);
                }
                runTask(new SoundPlayer(is));
            }
            return is;
        }


        /**
            Signals that a PooledThread has started. Creates the
            Thread's line and buffer.
        */
        protected void threadStarted() {
            // wait for the SoundManager constructor to finish
            synchronized (this) {
                try {
                    wait();
```

```
        }
        catch (InterruptedException ex) { }
    }

    // use a short, 100ms (1/10th sec) buffer for filters that
    // change in real-time
    int bufferSize = playbackFormat.getFrameSize() *
        Math.round(playbackFormat.getSampleRate() / 10);

    // create, open, and start the line
    SourceDataLine line;
    DataLine.Info lineInfo = new DataLine.Info(
        SourceDataLine.class, playbackFormat);
    try {
        line = (SourceDataLine)AudioSystem.getLine(lineInfo);
        line.open(playbackFormat, bufferSize);
    }
    catch (LineUnavailableException ex) {
        // the line is unavailable - signal to end this thread
        Thread.currentThread().interrupt();
        return;
    }

    line.start();

    // create the buffer
    byte[] buffer = new byte[bufferSize];

    // set this thread's locals
    localLine.set(line);
    localBuffer.set(buffer);
}


/**
    Signals that a PooledThread has stopped. Drains and
    closes the Thread's Line.
```

continues

Listing 4.10   SoundManager.java   *continued*

```
*/
protected void threadStopped() {
    SourceDataLine line = (SourceDataLine)localLine.get();
    if (line != null) {
        line.drain();
        line.close();
    }
}


/**
    The SoundPlayer class is a task for the PooledThreads to
    run. It receives the thread's Line and byte buffer from
    the ThreadLocal variables and plays a sound from an
    InputStream.
    <p>This class only works when called from a PooledThread.
*/
protected class SoundPlayer implements Runnable {

    private InputStream source;

    public SoundPlayer(InputStream source) {
        this.source = source;
    }

    public void run() {
        // get line and buffer from ThreadLocals
        SourceDataLine line = (SourceDataLine)localLine.get();
        byte[] buffer = (byte[])localBuffer.get();
        if (line == null || buffer == null) {
            // the line is unavailable
            return;
        }

        // copy data to the line
        try {
            int numBytesRead = 0;
```

```
            while (numBytesRead != -1) {
                // if paused, wait until unpaused
                synchronized (pausedLock) {
                    if (paused) {
                        try {
                            pausedLock.wait();
                        }
                        catch (InterruptedException ex) {
                            return;
                        }
                    }
                }
                // copy data
                numBytesRead =
                    source.read(buffer, 0, buffer.length);
                if (numBytesRead != -1) {
                    line.write(buffer, 0, numBytesRead);
                }
            }
        }
        catch (IOException ex) {
            ex.printStackTrace();
        }
    }

}
```

The SoundManager class extends the ThreadPool class, which we moved to the com.brackeen.javagamebook.util package.

The SoundManager class has an inner class, SoundPlayer, which does the work of copying sound data to a Line. SoundPlayer is an implementation of the Runnable interface, so it can be used as a task for a thread in the thread pool. An addition to SoundPlayer over SimpleSoundPlayer is that it stops copying data if the SoundManager is in the paused state. If it is in the paused state, SoundPlayer calls wait(), which causes the thread to wait idly until it is notified. SoundManager notifies all waiting threads when it is unpaused.

Thread-Local Variables

One thing you wanted to accomplish in SoundManager is to make sure each thread has its own Line and byte buffer so you can reuse them without having to create new objects every time a sound is played. To give each thread in the thread pool its own Line and byte buffer, you'll take advantage of thread-local variables.

Whereas local variables are variables that are local to a block of code, thread-local variables are variables that have a different value for every thread. In this example, the SoundManager class has the thread-local variables, localLine and localBuffer. Each thread that accesses these variables can have its own Line and byte buffer, and no other thread can access another thread's local variables. Thread-local variables are created with the ThreadLocal class.

For thread-local variables to work, you need to cheat a little here and update the ThreadPool class. You need a way to create the thread-local variables when a thread starts and to do any cleanup of the thread-local variables when the thread dies. To do this, in PooledThread, signal the ThreadPool class when each thread starts and stops:

```
public void run() {
    // signal that this thread has started
    threadStarted();

    while (!isInterrupted()) {

        // get a task to run
        Runnable task = null;
        try {
            task = getTask();
        }
        catch (InterruptedException ex) { }

        // if getTask() returned null or was interrupted,
        // close this thread.
        if (task == null) {
            break;
        }
```

```
        // run the task, and eat any exceptions it throws
        try {
            task.run();
        }
        catch (Throwable t) {
            uncaughtException(this, t);
        }
    }
    // signal that this thread has stopped
    threadStopped();
}
```

In the `ThreadPool` class, the `threadStarted()` and `threadStopped()` methods don't do anything, but in `SoundManager`, they're put to use. The `threadStarted()` method creates a new Line and a new byte buffer, and adds them to the thread-local variables. In the `threadStopped()` method, the Line is drained and closed.

Besides reducing the lag and enabling you to pause playing sounds, `SoundManager` provides easier methods for playing sound. It takes care of the creation of `ByteArrayInputStreams` or `FilteredSoundStreams`, so all you have to do is pass it a `Sound` object and an optional `SoundFilter`.

That's it for the nifty new sound manager. So far, you've learned to play sound, use sound filters, and even emulate 3D sound. Now you'll move on to the other sound topic: music.

Playing Music

Although background music isn't found in every game you play, it can play an important role in a game. Music can set the mood—for example, an action game could play fast-paced music, while slower music might be better suited for a game that requires more thought.

Also, music can change the player's emotions toward elements of the game. Is the music happy? Or is it dramatic? Happy music might be better suited for the easier levels, such as the first few levels of a game. Dramatic music could be played for the more difficult levels, such as when the player is fighting a powerful bad guy.

When you've decided on the type of music you want, the next step is to figure out where the music comes from. Nope, it doesn't come from those voices in your head. Instead, games typically play music in one of three ways:

➤ Streaming music from an audio track on a CD

➤ Playing compressed music such as MP3 or Ogg Vorbis

➤ Playing MIDI music

Playing CD Audio

Some CD-ROM games have plain old Red Book Audio (the standard audio CD format) right on the CD. The benefit here is you get great-quality sound and it's easy to implement: Just tell the sound card to start playing the CD, without any other involvement from the game. The other cool aspect is that players can slip the game CD into their audio CD player and groove to the game's tracks.

Unfortunately, CD audio takes up a lot of space, typically around 30MB for a three-minute song. If you have four three-minute songs, that's 120MB of space that could be used for more graphics or bigger levels. In addition, the Java Sound implementation doesn't support playback from a CD, so this option is out for you.

Playing MP3 and Ogg Vorbis

The second option is compressed music. MP3 and Ogg Vorbis formats are much smaller than that for CD audio, typically around 3MB for a three-minute song, and have near-CD quality. They've become increasingly more popular in games.

The drawback here is that decoding MP3 or Ogg Vorbis files takes quite a chunk of processor power. Sound cards can't play compressed music directly, so the music is decoded while it's played. This means the extra processor use can interfere with other parts of your game. On faster, modern machines, the decoding won't be noticeable, but on slower, older machines, the decoding could take 20% to 40% of the processor or more. That could make other parts of the game, such as animation, seem slow or jerky.

If the processor time doesn't matter to your game, you'll need to get an MP3 or Ogg Vorbis Java decoder. Java Zoom, at `www.javazoom.net`, has both. This site provides a plug-in through Java's Service Provider Interface that enables you to get an `AudioInputStream` that decodes an MP3 or Ogg Vorbis stream. Just include the necessary .jar file, and be sure to convert the `AudioInputStream`, like so:

```
// create the format used for playback
// (uncompressed, 44100Hz, 16-bit, mono, signed, little-endian)
AudioFormat playbackFormat =
    new AudioFormat(44100, 16, 1, true, false);

// open the source file
AudioInputStream source =
    AudioSystem.getAudioInputStream(new File("music.ogg"));

// convert to playback format
source = AudioSystem.getAudioInputStream(playbackFormat, source);
```

Also, be sure not to load the samples into memory. A compressed sound file might take up only 1MB for each minute of music, but the uncompressed samples would take 10MB for each minute. Instead, play any large sounds directly from the `AudioInputStream`, which streams the sound from disk.

But which one should your game use, MP3 or Ogg Vorbis? Although MP3 is incredibly popular, Ogg Vorbis is license-free and claims better sound quality. The people playing your game won't notice or care, so go with whichever one suits your needs better. You can find more information on Ogg Vorbis at `www.xiph.org/ogg/vorbis`. Also, be sure to look into MP3 licensing issues at `www.mp3licensing.com`.

Playing MIDI Music

Finally, there's MIDI music. MIDI music isn't sampled music like other sound formats; instead, it works more like a composer's sheet music, giving instructions on which note to play on each instrument. The audio system synthesizes to each note according to the pitch, instrument, and volume, among other parameters.

Because MIDI files contain instructions instead of samples, MIDI files are very small compared to sampled sound formats and are often measured in kilobytes rather than megabytes.

Because the music is synthesized, the quality might not be as high as that of sampled music. Some instruments won't sound realistic, or the music might sound a little too mechanical. A creative musician can usually mask the deficiencies of MIDI music, however.

The Java Sound API synthesizes MIDI music through the use of a soundbank, which is a collection of instruments. Unfortunately, although the Java SDK includes a soundbank, the Java runtime does not. If a soundbank isn't found, the hardware MIDI port, which has unreliable timing in Java Sound, is used. For this reason, it's recommended to use a soundbank.

The Java SDK includes a minimal-quality soundbank, and you can download higher-quality soundbanks from `http://java.sun.com/products/java-media/sound/soundbanks.html` and include them with your game.

The Java Sound API provides MIDI sound capabilities in the `javax.sound.midi` package. To play MIDI music, you need two objects in this package: `Sequence` and `Sequencer`. A `Sequence` object contains the MIDI data, and a `Sequencer` sends a `Sequence` to the MIDI synthesizer. Here's an example of playing a MIDI file:

```
// open the midi file
Sequence sequence = MidiSystem.getSequence(new File(filename));
// open the sequencer
Sequencer sequencer = MidiSystem.getSequencer();
sequencer.open();
// play the midi sequence
sequencer.setSequence(sequence);
sequencer.start();
```

By default, the Sequencer plays a Sequence once and then stops. But in a game, you usually want to loop the music. To loop a Sequence, you need to be notified when the music is done playing and start the Sequencer again.

An example of how to loop music is in the MidiPlayer class in Listing 4.11. It implements the MetaEventListener interface, which notifies the class when the Sequence is done playing via the end-of-track message.

Listing 4.11   MidiPlayer.java

```
package com.brackeen.javagamebook.sound;

import java.io.File;
import java.io.IOException;
import javax.sound.midi.*;

public class MidiPlayer implements MetaEventListener {

    // Midi meta event
    public static final int END_OF_TRACK_MESSAGE = 47;

    private Sequencer sequencer;
    private boolean loop;
    private boolean paused;

    /**
        Creates a new MidiPlayer object.
    */
    public MidiPlayer() {
        try {
            sequencer = MidiSystem.getSequencer();
            sequencer.open();
            sequencer.addMetaEventListener(this);
        }
        catch ( MidiUnavailableException ex) {
            sequencer = null;
        }
    }
```

continues

Listing 4.11 MidiPlayer.java *continued*

```java
/**
    Loads a sequence from the file system. Returns null if
    an error occurs.
*/
public Sequence getSequence(String filename) {
    try {
        return MidiSystem.getSequence(new File(filename));
    }
    catch (InvalidMidiDataException ex) {
        ex.printStackTrace();
        return null;
    }
    catch (IOException ex) {
        ex.printStackTrace();
        return null;
    }
}


/**
    Plays a sequence, optionally looping. This method returns
    immediately. The sequence is not played if it is invalid.
*/
public void play(Sequence sequence, boolean loop) {
    if (sequencer != null && sequence != null) {
        try {
            sequencer.setSequence(sequence);
            sequencer.start();
            this.loop = loop;
        }
        catch (InvalidMidiDataException ex) {
            ex.printStackTrace();
        }
    }
}
```

```java
/**
    This method is called by the sound system when a meta
    event occurs. In this case, when the end-of-track meta
    event is received, the sequence is restarted if
    looping is on.
*/
public void meta(MetaMessage event) {
    if (event.getType() == END_OF_TRACK_MESSAGE) {
        if (sequencer != null && sequencer.isOpen() && loop) {
            sequencer.start();
        }
    }
}


/**
    Stops the sequencer and resets its position to 0.
*/
public void stop() {
    if (sequencer != null && sequencer.isOpen()) {
        sequencer.stop();
        sequencer.setMicrosecondPosition(0);
    }
}


/**
    Closes the sequencer.
*/
public void close() {
    if (sequencer != null && sequencer.isOpen()) {
        sequencer.close();
    }
}


/**
```

continues

Listing 4.11   MidiPlayer.java   *continued*

```java
        Gets the sequencer.
    */
    public Sequencer getSequencer() {
        return sequencer;
    }


    /**
        Sets the paused state. Music may not immediately pause.
    */
    public void setPaused(boolean paused) {
        if (this.paused != paused && sequencer != null) {
            this.paused = paused;
            if (paused) {
                sequencer.stop();
            }
            else {
                sequencer.start();
            }
        }
    }


    /**
        Returns the paused state.
    */
    public boolean isPaused() {
        return paused;
    }

}
```

MidiPlayer also provides methods for opening Sequences and pausing the music. To pause, MidiPlayer calls the stop() method of the Sequencer object, which stops the Sequence without resetting its position. Calling start() resumes the paused sequence. All this happens in MidiPlayer's setPaused() method.

Creating Adaptive Music

Now that you can play MIDI music, let's discuss one of its advantages: easy implementation of adaptive music. *Adaptive music* is music that changes based on the state of the game. For instance, if the player is battling a large number of enemies, the music might be fast and loud. Conversely, the music might be quiet when the player is walking around exploring rooms alone.

The change in music could happen at any time—for example, the player could be strolling along one second, and then 100 robots could be trying to kill him the next. So, changing the music smoothly can be a challenge.

You can adapt songs to the game state in two ways:

➤ Change songs

➤ Modify the song currently playing

Because the actions of a player can change at any time, changing songs is a more difficult task. The change can't be abrupt, or it will be distracting. Songs can be designed so that they have "change points" to signify places where a song change can occur.

Also, songs need to transition smoothly. To do this, the first song can fade out while the next song is fading in. Also, while the first song is fading out, its tempo could change to match the tempo of the next song.

Or, you could just take the easy way out and insert a sound of a scratching phonograph needle.

The second option is to simply modify the exiting song. You can do this by changing the tempo or volume, or adding another instrument to it.

Adding or taking away an instrument is easy to do with MIDI sequences. MIDI music is typically organized into tracks, with each track playing a specific instrument. For instance, there might be one track for guitar, one for keyboards, and so on.

You can mute or unmute a track with one method:

```
sequencer.setTrackMute(trackNum, true);
```

Here, trackNum is an integer representing the track number you want to mute. If you don't know what track belongs to what instrument in your MIDI file, you might have to experiment by muting each track, one by one.

Try manipulating the MIDI music in the MidiTest class in Listing 4.12. It's a short test that uses MidiPlayer to start a song, first with the drum track off. After playing through once, it plays the song again with the drum track on.

Listing 4.12   MidiTest.java

```java
import java.io.File;
import java.io.IOException;
import javax.sound.midi.*;

import com.brackeen.javagamebook.sound.MidiPlayer;

/**
    An example that plays a Midi sequence. First, the sequence
    is played once with track 1 turned off. Then the sequence is
    played once with track 1 turned on. Track 1 is the drum track
    in the example midi file.
*/
public class MidiTest implements MetaEventListener {

    // The drum track in the example Midi file
    private static final int DRUM_TRACK = 1;

    public static void main(String[] args) {
        new MidiTest().run();
    }

    private MidiPlayer player;

    public void run() {
```

```
player = new MidiPlayer();

// load a sequence
Sequence sequence =
    player.getSequence("../sounds/music.midi");

// play the sequence
player.play(sequence, true);

// turn off the drums
System.out.println("Playing (without drums)...");
Sequencer sequencer = player.getSequencer();
sequencer.setTrackMute(DRUM_TRACK, true);
sequencer.addMetaEventListener(this);
}



/**
    This method is called by the sound system when a meta
    event occurs. In this case, when the end-of-track meta
    event is received, the drum track is turned on.
*/
public void meta(MetaMessage event) {
    if (event.getType() == MidiPlayer.END_OF_TRACK_MESSAGE) {
        Sequencer sequencer = player.getSequencer();
        if (sequencer.getTrackMute(DRUM_TRACK)) {
            // turn on the drum track
            System.out.println("Turning on drums...");
            sequencer.setTrackMute(DRUM_TRACK, false);
        }
        else {
            // close the sequencer and exit
            System.out.println("Exiting...");
            player.close();
            System.exit(0);
        }
    }
```

continues

Listing 4.12 MidiTest.java *continued*

```
      }

}
```

Just like when you play sampled sound, you must explicitly exit the VM when you're done. MidiTest exits the VM when it receives the second end-of-track message.

Summary

In this chapter, you learned the basics of sound, sound filters, and music. You made real-time echo and psuedo-3D filters, and you created a cool sound manager to handle game sound effects. You also made some adaptive music and learned how to play back MP3 and Ogg Vorbis sound files. Combining this knowledge with graphics and interactivity from the previous chapters, you're ready to create your own game.

Chapter 5

Creating a 2D Platform Game

This is where the fun starts.

The previous chapters covered the basics of using Java to create graphics, sound, and interactivity. In this chapter, you're going to use what you created in the previous chapters to create a real 2D platform game. *Platform games* are games in which the player runs and jumps from platform to platform, avoiding bad guys and collecting power-ups. To create a platform game, in this chapter you'll learn about tile-based maps, map files, collision detection, power-ups, simple bad guys, and parallax background scrolling. Check out the screenshot of the game you'll create in Figure 5.1.

> **NOTE**
> This chapter is less about Java-related technology and more about game-programming techniques, so not all the code for the game is presented here. Instead, you can get the code from the website, `www.brackeen.com/javagamebook`, as always.

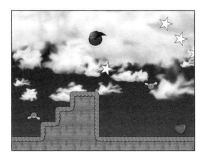

Figure 5.1   In this chapter, you'll create a 2D platform game with tile-based maps, bad guys, and power-ups.

Creating a Tile-Based Map

In a 2D platform game, the map of an entire level, or the *game map*, is usually several screens wide. Some maps are 20 screens wide; others are 100 or more. As the main character walks across the screen, the map scrolls.

As you can imagine, using one huge image for the game map is not the best idea in this situation. This would take up so much memory that most machines wouldn't be capable of loading the map. Plus, using a huge image doesn't help define which parts of the map the player can and cannot walk through—in other words, which parts are "solid" and which are "empty."

Instead of using a huge image for the entire map, you'll create a tile-based map. *Tile-based maps* break down the map into a grid, as shown in Figure 5.2. Each cell in the grid contains either a small tile image or nothing.

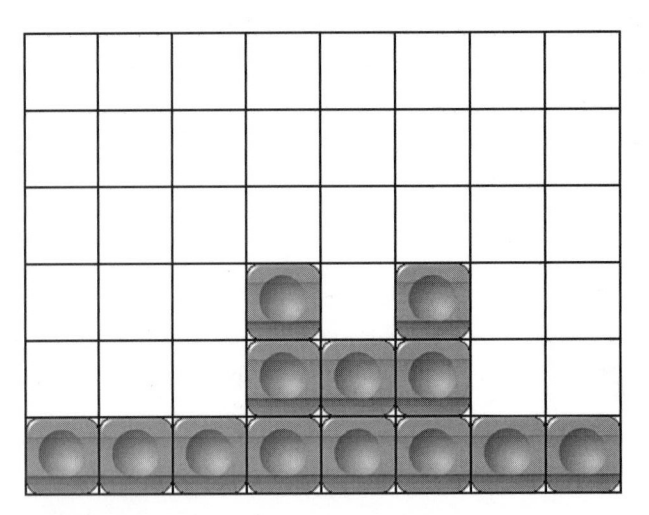

Figure 5.2   A tile-based map is composed of several image tiles on a grid.

Tile-based maps are like creating a game with building blocks. Only a few different block colors are used, but you have an unlimited amount of each color.

The tile map contains references to which image belongs to each cell in the grid. This way, you need only a few small images for the tiles, and you can make the maps as big as you want without worrying too much about memory constraints.

How big the tiles are is up to you. Most tile-based games use a tile size that is a power of 2, such as 16 or 32. In this game, you'll use a tile size of 64. Figure 5.3 shows the nine tiles used in the game.

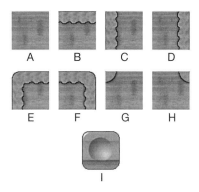

Figure 5.3   This tile-based game has nine different tiles.

Tile-based maps also have the nice side effect of being able to easily determine what's "solid" and what's "empty" in a map. That way, you know which part of the map the player can jump on, and you can make sure the player can't magically walk through walls. You will use this later in this chapter, in the "Collision Detection" section. But first, let's implement the tile map.

Implementing the Tile Map

The `TileMap` class in Listing 5.1 contains the tile map you'll use in the game. It holds a two-dimensional array of `Image` objects that define the tile map. Empty tiles are null.

Keep in mind that each entry in the `Image` array isn't a unique object; it's just a reference to an existing object. If one tile is in the map 12 times, the same `Image` object will be in the array 12 times. Object references are only 4 bytes on a 32-bit Java VM, so a one-dimensional 5,000-`Image` array takes up only about 20KB. (Actually, because Java doesn't really have two-dimensional arrays and has only arrays of arrays, a "two-dimensional" version adds up to about 30KB. Either way, it's a very small amount.)

Listing 5.1 TileMap.java

```java
package com.brackeen.javagamebook.tilegame;

import java.awt.Image;
import java.util.LinkedList;
import java.util.Iterator;

import com.brackeen.javagamebook.graphics.Sprite;

/**
    The TileMap class contains the data for a tile-based
    map, including Sprites. Each tile is a reference to an
    Image. Of course, Images are used multiple times in the tile
    map.
*/
public class TileMap {

    private Image[][] tiles;
    private LinkedList sprites;
    private Sprite player;

    /**
        Creates a new TileMap with the specified width and
        height (in number of tiles) of the map.
    */
    public TileMap(int width, int height) {
        tiles = new Image[width][height];
        sprites = new LinkedList();
    }


    /**
        Gets the width of this TileMap (number of tiles across).
    */
    public int getWidth() {
        return tiles.length;
    }
```

```
/**
    Gets the height of this TileMap (number of tiles down).
*/
public int getHeight() {
    return tiles[0].length;
}



/**
    Gets the tile at the specified location. Returns null if
    no tile is at the location or if the location is out of
    bounds.
*/
public Image getTile(int x, int y) {
    if (x < 0 || x >= getWidth() ||
        y < 0 || y >= getHeight())
    {
        return null;
    }
    else {
        return tiles[x][y];
    }
}



/**
    Sets the tile at the specified location.
*/
public void setTile(int x, int y, Image tile) {
    tiles[x][y] = tile;
}



/**
    Gets the player Sprite.
*/
public Sprite getPlayer() {
    return player;
```

continues

Listing 5.1 TileMap.java *continued*

```
    }


    /**
        Sets the player Sprite.
    */
    public void setPlayer(Sprite player) {
        this.player = player;
    }


    /**
        Adds a Sprite object to this map.
    */
    public void addSprite(Sprite sprite) {
        sprites.add(sprite);
    }


    /**
        Removes a Sprite object from this map.
    */
    public void removeSprite(Sprite sprite) {
        sprites.remove(sprite);
    }


    /**
        Gets an Iterator of all the Sprites in this map,
        excluding the player Sprite.
    */
    public Iterator getSprites() {
        return sprites.iterator();
    }

}
```

Besides the tiles, the `TileMap` contains the sprites in the game. Sprites can be anywhere on the map, not just on tile boundaries. See Figure 5.4 for a list of the sprites in the game.

The Hero   The Fly   The Grub

The Goal Music Note The Star

Figure 5.4   Besides the player, other sprites include two bad guys and three power-ups.

The `TileMap` class also treats the player as a special sprite because you usually want to treat it quite differently from the rest of the sprites.

Loading Tile Maps

Now that you have a place to store the tile map, you need to come up with a reasonable way to actually create the map.

Tile-based games always have more than one map or level, and this game is no exception. You'll want an easy way to create multiple maps so that when the player finishes one map, the player can then start the next map.

You could create maps by calling `TileMap`'s `addTile()` and `addSprite()` methods for every tile and sprite in the game. As you can imagine, this technique isn't very flexible. It makes editing levels far too difficult, and the code itself would not be very pretty to look at.

Many tile-based games have their own map editors for creating maps. These tile-based editors enable you to visually add tiles and sprites to the game, and are quick and easy to use. They usually store maps in an intermediate map file that the game can parse.

Creating a map editor is a bit of overkill in this case. Instead, you'll just define a text-based map file format that can be edited in an everyday text editor. Because tile maps are defined on a grid, each character in the text file will be either a tile or a sprite, as shown in the example in Listing 5.2.

Listing 5.2   map.txt

```
# Map file for tile-based game
# (Lines that start with '#' are comments)
# The tiles are:
#    (Space)  Empty tile
#    A..Z     Tiles A through Z
#    o        Star
#    !        Music Note
#    *        Goal
#    1        Bad Guy 1 (grub)
#    2        Bad Guy 2 (fly)
AD        IIIIIII           IIIIIIIIIIIIIIIIIIIIIIIIIIIIIIIIIII
AD                 o o o                I                      E
AD               IIIIIII                I                      C
AD                                      I           o o        C
AD             2   !       2                        IIIII      C
AD               IIIII                                         C
AD      III                       1   1 1          2          C
AD                      1      IIIIIIIIIIIII                   C
AD      1       EBBBBBBBBBBBBBBBF   o o o o o o          * C
AHBBBBBBBBBBBBBBBBBGAAAAAAAAAAAAAAAAAHBBBBBBBBBBBBBBBBBBBBBBBBBBBBBBBBBBBBBG
```

This map file is both visually understandable and easy to edit. Lines that start with # are comments, and all other lines define a row of tiles. The size of the map isn't fixed, so you can make maps bigger by adding more lines or making the lines longer.

Parsing the map file is easy and basically takes three steps:

1. Read every line, ignoring commented lines, and put each line in a list.

2. Create a TileMap object. The width of the TileMap is the length of the longest line in the list, and the height is the number of lines in the list.

3. Parse each character in each line, and add the appropriate tile or sprite to the map, depending on that character.

If a character is encountered that is "illegal," the tile is considered to be empty.

Here's all the parsing code, wrapped up in a `loadMap()` method in Listing 5.3.

Listing 5.3   `loadMap()` Method

```java
private TileMap loadMap(String filename) throws IOException {

    ArrayList lines = new ArrayList();
    int width = 0;
    int height = 0;

    // read every line in the text file into the list
    BufferedReader reader = new BufferedReader(
        new FileReader(filename));
    while (true) {
        String line = reader.readLine();
        // no more lines to read
        if (line == null) {
            reader.close();
            break;
        }

        // add every line except for comments
        if (!line.startsWith("#")) {
            lines.add(line);
            width = Math.max(width, line.length());
        }
    }

    // parse the lines to create a TileEngine
    height = lines.size();
    TileMap newMap = new TileMap(width, height);
    for (int y=0; y<height; y++) {
        String line = (String)lines.get(y);
        for (int x=0; x<line.length(); x++) {
            char ch = line.charAt(x);

            // check if the char represents tile A, B, C, etc.
            int tile = ch - 'A';
            if (tile >= 0 && tile < tiles.size()) {
```

continues

Listing 5.3   `loadMap()` **Method**   *continued*

```
            newMap.setTile(x, y, (Image)tiles.get(tile));
        }

        // check if the char represents a sprite
        else if (ch == 'o') {
            addSprite(newMap, coinSprite, x, y);
        }
        else if (ch == '!') {
            addSprite(newMap, musicSprite, x, y);
        }
        else if (ch == '*') {
            addSprite(newMap, goalSprite, x, y);
        }
        else if (ch == '1') {
            addSprite(newMap, grubSprite, x, y);
        }
        else if (ch == '2') {
            addSprite(newMap, flySprite, x, y);
        }
    }
}

// add the player to the map
Sprite player = (Sprite)playerSprite.clone();
player.setX(TileMapRenderer.tilesToPixels(3));
player.setY(0);
newMap.setPlayer(player);

return newMap;
}
```

One thing to note is the special case of adding sprites to the `TileMap`. For starters, you need to create a different `Sprite` object for each sprite in the game. To do this, you can clone sprites from a "host" sprite.

Second, a sprite might not necessarily be the same size as the tile size. So, in this case, you'll center and bottom-justify each sprite in the tile it's in. All this is taken care of in the addSprite() method in Listing 5.4.

Listing 5.4 addSprite() Method

```
private void addSprite(TileMap map,
    Sprite hostSprite, int tileX, int tileY)
{
    if (hostSprite != null) {
        // clone the sprite from the "host"
        Sprite sprite = (Sprite)hostSprite.clone();

        // center the sprite
        sprite.setX(
            TileMapRenderer.tilesToPixels(tileX) +
            (TileMapRenderer.tilesToPixels(1) -
            sprite.getWidth()) / 2);

        // bottom-justify the sprite
        sprite.setY(
            TileMapRenderer.tilesToPixels(tileY + 1) -
            sprite.getHeight());

        // add it to the map
        map.addSprite(sprite);
    }
}
```

In earlier demos in the book, the sprite's position was relative to the screen, but in this game, the sprite's position is relative to the tile map. You can use the TileMapRender.tilesToPixels() static function to convert tile positions to pixel positions in the map. This function multiplies the number of tiles by the tile size:

```
int pixelSize = numTiles * TILE_SIZE;
```

This way, sprites can move around to any position in the map and don't have to be justified with the tile boundaries.

That's about it. Now you have a flexible way to create maps and parse them to create `TileMap` objects. In this game, all the maps live in the map folder and are named map1.txt, map2.txt, and so on. Whenever you advance to the next map, the code just looks for the next map file; if it's not found, the code starts over with the first map file. This means you can just drop new map files in the map folder without having to tell the game how many maps exist.

Drawing Tile Maps

As mentioned before, the tile maps are much larger than the screen, so only a portion of the map is shown on the screen at a time. As the player moves, the map scrolls to keep the player in the middle of the screen, as shown in Figure 5.5.

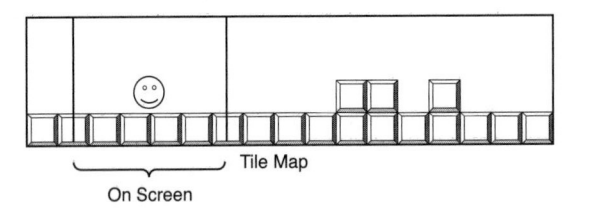

Figure 5.5   Only a small portion of the tile map is onscreen at a time, and the map scrolls to keep the player in the middle of the screen.

Therefore, before you draw the tiles, you need to figure out the position of the map onscreen. Start off by keeping the player in the middle of the screen, like this:

```
int offsetX = screenWidth / 2 -
    Math.round(player.getX()) - TILE_SIZE;
```

This formula assigns offsetX the horizontal position of the map onscreen. It's an easy formula, but you also need to make sure that when the player is near the far left or far right edges of the map, the scrolling stops so that the "void" beyond the edges of the map isn't shown. To do this, give the offsetX value a limit:

```
int mapWidth = tilesToPixels(map.getWidth());
offsetX = Math.min(offsetX, 0);
offsetX = Math.max(offsetX, screenWidth - mapWidth);
```

For convenience, also create the offsetY variable for the vertical scroll position. It keeps the map flush with the bottom of the screen, no matter how big the screen is:

```
int offsetY = screenHeight - tilesToPixels(map.getHeight());
```

Now you're ready to draw the tiles. You could just draw every single tile in the map, but instead, you just need to draw the visible tiles. Here, you get the first horizontal tile to draw based on offsetX and then calculate the last horizontal tile to draw based on the width of the screen. Then you draw the visible tiles:

```
int firstTileX = pixelsToTiles(-offsetX);
int lastTileX = firstTileX +
    pixelsToTiles(screenWidth) + 1;
for (int y=0; y<map.getHeight(); y++) {
    for (int x=firstTileX; x <= lastTileX; x++) {
        Image image = map.getTile(x, y);
        if (image != null) {
            g.drawImage(image,
                tilesToPixels(x) + offsetX,
                tilesToPixels(y) + offsetY,
                null);
        }
    }
}
```

That's it! The tile map is now drawing on the screen and scrolling smoothly wherever the player goes. But it would probably help if you actually draw the player, right? You'll do that next—and while you're at it, you'll draw all the other sprites, too.

Drawing Sprites

After drawing the tiles, you'll draw the sprites. Because you drew only the visible tiles, let's look into only drawing the visible sprites as well. Here are a few ideas:

➤ Partition the sprites into screen-size sections. Draw only the sprites that are in the sections visible on the screen. As the sprites move, make sure they are stored in the appropriate section.

➤ Keep the sprites in a list ordered by the sprites' horizontal position, from left to right. Keep track of the first visible sprite in the list, which can change as bad guys die or the screen scrolls. Draw sprites in the list from the first visible sprite until one is found that is not visible. As the sprites move, make sure the list is sorted.

➤ Implement the brute-force method of running through every sprite in the list, checking whether it's visible.

The first two ideas no doubt are useful if there are a lot of sprites in the map. However, in this case, there are not very many sprites in each map, so you can use the brute-force method and check to see if each sprite is visible. Actually, you can just run through the list, drawing every sprite:

```
Iterator i = map.getSprites();
while (i.hasNext()) {
    Sprite sprite = (Sprite)i.next();
    int x = Math.round(sprite.getX()) + offsetX;
    int y = Math.round(sprite.getY()) + offsetY;
    g.drawImage(sprite.getImage(), x, y, null);
}
```

This way, the graphics engine does the work, checking to see whether each image is visible before drawing it. It's not the most efficient solution, but it works.

Parallax Scrolling

Now that you've got the tiles and sprites drawn, you just need to draw one more thing: the background. When you draw the background, you need to decide how the background is drawn in comparison to the map. Here are a few ways to do this:

➤ Keep the background static so it doesn't scroll when the map scrolls.

➤ Scroll the background at the same rate as the map.

➤ Scroll the background at a slower rate than the map so the background appears to be farther away.

The third method is called *parallax scrolling* and is the method you'll use for the game. *Parallax* is the apparent change in position of an object when seen from a different point of view. For example, when you're driving in a car and look out the side window, the nearby objects, such as traffic signs, fly by rather quickly, but farther objects, such as mountains, slowly creep by. The farther away an object is, the less it appears to move as you move.

If you make the background move slower than the map, it will appear farther away and will give the game a bit of perspective.

As mentioned before, you don't want to use a huge image for the entire map. Likewise, you don't want to use a huge image for the entire background of the map. Because you're using parallax scrolling, you don't need to. You'll create a background image that is two screens wide, and it will scroll from the first screen to the second screen as the map scrolls from the left to the right. This is the key to implementing parallax scrolling in the game.

When the player is on the left part of the map, the leftmost part of the map is shown and the left part of the background is drawn (see Figure 5.6).

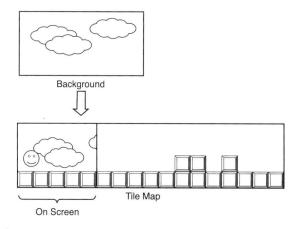

Figure 5.6   When the player is on the left part of the map,
the leftmost part of the background is drawn.

Drawing the left part of the background on the screen is easy enough:

```
int backgroundX = 0;
g.drawImage(background, backgroundX, 0, null);
```

Likewise, when the player is on the far right side of the map, the rightmost part of the background is shown (see Figure 5.7).

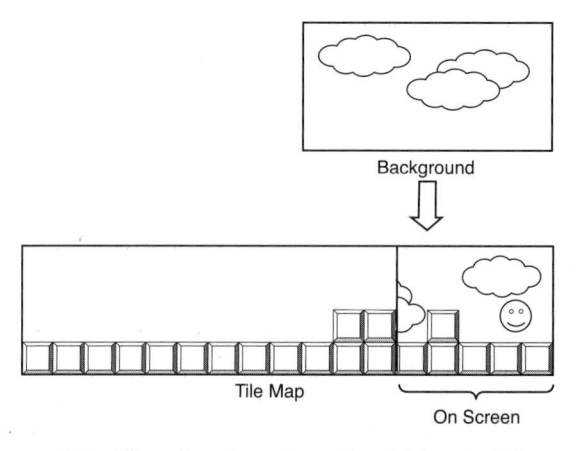

Figure 5.7   When the player is on the right part of the map,
the rightmost part of the background is drawn.

Here's how you draw the right part of the background on the screen:

```
int backgroundX = screenWidth - background.getWidth(null);
g.drawImage(background, backgroundX, 0, null);
```

Now, what about all the points in between the left and right parts of the map? Well, previously you calculated offsetX, which is the position of the map that the screen is drawing, so you just need a formula to convert offsetX to backgroundX. The range for offsetX is from 0 (left part of map drawn) to screenWidth–mapWidth (right part of map drawn). This matches with the range of backgroundX from 0 to screenWidth–background.getWidth(null). So, all you have to do interpolate these two discrete points:

```
int backgroundX = offsetX *
    (screenWidth - background.getWidth(null)) /
    (screenWidth - mapWidth);
g.drawImage(background, backgroundX, 0, null);
```

That was more simple than you thought, huh? With this formula, the background scrolls slowly as the player moves across the map. This formula assumes two things, however:

➤ The background is wider than the screen.

➤ The map is wider than the background.

One last thing to note is that you don't have to use an image as a background. You could just as easily use another `TileMap` so that you could be free to create as large a background as you want. Also, there doesn't have to be just one scrolling background. There could be two or more, each scrolling at different speeds, with the front layers having transparency so the back layers show through.

The background image itself could also be tiled. If you do this, make sure the right edge of the background matches up with the left edges, so the background appears seamless.

Power-Ups

Now that you have a formula for drawing the background, you can draw everything the game requires. The next step is to implement the sprites.

The first type of sprite you'll implement is the power-up. A power-up is a sprite that the player can pick up, often giving the player points, extra powers, or the ability to perform some other action.

The `PowerUp` class in Listing 5.5 defines the power-ups. It is an abstract class that extends `PowerUp`, but it contains static inner subclasses for each power-up in the game: the star, the music note, and the goal.

Listing 5.5   PowerUp.java

```java
package com.brackeen.javagamebook.tilegame.sprites;

import java.lang.reflect.Constructor;
import com.brackeen.javagamebook.graphics.*;

/**
    A PowerUp class is a Sprite that the player can pick up.
*/
public abstract class PowerUp extends Sprite {

    public PowerUp(Animation anim) {
        super(anim);
    }


    public Object clone() {
        // use reflection to create the correct subclass
        Constructor constructor = getClass().getConstructors()[0];
        try {
            return constructor.newInstance(
                new Object[] {(Animation)anim.clone()});
        }
        catch (Exception ex) {
            // should never happen
            ex.printStackTrace();
            return null;
        }
    }


    /**
        A Star PowerUp. Gives the player points.
    */
    public static class Star extends PowerUp {
        public Star(Animation anim) {
            super(anim);
        }
    }
```

```
/**
    A Music PowerUp. Changes the game music.
*/
public static class Music extends PowerUp {
    public Music(Animation anim) {
        super(anim);
    }
}


/**
    A Goal PowerUp. Advances to the next map.
*/
public static class Goal extends PowerUp {
    public Goal(Animation anim) {
        super(anim);
    }
}

}
```

One of the things you need to implement in all the sprites in the game is the `clone()` method, which is a way to make many copies of the same sprite. Instead of implementing a `clone()` method for every subclass of `PowerUp`, the `PowerUp` class contains a generic `clone()` method that uses reflection to clone the object, even if it is a subclass. It selects the first constructor of the object's class and then creates a new instance of that object using that constructor.

Notice that subclasses of `PowerUp` don't really do anything. They're merely placeholders so that you can tell which power-up is which. But what are they supposed to do?

➤ When the player acquires a star, a sound is played, but no other action is taken.

➤ When the player acquires a music note, the drum track in the background MIDI music is toggled on or off.

➤ Finally, when the player acquires the "goal" power-up, the next map is loaded.

All of the power-up actions take place in the collision-detection code (which we discuss later in this chapter). Whenever the player collides with a `PowerUp`, the `acquirePowerUp()` method is called to determine what to do with it:

```
public void acquirePowerUp(PowerUp powerUp) {
    // remove it from the map
    map.removeSprite(powerUp);

    if (powerUp instanceof PowerUp.Star) {
        // do something here, like give the player points
        soundManager.play(prizeSound);
    }
    else if (powerUp instanceof PowerUp.Music) {
        // change the music
        soundManager.play(prizeSound);
        toggleDrumPlayback();
    }
    else if (powerUp instanceof PowerUp.Goal) {
        // advance to next map
        soundManager.play(prizeSound,
            new EchoFilter(2000, .7f), false);
        map = resourceManager.loadNextMap();
    }
}
```

> **NOTE**
>
> Note that this is only one way to implement power-ups. Another way is to provide an `acquire()` method in the `PowerUp` class that is called when the player acquires the power-up. This way, each power-up class takes care of its own actions. However, the way this game is designed, the `PowerUp` object does not have access to things such as the sound manager or the map; the `PowerUp` objects do not perform any actions.

Simple Baddies

A game wouldn't be any fun without bad guys, right?

Hopefully, they don't have to be smart baddies because the two baddies in this game, the fly and the grub, aren't. All they do is move forward until they bump into a wall. Then they turn around and move forward again. And they do it over and over.

Animations

Before you implement the baddies, let's talk about their animations. You might notice, way back in Figure 5.4, that the player and the two baddies are facing only left. Instead of creating more PNG files for the players facing right, you can just make mirror images of the left-facing images.

Back in Chapter 2, "2D Graphics and Animation," you used the `AffineTransform` class to mirror an image whenever it is drawn. This time, you'll use the `AffineTransform` class to create mirror images on startup, saving them to another image. While you're at it, you'll create code to make horizontally mirrored, or flipped, images as well, as shown in Listing 5.6.

Listing 5.6   Creating Transformed Images

```
public Image getMirrorImage(Image image) {
    return getScaledImage(image, -1, 1);
}

public Image getFlippedImage(Image image) {
    return getScaledImage(image, 1, -1);
}

private Image getScaledImage(Image image, float x, float y) {

    // set up the transform
    AffineTransform transform = new AffineTransform();
    transform.scale(x, y);
    transform.translate(
        (x-1) * image.getWidth(null) / 2,
        (y-1) * image.getHeight(null) / 2);

    // create a transparent (not translucent) image
    Image newImage = gc.createCompatibleImage(
        image.getWidth(null),
        image.getHeight(null),
        Transparency.BITMASK);
```

continues

Listing 5.6 Creating Transformed Images *continued*

```
        // draw the transformed image
        Graphics2D g = (Graphics2D)newImage.getGraphics();
        g.drawImage(image, transform, null);
        g.dispose();

        return newImage;
    }
```

Now you can make sprites for when the player and baddies are moving to the right. Another sprite you might want is the one that shows a "dead" baddie. Again, you could create more PNG images for this, but instead, just use a flipped, or upside-down, version of the image to represent a dead baddie. That's where the getFlippedImage() method comes in.

Creature Class

Each baddie in the game can have four different animations:

➤ Moving left

➤ Moving right

➤ Dead, facing left

➤ Dead, facing right

To accommodate this, you need a new type of sprite object that can change its underlying animation whenever it changes direction or dies.

The Creature class, in Listing 5.7, accommodates this. Besides the four different animations, it keeps track of the state of the player, which is either STATE_NORMAL, STATE_DYING, or STATE_DEAD. It takes one second for a Creature to move from the "dying" state to the "dead" state.

Listing 5.7 Creature.java

```
package com.brackeen.javagamebook.tilegame.sprites;

import java.lang.reflect.Constructor;
import com.brackeen.javagamebook.graphics.*;
```

```
/**
    A Creature is a Sprite that is affected by gravity and can
    die. It has four Animations: moving left, moving right,
    dying on the left, and dying on the right.
*/
public abstract class Creature extends Sprite {

    /**
        Amount of time to go from STATE_DYING to STATE_DEAD.
    */
    private static final int DIE_TIME = 1000;

    public static final int STATE_NORMAL = 0;
    public static final int STATE_DYING = 1;
    public static final int STATE_DEAD = 2;

    private Animation left;
    private Animation right;
    private Animation deadLeft;
    private Animation deadRight;
    private int state;
    private long stateTime;

    /**
        Creates a new Creature with the specified Animations.
    */
    public Creature(Animation left, Animation right,
        Animation deadLeft, Animation deadRight)
    {
        super(right);
        this.left = left;
        this.right = right;
        this.deadLeft = deadLeft;
        this.deadRight = deadRight;
        state = STATE_NORMAL;
    }
```

continues

Listing 5.7 Creature.java *continued*

```java
public Object clone() {
    // use reflection to create the correct subclass
    Constructor constructor = getClass().getConstructors()[0];
    try {
        return constructor.newInstance(new Object[] {
                (Animation)left.clone(),
                (Animation)right.clone(),
                (Animation)deadLeft.clone(),
                (Animation)deadRight.clone()
            });
    }
    catch (Exception ex) {
        // should never happen
        ex.printStackTrace();
        return null;
    }
}


/**
    Gets the maximum speed of this Creature.
*/
public float getMaxSpeed() {
    return 0;
}


/**
    Wakes up the creature when the Creature first appears
    on screen. Normally, the creature starts moving left.
*/
public void wakeUp() {
    if (getState() == STATE_NORMAL && getVelocityX() == 0) {
        setVelocityX(-getMaxSpeed());
    }
}
```

```java
/**
    Gets the state of this Creature. The state is either
    STATE_NORMAL, STATE_DYING, or STATE_DEAD.
*/
public int getState() {
    return state;
}



/**
    Sets the state of this Creature to STATE_NORMAL,
    STATE_DYING, or STATE_DEAD.
*/
public void setState(int state) {
    if (this.state != state) {
        this.state = state;
        stateTime = 0;
        if (state == STATE_DYING) {
            setVelocityX(0);
            setVelocityY(0);
        }
    }
}



/**
    Checks if this creature is alive.
*/
public boolean isAlive() {
    return (state == STATE_NORMAL);
}



/**
    Checks if this creature is flying.
*/
public boolean isFlying() {
    return false;
```

continues

Listing 5.7   Creature.java   *continued*

```
    }


    /**
        Called before update() if the creature collided with a
        tile horizontally.
    */
    public void collideHorizontal() {
        setVelocityX(-getVelocityX());
    }


    /**
        Called before update() if the creature collided with a
        tile vertically.
    */
    public void collideVertical() {
        setVelocityY(0);
    }


    /**
        Updates the animation for this creature.
    */
    public void update(long elapsedTime) {
        // select the correct Animation
        Animation newAnim = anim;
        if (getVelocityX() < 0) {
            newAnim = left;
        }
        else if (getVelocityX() > 0) {
            newAnim = right;
        }
        if (state == STATE_DYING && newAnim == left) {
            newAnim = deadLeft;
        }
        else if (state == STATE_DYING && newAnim == right) {
```

```
            newAnim = deadRight;
        }

        // update the Animation
        if (anim != newAnim) {
            anim = newAnim;
            anim.start();
        }
        else {
            anim.update(elapsedTime);
        }

        // update to "dead" state
        stateTime += elapsedTime;
        if (state == STATE_DYING && stateTime >= DIE_TIME) {
            setState(STATE_DEAD);
        }
    }

}
```

The `Creature` class contains several methods to add functionality to the `Sprite` class:

➤ The `wakeUp()` method can be called when the baddie first appears on screen. In this case, it calls `setVelocityX(-getMaxSpeed())` to start the baddie moving, so baddies don't move until you first see them.

➤ The `isAlive()` and `isFlying()` methods are convenience methods to check the state of the baddie. Baddies that aren't alive don't hurt the player, and gravity doesn't apply to baddies that are flying.

➤ Finally, the methods `collideVertical()` and `collideHorizontal()` are called when the baddie collides with a tile. In the case of a vertical collision, the vertical velocity of the baddie is set to `0`. In the case of a horizontal collision, the baddie simply changes direction. That is the extent of the baddies' intelligence.

You'll notice that `Creature` is an abstract class, so you'll need to subclass it to get any use out of it. The first subclass you'll create is the `Grub` in Listing 5.8.

Listing 5.8 Grub.java

```
package com.brackeen.javagamebook.tilegame.sprites;

import com.brackeen.javagamebook.graphics.Animation;

/**
    A Grub is a Creature that moves slowly on the ground.
*/
public class Grub extends Creature {

    public Grub(Animation left, Animation right,
        Animation deadLeft, Animation deadRight)
    {
        super(left, right, deadLeft, deadRight);
    }


    public float getMaxSpeed() {
        return 0.05f;
    }

}
```

The code in the Grub class is very difficult to understand, so try to follow along. Okay, it's not difficult! The only thing it does is override the getMaxSpeed() method to set the speed of the grub to its slow pace.

The next baddie you'll create is the fly, in Listing 5.9.

Listing 5.9 Fly.java

```
package com.brackeen.javagamebook.tilegame.sprites;

import com.brackeen.javagamebook.graphics.Animation;

/**
    A Fly is a Creature that flies slowly in the air.
*/
```

```java
public class Fly extends Creature {

    public Fly(Animation left, Animation right,
        Animation deadLeft, Animation deadRight)
    {
        super(left, right, deadLeft, deadRight);
    }


    public float getMaxSpeed() {
        return 0.2f;
    }


    public boolean isFlying() {
        return isAlive();
    }

}
```

Just like the `Grub` class, `Fly` is a subclass of `Creature`. Besides defining the speed of the fly, the `isFlying()` method is overridden to return `true` as long as the fly is alive. That way, gravity applies to the fly only when it is dying or dead.

There's just one more subclass of `Creature`: the `Player` class in Listing 5.10. Although the player isn't a baddie, it needs the features of `Creature`, such as multiple animations and states.

Listing 5.10   Player.java

```java
package com.brackeen.javagamebook.tilegame.sprites;

import com.brackeen.javagamebook.graphics.Animation;

/**
    The Player.
*/
public class Player extends Creature {
```

Listing 5.10   Player.java   *continued*

```java
    private static final float JUMP_SPEED = -.95f;


    private boolean onGround;

    public Player(Animation left, Animation right,
        Animation deadLeft, Animation deadRight)
    {
        super(left, right, deadLeft, deadRight);
    }


    public void collideHorizontal() {
        setVelocityX(0);
    }


    public void collideVertical() {
        // check if collided with ground
        if (getVelocityY() > 0) {
            onGround = true;
        }
        setVelocityY(0);
    }


    public void setY(float y) {
        // check if falling
        if (Math.round(y) > Math.round(getY())) {
            onGround = false;
        }
        super.setY(y);
    }


    public void wakeUp() {
        // do nothing
    }
```

```
/**
    Makes the player jump if the player is on the ground or
    if forceJump is true.
*/
public void jump(boolean forceJump) {
    if (onGround || forceJump) {
        onGround = false;
        setVelocityY(JUMP_SPEED);
    }
}


public float getMaxSpeed() {
    return 0.5f;
}

}
```

Basically, the only feature `Player` adds to `Creature` is the ability to jump. Most of time, you don't want the player to be able jump if the player is not on the ground. The methods `setY()` and `collideVertical()` are overridden to keep track of whether the player is on the ground. If the player is on the ground, the player can jump. Alternatively, you can force a player to jump in midair by calling `jump(true)`.

Collision Detection

As mentioned before, you need to make sure the player (and the baddies) can't walk through walls but can jump up on platforms. In short, every time you move a creature, you need to check to see whether the creature collided with any tiles; if it did, you must adjust the creature's position accordingly. Because you're using tile-based maps, collision detection is an easy technique to implement.

We'll break this process down into parts: detecting a tile collision and correcting a sprite's position to avoid a collision.

Detecting a Collision

Theoretically, the sprite could move across several tiles at once and could be located in up to four different tiles at any one time. Therefore, you need to check every tile the sprite is currently in and every sprite the tile is going to be in.

Here's `getTileCollision()`, which achieves this task (see Listing 5.11). It checks to see if the sprite crosses any solid tiles in its path from its old position to its new position. If so, it returns the location of the tile the sprite collides with. Otherwise, it returns `null`.

Listing 5.11 `getTileCollision()` Method

```
Point pointCache = new Point();

...

/**
    If a collision is found, returns the tile location of the
    collision. Otherwise, returns null.
*/
public Point getTileCollision(Sprite sprite,
        float newX, float newY)
{
    float fromX = Math.min(sprite.getX(), newX);
    float fromY = Math.min(sprite.getY(), newY);
    float toX = Math.max(sprite.getX(), newX);
    float toY = Math.max(sprite.getY(), newY);

    // get the tile locations
    int fromTileX = TileMapRenderer.pixelsToTiles(fromX);
    int fromTileY = TileMapRenderer.pixelsToTiles(fromY);
    int toTileX = TileMapRenderer.pixelsToTiles(
        toX + sprite.getWidth() - 1);
    int toTileY = TileMapRenderer.pixelsToTiles(
        toY + sprite.getHeight() - 1);

    // check each tile for a collision
    for (int x=fromTileX; x<=toTileX; x++) {
```

```
        for (int y=fromTileY; y<=toTileY; y++) {
            if (x < 0 || x >= map.getWidth() ||
                map.getTile(x, y) != null)
            {
                // collision found, return the tile
                pointCache.setLocation(x, y);
                return pointCache;
            }
        }
    }

    // no collision found
    return null;
}
```

Also, `getTileCollision()` treats movement off the left or right edge of the map as a collision, to keep creatures on the map.

Note that this method isn't perfect when a sprite moves across several tiles in between frames (a case for a large amount of time between frames). You'll implement better sprite-to-environment collisions in Chapter 11, "Collision Detection," but this code will work for most cases.

Handling a Collision

Next, you'll correct the sprite's position after a collision is detected. Start with the example in Figure 5.8, with the sprite moving down and to the right.

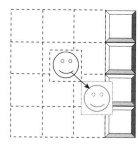

Figure 5.8   The sprite collides with a wall when it moves too far.

In this case, the sprite moves diagonally and collides with two sprites at the same time. Visually, it looks like an easy fix: Just scoot the sprite over to the left. But how can you calculate that the fix is to move left and not up, down, or to the right?

To calculate this, break the movement of the sprite into two parts: moving horizontally and moving vertically. First, move the sprite horizontally, as shown in Figure 5.9.

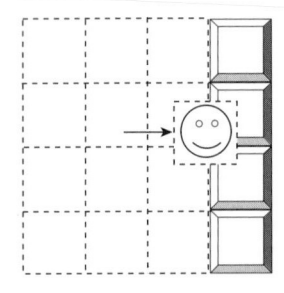

Figure 5.9 First, move the sprite horizontally. A collision is detected.

In this example, a collision with a tile is detected. To correct this, just move the sprite back the opposite way it came, lining up the sprite with the edge of the tile, as shown in Figure 5.10.

Figure 5.10 Second, correct the sprite's horizontal position so it doesn't collide with any tiles.

Now the player has moved horizontally, and its position has been corrected to avoid a collision. Next, apply the same technique for the vertical movement, as shown in Figure 5.11.

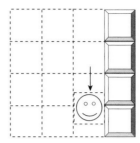

Figure 5.11   Finally, move the sprite vertically. In this case, there is no collision.

In this example, there is no collision when the sprite moves vertically, so you are done.

The code for this is in the updateCreature() method in Listing 5.12: to move the sprite's horizontal position and then its vertical position, checking and correcting for collisions all the way.

Listing 5.12   updateCreature() **Method**

```
private void updateCreature(Creature creature, long elapsedTime) {

    // apply gravity
    if (!creature.isFlying()) {
        creature.setVelocityY(creature.getVelocityY() +
            GRAVITY * elapsedTime);
    }

    // change x
    float dx = creature.getVelocityX();
    float oldX = creature.getX();
    float newX = oldX + dx * elapsedTime;
    Point tile =
        getTileCollision(creature, newX, creature.getY());
    if (tile == null) {
        creature.setX(newX);
    }
    else {
        // line up with the tile boundary
        if (dx > 0) {
            creature.setX(
```

continues

Listing 5.12 updateCreature() **Method** *continued*

```
                  TileMapRenderer.tilesToPixels(tile.x) -
                  creature.getWidth());
        }
        else if (dx < 0) {
            creature.setX(
                  TileMapRenderer.tilesToPixels(tile.x + 1));
        }
        creature.collideHorizontal();
    }

    // change y
    float dy = creature.getVelocityY();
    float oldY = creature.getY();
    float newY = oldY + dy * elapsedTime;
    tile = getTileCollision(creature, creature.getX(), newY);
    if (tile == null) {
        creature.setY(newY);
    }
    else {
        // line up with the tile boundary
        if (dy > 0) {
            creature.setY(
                  TileMapRenderer.tilesToPixels(tile.y) -
                  creature.getHeight());
        }
        else if (dy < 0) {
            creature.setY(
                  TileMapRenderer.tilesToPixels(tile.y + 1));
        }
        creature.collideVertical();
    }
}
```

The updateCreature() method also applies gravity to creatures that aren't flying. Gravity always affects the creatures, but if a creature is standing on a tile, the effect isn't visible because the creature collides with the tile it is standing on.

When a collision is detected and corrected for, the creature's `collideVertical()` or `collideHorizontal()` methods are called. Usually these methods change or halt the velocity of the creature so the collision won't happen again any time soon.

That's it! Now the player and the baddies can roam around the map without walking through tiles.

Sprite Collisions

Next, you need to detect when the player collides with other sprites, such as power-ups and bad guys. In this game, you'll ignore collisions between creatures and just detect collisions with the player. This is simply a matter of seeing whether the player's sprite boundary intersects with another sprite's boundary, as shown in the `isCollision()` method in Listing 5.13.

Listing 5.13   `isCollision()` Method

```
public boolean isCollision(Sprite s1, Sprite s2) {
    // if the Sprites are the same, return false.
    if (s1 == s2) {
        return false;
    }
    // if one of the Sprites is a dead Creature, return false
    if (s1 instanceof Creature && !((Creature)s1).isAlive()) {
        return false;
    }
    if (s2 instanceof Creature && !((Creature)s2).isAlive()) {
        return false;
    }

    // get the pixel location of the Sprites
    int s1x = Math.round(s1.getX());
    int s1y = Math.round(s1.getY());
    int s2x = Math.round(s2.getX());
    int s2y = Math.round(s2.getY());

    // check if the two Sprites' boundaries intersect
    return (s1x < s2x + s2.getWidth() &&
```

continues

Listing 5.13 `isCollision()` **Method** *continued*

```
            s2x < s1x + s1.getWidth() &&
            s1y < s2y + s2.getHeight() &&
            s2y < s1y + s1.getHeight());
}
```

Because the `TileMap` contains all the sprites in a list, you can just run through the list checking every sprite to see if it collided with the player, shown in Listing 5.14.

Listing 5.14 `getSpriteCollision()` **Method**

```
public Sprite getSpriteCollision(Sprite sprite) {

    // run through the list of Sprites
    Iterator i = map.getSprites();
    while (i.hasNext()) {
        Sprite otherSprite = (Sprite)i.next();
        if (isCollision(sprite, otherSprite)) {
            // collision found, return the Sprite
            return otherSprite;
        }
    }

    // no collision found
    return null;
}
```

What happens when a collision with a sprite is made is entirely up to you. If the sprite is a power-up, you can just give the player points, play a sound, or do whatever else the power-up is supposed to do.

If the sprite is a bad guy, you can either kill the bad guy or kill the player. In this case, you kill the creature if the player falls or jumps on it, or, in other words, when the vertical movement of the player is increasing:

```
boolean canKill = (oldY < player.getY());
```

In all other cases, such as when the player just walks up and touches a bad guy, the player dies.

In the future, you might want to add other ways to kill a bad guy, such as with an "invincible" power-up or by pushing a creature off a cliff.

Finishing Things Up and Making It Fast

Now you have just about everything you need for the game. Of course, some of the basics, such as keyboard input, sound, and music, are in the game, too, but these functions exist in classes not listed in this chapter. Besides the classes already listed in this chapter, there are three other classes:

➤ `GameManager`   Handles keyboard input, updates sprites, provides collision detection, and plays sound and music.

➤ `TileMapRenderer`   Draws the tile map, parallax background, and sprites.

➤ `ResourceManager`   Loads images, creates animations and sprites, and loads levels.

Don't worry; the source code for these classes is on the website, and the code relevant to this chapter was listed here and there.

To make the game run at a higher frame rate, a couple of changes were made to the `GameCore` class:

➤ A 16-bit color mode is the first choice to provide faster frame rates.

➤ The code to sleep for 20 milliseconds in the game loop was removed so that the game uses all the processor power possible.

Creating an Executable .jar File

Finally, when you're ready to pass out your game to friends, the last thing you want is to give them arcane instructions on how to run the code. Telling another programmer to type something like this at the command line might be okay:

```
java com.brackeen.javagamebook.tilegame.GameManager
```

But the casual user might not even know what a command line is or even what to do if problems occur. It's probably a good idea to make it easier by creating an executable .jar file. With an executable .jar file, all the user has to do is double-click the .jar file, and the game starts right up. Your programmer friends would probably appreciate the time it saves them as well.

If you're unfamiliar with what a .jar file is, it's a *Java archive* file—basically just a container for a group of classes. All the classes for your game are stored in the .jar file, which is usually compressed.

To make the .jar file executable, you specify which class to run in the .jar's *manifest file*. The manifest file is called META-INF/MANIFEST.MF inside the .jar. For this platform game, the manifest file looks something like this:

```
Manifest-Version: 1.0
Main-Class: com.brackeen.javagamebook.tilegame.GameManager
```

When you double-click a .jar file, the Java VM starts up and looks at the .jar file's manifest. If the `Main-Class` attribute is found, it runs the specified class. If there is no manifest or the `Main-Class` attribute doesn't exist, the VM just pretends that nothing happened and exits.

If you're using the jar tool to create .jar files, first create a manifest file in a text editor and then use the -m option to add the manifest file to your .jar.

If you're using Ant to build .jar files, Ant can create the manifest file automatically and add it to the .jar. Listing 5.15 shows a sample Ant target that creates an executable .jar file for the game.

Listing 5.15   Sample Ant Build Target for Making an Executable .jar

```
<target name="build" depends="compile">
  <jar jarfile="${basedir}/tilegame.jar">
    <manifest>
      <attribute name="Main-Class"
          value="com.brackeen.javagamebook.tilegame.GameManager"/>
    </manifest>
```

```
        <fileset dir="${destdir}" includes="**/*.class"/>
    </jar>
</target>
```

Manifests can also contain all sorts of other data. Check out the "Jar Guide" in the Java SDK documentation for all the information, and see ant.apache.org for more information on Ant.

Note, however, that not everyone will be able to execute a .jar by double-clicking on it. Linux users won't be able to, and someone on a Windows machine might have WinZip set up to open .jar files instead of the Java runtime. If you can't double-click the .jar, run this command at the console:

```
java -jar tilegame.jar
```

Also check out Chapter 18, "Game Design and the Last 10%," for information on other ways to deploy your game, such as using Java Web Start.

Ideas to Expand the Game

The tile game isn't perfect, and there are lots of ways to make it better. First, a few problems could be fixed:

➤ On Windows machines, the granularity of the system timer isn't accurate enough for smooth scrolling. You'll create a workaround for this in Chapter 16, "Optimization Techniques."

➤ Using sprite bounds for collision detection isn't accurate enough. Smaller collision bounds could be used instead. We present more ideas for this problem in Chapter 11.

➤ Also, you could use better collision handling for times when the sprite travels across large distances between frames. You'll implement this in Chapter 11 as well.

Furthermore, just by adding levels and more tile images, you could make the gameplay last much longer. You could also tweak the engine to make it faster and taller, with weaker gravity, or whatever suits your desires. Here are some other ideas that you could add to it:

➤ Add interactive tiles, such as being able to break tiles or open doors. This could add a puzzle element to the game.

➤ Add "walk-through" tiles that have a graphic but aren't solid. This could be useful for map decoration.

➤ Add more than one parallax-scrolling background, such as a transparent background of trees or mountains.

➤ Use a different sprite animation when the player is jumping.

➤ Create a more destructive environment by adding falling rocks or bottomless pits.

➤ Give the player variable-height jumping and running acceleration. The longer the jump key is held down, the higher the player jumps. Likewise, the longer the player moves, the faster the player goes.

➤ Add creature-to-creature collisions so that bad guys bump into one another instead of walk through each other.

➤ Use 3D sound to make the fly buzz when it gets closer to you, or make all sounds echo as if you're in a cave.

➤ Provide a better map-to-map transition, such as summing up the stars collected for the previous map and providing a "get ready" screen before the next map.

➤ Add more standard game options, such as pausing, key configuration, and menus.

➤ Add more bad guys, more graphics, more levels—more, more, more!

Summary

You've come a long way! It's only the fifth chapter of the book, but already you've created a fun 2D platform game with a tile-based map, collision detection, bad guys, power-ups, and parallax scrolling.

Chapter 6

Multi-Player Games

By Bret Barker

Multi-player computer games have been around for decades. Long ago, in the distant computing world of the 1970s, hackers wrote primitive network games on DEC VAXs and other minicomputers running early versions of UNIX, VMS, and other operating systems. By the 1980s, multi-user dungeons (MUDs) were gaining popularity, and every major online service of the time (CompuServe, Prodigy, and GEnie) had its own offering of online games.

In those days before the Internet boom, the audience was still very small because most homes were without Internet connections or even computers. All that changed in 1993 when Id Software released its first network-enabled first-person shooter (FPS), *Doom*. *Doom* allowed up to four players to shoot at each over a local area network (LAN), or two players to play via modem. The introduction of *Doom* brought about a new genre of high-speed multi-player games. *Doom* was followed by *Quake*, which gave rise to LAN parties and a new crop of companies (mostly defunct now) dedicated to providing dedicated, low-latency game server networks.

As more people swarmed to the Internet, an opportunity arose to provide games to a wider audience than the traditional hard-core gamers. The casual games genre was born, consisting of web-based or downloadable games that were a bit slower in pace. A number of companies sprung up in the late 1990s to serve this demographic, offering basic parlor games (chess, checkers, solitaire, blackjack, and so on), word and puzzle-style games, as well as some original games. Although these games are turn-based and relatively slow compared to FPS games, sites such as Pogo, Yahoo! Games, and MSN Gaming Zone serve a large player base and often have thousands of simultaneous players.

The other major genre addition of the 1990s was the massively multi-player online role-playing game (MMORPG), started by 3DO with its release of *Meridian 59* in 1996, but quickly eclipsed by EA's *Ultima Online* and Sony's *Everquest*. These games broke new ground with the number of simultaneous users supported and the vastness of their virtual worlds.

Each of these genres has come with its own set of design challenges. In this chapter, we explore the design of a generic multi-player game server and client. We discuss the use of the JDK 1.4 NIO packages through a simple client/server example, show you how to build a flexible multi-player game server framework, and discuss some advanced topics. In the end, you will have a good base of knowledge and code to serve as a starting point for building your own multi-player game server.

This chapter is a bit of a departure from those presented earlier. You won't be doing anything sexy here—no flashy graphics, no dazzling sound effects. Nope, the most exciting thing you'll see here is a message in the server log file that reads:

```
New connection from 10.0.0.1, 483 users online.
```

So, if sockets, logging, thread pool wraps, and remote admin consoles sound like fun to you, let's get to it!

Prerequisite Knowledge

It is assumed that you have working knowledge of a command shell, whether bash, tcsh, or the Windows shell (cmd). Note that if you are working on Windows, Cygwin (available at www.cygwin.com) will make life much easier because it provides a bash shell and a set of standard command-line utilities.

Server applications are meant to be run headless and to provide their output via log files. *Headless* refers to the lack of a GUI (the head) for the application. You'll want to become familiar with how to browse and search the logs using tools such as grep and tail.

For example, to view the last 50 lines of a log file, enter the following:

```
tail -n 50 server.log
```

To continuously watch an active log file, use the `-f` (follow) switch:

```
tail -f server.log
```

More recent versions of the GNU `tail` command have a `-F` switch that follows the same log file-name even when the underlying file is replaced. This is valuable for watching logs that rotate often.

`grep` is a tool used to find lines in text files that match a given pattern. By combining `tail` with `grep` using a pipe (`|`), you suddenly have a very powerful tool for analyzing your log files. Let's say you want to see only log messages that refer to client disconnections. The following command gives you just those lines from a running log:

```
tail -F server.log | grep disconnect
```

If you are analyzing old logs, you might want to combine `grep` with a `pager` command, such as `less`:

```
grep disconnect server.log | less
```

The man pages for these commands provide full details on their usage and options.

Additionally, familiarity with network diagnostic tools such as netstat and packet sniffers such as ethereal will aid immensely in debugging server operation and client/server communications.

The Revolution in Java's I/O Libraries

Network servers (and particularly game servers) must handle a large number of simultaneous clients. They must be capable of efficiently reading and writing a huge volume of messages to and from those clients.

Before the release of the JDK 1.4, Java did not have a built-in mechanism for handling nonblocking I/O operations. Server applications were forced to have at least one thread per connected client, sitting there waiting on a blocking socket `read()` method.

The drawbacks of this are fairly obvious, but let's enumerate a few of them. Operating systems have limits on the number of threads, either just by policy or intrinsically due to performance of the scheduler. Also, there is a minimum stack memory overhead for each thread, time associated with thread creation, and the overhead of saving and restoring thread state during context switches. All of these are good reasons to want to keep the number of threads to a minimum. When you need to serve hundreds or thousands of simultaneous users, one thread per user just won't cut it.

Fortunately, and only after significant pressure from the Java community, Sun introduced a new I/O system with the release of JDK 1.4. These New I/O (NIO) APIs reside in the `java.nio` package and its subpackages `java.nio.channels` and `java.nio.charset`.

Overview of the JDK 1.4 NIO Libraries

Java's NIO packages consist of a number of new classes designed specifically to provide a high-performance I/O system, as has long been available in C and other languages. In addition to the new classes, several of the original networking classes (such as `java.net.Socket`) were updated to cooperate with the new APIs.

Java's NIO classes fall into several categories: channels, buffers, and selectors. It is important to get comfortable with these classes because they are used to form the foundation of our applications. Let's start with an overview of these classes and then move on to an example of their use in an application.

Channels

Channels are abstract representations of operating system resources, such as files, pipes, and, most important for our discussion, network sockets.

Channels and buffers replace the functionality that Java's `Stream` classes provided in the earlier JDKs for dealing with network and file resources.

Interfaces

At the root of all channel classes is the `java.nio.channel.Channel` interface, which contains only two method prototypes:

```
public void close();
public boolean isOpen();
```

The `Channel` interface is extended by a number of subinterfaces. The first two of interest are `ReadableByteChannel` and `WritableByteChannel`, which add the following two methods:

```
public int read(ByteBuffer dst);
public int write(ByteBuffer src);
```

The first is used to read data from the channel into the given buffer, and the second is used to write data to the channel from the given buffer.

The `ByteChannel` interface merely combines `ReadableByteChannel` and `WritableByteChannel` into a single interface.

`GatheringByteChannel` and `ScatteringByteChannel` add the capability to write from or read to multiple buffers in a single operation. This is useful when reading a message's header and payload into two separate buffers. For instance, if you were reading HTTP post responses, you might want the HTTP header in one buffer and the `POST` data in another. The method signatures are shown here:

```
long write(ByteBuffer[] srcs);
long write(ByteBuffer[] srcs, long offset, long length);
long read(ByteBuffer[] dsts);
long read(ByteBuffer[] dsts, long offset, long length);
```

The return values from the `write` methods are the number of bytes actually written, which can be 0. The `read` methods return the number of bytes read, or `-1` to indicate end-of-stream. In many situations when the socket connection is terminated, this `-1` return value is your first indication of failure.

Classes

The following is a brief description of the classes in the `java.nio.channels` package that are of interest for server programming. For further details and descriptions of the remaining classes, see the API documentation.

ServerSocketChannel

This class is used in place of (and wraps an underlying) `java.net.ServerSocket`. You'll use a `ServerSocketChannel` for accepting incoming client socket connections.

A new `ServerSocketChannel` is created by invoking the static `open()` method. To put it into action, however, you must first configure its blocking mode and then bind it to an address and port.

A `SelectableChannel` can be in either blocking or nonblocking mode. If set to blocking, all I/O operations on the channel block until they complete. In nonblocking mode, I/O operations return immediately, possibly without actually performing any I/O. A `ServerSocketChannel` defaults to blocking operation. As such, the `ServerSocketChannel.accept()` method acts just like the old `ServerSocket.accept()`, blocking the current thread until a connection is made.

Here is a quick example of setting up a `ServerSocketChannel` for nonblocking operations:

```
// open a ServerSocketChannel and configure for non-blocking mode
ServerSocketChannel sSockChan;
sSockChan = ServerSocketChannel.open();
sSockChan.configureBlocking(false);
// bind to localhost on designated port
InetAddress addr = InetAddress.getLocalHost();
sSockChan.socket().bind(new InetSocketAddress(addr, PORT));
```

Later, in the ChatterBox sample application, you'll see how to register the channel with a selector and start accepting connections.

Access to the `ServerSocketChannel`'s underlying `ServerSocket` object is achieved via the `socket()` method:

```
public ServerSocket socket();
```

One additional method of note is the `validOps()` method, inherited from `SelectableChannel`, which returns the operations for which the channel

has been registered. For ServerSocketChannels, this always returns
SelectionKey.OP_ACCEPT. Refer to the java.nio.channels.SelectionKey
API documentation for further discussion of socket operations.

SocketChannel

A SocketChannel is used to represent each individual client's socket connection to
the server. Similar to ServerSocketChannel, SocketChannel replaces and wraps an
underlying java.net.Socket object.

> **NOTE**
> ServerSocketChannel and SocketChannel are for TCP connections only; for UDP
> connections, see the description of DatagramChannel in the next section.

SocketChannel has all the methods of ServerSocketChannel, plus additional
methods for reading and writing, and for methods for managing the connection of the
socket. On the server, sockets are opened when you accept a connection from your
ServerSocketChannel; on the client side, you use either the open(SocketAddress
address) method or the open() method followed by a call to
connect(SocketAddress address).

We'll use SocketChannels for all of the read and write operations between the client
and server, as you'll see later in this chapter.

DatagramChannel

This class is used to send and receive data using the User Datagram Protocol (UDP)
instead of TCP.

The User Datagram Protocol is defined in RFC 768 (www.faqs.org/ftp/
rfc/rfc768.txt). As opposed to TCP, UDP is an unreliable protocol. This means
that there is no guarantee that any packet sent will actually arrive at the destination,
nor that packets sent will arrive in the same order in which they were sent.

Most of the discussion in this chapter covers TCP because it is the easiest to deal with,
and most of our game messages need to be reliably delivered for the game to function
correctly.

UDP has its place, though, and can be very useful when a large number of events need to be sent very rapidly and you don't care whether they all make it. For example, in a multi-player FPS-style game, the position of each player must be continuously communicated to other players. The delay involved in TCP transmissions would be unacceptable for this task, especially in the hostile network conditions common on the Internet, where packets routinely are dropped and need to be resent. With UDP, however, you can blast the location data out and if the server gets packets that are out of order, it can simply dump them in the bit bucket and continue on because the player has already moved on, so to speak. Additionally, UDP packets are much smaller than TCP packets and, thus, make more efficient use of UDP bandwidth.

Buffers

A *buffer* is a finite block of memory used for temporary storage of primitive data types. You'll use buffers to hold data as it is moved in and out of SocketChannels.

Classes

The java.nio package is home to a number of buffer classes, one for each of Java's primitive data types:

- ➤ ByteBuffer
- ➤ CharBuffer
- ➤ DoubleBuffer (not to be confused with double-buffering, explained in Chapter 2, "2D Graphics and Animation")
- ➤ FloatBuffer
- ➤ IntBuffer
- ➤ LongBuffer
- ➤ ShortBuffer

Additionally, there is a special buffer class for memory-mapped files called MappedByteBuffer, which is useful when handling large files. A FileChannel's map() method is used to attach the buffer to the file.

All of the buffer classes belong to the `java.nio` package and derive from the abstract base class `Buffer`. `Buffer` defines methods for querying and manipulating the capacity, position, limit, and mark of the buffer:

➤ The capacity is the number of elements of the given primitive type that it can contain and is set at creation time using the `allocate()` methods of the subclasses. We discuss buffer allocation when we get to the specifics of `ByteBuffers` later.

➤ The limit is the roadblock for reading from and writing to the buffer. When reading, it is the index of the first element that cannot be read. When writing, it is the index of the first element that cannot be written.

➤ The position is, of course, the current position in the buffer, where the next element will be read or written.

➤ The mark is used for moving the position back to a set point when the `reset()` method is called.

These indicators are shown in Figure 6.1, in which the buffer is in a random valid state.

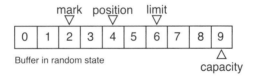

Figure 6.1   Buffer with mark, position, limit, and capacity indicated.

Filling and Draining

Buffers can be filled either by reading from a channel or with the various `put()` methods defined in the subclasses. For example, if you wanted to read a number of bytes `length` at offset o from a file into a `ByteBuffer`, you would use the `FileChannel.read(ByteBuffer src, int o, int length)` method.

Buffers can be drained either by writing from the buffer to a channel or with the various `get()` methods defined in the subclasses. For example, to write data to a `SocketChannel` from a `ByteBuffer`, you would call the `SocketChannel.write(ByteBuffer src)` method.

Remember that buffers are of fixed capacity, so they don't actually grow and shrink when filling or draining. Instead, only the aforementioned indicators (position, limit, and mark) are altered.

Manipulating Buffers

You should familiarize yourself with a few key methods to work with buffers:

➤ clear()

➤ flip()

➤ rewind()

➤ compact()

To prepare a buffer for filling, the clear() method is called, which sets the position to 0 and the limit to the capacity, as seen in Figure 6.2. Thus, following the clear() call, the buffer is ready to accept capacity elements from a channel read or put() operation.

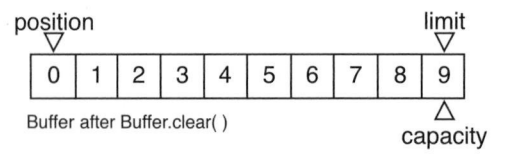

Figure 6.2 The buffer after calling Buffer.clear().

After a buffer is full (or at least contains as much data as required), the flip() method can be called to prepare the buffer for draining with a get() or channel write() operation. Flip() sets the limit to the current position and sets the position to 0. Figure 6.3 shows a buffer after data has been placed in it with a put() or channel write() and then shows the same buffer after calling flip().

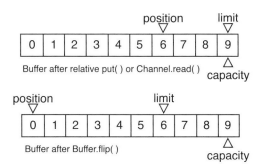

Figure 6.3   The buffer after calling `Buffer.flip()`.

`Buffer.rewind()` simply resets the position to 0, preparing the buffer for another draining, assuming it has already been flipped. This would be used, for example, to write some data to both a socket and a file, or to write the same data to multiple client channels. This scenario is depicted in Figure 6.4.

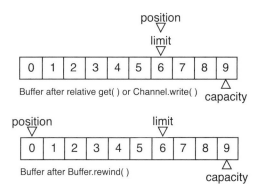

Figure 6.4   The buffer after calling `Buffer.rewind()`.

The `compact()` method moves the elements between the current position and the limit to the beginning of the buffer. The position is left at the end of the data after the move, and the limit is set to the capacity. We'll use this method later in the server, so keep an eye out for it.

Direct Versus Nondirect

One last thing to understand about Java's buffers is that they can be either direct or nondirect. Direct buffers are allocated as a native data structure that can transfer data to or from a native resource such as a socket without having to copy the data into a data structure inside the Java VM. This can have enormous positive impact on performance.

Likewise, when allocating buffers that will not interact with native resources, a nondirect buffer should be used. Other than allocation using either `allocate()` or `allocateDirect()`, there is no difference in the API when using a direct or nondirect buffer.

Selectors and *SelectionKeys*

One of the main features of the NIO libraries is the capability to perform nonblocking read and write operations on sockets. To take advantage of this, however, you need a way to handle multiple connections in an organized fashion. Selectors are the key to this, providing a mechanism for multiplexing access to the channels.

Multiplexing is a method of combining multiple communication signals into a single data stream by interleaving the signals in either the frequency or the time domain. In the case of channels and selectors, the selector listens for incoming data from all registered channels and presents it serially through the results of the `select()` method. This way, you need to talk to only a single `Selector` object to find out when any of the channels have data ready.

Channels are first registered with a selector, along with a set of operations that the selector should watch for, using the `SelectableChannel.register()` method. The operations are OP_ACCEPT, OP_CONNECT, OP_READ, and OP_WRITE; they are defined as constants in the `SelectionKey` class.

> **NOTE**
> It is okay to use a single selector for both the `ServerSocketChannel` and client `SocketChannels`, to listen for new connections and channels with data ready to read from a single source. However, in practice, we will separate the two types for clarity of the design.

When you are ready to look for activity on your registered channels, call one of the `select` methods of the selector. Three versions of the `select` method exist:

➤ select()   Blocks until at least one channel has activity in the interest set. The interest set is the set of operations (any of OP_ACCEPT, OP_CONNECT, OP_READ, or OP_WRITE) that the selector will watch for on the channel.

➤ select(long timeout)   Same as select(), but blocks for only a maximum of timeout milliseconds.

➤ selectNow()   Returns immediately, regardless of how many channels are ready—possibly zero.

When a select method is called, the operating system is queried about the registered channels, and any that have activity have their SelectionKeys added to the Selector's set of selected keys. The select methods all return an integer to indicate the number of selected keys, or 0 if none is ready.

After a select call, the ready SelectionKeys can be retrieved by calling Selector.selectedKeys(), which returns a Set. SelectionKeys are little more than holders for the channels they are linked to, but they provide one important feature that we'll use throughout your code. Each SelectionKey can hold on to any object as an attachment. We will use the attachment simply to store partially read messages from each channel, but you might find other good uses for it as well. Attachments can be provided when the channel is registered with the selector, or later using SelectionKey.attach(), and are retrieved using the attachment() method.

One other method of the Selector class bears mentioning: wakeup(). The wakeup() method is one of several ways to break a selector out of a blocking select() call. The other ways are either to call Thread.interrupt() on the blocked thread or to call the selector's close() method.

ChatterBox, A Basic Multi-Player Application

Now that we have the basics out of the way, let's get down to some real code. In this section, we'll build a working client/server application called ChatterBox. Although it is simple, it demonstrates how to put together what we've learned so far into something useful.

The Server: ChatterServer

ChatterServer is a multi-user chat application that allows for any number of users to connect to the server and send text messages to one another.

The server needs to perform the following main functions:

➤ Accept client connections

➤ Read messages from clients

➤ Write messages to clients

➤ Handle disconnections (graceful or otherwise)

Initial Setup

Before getting into the work functions, there is a bit of setup to do. In the constructor for ChatterServer is the following:

```
clients = new LinkedList();
writeBuffer = ByteBuffer.allocateDirect(255);
readBuffer = ByteBuffer.allocateDirect(255);
```

The LinkedList is for keeping track of the connected clients. Additionally, we allocate two ByteBuffers, one for reading from the channel and one for writing to the channel. Both buffers are allocated as direct buffers. Because we'll be passing data between sockets and the buffers, this allows the Java VM to use optimized operating system calls and to avoid passing the data across the boundary between native and Java code, as discussed earlier.

The server will listen on port 10997 for incoming client connections. The choice of port 10997 is arbitrary. You could, of course, set your server to communicate over any port you want, but it is good practice to respect the "well-known" port numbers (see www.iana.org/assignments/port-numbers). The port is set up in the initServerSocket() method, shown in Listing 6.1.

Listing 6.1   Initializing the Server

```
private static final int PORT = 10997;

private void initServerSocket() {
    try {
        sSockChan = ServerSocketChannel.open();
        sSockChan.configureBlocking(false);

        InetAddress addr = InetAddress.getLocalHost();
        sSockChan.socket().bind(new InetSocketAddress(addr, PORT));

        readSelector = Selector.open();
    }
    catch (Exception e) {
        log.error("error initializing server", e);
    }
}
```

First, we open a ServerSocketChannel and configure it for nonblocking operation. Then bind it to the IP address and port. Finally, a selector is opened, with which all new client channels will be registered.

The Main Loop

Now that everything is all set up, we can go ahead and start the run() method. For simplicity, your ChatterServer is implemented using a single thread, so we'll do all of our actions in one main loop. The run() method simply calls the acceptNewConnections() and readIncomingMessages() methods repeatedly.

Accepting Connections

Accepting incoming client connections is a simple matter of invoking the accept() method on the previously opened ServerSocketChannel. Listing 6.2 shows the acceptNewConnections() method from ChatterServer.

Listing 6.2   Accepting Client Connections

```
private void acceptNewConnections() {
    try {
        SocketChannel clientChannel;
        while ((clientChannel = sSockChan.accept()) != null) {
            addNewClient(clientChannel);
            sendBroadcastMessage("login from: " +
                clientChannel.socket().getInetAddress(),
                clientChannel);
            sendMessage(clientChannel, "\n\nWelcome to ChatterBox,
                there are " + clients.size() + " users online.\n");
            sendMessage(clientChannel, "Type 'quit' to exit.\n");
        }
    }
    catch (IOException ioe) {
        log.warn("error during accept(): ", ioe);
    }
    catch (Exception e) {
        log.error("exception in acceptNewConnections()", e);
    }
}

private void addNewClient(SocketChannel chan) {
    clients.add(chan);
    try {
        chan.configureBlocking( false);
        SelectionKey readKey = chan.register(readSelector,
            SelectionKey.OP_READ, new StringBuffer());
    }
    catch (ClosedChannelException cce) {}
    catch (IOException ioe) {}
}
```

The ServerSocketChannel is configured for nonblocking operation, so all calls to accept() will return immediately, regardless of whether a connection is pending. This avoids blocking the one and only server thread. If no connections are pending, this method will end quickly; otherwise, it will loop until all new connections are processed. For each connection, we first call addNewClient(), also shown in Listing 6.2, which does a few housekeeping tasks. The client channel is configured as non-blocking and then is registered with the selector. We are interested in knowing only when the channel has data available for reading, so SelectionKey.OP_READ is passed as the interest set. The last parameter is the attachment for the SelectionKey assigned to the channel. Here, a simple StringBuffer is used as the attachment that will hold partially read messages for this client.

Finally, a welcome message is sent to the new client and a broadcast message is sent to all connected clients notifying them of the new connection.

Writing Messages

ChatterServer has a sendMessage() method that is used to write messages to individual ChatterClients, as well as sendBroadcastMessage() for sending to all clients. Listing 6.3 shows the implementation along with the helper methods, prepWriteBuffer() and channelWrite().

Listing 6.3   Writing Messages

```
private void sendMessage(SocketChannel channel, String mesg) {
    prepWriteBuffer(mesg);
    channelWrite(channel, writeBuffer);
}

private void sendBroadcastMessage(String mesg, SocketChannel from)
{
    prepWriteBuffer(mesg);
    Iterator i = clients.iterator();
    while (i.hasNext()) {
        SocketChannel channel = (SocketChannel)i.next();
        if (channel != from)
            channelWrite(channel, writeBuffer);
    }
}

private void prepWriteBuffer(String mesg) {
    writeBuffer.clear();
```

continues

Listing 6.3 Writing Messages *continued*

```
        writeBuffer.put(mesg.getBytes());
        writeBuffer.putChar('\n');
        writeBuffer.flip();
    }

    private void channelWrite(SocketChannel channel,
                                 ByteBuffer writeBuffer) {
        long nbytes = 0;
        long toWrite = writeBuffer.remaining();

        try {
            while (nbytes != toWrite) {
                nbytes += channel.write(writeBuffer);

                try {
                    Thread.sleep(CHANNEL_WRITE_SLEEP);
                }
                catch (InterruptedException e) {}
            }
        }
        catch (ClosedChannelException cce) {}
        catch (Exception e) {}

        writeBuffer.rewind();
    }
```

In prepWriteBuffer(), we start by clearing the writeBuffer. Then fill it with data
from the String that is provided using the ByteBuffer.put() method. Then we call
writeBuffer.flip() to prepare the buffer for writing to the channel. Recall that the
flip() method sets the buffer's limit to the current position, which is at the end of the
data just inserted, and resets the position to 0.

ChannelWrite() consists of a loop around the Channel.write() call. The
reason for the loop is that the nonblocking SocketChannel will not necessarily
write the entire contents of the given buffer in one shot. It can write only as many
bytes as are available in the socket's output buffer. Note that you can change
the size of the socket buffers using Socket.setSendBufferSize() and

`Socket.setReceiveBufferSize()`. The defaults are operating system–dependent. In this ChatterBox application, it is likely that a message will get sent in one call to the `write()` method, but this is good practice and will definitely be required for the full client and server applications in which message sizes and volumes can be much larger.

Note at the end of `channelWrite()` that `writeBuffer.rewind()` is called. This sets up the buffer for subsequent channel writes by moving the buffer's position back to 0 while keeping the limit—and the buffer's contents—intact.

`sendBroadcastMessage()` calls `sendMessage()` for each client in the list, with the exception of the `from` client. There is no need for the originator of the message to be sent a copy.

Reading Messages

Receiving messages from clients is a bit more complicated than sending them. The complication arises not from pulling bytes from the channel, but from the need to determine when a full message has arrived. Listing 6.4 shows the full `read()` method of ChatterServer.

Listing 6.4   `ChatterServer.readIncomingMessages()`

```
private void readIncomingMessages() {
    try {
        readSelector.selectNow();
        Set readyKeys = readSelector.selectedKeys();
        Iterator i = readyKeys.iterator();
        while (i.hasNext()) {
            SelectionKey key = (SelectionKey) i.next();
            i.remove();
            SocketChannel channel = (SocketChannel) key.channel();
            readBuffer.clear();
            long nbytes = channel.read(readBuffer);
            // check for end-of-stream
            if (nbytes == -1) {
                log.info("disconnect: " +
                    channel.socket().getInetAddress() +
                    ", end-of-stream");
                channel.close();
```

continues

Listing 6.4   `ChatterServer.readIncomingMessages()`   *continued*

```
                        clients.remove(channel);
                        sendBroadcastMessage("logout: " +
                            channel.socket().getInetAddress() , channel);
                    }
                else {
                        StringBuffer sb = (StringBuffer)key.attachment();
                        readBuffer.flip( );
                        String str = asciiDecoder.decode( readBuffer).toString( );
                        readBuffer.clear( );
                        sb.append( str);

                        String line = sb.toString();
                        if ((line.indexOf("\n") != -1) ||
                            (line.indexOf("\r") != -1))
                            line = line.trim();
                            log.info ("got mesg: " + line);
                            if (line.startsWith("quit")) {
                                log.info("got quit msg, closing channel: " +
                                        channel.socket().getInetAddress());
                                channel.close();
                                clients.remove(channel);
                                sendBroadcastMessage("logout: " +
                                  channel.socket().getInetAddress(), channel);
                            }
                            else {
                                log.info("broadcasting: " + line);
                                sendBroadcastMessage(
                                    channel.socket().getInetAddress() +
                                    ": " + line, channel);
                                sb.delete(0, sb.length());
                            }
                        }
                    }
                }
            }
        }
```

```
    catch (IOException ioe) {
        log.warn("error during select(): ", ioe);
    }
    catch (Exception e) {
        log.error("exception in run()", e);
    }
}
```

First, we do a `selectNow()` on the `readSelector` to check whether any channels have activity that are of interest—in this case, any keys with `OP_READ` set. The `Selector.selectNow()` method returns immediately, regardless of how many (possibly zero) keys are ready. Again, the nonblocking call is used to avoid holding up the only thread. If we called `select()` instead, the call would block until data was incoming on the channel, and any pending outgoing messages would be stuck. Later, for the full server implementation, we'll dedicate a thread to socket reading and others for writing, so the blocking `select()` call will be used instead.

When we have a ready key, we get a reference to the `SocketChannel` and call its `read()` method, which fills the `readBuffer` with as many bytes as are available in the socket's input buffer. Before you can process that data, you first need to check for an end-of-stream condition. The `SocketChannel.read()` method returns `-1` to indicate that the end-of-stream has been reached, which basically means that the socket was closed.

Now that we know that some bytes are available, we grab the `StringBuffer`, previously stored as the `SelectionKey`'s attachment. Then append the contents of the `readBuffer` into the `StringBuffer` and check to see if there is a complete message.

The application terminates each message with the new line character \n, so the `String.indexOf()` method is used to check for the presence of that character. We talk more about message formats later in the "GameEvents" section of this chapter; for now, this tactic suffices.

Disconnections

Clients eventually close their connections to the server. This can happen for many reasons, both intentional and accidental, and in a variety of ways. We must take care to cover all cases and act accordingly.

A client might close its connection by sending a "quit" command to the server. The server checks for a "quit" message inside the `readIncomingMessages()` method and closes the client's channel. This is the preferred method because it allows both the client and the server to do any required cleanup.

Client connections can be terminated forcefully by the client application closing the channel or exiting abruptly, or because of network connectivity failures. The server's first indication is either in `readIncomingMessages()`, where the `channel.read()` returns the end-of-stream indicator as discussed earlier, or by catching a `ChannelClosedException` or `IOException` in the `sendMessage()` or `readIncomingMessages()` methods.

In either case, you need to be sure to close the channel, remove the client from the client list, and perform any other necessary cleanup.

> **NOTE**
> It is not necessary to unregister the channel from the selector. The channel implementation cancels its `SelectionKey` when it is closed, which causes it to be removed from the selector's key set. See the Selector API documentation for further details.

Building and Running the Server

Ah, our first real server program is complete. Let's get it built and fire it up for some testing. What's that, you say? We haven't written the client yet? No problem. As you'll see in a minute, because of our choice of a simple message format (new line terminated Strings), you can use any old Telnet client to talk to the server.

First, grab a copy of the code and then use Ant to build the ChatterBox application:

```
$ cd chap06
$ ant
```

The code is compiled and ready for testing. For this test, you need to have three separate terminal windows open (or use screen, if you fancy: `www.gnu.org/software/screen/`).

In the first terminal, run the server with the provided shell script:

```
$./bin/chatter_server.sh
```

You should see some initial log messages print to the screen.

Connecting with Telnet

The Telnet protocol is defined in RFC 854 (`www.faqs.org/rfcs/rfc854.html`), dating back to 1983. It was primarily designed to facilitate communication between local and remote terminals, usually for interactive shell sessions. Due to security concerns, this functionality has largely been replaced by the secure shell (ssh) protocols, but Telnet isn't dead yet. By having the server communicate with a very rudimentary subset of the Telnet protocol, we can take advantage of the ubiquity of Telnet clients on modern operating systems and use it as the test client.

From another terminal, Telnet to the server host IP (10.0.0.1, in this example), also providing the port number to connect to:

```
$ telnet 10.0.0.1 10997
Trying 10.0.0.1...
Connected to 10.0.0.1.
Escape character is '^]'.

Welcome to ChatterBox, there are 1 users online.

Type 'quit' to exit.
```

You are greeted by the welcome message and told how many users are online. In the server terminal, you should see log messages indicating that it has received the connection.

Now do the same from the third terminal. This time, after connecting, type a message and press Return. You should see the message echoed to the other client terminal. Go ahead, talk to yourself—it's okay.

```
$ telnet 10.0.0.1 10997
Trying 10.0.0.1...
Connected to 10.0.0.1.
Escape character is '^]'.

Welcome to ChatterBox, there are 2 users online.

Type 'quit' to exit.

hello there
/10.0.0.1: wassup?

quit
Connection closed by foreign host.
$
```

There you have it, a multi-user server application! I know, it's not very fun, is it? But we're getting there. The next thing to do is construct a real client application.

The Client: ChatterClient

ChatterClient is a relatively simple application and shares much with ChatterServer. It needs to perform only three tasks:

➤ Connect to the server.

➤ Send messages.

➤ Receive messages.

Setup

As with the server, we need to do a bit of initialization first. We set up two ByteBuffers just as we did for ChatterServer, one each for reading and writing. Additionally, before dropping into the main loop, a console input thread is started. This thread is responsible for reading user input from STDIN.

Making the Connection

First let's look at making a connection to the server. As discussed earlier, we'll use a `SocketChannel` to implement the socket connection. Listing 6.5 shows the `connect()` method.

Listing 6.5   `ChatterServer.connect()`

```
private void connect(String hostname) {
    try {
        readSelector = Selector.open();
        InetAddress addr = InetAddress.getByName(hostname);
        channel = SocketChannel.open(new InetSocketAddress(addr, PORT));
        channel.configureBlocking(false);
        channel.register(readSelector, SelectionKey.OP_READ,
            new StringBuffer());
    }
    catch (UnknownHostException uhe) {}
    catch (ConnectException ce) {}
    catch (Exception e) {}
}
```

First we open a new selector and get the IP address of the server using `InetAddress.getByName()`. Then we open the `SocketChannel` with that address and the port number we are using (10997). Next, the channel is configured to be in nonblocking mode. The last thing to do is register the channel with the selector, again using a `StringBuffer` as the attachment.

Note that in the ChatterBox example, we largely ignore exceptions for clarity. In production code, you must be careful to catch all exceptions and deal with them appropriately by trying to recover gracefully, logging error messages, alerting the user, or any combination of these.

The Main Loop

The client uses two threads, one for console input/writing (`InputThread`) and the main execution thread. The main loop, in the `run()` method, simply calls `readIncomingMessages()` repetitively to communicate with the server. Outgoing messages to the server are initiated from within `InputThread`.

Sending and Receiving Messages

As you'll see from the code, sending and receiving messages is nearly identical in both the client and the server. Later, in the game server framework, we'll separate common code such as this into a utility class, to avoid the redundancy.

Building and Running the Client

As with the server, use Ant to build the code:

```
$ cd chap06
$ ant
```

Then call the provided shell script to start the client. ChatterClient takes the host IP and port as parameters, so invoke it just like the previous Telnet example:

```
$ ./bin/chatter_client.sh 10.0.0.1 10997
```

The interaction is nearly identical as when using Telnet:

```
$ ./bin/chatter_client.sh 10.0.0.1 10997

Welcome to ChatterBox, there are 1 users online.

Type 'quit' to exit.

>
login from: /10.0.0.7
> hello
/10.0.0.7: wassup?
>
```

That's all for our first multi-user application. Now we can get on to bigger and better things!

Multi-Player Game Server Framework

In the last section, you learned how to build a basic client/server application using the NIO libraries. Now we're going to take the Chatterbox example to the next level and turn it into a full-featured multi-player game server framework.

Design Goals and Tactics

The design goals for the framework are as follows:

➤ **Simplicity.** The core classes should be as streamlined as possible.

➤ **Versatility/extensibility.** The game needs to support a variety of game styles, ideally within a single instance of the server.

➤ **Scalability.** The server needs to handle a large number of concurrent connections.

➤ **Performance.** The design must strive to provide the highest message throughput possible. Slow operations on events (such as those that require database or file access) must not block the flow of other events.

To achieve these goals, we're going to make several key refinements to the original example:

➤ Encapsulate the communication messages into GameEvents.

➤ Cleanly separate logic from mechanism.

➤ Separate the server process into various stages of a pipeline.

➤ Back each stage with a thread pool for concurrent operations.

➤ Separate each stage with a queue to buffer events.

➤ Provide a game logic plug-in architecture for supporting multiple games within the same server application.

Before we can tackle these lofty goals, we'll need to build some additional tools. Chapter 3, "Interactivity and User Interfaces," discussed threading in Java and introduced the `ThreadPool` class. In this section, we'll build a variation of that thread pool that uses a `BlockingQueue` of GameEvents.

The combination of a `ThreadPool` with a `BlockingQueue` is a design pattern called a *Wrap*. In the paper "A Design Framework for Highly Concurrent Systems" (Computer Science Division, University of California, Berkeley, 2002), Matt Welsh and co-authors explain it like this:

> The Wrap pattern involves "wrapping" a set of threads with a queue interface.... Each Thread processes a single task through some number of stages and may block one or more times. Applying Wrap places a single input queue in front of the set of threads, effectively creating a task handler out of them. This operation makes the processing within the task handler robust to load, as the number of threads inside of the task handler can now be fixed at a value that prevents thread overhead from degrading performance, and additional tasks that cannot be serviced by these threads will accumulate in the queue.

A `BlockingQueue` is simply a `Queue` data structure that has a blocking `deQueue()` method. In other words, when `deQueue()` is called, the running thread blocks until an element is available in the queue, possibly indefinitely. `BlockingQueues` are covered widely in books on threading, so we just refer you to the source code for our implementation (`com.hypefiend.javagamebook.common.EventQueue`) for more details. Wraps are very beneficial for our server application because we can have a number of threads waiting to perform a step in the pipeline, buffered from other stages of the pipeline by the incoming event queue. An important detail here is that the number of threads in each Wrap or stage of the pipeline becomes a tunable parameter of the system, enabling just the right number of threads to be allocated for a particular task to achieve maximum event throughput.

The Design

Our server design is modeled after the flow of data in the system, as shown in Figure 6.5.

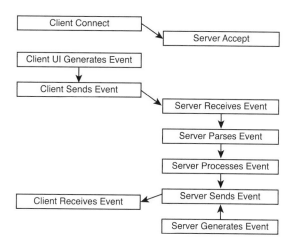

Figure 6.5   Client/server communication flow.

The sequence starts with the client connecting to the server and the server accepting that connection. Then the client sends events to the server. The server reads, parses, and processes the events. This processing often results in outgoing events being generated and sent to one or more clients. The clients then receive the events and process them, and the cycle repeats.

As you can see, most of the interaction is driven by the client, but the server might generate some events independent of client actions. For instance, this could be in response to timers on the server for signaling game end times or a system-wide administrative message.

Some design choices must be made that will help shape the application. The first is to decide on an event format because events are the application's primary data structure. After that, you'll need to determine exactly what classes and interfaces are required to implement the previously discussed sequence.

GameEvents

Communication between client and server, as well as between each stage of the pipeline, is done via events. The choice of event formats is important to the individual game designs but is transparent to the framework because we provide an interface to the events and for passing events between segments. This way, each game can have its own distinct event format.

There are many possible formats that can be used to transmit data in the system. The choice is highly dependent on the characteristics of the games to be hosted on the framework. At the most basic level, simple ASCII text messages can be used as in the ChatterBox application. However, an application with any real level of functionality requires a more complex structure. We discuss a couple of options here, but there are certainly other possibilities, and you should design an event format that is appropriate for your games. The design criteria for selecting an event format are listed here:

> **Size/compactness.** Because you are sending these events over the network, bandwidth can become an issue as you reach a high volume of messages. An arcade-style game requires a much larger quantity of messages than a card game.

> **Human readability.** Keeping the format humanly readable has its advantages in debugging but is at odds with the first criterion: size. A compromise approach is to use an abbreviated human-readable format to shorten the messages but maintain readability.

> **Serialization/parsing ease and speed.** Events must be converted from their object format into the over-the-wire format and back again. This process should both execute quickly and be easy to implement.

> **Size of serialization/parsing code.** Depending on the deployment scenario, the size of the client code can be a significant issue (for example, with a mobile device), so requiring a large code library to parse your events could be prohibitive.

> **Flexibility.** It needs to handle a variety of event types.

Let's take a look at a few of the common options available for event formats and see how they meet these criteria. Whichever format you choose, it is important to gather empirical data on the size and performance of a given method, to make sure it will meet your requirements for bandwidth, flexibility, and processor overhead—preferably before you start writing the main code for the project!

Serialized Java Objects

This method involves using Java's built-in serialization capabilities to convert a GameEvent object into a byte stream. The advantages are that it is easy to implement, size efficiency and serialization speed are reasonable, and very little additional code is required to perform the conversion because serialization has been built into Java's core libraries since JDK 1.1. This format is not humanly readable, however.

XML

XML is an increasingly popular format for all sorts of network communication and data storage needs. For GameEvents, it has the advantages of being easy to implement, very readable, and flexible for a variety of message types. The drawbacks can far outweigh these benefits, however. Serialized size is huge (unless using highly abbreviated element and attribute names), and parsing overhead could be too large when dealing with high event volumes. Also, the additional parsing code required on the client could be an issue. However, the 5k NanoXML parser (available at `http://nanoxml.n3.net`) provides a good option for size-constrained clients.

Custom Binary

This format basically involves writing out the fields of the GameEvent directly to a sequence of bytes, using as few bytes as possible for each primitive data type.

Certain techniques can be used to squeeze primitives down beyond their native size requirements—for example, using Run-Length Encoding (RLE) to compress Strings, bit-packing multiple Boolean values into a single byte, and quantizing and compressing integers.

This option can provide the best size, is fairly easy to write, and is quick to parse. Like serialized objects, it is completely unreadable. But if you need to squeeze the most out of your bandwidth, this is the only way to go.

Binary-Encoded XML

Programmers have realized that although the verbosity of XML is a good thing, it tends to hog bandwidth and storage. This is extremely important for wireless devices. The WAP Binary XML Format (`www.w3.org/TR/wbxml/`) is a World Wide Web Consortium recommendation that attempts to solve this problem.

That or similar encodings might provide a good compromise—not readable while in transit, but normal XML when decoded. The format provides efficient size for transport, but encoding/decoding can add substantial overhead.

Terminology

Before we get into the implementation, let's define a few terms that we'll be using in the framework:

➤ **GameName**. A class of game, such as Chess, TicTacToe, or SpaceWar.

➤ **Game**. A particular instance, or play, of a GameName.

➤ **GameID**. A unique identifier for a game.

➤ **Player**. An identifiable user connected to the server that might or might not be actively engaged in a game.

➤ **PlayerID**. Unique identifier for a player.

➤ **Session**. The time between a player login and logout. This can span more than one connection/disconnection cycle.

➤ **SessionID**. Unique identifier for a session.

➤ **EventType**. One of a set of event types that determines the purpose of the event, such as LOGIN, CHAT_MSG, or MOVE.

Class Diagrams

Class diagrams for both the server side and the client side of the Game Server Framework are shown in Figures 6.6 and 6.7.

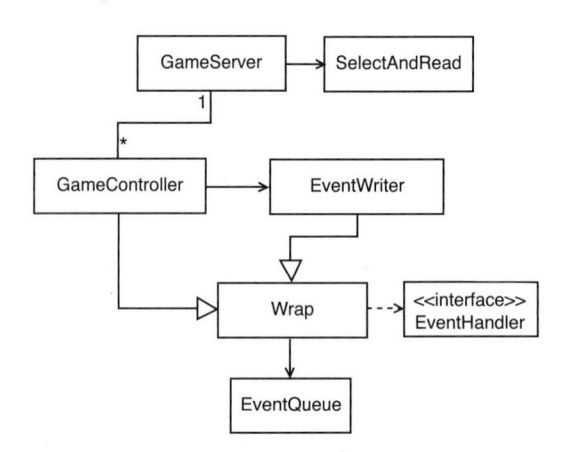

Figure 6.6 Server framework class diagram.

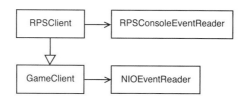

Figure 6.7   Client framework class diagram.

Common Classes and Interfaces

The framework contains a number of interfaces and classes that are shared between the client and the server. They are all contained in the com.hypefiend. javagamebook.common package:

> ➤ Attachment   Class that is used as our SelectionKey attachment. Holds the read buffer and handles checks for complete message payloads.

> ➤ EventHandler   Interface that defines only one method: handleGameEvent().

> ➤ EventQueue   The Blocking Queue, mentioned earlier.

> ➤ GameConfig   Class to hold configuration data for GameController classes.

> ➤ GameEvent   Interface for GameEvents that allows the framework to treat each game's events generically.

> ➤ GameEventDefault   A basic implementation of GameEvent, used in the sample game.

> ➤ Globals   A class that defines common constants for the client and server.

> ➤ NIOUtils   Contains a number of utility functions for dealing with channels and buffers.

> ➤ Player   Interface for players that allows the framework to treat each game's players generically.

> ➤ PlayerDefault   A basic implementation of Player, used in the sample game.

Some of these classes and interfaces require elaboration. Let's cover them in detail before we get on to the server-specific classes.

GameEvent Interface

For our framework, we define an interface for the events and provide a default implementation. It is expected, however, that games will either extend or replace the default implementation as needed.

Listing 6.6 shows the complete `GameEvent` interface.

Listing 6.6   `GameEvent` Interface

```
public interface GameEvent {
    public int getType();
    public void setType(int type);
    public String getGameName();
    public void setGameName(String gameName);
    public String getMessage();
    public void setMessage(String message);
    public String getPlayerId();
    public void setPlayerId(String id);
    public String getSessionId();
    public void setSessionId(String id);
    public String[] getRecipients();
    public void setRecipients(String[] recipients);
    public void read(ByteBuffer buff);
    public int write(ByteBuffer buff);
}
```

In addition to the `GameEvent` interface itself, an interface that will allow for the passing of events between stages of the server's event-handling pipeline is required. This `EventListener` interface consists of a single method only:

```
public void handleEvent(GameEvent event);
```

All server and client classes that accept incoming events must implement this interface.

GameEventDefault

The default `GameEvent` implementation, `GameEventDefault`, uses the `ByteBuffer` `put` and `get` methods directly to read and write event data as raw byte sequences. For example, to write the `eventType` member, we use this line:

```
buff.putInt(eventType);
```

To write String members, such as a message, we first write the number of bytes representing the String length and then the bytes of the String itself:

```
buff.putShort((short)str.length());
buff.put(str.getBytes());
```

Listing 6.7 shows the entire read() and write() methods of GameEventDefault.

Listing 6.7 GameEventDefault read and write Methods

```
public int write(ByteBuffer buff) {
    int pos = buff.position();
    buff.putInt(eventType);
    NIOUtils.putStr(buff, playerId);
    NIOUtils.putStr(buff, sessionId);
    buff.putInt(gameId);
    NIOUtils.putStr(buff, gameName);
    buff.putInt(numRecipients);
    for (int i = 0;i < numRecipients;i++)
        NIOUtils.putStr(buff, recipients[i]);
    NIOUtils.putStr(buff, message);

    return buff.position() - pos;
}

public void read(ByteBuffer buff) {
    eventType = buff.getInt();
    playerId = NIOUtils.getStr(buff);
    sessionId = NIOUtils.getStr(buff);
    gameId = buff.getInt();
    gameName = NIOUtils.getStr(buff);
    numRecipients = buff.getInt();
    recipients = new String[numRecipients];
    for (int i = 0;i < numRecipients;i++)
        recipients[i] = NIOUtils.getStr(buff);
    message = NIOUtils.getStr(buff);
}
```

Note that the `write` method returns an integer specifying the number of bytes written. This is important for the framework's over-the-wire event protocol.

Over-the-Wire Event Protocol

To accommodate a variety of event formats, we need to precede the event data with a small header when sending the events over the network.

This format of the header and payload is shown in Figure 6.8. First the `clientId`, the `GameName` hash code, and the `payloadSize` (in bytes) are sent, each of which is a 4-byte integer. Then the payload is sent, which is `payloadSize` bytes in length.

ClientId (4 bytes)	GameName hash code (4 bytes)	PayloadSize (4 bytes)	Payload (PayloadSize bytes)

Figure 6.8   Over-the-wire event format.

We discuss how to actually read and write this data, and instantiate the proper `GameEvents` on the receiving end when we introduce the `SelectAndRead` and `EventWriter` classes of the server implementation.

Server Implementation

The server side of the framework consists of a small number of classes, as follows:

- ➤ `EventWriter`
- ➤ `GameController`
- ➤ `GameServer`
- ➤ `SelectAndRead`

We cover each of these in detail because they form the foundation of the framework.

GameServer and *GameController*

The `GameServer` class is the centerpiece of the server application and contains the application's `main()` method. The duties of the `GameServer` are to accept incoming socket connections, keep track of connected clients, and manage the `GameControllers`.

The code for setting up the ServerSocket and accepting connections is similar to the code in ChatterServer, as can be seen in Listing 6.8.

Listing 6.8 GameServer initServerSocket() and run() Methods

```
private void initServerSocket() {
    try {
        sSockChan = ServerSocketChannel.open();
        sSockChan.configureBlocking(false);

        InetAddress addr = InetAddress.getLocalHost();
        sSockChan.socket().bind(new InetSocketAddress(addr, Globals.PORT));

        selector = Selector.open();
        SelectionKey acceptKey = sSockChan.register(selector,
            SelectionKey.OP_ACCEPT);
    }
    catch (Exception e) {
        log.error("error initializing ServerSocket", e);
    }
}

public void run() {
    init();
    log.info("******** GameServer running ********");
    running = true;
    int numReady = 0;

    while (running) {
        try {
            selector.select();
            Set readyKeys = selector.selectedKeys();
            Iterator i = readyKeys.iterator();
            while (i.hasNext()) {
                SelectionKey key = (SelectionKey) i.next();
                i.remove();

                ServerSocketChannel ssChannel =
                    (ServerSocketChannel) key.channel();
```

continues

Listing 6.8 `GameServer initServerSocket()` and `run()` Methods *continued*

```
                SocketChannel clientChannel = ssChannel.accept();

                selectAndRead.addNewClient(clientChannel);
                log.info("got connection from: " +
                    clientChannel.socket().getInetAddress());
            }
        }
        catch (IOException ioe) {
            log.warn("error during serverSocket select(): ", ioe);          }
        catch (Exception e) {
            log.error("exception in run()", e);
        }
    }
}
```

The `GameServer` code is similar to that of ChatterServer. There are a few differences worth noting, however. The first is that we use a selector for the `ServerSocketChannel`. Just as you can use a selector to multiplex client channels for reading, you can use selectors to multiplex `ServerSocketChannels`. This is used when a server application needs to listen on either multiple addresses or ports. Our framework doesn't use this capability currently, but we talk more about this later when discussing remote administration consoles.

The other difference in the `run()` method is that after a connection is accepted, it is passed off to a class called `SelectAndRead` for further processing.

SelectAndRead

Much like its name implies, `SelectAndRead` houses the selector that multiplexes client channels and reads GameEvents from those channels. Complete events are passed off to `GameControllers` based on the GameName hash code found in the event header.

New client connections are handed off to SelectAndRead from the GameServer via
SelectAndRead.addNewClient(). The SocketChannel for the client is added to a
LinkedList, and selector.wakeup() is called to interrupt SelectAndRead's
blocking select() call. This has the effect of breaking the SelectAndRead thread
out of the select() method and then calling checkNewConnections(), which runs
through the LinkedList of new client SocketChannels, registering them with the
selector. Listing 6.9 has the code for both methods.

Listing 6.9 SelectAndRead, addNewClient(), and checkNewConnections()

```
public void addNewClient(SocketChannel clientChannel) {
    synchronized (newClients) {
        newClients.addLast(clientChannel);
    }
    // force selector to return
    // so our new client can get in the loop right away
    selector.wakeup();
}

private void checkNewConnections() {
    synchronized (newClients) {
        while (newClients.size() > 0) {
            try {
                SocketChannel clientChannel =
                    (SocketChannel)newClients.removeFirst();
                clientChannel.configureBlocking( false);
                clientChannel.register( selector, SelectionKey.OP_READ,
                    new Attachment());
            }
            catch (ClosedChannelException cce) {
                log.error("channel closed", cce);
            }
            catch (IOException ioe) {
                log.error("ioexception on clientChannel", ioe);
            }
        }
    }
}
```

`SelectAndRead` uses similar methods to those found in ChatterServer for reading data from the client channels, with a few notable exceptions.

Instead of simply reading strings from the channel and checking for linefeeds to separate messages, it must now look for complete GameEvents.

Because the event format is implementation specific, the framework reads only the raw bytes of the event and delegates the job of instantiating the GameEvent to the GameController implementation via `createGameEvent()`. Listing 6.10 shows the `select()` method along with the methods for reading and delegating the GameEvent.

Listing 6.10   Reading GameEvents

```
private void select() {
    try {
        selector.select();
        Set readyKeys = selector.selectedKeys();
        Iterator i = readyKeys.iterator();
        while (i.hasNext()) {
            SelectionKey key = (SelectionKey) i.next();
            i.remove();
            SocketChannel channel = (SocketChannel) key.channel();
            Attachment attachment = (Attachment) key.attachment();

            long nbytes = channel.read(attachment.readBuff);
            // check for end-of-stream condition
            if (nbytes == -1) {
                log.info("disconnect: " +
                    channel.socket().getInetAddress() +
                    ", end-of-stream");
                channel.close();
            }

            // check for a complete event
            try {
                if (attachment.readBuff.position() >=
                    attachment.HEADER_SIZE) {
                    attachment.readBuff.flip();
```

```
                        // read as many events as are available in the buffer
                        while (attachment.eventReady()) {
                            GameEvent event = getEvent(attachment);
                            delegateEvent(event, channel);
                            attachment.reset();
                        }
                        // prepare for more channel reading
                        attachment.readBuff.compact();
                    }
                }
                catch (IllegalArgumentException e) {
                    log.error("illegal arguement exception", e);
                }
            }
        }
    catch (IOException ioe) {
        log.warn("error during select(): ", ioe);
    }
    catch (Exception e) {
        log.error("exception during select()", e);
    }
}


private GameEvent getEvent(Attachment attachment) {
    GameEvent event = null;
    ByteBuffer bb = ByteBuffer.wrap(attachment.payload);

    // get the controller and tell it to instantiate an event for us
    GameController gc =
        gameServer.getGameControllerByHash(attachment.gameNameHash);
    if (gc == null)
        return null;
    event = gc.createGameEvent();

    // read the event from the payload
    event.read(bb);
    return event;
}
```

continues

Listing 6.10   Reading GameEvents   *continued*

```
private void delegateEvent(GameEvent event, SocketChannel channel)
{
    if (event != null && event.getGameName() == null) {
        log.error("GameServer.handleEvent() : gameName is null");
        return ;
    }

    GameController gc;
    gc = gameServer.getGameController(event.getGameName());
    if (gc == null) {
        log.error("No GameController for gameName: "
            + event.getGameName());
        return ;
    }

    Player p = gameServer.getPlayerById(event.getPlayerId());
    if (p != null) {
        if (p.getChannel() != channel) {
            log.warn("player is on a new channel, must be reconnect.");
            p.setChannel(channel);
        }
    }
    else {
        // first time we see a playerId, create the Player object
        // and populate the channel, and also add to our lists
        p = gc.createPlayer();
        p.setPlayerId(event.getPlayerId());
        p.setChannel(channel);
        gameServer.addPlayer(p);

        gc.handleEvent(event);
    }
```

As `SelectAndRead` pulls data from the `SocketChannel`, it is stored temporarily in buffers in the `Attachment` class. The `Attachment` class is just a holding cell for this data and contains only methods for verifying that the header and payload data has been read.

After every read, the event header is checked; if there are at least `payloadSize` bytes in the `readBuffer`, the event is complete. The GameName hash code is used to fetch the instance of the appropriate `GameController` from the `GameServer`. Next, the `GameController`'s `createGameEvent()` method is called to instantiate a new event, and the event reads itself from the contents of `Attachment.readBuffer`.

A bit of complication with the way initial user connections are handled and players are created bears explanation. The `GameServer` is the keeper of the master player lists. When `SelectAndRead` gets a complete event, it first checks the playerId and asks the `GameServer` if it has seen that ID before. If it hasn't, this is a new connection and it first calls on the `GameController` to instantiate a new player using the `createPlayer()` method.

When the `GameController` gets a login event from a player, it must query the `GameServer` to get the player object that was previously instantiated. This seems a bit roundabout, but it enforces strict handling of player creation and tracking by the `GameServer`.

GameControllers

`GameControllers` encapsulate the server-side game logic and enable you to have a variety of different games running simultaneously in one `GameServer`. All `GameControllers` must extend the `GameController` base class, which, in turn, extends Wrap. Thus, each `GameController` has its own EventQueue and thread pool backing it.

The `GameServer`, `SelectAndRead`, and `GameEvent` implementations form a team that provides the foundation for handling the client/server communication and hides the details of the network implementation (in this case, NIO channels) from the rest of the system. In other words, `GameControllers` don't have to care how the events are read or written—they care only that incoming GameEvents appear in the EventQueue and outgoing events get dropped into the `EventWriter`'s EventQueue. You could rewrite the underlying network code to use UDP, HTTP, or other means of moving the events around without having to touch the `GameControllers`.

GameControllers are loaded dynamically by the GameServer during initialization. This approach prevents the GameServer from being tied to a fixed set of GameControllers. In fact, it doesn't even know their names until they are first loaded. Listing 6.11 shows the code in GameServer that loads the GameController instances.

Listing 6.11 GameServer, getGameController(), and loadGameController() Methods

```
private void loadGameControllers() {
    log.info("loading GameControllers");
    // grab all class files in the same directory as GameController
    String baseClass =
        "com/hypefiend/javagamebook/server/controller/GameController.class";
    File f = new File( this.getClass(
        ).getClassLoader().getResource(baseClass).getPath());
    File[] files = f.getParentFile().listFiles( );
    if (files == null) {
        log.error("error getting GameController directory");
        return ;
    }

    for ( int i = 0; ( i < files.length); i++) {
        String file = files[i].getName( );
        if (file.indexOf( ".class") == -1)
            continue;
        if (file.equals("GameController.class"))
            continue;
        try {
            String controllerClassName = CONTROLLER_CLASS_PREFIX +
                file.substring(0, file.indexOf(".class"));
            log.info("loading class: " + controllerClassName);
            Class cl = Class.forName(controllerClassName);
            // make sure it extends GameController
            if (!GameController.class.isAssignableFrom(cl)) {
                log.warn("class file does not extend GameController: " +
                    file);
                continue;
            }
```

```
            // get an instance and initialize
            GameController gc = (GameController) cl.newInstance();
            String gameName = gc.getGameName();
            gc.init(this, getGameConfig(gameName));

            // add to our controllers hash
            gameControllers.put("" + gameName.hashCode(), gc);
            log.info("loaded controller for gameName: " + gameName +
                ", hash: " + gameName.hashCode());
        }
        catch (Exception e) {
            log.error("instantiating GameController,file: " + file, e);
        }
    }
}
```

The hash code of the GameName is used as the key for storing the GameControllers in a Hashtable. This key is also used in the header in the over-the-wire protocol, as discussed earlier.

The GameController base class defines a few abstract methods that its subclasses must implement:

➤ protected abstract void initController(GameConfig gc)   This method is for GameControllers to perform any initialization that they require.

➤ public abstract String getGameName()   Must return the GameName for the controller.

➤ public abstract Player createPlayer()   Factory method that must return an object that implements the Player interface.

➤ public abstract GameEvent createGameEvent()   Factory method that must return an object that implements the GameEvent interface.

The two factory methods, `createPlayer()` and `createGameEvent()`, allow the core `GameServer` to instantiate these objects on behalf of the controllers as needed, without requiring knowledge of the implementation a particular controller is using.

`GameControllers` are responsible for pulling incoming events from their EventQueue (deposited there by the `SelectAndRead` class, as described previously), processing those events, and dropping outgoing events into the `EventWriter`'s EventQueue. The `processEvent()` method (from the `Wrap` class, which `GameController` extends) is called every time a GameEvent arrives in the EventQueue. The method has the following signature:

```
protected abstract void processEvent(GameEvent event);
```

> **NOTE**
> It is important to realize that by extending `Wrap`, all controllers are inherently multi-threaded and thus must use synchronization accordingly when processing events.

Having all controllers extend the `GameController` base class enables the framework to take care of some housekeeping, such as initialization and logging in a uniform manner across all controllers. The base class handles initialization of the `Wrap` and a Log4J category for the controller. The base implementation also manages the run cycle, pulling events from the incoming queue and passing them to the `processEvent()` method.

By restricting controllers to the method defined previously, the framework provides a very controlled atmosphere in which to run the game logic. Note that each controller gets a reference to the `GameServer` as well. You might find that you need additional latitude depending on the complexity of your games, so by all means, feel free to extend the powers given to the controllers. The idea is just to have a central place where you can make changes or additions that will affect all controllers, and to isolate the `GameController` logic code from the network communication code.

EventWriter

`EventWriter` is simply a `Wrap` that handles a queue of outgoing events. Events are written using the utility method in NIOUtils, `channelWrite()`. When sending broadcast events, it grabs the list of recipients from the GameEvent and then sends the event to each player in turn.

The Client

The game client uses much of the code in the common classes detailed earlier and adds two classes of its own: `GameClient` and `NIOEventReader`.

`GameClient` is an abstract base class for the client applications. Games can extend this class and need only implement the following methods:

> ➤ `getGameName`   Returns the game's GameName.
>
> ➤ `createGameEvent`   Factory method for creating game-specific GameEvents.
>
> ➤ `createLoginEvent`   Factory method for creating a game-specific GameEvent used to log in to the server.
>
> ➤ `createDisconnectEvent`   Factory method for creating a game-specific GameEvent for disconnections.
>
> ➤ `processIncomingEvents`   Handles incoming GameEvents from the GameServer.

`GameClient` also handles initial connections to the server and writing of outgoing events.

`NIOEventReader` is the client-side version of `SelectAndRead`. It is simplified because the client is reading from only a single `SocketChannel`, but otherwise it is nearly identical. `NIOEventReader` delegates event creation and processing to a `GameClient` instead of a `GameController`, as in `SelectAndRead`.

JDK 1.4 Client vs. JDK 1.1

Our `GameClient` and associated classes are built using JDK 1.4 NIO classes because that is our focus in this chapter. Depending on your deployment scenario, it might not be possible to use a 1.4 VM. It would not be difficult to make a version of the client that uses the older JDK libraries; the main things that would need to be changed are the `NIOEventReader` and the event-writing code in `GameClient`.

A Sample Game: RPS (Rock, Paper, Scissors)

With all the framework code in place, it is actually very simple to implement a game. You only need to create server- and client-side logic and associated data classes.

This sample game is a networked rock, paper, scissors (RPS) game. In this game, any number of players can connect to the server and challenge each other to a game. After they are joined in a game, the two clients can play as many rounds as they desire; when they are finished, the server returns the tally of how many games have been won, lost, or tied. Clients also can chat with one another before and during games.

Let's take a look at the classes needed to implement RPS.

Classes

We'll be using the `PlayerDefault` and `GameEventDefault` classes here, so we don't need to build custom Player or GameEvent implementations. For the server side, we need a `GameController`, `RPSController`. Additionally, we'll add a class to hold game data, `RPSGame`. For the client side, subclass `GameClient` with the `RPSClient` class and also add `RPSConsoleEventReader` for handling user input. Figure 6.9 shows the same class diagram from Figure 6.6, with the addition of the RPS classes.

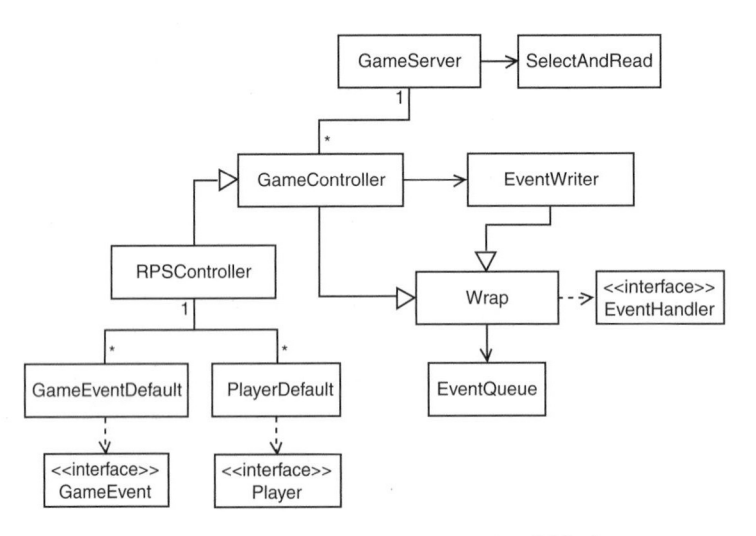

Figure 6.9   Game Server Framework plus RPS classes.

RPSController

The game logic will be very simple, yet still require a number of event types and add a good amount of logic code. RPSController keeps track of the RPS players and their games. We don't go into all the details of the logic here; we discuss just how the RPSController interacts with the framework.

Incoming client events are delivered to the controller's EventQueue and then are picked up by the run() method in the GameController base class and passed to the RPSController's processEvent() method.

To send events to clients, RPSController uses the sendEvent() or sendBroadcastEvent() methods of the base class. These methods call GameServer.write(), which drops the events into the EventQueue of the EventWriter class.

Note that the RPSController class is part of the com.hypefiend.javagamebook. server.controller package, whereas the other classes are in com.hypefiend. javagamebook.games.rps. This is a consequence of the method that the GameServer uses to dynamically load the GameControllers.

RPSGame

RPSGame represents a set of rock, paper, scissors games between a pair of players. It keeps track of the player's moves during each round and tallies wins, losses, and ties for each player.

RPSClient

For the client, we need to program only a bit of rudimentary logic to handle reading input from the console and to handle incoming events from the server, as well as do a bit of housekeeping to keep track of the player and game/challenge state.

Listing 6.12 shows the entire RPSClient code. As you can see, there isn't much to it. For most events, we simply write the contents of GameEvent.getMessage() to STD-OUT. Everything else is handled by the GameClient base class.

Listing 6.12   RPSClient.java

```
public class RPSClient extends GameClient {
    protected static Logger log = Logger.getLogger("RPSClient");
    protected RPSConsoleEventReader consoleReader;

    public static void main(String args[] ) {
        BasicConfigurator.configure();
        RPSClient gc = new RPSClient();
        gc.init(args);
        gc.start();
    }

    public void init(String args[]) {
        super.init(args);
        consoleReader = new RPSConsoleEventReader(this, inQueue, outQueue);
        consoleReader.start();
    }

    protected void shutdown() {
        consoleReader.shutdown();
        super.shutdown();
    }

    protected void processIncomingEvents() {
        GameEvent inEvent;
        while (inQueue.size() > 0) {
            try {
                inEvent = inQueue.deQueue();
                switch (inEvent.getType()) {
                case GameEventDefault.S_LOGIN_ACK_OK:
                    break;
                case GameEventDefault.SB_LOGIN:
                    stdOut( "login: " + inEvent.getMessage());
                    break;
                case GameEventDefault.SB_LOGOUT:
                    stdOut( "logout: " + inEvent.getMessage());
                    break;
```

```
                case GameEventDefault.SB_CHAT_MSG:
                    stdOut( inEvent.getPlayerId() + ": " +
                        inEvent.getMessage());
                    break;
                case GameEventDefault.S_DISCONNECT:
                    stdErr( "disconnected from server: " +
                        inEvent.getMessage());
                    shutdown();
                    break;
                case GameEventDefault.S_JOIN_GAME_ACK_OK:
                    stdOut( inEvent.getMessage());
                    inGame = true;
                    break;
                case GameEventDefault.S_JOIN_GAME_ACK_FAIL:
                    stdOut( inEvent.getMessage());
                    inGame = false;
                    break;
                case GameEventDefault.SB_PLAYER_QUIT:
                    stdOut( inEvent.getMessage());
                    inGame = false;
                    break;
                default:
                    stdOut( inEvent.getMessage());
                    break;
                }
            }
        catch (InterruptedException ie) {}
        }
}

public String getGameName() {
    return "RPS";
}

public GameEvent createGameEvent() {
    return new GameEventDefault();
}
```

continues

Listing 6.12 RPSClient.java *continued*

```
    public GameEvent createLoginEvent() {
        return new GameEventDefault(GameEventDefault.C_LOGIN);
    }

    public GameEvent createDisconnectEvent(String reason) {
        return new GameEventDefault(GameEventDefault.S_DISCONNECT, reason);
    }
}
```

RPSConsoleEventReader

ConsoleEventReader is a client class that is used to read input from the user via STDIN. We use a BufferedReader to read full lines of text, and use a StringTokenizer to break out commands from the String. Based on the tokens, a GameEvent is generated for the appropriate action and fed to the client's outgoing EventQueue.

Running the RPS Game

First, grab a copy of the code and then use Ant to build the game server and client:

```
$ cd chap06
$ ant
```

Just as you did with the ChatterBox example, you need three separate terminal windows open. In the first terminal, run the server with the provided shell script:

```
$ ./bin/server.sh
```

Then start the first client. The script takes two parameters: the IP address of the server and a player name:

```
$ ./bin/client.sh 10.0.0.1 bret
```

and the other client:

```
$ ./bin/client.sh 10.0.0.1 brackeen
```

Each client is shown the game welcome text, the help text, and the list of online players:

```
Welcome to the RPS (Rock, Paper, Scissors) Multi-player Game

commands:
'/quit'                                quit the application
'/help'                                show this help
'/players'                             list players online
'/newgame <opponent name>'             start a new game against
                                       opponent
'/move <(r)ock|(p)aper|(s)cissors>'    enter your move
'/endgame'                             end the game
all other input is treated as a chat message

players online:
brackeen
bret


brackeen >
```

Start a game by having the first player enter the newgame command. Note that all commands are preceded with a forward slash (like IRC commands), and all other input is treated as chat messages:

```
bret> /newgame brackeen
```

Both players are notified that a game has started. Now enter the moves

```
brackeen > /move rock
```

and

```
bret > /move paper
```

The results of the game are displayed to each player, like this:

```
Opponent chooses rock
You Win
bret vs. brackeen >
```

To play more games against the same player, simply keep entering moves. When you want to stop, you can enter the `endgame` command to see a tally of your wins, losses, and ties for this session:

```
bret vs. brackeen > /endgame

GameOver, player bret has quit.
Final tallies
bret wins: 1
brackeen wins: 3
ties: 1
```

To exit the client, enter the `quit` command.

That was fun, right? We've successfully created a multi-player game, based on an extensible Game Server Framework. You are encouraged to rummage through the rest of the code to get better acquainted with all the details.

Complete the Look: Building on the Framework

We haven't tackled a number of things with our framework so far that are required for a full-featured game system. We discuss some of them here but leave the implementation up to you.

Client GUI

We wrote only a console-based client for our RPS game because we wanted to focus on the networking and logic code. Clearly, though, most games these days require a graphical client. Adding a GUI and connecting it to the underlying code is fairly trivial. Our event-based design allows us to just have the GUI drop events into the outgoing `EventQueue` just like `RPSConsoleEventReader` does. Similarly, the `GameClient` can pass incoming events to a GUI if it implements the `EventHandler` interface.

Persistence

One important aspect of game servers we haven't touched on yet is persistence. Most games require at least some amount of game data to be stored, usually in a relational database. Typical needs are to store player data, high scores, game statistics, buddy lists, and other game-specific data.

Because we are using a standalone Java application as the `GameServer`, we don't have the luxury of relying on built-in persistence mechanisms that are found in modern J2EE application servers.

So what are the options? Many developers choose to go with the lowest common denominator of using the JDBC APIs directly. The benefit is speed, and if your data needs are small, this might be a fine choice. However, a recent trend has been toward the use of object/relational mapping APIs. Sun has a specification for Java Data Objects (JDO, available at `http://java.sun.com/products/jdo`). Two other competing APIs are Castor JDO (`www.castor.org`) and Jakarta OJB (`http://db.apache.org/ojb`), both of which are in active development.

Buddy Lists, Lobbies, and Chat

Multi-player servers need mechanisms for players to find friends, arrange games, and chat with one another. These are referred to collectively as community features.

Friend finding often involves a buddy list feature, similar to the functionality found in instant-messaging clients. This notifies you when a friend logs in and shows you which game lobby or server that person is on.

Player-matching features depend highly on the genre but often involve lobbies where players of similar skill, game interest, or other criteria can meet, chat, and challenge one another to games.

Chat is a requirement for just about any game genre. In addition to basic chat functionality, you need features for administrators to be able to kick out or ban users (features found in IRC servers). Players want the ability to ignore either certain players—or all chat—to avoid offensive or obnoxious players.

Server Administration

Like any server application, game servers require periodic monitoring and maintenance. Servers need to generate log files and require tools to manage their execution life cycle (startup/shutdown). Additionally, game servers might require mechanisms for game watching, kick/ban functionality, and remote management.

Logging

Logging is a very important aspect of any server application, especially for game servers. Every application needs at least an error log and a debugging log. Additionally, you might want chat logs (to see what those users are saying about you), game history logs, connection/access logs, or other game-specific logging.

JDK 1.4 includes a new logging API in the `java.util.logging` package. However, it is new on the scene, and many programmers are reluctant to ditch what has become the de facto standard for logging APIs, Log4J. Log4J began life in 1999 as a project as part of IBM's Alphaworks initiative and thrived there for a couple of years before being taken on as part of the Apache Jakarta Project (`http://jakarta.apache.org`). Log4J is highly configurable, easy to use, and efficient. Our examples use Log4J, but admittedly with only a very basic configuration.

It is equally important to generate logs from game clients. Usually, you will not want to see the data, but it is invaluable during testing. Even after deployment, if a user is having trouble, you can have that user send in his or her log file to help you diagnose the problem.

Depending on your distribution mechanism, you might be constrained in the size of your client application. In this case, the Log4J library might be too large, and you will want to search out a smaller alternative.

Whichever API you choose, it is important to log just the right amount of data. Too much will clutter your log files, making them difficult to read and hogging loads of disk space. Too little will leave you guessing when debugging.

Startup/Shutdown

Because the server must be running continuously, you need to accommodate starting and stopping the server automatically at system startup and shutdown. On UNIX-based platforms (Linux, Solaris, and so on) this is accomplished using a startup script. Listing 6.13 contains an example of an `init.d` script for Debian GNU/Linux, but it should work with a bit of modification on other Linux distributions and UNIX systems.

Listing 6.13   `init.d` Script

```
#! /bin/sh

PATH=/usr/local/gameserver/bin:/usr/local/java/bin:/usr/local/sbin:
/usr/local/bin:/sbin:/bin:/usr/sbin:/usr/bin
DAEMON=/usr/local/gameserver/bin/server.sh
NAME=gameserver
DESC=" Multi-player GameServer"

test -x $DAEMON || exit 0

set -e

case "$1" in
  start)
        echo -n "Starting $DESC: $NAME"
        start-stop-daemon --start --quiet --exec $DAEMON
        echo "."
        ;;
  stop)
        echo -n "Stopping $DESC: $NAME "
        start-stop-daemon --stop --quiet --pidfile /var/run/$NAME.pid
        rm /var/run/$NAME.pid
        echo "."
        ;;
  *)
        N=/etc/init.d/$NAME
        echo "Usage: $N {start|stop}" >&2
        exit 1
        ;;
```

continues

Listing 6.13   `init.d` Script   *continued*
```
esac

exit 0
```

The script is based on the `init.d` skeleton, found in /etc/init.d/skeleton on Debian systems. In addition to the init script, you need a way to drop the process ID (pid) into the /var/run/gameserver.pid file every time the server is started. This can be accomplished with a bit of Perl that parses the pid from the output of the `ps` command.

For Windows systems, the same result is achieved by making the server application into an NT service. A number of tools can be used for adapting a Java application into a service. One is at `http://wrapper.sourceforge.net`, but a quick Google search for Java Windows service will turn up many other options.

Java Shutdown Hooks

As of JDK 1.3, Java has had the capability to add what is called a *shutdown hook*. A shutdown hook enables you to register a Runnable object to be activated when the VM is terminated. This allows for a clean shutdown of the server application; it can save game state, gracefully disconnect users, close database connections or other open resources, and finally exit.

The paper "Revelations on Java Signal Handling and Termination" (IBM DeveloperWorks, `www.ibm.com/developerWorks`, January 2002) is an excellent resource in which author Chris White discusses shutdown hooks and signal handling in general.

Server Admin Consoles

An additional tool for monitoring and debugging your game server is an administration console. Administrative consoles can be either local or remote. A local console is implemented like `RPSConsoleEventReader`, reading commands from STDIN and turning that input into events. A remote console is a modified `GameClient`, similar to `RPSClient`, with either a command line or graphical UI.

In either case, the admin console sends GameEvents to `GameControllers` like any other client. The difference is that you first require users to be authenticated against the list of administrators and possibly remote IP addresses. The admin client might speak to the normal `GameController` or to a special `AdminController` that divides that functionality into a separate class.

An `AdminController` could provide a number of features to administrators, such as server performance monitoring, game watching, log viewing, and remote shutdown/restart.

For additional security, you might want to listen on another port for administrative access and then set up appropriate firewall rules to limit access to that port. The `GameServer` can then be configured with an additional `ServerSocketChannel` on that port and have it bound to the main selector.

Game Watching

Game watching and monitoring is the act of spying on a game while it is in progress. This can be invaluable for troubleshooting and analyzing player behavior.

Implementing this feature involves a slightly modified `GameClient` that takes actions for both players from the server and takes no game input from the user. Also, the `GameController` needs to be enhanced to allow admin clients to attach to a game and start receiving all events for that game. A small change to the `sendEvent()` and `sendBroadcastEvent()` methods could first check for the existence of an attached spy and send extra copies of all events for that game to the spy.

Advanced Topics

You must deal with some additional issues to deploy your multi-player game system in the real world. These include handling flaky client connections, dealing with network firewalls, and doing performance profiling and enhancement.

Disconnects and Reconnects

A major headache of game server development is dealing with client disconnections. Players don't take too kindly to a loss of network connection that forces them to forfeit a game.

Disconnections can happen for a number of reasons. If the client is on a modem connection, that client might get disconnected. On any connection, there could be heavy network congestion between the client and the server.

You must take care to recognize latent or disconnected clients quickly and to gracefully deal with them. Ideally, players should be able to reconnect and pick up where they left off in the game. Depending on the game genre, this might or might not be possible, but it should at least be considered.

Ping Events

A technique that is often used to keep tabs on client connections is to send periodic ping events (also called heartbeat events) between the client and server. Ping events are useful not only for detecting disconnects, but also for measuring latency of the client connection.

When a client fails to send a ping event for a certain period of time, you can assume the client is having a connection problem. A thread that monitors those events can then take appropriate action, such as notifying other players in the client's game.

The Reaper

The example framework currently allows clients to remain connected indefinitely. This can lead to problems if idle players are wasting valuable server resources or clogging game lobbies.

To avoid wasting server load on clients that are not active, it might be useful to disconnect idle clients after a fixed interval. This can be accomplished by having a period task (the Reaper) that checks the last action time of a client, which could be the time of the client's last non-ping event. Any clients that have not been active for the timeout period are sent a disconnect event and have their connection closed. `java.util.Timer` or a custom dedicated thread can be used to implement the Reaper.

HTTP Tunneling

In the not too distant past, it was possible to run a server on just about any port that you wished, and expect the majority of clients to be able to connect to it. However, the reality of the Internet today is that increasing security threats have sysadmins on the defensive. Because of this, a large number of businesses, home users, and even entire Internet access providers are blocking access to all unprivileged ports (greater than 1024) and even common ports such as 21 (FTP) and 25 (SMTP).

As a result, one of the few (mostly) ports guaranteed to be open is the HTTP port (80). So you simply run your server on port 80, right? Well, the trick here comes when using applets for the game client. For unsigned applets, network access is limited to the server from which it was downloaded (the origin server). So, if the applet needs to be downloaded from a web server running on port 80, how can our game server also be running on port 80?

Even worse, many firewalls do packet filtering and ensure that traffic on port 80 is indeed legitimate HTTP traffic. Currently, our game traffic looks nothing like the HTTP protocol.

To top it off, HTTP is a stateless transactional protocol. In other words, the basic flow is request, response, request, response, and so on. The client always sends a request to the server to get information. For the game server, however, we require that the server be capable of pushing information to the client at any given time; the assumption is that there is a two-way, always-connected pipe.

But don't despair: There are solutions to these problems, and we consider two of them here. First there are a couple of tricks needed for either method.

The first is to wrap the communications to look like valid HTTP communications. Instead of using the over-the-wire protocol header discussed earlier, events would get wrapped in HTTP request and response headers. Additionally, using either XML or other ASCII event formats would be more in tune with using HTTP, but it is still possible to use binary event payloads, if desired.

The second trick is to overcome the lack of full-duplex communication channels. This can be done by using a pair of connections, both originating from the client. Both use HTTP 1.1 keep-alive connections. We will call the first one the server push connection. The client opens this first, sends a single event to the server on it, and then reads events from the server only as they are available. We will call the second connection the client request connection, and it will be used for the client to send all further events to the server.

That defeats the packet filters, but the other issue is that you need to serve the applet files and all related resources (images, sounds, and so on) from the same address as your server communications. Here you have two options: Either actually serve both types of traffic from the same server, or trick the client into thinking that it is coming from the same server.

Option 1: Combo-Server

The first possible solution is to give your game server the functionality of a web server in addition to its normal responsibilities. When you receive a client request, you just need to determine whether it's game traffic. If so, you need to route it to the correct `GameController`; if not, you need to send it to a `DownloadController` that will handle the file serving.

A few problems arise with this first solution. The biggest one is that it is just not clean. You're writing a game server here. Why should you have to waste your time working on a finely tuned web server when Apache could do much better in its sleep?

What's a poor game developer to do? Unfortunately, not much, but a developer with a bit of cash to blow can buy a number of off-the-shelf solutions in the form of an URL-inspecting load balancer so that hardware can sniff your incoming messages and route them accordingly.

Option 2: URL-Based Load Balancing

For those not familiar with high-end network gear, URL-based load balancing is a feature present in many firewall and load-balancer appliances today. These devices enable you to route traffic coming into a single IP and port combination across a server farm based on a number of criteria. The URL-inspection feature allows that routing to be performed based on the contents of the URL string in an HTTP request.

Consider the following pseudo-code for the load-balancing logic:

```
if (URL_PATH matches "/GameServer*")
    originServer = "gameserver.hypefiend.com"
else
    originServer = "webserver.hypefiend.com"
```

So, a request like

```
GET /launchgame.html
```

or

```
GET /applet/gameapplet.jar
```

would get directed to webserver.hypefiend.com, which can be running a standard Apache or other web server on port 80 and can hold all of the game assets (web pages, graphics, applets, sounds).

On the other hand, requests such as this get directed to gameserver.hypefiend.com, running the game server, now having only to be a game server:

```
GET /GameServer/gamename=rps&playerid=bret
```

To the client (in this case, the Java VM), the process is transparent. Both the downloads and the game traffic seem to be coming from the same IP address and port.

A good load balancer is essential for any large system deployment, so this hardware might not really be an added expense.

We'll leave it as an exercise for you to adapt your GameServer to use HTTP tunneling instead of raw sockets connections. It's not a huge stretch—the same basic architecture and all of the GameController code can be left untouched. Mainly you need to do the following:

➤ Adapt SelectAndRead to recognize HTTP headers and pull event payloads from HTTP POST data.

➤ Adapt EventWriter to wrap responses with HTTP headers.

➤ Modify the GameServer and Player interface to allow for two connections per player.

Testing with Bots

To fulfill the design goal of handling a large number of simultaneous users, and to be able to test that functionality without having a small hoard of volunteer testers, you must find a way to simulate the load of a lot of users. To do this, you do what is commonly referred to as *bot testing*.

Bot testing involves crafting a version of the client application that can provide unattended simulation of a large number of users connected and playing games. Although this will not accurately simulate all aspects of a real high user load, it allows testing of a number of key performance, stability, and longevity factors. Things to look for during bot testing are listed here:

➤ The maximum number of simultaneous bot users the server supports

➤ The event throughput (events/sec) at various levels of simultaneous connections

➤ Connection delay at various levels of simultaneous connections

➤ CPU usage at various levels of simultaneous connections

➤ Event latency (the time it takes from the event being received to the time it starts processing)

➤ EventQueue backlogs (for tuning your Wrap pool sizes)

➤ Memory usage over time, carefully checking for any continuous growth that would indicate a leak (yes, it is possible in Java)

➤ Any unusual exceptions or other errors

➤ Any thread deadlocks

It is recommended that you have as many separate machines doing the bot testing as possible. The fewer number of connections per machine you have, the closer it will be to simulating real users. After all, many bots on the same machine actually send their packets to the server sequentially, not truly simultaneously.

Definitely avoid running the bots on the same machine as the GameServer. Doing so will severely skew any test results.

Those Pesky Modems

Bot testing on your local network or even on remote well-connected machines will not provide some things when your target user audience might be mostly connected by modems (sometimes as slow as 28.8; can you imagine?). Modem connections are notorious for having extremely high latency (typically in the 250ms range just to reach the ISP), sporadic throughput, packet loss, and frequent disconnects.

One trick that can be used to simulate at least some of these problems is to use a tool called a *modem-emulating proxy server*. A number of these tools are available, as a quick Google search will reveal. They provide a proxy server that limits the bandwidth of the connection and introduces artificial latency. One such application is called Sloppy (from slow proxy) and is available at `www.dallaway.com/sloppy/`. It proxies only HTTP communication, however, not generic TCP traffic, so unless you are using HTTP encapsulation, you'll need to find another tool.

Proxy servers get you only so far. It is highly recommended that if your audience will be using modems, you do regular and thorough testing using the same hardware, OS, ISP, and so on as your audience does. It might be painful, but your players will thank you.

Profiling and Performance Stats

To optimize your application, it is first necessary to evaluate the efficiency of your server implementation and identify the bottlenecks. To do this, you need empirical evidence. Most programmers have used profiling tools, which measure the amount of time that a program spends executing each method. Java includes profiling tools as part of the Java Runtime, and a number of third-party tools are available as well. However, usually it becomes necessary to augment those tools with some custom code for generating performance statistics that is unique to your application.

For instance, in our `GameServer`, knowing which methods your apps spend most of their time in is certainly useful, but the key metrics of interest are as follows:

> ➤ Event processing time
>
> ➤ Game logic times for each `GameEvent` type
>
> ➤ Event latency (time that an event waits in queue before processing)

➤ Database query times

➤ Time to add a new connection

An easy way to obtain these stats is to insert some code around your key methods to check times and record to a log file for further analysis. Listing 6.14 shows the `processEvent()` method from `RPSController` with added performance stat code.

Listing 6.14 `processEvent()` with Timing Code

```
Public void processevent(event) {
    long start = System.currentTimeMillis();

    switch (e.getType()) {
    case GameEventDefault.C_LOGIN:
        login(e);
        break;
    case GameEventDefault.C_LOGOUT:
        logout(e);
        break;
    case GameEventDefault.C_JOIN_GAME:
        join(e);
        break;
    case GameEventDefault.C_QUIT_GAME:
        quit(e);
        break;
    case GameEventDefault.C_CHAT_MSG:
        chat(e);
        break;
    case GameEventDefault.C_MOVE:
        move(e);
        break;
    case GameEventDefault.C_GET_PLAYERS:
        getPlayers(e);
        break;
    }

    // log the method name, the event type,
    // the duration in the queue, time to process,
```

```
        // and current queue size
        statslog.info("processEvent, " + event.getType() + "," +
            (start - event.getQueuedTime()) + "," +
            System.currentTimeMillis() - start) + "," +
            eventQueue.size();
}
```

If you tweak your Log4J Appender to output only the timestamp and the data that you provide, you will have a nice comma-separated value (CSV) file that you can analyze with external tools such as Excel or some Perl scripts.

Performance Tweaks

You can tweak performance of server applications in endless ways. The most important thing is not to spend time optimizing code that doesn't need it. It might seem obvious, but often what you think is your bottleneck really isn't. The only way to know for sure is to perform profiling to measure which code is actually wasting most of your CPU time.

That being said, because most of your server's effort involves handling GameEvents, there are a couple of simple rules for tweaking that part of the core system:

➤ **Make events smaller**. The smaller the event, the less time it takes to allocate, serialize, and transmit.

➤ **Send fewer events**. Every event counts, so if a client doesn't absolutely need the data, don't send it. For example, in GameController.sendBroadcastEvent(), we don't send the event to the originator of the message.

The Evil Trash Collector

By default, the Java VM runs a garbage-collection thread in the background that periodically fires up and does a full garbage-collection run. Another method is available, called incremental garbage collection, that is invoked with the -Xincgc command-line switch.

Incremental garbage collection avoids the "stall" that can happen as the garbage collection loads down the server in a short burst. Instead, the garbage collector runs more frequently but does less work in each cycle. As a result, there will not be such a sudden burst of work, but at the expense of worse overall performance of the GC.

Additionally, JDK 1.4.1 includes some experimental garbage-collection options: `-XX:+UseConcMarkSweepGC` and `-XX+UseParallelGC`. These options are nonstandard and should be used with caution, but they might provide great benefits to your application's performance. For more details, see `http://java.sun.com/docs/hotspot/VmOptions.html`.

Object Reuse

Speaking of garbage collection, the best route to avoiding it is to use fewer objects in the first place. There are a few tactics for doing this.

The first is basic optimization, going through and removing unnecessary allocations. On top of that, simple object reuse, as done with the outgoing chat events in the `RPSController`, can be helpful. But the best tactic for oft-created objects is to use an object pool.

Object pools, like thread pools and database connection pools, provide a mechanism for reusing objects. The pool is created with an initial number of objects of the given class. When you need an instance of the class, instead of using the `new` operator to create one, you call a method of the pool to fetch an instance.

Our game server could benefit greatly from pooling some objects, notably GameEvents. An active `GameServer` can be creating GameEvents at an astounding rate. But the life of these events is very short. They are created, sent to a client (or clients), and then destroyed.

Pooling GameEvents could make a drastic difference in the performance of a loaded game server. The hard part is figuring out how many objects are required in the pool, but this can be determined during automated testing, or the pool can be made adaptive using a low-priority background thread to adjust the size of the pool. Many web and application servers use that technique for managing their request-handling thread pools.

Other Tweaks

Here are some other suggestions for getting the most out of your game server:

➤ **Threads**. Keep the number of threads down. Performance stats help identify what `Wraps` need more or fewer threads by checking their average queue size. Every thread, idle or not, takes additional overhead, so start with the least amount you can.

➤ **Synchronization**. Keep it tight. Keep statements that don't need to be there out of the synchronized blocks.

➤ **Busy loops**. Avoid using busy wait loops, like this one:

```
while (true) {
    checkForSomeCondition();
    try {
        Thread.sleep(SLEEP_TIME);
    }
    catch(InterruptedException ie) {}
}
```

While waiting for something, use a blocking queue or similar construct. For executing periodic tasks, use `java.util.Timer`.

➤ **Logging**. Remove *all* logging statements, even ones that won't be logged, in tight inner loops. Keep a check on logging that *is* enabled in the live code. Too much logging kills a server's performance.

Summary

We covered a lot of ground in this chapter. You learned how to use the JDK 1.4 NIO APIs, and how to build a multi-user chat server. Then we detailed the design and implementation of a flexible Game Server Framework and built an exciting fast-action game on top of it. Hopefully, we've left you with enough understanding and ideas for you to build a multi-player game server for your own project.

Part II

3D Graphics and Advanced Techniques

Chapter 7

3D Graphics

Once I heard someone say there will never, ever be flying cars.

Of course, I was disappointed, and I'm still getting over it. This person elaborated that the reason there will never be flying cars is not because it won't ever be technically feasible to create a flying car: Most people just can't handle the additional concept of moving a vehicle up and down instead of moving just left, right, forward, and backward. We can handle movement only in two dimensions (not counting hills and valleys because we are just following the ground), and a third dimension is just too complicated for many people.

It's true that 3D concepts are complicated. So are 3D graphics. But hopefully, by the end of this chapter, you'll have enough knowledge of basic 3D graphics concepts that you'll be able to create your own flying cars—in a game, anyway.

Types of 3D Rendering

Two popular types of 3D rendering exist: ray tracing and polygon modeling.

Ray tracing is a bit like the real world, in that it models rays of light, only in reverse. Instead of modeling light rays from light sources to the eye, it does the opposite, modeling rays from the eye to the world. As you can imagine, modeling a ray of light for every pixel on the screen is computationally expensive. Although ray tracing is not common in real-time 3D graphics, it can give rather realistic results, and it was used in the movie *Ice Age*.

The 3D rendering technique common in real-time games and most movies with computer-generated imagery is polygon modeling. With *polygon modeling*, the virtual 3D world is interpreted as flat polygons. A polygon is a flat, closed shape with three or more sides (such as triangles, rectangles, and octagons). Using polygons speeds things up, but rounded objects such as spheres don't translate to a polygon model very well (unless you use enough polygons to make them appear round). Polygon modeling is less computationally expensive than ray tracing and can be sped up by a large magnitude using a 3D accelerator card. It is usually in the best interest of your game to take advantage of 3D accelerator cards because they are found on nearly every computer today.

In Java, there two common ways to take advantage of a 3D accelerator card: either with Java3D or with an OpenGL binding.

Java3D is a high-level API that handles things such as hidden surface removal, simple collision detection, and scene management. Programmers using Java3D can get up and running quickly without having to know a lot of 3D graphics programming techniques. Although Java3D is mostly written in Java, its core uses either OpenGL or DirectX to render 3D graphics.

Java3D is available for Windows and many flavors of UNIX but is not included in the Java 1.4.1 SDK. Also, because of licensing, Java3D is not available for all systems. Currently, Java3D is not available for Mac OS X.

OpenGL bindings, on the other hand, are usually free to use in commercial products and are available for a wider range of hardware, including Mac OS X. OpenGL is a low-level API, so it requires a more thorough knowledge of 3D graphics programming to take advantage of. The OpenGL bindings simply allow your Java code to access OpenGL functions.

A couple of popular OpenGL bindings are GL4Java (`www.jausoft.com/gl4java.html`) and LWJGL (`java-game-lib.sourceforge.net`). At this writing, GL4Java is available on more systems and enables you to also use the AWT and Swing at the same time; it hasn't been updated in more than a year, though, so the latest OpenGL features might not be available. LWJGL, or Light-Weight Java Game Library, uses NIO native buffers to interact with OpenGL, so it's a bit faster; it currently is being regularly maintained and updated, but it is not compatible with AWT or Swing.

In this chapter and the next, "Texture Mapping and Lighting," you'll create a lightweight, software-based 3D polygon renderer. A software-based renderer won't be as fast as a hardware-based renderer, so it might not be an ideal solution for large-scale games. But in the process of creating a software-based 3D renderer, you'll have a better understanding of how hardware-based renderers work, and you'll learn a lot of 3D graphics techniques that can be applied to a hardware-based solution.

Also, a software-based renderer is a great solution if you want to make a small downloadable game without requiring the user to download or install Java3D or an OpenGL binding.

Don't Forget Your Math

Before jumping into 3D graphics programming, let's tack a step back and talk about trigonometry and vectors. Hey, don't fall asleep—I'm serious. You'll use the trigonometry definitions and vector math basics a lot when dealing with 3D graphics.

Trigonometry and Right Triangles

You've probably seen the trigonometric definitions in Figure 7.1. The definitions show how the angles and side lengths of a right triangle relate to each other. Some people have these definitions memorized; for everyone else, Figure 7.1 is provided here for a quick reference.

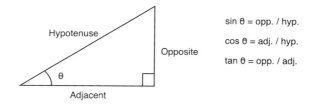

Figure 7.1   The definitions of the trigonometric functions.

Lots of 3D graphics problems can be solved using right triangles. A right triangle is a triangle that has one 90° angle. To "solve" a right triangle, or calculate the length of all the sides and angles, you need to know at least two pieces of information about it: either two sides or one side and one angle.

You're probably familiar with the equation $a^2+b^2=c^2$. In this equation, called the Pythagorean Theorem, a, b, and c are sides of a right triangle. The hypotenuse, or side opposite the right angle, is c. If you know the length of two sides of a triangle and need to know the third, this equation is for you.

However, if you know only one side and one angle, the trigonometric definitions in Figure 7.1 come in handy. The definitions of sine, cosine, and tangent show the relationship between the sides of a right triangle and its angles, and enable you to solve a triangle in various situations.

Vector Math

When working with 3D graphics, we denote a point in 3D space as the triplet (x, y, z). The tricky part, and the part important to understand, is that this triplet can be thought of as either a point in space or a vector. A *vector* is a magnitude and a direction, like a velocity, and is the basis of vector math. An example of a direction is east, and an example of a magnitude is 55 mph. So, if the x-axis points east, then the vector (55, 0, 0) could be interpreted as east at 55 mph. Likewise, if the z-axis points south, then the vector (0, 0, 55) could be interpreted as south at 55 mph.

In this book, you work with only 3D vectors, but keep in mind that vectors aren't limited to three dimensions; they can have two dimensions or even more than three. In the text, we denote vectors as an uppercase letter (as opposed to a real number, in lower case). Also, we denote a vector's components with a subscript:

$V = (V_x, \ V_y, \ V_z)$

Remember, a vector is a magnitude and a direction, and it doesn't have an origin. It doesn't matter what the origin is. In other words, traveling east at 55 mph in Los Angeles is the same as traveling east at 55 mph in Paris (except in Paris, you'll probably be using kilometers, but you get the idea). It's the same vector.

Now let's move on to some vector math. First, basic addition: Vectors can be added together, as shown in Figure 7.2. In this figure, the vectors U and V are added together (U+V), and U is subtracted from V (V–U). The vectors –U and –V are also shown: These vectors have the same magnitude but opposite direction of their positive counterparts.

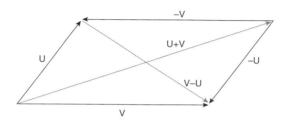

Figure 7.2   Vectors can be added together.

Mathematically, adding two 3D vectors is achieved by adding their components together:

$U+V = (U_x+V_x, \quad U_y+V_y, \quad U_z+V_z)$

For example, if a bird is traveling east at 55 mph and the wind is pushing the bird west at 10 mph, the result of the bird and wind vectors added together would be east at 45 mph. Note that adding two vectors results in a new vector with a different magnitude, a different direction, or both. Of course, the same works for subtraction. Next, you can multiply a vector by a scale. This changes its magnitude without changing its direction, and is achieved by multiplying every component by the scale:

$s\ V = (s\ V_x, \quad s\ V_y, \quad s\ V_z)$

So, multiplying east at 55 mph by 2 would mean east at 110 mph. Don't try that at home, kids.

A vector's magnitude, or length, is notated with bars around it. The length can be calculated using the three-dimensional version of the Pythagorean Theorem:

$|V| = (V_x^2+V_y^2+V_z^2)^{1/2}$

If a vector has a length of 1, it's called a unit vector, or a normalized vector. You can normalize a vector by dividing it by its length. A normalized vector is denoted with a party hat over it:

$$\hat{U} = U / |U|$$

Vectors may also wear party hats when they've had too much punch.

That's it for a quick introduction to vector math. We'll get into more vector math later in this chapter, but with the information we have so far, we'll go ahead and create a useful vector class. The Vector3D class, in Listing 7.1, uses floats to describe a 3D vector. We use floats for most 3D calculations in this book, mainly because they're less costly than doubles in most situations and give us enough precision for our needs.

Listing 7.1   Vector3D.java

```java
package com.brackeen.javagamebook.math3D;

/**
    The Vector3D class implements a 3D vector with the
    floating-point values x, y, and z. Vectors can be thought of
    either as a (x,y,z) point or as a vector from (0,0,0) to
    (x,y,z).
*/
public class Vector3D implements Transformable {

    public float x;
    public float y;
    public float z;


    /**
        Creates a new Vector3D at (0,0,0).
    */
    public Vector3D() {
        this(0,0,0);
    }
```

```
/**
    Creates a new Vector3D with the same values as the
    specified Vector3D.
*/
public Vector3D(Vector3D v) {
    this(v.x, v.y, v.z);
}



/**
    Creates a new Vector3D with the specified (x, y, z) values.
*/
public Vector3D(float x, float y, float z) {
    setTo(x, y, z);
}



/**
    Checks if this Vector3D is equal to the specified Object.
    They are equal only if the specified Object is a Vector3D
    and the two Vector3D's x, y, and z coordinates are equal.
*/
public boolean equals(Object obj) {
    Vector3D v = (Vector3D)obj;
    return (v.x == x && v.y == y && v.z == z);
}



/**
    Checks if this Vector3D is equal to the specified
    x, y, and z coordinates.
*/
public boolean equals(float x, float y, float z) {
    return (this.x == x && this.y == y && this.z == z);
}
```

continues

Listing 7.1 Vector3D.java *continued*

```java
/**
    Sets the vector to the same values as the specified
    Vector3D.
*/
public void setTo(Vector3D v) {
    setTo(v.x, v.y, v.z);
}




/**
    Sets this vector to the specified (x, y, z) values.
*/
public void setTo(float x, float y, float z) {
    this.x = x;
    this.y = y;
    this.z = z;
}




/**
    Adds the specified (x, y, z) values to this vector.
*/
public void add(float x, float y, float z) {
    this.x+=x;
    this.y+=y;
    this.z+=z;
}




/**
    Subtracts the specified (x, y, z) values to this vector.
*/
public void subtract(float x, float y, float z) {
    add(-x, -y, -z);
}
```

```
/**
    Adds the specified vector to this vector.
*/
public void add(Vector3D v) {
    add(v.x, v.y, v.z);
}



/**
    Subtracts the specified vector from this vector.
*/
public void subtract(Vector3D v) {
    add(-v.x, -v.y, -v.z);
}



/**
    Multiplies this vector by the specified value. The new
    length of this vector will be length()*s.
*/
public void multiply(float s) {
    x*=s;
    y*=s;
    z*=s;
}



/**
    Divides this vector by the specified value. The new
    length of this vector will be length()/s.
*/
public void divide(float s) {
    x/=s;
    y/=s;
    z/=s;
}
```

continues

Listing 7.1 Vector3D.java *continued*

```java
/**
    Returns the length of this vector as a float.
*/
public float length() {
    return (float)Math.sqrt(x*x + y*y + z*z);
}



/**
    Converts this Vector3D to a unit vector, or, in other
    words, a vector of length 1. Same as calling
    v.divide(v.length()).
*/
public void normalize() {
    divide(length());
}



/**
    Converts this Vector3D to a String representation.
*/
public String toString() {
    return "(" + x + ", " + y + ", " + z + ")";
}
}
```

There's nothing too difficult here. Vector3D has methods for adding, subtracting, multiplying, dividing, getting the length of, and normalizing vectors.

We use the Vector3D class for both vectors and points in space because some math calculations require treating a point as a vector, or vice versa. For example, you might want to get the vector between two points in space. In this case, if both points were a Vector3D, subtracting one from the other would result in the vector between them.

As said before, there's more to talk about with vector math, and there are a few more methods to add on to the Vector3D class. We get to this later in the chapter. For now, you have enough to move on to some 3D basics.

3D Basics

So what do those x, y, and z values in a 3D vector actually refer to anyway?

When you're doing 2D graphics work, it's common to use a 2D coordinate system that's the same as the screen: the origin in the upper-left corner, x increasing from left to right, and y increasing from top to bottom. In 3D graphics, the three axes won't map directly to any device coordinates, so the goal is to "translate" the 3D world onto the 2D coordinate system of the screen. In this book, we use the 3D coordinate system common in math textbooks, called the "right-handed" coordinate system, where the x-axis points "right," the y-axis points "up," and the z-axis points "back" (away from the viewer). This is also the system used by OpenGL. The right-handed coordinate system is shown in Figure 7.3.

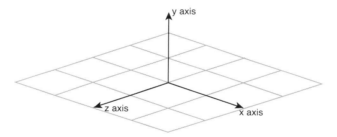

Figure 7.3   The right-handed coordinate system is common in 3D graphics and is the coordinate system we use in this book.

If, on your right hand, you point your index finder in the direction of the y-axis and your thumb in the direction of the x-axis, your middle finger points in the direction of the z-axis. The same thing works for your left hand and the left-handed coordinate system, shown in Figure 7.4.

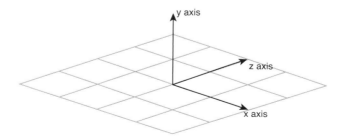

Figure 7.4   The left-handed coordinate system is an alternative way of viewing the 3D world.

Other 3D coordinate system variations include a rotation of either the left-handed or right-handed coordinate systems so that the z-axis points "up." Here, however, you'll work with only the right-handed system in Figure 7.3. Next, you'll learn about the concept of the camera and the view window. The *camera* is where the view is located relative to everything else in the world. The *view window* is a window in 3D space that is the same size of the 3D window onscreen. In games, the view window is typically the same dimension of the screen.

Locate the camera at the origin, (0,0,0) and the view window down the opposite direction of the z-axis, as shown in Figure 7.5. This makes the z-axis decrease with depth, which is a common way to represent the view window.

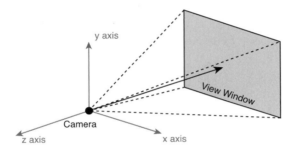

Figure 7.5 The camera, located at (0,0,0), looks toward the center of the view window in the opposite direction of the z-axis. The view window is commonly the entire screen.

It may sound crazy to keep the camera at (0,0,0), looking straight down the z-axis. Don't you want to move the camera and change the direction the camera is facing? When you turn 90° right, wouldn't you then be looking down the x-axis?

The answer is "sorta." Keeping the camera looking down the z-axis and fixed at (0,0,0) actually simplifies many calculations and is the common way to represent 3D graphics. We'll come up with a way to simulate camera movement later in the chapter, but for now, we focus on drawing a 3D world with a fixed camera.

Note that everything that is visible to the camera is inside what's called the *view frustum*, as shown in Figure 7.6. The view frustum shape is usually a four-sided pyramid, sometimes with part of its tip cut off by a front-clip plane. Only what's inside the frustum needs to be drawn.

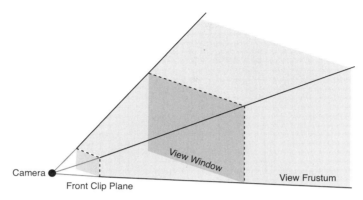

Figure 7.6   Everything that is visible is inside the view frustum.

Take a step back and look at want you want to do. You have a 3D world, and you want to display the objects inside the view frustum as a 2D image, with farther objects appearing smaller than closer ones. To actually draw something, you'll project the 3D world onto the view window, as shown in Figure 7.7.

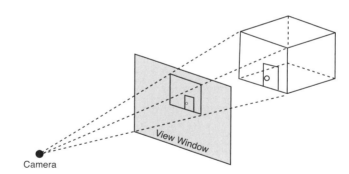

Figure 7.7   Objects in the 3D world are projected onto the view window. Thus, farther objects appear smaller.

When projecting a point in 3D to the view window, you can imagine a line from the 3D point being drawn to the camera (like the dotted lines in Figure 7.7). The intersection of this line with the view window is where the projected point lies. Because you treat the camera as a point, objects farther from the camera appear smaller than closer ones. This brings up to the next topic, which actually gets the math to project a point onto the view window.

3D Math

Projecting a point onto the view window reduces to a simple right triangle problem, as shown in Figure 7.8.

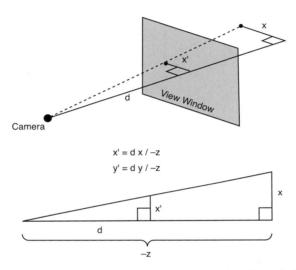

$$x' = d\,x\,/\,{-z}$$
$$y' = d\,y\,/\,{-z}$$

Figure 7.8 Projecting a point, (x, y, z), onto the view window.

In Figure 7.8, you find the 2D projected point, (x', y'), from the 3D point, (x, y, z). Remember that z decreases in the direction of the view, so the length along the z-axis from the origin to the 3D point is −z. In this figure, you deal only with the x coordinate, but the y coordinate can be calculated using the same technique.

The triangle formed by the lines x and −z is a similar triangle (the angles are the same) to the triangle formed by x' and d. To solve this, however, you need to know d, the distance from the camera to the view window, what we call the view distance.

The good news is, you can pick any value for d, the view distance, which will be constant in the normal course of a game. It depends on only how wide you want the view angle to be. For example, if the camera is very close to the view window (short view distance), the camera can see a wide angle of the 3D world. Likewise, if the camera is far from the view window (longer view distance), the camera will have "tunnel vision" because the view angle will be very small.

The size of the view angle is your choice. Typically, values for the horizontal view angle vary from 45° to 90°. In the examples in this book, we use 75°.

With the horizontal view angle, the view distance can be calculated as shown in Figure 7.9.

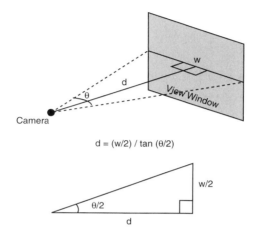

Figure 7.9 Calculating d, the distance between the camera and the view window, based on θ, the view angle, and w, the width of the view window.

Note that the view distance depends on the size of the window. So, if you give the player an option of changing the size of the window or screen on the fly, you must recalculate the view distance.

Now that you know the view distance, you can project a point to the view window using the formula from Figure 7.8. However, the 2D coordinate system of the view window isn't the same as the view window of the screen, as shown in Figure 7.10. You need one more step to convert view window coordinates to screen coordinates.

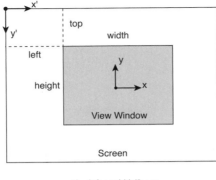

$$x' = \text{left} + \text{width}/2 + x$$
$$y' = \text{top} + \text{height}/2 - y$$

Figure 7.10 Converting a point on the view window, (x, y), to a point on the screen, (x', y').

That does it. With these equations, you can project a 3D point onto the screen. The view window and projection are summed up in the `ViewWindow` class in Listing 7.2.

Listing 7.2 ViewWindow.java

```
package com.brackeen.javagamebook.math3D;

import java.awt.Rectangle;

/**
    The ViewWindow class represents the geometry of a view window
    for 3D viewing.
*/
public class ViewWindow {

    private Rectangle bounds;
    private float angle;
    private float distanceToCamera;

    /**
        Creates a new ViewWindow with the specified bounds on the
        screen and horizontal view angle.
    */
    public ViewWindow(int left, int top, int width, int height,
        float angle)
```

```
{
    bounds = new Rectangle();
    this.angle = angle;
    setBounds(left, top, width, height);
}



/**
    Sets the bounds for this ViewWindow on the screen.
*/
public void setBounds(int left, int top, int width,
    int height)
{
    bounds.x = left;
    bounds.y = top;
    bounds.width = width;
    bounds.height = height;
    distanceToCamera = (bounds.width/2) /
        (float)Math.tan(angle/2);
}



/**
    Sets the horizontal view angle for this ViewWindow.
*/
public void setAngle(float angle) {
    this.angle = angle;
    distanceToCamera = (bounds.width/2) /
        (float)Math.tan(angle/2);
}



/**
    Gets the horizontal view angle of this view window.
*/
public float getAngle() {
    return angle;
}
```

continues

Listing 7.2   ViewWindow.java   *continued*

```java
/**
    Gets the width of this view window.
*/
public int getWidth() {
    return bounds.width;
}



/**
    Gets the height of this view window.
*/
public int getHeight() {
    return bounds.height;
}



/**
    Gets the y offset of this view window on the screen.
*/
public int getTopOffset() {
    return bounds.y;
}



/**
    Gets the x offset of this view window on the screen.
*/
public int getLeftOffset() {
    return bounds.x;
}



/**
    Gets the distance from the camera to this view window.
*/
public float getDistance() {
```

```
        return distanceToCamera;
    }




    /**
        Converts an x coordinate on this view window to the
        corresponding x coordinate on the screen.
    */
    public float convertFromViewXToScreenX(float x) {
        return x + bounds.x + bounds.width/2;
    }


    /**
        Converts a y coordinate on this view window to the
        corresponding y coordinate on the screen.
    */
    public float convertFromViewYToScreenY(float y) {
        return -y + bounds.y + bounds.height/2;
    }


    /**
        Converts an x coordinate on the screen to the
        corresponding x coordinate on this view window.
    */
    public float convertFromScreenXToViewX(float x) {
        return x - bounds.x - bounds.width/2;
    }


    /**
        Converts a y coordinate on the screen to the
        corresponding y coordinate on this view window.
    */
    public float convertFromScreenYToViewY(float y) {
        return -y + bounds.y + bounds.height/2;
```

continues

Listing 7.2 ViewWindow.java *continued*

```
    }


    /**
        Projects the specified vector to the screen.
    */
    public void project(Vector3D v) {
        // project to view window
        v.x = distanceToCamera * v.x / -v.z;
        v.y = distanceToCamera * v.y / -v.z;

        // convert to screen coordinates
        v.x = convertFromViewXToScreenX(v.x);
        v.y = convertFromViewYToScreenY(v.y);
    }
}
```

In the `ViewWindow` class, the projection occurs in the `project()` method, which projects a `Vector3D` to the `ViewWindow` and then translates it to screen coordinates. After calling the `project()` method, the x and y components of the `Vector3D` are the screen coordinates, and the z component can be ignored.

Huzzah, you can project points from 3D space onto the screen! Wait, that's boring. Points are one thing, but the goal is to create a polygon modeler. So let's talk about polygons.

Polygons

You can put solid polygons into two different categories: convex and concave, as show in Figure 7.11. *Concave* polygons have a part that bulges inward, like a cave. In the code in this chapter, you deal only with convex polygons because concave polygons have some complexities that make things harder than they should be. Of course, any concave polygon can be broken down into a series of convex polygons, so this isn't an issue if you want to simulate concave polygons in your game.

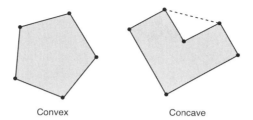

Convex   Concave

Figure 7.11   Two types of polygons: convex and concave. A polygon
is concave if any part of it bulges inward.

Looking at Figure 7.11, you can tell it's easy to describe a polygon mathematically:
Polygons are just a series of points, or vertices. Polygons appear solid only once they
are drawn on the screen. So, you start by creating the Polygon3D class in Listing 7.3,
which currently does nothing but manage a list of vertices.

Listing 7.3   Polygon3D.java

```java
package com.brackeen.javagamebook.math3D;

/**
    The Polygon3D class represents a polygon as a series of
    vertices.
*/
public class Polygon3D {

    private Vector3D[] v;
    private int numVertices;

    /**
        Creates an empty polygon that can be used as a "scratch"
        polygon for transforms, projections, etc.
    */
    public Polygon3D() {
        numVertices = 0;
        v = new Vector3D[0];
    }


    /**
```

continues

Listing 7.3 Polygon3D.java *continued*

```
        Creates a new Polygon3D with the specified vertices.
    */
    public Polygon3D(Vector3D v0, Vector3D v1, Vector3D v2) {
        this(new Vector3D[] { v0, v1, v2 });
    }


    /**
        Creates a new Polygon3D with the specified vertices. All
        the vertices are assumed to be in the same plane.
    */
    public Polygon3D(Vector3D v0, Vector3D v1, Vector3D v2,
        Vector3D v3)
    {
        this(new Vector3D[] { v0, v1, v2, v3 });
    }


    /**
        Creates a new Polygon3D with the specified vertices. All
        the vertices are assumed to be in the same plane.
    */
    public Polygon3D(Vector3D[] vertices) {
        this.v = vertices;
        numVertices = vertices.length;
    }


    /**
        Sets this polygon to the same vertices as the specified
        polygon.
    */
    public void setTo(Polygon3D polygon) {
        numVertices = polygon.numVertices;

        ensureCapacity(numVertices);
        for (int i=0; i<numVertices; i++) {
            v[i].setTo(polygon.v[i]);
```

```
        }
    }


    /**
        Ensures this polygon has enough capacity to hold the
        specified number of vertices.
    */
    protected void ensureCapacity(int length) {
        if (v.length < length) {
            Vector3D[] newV = new Vector3D[length];
            System.arraycopy(v,0,newV,0,v.length);
            for (int i=v.length; i<newV.length; i++) {
                newV[i] = new Vector3D();
            }
            v = newV;
        }
    }


    /**
        Gets the number of vertices this polygon has.
    */
    public int getNumVertices() {
        return numVertices;
    }


    /**
        Gets the vertex at the specified index.
    */
    public Vector3D getVertex(int index) {
        return v[index];
    }


    /**
        Projects this polygon onto the view window.
```

continues

Listing 7.3 Polygon3D.java *continued*

```
*/
    public void project(ViewWindow view) {
        for (int i=0; i<numVertices; i++) {
            view.project(v[i]);
        }
    }
}
```

The Polygon3D class uses an array of Vector3Ds to represent a 3D polygon. Like Vector3D, Polygon3D is just a start; you'll add to it later in this chapter.

The default, no-argument constructor creates a blank polygon with no vertices. A polygon that uses this constructor can be used as a "scratch" polygon. A scratch polygon is convenient in case you want to copy a polygon and modify it, preserving the original polygon. Call the setTo() method to set the scratch polygon to the polygon you want to copy and modify.

Notice that the Polygon3D class describes a polygon's shape, but not its color or texture. We get to textured polygons in the next chapter, but for now you'll create solid-colored polygons to draw. You can easily create a SolidPolygon3D class, which is a subclass of Polygon3D with additional methods to set or get the color of the polygon.

At this point, you could create a simple 3D demo, but first let's talk about 3D transforms to make the 3D demo more interesting.

3D Transforms

To get your polygons to move around in 3D space (and maybe do some tricks), you apply 3D transforms to them. 3D polygon transforms usually consist of translation, scaling, and rotation.

➤ Translation, or moving a polygon around in space, is achieved by adding the translation vector to each vertex in the polygon.

➤ Scaling, or making a polygon grow or shrink in size (without changing its shape), is trivial if the center of the polygon is the origin. In this case, multiplying the scale factor by each vertex scales the polygon. However, if the center of the polygon is not the origin, this can also translate the polygon as well as scale. Scaling isn't a requirement of our 3D engine, so we'll skip this one.

➤ Rotation involves rotating a polygon around the x-axis, the y-axis, the z-axis, or a combination thereof.

Rotations

First, take a look at the math involved in rotation—specifically, rotation around the z-axis. When you rotate around the z-axis, the z value of the point isn't changed, so it's just like doing a 2D rotation around the point (0,0), as in Figure 7.12. Every point in the polygon rotates around (0,0), which changes its position but not its distance from (0,0).

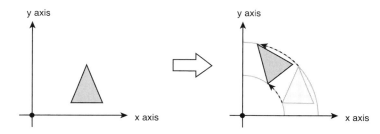

Figure 7.12   Rotation around the z-axis is a simple 2D rotation around the point (0,0).

If we treat x and y as a magnitude, r, and an angle around the z-axis, φ, then the x and y coordinates of the point that you want to rotate can be interpreted as follows:

```
x = r cos φ
```

```
y = r sin φ
```

Rotating counterclockwise by an angle, θ becomes this (a visual example is in Figure 7.13):

```
x' = r cos (φ+θ)
```

```
y' = r sin (φ+θ)
```

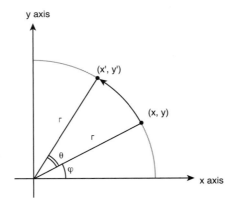

Figure 7.13 Rotating a point (x,y) by the angle θ. The angle of the original point (x,y) is φ, and the angle of the rotated point (x', y') is (φ+θ).

This reduces to the following:

```
x' = r cos φ cos θ - r sin φ sin θ
y' = r sin φ cos θ + r cos φ sin θ
```

Substituting the original formulas for x and y gives you this:

```
x' = x cos θ - y sin θ
y' = x sin θ + y cos θ
```

That's it. This formula enables you to rotate a point around the z-axis counterclockwise by the angle θ.

Rotating around the x-axis and the y-axis is similar. Here are all the rotation formulas:

To rotate counterclockwise around the x-axis:

```
x' = x
y' = y cos θ - z sin θ
z' = y sin θ + z cos θ
```

To rotate counterclockwise around the y-axis:

```
x' = z sin θ + x cos θ
y' = y
z' = z cos θ - x sin θ
```

To rotate counterclockwise around the z-axis:

```
x' = x cos θ - y sin θ
y' = x sin θ + y cos θ
z' = z
```

A complete rotation transform involves three rotations: one each for the x-, y-, and z-axes. When you transform a polygon, just apply these formulas to each point in the polygon.

Encapsulating Rotation and Translation Transforms

Even though these rotation formulas are simple, keep in mind that the functions `Math.sin()` and `Math.cos()` don't come cheap: They're implemented using a lot of calculations and involve JNI calls, so calling these functions for every `Vector3D` you want to transform isn't too efficient. Instead, you can precompute the value of the sine and cosine of each angle whenever the transform changes. Because the transform changes only once per frame, at most, this greatly reduces the number of `Math.sin()` and `Math.cos()` calls.

The `Transform3D` class in Listing 7.4 implements this. It contains all the information needed to apply translation and rotation transforms, but it doesn't actually apply transforms. Later, when you apply transforms, you can use the precomputed sine and cosine values to rotate all of your `Vector3D`s.

Listing 7.4   Transform3D.java

```java
package com.brackeen.javagamebook.math3D;

/**
    The Transform3D class represents a rotation and translation.
*/
```

Listing 7.4 Transform3D.java *continued*

```java
public class Transform3D {

    protected Vector3D location;
    private float cosAngleX;
    private float sinAngleX;
    private float cosAngleY;
    private float sinAngleY;
    private float cosAngleZ;
    private float sinAngleZ;

    /**
        Creates a new Transform3D with no translation or rotation.
    */
    public Transform3D() {
        this(0,0,0);
    }


    /**
        Creates a new Transform3D with the specified translation
        and no rotation.
    */
    public Transform3D(float x, float y, float z) {
        location = new Vector3D(x, y, z);
        setAngle(0,0,0);
    }


    /**
        Creates a new Transform3D
    */
    public Transform3D(Transform3D v) {
        location = new Vector3D();
        setTo(v);
    }


    public Object clone() {
```

```
        return new Transform3D(this);
    }


    /**
        Sets this Transform3D to the specified Transform3D.
    */
    public void setTo(Transform3D v) {
        location.setTo(v.location);
        this.cosAngleX = v.cosAngleX;
        this.sinAngleX = v.sinAngleX;
        this.cosAngleY = v.cosAngleY;
        this.sinAngleY = v.sinAngleY;
        this.cosAngleZ = v.cosAngleZ;
        this.sinAngleZ = v.sinAngleZ;
    }


    /**
        Gets the location (translation) of this transform.
    */
    public Vector3D getLocation() {
        return location;
    }

    public float getCosAngleX() {
        return cosAngleX;
    }

    public float getSinAngleX() {
        return sinAngleX;
    }

    public float getCosAngleY() {
        return cosAngleY;
    }

    public float getSinAngleY() {
```

continues

Listing 7.4 Transform3D.java *continued*

```java
            return sinAngleY;
    }

    public float getCosAngleZ() {
        return cosAngleZ;
    }

    public float getSinAngleZ() {
        return sinAngleZ;
    }

    public float getAngleX() {
        return (float)Math.atan2(sinAngleX, cosAngleX);
    }

    public float getAngleY() {
        return (float)Math.atan2(sinAngleY, cosAngleY);
    }

    public float getAngleZ() {
        return (float)Math.atan2(sinAngleZ, cosAngleZ);
    }

    public void setAngleX(float angleX) {
        cosAngleX = (float)Math.cos(angleX);
        sinAngleX = (float)Math.sin(angleX);
    }

    public void setAngleY(float angleY) {
        cosAngleY = (float)Math.cos(angleY);
        sinAngleY = (float)Math.sin(angleY);
    }

    public void setAngleZ(float angleZ) {
        cosAngleZ = (float)Math.cos(angleZ);
        sinAngleZ = (float)Math.sin(angleZ);
```

```
    }

    public void setAngle(float angleX, float angleY, float angleZ)
    {
        setAngleX(angleX);
        setAngleY(angleY);
        setAngleZ(angleZ);
    }

    public void rotateAngleX(float angle) {
        if (angle != 0) {
            setAngleX(getAngleX() + angle);
        }
    }

    public void rotateAngleY(float angle) {
        if (angle != 0) {
            setAngleY(getAngleY() + angle);
        }
    }

    public void rotateAngleZ(float angle) {
        if (angle != 0) {
            setAngleZ(getAngleZ() + angle);
        }
    }

    public void rotateAngle(float angleX, float angleY,
        float angleZ)
    {
        rotateAngleX(angleX);
        rotateAngleY(angleY);
        rotateAngleZ(angleZ);
    }
}
```

Applying Transforms

Actually applying the transforms occurs in some methods you'll add to the Vector3D class, shown here in Listing 7.5.

Listing 7.5   Transform Methods for Vector3D.java

```
/**
    Rotate this vector around the x-axis the specified amount,
    using precomputed cosine and sine values of the angle to
    rotate.
*/
public void rotateX(float cosAngle, float sinAngle) {
    float newY = y*cosAngle - z*sinAngle;
    float newZ = y*sinAngle + z*cosAngle;
    y = newY;
    z = newZ;
}



/**
    Rotate this vector around the y-axis the specified amount,
    using precomputed cosine and sine values of the angle to
    rotate.
*/
public void rotateY(float cosAngle, float sinAngle) {
    float newX = z*sinAngle + x*cosAngle;
    float newZ = z*cosAngle - x*sinAngle;
    x = newX;
    z = newZ;
}



/**
    Rotate this vector around the y-axis the specified amount,
    using precomputed cosine and sine values of the angle to
    rotate.
*/
public void rotateZ(float cosAngle, float sinAngle) {
    float newX = x*cosAngle - y*sinAngle;
```

```
    float newY = x*sinAngle + y*cosAngle;
    x = newX;
    y = newY;
}



/**
    Adds the specified transform to this vector. This vector
    is first rotated, then translated.
*/
public void add(Transform3D xform) {

    // rotate
    addRotation(xform);

    // translate
    add(xform.getLocation());
}



/**
    Subtracts the specified transform to this vector. This
    vector is translated, then rotated.
*/
public void subtract(Transform3D xform) {

    // translate
    subtract(xform.getLocation());

    // rotate
    subtractRotation(xform);
}



/**
    Rotates this vector with the angle of the specified
    transform.
*/
```

continues

Listing 7.5   Transform Methods for Vector3D.java   *continued*

```java
public void addRotation(Transform3D xform) {
    rotateX(xform.getCosAngleX(), xform.getSinAngleX());
    rotateZ(xform.getCosAngleZ(), xform.getSinAngleZ());
    rotateY(xform.getCosAngleY(), xform.getSinAngleY());
}


/**
    Rotates this vector with the opposite angle of the
    specified transform.
*/
public void subtractRotation(Transform3D xform) {
    // note that sin(-x) == -sin(x) and cos(-x) == cos(x)
    rotateY(xform.getCosAngleY(), -xform.getSinAngleY());
    rotateZ(xform.getCosAngleZ(), -xform.getSinAngleZ());
    rotateX(xform.getCosAngleX(), -xform.getSinAngleX());
}
```

In this code, you'll notice the methods to "add" and "subtract" a transform. Adding a transform applies the transform as is. Subtracting a transform applies the inverse of a transform: Instead of rotating by θ and adding location V, it rotates by $-\theta$ and subtracts location V. You'll use the subtract methods for free camera movement later in this chapter.

The add(Transform3D) and subtract(Transform3D) methods are also in the Polygon3D class. These methods simply transform every vertex in the polygon.

Rotation Order

Because each rotation occurs one axis at a time, the order of the axis rotation is important. Different rotation orders can have different end results. Here, when adding a transformation, the rotation occurs in the order x, z, y. Subtracting a transform rotates in the opposite order. This choice was arbitrary and provides predictable results for walking around a 3D scene in the style of a first-person shooter.

A Simple 3D Pipeline

At this point, you can outline a simple 3D pipeline for drawing a polygon:

1. Apply the transform.

2. Project it onto the view window.

3. Draw.

The `Simple3DTest1` class in Listing 7.6 implements this 3D pipeline. It transforms, projects, and draws two polygons that make up a tree.

Listing 7.6   Simple3DTest1.java

```
import com.brackeen.javagamebook.test.GameCore;

import java.awt.*;
import java.awt.event.KeyEvent;
import java.awt.geom.GeneralPath;

import com.brackeen.javagamebook.input.*;
import com.brackeen.javagamebook.math3D.*;

/**
    A 3D test to demonstrate drawing polygons.
*/
public class Simple3DTest1 extends GameCore {

    public static void main(String[] args) {
        new Simple3DTest1().run();
    }

    // create solid-colored polygons
    private SolidPolygon3D treeLeaves = new SolidPolygon3D(
        new Vector3D(-50, -35, 0),
        new Vector3D(50, -35, 0),
        new Vector3D(0, 150, 0));
```

continues

Listing 7.6 Simple3DTest1.java *continued*

```java
    private SolidPolygon3D treeTrunk = new SolidPolygon3D(
        new Vector3D(-5, -50, 0),
        new Vector3D(5, -50, 0),
        new Vector3D(5, -35, 0),
        new Vector3D(-5, -35, 0));

    private Transform3D treeTransform = new Transform3D(0,0,-500);
    private Polygon3D transformedPolygon = new Polygon3D();
    private ViewWindow viewWindow;

    private GameAction exit = new GameAction("exit");
    private GameAction zoomIn = new GameAction("zoomIn");
    private GameAction zoomOut = new GameAction("zoomOut");


    public void init() {
        super.init();

        InputManager inputManager = new InputManager(
            screen.getFullScreenWindow());
        inputManager.setCursor(InputManager.INVISIBLE_CURSOR);
        inputManager.mapToKey(exit, KeyEvent.VK_ESCAPE);
        inputManager.mapToKey(zoomIn, KeyEvent.VK_UP);
        inputManager.mapToKey(zoomOut, KeyEvent.VK_DOWN);

        // make the view window the entire screen
        viewWindow = new ViewWindow(0, 0,
            screen.getWidth(), screen.getHeight(),
            (float)Math.toRadians(75));

        // give the polygons color
        treeLeaves.setColor(new Color(0x008000));
        treeTrunk.setColor(new Color(0x714311));
    }


    public void update(long elapsedTime) {
        if (exit.isPressed()) {
```

```
            stop();
            return;
        }

        // cap elapsedTime
        elapsedTime = Math.min(elapsedTime, 100);

        // rotate around the y-axis
        treeTransform.rotateAngleY(0.002f*elapsedTime);

        // allow user to zoom in/out
        if (zoomIn.isPressed()) {
            treeTransform.getLocation().z += 0.5f*elapsedTime;
        }
        if (zoomOut.isPressed()) {
            treeTransform.getLocation().z -= 0.5f*elapsedTime;
        }
    }



    public void draw(Graphics2D g) {
        // erase background
        g.setColor(Color.black);
        g.fillRect(0, 0, screen.getWidth(), screen.getHeight());

        // draw message
        g.setColor(Color.white);
        g.drawString("Press up/down to zoom. Press Esc to exit.",
            5, fontSize);

        // draw the tree polygons
        trandformAndDraw(g, treeTrunk);
        trandformAndDraw(g, treeLeaves);
    }



/**
    Projects and draws a polygon onto the view window.
```

continues

Listing 7.6 Simple3DTest1.java *continued*

```java
*/
private void trandformAndDraw(Graphics2D g,
    SolidPolygon3D poly)
{
    transformedPolygon.setTo(poly);

    // translate and rotate the polygon
    transformedPolygon.add(treeTransform);

    // project the polygon to the screen
    transformedPolygon.project(viewWindow);

    // convert the polygon to a Java2D GeneralPath and draw it
    GeneralPath path = new GeneralPath();
    Vector3D v = transformedPolygon.getVertex(0);
    path.moveTo(v.x, v.y);
    for (int i=1; i<transformedPolygon.getNumVertices(); i++)
    {
        v = transformedPolygon.getVertex(i);
        path.lineTo(v.x, v.y);
    }
    g.setColor(poly.getColor());
    g.fill(path);
}
}
```

Simple3DTest1 draws a tree that constantly spins around the y-axis. You can move the tree closer to or farther from the camera by pressing the up/down keys. See the screenshot in Figure 7.14.

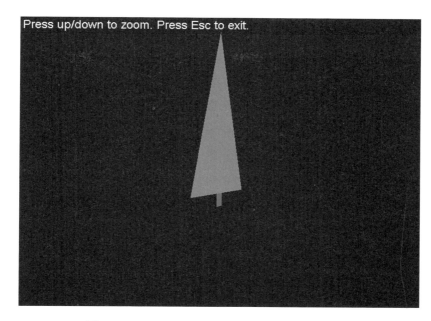

Figure 7.14   Screenshot of `Simple3DTest1`.

In `Simple3DTest1`, instead of using a plain `Polygon3D`, you use the `SolidPolygon3D` subclass.

The 3D polygons are drawn in the `transformAndDraw()` method. This method transforms and projects the polygon.

To draw a polygon, you first convert it to a `GeneralPath` (part of the `java.awt.geom` package). The `Graphics2D` interface provides methods to fill `GeneralPaths`, so the polygon drawing is done for you.

Notice that the tree polygons are never actually transformed. They are copied to a scratch polygon, which is then transformed. If the actual tree polygons were transformed, over time they would eventually accumulate floating-point errors. One transform isn't enough to create any noticeable error, but after many transforms, errors might start to creep in and could result in distorted polygons. So, copy the polygon to the scratch polygon and then transform the scratch polygon.

A few problems crop up with `Simple3DTest1`. Perhaps you noticed a few of them:

➤ The camera is fixed at (0,0,0). Even though the tree can move toward or away from this point along the z-axis, you want to be able to move the camera around freely.

➤ When the tree is very close to the camera, the polygons are drawn in strange ways. Also, if you zoom in too far (past the tree), the tree appears upside down! This occurs because the polygons aren't clipped to the view frustum.

➤ You can barely see it, but sometimes the polygons don't exactly line up with one another—you can sometimes see cracks or spaces between them. There are two reasons for this: First, `Graphics2D`, by default, fills the `GeneralPath` with its vertices rounded to integer coordinates instead of keeping the vertices at their floating-point coordinates. Second, two abutting polygons against each other creates unwanted T-junctions because they don't share common vertices. Forget about T-junctions for now; you'll fix them later in Chapter 10, "3D Scene Management Using BSP Trees."

➤ Finally, the tree is flat, which is kind of boring. Solid trees and other solid shapes would be more interesting.

Let's get started on fixing these problems! First up: free camera movement.

Camera Movement

In `Simple3DTest1`, you applied a transform to the tree polygons to make the tree move toward and away from the camera. Actually, could you really tell what was moving? Was it the tree or was it the camera?

It doesn't matter which was moving because, from the viewer's point of view, you perceive only the relative distance to the tree.

Instead of changing your 3D programming techniques to allow a camera anywhere in the world, use a `Transform3D` that represents the camera location, and apply the inverse of this transform (subtract) to every polygon in the scene. So basically, you move the world around, rather than moving the camera around. This way, you can keep your camera at (0,0,0) to simplify the math, but it will appear as if the camera is roaming wherever it wants.

For a camera transform example, let's say the virtual camera is at (10,50,500) and is looking to the left 5°. To apply the camera transform, displace every polygon by (–10,–50,–500) and rotate to the right 5°. In other words, just call the `subtract(Transform3D)` method for each polygon.

Rotation around each axis provides the following effects in your 3D coordinate system:

- ➤ Rotating around the x-axis is like looking up or down.

- ➤ Rotating around the y-axis is like turning your head left or right.

- ➤ Rotating around the z-axis is like tilting your head to the side.

In your camera code, you'll actually limit how much you can look up and look down. Also, you'll keep the camera tilting for demonstration purposes; allowing users to tilt their head in a normal 3D game usually isn't necessary.

Solid Objects and Back-Face Removal

The first demo, `Simple3DTest1`, draws every polygon in the order in which they appear in the polygon list. In this example, this technique doesn't have any negative impact because you are drawing a flat tree with no polygons that overlap.

If you were drawing a solid shape—that is, a group of polygons with a front, a back, and sides—you would need a better algorithm for determining which polygons to draw and in what order. Otherwise, polygons in the back could appear over polygons in the front, or polygons that are far away could appear on top of polygons that are close up. Needless to say, this would lead to a confusing 3D experience.

We get to ordering visible polygons in later chapters, but first let's talk about hidden surface-removal algorithms. This idea is to not draw polygons or parts of polygons that are either behind other polygons or otherwise aren't seen by the camera.

The first hidden surface-removal technique you'll use is called back-face removal, sometimes called back-face culling. Figure 7.15 shows the basic idea of back-face removal: Draw only polygons that are facing the camera.

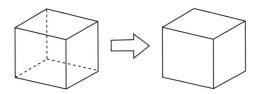

Figure 7.15   Removing back faces. Instead of all six sides of a cube being drawn, only the three sides that face the camera are drawn.

Removing back faces is a great trick and, on average, reduces by half the number of polygons that need to be drawn. Also, back-face removal draws convex polyhedrons perfectly with no extra effort. A convex polyhedron is a polyhedron, or 3D polygonal solid, with no inward bulges.

Back-face removal isn't a perfect solution for drawing all polygons, however. For convex polyhedrons or for several solid objects, you need another algorithm, such as z-buffering, which we get into in Chapter 9, "3D Objects."

To determine whether a polygon is a back face, let's first introduce the concept of a polygon normal. A polygon normal is the vector that is perpendicular, or orthogonal, to the polygon. Luckily, the normal also points in the direction the polygon is facing.

You can tell whether the polygon is facing the camera if the normal is less than 90° from the direction to the camera, as shown in Figure 7.16.

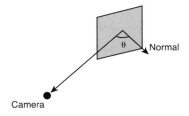

Figure 7.16   Determining whether a polygon is facing the camera.

Now you just need to calculate two things: the polygon normal and the angle between two vectors. Let's start with the angle between two vectors.

The Dot Product

To calculate the angle between two vectors, you can take advantage of the law of cosines, as shown in Figure 17.

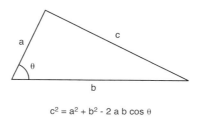

$$c^2 = a^2 + b^2 - 2\,a\,b\,\cos\theta$$

Figure 7.17   The law of cosines.

To make the law of cosines work with vectors, instead of the lengths a, b, and c, we'll use the vectors U, V, and (U–V). Thus, the law of cosines equation becomes this:

$$|U{-}V|^2 \;=\; |U|^2 + |V|^2 - 2\,|U|\,|V|\cos\theta$$

In this case, the exact angle isn't important. You need to know only whether the angle is less than 90°. If the angle is less than 90° (or "acute"), then the cosine of the angle will be greater than 0. In other words, $\cos\theta > 0$. Likewise, $2|U||V|\cos\theta > 0$. Let's solve the law of cosines with this in mind.

$$
\begin{aligned}
2|U||V|\cos\theta &= |U|^2 + |V|^2 - |U{-}V|^2 \\
&= |U|^2 + |V|^2 - (U_x{-}V_x)^2 - (U_y{-}V_y)^2 - (U_z{-}V_z)^2 \\
&= |U|^2 + |V|^2 - U_x{}^2 - V_x{}^2 - U_y{}^2 - V_y{}^2 - U_z{}^2 - V_z{}^2 \\
&\quad + 2U_xV_x + 2U_yV_y + 2U_zV_z \\
&= 2U_xV_x + 2U_yV_y + 2U_zV_z \\
|U||V|\cos\theta &= U_xV_x + U_yV_y + U_zV_z
\end{aligned}
$$

That certainly simplified a lot, didn't it? Just three multiplications and two additions are all it takes to determine whether an angle between two vectors is acute. It turns out (surprise, surprise) that this isn't the first time this has been done before. This equation is called the dot product and is one of the basics of vector math. It's often denoted as a dot, as in this example:

$$U \bullet V = U_x V_x + U_y V_y + U_z V_z = |U||V| \cos \theta$$

Therefore, with the dot product, you can easily tell whether the angle between two vectors is acute, obtuse, or a right angle:

```
If (U•V<0), then (θ>90°)
If (U•V=0), then (θ=90°)
If (U•V>0), then (θ<90°)
```

You'll use the dot product a lot in 3D graphics, so add a getDotProduct() method to the Vector3D class to calculate the dot product between two vectors:

```
/**
    Returns the dot product of this vector and the specified
    vector.
*/
public float getDotProduct(Vector3D v) {
    return x*v.x + y*v.y + z*v.z;
}
```

Looking back at the big picture of back-face removal, you can now tell whether the angle between a polygon normal and the vector to the camera is acute. Next, you need to find the polygon normal.

The Cross Product

Using the dot product, you can tell whether two vectors are orthogonal, or at right angles to each other, if their dot product is 0. This helps you find the normal of a polygon.

Okay, so now you want to find the normal of a specific polygon. Take any two vectors in this polygon (we'll call them U and V). The dot product between these vectors and the polygon's normal, N, will be 0:

```
U•N  =  0
V•N  =  0
```

Therefore:

$$U_xN_x + U_yN_y + U_zN_z = 0$$
$$V_xN_x + V_yN_y + V_zN_z = 0$$

This system of equations has infinite solutions, but one solution can be found by using determinants (determinants are one of those things you'll find in a linear algebra textbook):

$$N_x = U_yV_z - U_zV_y$$
$$N_y = U_zV_x - U_xV_z$$
$$N_z = U_xV_y - U_yV_x$$

That's it—you now have the normal. This solution is called the cross product and is donated by a cross:

$$U{\times}V = (U_yV_z - U_zV_y,\ U_zV_x - U_xV_z,\ U_xV_y - U_yV_x)$$

Just as with the dot product, you'll use the cross product often, so add a cross product to the `Vector3D` class:

```
/**
    Sets this vector to the cross product of the two
    specified vectors. Either of the specified vectors can
    be this vector.
*/
public void setToCrossProduct(Vector3D u, Vector3D v) {
    // assign to local vars first in case u or v is 'this'
    float x = u.y * v.z - u.z * v.y;
    float y = u.z * v.x - u.x * v.z;
    float z = u.x * v.y - u.y * v.x;
```

```
    this.x = x;
    this.y = y;
    this.z = z;
}
```

There's one catch, and maybe you thought of it. The normal is just a vector orthogonal to the polygon. How can you tell which way the normal is pointing? It could be pointing in the direction the polygon is facing, or it could be pointing in the opposite direction because both vectors are orthogonal to the polygon. And which side of the polygon is the "front" and which is the "back," anyway?

The answer is: It all depends on how the vertices in the polygon are defined. In the right-handed coordinate system, the front of the polygon is the side where the vertices of the polygon appear in counterclockwise order, as in Figure 7.18. If you looked at that polygon on the other side, the vertices would be in clockwise order.

So, be sure to define your polygons so that viewing them from the front makes the vertices appear in counterclockwise order.

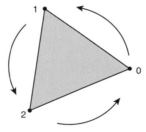

Figure 7.18   A polygon with its vertices appearing in
counterclockwise order is the "front" of the polygon.

Next, add some methods to the `Polygon3D` class to calculate the normal. The normal will be a member variable, so it doesn't have to be recalculated every time. Because each vertex in the polygon is a point, you use the vectors `temp1` and `temp2` to calculate two vectors in the polygon.

```
/**
    Calculates the unit-vector normal of this polygon.
    This method uses the first, second, and third vertices
    to calculate the normal, so if these vertices are
    collinear, this method will not work.
    Use setNormal() to explicitly set the normal.
    This method uses static objects in the Polygon3D class
    for calculations, so this method is not thread-safe across
    all instances of Polygon3D.
*/
public Vector3D calcNormal() {
    if (normal == null) {
        normal = new Vector3D();
    }
    temp1.setTo(v[2]);
    temp1.subtract(v[1]);
    temp2.setTo(v[0]);
    temp2.subtract(v[1]);
    normal.setToCrossProduct(temp1, temp2);
    normal.normalize();
    return normal;
}


/**
    Gets the normal of this polygon. Use calcNormal() if
    any vertices have changed.
*/
public Vector3D getNormal() {
    return normal;
}


/**
    Sets the normal of this polygon.
*/
public void setNormal(Vector3D n) {
    if (normal == null) {
```

```
        normal = new Vector3D(n);
    }
    else {
        normal.setTo(n);
    }
}
```

The `calcNormal()` method uses the first, second, and third vertices of the polygon to determine the normal. Of course, this won't work if these three vertices all fall on the same line (that is, if they are collinear). In the next chapter, we talk about bounding rectangles of polygons; you can use a bounding rectangle's normal in cases like this.

Finally, you can determine whether a polygon is facing the camera. Add another method to `Polygon3D`, called `isFacing()`, which checks whether the polygon is facing a specific point:

```
/**
    Tests if this polygon is facing the specified location.
    This method uses static objects in the Polygon3D class
    for calculations, so this method is not thread-safe across
    all instances of Polygon3D.
*/
public boolean isFacing(Vector3D u) {
    temp1.setTo(u);
    temp1.subtract(v[0]);
    return (normal.getDotProduct(temp1) >= 0);
}
```

`calcNormal()` and `isFacing()` use temporary static `Vector3D` objects, which pretty much makes `Polygon3D` not thread-safe. That's okay in this situation because you're calling these methods only in the main thread in the game.

More About the Dot and Cross Products

For reference, here are a few properties of the dot product and the cross product. You'll use a few of these in the next chapter. Here, A, B, and C are vectors and s is a real number.

Dot product:

```
A•B  =  B•A
(sA)•B  =  s(A•B)
A•B+A•C  =  A•(B+C)
```

Cross product:

```
A×B  =  -B×A
A×(B+C)  =  A×B+A×C
```

Scalar triple product:

```
(A×B)•C  =  (C×A)•B  =  (B×C)•A
```

Vector triple product:

```
A×(B×C)  =  B(A•C)-C(A•B)
```

Scan-Converting Polygons

In `Simple3DTest1`, you drew polygons by converting projected polygons to a `GeneralPath`. As you saw, this gave imperfect results because the vertices of the polygons were rounded to the nearest integer. To fix this, you'll create a custom scan converter that keeps the floating-point vertices. A *scan converter* converts a polygon into horizontal scans so that the polygon can be drawn as a series of horizontal lines. You'll reuse this custom scan converter later on for texture mapping.

It might sound silly to keep the vertices as floating points because the screen can handle only integer coordinates anyway. Eventually, the polygon will exist on all integer boundaries, but the trick is to convert from floating point to integers at a later time. By default, drawing with `GeneralPath` rounds each point to the nearest integer before drawing each edge of the polygon; you'll convert to integers after drawing each edge. This way, each edge of the polygon is more drawn more accurately.

Drawing the outline of a polygon is like a game of connect-the-dots: You just draw each edge, or every line from vertex to vertex. Filling a polygon with a solid color might initially seem more complicated. To make it easier, we break it down into smaller steps. Shown in Figure 7.19, a polygon is broken down into horizontal scans for every row of pixels. To fill the polygon, just draw a horizontal line for every scan.

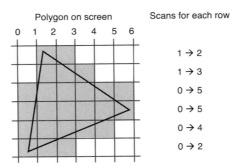

Figure 7.19 Converting a polygon to horizontal scans.

In Figure 7.19, every pixel under any part of the polygon is drawn. But what happens when two polygons are next to each other? In this scenario, polygons share edges, so some pixels will be drawn twice. It won't be clear which pixel belongs to which polygon.

To fix this situation, you'll differentiate between left and right edges of each polygon. Left edges of a polygon will use the `ceil()` function to round up, while right edges will round down using `ceil()-1`. This is shown in Figure 7.20.

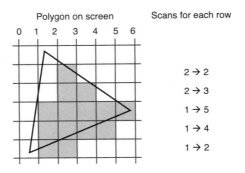

Figure 7.20 Converting a polygon to horizontal scans using a more conservative method.

Using the technique demonstrated in Figure 7.20, two adjacent polygons won't overlap each over.

Also, you'll use a custom ceil() function in the MoreMath class:

```
public static int ceil(float f) {
    if (f > 0) {
        return (int)f + 1;
    }
    else {
        return (int)f;
    }
}
```

This function converts a float to an int, whereas the Math.ceil() function takes a double as a parameter and returns a double. This way, you don't have to convert anything to or from a double.

Now you'll create a simple Scan class, shown in Listing 7.7.

Listing 7.7   Scan Class

```
/**
    A horizontal scan line.
*/
public class Scan {
    public int left;
    public int right;

    /**
        Sets the left and right boundaries for this scan if
        the x value is outside the current boundary.
    */
    public void setBoundary(int x) {
        if (x < left) {
            left = x;
        }
        if (x-1 > right) {
            right = x-1;
```

continues

Listing 7.7 Scan Class *continued*

```java
        }
    }


    /**
        Clears this scan line.
    */
    public void clear() {
        left = Integer.MAX_VALUE;
        right = Integer.MIN_VALUE;
    }


    /**
        Determines if this scan is valid (if left <= right).
    */
    public boolean isValid() {
        return (left <= right);
    }


    /**
        Sets this scan.
    */
    public void setTo(int left, int right) {
        this.left = left;
        this.right = right;
    }


    /**
        Checks if this scan is equal to the specified values.
    */
    public boolean equals(int left, int right) {
        return (this.left == left && this.right == right);
    }
}
```

The Scan class is an inner class of ScanConverter.

Each scan line has its own Scan object, and the scan converter scans every edge in the polygon. Every time it scans an edge on a particular scan line, the scan converter calls the Scan object's setBoundary() method. Calling this method could change the scan's left or right boundaries. If two different edges are scanned on the same line (and the edges have different locations), the left boundary will be less than the right boundary; thus, the scan will become valid. In other words, it requires more than one edge to create a valid scan.

To actually scan a polygon's edge, you'll use the equation of the line. Consider a projected edge of the polygon formed by the points (x1, y1) and (x2, y2). For every horizontal line (y), you can find the corresponding x value by using this equation:

```
(x-x1)/(x2-x1)  =  (y-y1)/(y2-y1)
x  =  (y-y1)(x2-x1)/(y2-y1)+x1
```

The ScanConverter class uses this equation. The ScanConverter class also keeps track of the ViewWindow (in case it changes size), a list of Scans for every horizontal line in the ViewWindow, and a top and bottom value for the top and bottom values of the last scanned polygon. The member variables of the ScanConverter are these:

```
ViewWindow view;
Scan[] scans;
int top;
int bottom;
```

The method used to scan a polygon in the ScanConverter class is in Listing 7.8.

Listing 7.8   Simple Polygon Scan Conversion

```
int minX = view.getLeftOffset();
int maxX = view.getLeftOffset() + view.getWidth() - 1;
int minY = view.getTopOffset();
int maxY = view.getTopOffset() + view.getHeight() - 1;

int numVertices = polygon.getNumVertices();
for (int i=0; i<numVertices; i++) {
```

continues

Listing 7.8 Simple Polygon Scan Conversion *continued*

```
Vector3D v1 = polygon.getVertex(i);
Vector3D v2;
if (i == numVertices - 1) {
    v2 = polygon.getVertex(0);
}
else {
    v2 = polygon.getVertex(i+1);
}

// ensure v1.y < v2.y
if (v1.y > v2.y) {
    Vector3D temp = v1;
    v1 = v2;
    v2 = temp;
}
float dy = v2.y - v1.y;

// ignore horizontal lines
if (dy == 0) {
    continue;
}

int startY = Math.max(MoreMath.ceil(v1.y), minY);
int endY = Math.min(MoreMath.ceil(v2.y)-1, maxY);
float dx = v2.x - v1.x;

float gradient = dx / dy;

// scan-convert this edge (line equation)
for (int y=startY; y<=endY; y++) {
    int x = MoreMath.ceil(v1.x + (y - v1.y) * gradient);
    // ensure x within view bounds
    x = Math.min(maxX+1, Math.max(x, minX));
    scans[y].setBoundary(x);
}
```
}

The `ScanConverter` class converts a projected polygon to a series of horizontal scans. It also ensures that all the scans are in the view window.

Note that the `ScanConverter` works only with convex polygons. Concave polygons could have some inward bulges that the `ScanConverter` misses.

Here's how to iterate through all the scans:

```
int y = scanConverter.getTopBoundary();
while (y <= scanConverter.getBottomBoundary()) {
    ScanConverter.Scan scan = scanConverter.getScan(y);
    if (scan.isValid()) {
        g.drawLine(scan.left, y, scan.right, y);
    }
    y++;
}
```

Optimizing Scan Conversion with Fixed-Point Math

This basic scan converter works, but it's going to be a little slower than it could be. This will be particularly noticeable when there are lots of polygons on screen.

One reason this code isn't fast enough is because you are doing a lot of math with floats for every horizontal scan line. To speed up the scan conversion, you can use integers instead of floats and try to limit the amount of math involved per scan line.

Of course, integers don't give the desired accuracy, so you'll have to be a little creative on how you interpret the integers. To do this, multiply each floating point value by a scale to get the value in integer range. For example, for a scale of 1,000, multiplying 10.5 times 1,000 gives the integer value 10,500.

What value to use as a scale is important. If you use a power of 2, you can convert between scaled and unscaled integers by using bit shifting.

In the examples, we use a scale of 2^{16}. Because integers are 32 bits long, this leaves the most significant 16 bits as the integer part and the least significant 16 bits as the fractional part. This number representation technique is often called fixed-point because the decimal point is fixed somewhere within the integer.

Let's start with some constants that define the scaled, fixed-point integers:

```
final int SCALE_BITS = 16;
final int SCALE = 1 << SCALE_BITS;
final int SCALE_MASK = SCALE - 1;
```

The `<<` operator is a bit shift, and `1 << 16` is equivalent to 2^{16}. With these constants, you can go ahead and lay out the code to convert to and from a fixed point.

Convert a floating-point number to a fixed-point number:

```
int fixed = (int)(value * SCALE);
```

Convert a fixed-point number to a floating-point number:

```
float value = (float)fixed / SCALE;
```

Convert an integer to a fixed-point number:

```
int fixed = value << SCALE_BITS;
```

Convert a fixed-point number to an integer:

```
int value = fixed >> SCALE_BITS;
```

Get the fractional part of a fixed-point number:

```
float frac = (float)(fixed & SCALE_MASK) / SCALE;
```

Adding and subtracting two fixed-point numbers is performed just like normal addition and subtraction. Multiplication by a fixed-point number and a normal integer works the same as well.

However, multiplication or division of two fixed-point numbers is a bit different. Multiplying two 32-bit numbers creates a 64-bit result, so for two fixed-point numbers, this effectively doubles the number of bits in the fractional part of the result. To fix this, you have to do multiplication in a 64-bit number (a long) so you don't chop off the bits you need. Then you need to shift it back down to convert back to your normal fixed-point number:

```
int fixed = (int) (((long)fixed1 * fixed2) >> SCALE_BITS);
```

Likewise, division has a similar effect but can be easily remedied:

```
int fixed = (int) (((long)fixed1 << SCALE_BITS) / fixed2);
```

You actually won't need to multiply or divide two fixed-point numbers in your code, but they are here for reference.

Okay, now that you understand fixed-point numbers, here's the optimized scan converter:

```
int minX = view.getLeftOffset();
int maxX = view.getLeftOffset() + view.getWidth() - 1;
int minY = view.getTopOffset();
int maxY = view.getTopOffset() + view.getHeight() - 1;

int numVertices = polygon.getNumVertices();
for (int i=0; i<numVertices; i++) {
    Vector3D v1 = polygon.getVertex(i);
    Vector3D v2;
    if (i == numVertices - 1) {
        v2 = polygon.getVertex(0);
    }
    else {
        v2 = polygon.getVertex(i+1);
    }

    // ensure v1.y < v2.y
    if (v1.y > v2.y) {
        Vector3D temp = v1;
        v1 = v2;
        v2 = temp;
    }
    float dy = v2.y - v1.y;

    // ignore horizontal lines
    if (dy == 0) {
        continue;
```

```
    }

    int startY = Math.max(MoreMath.ceil(v1.y), minY);
    int endY = Math.min(MoreMath.ceil(v2.y)-1, maxY);
    top = Math.min(top, startY);
    bottom = Math.max(bottom, endY);
    float dx = v2.x - v1.x;

    // special case: vertical line
    if (dx == 0) {
        int x = MoreMath.ceil(v1.x);
        // ensure x within view bounds
        x = Math.min(maxX+1, Math.max(x, minX));
        for (int y=startY; y<=endY; y++) {
            scans[y].setBoundary(x);
        }
    }
    else {
        // scan-convert this edge (line equation)
        float gradient = dx / dy;

        // trim start of line
        float startX = v1.x + (startY - v1.y) * gradient;
        if (startX < minX) {
            int yInt = (int)(v1.y + (minX - v1.x) /
                gradient);
            yInt = Math.min(yInt, endY);
            while (startY <= yInt) {
                scans[startY].setBoundary(minX);
                startY++;
            }
        }
        else if (startX > maxX) {
            int yInt = (int)(v1.y + (maxX - v1.x) /
                gradient);
            yInt = Math.min(yInt, endY);
            while (startY <= yInt) {
                scans[startY].setBoundary(maxX+1);
```

```
                    startY++;
            }
    }

    if (startY > endY) {
        continue;
    }


    // trim back of line
    float endX = v1.x + (endY - v1.y) * gradient;
    if (endX < minX) {
        int yInt = MoreMath.ceil(v1.y + (minX - v1.x) /
            gradient);
        yInt = Math.max(yInt, startY);
        while (endY >= yInt) {
            scans[endY].setBoundary(minX);
            endY--;
        }
    }
    else if (endX > maxX) {
        int yInt = MoreMath.ceil(v1.y + (maxX - v1.x) /
            gradient);
        yInt = Math.max(yInt, startY);
        while (endY >= yInt) {
            scans[endY].setBoundary(maxX+1);
            endY--;
        }
    }


    if (startY > endY) {
        continue;
    }


    // line equation using integers
    int xScaled = (int)(SCALE * v1.x +
        SCALE * (startY - v1.y) * dx / dy) + SCALE_MASK;
    int dxScaled = (int)(dx * SCALE / dy);
```

```
        for (int y=startY; y<=endY; y++) {
            scans[y].setBoundary(xScaled >> SCALE_BITS);
            xScaled+=dxScaled;
        }
    }
}
```

Of course, fixed-point numbers don't have the precision or range that floating-point numbers do. Because the scan values can be out of range of the fixed-point number representation, in this code you trim the left and right parts of the scan if they are not within the view. Also, instead of recalculating the intersection at every point, you use the line's slope (dxScaled) to increase the x value (xScaled) for every line.

The complete ScanConverter is probably not completely optimized; someone out there surely could make it even faster. One idea is to actually clip the 2D polygons to be within the view before scan converting so you don't scan off-screen polygons or the parts of polygons that are not visible. But this ScanConverter works well.

3D Clipping

Last in the fixes to Simple3DTest1 is to add 3D clipping. You might remember that the tree polygon looked very strange when it was close to the camera, and the tree appeared upside down when it was behind the camera. To fix this, you're going to clip the polygons to the view frustum.

The view frustum is a pyramid formed by four planes. You could clip a polygon to each of the planes. Alternatively, you could clip a polygon to a front clip plane and let 2D clipping handle the rest. This works well and is the method you'll use.

Three situations arise when clipping a polygon to a plane: Either the polygon is completely in front of the plane, completely behind it, or intersecting the plane. If it's behind the plane, you can ignore the polygon. If it intersects the plane, you need to clip the polygon to the plane so that you draw only the portion of the polygon in front of the plane. Clipping a convex polygon to a plane creates another convex polygon, so you're not creating any concave polygons in this process.

Let's start with Figure 7.21. Here, a polygon intersects the clip plane. In the figure, the front of the plane is on top of the dotted line.

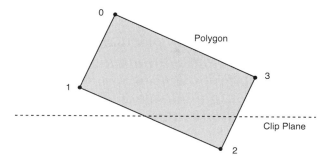

Figure 7.21   Clipping, step 1: A polygon intersects the clip plane.

In the next step, in Figure 7.22, you add vertices to the polygon where the polygon's edges and the clip plane intersect.

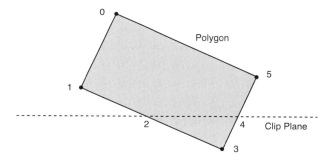

Figure 7.22   Clipping, step 2: Add vertices at the intersection of the clip plane and the polygon's edges.

At this stage, every edge of the polygon is either completely in front of or completely behind the clip plane. The last step is to just remove the edges behind the clip plane, or to simply remove all vertices that are behind the clip plane, as shown in Figure 7.23.

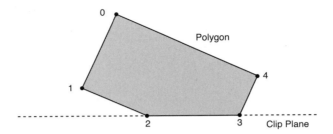

Figure 7.23 Clipping, step 3: Remove all vertices behind the clip plane.

Because the front clip plane is parallel to the view window, all that's left is to pick a location of the clip plane. You might first pick z=0, but this can lead to some divide-by-zero problems. In the demos in this book, we use z=−1.

To find the intersection of a polygon edge with the clip plane, again you use the equation of the line. Knowing the location of the clip plane z, you get the equations to find the point of intersection:

```
x = (z-z1)(x2-x1)/(z2-z1)+x1
y = (z-z1)(y2-y1)/(z2-z1)+y1
z = z
```

The clipping algorithms is implemented in the `clip()` method, shown here and added to the `Polygon3D` class:

```
/**
    Clips this polygon so that all vertices are in front of
    the clip plane, clipZ (in other words, all vertices
    have z <= clipZ).
    The value of clipZ should not be 0, as this causes
    divide-by-zero problems.
    Returns true if the polygon is at least partially in
    front of the clip plane.
*/
public boolean clip(float clipZ) {
    ensureCapacity(numVertices * 3);

    boolean isCompletelyHidden = true;
```

```
// insert vertices so all edges are either completely
// in front of or behind the clip plane
for (int i=0; i<numVertices; i++) {
    int next = (i + 1) % numVertices;
    Vector3D v1 = v[i];
    Vector3D v2 = v[next];
    if (v1.z < clipZ) {
        isCompletelyHidden = false;
    }
    // ensure v1.z < v2.z
    if (v1.z > v2.z) {
        Vector3D temp = v1;
        v1 = v2;
        v2 = temp;
    }
    if (v1.z < clipZ && v2.z > clipZ) {
        float scale = (clipZ-v1.z) / (v2.z - v1.z);
        insertVertex(next,
            v1.x + scale * (v2.x - v1.x) ,
            v1.y + scale * (v2.y - v1.y),
            clipZ);
        // skip the vertex we just created
        i++;
    }
}

if (isCompletelyHidden) {
    return false;
}

// delete all vertices that have z > clipZ
for (int i=numVertices-1; i>=0; i--) {
    if (v[i].z > clipZ) {
        deleteVertex(i);
    }
}

return (numVertices >= 3);
}
```

```
/**
    Inserts a new vertex at the specified index.
*/
protected void insertVertex(int index, float x, float y,
    float z)
{
    Vector3D newVertex = v[v.length-1];
    newVertex.x = x;
    newVertex.y = y;
    newVertex.z = z;
    for (int i=v.length-1; i>index; i--) {
        v[i] = v[i-1];
    }
    v[index] = newVertex;
    numVertices++;
}


/**
    Delete the vertex at the specified index.
*/
protected void deleteVertex(int index) {
    Vector3D deleted = v[index];
    for (int i=index; i<v.length-1; i++) {
        v[i] = v[i+1];
    }
    v[v.length-1] = deleted;
    numVertices--;
}
```

The clipping technique implemented is relatively simple, considering that you're clipping to only a vertical, front clip plane. Optionally, you might also want to clip to a vertical back clip plane (so polygons very far away aren't drawn). Of course, clipping to the left, right, top, and bottom planes of the view frustum relieves the scan converter of some work, but just clipping to the front clip plane provides the correct results.

Final Rendering Pipeline

Now you must extend the simple 3D pipeline used for `Simple3DTest1` and add back-face removal, clipping, and scan converting:

1. Check if facing camera.

2. Apply transform.

3. Clip.

4. Project onto view window.

5. Scan-convert.

6. Draw.

To draw using this new 3D pipeline, you'll create the abstract `PolygonRenderer`, shown in Listing 7.9.

Listing 7.9   PolygonRenderer.java

```
package com.brackeen.javagamebook.graphics3D;

import java.awt.Graphics2D;
import java.awt.Color;
import com.brackeen.javagamebook.math3D.*;

/**
    The PolygonRenderer class is an abstract class that transforms
    and draws polygons onto the screen.
*/
public abstract class PolygonRenderer {

    protected ScanConverter scanConverter;
    protected Transform3D camera;
    protected ViewWindow viewWindow;
    protected boolean clearViewEveryFrame;
    protected Polygon3D sourcePolygon;
    protected Polygon3D destPolygon;
```

continues

Listing 7.9 PolygonRenderer.java *continued*

```java
/**
    Creates a new PolygonRenderer with the specified
    Transform3D (camera) and ViewWindow. The view is cleared
    when startFrame() is called.
*/
public PolygonRenderer(Transform3D camera,
    ViewWindow viewWindow)
{
    this(camera, viewWindow, true);
}



/**
    Creates a new PolygonRenderer with the specified
    Transform3D (camera) and ViewWindow. If
    clearViewEveryFrame is true, the view is cleared when
    startFrame() is called.
*/
public PolygonRenderer(Transform3D camera,
    ViewWindow viewWindow, boolean clearViewEveryFrame)
{
    this.camera = camera;
    this.viewWindow = viewWindow;
    this.clearViewEveryFrame = clearViewEveryFrame;
    init();
}



/**
    Create the scan converter and dest polygon.
*/
protected void init() {
    destPolygon = new Polygon3D();
    scanConverter = new ScanConverter(viewWindow);
}
```

```java
/**
    Gets the camera used for this PolygonRenderer.
*/
public Transform3D getCamera() {
    return camera;
}



/**
    Indicates the start of rendering of a frame. This method
    should be called every frame before any polygons are drawn.
*/
public void startFrame(Graphics2D g) {
    if (clearViewEveryFrame) {
        g.setColor(Color.black);
        g.fillRect(viewWindow.getLeftOffset(),
            viewWindow.getTopOffset(),
            viewWindow.getWidth(), viewWindow.getHeight());
    }
}



/**
    Indicates the end of rendering of a frame. This method
    should be called every frame after all polygons are drawn.
*/
public void endFrame(Graphics2D g) {
    // do nothing, for now.
}



/**
    Transforms and draws a polygon.
*/
public boolean draw(Graphics2D g, Polygon3D poly) {
    if (poly.isFacing(camera.getLocation())) {
        sourcePolygon = poly;
        destPolygon.setTo(poly);
```

continues

Listing 7.9   PolygonRenderer.java   *continued*

```
            destPolygon.subtract(camera);
            boolean visible = destPolygon.clip(-1);
            if (visible) {
                destPolygon.project(viewWindow);
                visible = scanConverter.convert(destPolygon);
                if (visible) {
                    drawCurrentPolygon(g);
                    return true;
                }
            }
        }
        return false;
    }


    /**
        Draws the current polygon. At this point, the current
        polygon is transformed, clipped, projected,
        scan-converted, and visible.
    */
    protected abstract void drawCurrentPolygon(Graphics2D g);
}
```

The PolygonRenderer class is an abstract class that provides a framework to render polygons. Its main purpose is to implement the rendering pipeline for a polygon in the draw() method. Any subclasses need to implement the drawCurrentPolygon() method to actually draw the final, scan-converted polygon. Also, the renderer can optionally clear the view before drawing every frame, provided the startFrame() method is called. You'll want to clear the view because the examples don't have polygons that fill the entire screen. For 3D scenes in which every pixel is covered by a polygon, there's no reason to clear the view.

You'll create a few different PolygonRenderer subclasses for different types of polygons in the next chapter, "Texture Mapping and Lighting." Currently, you are dealing only with solid-colored polygons, so you'll create a SolidPolygonRenderer subclass, whose drawCurrentPolygon() method is shown in Listing 7.10.

Listing 7.10 `SolidPolygonRenderer.drawCurrentPolygon`

```
protected void drawCurrentPolygon(Graphics2D g) {

    // set the color
    if (sourcePolygon instanceof SolidPolygon3D) {
        g.setColor(((SolidPolygon3D)sourcePolygon).getColor());
    }
    else {
        g.setColor(Color.GREEN);
    }

    // draw the scans
    int y = scanConverter.getTopBoundary();
    while (y<=scanConverter.getBottomBoundary()) {
        ScanConverter.Scan scan = scanConverter.getScan(y);
        if (scan.isValid()) {
            g.drawLine(scan.left, y, scan.right, y);
        }
        y++;
    }
}
```

The `SolidPolygonRenderer` class implements the `drawCurrentPolygon()` method, which draws a polygon from the scan list in the `ScanConverter`. Note that this method is called only from the `draw()` method, which means that when it is called, the current `destPolygon` is transformed, clipped, projected, scan-converted, and visible in the view window. The source polygon is also available to get any necessary data out of it.

If the source polygon isn't an instance of the `SolidPolygon3D` class, (in other words, if the polygon has no color associated with it), the polygon is filled with green.

Now you'll create another test to try out the new renderer. This new test, called `Simple3DTest2`, creates a 3D convex polyhedron that looks strangely like a house. It has a couple front-facing polygons that imitate a door and a window, as shown in Figure 7.24.

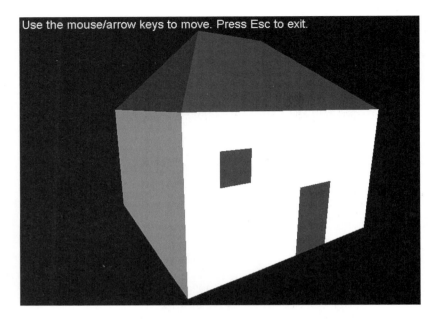

Figure 7.24 Screenshot of `Simple3DTest2`, which includes clipping, back-face removal, a custom polygon renderer, and free camera movement.

`Simple3DTest2` enables the user to wander freely around the house, looking up, down, left, and right, and moving anywhere, even within the house. Note that if you actually go in the house, you won't see anything because every polygon is facing away from the camera.

The entire `Simple3DTest2` code is too long to list here (a bulk of if is just creating polygons), but we'll talk about the relevant parts here. `Simple3DTest2` uses the `SolidPolygonRenderer` to draw every polygon in the list of polygons:

```
public void draw(Graphics2D g) {

    // draw polygons
    polygonRenderer.startFrame(g);
    for (int i=0; i<polygons.size(); i++) {
        polygonRenderer.draw(g, (Polygon3D)polygons.get(i));
    }
```

```
        polygonRenderer.endFrame(g);

        drawText(g);
    }
```

Simple3DTest2 also draws some onscreen instructions and can optionally display the frame rate of the renderer:

```
private boolean drawFrameRate = false;
private boolean drawInstructions = true;

private int numFrames;
private long startTime;
private float frameRate;

...

public void drawText(Graphics g) {

    // draw text
    g.setColor(Color.WHITE);
    if (drawInstructions) {
        g.drawString("Use the mouse/arrow keys to move. " +
            "Press Esc to exit.", 5, fontSize);
    }
    // (you may have to turn off the BufferStrategy in
    // ScreenManager for more accurate tests)
    if (drawFrameRate) {
        calcFrameRate();
        g.drawString(frameRate + " frames/sec", 5,
            screen.getHeight() - 5);
    }
}


public void calcFrameRate() {
    numFrames++;
    long currTime = System.currentTimeMillis();
```

```
    // calculate the frame rate every 500 milliseconds
    if (currTime > startTime + 500) {
        frameRate = (float)numFrames * 1000 /
            (currTime - startTime);
        startTime = currTime;
        numFrames = 0;
    }
}
```

The frame rate is recalculated every 500ms and just involves dividing the number of frames drawn by the amount of time that has passed. An alternative way to calculate the frame rate is to just keep a running average, but this doesn't give a good look at the current frame rate because the frame rate can vary from time to time based on how much the renderer has to draw.

The camera's transform is updated in the update() method of Simple3DTest2:

```
public void update(long elapsedTime) {
    if (exit.isPressed()) {
        stop();
        return;
    }

    // check options
    if (largerView.isPressed()) {
        setViewBounds(viewWindow.getWidth() + 64,
            viewWindow.getHeight() + 48);
    }
    else if (smallerView.isPressed()) {
        setViewBounds(viewWindow.getWidth() - 64,
            viewWindow.getHeight() - 48);
    }
    if (frameRateToggle.isPressed()) {
        drawFrameRate = !drawFrameRate;
    }

    // cap elapsedTime
    elapsedTime = Math.min(elapsedTime, 100);
```

```
float angleChange = 0.0002f*elapsedTime;
float distanceChange = .5f*elapsedTime;

Transform3D camera = polygonRenderer.getCamera();
Vector3D cameraLoc = camera.getLocation();

// apply movement
if (goForward.isPressed()) {
    cameraLoc.x -= distanceChange * camera.getSinAngleY();
    cameraLoc.z -= distanceChange * camera.getCosAngleY();
}
if (goBackward.isPressed()) {
    cameraLoc.x += distanceChange * camera.getSinAngleY();
    cameraLoc.z += distanceChange * camera.getCosAngleY();
}
if (goLeft.isPressed()) {
    cameraLoc.x -= distanceChange * camera.getCosAngleY();
    cameraLoc.z += distanceChange * camera.getSinAngleY();
}
if (goRight.isPressed()) {
    cameraLoc.x += distanceChange * camera.getCosAngleY();
    cameraLoc.z -= distanceChange * camera.getSinAngleY();
}
if (goUp.isPressed()) {
    cameraLoc.y += distanceChange;
}
if (goDown.isPressed()) {
    cameraLoc.y -= distanceChange;
}

// look up/down (rotate around x)
int tilt = tiltUp.getAmount() - tiltDown.getAmount();
tilt = Math.min(tilt, 200);
tilt = Math.max(tilt, -200);

// limit how far you can look up/down
float newAngleX = camera.getAngleX() + tilt * angleChange;
newAngleX = Math.max(newAngleX, (float)-Math.PI/2);
```

```
newAngleX = Math.min(newAngleX, (float)Math.PI/2);
camera.setAngleX(newAngleX);

// turn (rotate around y)
int turn = turnLeft.getAmount() - turnRight.getAmount();
turn = Math.min(turn, 200);
turn = Math.max(turn, -200);
camera.rotateAngleY(turn * angleChange);

// tilet head left/right (rotate around z)
if (tiltLeft.isPressed()) {
    camera.rotateAngleZ(10*angleChange);
}
if (tiltRight.isPressed()) {
    camera.rotateAngleZ(-10*angleChange);
}
}
```

The update() method takes both the keyboard and mouse as input, and moves the camera accordingly. It uses the mouselook feature you developed in Chapter 3, "Interactivity and User Interfaces," to enable the user to look around the 3D world. Also, it limits how far up and down the user can look so the player doesn't have to bend his or her head all the way back and around again.

Here's a list of all the controls in the demo:

Mouse move	Turn left/right; look up/down
Arrow keys; W, S, A, D	Move forward, back, left, right
Page up/down	Move up/down
Insert/delete	Tilt left/right
+	Increase view window size
−	Decrease view window size
R	Show frame rate
Esc	Exit

Using +/– to change the view window is handy in case a demo is running too slowly at full screen and you want to decrease the view window to make it run faster.

```
/**
    Sets the view bounds, centering the view on the screen.
*/
public void setViewBounds(int width, int height) {
    width = Math.min(width, screen.getWidth());
    height = Math.min(height, screen.getHeight());
    width = Math.max(64, width);
    height = Math.max(48, height);
    viewWindow.setBounds((screen.getWidth() - width) /2,
        (screen.getHeight() - height) /2, width, height);
}
```

When you run the demo, you'll also notice that the sides of the house are a shade darker than the rest. No, this isn't a secret shading feature of the 3D engine I forgot to mention—those polygons are just given a darker color by hand. In the next chapter, we get into real lighting and shading.

Summary

Well, that's it for the start of 3D graphics. We've still got a lot to talk about with 3D, such as texture mapping, lighting, and scene management, but we get to these topics in the next three chapters.

As usual, in this chapter, we've covered a lot of ground. Vector math, fixed-point math, dot products, cross products, polygon normals, view windows, back-face removal, transforms, projections, clipping, scan-converting, and polygon filling are a few things you've learned about. Along the way you've been using code from previous chapters, such as full-screen graphics and keyboard and mouse input (including mouselook). Also, you've created a basic 3D engine framework you'll use in chapters to come.

Chapter 8

Texture Mapping and Lighting

When Super Nintendo came out when I was just a kid, I knew I had to have one. Super Nintendo was quite a step up from the previous Nintendo Entertainment System, complete with superior 2D graphics, cooler games, and whatever other whiz-bang feature was popular at the time. Soon enough, Christmas came around and I had one sitting under the tree.

Later, my mom's friend came over with her son who was a few years younger than me. He was too young to be my peer, but, of course, it was my duty to entertain him anyway. We turned on my brand-new game system and began playing a generic 2D side-scrolling game.

The game's parallax scrolling techniques made his jaw drop. Trees in the foreground were scrolling by quickly while the mountains in the back were slowly creeping, all with sharp and realistic textures. Never had he seen anything like it before. He shook his head and exclaimed, "Now that's 3D!"

But, of course, it wasn't 3D. It was just an effect that simulated depth in a very two-dimensional scene—but simulated it well enough to impress a young boy. I didn't explain to him that the game wasn't really 3D because I realized something important: As long as a game is drawing onto a 2D surface such as a TV or computer monitor, the game is really just simulating a 3D scene. It's just a 2D picture, but the idea is to simulate 3D as realistically as possible. 3D is in the eye of the beholder.

That brings us to the topics of this chapter: texture mapping and lighting. The demos from Chapter 7, "3D Graphics," gave depth, but everything on the screen was made up of simple, solid-colored polygons, which looked very abstract. In this chapter, you'll give polygons textures and shading, creating a more realistic experience. By the end of this chapter, you should be able to run the demos and finally say, "Now *that's* 3D!"

Specifically, you'll create a software-based texture-mapper and implement lighting using a shade map, a technique popularized by games such as the original *Quake*. Despite its drawbacks, a software renderer in Java has a few advantages over a hardware renderer, such as not requiring a hardware-dependent API or having to worry about out-of-date or buggy 3D drivers. Plus, building a 3D texture-mapping engine is just plain fun. Eventually, you might want to use a hardware-based 3D renderer to deliver maximum performance in a game, but the techniques you'll learn in this chapter will enable you to understand and control any 3D renderer more thoroughly, whether it's hardware-based or not.

Perspective-Correct Texture Mapping Basics

The goal of this section is to create a texture-mapper that is perspective-correct so that as the polygon gets smaller with distance, so does the texture.

Notice that a texture can be smaller than the actual polygon you're mapping to. In this case, the texture is tiled onto the polygon, as shown in Figure 8.1.

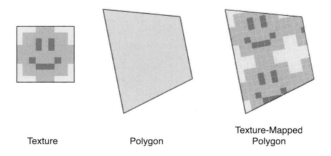

Texture   Polygon   Texture-Mapped
                                   Polygon

Figure 8.1   When mapping a texture that is smaller than a polygon, the texture is tiled across it.

A pixel in a texture is commonly called a *texel*, short for "texture element." Keep in mind that your textures will be scaled based on how close the camera is to the polygon, so the texels will scale as well. In other words, a texel is rarely the same size as a pixel in the view window.

You can do texture mapping in two ways: Map every texel to a pixel, or map every pixel to a texel. Mapping each texel to a pixel is more work than it's worth because sometimes not every texel in a texture is drawn (such as when you view a texture from an angle or from far away). Also, texels themselves can be rotated and scaled based on the texture orientation. Basically, if you map texels to pixels, you're drawing a solid polygon for each texel and doing some overdrawing (drawing some pixels more than once) along the way.

Instead, you'll map pixels to texels, with the goal of drawing every pixel in the view window only once. In other words, for every pixel in the view window, you'll find the appropriate texel to draw.

With this goal in mind, a good stage to do the texture mapping within the rendering pipeline is after the polygon has been scan-converted, just like you did with the solid-fill polygon renderer in the previous chapter.

Deriving the Texture Mapping Equations

I could just give you the equations commonly used for texture mapping (which are easy to find on the Internet). However, I'm going to start by giving you more background on how these equations are derived—you know, in case you're curious. Let's get started with some vector math. If you're unfamiliar with the basics of vector math, be sure to check out the introduction in the previous chapter.

First, let's define how a texture is oriented on the polygon. You want a texture to be able to be offset or rotated anywhere in the polygon, so you do this with the following vectors (shown in Figure 8.2):

- ➤ O, the origin

- ➤ U, a vector representing the texture's x direction

- ➤ V, a vector representing the texture's y direction

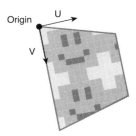

Figure 8.2 A texture's orientation within a polygon is defined by an origin and two direction vectors.

In this configuration, the texture could be oriented in any direction. Also, the texture origin doesn't necessarily have to be within the polygon bounds.

Let's make a couple rules, though. Keep the U and V vectors *orthogonal* to each other (in other words, at right angles to each other) because you really don't need to skew any textures onto a surface. Also, you should make sure the U and V vectors are on the same plane as the polygon. Otherwise, if the U or V vectors were pointing outward from the polygon, you could get some strange results, such as polygons that have textures that appear at an angle when you're looking at them head on.

Now look at the O, U, and V vectors more closely and how they relate to what we want to do. Remember, you want to map every pixel to a texel. Before you know what texel to draw, you need to know the exact point on the polygon, P, for a point on the view window, W. Let's skip a step and assume you already have a point on the polygon, P, and you want to determine the (x,y) texture coordinate (see Figure 8.3).

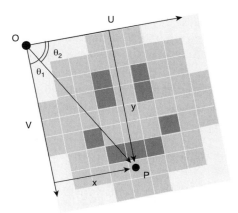

Figure 8.3 How a point on the polygon, P, relates to the texture's orientation.

From Figure 8.3, you can get the equations for x and y, which are the location within the texture:

```
x  =  |P-O|cos θ₂
y  =  |P-O|cos θ₁
```

In these equations, $|P-O|$ is the distance from O to P, θ_1 is the angle between (P–O) and V, and θ_2 is the angle between (P–O) and U.

Going a step further, if U and V are unit vectors, you can use the dot product to simplify things:

```
x  =  U•(P-O)
y  =  V•(P-O)
```

Remember, it's okay if the (x,y) texture coordinates are negative or otherwise are not within the texture bounds; you're going to tile the texture across the polygon.

Now let's go back a step and find the point P on the polygon from the point on the view window, W (see Figure 8.4). You already know which polygon W points to because, at the texture-mapping stage, the polygon is already projected onto the view window.

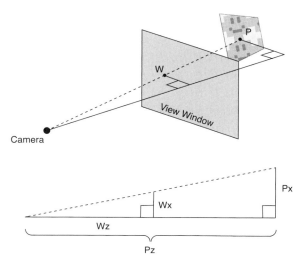

Figure 8.4 Projecting a point on the polygon, P, onto a point on the view window, W.

Looking at the problem in reverse, W is simply the projection of P to the view window, which is solved with the standard projection equations from Chapter 7:

$$
\begin{aligned}
W_x &= d\ P_x/P_z \\
W_y &= d\ P_y/P_z \\
W_z &= d\ P_z/P_z
\end{aligned}
$$

W_z is equal to d, the distance from the camera to the view window. Converting this to vector form, you get this:

$$
W = (d/P_z)\,P
$$

You need to find P, so solve this formula for P:

$$
P = (P_z/d)\,W
$$

So, to find P, you need to find P_z, which is the distance from the camera to the polygon along the z-axis.

To find P_z, you need information on the plane formed by the polygon. Use the equation of the plane, which basically just says that the normal of the plane, N, and any line in the plane are orthogonal to each other. The line to use is (P–O) from Figure 8.3 because this vector is in the same plane as the polygon. Let's begin:

$$
\begin{aligned}
N \bullet (P-O) &= 0 \\
N \bullet O &= N \bullet P
\end{aligned}
$$

Here insert the previous equation for P and solve for P_z:

$$
\begin{aligned}
N \bullet O &= N \bullet ((P_z/d)\,W) \\
N \bullet O &= (P_z/d)\,(N \bullet W) \\
P_z &= d\ (N \bullet O)/(N \bullet W)
\end{aligned}
$$

Now plug P_z back into the previous formula and get P:

$$
P = W(N \bullet O)/(N \bullet W)
$$

Therefore

```
x  =  U• (W (N•O) / (N•W) −O)
```

and

```
y  =  V• (W (N•O) / (N•W) −O)
```

Now you have some texture mapping equations. However, these are pretty nasty-looking equations. Luckily, they reduce a bit when you apply some of the rules of vector math. Let's start with the x coordinate:

```
x  =  U• (W (N•O) −O (N•W) ) / (N•W)
```

First, apply the vector triple product definition A×B×C = B(A·C)−C(A·B)

```
x  =  U• (N×W×O) / (N•W)
```

Next, apply the scalar triple product definition A·B×C = A×B·C

```
x  =  (U×N×W•O) / (N•W)
```

If you assume that U×N = −V and N = U×V (that the polygon normal and the two texture directions are all orthogonal to each other), then:

```
x  =  (−V×W•O) / (U×V•W)
```

Finally, you get this:

```
x  =  (V×O•W) / (U×V•W)
y  =  (O×U•W) / (U×V•W)
```

This is much easier, but you can continue simplifying. Notice that when you're texture-mapping a specific polygon, the only thing that's going to change as you render a polygon is W. The vectors O, U, and V don't change, so you can precompute those cross-products beforehand for each polygon:

$$A = V \times O$$
$$B = O \times U$$
$$C = U \times V$$

So when you're texture mapping, you just calculate this:

$$x = A \bullet W / C \bullet W$$
$$y = B \bullet W / C \bullet W$$

Whew! That's it—you've found some texture mapping equations. Now you'll put these equations to use and create a texture-mapper.

A Simple Texture-Mapper

First, to describe the texture orientation, you'll create a `Rectangle3D` class, in Listing 8.1, which is a freely oriented rectangle in 3D space. In other words, it doesn't have to be aligned with an axis like the `Rectangle2D` class in `java.awt.geom`.

Listing 8.1   Rectangle3D.java

```
package com.brackeen.javagamebook.math3D;

/**
    A Rectangle3D is a rectangle in 3D space, defined as an origin
    and vectors pointing in the directions of the base (width) and
    side (height).
*/
public class Rectangle3D {

    private Vector3D origin;
    private Vector3D directionU;
    private Vector3D directionV;
    private Vector3D normal;
    private float width;
    private float height;
```

```
/**
    Creates a rectangle at the origin with a width and height
    of zero.
*/
public Rectangle3D() {
    origin = new Vector3D();
    directionU = new Vector3D(1,0,0);
    directionV = new Vector3D(0,1,0);
    width = 0;
    height = 0;
}




/**
    Creates a new Rectangle3D with the specified origin,
    direction of the base (directionU) and direction of
    the side (directionV).
*/
public Rectangle3D(Vector3D origin, Vector3D directionU,
    Vector3D directionV, float width, float height)
{
    this.origin = new Vector3D(origin);
    this.directionU = new Vector3D(directionU);
    this.directionU.normalize();
    this.directionV = new Vector3D(directionV);
    this.directionV.normalize();
    this.width = width;
    this.height = height;
}




/**
    Sets the values of this Rectangle3D to the specified
    Rectangle3D.
*/
public void setTo(Rectangle3D rect) {
    origin.setTo(rect.origin);
    directionU.setTo(rect.directionU);
```

continues

Listing 8.1 Rectangle3D.java *continued*

```java
        directionV.setTo(rect.directionV);
        width = rect.width;
        height = rect.height;
    }


    /**
        Gets the origin of this Rectangle3D.
    */
    public Vector3D getOrigin() {
        return origin;
    }


    /**
        Gets the direction of the base of this Rectangle3D.
    */
    public Vector3D getDirectionU() {
        return directionU;
    }


    /**
        Gets the direction of the side of this Rectangle3D.
    */
    public Vector3D getDirectionV() {
        return directionV;
    }


    /**
        Gets the width of this Rectangle3D.
    */
    public float getWidth() {
        return width;
    }
```

```java
/**
    Sets the width of this Rectangle3D.
*/
public void setWidth(float width) {
    this.width = width;
}



/**
    Gets the height of this Rectangle3D.
*/
public float getHeight() {
    return height;
}



/**
    Sets the height of this Rectangle3D.
*/
public void setHeight(float height) {
    this.height = height;
}



/**
    Calculates the normal vector of this Rectangle3D.
*/
protected Vector3D calcNormal() {
    if (normal == null) {
        normal = new Vector3D();
    }
    normal.setToCrossProduct(directionU, directionV);
    normal.normalize();
    return normal;
}



/**
```

continues

Listing 8.1 Rectangle3D.java *continued*

```
        Gets the normal of this Rectangle3D.
    */
    public Vector3D getNormal() {
        if (normal == null) {
            calcNormal();
        }
        return normal;
    }



    /**
        Sets the normal of this Rectangle3D.
    */
    public void setNormal(Vector3D n) {
        if (normal == null) {
            normal = new Vector3D(n);
        }
        else {
            normal.setTo(n);
        }
    }


    public void add(Vector3D u) {
        origin.add(u);
        // don't translate direction vectors or size
    }

    public void subtract(Vector3D u) {
        origin.subtract(u);
        // don't translate direction vectors or size
    }

    public void add(Transform3D xform) {
        addRotation(xform);
        add(xform.getLocation());
    }
```

```java
    public void subtract(Transform3D xform) {
        subtract(xform.getLocation());
        subtractRotation(xform);
    }

    public void addRotation(Transform3D xform) {
        origin.addRotation(xform);
        directionU.addRotation(xform);
        directionV.addRotation(xform);
    }

    public void subtractRotation(Transform3D xform) {
        origin.subtractRotation(xform);
        directionU.subtractRotation(xform);
        directionV.subtractRotation(xform);
    }

}
```

Simply put, the `Rectangle3D` class keeps track of three vectors (the origin, U, and V) and the rectangle's normal.

Now you'll create a `SimpleTexturedPolygonRenderer` class, shown in Listing 8.2. This is a very straightforward subclass of the `PolygonRenderer` you created in Chapter 7, and it simply follows the texture mapping equations.

Listing 8.2   SimpleTexturedPolygonRenderer.java

```java
package com.brackeen.javagamebook.graphics3D;

import java.awt.*;
import java.awt.image.*;
import java.io.File;
import java.io.IOException;
import javax.imageio.ImageIO;
import com.brackeen.javagamebook.math3D.*;

/**
    The SimpleTexturedPolygonRenderer class demonstrates
```

continues

Listing 8.2 SimpleTexturedPolygonRenderer.java *continued*

```
    the fundamentals of perspective-correct texture mapping.
    It is very slow and maps the same texture for every polygon.
*/
public class SimpleTexturedPolygonRenderer extends PolygonRenderer
{
    protected Vector3D a = new Vector3D();
    protected Vector3D b = new Vector3D();
    protected Vector3D c = new Vector3D();
    protected Vector3D viewPos = new Vector3D();
    protected Rectangle3D textureBounds = new Rectangle3D();
    protected BufferedImage texture;

    public SimpleTexturedPolygonRenderer(Transform3D camera,
        ViewWindow viewWindow, String textureFile)
    {
        super(camera, viewWindow);
        texture = loadTexture(textureFile);
    }


    /**
        Loads the texture image from a file. This image is used
        for all polygons.
    */
    public BufferedImage loadTexture(String filename) {
        try {
            return ImageIO.read(new File(filename));
        }
        catch (IOException ex) {
            ex.printStackTrace();
            return null;
        }
    }


    protected void drawCurrentPolygon(Graphics2D g) {
```

```
// Calculate texture bounds.
// Ideally texture bounds are pre-calculated and stored
// with the polygon. Coordinates are computed here for
// demonstration purposes.
Vector3D textureOrigin = textureBounds.getOrigin();
Vector3D textureDirectionU = textureBounds.getDirectionU();
Vector3D textureDirectionV = textureBounds.getDirectionV();

textureOrigin.setTo(sourcePolygon.getVertex(0));

textureDirectionU.setTo(sourcePolygon.getVertex(3));
textureDirectionU.subtract(textureOrigin);
textureDirectionU.normalize();

textureDirectionV.setTo(sourcePolygon.getVertex(1));
textureDirectionV.subtract(textureOrigin);
textureDirectionV.normalize();

// transform the texture bounds
textureBounds.subtract(camera);

// start texture-mapping calculations
a.setToCrossProduct(textureBounds.getDirectionV(),
    textureBounds.getOrigin());
b.setToCrossProduct(textureBounds.getOrigin(),
    textureBounds.getDirectionU());
c.setToCrossProduct(textureBounds.getDirectionU(),
    textureBounds.getDirectionV());

int y = scanConverter.getTopBoundary();
viewPos.z = -viewWindow.getDistance();

while (y<=scanConverter.getBottomBoundary()) {
    ScanConverter.Scan scan = scanConverter.getScan(y);

    if (scan.isValid()) {
        viewPos.y =
            viewWindow.convertFromScreenYToViewY(y);
```

continues

Listing 8.2 SimpleTexturedPolygonRenderer.java *continued*

```java
                    for (int x=scan.left; x<=scan.right; x++) {
                        viewPos.x =
                            viewWindow.convertFromScreenXToViewX(x);

                        // compute the texture location
                        int tx = (int)(a.getDotProduct(viewPos) /
                            c.getDotProduct(viewPos));
                        int ty = (int)(b.getDotProduct(viewPos) /
                            c.getDotProduct(viewPos));

                        // get the color to draw
                        try {
                            int color = texture.getRGB(tx, ty);

                            g.setColor(new Color(color));
                        }
                        catch (ArrayIndexOutOfBoundsException ex) {
                            g.setColor(Color.red);
                        }

                        // draw the pixel
                        g.drawLine(x,y,x,y);
                    }
                }
                y++;
            }
        }
    }
}
```

This class uses a `BufferedImage` to store the texture. During the rendering process, it creates a new `Color` object for every pixel. Because the `Graphics2D` class has no `drawPixel()` method, you use `drawLine()` to draw a 1-pixel-long line. One thing to note is that the renderer does not tile textures; it requires the texture be the same size as the polygon. We get to texture tiling in the next section, but for now, this is a start. Now let's create a simple test to try it out.

The TextureMapTest1 class in Listing 8.3 creates a single polygon and draws it on the screen, allowing the user to wander around it.

Listing 8.3   TextureMapTest1.java

```
import com.brackeen.javagamebook.math3D.*;
import com.brackeen.javagamebook.graphics3D.*;
import com.brackeen.javagamebook.test.GameCore3D;

public class TextureMapTest1 extends GameCore3D {

    public static void main(String[] args) {
        new TextureMapTest1().run();
    }

    public void createPolygons() {
        Polygon3D poly;

        // one wall for now
        poly = new Polygon3D(
            new Vector3D(-128, 256, -1000),
            new Vector3D(-128, 0, -1000),
            new Vector3D(128, 0, -1000),
            new Vector3D(128, 256, -1000));
        polygons.add(poly);
    }

    public void createPolygonRenderer() {
        viewWindow = new ViewWindow(0, 0,
            screen.getWidth(), screen.getHeight(),
            (float)Math.toRadians(75));

        Transform3D camera = new Transform3D(0,100,0);
        polygonRenderer = new SimpleTexturedPolygonRenderer(
            camera, viewWindow, "../images/test_pattern.png");
    }

}
```

`TextureMapTest1` extends the `GameCore3D` class, which is pretty much the same as `Simple3DTest2` from the previous chapter. All `TextureMapTest1` does is create a polygon and a polygon renderer, and lets the user wander around the world. See Figure 8.5 to see what it looks like.

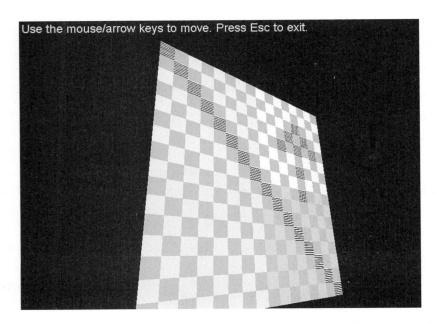

Figure 8.5 The `TextureMapTest1` demo draws a test-pattern texture over a polygon.

The texture in `TextureMapTest1` is a simple asymmetrical test pattern that can be use to ensure the texture is mapped correctly onto the polygon. It is easy to tell which side is left or right and which side is up and down, so you know if you've got all of your math right. If the arrow in the texture was pointing the wrong away or if the image was flipped, you would know the equations might be off or that you're missing a sign somewhere.

Problems with the First Texture-Mapper

When you run the test, you'll probably notice that it is excruciatingly slow. It might take more than 1 second to draw a single frame, depending on the speed of your machine. There are several reasons for this slow behavior:

➤ Creating a new `Color` object for every pixel is too much overhead per pixel. It also gives the garbage collector more work to do.

➤ Calling the `setColor()` and `drawLine()` methods is also too much overhead per pixel.

➤ The `BufferedImage`'s `getRGB()` method must convert a pixel to 24-bit color if it's not already in this format.

➤ You're performing too many calculations per pixel.

➤ Catching a thrown `ArrayIndexOutOfBoundsException` is actually slower than manually checking the array bounds. However, this really isn't an issue in this case because the test is set up to avoid these exceptions.

Note that none of these issues is a problem for normal tasks—don't think that creating `Color` objects or catching exceptions are slow in general. For most purposes, these things are fine; they happen to be slow only when you try to do these things for every pixel on screen at a high frame rate. To get an idea of the magnitude of what you're trying to accomplish, with a 640×480 screen at 60 frames per second, you're drawing 18,432,000 pixels every second. So, it's important to use the fastest method possible for drawing a single pixel, which means you should avoid some programming techniques that would be acceptable in other situations.

Optimizing Texture Mapping

Unfortunately, the `Graphics2D` interface doesn't provide a fast interface for drawing one pixel at a time, each with a different color. And there are currently no interfaces in Java to directly access video memory. Theoretically, this could be accomplished using a `ByteBuffer` that points directly to video memory, but you'd still have the JNI overhead of drawing one pixel at a time.

To make up for this, you'll first draw pixels to a `BufferedImage` and then to the `BufferedImage` to the screen. This is like the concept of double buffering discussed in Chapter 2, "2D Graphics and Animation." With `BufferedImages`, you can extract the data from the image as an array and copy pixel data directly to it. Copying an element to an array is one of the fastest operations you can do.

The drawback here is the extra time it takes to copy the image to video memory using a `Graphics.drawImage()` call. This takes about 5% to 10% of the processor on the machines I have tested. Still, the benefits outweigh the costs.

One decision to make is what color depth to use for the `BufferedImage`. Of course, the `BufferedImage` should have the same color depth and pixel layout as the display so that the image can be blitted to the screen quickly without any color conversion. So, you must decide on a display depth of 8-bit, 16-bit, or 24-bit color. With 8-bit color depth, you're forced to use a particular color palette, which visually limits things such as shading. 24-bit (or 32-bit) color gives you the best color quality, but 16-bit color is a faster choice because there is less data to push around. 16-bit color has less color quality than 24-bit color, but it is good enough for a 3D game with texture mapping and lighting. With a 16-bit `BufferedImage`, you can extract the `BufferedImage`'s underlying array like this:

```
BufferedImage doubleBuffer;
short[] doubleBufferData;
...
// get the buffer data
DataBuffer dest = doubleBuffer.getRaster().getDataBuffer();
doubleBufferData = ((DataBufferUShort)dest).getData();
```

Next we discuss the storage format of textures.

Texture Storage

Just as the double buffer has the same color depth and pixel format as the display, you want the textures to have the same color depth and pixel format. You could use `BufferedImages` for textures as you did in the first example, but you really don't need all the functionality that a `BufferedImage` provides. Instead, create an abstract `Texture` class, in Listing 8.4, that simply enables the caller to get the color at a particular (x,y) location within the texture.

Listing 8.4   Texture.java

```
/**
    The Texture class is an abstract class that represents a
    16-bit color texture.
```

```java
*/
public abstract class Texture {

    protected int width;
    protected int height;

    /**
        Creates a new Texture with the specified width and height.
    */
    public Texture(int width, int height) {
        this.width = width;
        this.height = height;
    }


    /**
        Gets the width of this Texture.
    */
    public int getWidth() {
        return width;
    }


    /**
        Gets the height of this Texture.
    */
    public int getHeight() {
        return height;
    }


    /**
        Gets the 16-bit color of this Texture at the specified
        (x,y) location.
    */
    public abstract short getColor(int x, int y);

}
```

The Texture class is abstract, so you have to extend it to get any use out of it. The getColor() method needs to be implemented to return the 16-bit color value of the texture at the specified (x,y) location within the texture.

Remember that you want to be able to tile a texture across a polygon if you have to. You can do this easily if you restrict the width and height of each texture to be a power of 2, such as 16, 32, 128, and so on. For example, let's say you have a texture with a width of 32 pixels. The value of 32 in binary is represented (in 8 bits) as this:

```
00100000
```

This number minus one, 31, is called the mask. For a power of 2, subtracting 1 has the same effect as converting the 1 to a 0 and the following 0s to 1s. It is represented in binary as follows:

```
00011111
```

This mask represents all the valid bits for this range of numbers—or, in this case, the texture x coordinate. If you perform a bitwise AND operation (using &) with the incoming texture x coordinate, you chop off the unwanted upper bits and get a value within the range you need: 0 to 31. Remember, this works only for powers of 2. This idea is summed up in the PowerOf2Texture class shown in Listing 8.5.

Listing 8.5 PowerOf2Texture.java

```java
package com.brackeen.javagamebook.graphics3D.texture;

/**
    The PowerOf2Texture class is a Texture with a width and height
    that are a power of 2 (32, 128, etc.).
*/
public class PowerOf2Texture extends Texture {

    private short[] buffer;
    private int widthBits;
    private int widthMask;
    private int heightBits;
    private int heightMask;
```

```
/**
    Creates a new PowerOf2Texture with the specified buffer.
    The width of the bitmap is 2 to the power of widthBits, or
    (1 << widthBits). Likewise, the height of the bitmap is 2
    to the power of heightBits, or (1 << heightBits).
*/
public PowerOf2Texture(short[] buffer,
    int widthBits, int heightBits)
{
    super(1 << widthBits, 1 << heightBits);
    this.buffer = buffer;
    this.widthBits = widthBits;
    this.heightBits = heightBits;
    this.widthMask = getWidth() - 1;
    this.heightMask = getHeight() - 1;
}


/**
    Gets the 16-bit color of the pixel at location (x,y) in
    the bitmap.
*/
public short getColor(int x, int y) {
    return buffer[
        (x & widthMask) +
        ((y & heightMask) << widthBits)];
}

}
```

The `PowerOf2Texture` class keeps track of a short array to hold the texture and also the width and height mask. The `getColor()` method uses the masks to get the correct x and y values so you can tile the texture across the polygon.

Finally, you need an easy way to extract data from `BufferedImages` to create your textures. To do this, add a static `createTexture()` method to the `Texture` class. For now, it creates only `PowerOf2Texture`, but later you'll extend it to create other texture types.

```
/**
    Creates a Texture from the specified image.
*/
public static Texture createTexture(BufferedImage image) {
    int type = image.getType();
    int width = image.getWidth();
    int height = image.getHeight();

    if (!isPowerOfTwo(width) || !isPowerOfTwo(height)) {
        throw new IllegalArgumentException(
            "Size of texture must be a power of two.");
    }

    // convert image to an 16-bit image
    if (type != BufferedImage.TYPE_USHORT_565_RGB) {
        BufferedImage newImage = new BufferedImage(
            image.getWidth(), image.getHeight(),
            BufferedImage.TYPE_USHORT_565_RGB);
        Graphics2D g = newImage.createGraphics();
        g.drawImage(image, 0, 0, null);
        g.dispose();
        image = newImage;
    }

    DataBuffer dest = image.getRaster().getDataBuffer();
    return new PowerOf2Texture(
        ((DataBufferUShort)dest).getData(),
        countbits(width-1), countbits(height-1));
}
```

In this function you assume that the 16-bit display has the same pixel format as the BufferedImage type TYPE_USHORT_565_RGB. So far, I haven't found a 16-bit display that doesn't have this pixel format, but theoretically one could exist. Alternatively, you can always use the createCompatibleImage() method from GraphicsConfiguration to create an image compatible with the display.

Next, you create a new PolygonRenderer class, called FastTexturedPolygonRendrer. This new class has the same setup routines as

`SimpleTexturedPolygonRenderer`, calculating the A, B, and C vectors. It also preps the `doubleBufferData` array, which is the array you copy pixels to. At the end of each frame, the double buffer is blitted to the display.

This class also contains an inner class called `ScanRenderer`. `ScanRenderer` is an abstract class that contains a method to draw a horizontal scan of a polygon:

```
/**
    The ScanRenderer class is an abstract inner class of
    FastTexturedPolygonRenderer that provides an interface for
    rendering a horizontal scan line.
*/
public abstract class ScanRenderer {

    protected Texture currentTexture;

    public void setTexture(Texture texture) {
        this.currentTexture = texture;
    }

    public abstract void render(int offset,
        int left, int right);

}
```

You'll create a few different `ScanRenderers` for different types of drawing techniques.

Raw Optimization

The simplest `ScanRenderer` you can create is one that performs only a polygon-fill routine, and it's also the fastest (aside from one that does nothing):

```
public void render(int offset, int left, int right) {
    for (int x=left; x<=right; x++) {
        doubleBufferData[offset++] = (short)0x0007;
    }
}
```

Now that you have the general idea, create a `ScanRenderer` that performs the same calculations as the `SimpleTexturedPolygonRenderer`:

```
public void render(int offset, int left, int right) {
    for (int x=left; x<=right; x++) {
        int tx = (int)(a.getDotProduct(viewPos) /
            c.getDotProduct(viewPos));
        int ty = (int)(b.getDotProduct(viewPos) /
            c.getDotProduct(viewPos));
        doubleBufferData[offset++] =
            currentTexture.getColor(tx, ty);
        viewPos.x++;
    }
}
```

Poof, you have a much faster texture-mapper! You're copying pixel data from the texture to the double buffer much faster now. I tested this scan renderer on two machines by moving the camera close enough to a textured polygon so that it fills an entire 640×480 screen. On a 2.4GHz Pentium 4, this resulted in a speedup of 46 times, and on an 867MHz G4, this resulted in a speedup of 144 times. Not bad at all. This is a great start, but it could be better. You might look at this and think, okay, just some multiplication and a couple divides—no big deal. But keep in mind that you're doing those multiplications for every pixel on the screen.

Here you can apply one of the simplest forms of optimization, which is moving expensive code out of the loop. In this case, you really don't need to calculate four dot products for every pixel because the a, b, and c vectors aren't going to change. Also, you know that `viewPos.x` will increase by 1 for every pixel, so you can predict how the dot products will change. Here's a next iteration of the `ScanRenderer` that performs these optimizations:

```
public void render(int offset, int left, int right) {
    float u = a.getDotProduct(viewPos);
    float v = b.getDotProduct(viewPos);
    float z = c.getDotProduct(viewPos);
    float du = a.x;
    float dv = b.x;
```

```
    float dz = c.x;
    for (int x=left; x<=right; x++) {
        doubleBufferData[offset++] = currentTexture.getColor(
            (int)(u/z), (int)(v/z));
        u+=du;
        v+=dv;
        z+=dz;
    }
}
```

Compared to the last scan renderer, this optimization resulted in a speedup of 1.6 times on the Pentium 4, and a similar speedup of 1.4 times on the G4.

Next, you take advantage of a trick used with scan converting in the previous chapter: You use integers instead of floats. Converting every pixel from a float to an integer can be expensive, so instead use integers the entire time:

```
public static final int SCALE_BITS = 12;
public static final int SCALE = 1 << SCALE_BITS;


...


public void render(int offset, int left, int right) {
    int u = (int)(SCALE * a.getDotProduct(viewPos));
    int v = (int)(SCALE * b.getDotProduct(viewPos));
    int z = (int)(SCALE * c.getDotProduct(viewPos));
    int du = (int)(SCALE * a.x);
    int dv = (int)(SCALE * b.x);
    int dz = (int)(SCALE * c.x);
    for (int x=left; x<=right; x++) {
        doubleBufferData[offset++] =
            currentTexture.getColor(u/z, v/z);
        u+=du;
        v+=dv;
        z+=dz;
    }
}
```

The Pentium 4 handles floating-point operations pretty well, so there was no speedup there. The G4, however, resulted in a speedup of 1.2 times over the last scan renderer.

This has got you pretty close to the wire. The only things you're doing are a couple array references, some integer addition, and a couple of integer divides.

When you look at this, you might notice the biggest bottleneck: those two divides. Addition is cheap, but division can take several clock cycles.

But those divides are required, right? You can't get rid of these divides without sacrificing texture mapping quality.

That's the key: sacrificing quality. Luckily, you can sacrifice a bit of quality in a way that is visually acceptable and get a performance boost in the process.

The idea is to calculate only the correct texture coordinates every few pixels and then interpolate between these correct values. In mathematics, *interpolating* between two values means estimating a value between two known values. In the next ScanRenderer, you compute the correct texture coordinates every 16 pixels (or less than 16, if there are fewer pixels left in the scan). This way, between those 16 pixels, you need only a few additions and bit shifts.

```
public static final int INTERP_SIZE_BITS = 4;
public static final int INTERP_SIZE = 1 << INTERP_SIZE_BITS;


. . .


public void render(int offset, int left, int right) {
    float u = SCALE * a.getDotProduct(viewPos);
    float v = SCALE * b.getDotProduct(viewPos);
    float z = c.getDotProduct(viewPos);
    float du = INTERP_SIZE * SCALE * a.x;
    float dv = INTERP_SIZE * SCALE * b.x;
    float dz = INTERP_SIZE * c.x;
    int nextTx = (int)(u/z);
    int nextTy = (int)(v/z);
    int x = left;
    while (x <= right) {
```

```
int tx = nextTx;
int ty = nextTy;
int maxLength = right-x+1;
if (maxLength > INTERP_SIZE) {
    u+=du;
    v+=dv;
    z+=dz;
    nextTx = (int)(u/z);
    nextTy = (int)(v/z);
    int dtx = (nextTx-tx) >> INTERP_SIZE_BITS;
    int dty = (nextTy-ty) >> INTERP_SIZE_BITS;
    int endOffset = offset + INTERP_SIZE;
    while (offset < endOffset) {
        doubleBufferData[offset++] =
            texture.getColor(
            tx >> SCALE_BITS, ty >> SCALE_BITS);
        tx+=dtx;
        ty+=dty;
    }
    x+=INTERP_SIZE;
}
else {
    // variable interpolation size
    int interpSize = maxLength;
    u += interpSize * SCALE * a.x;
    v += interpSize * SCALE * b.x;
    z += interpSize * c.x;
    nextTx = (int)(u/z);
    nextTy = (int)(v/z);
    int dtx = (nextTx-tx) / interpSize;
    int dty = (nextTy-ty) / interpSize;
    int endOffset = offset + interpSize;
    while (offset < endOffset) {
        doubleBufferData[offset++] =
            texture.getColor(
            tx >> SCALE_BITS, ty >> SCALE_BITS);
        tx+=dtx;
        ty+=dty;
    }
```

```
            x+=interpSize;
        }
    }
}
```

On the two test machines, this scan renderer resulted in a speedup of 1.6 times on the Pentium 4 and a speedup of 1.4 times on the G4.

As mentioned before, this `ScanRenderer` does sacrifice some image quality, but most of the time it's not noticeable. It is noticeable if the depth of the polygon greatly changes along the horizontal scan line. So, when you're looking straight at a polygon, the depth of the polygon doesn't change when scanning from left to right, so it looks fine. Also, floors will look fine because their depth doesn't change from left to right. However, when you're looking at a vertical polygon at the side, the depth changes a lot; the textures may be slightly off and even look a little warped. This is particularly noticeable on low-resolution screens, where 16 pixels cover a larger amount of space.

An idea to limit the distortion is to use a variable interpolation size, depending on the change of depth of the polygon. Little or no change in depth could give you a larger interpolation size, and a larger change in depth would require a smaller interpolation. I'll leave this enhancement to you, as an exercise for the reader!

Method Inlining

There's one other optimization to mention: inlining methods. Calling a method has a certain overhead, but here you are calling `texture.getColor()` for every pixel. Luckily, the *HotSpot VM* (the default VM included with the Java 1.4 runtime) is smart enough to inline certain methods. Inlining a method basically moves the code from the method to the caller's code, effectively eliminating the method call. HotSpot inlines short methods that it determines are nonvirtual. (Remember, a nonvirtual method is one that doesn't have any subclasses that override it.) In the case of `Texture`, only the `PowerOf2Texture` class implements the `getColor()` method, and the method is short enough that HotSpot will inline it.

Later in this chapter, however, you'll have other `Texture` subclasses, such as `ShadedTexture`. When you have another class that implements the `getColor()` method, HotSpot won't inline it in the method, and you'll be stuck with method overhead for every pixel.

I tried to trick HotSpot into inlining that method by declaring a final local variable, with the idea that HotSpot would know the final local variable's class and could inline the method:

```
final Texture texture = currentTexture;
```

Because this local variable is final, its class never changes, so I thought HotSpot might be capable of inlining its getColor() method. It would have been nice if this had worked, but it didn't. At the moment, I don't see why HotSpot can't do inlining in this case, but it doesn't, so we must find another solution.

A solution that does work is to create a different ScanRenderer for each type of texture. The code for each of the renderers is exactly the same, except for a local variable, texture, that is created to explicitly reference the texture:

```
public class PowerOf2TextureRenderer extends ScanRenderer {

    public void render(int offset, int left, int right) {
        PowerOf2Texture texture = (PowerOf2Texture)currentTexture;
        ...
        // texture-mapping code goes here
    }
}
```

In the case of PowerOf2TextureRenderer, HotSpot now knows that the texture is a PowerOf2Texture and can inline the getColor() method accordingly. It's not the cleanest solution in terms of solid, object-oriented code—if you change one ScanRenderer, you have to change them all—but it works. Another drawback is that you need to make the PowerOf2Texture class (and any other Texture that has a ScanRenderer) final so that no other classes can subclass them and cause HotSpot to stop inlining.

Sometimes you have to work with what you've got, and this is one of those times. Programmers of Assembly language, C, and C++ sometimes have to do crazy things to optimize for a certain piece of hardware or operating system, and Java programmers sometimes have to do crazy things for the VM.

On the two test machines, the inlining optimization resulted in a speedup of 2.3 times on the Pentium 4 and a more modest speedup of 1.3 times on the G4. Overall, compared to the original slow texture-mapper, this renderer is 284 times faster on the Pentium 4 and 436 times faster on the G4. Nice!

Fast Texture Mapping Demo

Okay, so now you have a Texture class and a FastTexturedPolygonRenderer, so let's make another demo. The TextureMapTest2, shown in Figure 8.6, creates a convex polyhedron with textures mapped on all sides.

Figure 8.6　The TextureMapTest2 demo draws a texture-mapped polyhedron at a much faster frame rate than the TextureMapTest1 demo.

TextureMapTest2 uses a TexturedPolygon3D class, which is just like a regular Polygon3D except that it has fields for the polygon's texture and texture bounds.

The source code for TextureMapTest2 mostly just creates a bunch of polygons. A method in TextureMapTest2 worth mentioning is the setTexture() method:

```
public void setTexture(TexturedPolygon3D poly, Texture texture) {
    Vector3D origin = poly.getVertex(0);

    Vector3D dv = new Vector3D(poly.getVertex(1));
    dv.subtract(origin);

    Vector3D du = new Vector3D();
    du.setToCrossProduct(poly.getNormal(), dv);

    Rectangle3D textureBounds = new Rectangle3D(origin, du, dv,
        texture.getWidth(), texture.getHeight());

    poly.setTexture(texture, textureBounds);
}
```

This method creates the texture bounds for a polygon. Using this method means you don't have to explicitly create the texture bounds for every polygon.

The good news is that `TextureMapTest2` is much, much faster! As usual, press R to see the frame rate on your system. Next, we move on to sprucing up this demo a bit by adding some shading.

Simple Lighting

The goal of this section is to add some realistic shading to the polygons. In the previous chapter, the last demo was a solid-colored 3D house. The sides of the house were a shade darker than the front, so basically we faked the polygon shading. Here, we do real shading with light sources instead of coloring the polygons by hand.

Diffuse Reflection

The form of lighting you'll use here is diffuse reflection using Lambert's law. This law basically says that the intensity of reflected light depends on the angle between the normal of the surface and the direction of the light source, as shown in Figure 8.7.

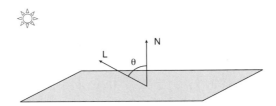

Figure 8.7 Diffuse reflection lights a polygon based on the angle between the polygon's normal and the direction of the light source.

The smaller the angle is, the more light is reflected. Likewise, larger angles reflect smaller amounts of light. Assuming the normal and direction of the light source are normalized, this can be expressed mathematically using the following equation, where i is the intensity of the reflection.

```
i = N•L
```

An easy way to see diffuse reflection work in the real world is to look at a room with one light source: For example, a dark room in which the walls and ceiling are the same color and a light is emitted from a light source near the ceiling. If you look at a corner between a wall and a ceiling, the ceiling near the corner will be darker than the wall. This is because the wall receives light directly from the light source, while the ceiling receives light from a larger angle. Thus, the ceiling appears a darker shade.

Ambient Lighting

Also, during the day in a typical room, you might not need any lights on because the sunlight comes in a window and bounces around the room, lighting everything in the room. Modeling light that bounces around the room is a bit difficult to calculate, so instead you can approximate this effect with ambient lighting. Ambient light limits the minimum light intensity an object can have. For example, in a sunlit room you might want everything in the room to have a minimum light intensity of 0.7. You can express this easily by giving a polygon an ambient light intensity:

```
i = a+N•L
```

The ambient light intensity should be between 0 and 1.

Light Source Intensity

Just like a polygon can have an ambient light intensity, the light source itself can have an intensity value. This is like the difference between a 60W and 100W light bulb. Using l to describe the light source intensity, the equation becomes this:

```
i = a+l(N•L)
```

Distance Falloff

Taking the light source intensity a step further, you can make the intensity of the light diminish with distance. That is, the farther away from a light source an object is, the dimmer the light source appears. The falloff distance is the distance that a light source is no longer visible. Using l as the light source intensity, f as the falloff distance, and d as the distance from the object to the light source, the equation becomes this:

```
l' = l(f-d)/(f+d)
i = a+l'(N•L)
```

Implementing a Point Light

We express a light source with an intensity and optional falloff distance in the PointLight3D class in Listing 8.6.

Listing 8.6   PointLight3D.java

```java
package com.brackeen.javagamebook.math3D;

/**
    A PointLight3D is a point light that has an intensity
    (between 0 and 1) and optionally a distance falloff value,
    which causes the light to diminish with distance.
*/
public class PointLight3D extends Vector3D {

    public static final float NO_DISTANCE_FALLOFF = -1;

    public float intensity;
    public float distanceFalloff;
```

continues

Listing 8.6   PointLight3D.java   *continued*

```
    . . .

    /**
        Gets the intensity of this light from the specified
        distance.
    */
    public float getIntensity(float distance) {
        if (distanceFalloff == NO_DISTANCE_FALLOFF) {
            return intensity;
        }
        else if (distance >= distanceFalloff) {
            return 0;
        }
        else {
            return intensity * (distanceFalloff - distance)
                / (distanceFalloff + distance);
        }
    }

}
```

The `PointLight3D` class is a `Vector3D` that contains an intensity and distance falloff value for the light. Its `getIntensity()` method gets the light intensity for a particular distance.

Implementing Texture Lighting

The problem to solve here is to actually implement lighting on a texture. Basically, you have an intensity value from 0 to 1 for a polygon, and you need to apply that intensity value to the texture. A value of 1 leaves the texture unchanged, and values less than 1 modify the texture to be increasingly darker, all the way to an intensity of 0 that modifies the texture to be almost completely black.

You can't simply multiply the intensity value by the 16-bit color value because the 16-bit color value is a packed data structure. Really, you'd have to extract the red, green, and blue values; then multiply each by the light intensity; and then convert them back to a 16-bit color value. That's a bit too much work to do for every pixel.

Alternatively, you could limit the number of intensity values to, say, 64 and simply load 64 different versions of each texture, from dark to light. Then you could select the correct texture for each polygon depending on intensity value.

This works and is fast, but it's a waste of memory. A 128×128 16-bit texture takes up 32K of memory, so if you had 64 versions, that would be 2MB! Obviously, this severely limits the number of textures you can have in memory.

Another approach is, instead of having 64 versions of the texture, to have just 1 version of the texture and 64 versions of its color palette. You can do this by first requiring that all textures are 8-bit color; thus, each texture has its own small 256-color palette. Then, instead of creating 64 versions of the texture, you just create 64 versions of the palette.

The basic idea is shown in a simplified version in Figure 8.8.

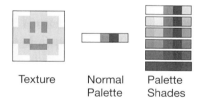

Texture   Normal   Palette
Palette   Shades

Figure 8.8   To light a texture, keep a normal, full-lit copy of the texture and several versions of the texture's color palette, ranging from the normal palette to an almost completely dark palette.

If the palettes themselves represent 16-bit color, then having 64 256-color palettes creates an overhead of only 32K. For an 8-bit 128×128 texture, that means a total of just 80K of memory, much more conservative than the previous 2MB idea.

To implement this concept, create the `ShadedTexture` class shown in Listing 8.7.

Listing 8.7   ShadedTexture.java

```java
package com.brackeen.javagamebook.graphics3D.texture;

import java.awt.Color;
import java.awt.image.IndexColorModel;

/**
    The ShadedTexture class is a Texture that has multiple
    shades. The texture source image is stored as a 8-bit image
    with a palette for every shade.
*/
public final class ShadedTexture extends Texture {

    public static final int NUM_SHADE_LEVELS = 64;
    public static final int MAX_LEVEL = NUM_SHADE_LEVELS-1;

    private static final int PALETTE_SIZE_BITS = 8;
    private static final int PALETTE_SIZE = 1 << PALETTE_SIZE_BITS;

    private byte[] buffer;
    private IndexColorModel palette;
    private short[] shadeTable;
    private int defaultShadeLevel;
    private int widthBits;
    private int widthMask;
    private int heightBits;
    private int heightMask;

    /**
        Creates a new ShadedTexture from the specified 8-bit image
        buffer and palette. The width of the bitmap is 2 to the
        power of widthBits, or (1 << widthBits). Likewise, the
        height of the bitmap is 2 to the power of heightBits, or
        (1 << heightBits). The texture is shaded from its
        original color to black.
    */
    public ShadedTexture(byte[] buffer,
```

```java
    int widthBits, int heightBits,
    IndexColorModel palette)
{
    this(buffer, widthBits, heightBits, palette, Color.BLACK);
}



/**
    Creates a new ShadedTexture from the specified 8-bit image
    buffer, palette, and target shaded. The width of the
    bitmap is 2 to the power of widthBits, or (1 << widthBits).
    Likewise, the height of the bitmap is 2 to the power of
    heightBits, or (1 << heightBits). The texture is shaded
    from its original color to the target shade.
*/
public ShadedTexture(byte[] buffer,
    int widthBits, int heightBits,
    IndexColorModel palette, Color targetShade)
{
    super(1 << widthBits, 1 << heightBits);
    this.buffer = buffer;
    this.widthBits = widthBits;
    this.heightBits = heightBits;
    this.widthMask = getWidth() - 1;
    this.heightMask = getHeight() - 1;
    this.buffer = buffer;
    this.palette = palette;
    defaultShadeLevel = MAX_LEVEL;

    makeShadeTable(targetShade);
}



/**
    Creates the shade table for this ShadedTexture. Each entry
    in the palette is shaded from the original color to the
    specified target color.
```

continues

Listing 8.7   ShadedTexture.java   *continued*

```java
    */
    public void makeShadeTable(Color targetShade) {

        shadeTable = new short[NUM_SHADE_LEVELS*PALETTE_SIZE];

        for (int level=0; level<NUM_SHADE_LEVELS; level++) {
            for (int i=0; i<palette.getMapSize(); i++) {
                int red = calcColor(palette.getRed(i),
                    targetShade.getRed(), level);
                int green = calcColor(palette.getGreen(i),
                    targetShade.getGreen(), level);
                int blue = calcColor(palette.getBlue(i),
                    targetShade.getBlue(), level);

                int index = level * PALETTE_SIZE + i;
                // RGB 5:6:5
                shadeTable[index] = (short)(
                            ((red >> 3) << 11) |
                            ((green >> 2) << 5) |
                            (blue >> 3));
            }
        }
    }


    private int calcColor(int palColor, int target, int level) {
        return (palColor - target) * (level+1) /
            NUM_SHADE_LEVELS + target;
    }



    /**
        Sets the default shade level that is used when getColor()
        is called.
    */
    public void setDefaultShadeLevel(int level) {
        defaultShadeLevel = level;
    }
```

```
    /**
        Gets the default shade level that is used when getColor()
        is called.
    */
    public int getDefaultShadeLevel() {
        return defaultShadeLevel;
    }


    /**
        Gets the 16-bit color of this Texture at the specified
        (x,y) location, using the default shade level.
    */
    public short getColor(int x, int y) {
        return getColor(x, y, defaultShadeLevel);
    }


    /**
        Gets the 16-bit color of this Texture at the specified
        (x,y) location, using the specified shade level.
    */
    public short getColor(int x, int y, int shadeLevel) {
        return shadeTable[(shadeLevel << PALETTE_SIZE_BITS) |
            (0xff & buffer[
            (x & widthMask) |
            ((y & heightMask) << widthBits)])];
    }
}
```

In the ShadedTexture class, the texture itself is stored in the buffer byte array. The byte array is useless by itself because it does not contain any color data; it contains only indices into a 256-color palette. Sixty-four versions of this 256-color palette are stored in the shadeTable array. The shade table is created in the makeShadeTable() method. In the getColor() method, the shadeTable is used to convert an index in the 8-bit buffer to a 16-bit color in the palette.

Also, you'll notice that the shade table is created with a default shade value of black, so all the textures fade from the normal palette at 1 to black at 0. You could use other colors to create some other effects. Another idea is to create a spotlight effect by fading from the normal palette at 0 and full white at 1.

Now let's try out the new shaded textures. Create a ShadedTexturedPolygonRenderer class (see Listing 8.8) to draw ShadedTextures, calculating the light intensity for each polygon on the fly.

Listing 8.8   ShadedTexturedPolygonRenderer.java

```
package com.brackeen.javagamebook.graphics3D;

import java.awt.*;
import java.awt.image.*;
import com.brackeen.javagamebook.math3D.*;
import com.brackeen.javagamebook.graphics3D.texture.*;

/**
    The ShadedTexturedPolygonRenderer class is a PolygonRenderer
    that renders ShadedTextured dynamically with one light source.
    By default, the ambient light intensity is 0.5 and there
    is no point light.
*/
public class ShadedTexturedPolygonRenderer
    extends FastTexturedPolygonRenderer
{

    private PointLight3D lightSource;
    private float ambientLightIntensity = 0.5f;
    private Vector3D directionToLight = new Vector3D();

    public ShadedTexturedPolygonRenderer(Transform3D camera,
        ViewWindow viewWindow)
    {
        this(camera, viewWindow, true);
    }
```

```java
public ShadedTexturedPolygonRenderer(Transform3D camera,
    ViewWindow viewWindow, boolean clearViewEveryFrame)
{
    super(camera, viewWindow, clearViewEveryFrame);
}



/**
    Gets the light source for this renderer.
*/
public PointLight3D getLightSource() {
    return lightSource;
}



/**
    Sets the light source for this renderer.
*/
public void setLightSource(PointLight3D lightSource) {
    this.lightSource = lightSource;
}



/**
    Gets the ambient light intensity.
*/
public float getAmbientLightIntensity() {
    return ambientLightIntensity;
}



/**
    Sets the ambient light intensity, generally between 0 and
    1.
*/
public void setAmbientLightIntensity(float i) {
    ambientLightIntensity = i;
}
```

continues

Listing 8.8   ShadedTexturedPolygonRenderer.java   *continued*

```java
protected void drawCurrentPolygon(Graphics2D g) {
    // set the shade level of the polygon before drawing it
    if (sourcePolygon instanceof TexturedPolygon3D) {
        TexturedPolygon3D poly =
            ((TexturedPolygon3D)sourcePolygon);
        Texture texture = poly.getTexture();
        if (texture instanceof ShadedTexture) {
            calcShadeLevel();
        }
    }
    super.drawCurrentPolygon(g);
}


/**
    Calculates the shade level of the current polygon
*/
private void calcShadeLevel() {
    TexturedPolygon3D poly = (TexturedPolygon3D)sourcePolygon;
    float intensity = 0;
    if (lightSource != null) {

        // average all the vertices in the polygon
        directionToLight.setTo(0,0,0);
        for (int i=0; i<poly.getNumVertices(); i++) {
            directionToLight.add(poly.getVertex(i));
        }
        directionToLight.divide(poly.getNumVertices());

        // make the vector from the average vertex
        // to the light
        directionToLight.subtract(lightSource);
        directionToLight.multiply(-1);
```

```
        // get the distance to the light for falloff
        float distance = directionToLight.length();

        // compute the diffuse reflect
        directionToLight.normalize();
        Vector3D normal = poly.getNormal();
        intensity = lightSource.getIntensity(distance)
            * directionToLight.getDotProduct(normal);
        intensity = Math.min(intensity, 1);
        intensity = Math.max(intensity, 0);
    }

    intensity+=ambientLightIntensity;
    intensity = Math.min(intensity, 1);
    intensity = Math.max(intensity, 0);
    int level =
        Math.round(intensity*ShadedTexture.MAX_LEVEL);
    ((ShadedTexture)poly.getTexture()).
        setDefaultShadeLevel(level);
    }

}
```

The ShadedTexturedPolygonRenderer class calculates the shade level for every polygon in the calcShadeLevel() method. This class is just a demonstration; really you'd want to recalculate the shade level for a polygon only if a light source changed or a polygon moved. Also, ShadedTexturedPolygonRenderer uses only one point light, and the ambient light intensity is the same for every polygon.

Despite its simplicity, this class enables you to change the light intensity of the light source on the fly, which is a neat feature. You'll create the ShadingTest1 class to take advantage of the new renderer. A screenshot from ShadingTest1 is shown in Figure 8.9.

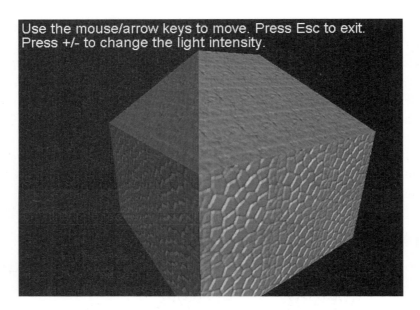

Use the mouse/arrow keys to move. Press Esc to exit.
Press +/- to change the light intensity.

Figure 8.9 `ShadingTest1` gives each polygon a different shade based on a light source. The light source intensity can be dynamically changed.

`ShadingTest1` is just like `TextureMapTest2`, except that it uses `ShadedTexturedPolygonRenderer` and enables you to change the light intensity with the +/– keys.

Advanced Lighting Using a Shade Map

The previous demo was cool and all, but making an entire polygon all the same shade isn't very accurate. Different parts of the polygon might have different angles and distances to the light source, as shown in Figure 8.10. This is especially true if the polygon is large.

Figure 8.10 Lighting a polygon with just one shade isn't accurate because different parts of the polygon might have different angles and distances to the light source.

To create a more realistic lighting effect, you could just break down all the polygons into smaller 16×16 polygons. Or, instead of breaking down polygons, another idea is to calculate a different light intensity value for every texel on the polygon. As you can imagine, calculating the light intensity for every texel is too expensive to do on the fly, especially if there are lots of lights in the world. Instead, you'll calculate the light intensities before the game starts and store these values in a polygon's shade map.

To reduce the memory requirements of the shade map, you could calculate only the correct light intensity every few pixels—for example, on a 16×16 grid. This will keep the shade map relatively small compared to the overall size of the polygon.

Finding the Bounding Rectangle

This shade map will be a rectangular map that covers the entire surface of the polygon. There are a couple ways to find this rectangular shape, and one of these ways is to find the minimum bounding rectangle of a polygon, shown in Figure 8.11. The minimum bounding rectangle is the smallest rectangle needed to cover a polygon, and one edge of the rectangle shares at least one edge of the polygon.

Figure 8.11   The minimum bounding rectangle of a polygon always shares at least one edge of the polygon.

However, you really need the rectangle to share the same orientation of the polygon's texture bounds so the shade map lines up properly with the texture map. This is the solution you'll use, but keep in mind that this solution has one drawback: It can waste some memory. For example, in Figure 8.12, the rectangular bounds that are aligned with the texture bounds have a much larger area than the polygon area.

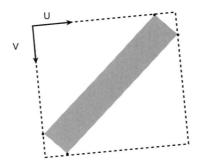

Figure 8.12 The bounding rectangle of a polygon that is aligned with the texture coordinates can waste memory.

Add a `calcBoundingRectangle()` method in `TexturedPolygon3D` to calculate the bounds of a polygon that is aligned with the texture bounds. This method uses dot products to find the desired length of the sides of the rectangle to cover every vertex of the polygon.

```
/**
    Calculates the bounding rectangle for this polygon that
    is aligned with the texture bounds.
*/
public Rectangle3D calcBoundingRectangle() {

    Vector3D u = new Vector3D(textureBounds.getDirectionU());
    Vector3D v = new Vector3D(textureBounds.getDirectionV());
    Vector3D d = new Vector3D();
    u.normalize();
    v.normalize();

    float uMin = 0;
    float uMax = 0;
    float vMin = 0;
    float vMax = 0;
    for (int i=0; i<getNumVertices(); i++) {
        d.setTo(getVertex(i));
        d.subtract(getVertex(0));
```

```
        float uLength = d.getDotProduct(u);
        float vLength = d.getDotProduct(v);
        uMin = Math.min(uLength, uMin);
        uMax = Math.max(uLength, uMax);
        vMin = Math.min(vLength, vMin);
        vMax = Math.max(vLength, vMax);
    }

    Rectangle3D boundingRect = new Rectangle3D();
    Vector3D origin = boundingRect.getOrigin();
    origin.setTo(getVertex(0));
    d.setTo(u);
    d.multiply(uMin);
    origin.add(d);
    d.setTo(v);
    d.multiply(vMin);
    origin.add(d);
    boundingRect.getDirectionU().setTo(u);
    boundingRect.getDirectionV().setTo(v);
    boundingRect.setWidth(uMax - uMin);
    boundingRect.setHeight(vMax - vMin);

    // explicitly set the normal since the texture directions
    // could create a normal negative to the polygon normal
    boundingRect.setNormal(getNormal());

    return boundingRect;
}
```

Applying the Shade Map

The next step is to determine when to apply the shade map to a polygon. One idea is to combine the shade map with the polygon's texture to create a shaded surface, as shown in Figure 8.13.

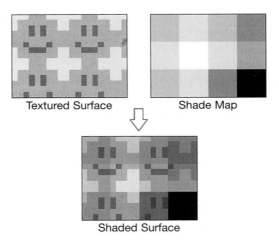

Figure 8.13 The shade map covers the entire surface of the polygon and is merged with the texture to create a shaded surface.

This basic technique creates a shaded surface that looks a little blocky around the shaded edges. To fix this, you can interpolate between shade values to create something that looks like Figure 8.14.

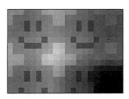

Figure 8.14 Interpolating the shade map gives the final surface a smoother look.

Instead of first creating a surface, another technique is to perform shading at the same time as texture mapping. This technique is feasible, but it cannot be optimized very well using shade map interpolation because calculating the interpolated shade value can be slow if performed for every pixel on screen.

Using surfaces, on the other hand, is just as fast as texture mapping after the surfaces are built. Surfaces can use a large amount of memory, but we cover memory issues later. For now, let's write some code to create shade maps and shaded surfaces.

First, to further define the geometry polygon's bounds, shade maps, and surfaces, take a look at Figure 8.15. In this figure, the surface bounds are slightly larger than the polygon bounds, to make up for any floating-point error during texture mapping. Floating-point error could make the resulting (x,y) surface coordinates incorrect by a texel or so. You don't want the texture mapping to calculate a value outside the bounds of the surface, and making sure the surface is slightly larger than the polygon bounds helps alleviate this issue. Also note that the shade map is aligned with the polygon bounds, not the surface bounds.

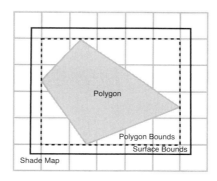

Figure 8.15   The shade map is given a small border around the edges to make up for any floating-point imprecision when texture mapping. The shade map is aligned with the polygon bounds, not the surface bounds.

Building the Shade Map

Now we move on to building the shade map. Remember, you need to build the shade map only once for each polygon, unless the lights change or a polygon moves. In the renderer, you'll keep the shade map static, so you don't ever have to recalculate it. The code for building a shade map is in Listing 8.9, in the `ShadedSurface` class. The `ShadedSurface` class is a subclass of `Texture` that contains a source texture, the surface data, and a shade map.

Listing 8.9   Building the Shade Map in ShadedSurface.java

```
public static final int SURFACE_BORDER_SIZE = 1;
public static final int SHADE_RES_BITS = 4;
public static final int SHADE_RES = 1 << SHADE_RES_BITS;
```

continues

Listing 8.9 Building the Shade Map in ShadedSurface.java *continued*

```java
public static final int SHADE_RES_MASK = SHADE_RES - 1;
public static final int SHADE_RES_SQ = SHADE_RES*SHADE_RES;
public static final int SHADE_RES_SQ_BITS = SHADE_RES_BITS*2;

...

/**
    Builds the shade map for this surface from the specified
    list of point lights and the ambient light intensity.
*/
public void buildShadeMap(List pointLights,
    float ambientLightIntensity)
{

    Vector3D surfaceNormal = surfaceBounds.getNormal();

    int polyWidth = (int)surfaceBounds.getWidth() -
        SURFACE_BORDER_SIZE*2;
    int polyHeight = (int)surfaceBounds.getHeight() -
        SURFACE_BORDER_SIZE*2;
    // assume SURFACE_BORDER_SIZE is <= SHADE_RES
    shadeMapWidth = polyWidth / SHADE_RES + 4;
    shadeMapHeight = polyHeight / SHADE_RES + 4;
    shadeMap = new byte[shadeMapWidth * shadeMapHeight];

    // calculate the shade map origin
    Vector3D origin = new Vector3D(surfaceBounds.getOrigin());
    Vector3D du = new Vector3D(surfaceBounds.getDirectionU());
    Vector3D dv = new Vector3D(surfaceBounds.getDirectionV());
    du.multiply(SHADE_RES - SURFACE_BORDER_SIZE);
    dv.multiply(SHADE_RES - SURFACE_BORDER_SIZE);
    origin.subtract(du);
    origin.subtract(dv);

    // calculate the shade for each sample point.
    Vector3D point = new Vector3D();
    du.setTo(surfaceBounds.getDirectionU());
```

```
        dv.setTo(surfaceBounds.getDirectionV());
        du.multiply(SHADE_RES);
        dv.multiply(SHADE_RES);
        for (int v=0; v<shadeMapHeight; v++) {
            point.setTo(origin);
            for (int u=0; u<shadeMapWidth; u++) {
                shadeMap[u + v * shadeMapWidth] =
                    calcShade(surfaceNormal, point,
                    pointLights, ambientLightIntensity);
                point.add(du);
            }
            origin.add(dv);
        }
    }



    /**
        Determine the shade of a point on the polygon.
        This computes the Lambertian reflection for a point on
        the plane. Each point light has an intensity and a
        distance falloff value, but no specular reflection or
        shadows from other polygons are computed. The value
        returned is from 0 to ShadedTexture.MAX_LEVEL.
    */
    protected byte calcShade(Vector3D normal, Vector3D point,
        List pointLights, float ambientLightIntensity)
    {
        float intensity = 0;
        Vector3D directionToLight = new Vector3D();

        for (int i=0; i<pointLights.size(); i++) {
            PointLight3D light = (PointLight3D)pointLights.get(i);
            directionToLight.setTo(light);
            directionToLight.subtract(point);

            float distance = directionToLight.length();
            directionToLight.normalize();
            float lightIntensity = light.getIntensity(distance)
```

continues

Listing 8.9   Building the Shade Map in ShadedSurface.java   *continued*

```
                  * directionToLight.getDotProduct(normal);
        lightIntensity = Math.min(lightIntensity, 1);
        lightIntensity = Math.max(lightIntensity, 0);
        intensity += lightIntensity;
    }

    intensity = Math.min(intensity, 1);
    intensity = Math.max(intensity, 0);

    intensity+=ambientLightIntensity;

    intensity = Math.min(intensity, 1);
    intensity = Math.max(intensity, 0);
    int level = Math.round(intensity*ShadedTexture.MAX_LEVEL);
    return (byte)level;
}
```

This code is fairly straightforward. The `buildShadeMap()` method builds a shade map for a surface, and the `calcShade()` method calculates the light intensity value for a point on the shade map.

In the renderer, you create all the shade maps before the game starts, but another idea is to store the shade maps in a file and load the shade maps from this file. This way, the shade maps don't have to be recalculated at startup.

Building the Surface

Next, we move on to building the surface, shown in Listing 8.10. This involves two separate methods: one to interpolate between values in the shade map, and another to actually draw the texture with the correct shade onto the surface.

Listing 8.10   Building the Surface in ShadedSurface.java

```
/**
    Builds the surface. First, this method calls
    retrieveSurface() to see if the surface needs to be
    rebuilt. If not, the surface is built by tiling the
    source texture and apply the shade map.
```

```
*/
public void buildSurface() {

    if (retrieveSurface()) {
        return;
    }

    int width = (int)surfaceBounds.getWidth();
    int height = (int)surfaceBounds.getHeight();

    // create a new surface (buffer)
    newSurface(width, height);

    // builds the surface.
    // assume surface bounds and texture bounds are aligned
    // (possibly with different origins)
    Vector3D origin = sourceTextureBounds.getOrigin();
    Vector3D directionU = sourceTextureBounds.getDirectionU();
    Vector3D directionV = sourceTextureBounds.getDirectionV();

    Vector3D d = new Vector3D(surfaceBounds.getOrigin());
    d.subtract(origin);
    int startU = (int)((d.getDotProduct(directionU) -
        SURFACE_BORDER_SIZE));
    int startV = (int)((d.getDotProduct(directionV) -
        SURFACE_BORDER_SIZE));
    int offset = 0;
    int shadeMapOffsetU = SHADE_RES - SURFACE_BORDER_SIZE -
        startU;
    int shadeMapOffsetV = SHADE_RES - SURFACE_BORDER_SIZE -
        startV;

    for (int v=startV; v<startV + height; v++) {
        sourceTexture.setCurrRow(v);
        int u = startU;
        int amount = SURFACE_BORDER_SIZE;
        while (u < startU + width) {
            getInterpolatedShade(u + shadeMapOffsetU,
```

continues

Listing 8.10   Building the Surface in ShadedSurface.java   *continued*

```
                    v + shadeMapOffsetV);

            // keep drawing until we need to recalculate
            // the interpolated shade. (every SHADE_RES pixels)
            int endU = Math.min(startU + width, u + amount);
            while (u < endU) {
                buffer[offset++] =
                    sourceTexture.getColorCurrRow(u,
                        shadeValue >> SHADE_RES_SQ_BITS);
                shadeValue+=shadeValueInc;
                u++;
            }
            amount = SHADE_RES;
        }
    }
}


/**
    Gets the shade (from the shade map) for the specified
    (u,v) location. The u and v values should be
    left-shifted by SHADE_RES_BITS, and the extra bits are
    used to interpolate between values. For an interpolation
    example, a location halfway between shade values 1 and 3
    would return 2.
*/
public int getInterpolatedShade(int u, int v) {

    int fracU = u & SHADE_RES_MASK;
    int fracV = v & SHADE_RES_MASK;

    int offset = (u >> SHADE_RES_BITS) +
        ((v >> SHADE_RES_BITS) * shadeMapWidth);

    int shade00 = (SHADE_RES-fracV) * shadeMap[offset];
    int shade01 = fracV * shadeMap[offset + shadeMapWidth];
    int shade10 = (SHADE_RES-fracV) * shadeMap[offset + 1];
```

```
    int shade11 = fracV * shadeMap[offset + shadeMapWidth + 1];

    shadeValue = SHADE_RES_SQ/2 +
        (SHADE_RES-fracU) * shade00 +
        (SHADE_RES-fracU) * shade01 +
        fracU * shade10 +
        fracU * shade11;

    // the value to increment as u increments
    shadeValueInc = -shade00 - shade01 + shade10 + shade11;

    return shadeValue >> SHADE_RES_SQ_BITS;
}



/**
    Gets the shade (from the built shade map) for the
    specified (u,v) location.
*/
public int getShade(int u, int v) {
    return shadeMap[u + v * shadeMapWidth];
}
```

Ideally, building surfaces needs to be fast because you're going to be building surfaces on the fly within the game. So, there's no optimizations applied to the buildSurface() method.

For example, we've added a couple methods to the ShadedTexture class called setCurrRow() and getColorCurrRow(). Because you are building the surface one row at a time, you can use these methods instead of the getColor() method so the row offset doesn't have to be recalculated for every texel.

The getInterpolatedShade() method gets the shade value at the specified location. You don't need to call this method for every texel, either, because you're building each row in the surface horizontally. You can use the shadeValueInc value to increment shadeValue for every texel. This way, you need to get the correct interpolated shade value only every 16 texels, similarly to how you optimized texture mapping.

Finally, Listing 8.11 shows the code for actually creating a ShadedSurface.

Listing 8.11   Creating a ShadedSurface Instance in ShadedSurface.java

```
/**
    Creates a ShadedSurface for the specified polygon. The
    shade map is created from the specified list of point
    lights and ambient light intensity.
*/
public static void createShadedSurface(
    TexturedPolygon3D poly, ShadedTexture texture,
    Rectangle3D textureBounds,
    List lights, float ambientLightIntensity)
{

    // create the surface bounds
    poly.setTexture(texture, textureBounds);
    Rectangle3D surfaceBounds = poly.calcBoundingRectangle();

    // give the surfaceBounds a border to correct for
    // slight errors when texture mapping
    Vector3D du = new Vector3D(surfaceBounds.getDirectionU());
    Vector3D dv = new Vector3D(surfaceBounds.getDirectionV());
    du.multiply(SURFACE_BORDER_SIZE);
    dv.multiply(SURFACE_BORDER_SIZE);
    surfaceBounds.getOrigin().subtract(du);
    surfaceBounds.getOrigin().subtract(dv);
    int width = (int)Math.ceil(surfaceBounds.getWidth() +
        SURFACE_BORDER_SIZE*2);
    int height = (int)Math.ceil(surfaceBounds.getHeight() +
        SURFACE_BORDER_SIZE*2);
    surfaceBounds.setWidth(width);
    surfaceBounds.setHeight(height);

    // create the shaded surface texture
    ShadedSurface surface = new ShadedSurface(width, height);
    surface.setTexture(texture, textureBounds);
    surface.setSurfaceBounds(surfaceBounds);
```

```
    // create the surface's shade map
    surface.buildShadeMap(lights, ambientLightIntensity);

    // set the polygon's surface
    poly.setTexture(surface, surfaceBounds);
}
```

Caching Surfaces

Keep in mind that surfaces take up a lot of memory, so precreating a surface for every polygon in a game might not be feasible. Instead, you have to create a surface on the fly, and only for the polygons that are visible.

Because building a surface is expensive, it's not a great idea to create every surface for every frame. Instead, the polygon renderer caches surfaces in a "visible" list. Only those surfaces that appear in the current frame are kept in the list, and the others are removed from memory to make room for more surfaces.

This works for a lot of conditions, but you're probably thinking of cases in which a polygon appears often but is not necessarily in every frame. For example, if the player is turning quickly left and right, getting a look at everything around, a surface could appear and reappear, being re-created every time it appears.

In situations like these, the garbage collector probably never even got a chance to throw away the surface memory in the first place. Wouldn't it be great if, instead of rebuilding a surface, you just asked the garbage collector to give it back to you if it wasn't already garbage-collected? Well, you can. This is accomplished using soft references.

A SoftReference object enables you to reference an object softly, as opposed to referencing it using a normal, strong reference. If only a soft reference to an object exists (that is, an object is *softly reachable*), the garbage collector has the option to clean it up. Usually, the garbage collector cleans up other objects before it cleans up softly reachable ones. Also, all softly reachable objects are cleaned before the VM throws an OutOfMemoryException.

In the ShadedSurface class, you create a new SoftReference to the surface's buffer like this:

```
/**
    Creates a new surface and add a SoftReference to it.
*/
protected void newSurface(int width, int height) {
    buffer = new short[width*height]
    bufferReference = new SoftReference(buffer);
}
```

Later, if the polygon renderer determines that the surface is no longer visible, the strong reference is removed:

```
/**
    Clears this surface, allowing the garbage collector to
    remove it from memory if needed.
*/
public void clearSurface() {
    buffer = null;
}
```

At this point, the buffer array is softly reachable, so the garbage collector has the option of removing it permanently from memory.

Later, if you want the surface back, first you can test whether it's retrievable from the garbage collector. If so, SoftReference's get() method returns the object, which you then assign back to a strong reference.

```
/**
    If the buffer has been previously built and cleared but
    not yet removed from memory by the garbage collector,
    then this method attempts to retrieve it. Returns true if
    successful.
*/
public boolean retrieveSurface() {
    if (buffer == null) {
        buffer = (short[])bufferReference.get();
```

```
        }
        return !(buffer == null);
}
```

If the object was already garbage-collected, the `get()` method returns null and you need to rebuild the surface.

So basically, you've implemented the equivalent of digging a surface out of the trashcan.

Sun recommends that garbage collectors don't throw away recently used or recently created softly reachable objects, but it's not a requirement of the garbage collectors. You might need to implement another level of caching yourself, but using soft references is a good idea nonetheless.

That's it for shaded surfaces. For good measure, the rest of the `ShadedSurface` class is in Listing 8.12.

Listing 8.12   Remaining Methods of ShadedSurface.java

```
package com.brackeen.javagamebook.graphics3D.texture;

import java.lang.ref.SoftReference;
import java.util.List;
import com.brackeen.javagamebook.math3D.*;

/**
    A ShadedSurface is a preshaded Texture that maps onto a
    polygon.
*/
public final class ShadedSurface extends Texture {

    public static final int SURFACE_BORDER_SIZE = 1;

    public static final int SHADE_RES_BITS = 4;
    public static final int SHADE_RES = 1 << SHADE_RES_BITS;
    public static final int SHADE_RES_MASK = SHADE_RES - 1;
    public static final int SHADE_RES_SQ = SHADE_RES*SHADE_RES;
    public static final int SHADE_RES_SQ_BITS = SHADE_RES_BITS*2;
```

continues

Listing 8.12 Remaining Methods of ShadedSurface.java *continued*

```java
private short[] buffer;
private SoftReference bufferReference;
private boolean dirty;
private ShadedTexture sourceTexture;
private Rectangle3D sourceTextureBounds;
private Rectangle3D surfaceBounds;
private byte[] shadeMap;
private int shadeMapWidth;
private int shadeMapHeight;

// for incrementally calculating shade values
private int shadeValue;
private int shadeValueInc;

/**
    Creates a ShadedSurface with the specified width and
    height.
*/
public ShadedSurface(int width, int height) {
    this(null, width, height);
}


/**
    Creates a ShadedSurface with the specified buffer,
    width, and height.
*/
public ShadedSurface(short[] buffer, int width, int height) {
    super(width, height);
    this.buffer = buffer;
    bufferReference = new SoftReference(buffer);
    sourceTextureBounds = new Rectangle3D();
    dirty = true;
}


/**
    Gets the 16-bit color of the pixel at location (x,y) in
```

```
    the bitmap. The x and y values are assumed to be within
    the bounds of the surface; otherwise an
    ArrayIndexOutOfBoundsException occurs.
*/
public short getColor(int x, int y) {
    return buffer[x + y * width];
}



/**
    Gets the 16-bit color of the pixel at location (x,y) in
    the bitmap. The x and y values are checked to be within
    the bounds of the surface, and if not, the pixel on the
    edge of the texture is returned.
*/
public short getColorChecked(int x, int y) {
    if (x < 0) {
        x = 0;
    }
    else if (x >= width) {
        x = width-1;
    }
    if (y < 0) {
        y = 0;
    }
    else if (y >= height) {
        y = height-1;
    }
    return getColor(x,y);
}



/**
    Marks whether this surface is dirty. Surfaces marked as
    dirty may be cleared externally.
*/
public void setDirty(boolean dirty) {
    this.dirty = dirty;
```

continues

Listing 8.12 Remaining Methods of ShadedSurface.java *continued*

```java
    }


    /**
        Checks whether this surface is dirty. Surfaces marked as
        dirty may be cleared externally.
    */
    public boolean isDirty() {
        return dirty;
    }


    /**
        Sets the source texture for this ShadedSurface.
    */
    public void setTexture(ShadedTexture texture) {
        this.sourceTexture = texture;
        sourceTextureBounds.setWidth(texture.getWidth());
        sourceTextureBounds.setHeight(texture.getHeight());
    }


    /**
        Sets the source texture and source bounds for this
        ShadedSurface.
    */
    public void setTexture(ShadedTexture texture,
        Rectangle3D bounds)
    {
        setTexture(texture);
        sourceTextureBounds.setTo(bounds);
    }


    /**
        Sets the surface bounds for this ShadedSurface.
    */
    public void setSurfaceBounds(Rectangle3D surfaceBounds) {
```

```
        this.surfaceBounds = surfaceBounds;
    }



    /**
        Gets the surface bounds for this ShadedSurface.
    */
    public Rectangle3D getSurfaceBounds() {
        return surfaceBounds;
    }

}
```

We've talked about nearly everything in the `ShadedSurface` class except the dirty flag. The dirty flag is irrelevant to the `ShadedSurface` itself—`ShadedSurface` doesn't care whether the flag is dirty. The dirty flag can be used externally to mark whether the surface data should be cleared. This idea is shown in the `ShadedSurfacePolygonRenderer` in Listing 8.13. It's not much different from any other renderer, except that it keeps a list of every surface that has been built. As discussed earlier, you build only the visible surfaces. If a surface is not visible (it is marked as dirty), the surface data is cleared and the surface is removed from the list.

Listing 8.13   ShadedSurfacePolygonRenderer.java

```
package com.brackeen.javagamebook.graphics3D;

import java.awt.*;
import java.awt.image.*;
import java.util.List;
import java.util.LinkedList;
import java.util.Iterator;

import com.brackeen.javagamebook.math3D.*;
import com.brackeen.javagamebook.graphics3D.texture.*;

/**
    The ShadedSurfacePolygonRenderer is a PolygonRenderer that
    renders polygons with ShadedSurfaces. It keeps track of
```

continues

Listing 8.13   ShadedSurfacePolygonRenderer.java   *continued*

```java
    built surfaces and clears any surfaces that weren't used
    in the last rendered frame, to save memory.
*/
public class ShadedSurfacePolygonRenderer
    extends FastTexturedPolygonRenderer
{

    private List builtSurfaces = new LinkedList();

    public ShadedSurfacePolygonRenderer(Transform3D camera,
        ViewWindow viewWindow)
    {
        this(camera, viewWindow, true);
    }

    public ShadedSurfacePolygonRenderer(Transform3D camera,
        ViewWindow viewWindow, boolean eraseView)
    {
        super(camera, viewWindow, eraseView);
    }

    public void endFrame(Graphics2D g) {
        super.endFrame(g);

        // clear all built surfaces that weren't used this frame.
        Iterator i = builtSurfaces.iterator();
        while (i.hasNext()) {
            ShadedSurface surface = (ShadedSurface)i.next();
            if (surface.isDirty()) {
                surface.clearSurface();
                i.remove();
            }
            else {
                surface.setDirty(true);
            }
        }
    }
}
```

```java
protected void drawCurrentPolygon(Graphics2D g) {
    buildSurface();
    super.drawCurrentPolygon(g);
}



/**
    Builds the surface of the polygon if it has a
    ShadedSurface that is cleared.
*/
protected void buildSurface() {
    // build surface, if needed
    if (sourcePolygon instanceof TexturedPolygon3D) {
        Texture texture =
            ((TexturedPolygon3D)sourcePolygon).getTexture();
        if (texture instanceof ShadedSurface) {
            ShadedSurface surface =
                (ShadedSurface)texture;
            if (surface.isCleared()) {
                surface.buildSurface();
                builtSurfaces.add(surface);
            }
            surface.setDirty(false);
        }
    }
}

}
```

The `ShadedSurfacePolygonRenderer` calls the `buildSurface()` method for every polygon. If the surface is cleared, it is built (or retrieved from the garbage collector) and added to the list of built surfaces.

Shaded Surface Demo

Now you'll create a demo using the shaded surfaces. The `ShadingTest2` class is the same as the `TextureMapTest2`, except it creates a few `PointLight3Ds` and uses the `ShadedSurfacePolygonRenderer`. A screenshot from `ShadingTest2` is shown in Figure 8.16.

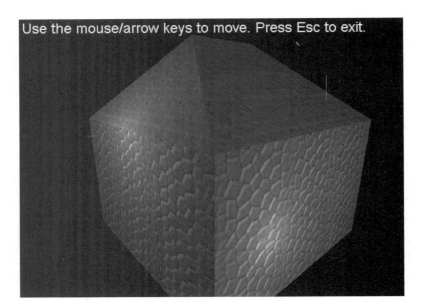

Figure 8.16 `ShadingTest2` demonstrates shaded surfaces.

As usual, you can walk around the house and see it from all sides. The house has low ambient light intensity and a couple of strong point lights to show off some of the realistic, dramatic lighting you can create.

Additional Concepts

In this section, we go through a few ideas that could extend the texture mapping and lighting you created in this chapter.

We've really just scratched the surface with, well, surfaces. With the shaded surfaces, you applied shading only to the texture, but you could also do all sorts of other effects, including effects created on the fly. For example, you could apply a "burn" effect if the player uses a flame thrower on the wall, or add an occasional surface "crack" to break up texture monotony, or show robot blast marks on the floor when you destroy a robot.

Depth Cueing

Another lighting trick is to have objects farther away appear darker than those close up so the amount of light you see diminishes with distance. This technique, called *depth cueing*, was popularized by games such as *Doom* and was a common effect on the Nintendo 64. In games such as *Doom*, the textures fade to black with distance, but there's really no reason to restrict the depth cueing to black. Several games for Nintendo 64 created a "fog" effect, with everything fading to a grayish hue.

Fake Shadows

In the next chapter, "3D Objects," you'll create individual objects that can roam around your 3D world. Sometimes, however, it's difficult to tell where an object is in relation to the floor, and an object can sometimes look like it is floating. To fix this visual quirk, a common technique is to draw a circular, fake shadow underneath the object. It's a "fake" shadow because it does not represent the object's shape (you won't see a shade for a robot's extended arm, for example), but it's a quick way to give a visual cue on the location of the objects.

MIP Mapping

With your surfaces, it's a big of an overkill to create a large surface for a polygon that is very far away. Really, it would make more sense if polygons that are far away from the camera have surfaces that are smaller sizes.

This technique is called *MIP mapping*. For the curious, *MIP* is an acronym for *Multum in Parvum*, which is Latin for "many in one." Far polygons have smaller surfaces, and as the surface gets closer to the camera, larger surfaces are created, if necessary. This technique can save a lot of memory and makes surfaces farther from the camera look smoother.

Bilinear Interpolation

When you run the demos in this chapter, you'll notice that when you're very close to a texture, the texels look blocky. Likewise, when you're far from a texture, slight artifacts creep up because not every texel in the surface is drawn to the screen. This is especially noticeable if the textures have sharp lines.

Bilinear interpolation eases both of these issues. Just as you interpolated between adjacent different values in the shade map, you can interpolate between adjacent texels in the texture, smoothing it out so that close-up textures don't look as blocky and so that textures farther away don't have as many artifacts.

I created the textures in this book to have no or very few sharp lines, so this effect of seeing artifacts when you're far away from a texture is minimized, even though bilinear interpolation would still look nicer. If you use something like the "test pattern" texture, you'll notice all sorts of strange-looking artifacts. Bilinear interpolation would greatly help to eliminate those artifacts.

Trilinear Interpolation

Trilinear interpolation is basically the combination of bilinear interpolation and MIP mapping. Instead of just interpolating between adjacent texels in a texture, this technique interpolates between adjacent MIP maps (one MIP map farther away from the camera and one MIP map closer). This eliminates any noticeable change when you move from one MIP map to another because two MIP maps are used and interpolated between.

Normal Maps and Depth Maps

Some of the textures used in this chapter had a bit of "fake" lighting built right into the texture to give the textures a bit of depth, like rocks jutting out with light and shadow around the rock edges.

Of course, this fake lighting isn't accurate because it doesn't take into consideration the lighting of the surrounding environment. The "fake" lighting could assume there is a light source in the upper-left corner, but in the environment, the light source could come from a different direction.

Some 3D accelerator cards can use normal maps and depth maps to create textures that respect the surrounding lighting.

Instead of a texture map, you'll have three maps: a color map (with no lighting in it), a depth map (to specify the "depth" of each pixel in the color map), and a normal map (to specify the normal vector of each pixel in the color map). Using the color, height, and normal vector, the correct lighting for each pixel can be calculated, resulting in a texture that respects the lighting of the surrounding environment.

Even though this is an expensive process, some 3D accelerated cards can combine these three maps quickly in real time.

Other Types of Lights

One last thing to mention is light sources. The only light source you used here was point lights that radiate in all directions equally, like the sun. To extend the lighting architecture, it would be great to add colored lights, cone lights (lights that radiate in a cone rather than in all directions), or an area light, which might come from a rectangular source and radiate out like a pyramid.

Also, although you can't see it in this demo, the lights can actually pass though a polygon to hit another polygon on the other side. It would be great to eliminate this by making sure that any light ray that hits a surface doesn't hit any other surface first.

Summary

In this chapter, we covered a lot of concepts, including fast texture mapping, diffuse lighting, and lighting using a shade map. Along the way, we also talked about heavy optimization techniques, efficient storage of shaded textures, and caching surfaces using soft references. We also glanced over some additional ideas on how to make the renderers created even better by adding things such as advanced lighting, MIP mapping, and bilinear interpolation.

In the next chapter we focus on animating 3D game objects, and we finally extend the renderer to be able to work with objects other than convex polyhedrons by using a z-buffer.

Chapter 9

3D Objects

In a typical game, the player will find objects to bump into, grab, jump over, jump on, eat, catch, dodge, nudge, fight with, throw, shoot, or whatever else you can think of.

In this chapter, you'll create a 3D object-animation system to move and rotate objects in the world. To draw the 3D objects, you'll use z-buffering to draw polygons in the correct z-order. You'll also create a parser to read 3D objects from OBJ files so you don't have to define lots of polygons in Java code. Finally, you'll put everything together by creating a few simple game objects and a game object manager. Using these techniques takes you a step closer to creating a real 3D game that gives the player some objects to interact with.

Hidden Surface Removal

The problem with drawing polygons is that you need to draw them in such a way that you don't see polygons that are hidden or are partially obscured by other polygons. This problem is generally solved with a correct hidden surface–removal algorithm or a combination of several hidden surface–removal algorithms.

In previous chapters, you used only back-face removal and clipping as your hidden surface–removal algorithms. With back-face removal, you can draw only convex polyhedrons. In this section, we present a few other hidden surface–removal techniques that enable you to draw polygons that form any shape.

Keep in mind that different hidden surface–removal algorithms work better for different situations. What works for a static world might not work for a moving 3D object, for example. In this chapter, we chose an algorithm that works better for 3D objects that can move and rotate around the world.

Painter's Algorithm

A basic hidden surface–removal algorithm is the *painter's algorithm*. When painting on a canvas, a painter first draws the background, then objects closer to the foreground, and so on until the foremost object is painted. With this technique, anything drawn in the foreground is painted over what is already on the canvas. For 3D graphics, the idea translates to drawing polygons in a back-to-front order.

To implement the painter's algorithm, all the polygons are first sorted from back to front, relative to the camera. The difficulty here is getting a correct sorting algorithm. You could just sort by the midpoint of each polygon, but this doesn't work in all cases. Consider the two projected polygons in Figure 9.1, for example.

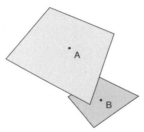

Figure 9.1   Looking at these two projected polygons, the painter's algorithm says that polygon B should be drawn first because it's behind polygon A.

With the two projected polygons in Figure 9.1, you can easily tell that polygon A is in front of polygon B, so polygon B should be drawn first. However, a problem arises when measuring the distance to the camera. By using the midpoints of the polygons, the midpoint of polygon A could actually be behind the midpoint of polygon B, in which case polygon A would be drawn first. Obviously, this is the incorrect behavior.

Another problem with the painter's algorithm is that drawing back to front can involve a lot of overdraw (drawing each pixel more than once), so it's not the ideal solution for drawing an entire scene.

Reverse Painter's Algorithm

The problem of overdraw with the painter's algorithm can be fixed with the *reverse painter's algorithm*. The reverse algorithm draws polygons from front to back rather than back to front. In this algorithm, you don't draw any pixel that's already been drawn, so you can use this algorithm without any overdraw. You just continue drawing polygons until the entire view window is filled. However, the reverse painter's algorithm still needs a polygon-sorting technique that is correct 100% of the time. Also, it works only if polygons completely surround the camera (as with enclosed areas) so that they can fill the view.

Z-Buffer

Z-buffering, also called *depth buffering*, doesn't have the problems of the painter's algorithm and is fairly easy to implement. With z-buffering, the depth of each pixel in the polygon is recorded in a buffer the same size as the view window. A pixel is drawn only if the depth of that pixel is closer than the depth currently in that location in the z-buffer. This results in a pixel-perfect 3D scene, no matter what order the polygons are drawn. The idea is shown in Figure 9.2.

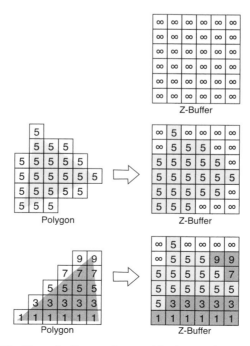

Figure 9.2 The z-buffer can be used to draw polygons correctly.
The numbers represent the depth of each pixel in the polygons.

In the example in Figure 9.2, the z-buffer starts off empty, with the depth of each pixel set to infinity. Every pixel of the first polygon is closer than the values in the z-buffer, so every pixel is drawn and the z-buffer is set to the polygon's depth values. The second polygon actually intersects the first, so the part of the second polygon behind the first polygon isn't drawn.

Z-buffering does have the drawback of requiring the extra memory for the buffer. With a 16-bit depth, a 1,024×768 screen would require 1.5MB of memory. That's not bad compared to the amount of memory most computers have today.

The major drawback is the extra time it takes to draw polygons. Checking the z-buffer for every pixel you draw gives you a bit of an overhead. This is especially noticeable if z-buffering is used for every pixel on the screen. In my tests with the examples in this book, it's two to three times slower than plain texture mapping if every pixel on the screen is drawn.

However, because 3D objects usually take up only small amounts of visual screen space, the overhead won't be as bad as using z-buffering for the entire world.

Z-Buffer Using 1/z

One problem with z-buffering is that the z-buffer has the same accuracy no matter how far away the polygon is from the camera. For example, if your z-buffer has 1-unit (or 1-texel) accuracy, overlapping polygons close to the camera won't merge very well—part of a polygon might have a depth of 10.7, not 11. You really need something more granular for polygons close to the camera. You can fix this in a couple ways:

➤ Use 32-bit floats (or 32-bit fixed points) for z-buffer depth. This is more accurate but takes up twice the memory and can be slower.

➤ Use the inverse of the depth, or 1/z.

When using z-buffering, you don't really need the exact depth value for every pixel in a polygon. All you really need is to compare depths between pixels correctly, and using 1/z still lets you do that. Also, 1/z is linear in screen space, as shown with the example polygon in Figure 9.3. This gives you a couple advantages:

➤ Using 1/z gives you high depth precision for objects close to the camera, where you need it most.

➤ Because 1/z changes linearly with screen space, as opposed to the actual z-depth, it's easy to set the depth for a horizontal scan—easier than texture mapping (which is not linear with screen space). You don't have to interpolate every 16 pixels like you did with texture mapping, so it's fast and accurate.

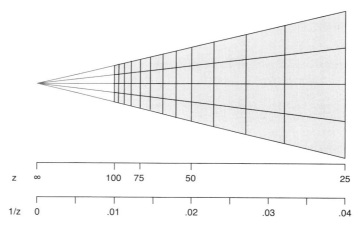

Figure 9.3   1/z is linear in screen space.

Z-buffering using 1/z is the technique used for the 3D objects in this book. Because you're using 16-bit integer values for the depth, you'll want to keep the depth between 0 and Short.MAX_VALUE. Assume that $z \geq 1$, and use something like this:

```
Short.MAX_VALUE / z
```

Using this formula means that the greater the value is, the closer the depth is; 0 is infinite depth.

Now you'll implement a z-buffer. The ZBuffer class, shown in Listing 9.1, creates a basic 16-bit z-buffer designed to work with 1/z values.

Listing 9.1 ZBuffer.java

```java
package com.brackeen.javagamebook.graphics3D;

/**
    The ZBuffer class implements a z-buffer, or depth-buffer,
    that records the depth of every pixel in a 3D view window.
    The value recorded for each pixel is the inverse of the
    depth (1/z), so there is higher precision for close objects
    and a lower precision for far-away objects (where high
    depth precision is not as visually important).
*/
public class ZBuffer {

    private short[] depthBuffer;
    private int width;
    private int height;

    /**
        Creates a new z-buffer with the specified width and height.
    */
    public ZBuffer(int width, int height) {
        depthBuffer = new short[width*height];
        this.width = width;
        this.height = height;
        clear();
    }


    /**
        Gets the width of this z-buffer.
    */
    public int getWidth() {
        return width;
    }


    /**
```

```
        Gets the height of this z-buffer.
*/
public int getHeight() {
    return height;
}



/**
    Clears the z-buffer. All depth values are set to 0.
*/
public void clear() {
    for (int i=0; i<depthBuffer.length; i++) {
        depthBuffer[i] = 0;
    }
}



/**
    Sets the depth of the pixel at specified offset,
    overwriting its current depth.
*/
public void setDepth(int offset, short depth) {
    depthBuffer[offset] = depth;
}



/**
    Checks the depth at the specified offset, and if the
    specified depth is lower (is greater than or equal to the
    current depth at the specified offset), then the depth is
    set and this method returns true. Otherwise, no action
    occurs and this method returns false.
*/
public boolean checkDepth(int offset, short depth) {
    if (depth >= depthBuffer[offset]) {
        depthBuffer[offset] = depth;
        return true;
    }
```

continues

Listing 9.1 ZBuffer.java *continued*

```
        else {
            return false;
        }
    }
}


}
```

Note that the ZBuffer class has two methods to manipulate the ZBuffer at a particular offset: setDepth() and checkDepth(). The setDepth() method just sets the depth at the specified offset in the z-buffer, erasing whatever value is already there. The checkDepth() method sets the depth only if the value is greater than the current depth at that offset; it returns true if this is the case, and false otherwise.

Finally, the clear() method sets every value in the z-buffer to 0, the equivalent of infinite depth. In this case, you need to call clear() every frame.

Calculating the Z-Depth

Next, you'll get the equations for calculating the depth for every point in the polygon.

Actually, you already have the equation. As you might recall from Chapter 8, "Texture Mapping and Lighting," you needed P_z, the depth of the polygon at a specific point on the view window, W, to figure out how to texture-map:

P_z = d(U×V•O)/(U×V•W)

Here, d is the distance from the camera to the view window, U and V are the texture x and y directions, and O is the texture origin (or any point on the polygon's plane). So, you're all set. (Aren't you glad you derived the equations for texture mapping in that chapter?) The inverse of this equation becomes this:

1/z = (U×V•W)/(d(U×V•O))

Most of this you can calculate for the entire polygon rather than for every pixel:

```
float w = SCALE * MIN_DISTANCE * Short.MAX_VALUE /
    (viewWindow.getDistance() *
    c.getDotProduct(textureBounds.getOrigin()));
```

Remember that the vector C is set to U×V, so you don't have to recalculate U×V.

In the equation, multiply the value by SCALE to get it ready to convert to fixed-point.

Also, multiply by MIN_DISTANCE, which is the minimum distance you want z-buffering to work. This value is set to 12. This gives a little more accuracy for objects drawn far away, but it makes objects drawn with a distance less than 12 have incorrect depths. This is okay because you'll never see objects closer than a distance of 12 when you implement collision detection in Chapter 11, "Collision Detection."

Finally, when you are texture mapping, before you texture map a horizontal scan, calculate the depth of the first pixel (depth) and the change in depth (dDepth):

```
float z = c.getDotProduct(viewPos);
float dz = c.x;
...
int depth = (int)(w*z);
int dDepth = (int)(w*dz);
```

Then, for every pixel in the scan, check the depth, set the pixel if the depth is set, and increment the depth:

```
...
if (zBuffer.checkDepth(offset, (short)(depth >> SCALE_BITS))) {
    doubleBufferData[offset] =
        texture.getColor(tx >> SCALE_BITS, ty >> SCALE_BITS);
}
depth+=dDepth;
...
```

That's it for drawing with the z-buffer. We sum up the process of calculating the depth for every pixel in a polygon in the ZBufferedRenderer class, which is a subclass of ShadedSurfacePolygonRenderer. This class is just like its parent class, except that when it renders, it checks the depth for every pixel is draws. It also clears the z-buffer at the start of every frame (or creates a new one if the size of the view window changed):

```
public void startFrame(Graphics2D g) {
    super.startFrame(g);
    // initialize depth buffer
    if (zBuffer == null ||
        zBuffer.getWidth() != viewWindow.getWidth() ||
        zBuffer.getHeight() != viewWindow.getHeight())
    {
        zBuffer = new ZBuffer(
            viewWindow.getWidth(), viewWindow.getHeight());
    }
    else if (clearViewEveryFrame) {
        zBuffer.clear();
    }
}
```

That's it for z-buffering. Now we move on to actually taking advantage of it by creating 3D objects that move around the world.

3D Animation

In the first demo in Chapter 7, "3D Graphics," you created a simple tree that moved toward and away from the camera, rotating around the y-axis the entire time. In that demo, you didn't have camera movement yet; instead, you applied a transform to the polygons of tree.

You'll apply this same concept to move and rotate any 3D object in a game: Every 3D object gets its own transform. By "3D object," I mean a group of polygons that are related to each other—often called a *polygon mesh* or *polygon model*. This polygon group can move independently of the world. For example, all the polygons that make up a robot would belong to a 3D object, and they would share the same transform.

This technique involves keeping a 3D object in its own coordinate system that is different from the world coordinate system, as shown in Figure 9.4.

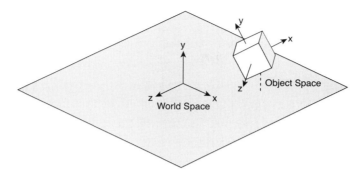

Figure 9.4   3D objects can have a different coordinate system than the world.

Instead of explicitly moving or rotating the polygons in a 3D object, the polygons are static and only the object's transform is changed. As mentioned in previous chapters, if you were to actually move and rotate a 3D object's polygons, over time floating-point errors would accumulate and you could end up with a distorted object. Instead, during the rendering process, copy each polygon to a scratch polygon and transform it by its object transform, just like you did to the tree from Chapter 7.

To accomplish independent movement in your 3D engine, just give each object its own Transform3D, the transform class from Chapter 7.

However, you really want an easy way to apply motion to an object, so extend the Transform3D class to add different types of motion.

Keep in mind that there are two types of motion: spatial motion (displacing the object) and angular motion (rotating the object in space). And there are three types of angular motion, one for each of the x-, y-, and z-axes.

Also, you want different objects to move and rotate at different speeds, and sometimes you want to tell an object to move or rotate for a certain period of time and then stop. For example, you might want to tell a robot to turn until facing a certain direction and then stop or move to be close to a player and then stop. With this in mind, let's go over some high-level goals to accomplish with object motion:

➤ Move an object to location (x,y,z) at speed s.

➤ Move an object in the direction (x,y,z) at speed s for the next t seconds, or forever.

➤ Rotate an object around an axis at speed s for the next t seconds, or forever.

➤ Rotate an object to face direction $3\pi/4$ radians at speed s.

➤ Stop all motion of an object.

All of the moving and rotating goals can be translated, at minimum, to "move at speed x for time t." At the end of the specified amount of time, the movement is stopped. (Optionally, some motion goals have no time limit, so you need to provide a way to keep that motion going forever.) Also, in addition to speed and amount of time, spatial movement requires a direction.

You can accomplish these goals in a subclass of `Transform3D` called `MovingTransform3D`. The bulk of this generic movement is in `MovingTransform3D`'s `Movement` inner class shown in Listing 9.2.

Listing 9.2   The `Movement` Inner Class of `MovingTransform3D`

```
/**
    The Movement class contains a speed and an amount of time
    to continue that speed.
*/
protected static class Movement {
    // change per millisecond
    float speed;
    long remainingTime;

    /**
        Sets this movement to the specified speed and time
        (in milliseconds).
    */
    public void set(float speed, long time) {
        this.speed = speed;
        this.remainingTime = time;
    }


    public boolean isStopped() {
        return (speed == 0) || (remainingTime == 0);
```

```
    }


    /**
        Gets the distance traveled in the specified amount of
        time in milliseconds.
    */
    public float getDistance(long elapsedTime) {
        if (remainingTime == 0) {
            return 0;
        }
        else if (remainingTime != FOREVER) {
            elapsedTime = Math.min(elapsedTime, remainingTime);
            remainingTime-=elapsedTime;
        }
        return speed * elapsedTime;
    }
}
```

The Movement inner class just keeps track of the speed and remaining time of a generic type of movement. Optionally, the remaining time can be FOREVER, in which case the movement never stops. For example, a projectile shot into the sky will never stop moving (unless you tell it to). The getDistance() method gets the distance traveled based on the specified amount of elapsed time (remember, distance = speed × time). Also in this method, remainingTime is decreased by elapsedTime until it reaches 0.

Here you keep track of the remaining time left in the movement rather than the absolute end time. If you keep track of the absolute end time, things that manipulate the flow of time, such as pausing the game or saving and reloading the game later, would cause the movement to be incorrect. For example, if at 7:58 p.m. you said "move forward until 8:00 p.m.," but the user paused the game from 7:59 p.m. until 8:01 p.m., when the user resumed the game, the movement would stop, which would be incorrect; the movement occurred for one minute when you really wanted the movement to occur for two minutes.

You'll use one instance of the Movement class here for spatial movement and three instances for angular movement (one for each axis). First, let's talk about and implement spatial movement.

Spatial Movement

Just like you did for sprites way back in Chapter 2, "2D Graphics and Animation," you'll give transforms a velocity to apply spatial movement. First define a couple fields in the `MovingTransform3D` class for the velocity of the transform:

```
// velocity (units per millisecond)
private Vector3D velocity;
private Movement velocityMovement;
```

Because the velocity vector is both a magnitude and a direction, you don't really need the speed field of the `Movement` class in this case. So, for velocity, the speed of the `Movement` is set to `1` as long as the velocity magnitude isn't `0`. Otherwise, the speed is set to `0`.

Now let's create a few methods to explicitly set the velocity of the transform:

```
/**
    Sets the velocity to the specified vector.
*/
public void setVelocity(Vector3D v) {
    setVelocity(v, FOREVER);
}


/**
    Sets the velocity. The velocity is automatically set to
    zero after the specified amount of time has elapsed. If
    the specified time is FOREVER, then the velocity is never
    automatically set to zero.
*/
public void setVelocity(Vector3D v, long time) {
    if (velocity != v) {
        velocity.setTo(v);
    }
    if (v.x == 0 && v.y == 0 && v.z == 0) {
        velocityMovement.set(0, 0);
    }
    else {
```

```
        velocityMovement.set(1, time);
    }

}

/**
    Adds the specified velocity to the current velocity. If
    this MovingTransform3D is currently moving, its time
    remaining is not changed. Otherwise, the time remaining
    is set to FOREVER.
*/
public void addVelocity(Vector3D v) {
    if (isMoving()) {
        velocity.add(v);
    }
    else {
        setVelocity(v);
    }
}
/**
    Returns true if currently moving.
*/
public boolean isMoving() {
    return !velocityMovement.isStopped() &&
        !velocity.equals(0,0,0);
}
```

The setVelocity() methods set the velocity to be applied for a specific amount of time, or FOREVER, with the idea that the movement stops after the time is up. You can add to the velocity using the addVelocity() method (for example, if you want to add gravity to an already moving object). Finally, you can check whether the transform is moving with the isMoving() method.

Next you'll write a method to explicitly define where to move:

```
/**
    Sets the velocity to move to the following destination
    at the specified speed.
```

```
*/
public void moveTo(Vector3D destination, float speed) {
    temp.setTo(destination);
    temp.subtract(location);

    // calc the time needed to move
    float distance = temp.length();
    long time = (long)(distance / speed);

    // normalize the direction vector
    temp.divide(distance);
    temp.multiply(speed);

    setVelocity(temp, time);
}
```

The moveTo() method is really a convenience method that calculates the velocity (both magnitude and direction) and the amount of time to move to reach the goal location based on the specified speed. It uses a scratch vector, temp, and calls the setVelocity() method to set the velocity. This way you can just tell an object where to move without calculating the direction and amount of time.

Angular Movement

The *angular movement*, or *rotation*, is similar to the velocity, except that you don't need a velocity vector; you need just three Movement instances:

```
// angular velocity (radians per millisecond)
private Movement velocityAngleX;
private Movement velocityAngleY;
private Movement velocityAngleZ;
```

The angular movement is pretty much the same for each axis, so we just focus on the y-axis here. First, here are the basic methods to set the angular velocity and check whether the object is currently rotating around the y-axis:

```
/**
    Sets the angular speed of the y axis.
*/
```

```
public void setAngleVelocityY(float speed) {
    setAngleVelocityY(speed, FOREVER);
}



/**
    Sets the angular speed of the y axis over the specified
    time.
*/
public void setAngleVelocityY(float speed, long time) {
    velocityAngleY.set(speed, time);
}



/**
    Returns true if the y axis is currently turning.
*/
public boolean isTurningY() {
    return !velocityAngleY.isStopped();
}
```

When using the setAngleVelocityY() methods, a positive speed is equivalent to turning counterclockwise, and a negative speed is the same as turning clockwise.

The trickier part is telling the object which direction to face. Whenever you want an object to face a certain direction, you need to calculate which is faster: turning clockwise or turning counterclockwise.

A lot of the time, the solution is trivial, but not all the time. Take Figure 9.5, for example. In this figure, the start location is on one end of the scale near $-\pi$, and the end location is on the other end of the scale near π. When you look at these angles on the circle, it's easy to tell which direction to turn. But it's not as obvious when you look at the angles on a linear scale from $-\pi$ to π, as shown in the bottom of Figure 9.2. (Likewise, you don't want the object to turn a full circle if you tell it to turn from $-\pi$ to π.)

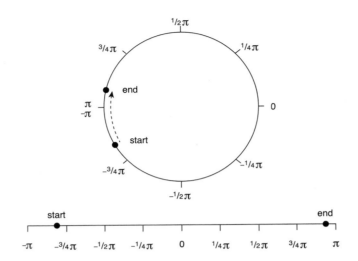

Figure 9.5 Finding the shortest angular distance between two angles.

To solve this, calculate both distances: the angular distance to the goal by turning clockwise, and the angular distance to the goal by turning counterclockwise. Whichever is shortest is the way to turn. This is shown here in the turnTo() method:

```
/**
    Turns the y axis to the specified angle with the specified
    speed.
*/
public void turnYTo(float angleDest, float speed) {
    turnTo(velocityAngleY, getAngleY(), angleDest, speed);
}



/**
    Turns the y axis to face the specified (x,z) vector
    direction with the specified speed.
*/
public void turnYTo(float x, float z, float angleOffset,
    float speed)
{
    turnYTo((float)Math.atan2(-z,x) + angleOffset, speed);
}
```

```
/**
    Turns the movement angle from the startAngle to the
    endAngle with the specified speed.
*/
protected void turnTo(Movement movement,
    float startAngle, float endAngle, float speed)
{
    startAngle = ensureAngleWithinBounds(startAngle);
    endAngle = ensureAngleWithinBounds(endAngle);
    if (startAngle == endAngle) {
        movement.set(0,0);
    }
    else {

        float distanceLeft;
        float distanceRight;
        float pi2 = (float)(2*Math.PI);

        if (startAngle < endAngle) {
            distanceLeft = startAngle - endAngle + pi2;
            distanceRight = endAngle - startAngle;
        }
        else {
            distanceLeft = startAngle - endAngle;
            distanceRight = endAngle - startAngle + pi2;
        }

        if (distanceLeft < distanceRight) {
            speed = -Math.abs(speed);
            movement.set(speed, (long)(distanceLeft / -speed));
        }
        else {
            speed = Math.abs(speed);
            movement.set(speed, (long)(distanceRight / speed));
        }
    }
}
```

```
/**
    Ensures the specified angle is with -pi and pi. Returns
    the angle, corrected if it is not within these bounds.
*/
protected float ensureAngleWithinBounds(float angle) {
    if (angle < -Math.PI || angle > Math.PI) {
        // transform range to (0 to 1)
        double newAngle = (angle + Math.PI) / (2*Math.PI);
        // validate range
        newAngle = newAngle - Math.floor(newAngle);
        // transform back to (-pi to pi) range
        newAngle = Math.PI * (newAngle * 2 - 1);
        return (float)newAngle;
    }
    return angle;
}
```

Because the turnTo() method requires that angles be between $-\pi$ and π, it calls the ensureAngleWithinBounds() method to translate the angle to be within this range, if necessary.

That's it for MovingTransform3D. The rest of the class is listed here in Listing 9.3.

Listing 9.3   The Rest of MovingTransform3D.java

```
package com.brackeen.javagamebook.math3D;

/**
    A MovingTransform3D is a Transform3D that has a location
    velocity and an angular rotation velocity for rotation around
    the x, y, and z axes.
*/
public class MovingTransform3D extends Transform3D {

    public static final int FOREVER = -1;

    // Vector3D used for calculations
    private static Vector3D temp = new Vector3D();
```

```java
// velocity (units per millisecond)
private Vector3D velocity;
private Movement velocityMovement;

// angular velocity (radians per millisecond)
private Movement velocityAngleX;
private Movement velocityAngleY;
private Movement velocityAngleZ;

/**
    Creates a new MovingTransform3D
*/
public MovingTransform3D() {
    init();
}



/**
    Creates a new MovingTransform3D, using the same values as
    the specified Transform3D.
*/
public MovingTransform3D(Transform3D v) {
    super(v);
    init();
}


protected void init() {
    velocity = new Vector3D(0,0,0);
    velocityMovement = new Movement();
    velocityAngleX = new Movement();
    velocityAngleY = new Movement();
    velocityAngleZ = new Movement();
}


public Object clone() {
    return new MovingTransform3D(this);
```

continues

Listing 9.3   The Rest of MovingTransform3D.java   *continued*

```
        }


    /**
        Updates this Transform3D based on the specified elapsed
        time. The location and angles are updated.
    */
    public void update(long elapsedTime) {
        float delta = velocityMovement.getDistance(elapsedTime);
        if (delta != 0) {
            temp.setTo(velocity);
            temp.multiply(delta);
            location.add(temp);
        }

        rotateAngle(
            velocityAngleX.getDistance(elapsedTime),
            velocityAngleY.getDistance(elapsedTime),
            velocityAngleZ.getDistance(elapsedTime));
    }


    /**
        Stops this Transform3D. Any moving velocities are set to
        zero.
    */
    public void stop() {
        velocity.setTo(0,0,0);
        velocityMovement.set(0,0);
        velocityAngleX.set(0,0);
        velocityAngleY.set(0,0);
        velocityAngleZ.set(0,0);
    }


    /**
        Gets the amount of time remaining for this movement.
```

```
    */
    public long getRemainingMoveTime() {
        if (!isMoving()) {
            return 0;
        }
        else {
            return velocityMovement.remainingTime;
        }
    }
}
```

Note that a MovingTransform3D's update() method should be called for every frame. This is the method that does all the work, updating the transform location and (x,y,z) angles.

Also, because the polygons are static, you need to apply the MovingTransform3D whenever the polygons are drawn. Next, you'll create a class to group related polygons and apply transforms to the polygons.

Polygon Groups

In this section, you'll implement a container for groups of polygons, where every polygon group has its own transform.

So far we've talked only about moving a 3D object as a whole. In real life, however, you might want different parts of a 3D object to move independently of one another. For example, a robot's arm might move separately from its body, and its fingers might move separately from its arm. And when the robot moves, its arm moves with it (unless the player "amputated" the arm at an earlier point of time, of course).

To allow for movement like this, you'll allow polygon groups to have child polygon groups, each with their own transform, effectively giving each polygon group its own coordinate system. See Figure 9.6, for example. In this figure, the 3D object is actually composed of two polygon groups: the "turret" and the "base." This way, the turret can rotate and move independently from the base.

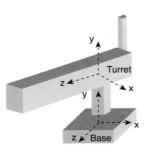

Figure 9.6 3D objects can be composed of multiple child polygon groups with their own coordinate system. In this example, the turret can move independently of the base.

Also in this example, the turret's location is centered right above the base group. This way, when the turret rotates left or right, it rotates around the base of the object. You wouldn't want the turret to rotate around, say, the antennae, because then it wouldn't appear that the turret was actually connected to the base.

The turret and the base have their own transforms, and the entire object has its own transform as well. This way of representing polygon groups creates a hierarchy of transforms, as shown in Figure 9.7.

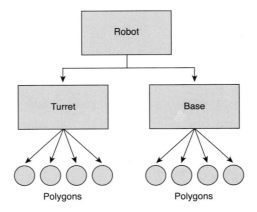

Figure 9.7 The 3D object is represented as a hierarchy of polygon groups (rectangles) and polygons (circles).

When you draw a polygon, first you apply its parent's transform, then that parent's transform, and so on all the way until you reach the root transform.

Some code to implement these polygon groups is here in the `PolygonGroup` class in Listing 9.4.

Listing 9.4   PolygonGroup.java

```java
package com.brackeen.javagamebook.math3D;

import java.util.List;
import java.util.ArrayList;

/**
    The PolygonGroup is a group of polygons with a
    MovingTransform3D. PolygonGroups can also contain other
    PolygonGroups.
*/
public class PolygonGroup {

    private String name;
    private List objects;
    private MovingTransform3D transform;

    /**
        Creates a new, empty PolygonGroup.
    */
    public PolygonGroup() {
        this("unnamed");
    }


    /**
        Creates a new, empty PolygonGroup with the specified name.
    */
    public PolygonGroup(String name) {
        setName(name);
        objects = new ArrayList();
        transform = new MovingTransform3D();
    }
```

continues

Listing 9.4 PolygonGroup.java *continued*

```java
/**
    Gets the MovingTransform3D for this PolygonGroup.
*/
public MovingTransform3D getTransform() {
    return transform;
}


/**
    Gets the name of this PolygonGroup.
*/
public String getName() {
    return name;
}


/**
    Sets the name of this PolygonGroup.
*/
public void setName(String name) {
    this.name = name;
}


/**
    Adds a polygon to this group.
*/
public void addPolygon(Polygon3D o) {
    objects.add(o);
}


/**
    Adds a PolygonGroup to this group.
*/
public void addPolygonGroup(PolygonGroup p) {
    objects.add(p);
```

```
    }


/**
    Clones this polygon group. Polygon3Ds are shared between
    this group and the cloned group; Transform3Ds are copied.
*/
public Object clone() {
    PolygonGroup group = new PolygonGroup(name);
    group.setFilename(filename);
    for (int i=0; i<objects.size(); i++) {
        Object obj = objects.get(i);
        if (obj instanceof Polygon3D) {
            group.addPolygon((Polygon3D)obj);
        }
        else {
            PolygonGroup grp = (PolygonGroup)obj;
            group.addPolygonGroup((PolygonGroup)grp.clone());
        }
    }
    group.transform = (MovingTransform3D)transform.clone();
    return group;
}


/**
    Gets the PolygonGroup in this group with the specified
    name, or null if none is found.
*/
public PolygonGroup getGroup(String name) {
    // check for this group
    if (this.name != null && this.name.equals(name)) {
        return this;
    }
    for (int i=0; i<objects.size(); i++) {
        Object obj = objects.get(i);
        if (obj instanceof PolygonGroup) {
            PolygonGroup subgroup =
```

continues

Listing 9.4 PolygonGroup.java *continued*

```
                            ((PolygonGroup)obj).getGroup(name);
                    if (subgroup != null) {
                        return subgroup;
                    }
                }
            }
        }

        // group not found
        return null;
    }


    /**
        Updates the MovingTransform3Ds of this group and any
        subgroups.
    */
    public void update(long elapsedTime) {
        transform.update(elapsedTime);
        for (int i=0; i<objects.size(); i++) {
            Object obj = objects.get(i);
            if (obj instanceof PolygonGroup) {
                PolygonGroup group = (PolygonGroup)obj;
                group.update(elapsedTime);
            }
        }
    }

}
```

The PolygonGroup class keeps track of a list of objects that are either Polygon3Ds or PolygonGroups, so any polygon group can have child polygon groups.

PolygonGroups can optionally have a name. The getGroup() method allows you to find a PolygonGroup by its name. For example, you would use this if you wanted to find the child PolygonGroup named turret to get its transform. This method looks at the polygon group itself and all child polygon groups, and returns null if no polygon group with the specified name is found.

The `update()` method simply updates the `PolygonGroups` transform and the transform of any child `PolygonGroups`.

The `clone()` method clones a `PolygonGroup`. You use this, for example, to create several different robots for a game. This method creates new `MovingTransform3Ds` for the new `PolygonGroup`, but the same polygons are used (because they are static anyway).

Iterating All the Polygons in a Group

When you're drawing a `PolygonGroup`, you really don't care which polygon belongs to which (child) group; you just want to draw each polygon the group contains, including polygons from child groups. Also, you want to draw the polygons only after they have been transformed.

Here you'll create a few methods in the `PolygonGroup` class to iterate over every polygon. Each polygon is responsible for iterating over all its polygons. If a group has any child groups, each child group is responsible for iterating over its own polygons.

```
private int iteratorIndex;

...

/**
    Resets the polygon iterator for this group.
*/
public void resetIterator() {
    iteratorIndex = 0;
    for (int i=0; i<objects.size(); i++) {
        Object obj = objects.get(i);
        if (obj instanceof PolygonGroup) {
            ((PolygonGroup)obj).resetIterator();
        }
    }
}


/**
    Checks if there is another polygon in the current
```

```
        iteration.
    */
    public boolean hasNext() {
        return (iteratorIndex < objects.size());
    }



    /**
        Gets the next polygon in the current iteration, applying
        the MovingTransform3Ds to it, and storing it in 'cache'.
    */
    public void nextPolygonTransformed(Polygon3D cache) {
        Object obj = objects.get(iteratorIndex);

        if (obj instanceof PolygonGroup) {
            PolygonGroup group = (PolygonGroup)obj;
            group.nextPolygonTransformed(cache);
            if (!group.hasNext()) {
                iteratorIndex++;
            }
        }
        else {
            iteratorIndex++;
            cache.setTo((Polygon3D)obj);
        }

        cache.add(transform);
    }
```

In these methods, each PolygonGroup has an iteratorIndex to indicate which polygon or child group is next to return from the list.

The nextPolygonTransformed() method returns the polygon at the current iteratorIndex. If the object in the list at iteratorIndex is a PolygonGroup, that group's nextPolygonTransformed() is called.

Also, the nextPolygonTransformed() applies the group's transform. So, a child group applies its transform, followed by its parent group. This way, the entire hierarchy of transforms is applied to each polygon.

To draw all the polygons in a group, add another `draw()` method to the ZBufferedRenderer class:

```
public boolean draw(Graphics2D g, PolygonGroup group) {
    boolean visible = false;
    group.resetIterator();
    while (group.hasNext()) {
        group.nextPolygonTransformed(temp);
        visible |= draw(g, temp);
    }
    return visible;
}
```

Okay, you've accomplished a lot so far: You've created a z-buffer, moving transforms, polygon groups, and a polygon renderer to render polygon groups using the z-buffer.

Next, you'll come up with a way to read polygon models from an external file.

Loading Polygon Groups from an OBJ File

Now that you can draw more complex polygon models, it's getting to the point that it is too complicated to write Java code for all the polygons you want to create. In this section, you'll create a parser to read Alias|Wavefront OBJ files, a popular text-based format commonly used for 3D objects.

Using a popular format such as the OBJ format means that 3D artists can create 3D objects in existing 3D design software and put them right in your game. Also, because the format is text based, people without access to this type of 3D design software can use a text editor to modify exiting OBJ files or create new ones.

In the code in this book, we actually support only a subset of the OBJ file specification, but the code will be capable of reading existing OBJ files without a problem. Do a search on the web for "obj file format" if you're curious about the complete file format specification.

The OBJ File Format

The OBJ format is a text format that contains one command per line. Lines beginning with # are comments, and blank lines are ignored. You'll support five keywords in your parser:

`mtllib <filename>`	Loads materials from an external .mtl file.
`v <x> <y> <z>`	Defines a vertex with floating-point coordinates (x,y,z).
`f <v1> <v2> <v3> ...`	Defines a new face. A *face* is a flat, convex polygon with vertices listed in counterclockwise order. The face can have any number of vertices. For each vertex, positive numbers indicate the index of the vertex that is defined in the file. Negative numbers indicate the vertex defined relative to the last vertex read. For example, 1 indicates the first vertex in the file, -1 is the last vertex read, and -2 is the vertex before last.
`g <name>`	Defines a new group by name. The subsequent faces are added to this group.
`usemtl <name>`	Uses the named material (loaded from an .mtl file) for subsequent faces.

The MTL format defines materials—or, in this case, textures. We talk about MTL files in a little bit, but first let's create an example OBJ file that's the shape of a cube, shown here in Listing 9.5.

Listing 9.5   cube.obj

```
# load materials
mtllib textures.mtl

# define vertices
v 16 32 16
v 16 32 -16
v 16 0 16
v 16 0 -16
v -16 32 16
v -16 32 -16
v -16 0 16
v -16 0 -16
```

```
# name the group
g myCube
# define the material
usemtl texture_A
# define the polygons
f 1 3 4 2
f 6 8 7 5
f 2 6 5 1
f 3 7 8 4
f 1 5 7 3
f 4 8 6 2
```

This sample OBJ file lists the eight vertices and six polygons that make up a cube. You'll use an object like this in the demo at the end of the chapter.

Now let's create an OBJ file parser. The first part of the parser, the ObjectLoader, is in Listing 9.6. It doesn't actually parse OBJ files yet, but it sets up a system of managing materials, vertices, and polygon groups. Also, it provides a basic parsing framework to ignore comments and blank lines, and send other lines to a separate line parser.

Listing 9.6   ObjectLoader.java

```java
package com.brackeen.javagamebook.math3D;

import java.io.*;
import java.util.*;
import com.brackeen.javagamebook.graphics3D.texture.*;

/**
    The ObjectLoader class loads a subset of the
    Alias|Wavefront OBJ file specification.
*/
public class ObjectLoader {

    /**
        The Material class wraps a ShadedTexture.
    */
    public static class Material {
        public File sourceFile;
```

continues

Listing 9.6 ObjectLoader.java *continued*

```java
        public ShadedTexture texture;
    }


    /**
        A LineParser is an interface to parse a line in a text
        file. Separate LineParsers are used for OBJ and MTL
        files.
    */
    protected interface LineParser {
        public void parseLine(String line) throws IOException,
            NumberFormatException, NoSuchElementException;
    }

    protected File path;
    protected List vertices;
    protected Material currentMaterial;
    protected HashMap materials;
    protected List lights;
    protected float ambientLightIntensity;
    protected HashMap parsers;
    private PolygonGroup object;
    private PolygonGroup currentGroup;

    /**
        Creates a new ObjectLoader.
    */
    public ObjectLoader() {
        materials = new HashMap();
        vertices = new ArrayList();
        parsers = new HashMap();
        parsers.put("obj", new ObjLineParser());
        parsers.put("mtl", new MtlLineParser());
        currentMaterial = null;
        setLights(new ArrayList(), 1);
    }

    /**
```

```
        Sets the lights used for the polygons in the parsed
        objects. After calling this method, calls to loadObject
        use these lights.
*/
public void setLights(List lights,
    float ambientLightIntensity)
{
    this.lights = lights;
    this.ambientLightIntensity = ambientLightIntensity;
}



/**
    Loads an OBJ file as a PolygonGroup.
*/
public PolygonGroup loadObject(String filename)
    throws IOException
{
    File file = new File(filename);
    object = new PolygonGroup();
    object.setFilename(file.getName());
    path = file.getParentFile();

    vertices.clear();
    currentGroup = object;
    parseFile(filename);

    return object;
}



/**
    Gets a Vector3D from the list of vectors in the file.
    Negative indices count from the end of the list, positive
    indices count from the beginning. 1 is the first index,
    -1 is the last. 0 is invalid and throws an exception.
*/
protected Vector3D getVector(String indexStr) {
```

continues

Listing 9.6 ObjectLoader.java *continued*

```java
        int index = Integer.parseInt(indexStr);
        if (index < 0) {
            index = vertices.size() + index + 1;
        }
        return (Vector3D)vertices.get(index-1);
    }



    /**
        Parses an OBJ (ends with ".obj") or MTL file (ends with
        ".mtl").
    */
    protected void parseFile(String filename)
        throws IOException
    {
        // get the file relative to the source path
        File file = new File(path, filename);
        BufferedReader reader = new BufferedReader(
            new FileReader(file));

        // get the parser based on the file extension
        LineParser parser = null;
        int extIndex = filename.lastIndexOf('.');
        if (extIndex != -1) {
            String ext = filename.substring(extIndex+1);
            parser = (LineParser)parsers.get(ext.toLowerCase());
        }
        if (parser == null) {
            parser = (LineParser)parsers.get("obj");
        }

        // parse every line in the file
        while (true) {
            String line = reader.readLine();
            // no more lines to read
            if (line == null) {
                reader.close();
```

```
            return;
        }

        line = line.trim();

        // ignore blank lines and comments
        if (line.length() > 0 && !line.startsWith("#")) {
            // interpret the line
            try {
                parser.parseLine(line);
            }
            catch (NumberFormatException ex) {
                throw new IOException(ex.getMessage());
            }
            catch (NoSuchElementException ex) {
                throw new IOException(ex.getMessage());
            }
        }

    }
  }

}
```

The ObjectLoader class has an inner interface called LineParser. This interface provides a method to parse a line in a file, and it has two implementing classes: ObjLineParser and MtlLineParser.

The parseFile() method parses either an OBJ file or an MTL file one line at a time, ignoring blank lines and comments. It uses the appropriate LineParser to parse each line, depending on the extension of the filename (either .obj or .mtl).

The getVector() method is a convenience method to get the vertex at the specified index. Remember, indices start at 1, and negative indices count backward from the last vertex.

Finally, the loadObject() method is designed to load an OBJ file and return a PolygonGroup.

Of course, none of this works without `ObjLineParser`, shown here in Listing 9.7.

Listing 9.7 `ObjLineParser` Inner Class of `ObjectLoader`

```
/**
    Parses a line in an OBJ file.
*/
protected class ObjLineParser implements LineParser {

    public void parseLine(String line) throws IOException,
        NumberFormatException, NoSuchElementException
    {
        StringTokenizer tokenizer = new StringTokenizer(line);
        String command = tokenizer.nextToken();
        if (command.equals("v")) {
            // create a new vertex
            vertices.add(new Vector3D(
                Float.parseFloat(tokenizer.nextToken()),
                Float.parseFloat(tokenizer.nextToken()),
                Float.parseFloat(tokenizer.nextToken())));
        }
        else if (command.equals("f")) {
            // create a new face (flat, convex polygon)
            List currVertices = new ArrayList();
            while (tokenizer.hasMoreTokens()) {
                String indexStr = tokenizer.nextToken();

                // ignore texture and normal coords
                int endIndex = indexStr.indexOf('/');
                if (endIndex != -1) {
                    indexStr = indexStr.substring(0, endIndex);
                }

                currVertices.add(getVector(indexStr));
            }

            // create textured polygon
            Vector3D[] array =
                new Vector3D[currVertices.size()];
```

```
        currVertices.toArray(array);
        TexturedPolygon3D poly =
            new TexturedPolygon3D(array);

        // set the texture
        ShadedSurface.createShadedSurface(
            poly, currentMaterial.texture,
            lights, ambientLightIntensity);

        // add the polygon to the current group
        currentGroup.addPolygon(poly);
    }
    else if (command.equals("g")) {
        // define the current group
        if (tokenizer.hasMoreTokens()) {
            String name = tokenizer.nextToken();
            currentGroup = new PolygonGroup(name);
        }
        else {
            currentGroup = new PolygonGroup();
        }
        object.addPolygonGroup(currentGroup);
    }
    else if (command.equals("mtllib")) {
        // load materials from file
        String name = tokenizer.nextToken();
        parseFile(name);
    }
    else if (command.equals("usemtl")) {
        // define the current material
        String name = tokenizer.nextToken();
        currentMaterial = (Material)materials.get(name);
        if (currentMaterial == null) {
            System.out.println("no material: " + name);
        }
    }
    else {
        // unknown command - ignore it
```

continues

Listing 9.7 `ObjLineParser` Inner Class of `ObjectLoader`   *continued*

```
            }


        }
    }
```

The `ObjLineParser` class uses a `StringTokenizer` to get space-delimited words from the line you're parsing. Parsing the line is pretty straightforward. The v command creates a new vertex, the f command creates a new polygon (with a `ShadedSurface`), the g command creates a new `PolygonGroup`, and the `usemtl` command sets the current material. The `mtllib` command actually triggers another call to `parseFile()` to load an MTL file.

Something to note about the f command is that for each vertex, it ignores any "/" symbols and the characters that follow. This is because the OBJ file specification uses additional vertices after the slash to define a polygon normal or texture coordinates. We're not using these extra vertices here, so we ignore the "/" symbol and the following characters for each word. This way we can read OBJ files that include this feature.

There's one more thing to do to complete the OBJ file reader: Create an MTL file reader.

The MTL File Format

The MTL file format is designed to define materials such as solid colors, reflective surfaces (such as shiny objects or mirrors), bump mapping (simulating material depth), and textures. It has all sorts of options and commands, but in this case, you're going to use only texture mapping. Here are the commands you'll use from the MTL file:

`newmtl <name>`	Defines a new material by name
`map_Kd <filename>`	Gives the material a texture map

No problem here. The `MtlLineParser` you create will read textures and create new `Material` objects (see Listing 9.8).

Listing 9.8   `MtlLineParser` Inner Class of `ObjectLoader`

```java
/**
    Parses a line in a material MTL file.
*/
protected class MtlLineParser implements LineParser {

    public void parseLine(String line)
        throws NoSuchElementException
    {
        StringTokenizer tokenizer = new StringTokenizer(line);
        String command = tokenizer.nextToken();

        if (command.equals("newmtl")) {
            // create a new material if needed
            String name = tokenizer.nextToken();
            currentMaterial = (Material)materials.get(name);
            if (currentMaterial == null) {
                currentMaterial = new Material();
                materials.put(name, currentMaterial);
            }
        }
        else if (command.equals("map_Kd")) {
            // give the current material a texture
            String name = tokenizer.nextToken();
            File file = new File(path, name);
            if (!file.equals(currentMaterial.sourceFile)) {
                currentMaterial.sourceFile = file;
                currentMaterial.texture = (ShadedTexture)
                    Texture.createTexture(file.getPath(),true);
            }
        }
        else {
            // unknown command - ignore it
        }
    }
}
```

That's it for loading OBJ files. You've created an OBJ loader that reads only a subset of the OBJ format, but it will be just what you need for the 3D objects in this book. If you want to extend the OBJ loader to read a broader set of OBJ commands, search the web for "OBJ file format," and you'll find plenty of resources to get you started.

Game Objects

In this section, you'll make a container for a `PolygonGroup` called a `GameObject`, which will be the base class for all objects in the games and demos in this book. The idea is that a game object can manipulate its own state, including the polygon group's transform. Really, the `GameObject` by itself doesn't do anything, and it needs to be extended to accomplish anything cool.

The `GameObject` class you'll create in this chapter will be just a start; you'll add on to it in later chapters when we discuss collision detection, path finding, and artificial intelligence.

First, let's look the basic states of any game object. A *game object* can be anything, such as a static object, a projectile, a power-up, or an enemy. During the course of a game, a game object could be idle (not moving) or active (potentially moving around). Also, some objects can be destroyed, such as when an enemy is blasted or when a projectile collides with a wall. With this in mind, we give game objects three possible states: `IDLE`, `ACTIVE`, and `DESTROYED`, as shown in Figure 9.8.

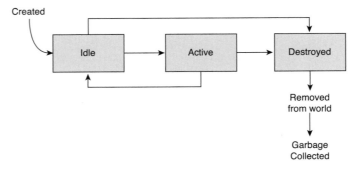

Figure 9.8 The game object life cycle.

When a game object is first created, it's in the IDLE state and can move to the ACTIVE state at any time. Likewise, when it's in the ACTIVE state it can return to the IDLE state at any time.

From either the IDLE state or the ACTIVE state, a game object can change to the DESTROYED state. When in the DESTROYED state, a game object shouldn't return to any other state. The game manager should remove the DESTROYED game object from the world, and afterward the game object should be garbage-collected (assuming no other references to the game object exist).

Different types of game objects follow this game object life cycle in different ways. For example, a static object could stay in the IDLE state for the entire game. A projectile might immediately jump to the ACTIVE state and stay there until it hits something, in which case it becomes DESTROYED. An enemy might start in the IDLE state and move to the ACTIVE state when it becomes visible. For example, if the enemy goes off the screen for a while, it might become IDLE again. Finally, an enemy moves to the DESTROYED state when the player blasts it enough times.

With all this in mind, you'll create the GameObject class (see Listing 9.9). This class manages the state and provides several convenience methods for the game object's PolygonGroup and transform.

Listing 9.9 GameObject.java

```
package com.brackeen.javagamebook.game;

import com.brackeen.javagamebook.math3D.*;

/**
    A GameObject class is a base class for any type of object in
a
    game that is represented by a PolygonGroup. For example, a
    GameObject can be a static object (like a crate), a moving
    object (like a projectile or a bad guy), or any other type of
    object (like a power-up). GameObjects have three basic
    states: STATE_IDLE, STATE_ACTIVE, or STATE_DESTROYED.
*/
public class GameObject {
```

continues

Listing 9.9 GameObject.java *continued*

```java
    protected static final int STATE_IDLE = 0;
    protected static final int STATE_ACTIVE = 1;
    protected static final int STATE_DESTROYED = 2;

    private PolygonGroup polygonGroup;
    private int state;

    /**
        Creates a new GameObject represented by the specified
        PolygonGroup. The PolygonGroup can be null.
    */
    public GameObject(PolygonGroup polygonGroup) {
        this.polygonGroup = polygonGroup;
        state = STATE_IDLE;
    }



    /**
        Shortcut to get the location of this GameObject from the
        Transform3D.
    */
    public Vector3D getLocation() {
        return polygonGroup.getTransform().getLocation();
    }



    /**
        Gets this object's transform.
    */
    public MovingTransform3D getTransform() {
        return polygonGroup.getTransform();
    }



    /**
        Gets this object's PolygonGroup.
    */
```

```java
public PolygonGroup getPolygonGroup() {
    return polygonGroup;
}


/**
    Sets the state of this object. Should be either
    STATE_IDLE, STATE_ACTIVE, or STATE_DESTROYED.
*/
protected void setState(int state) {
    this.state = state;
}


/**
    Sets the state of the specified object. This allows
    any GameObject to set the state of any other GameObject.
    The state should be either STATE_IDLE, STATE_ACTIVE, or
    STATE_DESTROYED.
*/
protected void setState(GameObject object, int state) {
    object.setState(state);
}


/**
    Returns true if this GameObject is idle.
*/
public boolean isIdle() {
    return (state == STATE_IDLE);
}


/**
    Returns true if this GameObject is active.
*/
public boolean isActive() {
    return (state == STATE_ACTIVE);
```

continues

Listing 9.9 GameObject.java *continued*

```java
    }


    /**
        Returns true if this GameObject is destroyed.
    */
    public boolean isDestroyed() {
        return (state == STATE_DESTROYED);
    }


    /**
        If this GameObject is in the active state, this method
        updates its PolygonGroup. Otherwise, this method does
        nothing.
    */
    public void update(GameObject player, long elapsedTime) {
        if (isActive()) {
            polygonGroup.update(elapsedTime);
        }
    }


    /**
        Notifies this GameObject whether it was visible or not
        on the last update. By default, if this GameObject is
        idle and notified as visible, it changes to the active
        state.
    */
    public void notifyVisible(boolean visible) {
        if (visible && isIdle()) {
            state = STATE_ACTIVE;
        }
    }
}
```

In this default game object, the game object's polygon group is updated only if it's in the ACTIVE state. A reference to the player's game object is a parameter in this method, so any game object can know the location of the player. Obviously, it is pretty common for enemies to want to know where the player is.

Also, notice the notifyVisible() method. This method is designed to tell an object whether it's visible in every frame. If it's visible and the current state is IDLE, the game object automatically changes to the ACTIVE state.

The rules of the game object life cycle are not strictly enforced in this class: You could theoretically move a game object state out of the DESTROYED state back to the ACTIVE state, but this could be pointless if the game object was already removed from the world.

Managing Game Objects

To keep track of all the objects in the world, you'll create the GameObjectManager interface, shown in Listing 9.10. We use a rather simple implementation of this interface in this chapter, but in later chapters you'll create a new implementation.

The GameObjectManager interface provides methods to keep track of every object in the world. Also, it has two methods, markVisible() and markAllVisible(), to mark which objects are visible to be drawn. The markVisible() method takes a Rectangle as a parameter, which specifies a 2D area (bird's-eye view) that is visible. Only objects marked as visible should be drawn; after they are drawn, all the objects are marked as invisible again.

Listing 9.10   GameObjectManager.java

```
package com.brackeen.javagamebook.game;

import java.awt.Rectangle;
import java.awt.Graphics2D;
import com.brackeen.javagamebook.game.GameObjectRenderer;

/**
    The GameObjectManager interface provides methods to keep
```

continues

Listing 9.10 GameObjectManager.java *continued*

```
      track of and draw GameObjects.
*/
public interface GameObjectManager {


    /**
        Marks all objects within the specified 2D bounds
        as potentially visible (should be drawn).
    */
    public void markVisible(Rectangle bounds);


    /**
        Marks all objects as potentially visible (should be drawn).
    */
    public void markAllVisible();


    /**
        Adds a GameObject to this manager.
    */
    public void add(GameObject object);


    /**
        Adds a GameObject to this manager, specifying it as the
        player object. An existing player object, if any,
        is not removed.
    */
    public void addPlayer(GameObject player);


    /**
        Gets the object specified as the Player object, or null
        if no player object was specified.
    */
```

```
        public GameObject getPlayer();


        /**
            Removes a GameObject from this manager.
        */
        public void remove(GameObject object);


        /**
            Updates all objects based on the amount of time passed
            from the last update.
        */
        public void update(long elapsedTime);


        /**
            Draws all visible objects.
        */
        public void draw(Graphics2D g, GameObjectRenderer r);

}
```

The draw() method in GameObjectManager draws every visible object managed
by the game object manager and marks every object as invisible. It uses a
GameObjectRenderer to draw the objects, which is just an interface to draw an
object, as shown in Listing 9.11. The ZBufferedRenderer class implements this
interface.

Listing 9.11   GameObjectRenderer.java

```
package com.brackeen.javagamebook.game;

import java.awt.Graphics2D;
import com.brackeen.javagamebook.game.GameObject;

/**
    The GameObjectRenderer interface provides a method for
    drawing a GameObject.
```

continues

Listing 9.11 GameObjectRenderer.java *continued*

```
*/
public interface GameObjectRenderer {

    /**
        Draws the object and returns true if any part of the
        object is visible.
    */
    public boolean draw(Graphics2D g, GameObject object);

}
```

The `SimpleGameObjectManager` implements the `GameObjectManager` interface by just keeping all the objects in a list. When an object is marked as visible, it's put in a "visible" list, which is cleared after all the objects in the visible list are drawn. You'll create a more advanced `GameObjectManager` later in Chapter 11, but this will work fine for now.

Putting It All Together

You've created a lot of stuff in this chapter. Now you are near the end of the chapter, so let's create a demo that uses it all.

The demo is a walkthrough with three different types of game objects: static boxes, projectiles, and bots. Each of these objects has its own OBJ file to define its 3D models.

The static boxes are just `GameObjects` and don't do anything special; they are just there to look at.

The `Bot` object is shown in Listing 9.12. It looks just like the example from Figure 9.6: a turret and a base. The turret moves independently of the base and turns to face the player at all times.

Listing 9.12   Bot.java

```java
import com.brackeen.javagamebook.math3D.*;
import com.brackeen.javagamebook.game.GameObject;

/**
    The Bot game object is a small static bot with a turret
    that turns to face the player.
*/
public class Bot extends GameObject {

    private static final float TURN_SPEED = .0005f;
    private static final long DECISION_TIME = 2000;

    protected MovingTransform3D mainTransform;
    protected MovingTransform3D turretTransform;
    protected long timeUntilDecision;
    protected Vector3D lastPlayerLocation;

    public Bot(PolygonGroup polygonGroup) {
        super(polygonGroup);
        mainTransform = polygonGroup.getTransform();
        PolygonGroup turret = polygonGroup.getGroup("turret");
        if (turret != null) {
            turretTransform = turret.getTransform();
        }
        else {
            System.out.println("No turret defined!");
        }
        lastPlayerLocation = new Vector3D();
    }

    public void notifyVisible(boolean visible) {
        if (!isDestroyed()) {
            if (visible) {
                setState(STATE_ACTIVE);
            }
            else {
                setState(STATE_IDLE);
```

continues

Listing 9.12   Bot.java   *continued*

```
                }
            }
        }

    public void update(GameObject player, long elapsedTime) {
        if (turretTransform == null || isIdle()) {
            return;
        }

        Vector3D playerLocation = player.getLocation();
        if (playerLocation.equals(lastPlayerLocation)) {
            timeUntilDecision = DECISION_TIME;
        }
        else {
            timeUntilDecision-=elapsedTime;
            if (timeUntilDecision <= 0 ||
                !turretTransform.isTurningY())
            {
                float x = player.getX() - getX();
                float z = player.getZ() - getZ();
                turretTransform.turnYTo(x, z,
                    -mainTransform.getAngleY(), TURN_SPEED);
                lastPlayerLocation.setTo(playerLocation);
                timeUntilDecision = DECISION_TIME;
            }
        }
        super.update(player, elapsedTime);
    }
}
```

In the Bot object, you don't check the player's location every frame; instead, you check only every two seconds (the amount of time is defined in DECISION_TIME). This way, the bot calculates what to do only every four seconds, and we've "dumbed down" the bot a little bit by making it sometimes lag behind the player.

Next up is the `Blast` game object, shown in Listing 9.13. The `Blast` object is a projectile that the player can fire. It simply travels in a straight line (while spinning) and destroys itself after five seconds. The SPEED and ROT_SPEED fields define how fast it moves and spins.

Listing 9.13   Blast.java

```java
import com.brackeen.javagamebook.math3D.*;
import com.brackeen.javagamebook.game.GameObject;


/**
    The Blast GameObject is a projectile, designed to travel
    in a straight line for five seconds, then die. Blasts
    destroy Bots instantly.
*/
public class Blast extends GameObject {

    private static final long DIE_TIME = 5000;
    private static final float SPEED = 1.5f;
    private static final float ROT_SPEED = .008f;


    private long aliveTime;

    /**
        Create a new Blast with the specified PolygonGroup
        and normalized vector direction.
    */
    public Blast(PolygonGroup polygonGroup, Vector3D direction) {
        super(polygonGroup);
        MovingTransform3D transform = polygonGroup.getTransform();
        Vector3D velocity = transform.getVelocity();
        velocity.setTo(direction);
        velocity.multiply(SPEED);
        transform.setVelocity(velocity);
        //transform.setAngleVelocityX(ROT_SPEED);
        transform.setAngleVelocityY(ROT_SPEED);
        transform.setAngleVelocityZ(ROT_SPEED);
        setState(STATE_ACTIVE);
```

continues

Listing 9.13 Blast.java *continued*

```
    }


    public void update(GameObject player, long elapsedTime) {
        aliveTime+=elapsedTime;
        if (aliveTime >= DIE_TIME) {
            setState(STATE_DESTROYED);
        }
        else {
            super.update(player, elapsedTime);
        }
    }

}
```

Now that you've got all the game objects, you can create the `GameObjectTest`. As usual, this class extends the `GameCore3D` class and just overrides a couple methods. First, the `createPolygon()` method loads the OBJ files and sets up the game objects:

```
public void createPolygons() {

    // create floor
    Texture floorTexture = Texture.createTexture(
        "../images/roof1.png", true);
    ((ShadedTexture)floorTexture).setDefaultShadeLevel(
        ShadedTexture.MAX_LEVEL*3/4);
    Rectangle3D floorTextureBounds = new Rectangle3D(
        new Vector3D(0,0,0),
        new Vector3D(1,0,0),
        new Vector3D(0,0,1),
        floorTexture.getWidth(),
        floorTexture.getHeight());
    float s = GAME_AREA_SIZE;
    floor = new TexturedPolygon3D(new Vector3D[] {
        new Vector3D(-s, 0, s),
        new Vector3D(s, 0, s),
        new Vector3D(s, 0, -s),
```

```
        new Vector3D(-s, 0, -s)});
    floor.setTexture(floorTexture, floorTextureBounds);


    // set up the local lights for the model.
    float ambientLightIntensity = .5f;
    List lights = new LinkedList();
    lights.add(new PointLight3D(-100,100,100, .5f, -1));
    lights.add(new PointLight3D(100,100,0, .5f, -1));

    // load the object models
    ObjectLoader loader = new ObjectLoader();
    loader.setLights(lights, ambientLightIntensity);
    try {
        robotModel = loader.loadObject("../images/robot.obj");
        powerUpModel = loader.loadObject("../images/cube.obj");
        blastModel = loader.loadObject("../images/blast.obj");
    }
    catch (IOException ex) {
        ex.printStackTrace();
    }


    // create game objects
    gameObjectManager = new SimpleGameObjectManager();
    gameObjectManager.addPlayer(new GameObject(
        new PolygonGroup("Playerv")));
    gameObjectManager.getPlayer().getLocation().y = 5;
    for (int i=0; i<NUM_BOTS; i++) {
        Bot object = new Bot((PolygonGroup)robotModel.clone());
        placeObject(object);
    }
    for (int i=0; i<NUM_POWER_UPS; i++) {
        GameObject object =
            new GameObject((PolygonGroup)powerUpModel.clone());
        placeObject(object);
    }
}
```

```
// randomly place objects in game area
public void placeObject(GameObject object) {
    float size = GAME_AREA_SIZE;
    object.getLocation().setTo(
        (float)(Math.random()*size-size/2),
        0,
        (float)(Math.random()*size-size/2));
    gameObjectManager.add(object);
}
```

Another method of interest in `GameObjectTest` is the `updateWorld()` method, which was changed from `GameCore3D` to use transforms for player movement. It adds the capability to fire a projectile:

```
public void updateWorld(long elapsedTime) {

    float angleVelocity;

    // cap elapsedTime
    elapsedTime = Math.min(elapsedTime, 100);

    GameObject player = gameObjectManager.getPlayer();
    MovingTransform3D playerTransform = player.getTransform();
    Vector3D velocity = playerTransform.getVelocity();

    playerTransform.stop();
    float x = -playerTransform.getSinAngleY();
    float z = -playerTransform.getCosAngleY();
    if (goForward.isPressed()) {
        velocity.add(x, 0, z);
    }
    if (goBackward.isPressed()) {
        velocity.add(-x, 0, -z);
    }
    if (goLeft.isPressed()) {
        velocity.add(z, 0, -x);
    }
    if (goRight.isPressed()) {
```

```
        velocity.add(-z, 0, x);
}
if (fire.isPressed()) {
    float cosX = playerTransform.getCosAngleX();
    float sinX = playerTransform.getSinAngleX();
    Blast blast = new Blast(
        (PolygonGroup)blastModel.clone(),
        new Vector3D(cosX*x, sinX, cosX*z));
    // blast starting location needs work. Looks like
    // the blast is coming out of your forehead when
    // you're shooting down.
    blast.getLocation().setTo(
        player.getX(),
        player.getY() + BULLET_HEIGHT,
        player.getZ());
    gameObjectManager.add(blast);
}


velocity.multiply(PLAYER_SPEED);
playerTransform.setVelocity(velocity);

// look up/down (rotate around x)
angleVelocity = Math.min(tiltUp.getAmount(), 200);
angleVelocity += Math.max(-tiltDown.getAmount(), -200);
playerTransform.setAngleVelocityX(angleVelocity *
    PLAYER_TURN_SPEED / 200);

// turn (rotate around y)
angleVelocity = Math.min(turnLeft.getAmount(), 200);
angleVelocity += Math.max(-turnRight.getAmount(), -200);
playerTransform.setAngleVelocityY(angleVelocity *
    PLAYER_TURN_SPEED / 200);

// for now, mark the entire world as visible in this frame.
gameObjectManager.markAllVisible();

// update objects
```

```
        gameObjectManager.update(elapsedTime);

        // limit look up/down
        float angleX = playerTransform.getAngleX();
        float limit = (float)Math.PI / 2;
        if (angleX < -limit) {
            playerTransform.setAngleX(-limit);
        }
        else if (angleX > limit) {
            playerTransform.setAngleX(limit);
        }

        // set the camera to be 100 units above the player
        Transform3D camera = polygonRenderer.getCamera();
        camera.setTo(playerTransform);
        camera.getLocation().add(0,100,0);

    }
```

Also, I snuck a cool effect into the GameCore3D class to make the instructions at the top of the screen fade out after a few seconds. On previous demos, the text, "Use the mouse/keys to move. Press Esc to exit." always appeared at the top of the screen, but in this demo, the text fades away after a few seconds. The fading is accomplished by using a translucent color:

```
// fade out the text over 500 ms
long fade = INSTRUCTIONS_TIME - drawInstructionsTime;
if (fade < 500) {
    fade = fade * 255 / 500;
    g.setColor(new Color(0xffffff | ((int)fade << 24), true));
}
else {
    g.setColor(Color.WHITE);
}
```

That's it for GameObjectTest. Check out the screenshot in Figure 9.9.

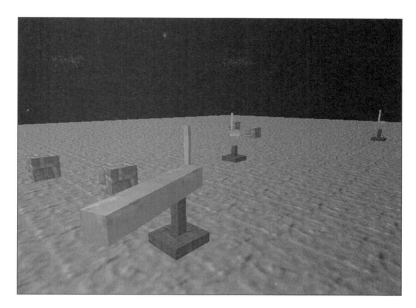

Figure 9.9   This screenshot from `GameObjectTest` shows polygons drawn in correct z-order.

One thing about this demo is that's it's easy to forget that you actually used z-buffering. If you're curious what it would look like without z-buffering, modify `ZBuffer`'s `checkDepth()` method to always return `true`. This draws polygons out of order and gives some strange-looking results.

In the `GameObjectTest` demo, when you look straight down so that the green floor covers the entire screen, you might notice that the frame rate is much slower than in demos from previous chapters. This is because the z-buffer is being checked and set for every pixel on the screen, which is a bit of an overhead. As mentioned before, z-buffering is fine for game objects because they appear in only smaller portions of the screen at a time. In the next chapter, on BSP trees, you'll learn about a better algorithm to draw the static polygons of the world much faster and merge 3D objects into the scene.

Future Enhancements

Here are a few more ideas for extending the code in this chapter:

➤ Add acceleration to the `MovingTransform3D`. This way, objects would smoothly speed up until the desired velocity is reached and then sustain that velocity. This would give a more realistic feel to the player movement.

➤ Add circular movement to `MovingTransform3D`. This way, objects could "orbit" around other objects.

➤ Allow `GameObjects` using a `MovingTransform3D` to make smooth turns around corners. The player can make smooth turns using the keyboard and mouse, but game objects are a different story. Instead of walking forward, stopping, turning, and then starting to walk again, it would be cool if the object could turn while moving. The object might have to slow down to limit the turn radius (just like you slow down to make a turn while driving a car).

➤ Extend OBJ and MTL support. Solid colors defined in the MTL could be easily implemented by creating a subclass of `Texture` that represents just one color.

➤ Add more imagination! You can do a lot more with game objects, such as making baddies that move around in a circle, robots that actually move their legs to walk, or ghosts that chase players only when they aren't looking. You'll be able to do even more with game objects when we tackle collision detection in Chapter 11.

Summary

We've still got one more hidden surface–removal algorithm to talk about in this book: BSP trees. Using a z-buffer is great for 3D moving objects, but drawing every pixel on the screen using the z-buffer can be a bit too slow. You'll fix this in the next chapter with BSP trees.

But in this chapter, as usual, we've tackled a lot of concepts. You learned about some hidden surface–removal techniques and implemented a z-buffer using 1/z as the depth. Of course, you created a renderer to draw polygons using the z-buffer. Also, you created a system to perform 3D object animation on polygon groups and created a parser to load 3D models from OBJ files. Finally, you created a base class for game objects, created a couple sample game objects, and tried everything out with a demo. With all these concepts, you've created some impressive results; in the next chapters, you'll extend these concepts even further.

Chapter 10

3D Scene Management Using BSP Trees

In the real world—not the gaming world, actually—a lot of effort has been put into designing buildings that withstand earthquakes.

Of course, you wouldn't want to construct a building with earthquake reinforcement in, say, Kansas. That would be a bit of overkill. But earthquake reinforcement makes sense in places such as Los Angeles and Tokyo. You've got to design your buildings for what works best in their environments.

That brings us to the topic of this chapter. In 3D rendering, you want to design your polygon-management technique, also called scene management, for what works best in your game environment. If you can assume that the polygons in the scene are stationary, you can apply some techniques to speed up the rendering.

The technique you'll use in this chapter is organizing polygons in a data structure called a *binary space partitioned tree*, or BSP tree. A BSP tree enables you to store polygons in a way so that you can quickly draw the scene, and later they will help with collision detection and path finding.

BSP Tree Intro

In the last chapter, "3D Objects," you created a z-buffer to correctly draw polygons in a scene. This created a perfectly drawn scene, with polygons close to the camera drawn in front of polygons farther away. But the drawback was checking and setting the z-buffer for every pixel: It was too much overhead for every pixel on the screen, and overdraw was often involved. The more polygons you have, the more z-buffer checking and potential overdraw you have. Obviously, this doesn't scale well.

What you really want is an alternative to the z-buffer with the following goals:

➤ To potentially manage a large number of polygons

➤ To quickly decide which polygons are visible from any location in the scene

➤ To draw only the visible polygons (and to not draw parts of polygons that aren't visible)

➤ To draw every pixel only once (no overdraw)

At first, those seem like some difficult goals to accomplish. Of course, the technique you use to solve these goals really depends on the type of game you have. For example, a driving game in which you spend a lot of time looking at wide open spaces would probably use a different technique than an indoor game in which you spend a lot of time looking at walls, floors, and ceilings.

You can organize polygons in many different ways to make it easy to decide which polygons are visible. Besides BSP trees, some other types of polygon-organization techniques are octrees and scene graphs. BSP trees enable you to draw all polygons from front-to-back order from any location in the scene.

By extension, using BSP trees solves all of the previous goals. However, the BSP tree isn't perfect. Here are a couple drawbacks:

➤ The world must be static (no moving walls here). However, 3D game objects can move around, so you can use 3D game objects for things such as monsters and doors.

➤ It's computationally expensive to build the tree. However, the ideal solution is to build the tree beforehand, loading the built tree at startup time.

Games such as *Doom* were the first to implement BSP trees. *Doom* used a 2D BSP tree with variable-height floors and ceilings, and the rendering engine had a restriction that a player could not look up and down in the game. In the code you make in this chapter, you also use a 2D BSP tree with variable-height floors and ceilings, but you use the 3D rendering engine from the previous chapters so the player can look up and down.

Even though we demonstrate a 2D BSP tree in this chapter, a 3D BSP tree, used in many modern games, is not that much more difficult to master. A 2D BSP tree just makes the examples and equations a bit easier to follow, and other topics such as collision detection and path finding are easier to describe.

The drawback to using a 2D BSP tree is that you can make a world with only vertical walls and horizontal floors and ceilings. However, you still can make some cool worlds with this limitation.

Binary Tree Basics

A BSP tree is a binary tree, so first let's run through some basic binary tree terminology and concepts.

A binary tree is a data structure that contains nodes in a hierarchical structure. Binary trees have the following properties:

➤ Each node has, at most, two children, often called the left child and the right child.

➤ The nodes have data associated with them.

➤ A node with no children is called a *leaf.*

➤ The node with no parent is called the *root node*.

➤ A sorted binary tree, often called a *binary search tree*, contains nodes sorted by their data.

Check out the example sorted binary tree in Figure 10.1. This is a sorted binary tree, and it contains a list of numbers—1, 3, 5, 6, 8, and 9. Okay, now bear with me in an explanation of a sorted binary tree. For every node, all values less than that node's value are on the left side of that node, and all values greater than that node's value are on the right side of that node. For example, because the root node has the value of 5, every number that is less than 5 is on the left side of the tree, and every number that is greater than 5 is on the right side of the tree. Study the example in Figure 10.1 until you understand this.

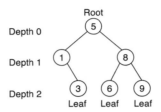

Figure 10.1   This example binary tree has three leaves and a depth of 2.

Also in Figure 10.1 you'll see that this tree has a depth of 2. The depth, sometimes called the height, is the number of the root's child generations. The example is also well balanced, which means that for every node, the depth of its left side is at most one away from the depth of its right side. A well-balanced sorted binary tree can be quickly searched, without having to look at every piece of data.

Now you'll implement a simple binary tree and later use the same concepts to make a BSP tree. You'll use integers as the binary tree's data, just like in the example. Let's start with a node:

```
public class Node {
    Node left;
    Node right;
    int value;

    public Node(int value) {
        this.value = value;
    }
}
```

The Node class has an integer value and references to the left and right children (which are initially null, so it has no children). Remember, a node can be a root, a leaf, or just a plain node. Creating a new Node is easy—here, you create a root node:

```
Node root = new Node(5);
```

Next, you write a method, insertSorted(), to insert a new value into a sorted tree.

```
public void insertSorted(Node node, int value) {
    if (value < node.value) {
        if (node.left != null) {
            insertSorted(node.left, value);
        }
        else {
            node.left = new Node(value);
        }
    }
    else if (value > node.value) {
        if (node.right != null) {
            insertSorted(node.right, value);
        }
        else {
            node.right = new Node(value);
        }
    }
    else {
        // do nothing - value already in tree
    }
}
```

To insert the value 8 into the tree, call the following:

```
insertSorted(root, 8);
```

This method uses *recursion* (or, calls itself) to insert values into the tree. A child node is really a binary tree itself—often called a *subtree*—so calling something such as insertSorted(node.left, value) just inserts the value into the node's left subtree.

Notice that this method doesn't allow duplicates into the tree: If a value is already in the tree, it's not inserted again.

Finally, you make a method to print every value in the order they are in the tree. This is called an in-order traversal because, you guessed it, the values are traversed in order.

```
public void printInOrder(Node node) {
    if (node != null) {
        printInOrder(node.left);
        System.out.println(node.value);
        printInOrder(node.right);
    }
}
```

To print every value in a tree in order, do this:

```
printInOrder(root);
```

Again, this method uses recursion. This method basically says: "For this node, print its left subtree, then print its value, and then print its right subtree."

That's it for a quick introduction of binary trees. Next, we move on to the main subject of this chapter and introduce the concept of a BSP tree.

The One-Dimensional BSP Tree

Eventually, this chapter will focus on 2D BSP trees, but understanding how a 2D or 3D BSP tree works can be difficult at first. So, I'd like to make things a little easier by first explaining a one-dimensional BSP tree. This example might seem trivial, but it will give you the idea of how BSP trees work.

In short, a BSP tree's node divides a world into halves—or, in other words, it is a *binary space partition*. Using a BSP tree allows you to sort polygons front to back from the camera's location.

Now imagine the player is standing in a simple world with a row of houses, as shown in Figure 10.2. Note that the houses are sorted by their numbers. Also, the houses have the same numbers as in the example in Figure 10.1.

Figure 10.2 The player is standing at position 7 in a row of houses.

Now assume that each house is a node partition. In this one-dimensional example, each house partitions the world into two spaces: the left space (everything to the left of the house) and the right space (everything to the right of the house).

Building the tree follows the same process you used to build a sorted binary tree in the previous section. The resulting binary tree in this example could look just like the one in Figure 10.1.

Now let's say you want to draw these houses in a 3D world. You want to draw the houses front to back from the camera's location, to eliminate overdraw and avoid the speed shortcomings of a z-buffer. So, in this example, you want to draw the houses closer to the player before drawing the farther ones.

Looking at Figure 10.2, the order to draw the houses in front to back order is broken down into two simple rules:

➤ Draw houses to the left of the camera in reverse order: (6, 5, 3, 1).

➤ Draw houses to the right of the camera in order: (8, 9).

From a 3D perspective, the houses on the left side will never overlap the houses on the right side. Therefore, it doesn't matter whether the order in which you draw the houses is first the left side and then the right (6, 5, 3, 1, 8, 9) or whether the two sides are mixed in some variation (6, 8, 5, 9, 3, 1). It matters only if each side is drawn in order. So, this technique works no mater which way the player is facing.

You'll implement these two rules with a variation of the printInOrder() method you created in the previous section, creating a printFrontToBack() method.

```java
public void printFrontToBack(Node node, int camera) {
    if (node == null) return;
    if (camera < node.value) {
        // print in order
        printFrontToBack(node.left, camera);
        System.out.println(node.value);
        printFrontToBack(node.right, camera);
    }
    else if (camera > node.value) {
        // print in reverse order
```

```
            printFrontToBack(node.right, camera);
            System.out.println(node.value);
            printFrontToBack(node.left, camera);
        }
        else {
            // order doesn't matter
            printFrontToBack(node.left, camera);
            printFrontToBack(node.right, camera);
        }
    }
}
```

This method is similar to the printInOrder() method, except that it prints in reverse order if the node's value is less than the camera's value. Let's walk through this method by looking at Figure 10.3.

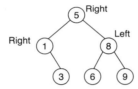

Figure 10.3 Traversing the tree from position 7.

With the binary tree from Figure 10.3, calling printFrontToBack() with camera location 7 follows these steps:

1. At the root node, 7 is greater than 5, so traverse the right node.

2. At node 8, 7 is less than 8, so traverse the left node.

3. Node 6 is a leaf, so print 6 and return to the parent.

4. Print 8 and traverse its right node.

5. Node 9 is a leaf, so print 9 and return to the parent.

6. You're finished traversing node 8, so return to the parent.

7. Print 5 and traverse its left node.

8. At node 1, 7 is greater than 1, so traverse the right node.

9. Node 3 is a leaf, so print 3 and return to the parent.

10. Node 1 does not have a left child, so print 1 and return.

11. You're finished traversing the root.

So, calling `printFrontToBack()` with camera location 7 prints the order (6, 8, 9, 5, 3, 1). Everything on the left is printed in front-to-back order (6, 5, 3, 1), and everything on the right it printed in front-to-back order (8, 9), which is just what we wanted.

Problem solved! Next, let's extend this idea to two dimensions.

The Two-Dimensional BSP Tree

To start, you'll go through an example of building and traversing a 2D BSP tree; afterward, you'll create an implementation.

Take a look at the example 2D floor plan in Figure 10.4. You'll build a BSP tree based on this floor plan.

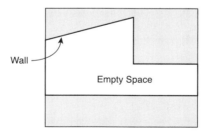

Figure 10.4   The 2D floor plan shows a simple room with four walls.

In the one-dimensional example, each house was a partition, so partitions were points. In 2D, partitions are lines, and in 3D—surprise!—the partitions are planes.

Lines easily partition a 2D area into two halves, but to actually build a BSP tree, you need to know what's to the "left" of the line and what's to the "right."

Actually, the terms *left* and *right* are a bit inaccurate in this case. These terms work fine for a one-dimensional world, but in 2D, lines can be oriented in any way. A vertical line divides the world into "left" and "right," but a horizontal line divides the world into "north" and "south."

Instead, we use the terms *front* and *back*. Line segments have a front and back just like polygons do, with the normal pointing in the direction of the front side, as shown in Figure 10.5. The front side is the visible side. This means you can use walls as the partitions.

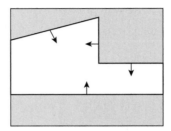

Figure 10.5   Line segments representing walls have a front and a back.

Because the partitions have a front and a back, you'll always be able to tell where the camera is in relation to each line: The camera is either in front of or in back of every partition.

With this knowledge, let's walk through an example of building a BSP tree. If you're still a bit fuzzy on how line partitions divide the space, this example will help.

BSP Tree-Building Example

As an example, you'll build the floor plan from Figure 10.5 by adding one wall at a time. The order in which you add walls will be arbitrary.

In Figure 10.6, the first partition, wall A, is added to the tree. Notice that the partition formed by wall A extends beyond wall A, shown as a dotted line.

Here, the leaves of the BSP tree are the empty spaces. These empty spaces are the same shape as the floor and ceiling polygons. You want your floors and ceilings to have different heights (so you can create things such as platforms and stairs), so keep floor and ceiling height information in these leaves. In Figure 10.6, start with leaf 1, which represents the entire empty area. The first partition, wall A, splits this leaf into two, creating leaves 1 and 2.

The empty spaces will always be convex because splitting a convex shape along a line always creates two convex shapes. So, the floor and ceiling polygons will be convex as well.

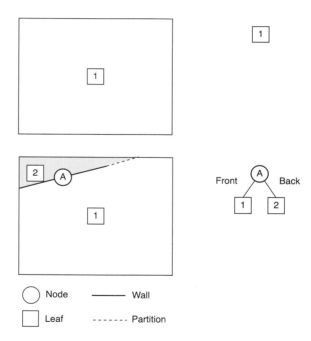

Figure 10.6 Building a BSP tree, part 1. The first wall is added.

Next, in Figure 10.7, walls B and C are added to the tree. Wall B is in front of A, so it is added to the front node of A. This splits leaf 1 into two leaves (1 and 3). Wall C is in front of A and in back of B, so it is added to the back node of B and splits leaf 3 into two leaves (3 and 4).

Notice that when you add wall B, leaf 3 is bounded by both wall B and the partition formed by wall A.

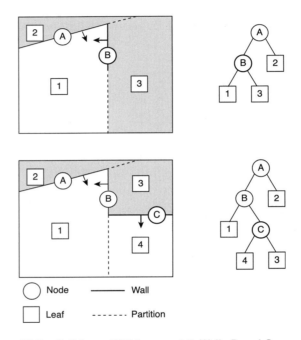

Figure 10.7 Building a BSP tree, part 2. Walls B and C are added.

The BSP building continues in Figure 10.8. There's just one more wall to add: wall D. But wall D actually spans the partition formed by wall B. Walls can't exist in two different locations in the tree, so wall D is split into two walls: D1 and D2.

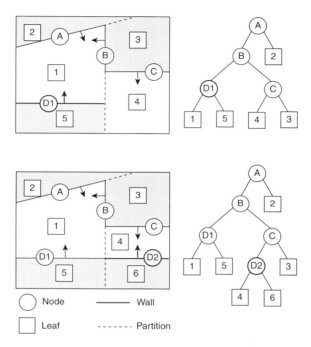

Figure 10.8   Building a BSP tree, part 3. Line D is split along the partition formed by line B.

That's it—you now have a built tree.

Going through the process of building the tree, you probably noticed that the tree would be different if the walls were added in a different order. For example, if the walls were added in the order D, B, C, A, you would get the tree in Figure 10.9. This tree didn't require any walls to be split, so there are fewer nodes. Also, the tree has a shorter depth. However, the tree isn't well balanced—all the walls are in the front of the first node.

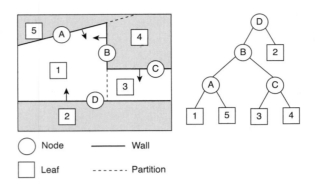

Figure 10.9 This alternate BSP tree is shorter and has fewer nodes.

When you have enough polygons, shorter, balanced trees will make for faster searches. So, the order in which you add walls to the tree is important.

An algorithm to decide the order in which you choose partitions should keep two things in mind:

1. **Minimize splits.** Fewer splits mean fewer polygons and less tree traversal.

2. **Keep the tree as balanced as possible.** Shorter, balanced trees means less tree traversal for unbalanced trees.

Sometimes these goals are mutually exclusive: Keeping the tree balanced can create more splits, and minimizing splits can create an unbalanced tree. Finding the right algorithm can be complicating. We present a couple of ideas here.

First, you could just minimize the number of splits, ignoring the balance of the tree. Here, every time you choose a partition, you would choose the one resulting in the minimum number of splits. For example, you wouldn't choose wall B before wall D because wall B splits wall D.

Second, you could just try to keep the tree as balanced as possible, ignoring the number of splits. Here you would always choose a partition that keeps the same number of walls (plus or minus one) on either side of the partition. For example, you could choose wall B as the first partition because two partitions would be on either side of it (even though it splits wall D).

Or, you could combine these two ideas. For a set of partitions that keep the tree relatively well balanced (with a certain degree), choose the partition with the minimum number of splits.

In this chapter, we don't get into the algorithms for picking partitions, so we leave that as an exercise for the reader. Instead, for a list of walls, just pick the first wall as the partition. This isn't the most ideal solution for large maps with lots of polygons, but it works fine for these examples.

BSP Tree-Traversing Example

Traversing the BSP tree is similar to how you traversed the one-dimensional BSP tree. Two rules apply:

> ➤ Draw polygons in front of the camera in order (front node, current node, back node).

> ➤ Draw polygons in back of the camera in reverse order (back node, current node, front node).

Take a look at the example in Figure 10.10. Imagine the camera is at the location marked with a star. This traversal algorithm traverses the nodes in this order: 4, D2, 6, C, 3, B, 1, D1, 5, A, 2. The polygons are traversed front to back, which is just what you want.

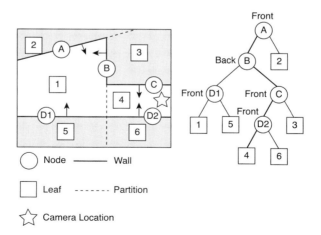

Figure 10.10   Traversing the tree from the star's location.

Also with this algorithm, the first leaf traversed is the leaf that the camera is in. Because horizontal polygons can have different heights, if you know the leaf the player is in, you can determine at what height the player should be located. For example, if the player is 100 units tall and the player is in a leaf with a floor at y=200, the player's camera will be y=300.

Now with the idea of building and traversing the polygons in a BSP tree, we move on a step deeper and write the code for a 2D BSP tree renderer.

Implementing a 2D BSP Tree

To start, you'll create the simple BSPTree class shown in Listing 10.1. This class defines the data structure of the tree as nodes and leaves. As usual, this code is just a start, and you'll add more methods to it later.

Listing 10.1 BSPTree.java

```java
package com.brackeen.javagamebook.bsp2D;

import java.awt.Rectangle;
import java.util.List;

/**
    The BSPTree class represents a 2D Binary Space Partitioned
    tree of polygons. The BSPTree is built using a BSPTreeBuilder
    class, and can be traversed using BSPTreeTraverser class.
*/
public class BSPTree {

    /**
        A Node of the tree. All children of the node are either
        to the front or back of the node's partition.
    */
    public static class Node {
        public Node front;
        public Node back;
        public BSPLine partition;
```

```
        public List polygons;
    }



    /**
        A Leaf of the tree. A leaf has no partition or front or
        back nodes.
    */
    public static class Leaf extends Node {
        public float floorHeight;
        public float ceilHeight;
        public Rectangle bounds;
        public boolean isBack;
    }

    private Node root;

    /**
        Creates a new BSPTree with the specified root node.
    */
    public BSPTree(Node root) {
        this.root = root;
    }



    /**
        Gets the root node of this tree.
    */
    public Node getRoot() {
        return root;
    }
}
```

The BSPTree class contains the inner class Node, which is a node in the tree. The node contains references to front and back nodes, a partition, and a list of polygons. The partition is a BSPLine, which we discuss in the next section. For nodes that aren't leaves, the list of polygons is a list of all the wall polygons collinear with the partition. For leaves (open spaces), this list contains floor and ceiling polygons.

The inner class Leaf is a subclass of Node. It contains the height of the floor and ceiling, which you'll use later to keep the player and objects at the correct height. It also contains the rectangular bounds of the leaf, which you'll use to determine object visibility (in other words, if the leaf is visible, objects within its bounds are visible).

The BSP Line

The line you'll use for partitions (and a few other uses) is the BSPLine in Listing 10.2.

Listing 10.2   BSPLine.java

```
package com.brackeen.javagamebook.bsp2D;

import java.awt.geom.*;
import com.brackeen.javagamebook.math3D.*;

public class BSPLine extends Line2D.Float {

    /**
        X coordinate of the line normal.
    */
    public float nx;

    /**
        Y coordinate of the line normal.
    */
    public float ny;
}
```

The BSPLine is a subclass of Line2D.Float. The Line2D.Float class is part of the java.awt.geom package that has floating-point fields x1, y1, x2, and y2 that define a line segment. In BSPLine, you also include the values for the line's normal, or the direction perpendicular to the line. The normal points in the direction of the "front" of the partition. This class is just a start; you'll add a bunch of methods to BSPLine as you move forward.

Determining the Side of a Point Relative to a Line

One thing you need to determine is whether polygons are in front of a line, in back of a line, or spanning a line. You do this just like you did polygon clipping in Chapter 7, "3D Graphics": one point at a time. For each point in a polygon, you determine whether the point is in front of or in back of the line.

You also need to know whether a point is actually on a line (in other words, is collinear with a line). For example, a polygon might have some points collinear with a line and other points in front. In this case, the polygon would be considered in front of the line, even though parts of it are collinear.

Finding whether a point is in front or back of a line is similar to how you determined whether a point was in front or in back of a polygon, only in 2D: Just find the dot product between the vector to the point and the normal of the line. If this value is less than 0, the point is in back; if it is greater than 0, the point is in front; and if it is equal to 0, the point is collinear.

One problem is that, due to floating-point inaccuracy, it is pretty rare for a point to actually be collinear. (Even 64-bit doubles won't be accurate enough; you really need infinite precision to be accurate 100% of the time.) This can cause problems if, say, a collinear point is calculated as being in back of the line while other points in a polygon are in front. In this case, the polygon would be considered to be spanning the line, which is inaccurate.

To fix this, you must sometimes treat lines as being "thick," as shown in Figure 10.11.

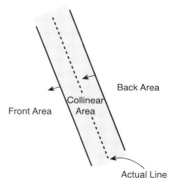

Figure 10.11   Finding the side of point relative to a "thick" line.

In Figure 10.11, the actual line (shown as a dotted line) has both a "front" line and a "back" line. If a point is between these two lines, the point is considered collinear. This way, you create a collinear area and make up for floating-point inaccuracy.

If you assume that the normal to the line is a unit normal (has a length of 1), we can easily "shift" the line forward and backward, and determine the side the point is on for both of these lines. If you want a 1-unit-wide line, shift the line by half of the length of the normal. This is shown in the getSideThick() method in Listing 10.3.

Listing 10.3 getSide() Methods of BSPLine.java

```
public static final int BACK = -1;
public static final int COLLINEAR = 0;
public static final int FRONT = 1;
public static final int SPANNING = 2;

. . .

/**
    Normalizes the normal of this line (make the normal's
    length 1).
*/
public void normalize() {
    float length = (float)Math.sqrt(nx * nx + ny * ny);
    nx/=length;
    ny/=length;
}


/**
    Gets the side of this line the specified point is on.
    Because of floating point inaccuracy, a collinear line
    will be rare. For this to work correctly, the normal of
    this line must be normalized, either by setting this line
    to a polygon or by calling normalize().
    Returns either FRONT, BACK, or COLLINEAR.
*/
```

```
public int getSideThin(float x, float y) {
    // dot product between vector to the point and the normal
    float side = (x - x1)*nx + (y - y1)*ny;
    return (side < 0)?BACK:(side > 0)?FRONT:COLLINEAR;
}



/**
    Gets the side of this line the specified point is on.
    This method treats the line as 1-unit thick, so points
    within this 1-unit border are considered collinear.
    For this to work correctly, the normal of this line
    must be normalized, either by setting this line to a
    polygon or by calling normalize().
    Returns either FRONT, BACK, or COLLINEAR.
*/
public int getSideThick(float x, float y) {
    int frontSide = getSideThin(x-nx/2, y-ny/2);
    if (frontSide == FRONT) {
        return FRONT;
    }
    else if (frontSide == BACK) {
        int backSide = getSideThin(x+nx/2, y+ny/2);
        if (backSide == BACK) {
            return BACK;
        }
    }
    return COLLINEAR;
}
```

The methods in Listing 10.3 are in the BSPLine class. The getSideThin() method treats the line normally, while getSideThick() treats the line as being 1 unit thick. Both methods return either FRONT, BACK, or COLLINEAR.

Now that you have these methods, finding the side of another line or a polygon is trivial. These methods are shown in Listing 10.4.

Listing 10.4 More `getSide()` Methods of BSPLine.java

```java
/**
    Gets the side of this line that the specified line segment
    is on. Returns either FRONT, BACK, COLLINEAR, or SPANNING.
*/
public int getSide(Line2D.Float segment) {
    if (this == segment) {
        return COLLINEAR;
    }
    int p1Side = getSideThick(segment.x1, segment.y1);
    int p2Side = getSideThick(segment.x2, segment.y2);
    if (p1Side == p2Side) {
        return p1Side;
    }
    else if (p1Side == COLLINEAR) {
        return p2Side;
    }
    else if (p2Side == COLLINEAR) {
        return p1Side;
    }
    else {
        return SPANNING;
    }
}


/**
    Gets the side of this line that the specified polygon
    is on. Returns either FRONT, BACK, COLLINEAR, or SPANNING.
*/
public int getSide(BSPPolygon poly) {
    boolean onFront = false;
    boolean onBack = false;

    // check every point
    for (int i=0; i<poly.getNumVertices(); i++) {
        Vector3D v = poly.getVertex(i);
        int side = getSideThick(v.x, v.z);
```

```
        if (side == BSPLine.FRONT) {
            onFront = true;
        }
        else if (side == BSPLine.BACK) {
            onBack = true;
        }
    }

    // classify the polygon
    if (onFront && onBack) {
        return BSPLine.SPANNING;
    }
    else if (onFront) {
        return BSPLine.FRONT;
    }
    else if (onBack) {
        return BSPLine.BACK;
    }
    else {
        return BSPLine.COLLINEAR;
    }
}
```

The methods in Listing 10.4 are also in the BSPLine class. Both of these methods use "thick" lines. A polygon or line is considered to be SPANNING only if one point is front while another is in back. Later, you'll split spanning polygons in two so that one polygon is in front of the line and one is in back.

The BSP Polygon

In previous chapters, you used the TexturedPolygon3D class for all polygons. In this chapter, you extend this class for polygons within a BSP tree. This class, BSPPolygon in Listing 10.5, is a subclass of TexturedPolygon3D that contains information on whether the polygon is a floor/ceiling or a wall; if it's a wall, it contains a BSPLine that represents the wall. Also, it contains an ambient light intensity so that every polygon can have a different ambient light intensity.

Listing 10.5 BSPPolygon.java

```java
package com.brackeen.javagamebook.bsp2D;

import com.brackeen.javagamebook.math3D.*;

/**
    A BSPPolygon is a TexturedPolygon3D with a type
    (TYPE_FLOOR, TYPE_WALL), an ambient light intensity value, and
    a BSPLine representation if the type is TYPE_WALL.
*/
public class BSPPolygon extends TexturedPolygon3D {

    public static final int TYPE_FLOOR = 0;
    public static final int TYPE_WALL = 1;

    private int type;
    private float ambientLightIntensity;
    private BSPLine line;


    . . .
}
```

It's not shown here, but the BSPPolygon class also has the conventional get and set methods to get and set the type, ambient light intensity, and BSPLine.

Traversing a BSP Tree

You need two ways to traverse a BSP tree, just like you did for the 1D BSP tree example: in-order and front-to-back order. Sometimes you just need to traverse every polygon in the tree (such as during the building process), so you need something like an in-order traversal. When you're drawing, you need a front-to-back traversal.

You'll create a BSPTreeTraverser class that actually performs traversals. First, though, you'll create a listener interface so that the BSPTreeTraverser can notify a listener when the polygons in a node are traversed. This BSPTreeTraverseListener interface, shown in Listing 10.6, typically is used for a polygon renderer and when working with all polygons in the tree.

Listing 10.6   BSPTreeTraverseListener.java

```
package com.brackeen.javagamebook.bsp2D;

/**
    A BSPTreeTraverseListener is an interface for a
    BSPTreeTraverser to signal visited polygons.
*/
public interface BSPTreeTraverseListener {

    /**
        Visits a BSP polygon. Called by a BSPTreeTraverer.
        If this method returns true, the BSPTreeTraverer will
        stop the current traversal. Otherwise, the BSPTreeTraverer
        will continue if there are polygons in the tree that
        have not yet been traversed.
    */
    public boolean visitPolygon(BSPPolygon poly,
        boolean isBackLeaf);

}
```

In Listing 10.6, the `BSPTreeTraverseListener` interface provides a `visitPolygon()` method that is called whenever a polygon is visited. If the implementation of this method returns `true`, the traversal stops. This way, you can stop a traversal at any time. When drawing, you don't need to continue traversing the tree after the screen is filled, so you can stop the traversal at that point. Of course, this method provides a polygon as a parameter, but in reality, you're traversing nodes. So, in `BSPTreeTraverser`, you provide a method to visit a node and visit every polygon in a node, as shown in Listing 10.7.

Listing 10.7   `visitNode()` Method of BSPTreeTraverser.java

```
private boolean traversing;
private BSPTreeTraverseListener listener;
private GameObjectManager objectManager;

...
```

continues

Listing 10.7 `visitNode()` Method of BSPTreeTraverser.java *continued*

```java
/**
    Visits a node in the tree. The BSPTreeTraverseListener's
    visitPolygon() method is called for every polygon in
    the node.
*/
private void visitNode(BSPTree.Node node) {
    if (!traversing || node.polygons == null) {
        return;
    }

    boolean isBack = false;
    if (node instanceof BSPTree.Leaf) {
        BSPTree.Leaf leaf = (BSPTree.Leaf)node;
        isBack = leaf.isBack;
        // mark the bounds of this leaf as visible in
        // the game object manager.
        if (objectManager != null && leaf.bounds != null) {
            objectManager.markVisible(leaf.bounds);
        }
    }

    // visit every polygon
    for (int i=0; traversing && i<node.polygons.size(); i++) {
        BSPPolygon poly = (BSPPolygon)node.polygons.get(i);
        traversing = listener.visitPolygon(poly, isBack);
    }
}
```

This method just visits every polygon in a node. Also, if there is a `GameObjectManager` (from Chapter 9, "3D Objects"), this method notifies the manager that the objects within the leaf's bounds are visible.

Now let's actually perform some traversals.

In-Order Traversal

First, do a simple in-order traversal, as shown in Listing 10.8.

Listing 10.8   In-Order `traverse()` Method of BSPTreeTraverser.java

```java
/**
    Traverses a tree in-order.
*/
public void traverse(BSPTree tree) {
    traversing = true;
    traverseInOrder(tree.getRoot());
}



/**
    Traverses a node in-order.
*/
private void traverseInOrder(BSPTree.Node node) {
    if (traversing && node != null) {
        traverseInOrder(node.front);
        visitNode(node);
        traverseInOrder(node.back);
    }
}
```

There's nothing really new in these methods, except that the traversal stops if the `traversing` Boolean is set to `false`.

As usual, you're using recursion to traverse the tree. If you're wondering about recursion speed, don't worry about it in this case. With binary trees traversal in Java, you won't see any significant speed improvement if you don't use recursion.

Some people try to eliminate recursion because it adds extra overhead. For example, computing Fibonacci numbers is much faster if you don't use recursion because, without recursion, you can eliminate both method-calling overhead and stack overhead.

For binary tree traversal, you can do without recursion by implementing your own stack. However, your stack probably won't be any faster than the VM's stack. So go ahead and use recursion in this case, to keep the code clean and more readable.

Front-to-Back Traversal

Next, you'll create a traverse method to traverse nodes in draw order, from front to back. This is just like the 1D BSP example and is shown in Listing 10.9.

Listing 10.9 Draw Order `traverse()` Method of BSPTreeTraverser.java

```java
private float x;
private float z;

...

/**
    Traverses a tree in draw order (front to back) using
    the specified view location.
*/
public void traverse(BSPTree tree, Vector3D viewLocation) {
    x = viewLocation.x;
    z = viewLocation.z;
    traversing = true;
    traverseDrawOrder(tree.getRoot());
}

/**
    Traverses a node in draw order (front to back) using
    the current view location.
*/
private void traverseDrawOrder(BSPTree.Node node) {
    if (traversing && node != null) {
        if (node instanceof BSPTree.Leaf) {
            // no partition, just handle polygons
            visitNode(node);
        }
        else if (node.partition.getSideThin(x,z)==BSPLine.FRONT)
{
            traverseDrawOrder(node.front);
            visitNode(node);
            traverseDrawOrder(node.back);
```

```
        }
        else {
            traverseDrawOrder(node.back);
            visitNode(node);
            traverseDrawOrder(node.front);
        }
    }
}
```

The `traverse()` method in Listing 10.9 traverses nodes from front to back relative to the specified location. For each node, `visitNode()` is called, which notifies the listener that a polygon was traversed.

That's it for traversing. Of course, you need to implement a `BSPTreeTraverseListener` class and a few other things before you can actually draw any polygons. But first, let's take a step back and look at building a tree.

Building a Tree

Let's break down BSP tree building into two parts: building the tree and clipping a polygon to a line.

Building a tree is a recursive process just like traversing the tree. The basic idea is to take a node with a list of polygons, choose a partition, build the front node using the polygons in front of the partition, and then build the back node using the polygons in back of the partition. This is shown in the `BSPTreeBuilder` class in Listing 10.10.

Listing 10.10   BSPTreeBuilder.java

```
/**
    Builds a BSP tree.
*/
public BSPTree build(List polygons) {
    currentTree = new BSPTree(createNewNode(polygons));
    buildNode(currentTree.getRoot());
    return currentTree;
}
```

continues

Listing 10.10 BSPTreeBuilder.java *continued*

```java
/**
    Builds a node in the BSP tree.
*/
protected void buildNode(BSPTree.Node node) {

    // nothing to build if it's a leaf
    if (node instanceof BSPTree.Leaf) {
        return;
    }

    // classify all polygons relative to the partition
    // (front, back, or collinear)
    ArrayList collinearList = new ArrayList();
    ArrayList frontList = new ArrayList();
    ArrayList backList = new ArrayList();
    List allPolygons = node.polygons;
    node.polygons = null;
    for (int i=0; i<allPolygons.size(); i++) {
        BSPPolygon poly = (BSPPolygon)allPolygons.get(i);
        int side = node.partition.getSide(poly);
        if (side == BSPLine.COLLINEAR) {
            collinearList.add(poly);
        }
        else if (side == BSPLine.FRONT) {
            frontList.add(poly);
        }
        else if (side == BSPLine.BACK) {
            backList.add(poly);
        }
        else if (side == BSPLine.SPANNING) {
            BSPPolygon front = clipBack(poly, node.partition);
            BSPPolygon back = clipFront(poly, node.partition);
            if (front != null) {
                frontList.add(front);
            }
            if (back != null) {
                backList.add(back);
```

```
                }

            }
        }

        // clean and assign lists
        collinearList.trimToSize();
        frontList.trimToSize();
        backList.trimToSize();
        node.polygons = collinearList;
        node.front = createNewNode(frontList);
        node.back = createNewNode(backList);

        // build front and back nodes
        buildNode(node.front);
        buildNode(node.back);
        if (node.back instanceof BSPTree.Leaf) {
            ((BSPTree.Leaf)node.back).isBack = true;
        }
    }


    /**
        Creates a new node from a list of polygons. If none of
        the polygons are walls, a leaf is created.
    */
    protected BSPTree.Node createNewNode(List polygons) {

        BSPLine partition = choosePartition(polygons);

        // no partition available, so it's a leaf
        if (partition == null) {
            BSPTree.Leaf leaf = new BSPTree.Leaf();
            leaf.polygons = polygons;
            buildLeaf(leaf);
            return leaf;
        }
        else {
```

continues

Listing 10.10   BSPTreeBuilder.java   *continued*

```
        BSPTree.Node node = new BSPTree.Node();
        node.polygons = polygons;
        node.partition = partition;
        return node;
    }
}


/**
    Chooses a line from a list of polygons to use as a
    partition. This method just returns the line formed by
    the first vertical polygon, or null if none is found. A
    smarter method would choose a partition that minimizes
    polygon splits and provides a more balanced, complete tree.
*/
protected BSPLine choosePartition(List polygons) {
    for (int i=0; i<polygons.size(); i++) {
        BSPPolygon poly = (BSPPolygon)polygons.get(i);
        if (poly.isWall()) {
            return new BSPLine(poly);
        }
    }
    return null;
}


/**
    Builds a leaf in the tree, calculating extra information
    like leaf bounds, floor height, and ceiling height.
*/
protected void buildLeaf(BSPTree.Leaf leaf) {

    if (leaf.polygons.size() == 0) {
        // leaf represents an empty space
        leaf.ceilHeight = Float.MAX_VALUE;
        leaf.floorHeight = Float.MIN_VALUE;
        leaf.bounds = null;
```

```
        return;
    }

    float minX = Float.MAX_VALUE;
    float maxX = Float.MIN_VALUE;
    float minY = Float.MAX_VALUE;
    float maxY = Float.MIN_VALUE;
    float minZ = Float.MAX_VALUE;
    float maxZ = Float.MIN_VALUE;

    // find min y, max y, and bounds
    Iterator i = leaf.polygons.iterator();
    while (i.hasNext()) {
        BSPPolygon poly = (BSPPolygon)i.next();
        for (int j=0; j<poly.getNumVertices(); j++) {
            Vector3D v = poly.getVertex(j);
            minX = Math.min(minX, v.x);
            maxX = Math.max(maxX, v.x);
            minY = Math.min(minY, v.y);
            maxY = Math.max(maxY, v.y);
            minZ = Math.min(minZ, v.z);
            maxZ = Math.max(maxZ, v.z);
        }
    }

    // find any platform within the leaf
    i = leaf.polygons.iterator();
    while (i.hasNext()) {
        BSPPolygon poly = (BSPPolygon)i.next();
        // if a floor
        if (poly.getNormal().y == 1) {
            float y = poly.getVertex(0).y;
            if (y > minY && y < maxY) {
                minY = y;
            }
        }
    }
```

continues

Listing 10.10 BSPTreeBuilder.java *continued*

```
      // set the leaf values
      leaf.ceilHeight = maxY;
      leaf.floorHeight = minY;
      leaf.bounds = new Rectangle(
          (int)Math.floor(minX), (int)Math.floor(minZ),
          (int)Math.ceil(maxX-minX+1),
          (int)Math.ceil(maxZ-minZ+1));
}
```

In this code, the build() method creates a new node that contains every polygon. Note that this method takes only BSPPolygons; because you're using a 2D BSP tree, this way you can easily tell whether a polygon is a vertical wall or a horizontal floor/ceiling. The createNewNode() method creates a new node containing every polygon in the specified list.

The buildNode() method builds a node based on the node's partition. This method classifies every polygon as being either in front, in back, spanning, or collinear with the node's partition. Then it puts each polygon in the proper child node. So, polygons to the front of the partition are placed in the node's "front" child node, and polygons in back of the partition are places in the node's "back" child node. Polygons that span the partition are split by using the clipFront() and clipBack() methods, which we discuss shortly.

The choosePartition() method chooses a partition from a list of polygons. As mentioned earlier, you won't be making a "smart" decision about what to choose as a partition; instead, you'll just choose the first wall in the list as a partition. Optimizing this method can be an exercise for the reader.

The buildLeaf() method simply calculates the floor height, ceiling height, and 2D bounds of the polygons within the leaf.

That's actually the bulk of building a BSP tree right there. Next, you need to write the methods to clip a polygon to a line.

Finding the Intersection of Two Lines

When you clip a polygon to a line, you actually ignore the y component of the polygon to make it a 2D clip. The clip will be similar to how you did polygon clipping in Chapter 7, but you need to find the intersection of an edge of the polygon with a line. In other words, you need to find the intersection of two lines.

The idea behind finding the intersection is shown in Figure 10.12.

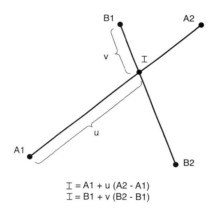

$$I = A1 + u (A2 - A1)$$
$$I = B1 + v (B2 - B1)$$

Figure 10.12   Finding the intersection of two lines.

In Figure 10.12, the point I is the intersection between the two lines. The value u is a fraction of the intersection within line A, so if the two line segments intersect, u will be between `0.0` and `1.0`. The same thing applies for value v in line B.

The equations in Figure 10.12 are just the basic equations of a line, but you can use these formulas to get the intersection. If you solve for u, you get this:

```
numerator   =  (B2y-B1y) (A2x-A1x) - (B2x-B1x) (A2y-A1y)
denominator =  (B2y-B1y) (A2x-A1x) - (B2x-B1x) (A2y-A1y)
u = numerator/denominator
```

Then, with u, you can find the intersection point:

```
x  =  A1x+u (A2x-A1x)
y  =  A1y+u (A2y-A1y)
```

We sum up these equations in the getIntersection() methods in BSPLine, as shown in Listing 10.11.

Listing 10.11   Intersection Methods of BSPLine.java

```java
/**
    Returns the fraction of intersection along this line.
    Returns a value from 0 to 1 if the segments intersect.
    For example, a return value of 0 means the intersection
    occurs at point (x1, y1), 1 means the intersection
    occurs at point (x2, y2), and .5 means the intersection
    occurs halfway between the two endpoints of this line.
    Returns -1 if the lines are parallel.
*/
public float getIntersection(Line2D.Float line) {
    // The intersection point I, of two vectors, A1->A2 and
    // B1->B2, is:
    // I = A1 + u * (A2 - A1)
    // I = B1 + v * (B2 - B1)
    //
    // Solving for u gives us the following formula.
    // u is returned.
    float denominator = (line.y2 - line.y1) * (x2 - x1) -
        (line.x2 - line.x1) * (y2 - y1);

    // check if the two lines are parallel
    if (denominator == 0) {
        return -1;
    }

    float numerator = (line.x2 - line.x1) * (y1 - line.y1) -
        (line.y2 - line.y1) * (x1 - line.x1);

    return numerator / denominator;
}


/**
```

```
    Returns the intersection point of this line with the
    specified line.
*/
public Point2D.Float getIntersectionPoint(Line2D.Float line) {
    return getIntersectionPoint(line, null);
}



/**
    Returns the intersection of this line with the specified
    line. If intersection is null, a new point is created.
*/
public Point2D.Float getIntersectionPoint(Line2D.Float line,
    Point2D.Float intersection)
{
    if (intersection == null) {
        intersection = new Point2D.Float();
    }
    float fraction = getIntersection(line);
    intersection.setLocation(
        x1 + fraction * (x2 - x1),
        y1 + fraction * (y2 - y1));
    return intersection;
}
```

The getIntersection() method calculates u, or the fraction of intersection along the line. The getIntersectionPoint() method calculates the (x,y) values of the intersection and creates a new Point2D.Float if one isn't specified.

If you were dealing with a 3D BSP tree, you would have to clip polygons to a plane rather than a line. This would involve clipping each edge of the polygon to the plane, so it could be accomplished with a line-to-plane intersection instead of a line-to-line intersection.

Now that you can compute intersections, you can move on to clipping polygons.

Clipping Polygons by a Line

Clipping polygons to a line is similar to the clipping you did in Chapter 7 and is a simple 2D clip. These methods, shown in Listing 10.12, just clip a polygon to a line, ignoring the y component of the polygon.

Listing 10.12 Clip Methods of BSPBuilder.java

```
/**
    Clips away the part of the polygon that lies in front
    of the specified line. The returned polygon is the part
    of the polygon in back of the line. Returns null if the
    line does not split the polygon. The original
    polygon is untouched.
*/
protected BSPPolygon clipFront(BSPPolygon poly, BSPLine line) {
    return clip(poly, line, BSPLine.FRONT);
}



/**
    Clips away the part of the polygon that lies in back
    of the specified line. The returned polygon is the part
    of the polygon in front of the line. Returns null if the
    line does not split the polygon. The original
    polygon is untouched.
*/
protected BSPPolygon clipBack(BSPPolygon poly, BSPLine line) {
    return clip(poly, line, BSPLine.BACK);
}



/**
    Clips a BSPPolygon so that the part of the polygon on the
    specified side (either BSPLine.FRONT or BSPLine.BACK)
    is removed, and returns the clipped polygon. Returns null
    if the line does not split the polygon. The original
    polygon is untouched.
*/
```

```java
protected BSPPolygon clip(BSPPolygon poly, BSPLine line,
    int clipSide)
{
    ArrayList vertices = new ArrayList();
    BSPLine polyEdge = new BSPLine();

    // add vertices that aren't on the clip side
    Point2D.Float intersection = new Point2D.Float();
    for (int i=0; i<poly.getNumVertices(); i++) {
        int next = (i+1) % poly.getNumVertices();
        Vector3D v1 = poly.getVertex(i);
        Vector3D v2 = poly.getVertex(next);
        int side1 = line.getSideThin(v1.x, v1.z);
        int side2 = line.getSideThin(v2.x, v2.z);
        if (side1 != clipSide) {
            vertices.add(v1);
        }

        if ((side1 == BSPLine.FRONT && side2 == BSPLine.BACK) ||
            (side2 == BSPLine.FRONT && side1 == BSPLine.BACK))
        {
            // ensure v1.z < v2.z
            if (v1.z > v2.z) {
                Vector3D temp = v1;
                v1 = v2;
                v2 = temp;
            }
            polyEdge.setLine(v1.x, v1.z, v2.x, v2.z);
            float f = polyEdge.getIntersection(line);
            Vector3D tPoint = new Vector3D(
                v1.x + f * (v2.x - v1.x),
                v1.y + f * (v2.y - v1.y),
                v1.z + f * (v2.z - v1.z));
            vertices.add(tPoint);
            // remove any created t-junctions
            removeTJunctions(v1, v2, tPoint);
        }

    }
```

continues

Listing 10.12 Clip Methods of BSPBuilder.java *continued*

```
        // Remove adjacent equal vertices. (A->A) becomes (A)
        for (int i=0; i<vertices.size(); i++) {
            Vector3D v = (Vector3D)vertices.get(i);
            Vector3D next = (Vector3D)vertices.get(
                (i+1) % vertices.size());
            if (v.equals(next)) {
                vertices.remove(i);
                i--;
            }
        }

        if (vertices.size() < 3) {
            return null;
        }

        // make the polygon
        Vector3D[] array = new Vector3D[vertices.size()];
        vertices.toArray(array);
        return poly.clone(array);
    }
```

A couple extra steps are needed when clipping a polygon. First, remove adjacent vertices that are equal. For example, if two vertices next to each other are the same, their edge will have a length of 0. One of these equal vertices is removed.

Also remove any T-junctions that you create. What are T-junctions? Glad you asked! Let's talk about it.

Removing T-Junction Gaps

Figure 10.13 shows an example T-junction gap. Due to floating-point inaccuracy, T-junctions can sometimes lead to gaps between polygons, sometimes only when viewed from certain angles. In this example, the large polygon has only three vertices. When the three polygons are transformed, a gap shows up between them. Most of the time, this gap isn't visible. However, occasionally, the gap appears as a missing pixel or two, or even a speckled line of missing pixels.

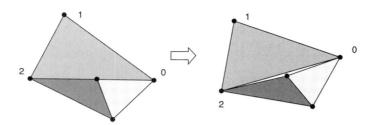

Figure 10.13   The large polygon has only three vertices. Due to floating-point inaccuracy, T-junctions can sometimes lead to gaps between polygons, sometimes only when viewed from certain angles.

Unfortunately, this is another problem for which you need infinite floating-point precision to solve it correctly. But, as usual, there is a workaround!

To eliminate the gap between the T-junctions, you can add another vertex to the spanning polygon at the point of intersection. This is shown in Figure 10.14.

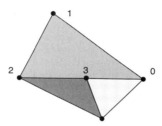

Figure 10.14   To eliminate T-junction gaps, the large polygon has a fourth vertex it shares with the other two polygons.

So, to eliminate T-junction gaps, the code inserts vertices into polygon edges whenever a polygon split occurs. This way, building the BSP tree never creates new T-junctions when it splits polygons. The idea is simple enough and is shown in the code in Listing 10.13.

Listing 10.13   T-Junction Removal Methods of BSPBuilder.java

```
/**
    Remove any T-Junctions from the current tree along the
    line specified by (v1, v2). Find all polygons with this
    edge and insert the T-intersection point between them.
```

continues

Listing 10.13 T-Junction Removal Methods of BSPBuilder.java *continued*

```java
*/
protected void removeTJunctions(final Vector3D v1,
    final Vector3D v2, final Vector3D tPoint)
{
    BSPTreeTraverser traverser = new BSPTreeTraverser(
        new BSPTreeTraverseListener() {
            public boolean visitPolygon(BSPPolygon poly,
                boolean isBackLeaf)
            {
                removeTJunctions(poly, v1, v2, tPoint);
                return true;
            }
        }
    );
    traverser.traverse(currentTree);
}


/**
    Remove any T-Junctions from the specified polygon. The
    T-intersection point is inserted between the points
    v1 and v2 if there are no other points between them.
*/
protected void removeTJunctions(BSPPolygon poly,
    Vector3D v1, Vector3D v2, Vector3D tPoint)
{
    for (int i=0; i<poly.getNumVertices(); i++) {
        int next = (i+1) % poly.getNumVertices();
        Vector3D p1 = poly.getVertex(i);
        Vector3D p2 = poly.getVertex(next);
        if ((p1.equals(v1) && p2.equals(v2)) ||
            (p1.equals(v2) && p2.equals(v1)))
        {
            poly.insertVertex(next, tPoint);
            return;
        }
    }
}
```

In Listing 10.13, you take the brute-force approach to finding matching T-junctions: Just check every edge of every polygon in the tree. Admittedly, this could be accomplished faster by just searching for polygons that share an edge with the line of the T-junction, but this works as well.

Notice that the BSP tree building removes only T-junctions that are created from clipped polygons. In other words, it assumes that polygons passed to the BSP builder don't have any T-junctions.

Taking a step back, you have everything you need for building: the building algorithm and polygon clipping. You also have BSP traversal, so let's make a short demo to try everything out.

Testing the BSP Tree

At this point, even though you can't draw polygons in the BSP tree in a 3D scene yet, you can create a test demo for the BSP tree. The BSPTest2D does this, drawing a bird's-eye view of a 3D scene just like in the previous examples and figures. Like in previous chapters, this demo extends the GameCore class, and its interesting methods are shown here in Listing 10.14.

Listing 10.14   BSP Building in BSPTest2D.java

```
public void createPolygons() {
    // The floor polygon
    BSPPolygon floor = new BSPPolygon(new Vector3D[] {
        new Vector3D(0,0,0), new Vector3D(0,0,600),
        new Vector3D(800,0,600), new Vector3D(800,0,0)
        }, BSPPolygon.TYPE_FLOOR);
    polygons.add(floor);

    // vertices defined from left to right as the viewer
    // looks at the wall
    BSPPolygon wallA = createPolygon(
        new BSPLine(0, 150, 500, 75), 0, 300);
    BSPPolygon wallB = createPolygon(
        new BSPLine(500, 75, 500, 300), 0, 300);
    BSPPolygon wallC = createPolygon(
```

continues

Listing 10.14 BSP Building in BSPTest2D.java *continued*

```
        new BSPLine(500, 300, 800, 300), 0, 300);
    BSPPolygon wallD = createPolygon(
        new BSPLine(800, 450, 0, 450), 0, 300);
    polygons.add(wallA);
    polygons.add(wallB);
    polygons.add(wallC);
    polygons.add(wallD);
}

public BSPPolygon createPolygon(BSPLine line, float bottom,
    float top)
{
    return new BSPPolygon(new Vector3D[] {
        new Vector3D(line.x1, bottom, line.y1),
        new Vector3D(line.x2, bottom, line.y2),
        new Vector3D(line.x2, top, line.y2),
        new Vector3D(line.x1, top, line.y1)
        }, BSPPolygon.TYPE_WALL);
}

public void buildTree() {
    BSPTreeBuilder builder = new BSPTreeBuilder();
    bspTree = builder.build(polygons.subList(0, numWalls+1));
}
```

In Listing 10.14, BSPPolygons are created to match the previous floor plan example. One giant floor that covers the entire area is created, which is unrealistic in the real-world (you wouldn't want nonvisible floors that are behind walls), but this works well as an example.

The rest of BSPTest2D draws the polygons from a bird's-eye perspective, as shown in the screenshot in Figure 10.15.

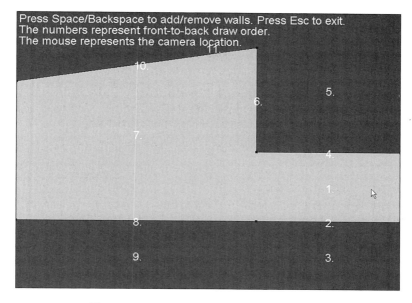

Figure 10.15   Screenshot of `BSPTest2D`.

In Figure 10.15, the mouse represents the camera's location, and the numbers represent the order in which the polygons are drawn from the camera location.

That's it! As you can see in the demo, building and traversal work great. Now you can move on to the goal of this chapter: actually drawing the polygons in the BSP tree.

Drawing Polygons Front to Back

Now that you have a BSP tree to traverse polygons from front to back, to draw polygons front to back you need to do two things:

➤ Avoid drawing over pixels that are already on the screen.

➤ Easily check whether the view is filled (whether every pixel is drawn).

You could just check and set the z-buffer—but, hey, that's what you're trying to avoid. Also, checking whether the view is filled by testing if every pixel is drawn is still too much of a hassle. And really, because you're drawing front to back, you just need a 1-bit z-buffer because when a pixel is drawn, it would never be overdrawn.

Because you're converting polygons to horizontal scans anyway, you can easily keep track of which scans in the view window have already been drawn. To do this, keep a list of scans for each horizontal row of pixels in the view window, as shown in Figure 10.16.

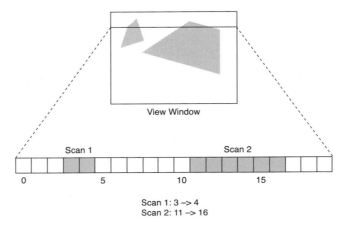

Figure 10.16   Every horizontal line in the view window contains a list of scans already drawn.

When you draw a new polygon, after scan-converting you add that scan to the list of scans in the view window. An example of this is in Figure 10.17. In this figure, the polygon scan is shortened so that it is not drawn over what is already in the view. Also, the list of scans in the view window for that row is merged to become one scan.

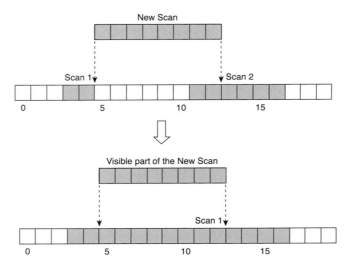

Figure 10.17   In this example, a new scan is added to the list of scans. The result is that the new scan is truncated to show only what is visible, and the two existing scans are merged.

Using this technique, you can easily check whether the view is filled by checking whether each horizontal scan is filled with one scan.

First, write some code to manage a row of scans. This is shown in the SortedScanList in Listing 10.15, which is an inner class of SortedScanConverter.

Listing 10.15 SortedScanList Inner Class of SortedScanConverter

```
/**
    The SortedScanList class represents a series of scans
    for a row. New scans can be added and clipped to what's
    visible in the row.
*/
private static class SortedScanList {

    private int length;
    private Scan[] scans;

    /**
        Creates a new SortedScanList with the default
        capacity (number of scans per row).
    */
    public SortedScanList() {
        this(DEFAULT_SCANLIST_CAPACITY);
    }


    /**
        Creates a new SortedScanList with the specified
        capacity (number of scans per row).
    */
    public SortedScanList(int capacity) {
        scans = new Scan[capacity];
        for (int i=0; i<capacity; i++) {
            scans[i] = new Scan();
        }
        length = 0;
```

continues

```java
}


/**
    Clears this list of scans.
*/
public void clear() {
    length = 0;
}


/**
    Returns the number of scans in this list.
*/
public int getNumScans() {
    return length;
}


/**
    Gets the nth scan in this list.
*/
public Scan getScan(int index) {
    return scans[index];
}


/**
    Checks if this scan list has only one scan and if that
    scan is equal to the specified left and right values.
*/
public boolean equals(int left, int right) {
    return (length == 1 && scans[0].equals(left,right));
}


/**
```

```
        Add and clip the scan to this row, putting what is
        visible (the difference) in the specified
        SortedScanList.
*/
public void add(int left, int right, SortedScanList diff) {
    for (int i=0; i<length && left <= right; i++) {
        Scan scan = scans[i];
        int maxRight = scan.left - 1;
        if (left <= maxRight) {
            if (right < maxRight) {
                diff.add(left, right);
                insert(left, right, i);
                return;
            }
            else {
                diff.add(left, maxRight);
                scan.left = left;
                left = scan.right + 1;
                if (merge(i)) {
                    i--;
                }
            }
        }
        else if (left <= scan.right) {
            left = scan.right + 1;
        }
    }
    if (left <= right) {
        insert(left, right, length);
        diff.add(left, right);
    }

}


// add() helper methods

private void growCapacity() {
    int capacity = scans.length;
```

continues

Listing 10.15 `SortedScanList` Inner Class of `SortedScanConverter` *continued*

```
        int newCapacity = capacity*2;
        Scan[] newScans = new Scan[newCapacity];
        System.arraycopy(scans, 0, newScans, 0, capacity);
        for (int i=length; i<newCapacity; i++) {
            newScans[i] = new Scan();
        }
        scans = newScans;
    }

    private void add(int left, int right) {
        if (length == scans.length) {
            growCapacity();
        }
        scans[length].setTo(left, right);
        length++;
    }

    private void insert(int left, int right, int index) {
        if (index > 0) {
            Scan prevScan = scans[index-1];
            if (prevScan.right == left - 1) {
                prevScan.right = right;
                return;
            }
        }

        if (length == scans.length) {
            growCapacity();
        }
        Scan last = scans[length];
        last.setTo(left, right);
        for (int i=length; i>index; i--) {
            scans[i] = scans[i-1];
        }
        scans[index] = last;
        length++;
    }
```

```
    private void remove(int index) {
        Scan removed = scans[index];
        for (int i=index; i<length-1; i++) {
            scans[i] = scans[i+1];
        }
        scans[length-1] = removed;
        length--;
    }


    private boolean merge(int index) {
        if (index > 0) {
            Scan prevScan = scans[index-1];
            Scan thisScan = scans[index];
            if (prevScan.right == thisScan.left-1) {
                prevScan.right = thisScan.right;
                remove(index);
                return true;
            }
        }
        return false;
    }

}
```

This code manages a list of scans and merges adjacent scans when possible. The public add() method enables you to add a polygon scan and get the visible difference in the diff argument.

To take advantage of this scan list class, create a new ScanConverter, shown in Listing 10.16. This can be used instead of the normal ScanConverter from Chapter 7.

Listing 10.16   SortedScanConverter.java

```
package com.brackeen.javagamebook.graphics3D;

import com.brackeen.javagamebook.math3D.*;

/**
    A ScanConverter used to draw sorted polygons from
```

continues

Listing 10.16 SortedScanConverter.java *continued*

```
       front to back with no overdraw. Polygons are added and clipped
       to a list of what's in the view window. Call clear() before
       drawing every frame.
*/
public class SortedScanConverter extends ScanConverter {

    protected static final int DEFAULT_SCANLIST_CAPACITY = 8;

    private SortedScanList[] viewScans;
    private SortedScanList[] polygonScans;
    private boolean sortedMode;

    /**
        Creates a new SortedScanConverter for the specified
        ViewWindow. The ViewWindow's properties can change in
        between scan conversions. By default, sorted mode is
        off, but can be turned on by calling setSortedMode().
    */
    public SortedScanConverter(ViewWindow view) {
        super(view);
        sortedMode = false;
    }


    /**
        Clears the current view scan. Call this method every frame.
    */
    public void clear() {
        if (viewScans != null) {
            for (int y=0; y<viewScans.length; y++) {
                viewScans[y].clear();
            }
        }
    }


    /**
```

```
        Sets sorted mode, so this scan converter can assume
        the polygons are drawn front to back, and should be
        clipped against polygons already scanned for this view.
    */
    public void setSortedMode(boolean b) {
        sortedMode = b;
    }


    /**
        Gets the nth scan for the specified row.
    */
    public Scan getScan(int y, int index) {
        return polygonScans[y].getScan(index);
    }


    /**
        Gets the number of scans for the specified row.
    */
    public int getNumScans(int y) {
        return polygonScans[y].getNumScans();
    }


    /**
        Checks if the view is filled.
    */
    public boolean isFilled() {
        if (viewScans == null) {
            return false;
        }

        int left = view.getLeftOffset();
        int right = left + view.getWidth() - 1;
        for (int y=view.getTopOffset(); y<viewScans.length; y++)
{
```

continues

Listing 10.16 SortedScanConverter.java *continued*

```
            if (!viewScans[y].equals(left, right)) {
                return false;
            }
        }
        return true;
    }


    protected void ensureCapacity() {
        super.ensureCapacity();
        int height = view.getTopOffset() + view.getHeight();
        int oldHeight = (viewScans == null)?0:viewScans.length;
        if (height != oldHeight) {
            SortedScanList[] newViewScans =
                new SortedScanList[height];
            SortedScanList[] newPolygonScans =
                new SortedScanList[height];
            if (oldHeight != 0) {
                System.arraycopy(viewScans, 0, newViewScans, 0,
                    Math.min(height, oldHeight));
                System.arraycopy(polygonScans, 0, newPolygonScans,
                    0, Math.min(height, oldHeight));
            }
            viewScans = newViewScans;
            polygonScans = newPolygonScans;
            for (int i=oldHeight; i<height; i++) {
                viewScans[i] = new SortedScanList();
                polygonScans[i] = new SortedScanList();
            }
        }
    }


    /**
        Scan-converts a polygon, and if sortedMode is on, adds
        and clips it to a list of what's in the view window.
    */
```

```
    public boolean convert(Polygon3D polygon) {
        boolean visible = super.convert(polygon);
        if (!sortedMode || !visible) {
            return visible;
        }

        // clip the scan to what's already in the view
        visible = false;
        for (int y=getTopBoundary(); y<=getBottomBoundary(); y++)
{

            Scan scan = getScan(y);
            SortedScanList diff = polygonScans[y];
            diff.clear();
            if (scan.isValid()) {
                viewScans[y].add(scan.left, scan.right, diff);
                visible |= (polygonScans[y].getNumScans() > 0);
            }
        }

        return visible;

    }
}
```

The SortedScanConverter assumes the polygons are drawn in a front-to-back order as long as it's in sorted mode. A scan list is kept for every row of pixels in the view window. Also, a scan list is kept for every row of pixels for the current polygon. The isFilled() method checks the scan lists for the view window to see if the view window is filled.

One thing to note is that the isFilled() method might be too expensive to call after drawing every polygon. Alternatively, this method can be called every three polygons or so. The drawback is that the tree traversal could go on longer than you need (and a couple extra polygons could get scan-converted), but overall, it is faster than calling isFilled() after drawing every polygon.

Using `SortedScanConverter` is similar to using `ScanConverter`, except that each row can have multiple scans. Here's an example:

```
int y = scanConverter.getTopBoundary();
while (y <= scanConverter.getBottomBoundary()) {
    for (int i=0; i<scanConverter.getNumScans(y); i++) {
        ScanConverter.Scan scan = scanConverter.getScan(y, i);

        if (scan.isValid()) {
            int offset = (y - viewWindow.getTopOffset()) *
                viewWindow.getWidth() +
                (scan.left - viewWindow.getLeftOffset());

            scanRenderer.render(offset, scan.left, scan.right);
        }
    }
    y++;
}
```

Using this `SortedScanConverter`, you can now draw polygons from front to back and test whether the view window is filled. Let's make a demo.

First BSP Example

You'll encapsulate the BSP drawing in the `SimpleBSPRenderer` class, which is a subclass of `ShadedSurfacePolygonRenderer`. This new class has one method for drawing polygons in a tree and also is a `BSPTraverseListener`, as shown here:

```
/**
    Draws the visible polygons in a BSP tree based on
    the camera location. The polygons are drawn front to back.
*/
public void draw(Graphics2D g, BSPTree tree) {
    currentGraphics2D = g;
    traverser.traverse(tree, camera.getLocation());
}
```

```
// from the BSPTreeTraverseListener interface
public boolean visitPolygon(BSPPolygon poly, boolean isBack) {
    draw(currentGraphics2D, poly);
    return !((SortedScanConverter)scanConverter).isFilled();
}
```

Next, create the basic demo in a class called `BSPTest3D`. The `BSPTest3D` class is similar to `BSPTest2D`, except that it draws polygons using the `SimpleBSPRenderer`:

```
public void draw(Graphics2D g) {

    // draw polygons
    polygonRenderer.startFrame(g);
    ((SimpleBSPRenderer)polygonRenderer).draw(g, bspTree);
    polygonRenderer.endFrame(g);

    super.drawText(g);
}
```

That's it for the demo. Finally, you can see your example floor plan in 3D. Check out the screenshot in Figure 10.18.

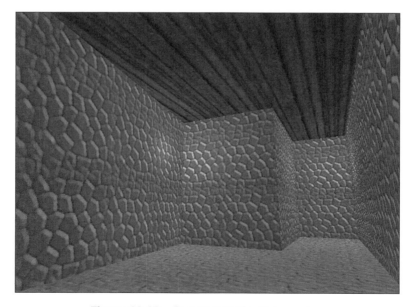

Figure 10.18   Screenshot of `BSPTest3D`.

This demo works fine, but there are a couple problems:

➤ You can draw 3D objects such as monsters and treasures, but they won't be merged correctly with the scene because object drawing relies on z-buffering.

➤ Creating polygons in code will quickly become a drag. You need an easier way.

So, let's work on solving these issues, shall we?

Drawing Objects in the Scene

Because you already have z-buffering to draw 3D objects, it would be easy to just continue to use z-buffering when you draw 3D objects in the 3D scene. However, you need to ensure that polygons are drawn correctly in the scene. For example, polygons that are partly behind walls should show only the visible part of the polygon. But—gasp—you want to avoid z-buffering, right?

Well, sort of. The easiest way to solve this problem is to just use z-buffering, but not the same z-buffering you used before. When you draw the polygons in the BSP tree, you draw each pixel in the view only once. So, for each pixel, you never have to check the z-buffer; you only have to set it. In other words, setting the z-buffer only once for every pixel won't have the performance impact of plain z-buffering.

Here's the basic flow:

1. Draw polygons in the BSP tree, setting the z-buffer.
2. Draw polygons in the 3D objects, checking and setting the z-buffer.

On machines I've tested, setting the z-buffer for polygons in a BSP tree takes about 3–10% of the processor, depending on the machine. In spite of the performance impact, it gives perfect merging of 3D objects in the scene. Also, it's a common way to do 3D rendering, ever since this technique was used in the original *Quake*.

One thing to note is that you can set the z-buffer separately from texture mapping. To do this, create a polygon renderer class called BSPRenderer that sets the z-buffer for every polygon scan that is drawn, as shown here:

```
/**
    Sets the z-depth for the current polygon scan.
*/
private void setScanDepth(int offset, int width) {
    float z = c.getDotProduct(viewPos);
    float dz = c.x;
    int depth = (int)(w*z);
    int dDepth = (int)(w*dz);
    int endOffset = offset + width;

    // depth will be constant for many floors and ceilings
    if (dDepth == 0) {
        short d = (short)(depth >> SCALE_BITS);
        while (offset < endOffset) {
            zBuffer.setDepth(offset++, d);
        }
    }
    else {
        while (offset < endOffset) {
            zBuffer.setDepth(offset++,
                (short)(depth >> SCALE_BITS));
            depth += dDepth;
        }
    }
}
```

This BSPRenderer also draws 3D objects using plain check-and-set z-buffering.

Okay, now you can draw 3D objects. One last step: loading maps from a file.

Loading Maps from a File

It's generally a good idea to separate content from code. In this case, the polygons and objects that make up the map are the content.

In the previous chapter, you used the common Alias|Wavefront OBJ file format to define groups of polygons. In this chapter, you do something similar for maps, with the following goals in mind:

➤ To easily define a 2D map with variable-height floors and ceilings

➤ To define point lights and ambient light intensity

➤ To define starting locations of 3D objects and the player

➤ To easily edit maps

To accomplish these goals, I created a simple file format similar to the OBJ format, called the *MAP format*. Like the OBJ file format, MAP is a text-based format with one command per line, and comments are marked as lines that start with #. The commands are shown in Table 10.1.

Table 10.1 MAP Format Commands

`mtllib <filename>`	Loads materials from an external .mtl file.
`usemtl <name>`	Uses the named material (loaded from an .mtl file) for subsequent polygons.
`v <x> <y> <z>`	Defines a vertex with floating-point coordinates (x,y,z).
`ambientLightIntensity <v>`	Defines the ambient light intensity for the next room, from 0 to 1.
`pointlight [v] [intensity] [falloff]`	Defines a point light located at the specified vector. Optionally, light intensity and fall-off distance can be specified.
`room [name]`	Defines a new room, optionally giving the room a name. A room consists of vertical walls, a horizontal floor, and a horizontal ceiling. Concave rooms are currently not supported but can be simulated by adjacent convex rooms.
`floor [height]`	Defines the height of the floor of the current room, using the current material. The current material can be null, in which case no floor polygon is created. The floor can be above the ceiling, in which case a pillar or block structure is created rather than a room.
`ceil [height]`	Defines the height of the ceiling of the current room, using the current material. The current material can be null, in which case no ceiling polygon is created. The ceiling can be below the floor, in which case a pillar or block structure is created rather than a room.
`wall [x] [z] [bottom] [top]`	Defines a wall vertex in a room using the specified x and z coordinates. Walls should be defined in clockwise order. If bottom and top are not defined, the floor and ceiling height are used. If the current material is null, or if bottom is equal to top, no wall polygon is created.

`obj [uniqueName]` `[filename] [v] [angle]`	Defines an object from an external OBJ file. The unique name allows this object to be uniquely identified, but it can be null if no unique name is needed. The filename is an external OBJ file. Optionally, the starting angle, in radians, around the y-axis can be specified.
`player [v] [angle]`	Specifies the starting location of the player and optionally a starting angle, in radians, around the y-axis.

The MAP format groups polygons into rooms. Everything is a room: hallways, rooms, even inside-out rooms such as pillars and steps. Also, you can define variable-height floors and ceilings.

Using this MAP format, you can create maps in a text editor instead of creating polygons by hand in the code itself. Here's an example map in Listing 10.17, which creates a room just like the floor plan used in this chapter.

Listing 10.17   basic.map

```
# load materials
mtllib textures.mtl

# define a room
ambientLightIntensity .5
room MainRoom

usemtl roof1
floor 0

usemtl roof2
ceil 300

# define walls
# a wall is defined from this vertex to the next vertex
usemtl wall1
wall 0 150
wall 0 450
wall 800 450
wall 800 300
wall 500 300
wall 500 75
```

continues

Listing 10.17   basic.map   *continued*

```
# define lights
v 400 200 100
pointlight -1 1 300
v 700 200 400
pointlight -1 .5 1000
v 65 200 385
pointlight -1 1 100


# specify the starting location of the player
v 400 0 300
player -1
```

This floor plan doesn't have any objects, but if you were to add some, it would look like this:

```
v -700 0 550
obj bot1 robot.obj -1 1.57
```

To read MAP files, there's a MapLoader class that is a subclass of ObjectLoader. Its parsing routines use a RoomDef class, shown in Listing 10.18, to define the rooms.

Listing 10.18   RoomDef.java

```java
package com.brackeen.javagamebook.bsp2D;

import java.util.*;
import com.brackeen.javagamebook.math3D.*;
import com.brackeen.javagamebook.graphics3D.texture.*;

/**
    The RoomDef class represents a convex room with walls, a
    floor, and a ceiling. The floor may be above the ceiling, in
    which case the RoomDef is a "pillar" or "block" structure,
    rather than a "room". RoomDefs are used as a shortcut
    to create the actual BSPPolygons used in the 2D BSP tree.
```

```
*/
public class RoomDef {

    private HorizontalAreaDef floor;
    private HorizontalAreaDef ceil;
    private List vertices;
    private float ambientLightIntensity;


    /**
        The HorizontalAreaDef class represents a floor or ceiling.
    */
    private static class HorizontalAreaDef {
        float height;
        Texture texture;
        Rectangle3D textureBounds;

        public HorizontalAreaDef(float height, Texture texture,
            Rectangle3D textureBounds)
        {
            this.height = height;
            this.texture = texture;
            this.textureBounds = textureBounds;
        }
    }


    /**
        The Vertex class represents a Wall vertex.
    */
    private static class Vertex {
        float x;
        float z;
        float bottom;
        float top;
        Texture texture;
        Rectangle3D textureBounds;
```

continues

Listing 10.18 RoomDef.java *continued*

```java
        public Vertex(float x, float z, float bottom, float top,
            Texture texture, Rectangle3D textureBounds)
        {
            this.x = x;
            this.z = z;
            this.bottom = bottom;
            this.top = top;
            this.texture = texture;
            this.textureBounds = textureBounds;
        }

        public boolean isWall() {
            return (bottom != top) && (texture != null);
        }
    }
}
```

The `RoomDef` class just keeps track of everything for a room defined in a map: wall vertices, the floor height, the ceiling height, and textures. Also, it has methods to create polygons out of the rooms, but those methods aren't shown here because they really don't do anything special. Some other code not shown here is the `MapLoader` because it's very similar to the `ObjectLoader`.

At first, you might think it would be okay to have concave rooms because the BSP partitions will break down the rooms into convex polygons anyway. However, concave rooms have a complexity that our BSP building code wasn't designed for, as shown in Figure 10.19. In this figure, a partition splits a concave polygon, which results in four separate polygons. So, note that rooms in the map file should always be convex.

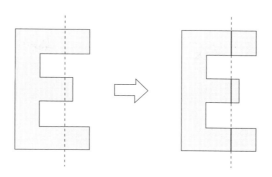

Figure 10.19 Splitting concave polygons along a line can create more than two polygons. In this case, four polygons are created.

Putting It All Together

That's it for BSP trees. As a final demo, I created the `BSPMapTest` that puts everything together: drawing polygons from the BSP tree, drawing 3D object polygons, and loading maps from a file. Check out the screenshots in Figures 10.20 and 10.21.

Figure 10.20 Screenshot of `BSPMapTest`.

Figure 10.21   Screenshot of `BSPMapTest`.

This demo isn't perfect. The major problem with this demo is there is no collision handling: you can walk right through walls. Likewise, you can't walk up stairs yet, and you just stay at the same height the entire time. We'll fix this in the next chapter, "Collision Detection."

Enhancements

The 2D BSP tree that you created in this chapter is pretty cool and gives you the ability to create some cool scenes, but there's always room for improvement. Here are a few ideas for enhancement:

➤ When building the tree, create a better partition-selection algorithm that creates a more balanced tree and minimizes polygon splits.

➤ Save the built BSP tree to a file so you don't have to calculate it at startup every time.

➤ Use a 3D BSP tree instead of a 2D one so you can have polygons that aren't horizontal or vertical, such as ramps and sloping ceilings.

➤ Use the z-buffer to draw particles for effects such as explosions.

Summary

In this chapter, we covered the complicated issue of BSP trees, including building 2D BSP trees, drawing polygons front to back, drawing 3D objects, and loading maps from a file. Along the way, we covered topics such as the basics of binary trees, line intersections, "thick" lines, and how to eliminate T-junction gaps.

At this point, you have a pretty cool 3D rendering engine and can move on to some other game-programming topics, such as collision detection, path finding, and AI.

Chapter 11

Collision Detection

Remember Pong?

Whether it's a pong ball bouncing off a paddle, a laser hitting a robot, an adventurer falling down a pit, the hero finding some ammo, two monsters ramming into one another, or just the player walking into a wall, you're going to need some sort of collision detection in almost any game.

In Chapter 5, "Creating a 2D Platform Game," you made some basic 2D collision detection that worked well for a 2D tile-based game. In this chapter, you'll expand on the ideas presented there, provide more thorough object-to-object collision detection, and provide collision detection against polygons stored in BSP trees.

Also, and just as important, we'll show different ways of handling a collision after it's detected, such as sliding along walls or letting game objects handle their own collision behavior.

Collision Basics

Collision detection is really more than just detection. We break down collisions into three areas of interest:

> ➤ **Deciding what collisions to test.** It seems kind of ridiculous to test whether two objects collide if they are on opposite sides of the world. Also, a world with 1,000 moving objects would require you to test each

object against every other object, or 999,000 tests in all. So, you should try to limit the number of objects you need to test as much as possible. An easy way to do this is only test objects that are close.

➤ **Detecting a collision.** Collision detection really depends on how accurate you want the collisions to be. You could provide perfect collision detection and test every polygon in one object with every polygon in another object, but just imagine the amount of computation involved. Likewise, for the 2D world, you could test every pixel from one sprite to every pixel from another sprite. Usually, games settle with collision-detection techniques that are slightly inaccurate but can be processed quickly.

➤ **Handling a collision.** If an object collides with something, the collision will be handled in different ways depending on the type of collision. For example, a projectile colliding with a robot might destroy both the projectile and the robot. An object bumping against a wall might slide against the wall. And so on.

In summary, a game should try for these collision-detection goals:

➤ Eliminate as many collision tests as possible.

➤ Quickly decide whether there is a collision.

➤ Provide collision detection that is accurate enough for the game.

➤ Handle the collision in a way that doesn't distract the user from the game.

The last goal is basically saying you don't want to restrict the player's movement too much during the course of a game. For example, you don't want to completely stop a player during a wall collision. Instead, let the player slide against the wall or gently bump off it.

Also, you don't want your collision detection to be inaccurate to the point that the player can cheat by squeezing through the wall at certain locations in the map, for example.

Let's start with a simple collision-detection algorithm. Consider that everything that moves in the game is an object, whether it's a monster, the player, a projectile, or whatever. For each object, follow these steps:

1. Update the object's location.

2. Check for any collisions with other objects or with the environment.

3. If a collision is found, revert the object to its previous location.

Notice that you check for a collision after each object moves. Alternatively, you could just move all the objects first and then check collisions afterward. However, you'd have to store the object's previous location with the object, and problems could occur if three or more objects collide.

Also, this basic algorithm just reverts an object to its previous location if a collision occurred. Normally, you want to use other types of collision handling based on the type of collision.

With this algorithm in mind, let's get started with object-to-object collisions.

Object-to-Object Collisions

Ideally, no matter how accurate you want the collision detection to be, it's a good idea to both eliminate as many object-to-object tests as possible and do a few other tests first to ensure that two objects have a good chance of colliding.

Eliminating Tests

Obviously, if an object doesn't move from one frame to the next, you don't need to do any collision tests for that object. For example, a crate that just sits there will never collide with anything. Other objects will collide with the crate, but those collisions are handled by the other objects.

To help eliminate collision tests further, you really should test only objects that are in the same proximity.

One way to do this is to arrange objects on a grid, like in Figure 11.1. Each object exists in one cell on the grid. Even though an object's bounds could extend to other cells, the object exists in only one cell. This way, an object needs to test for collisions only with objects in its own cell and its surrounding cells.

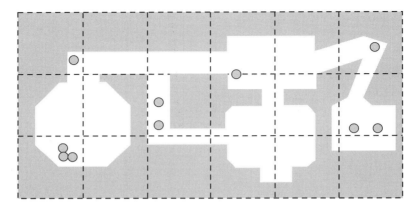

Figure 11.1 To reduce the number of object-to-object collision tests, you can isolate objects on a grid and only test an object against other objects that are in the same cell and its surrounding cells.

Other ways to isolate objects include 1D or 3D versions of the grid concept. For example, in a side-scrolling game, objects could be in a list sorted by their x location, so only neighboring objects in the list test for collisions. For a 3D game, objects could be isolated in a 3D grid instead of a 2D grid, so each cell would be a cube instead of a square. In this chapter, for collision with the 3D engine, we use the 2D version.

Isolating objects on a gird also has the benefit of easily applying object culling. For example, with a top-down engine, you would draw only the objects in visible cells. For a BSP tree, you would draw only the objects in cells that have visible leaves.

The code for arranging objects in a grid is trivial and is implemented for this chapter in the `GridGameObjectManager` class. When an object is updated, the `checkObjectCollision()` method is called (see Listing 11.1). This method checks for a collision with any objects in the object's surrounding cells.

Listing 11.1 Checking Surrounding Cells (GridGameObjectManager.java)

```
/**
    The Cell class represents a cell in the grid. It contains
    a list of game objects and a visible flag.
*/
private static class Cell {
    List objects;
    boolean visible;
```

```
    Cell() {
        objects = new ArrayList();
        visible = false;
    }
}


...


/**
    Checks to see if the specified object collides with any
    other object.
*/
public boolean checkObjectCollision(GameObject object,
    Vector3D oldLocation)
{

    boolean collision = false;

    // use the object's (x,z) position (ground plane)
    int x = convertMapXtoGridX((int)object.getX());
    int y = convertMapYtoGridY((int)object.getZ());

    // check the object's surrounding 9 cells
    for (int i=x-1; i<=x+1; i++) {
        for (int j=y-1; j<=y+1; j++) {
            Cell cell = getCell(i, j);
            if (cell != null) {
                collision |= collisionDetection.checkObject(
                    object, cell.objects, oldLocation);
            }
        }
    }

    return collision;
}
```

This code calls the chectObject() method of the CollisionDetection class, which
detects a collision between an object and a list of objects. You'll implement this class next.

Bounding Spheres

An inaccurate but fast technique for performing collision detection is the use of *bounding spheres*, such as the one in Figure 11.2.

Figure 11.2 A bounding sphere can be used for collision detection.

This idea is that if two objects' spheres collide, the collision is treated as if the two objects collide. A first try at testing whether two objects' spheres collide works something like this:

```
dx = objectA.x - objectB.x;
dy = objectA.y - objectB.y;
dz = objectA.z - objectB.z;
minDistance = objectA.radius + objectB.radius
if (Math.sqrt(dx*dx + dy*dy + dz*dz) < minDistance) {
    // collision found
}
```

However, that `Math.sqrt()` function call involves a lot of computation. Instead, you could square both sides of the equation to get something a bit simpler:

```
if (dx*dx + dy*dy + dz*dz < minDistance*minDistance) {
    // collision found
}
```

If your game is in a 2D world instead of 3D, you can test for circles instead of spheres, taking the z coordinate out of the equation.

Testing bounding spheres is easy, but it's not very accurate. For example, in Figure 11.3, the bounding sphere of the player collides with the bounding sphere of the robot, even though the player and the robot don't actually collide.

Figure 11.3   Bounding sphere inaccuracy: The two spheres collide, but the objects don't.

Of course, having this amount of inaccuracy is fine for many games. For example, for a fast-moving action game in which you're running around picking up food or ammo, you probably won't care whether you pick up the item a little before you actually touch the item. But for other situations, the inaccuracy can be annoying, such as when you get wounded by a creature that you know didn't touch you.

After an initial bounding sphere collision tests positive, you could go a step further and perform a second set of more comprehensive tests, such as checking every polygon of the object against every polygon of the other object.

Another method is to use a second set of spheres as a more accurate set of tests, as in Figure 11.4. In this figure, the robot has three bounding spheres that more accurately describe the robot's shape. After the bounding spheres of two objects test positive for a collision, their second set of spheres could be tested. If any of the player's secondary spheres collide with any of the robot's secondary spheres, then a collision occurs.

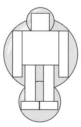

Figure 11.4   Multiple spheres can be used for more accurate boundary tests.

So, you effectively have two levels of spheres for each object. Of course, you don't have to stop at just two levels of sphere testing. You could have many more, with each level having more spheres, therefore getting more accurate. This is commonly called a sphere tree or sphere subdivision. This way, you can quickly reject noncolliding objects and have more accurate tests for potential collisions. This also lets you know which part of your object was hit, allowing you to act accordingly. For example, you could have just your robot's lower leg fall off if a missile strikes it.

Note that sphere trees need to rotate with the object as the object rotates. For example, the spheres need to follow a robot's arm as it moves around. In the code from Chapter 9, "3D Objects," we defined 3D objects as nested polygon groups. Because this is already a tree structure, to implement sphere trees you could give each polygon group its own set of spheres and ensure that the group's transform is applied to the spheres. You won't actually implement sphere trees in this chapter, but it's food for thought.

To sum it up, for a typical frame, most of the objects require no collision test, some objects require a simple collision test, and a few objects require the more complex, computationally expensive collision tests.

Bounding Cylinders

An alternative to bounding spheres is *upright bounding cylinders*, shown in Figure 11.5. This reduces collision tests to a 2D circle test and a 1D vertical test.

Figure 11.5 An upright bounding cylinder can be used for collision detection.

Upright bounding cylinders tend to describe tall, thin objects (such as players or monsters) more accurately than just one sphere. In this chapter, for the 3D engine, you'll implement upright bounding cylinders for object-to-object collision detection.

All the basic collision-detection code in this chapter goes in the `CollisionDetection` class. The methods for handling object-to-object collision in this class are shown in Listing 11.2.

Listing 11.2   Checking Objects (CollisionDetection.java)

```
/**
    Checks if the specified object collisions with any other
    object in the specified list.
*/
public boolean checkObject(GameObject objectA, List objects,
    Vector3D oldLocation)
{
    boolean collision = false;
    for (int i=0; i<objects.size(); i++) {
        GameObject objectB = (GameObject)objects.get(i);
        collision |= checkObject(objectA, objectB,
            oldLocation);
    }
    return collision;
}



/**
    Returns true if the two specified objects collide.
    Object A is the moving object, and Object B is the object
    to check. Uses bounding upright cylinders (circular base
    and top) to determine collisions.
*/
public boolean checkObject(GameObject objectA,
    GameObject objectB, Vector3D oldLocation)
{
    // don't collide with self
    if (objectA == objectB) {
        return false;
    }

    PolygonGroupBounds boundsA = objectA.getBounds();
    PolygonGroupBounds boundsB = objectB.getBounds();

    // first, check y axis collision (assume height is pos)
    float Ay1 = objectA.getY() + boundsA.getBottomHeight();
    float Ay2 = objectA.getY() + boundsA.getTopHeight();
```

continues

Listing 11.2   Checking Objects (CollisionDetection.java)   *continued*

```java
        float By1 = objectB.getY() + boundsB.getBottomHeight();
        float By2 = objectB.getY() + boundsB.getTopHeight();
        if (By2 < Ay1 || By1 > Ay2) {
            return false;
        }


        // next, check 2D, x/z plane collision (circular base)
        float dx = objectA.getX() - objectB.getX();
        float dz = objectA.getZ() - objectB.getZ();
        float minDist = boundsA.getRadius() + boundsB.getRadius();
        float distSq = dx*dx + dz*dz;
        float minDistSq = minDist * minDist;
        if (distSq < minDistSq) {
            return handleObjectCollision(objectA, objectB, distSq,
                minDistSq, oldLocation);
        }
        return false;
    }


    /**
        Handles an object collision. Object A is the moving
        object, and Object B is the object that Object A collided
        with. For now, just notifies Object A of the collision.
    */
    protected boolean handleObjectCollision(GameObject objectA,
        GameObject objectB, float distSq, float minDistSq,
        Vector3D oldLocation)
    {
        objectA.notifyObjectCollision(objectB);
        return true;
    }
```

In this code, game objects have a `PolygonGroupBounds` object that bounds a polygon group as a cylinder. The bounds consist of the cylinder's radius, bottom height (often 0), and top height.

The checkObject() method just checks whether two bounding cylinders collide; if they do, the handleObjectCollision() method is called.

The handleObjectCollision() method just notifies the moving object that a collision occurred through the notifyObjectCollision() method. This and other notify methods exist in the GameObject class, but they don't do anything by default— subclasses of GameObject can override notify methods if they want. For example, in the Blast class, the notifyObjectCollision() method is used to destroy a bot if it collides with one:

```
public void notifyObjectCollision(GameObject object) {
    // destroy bots and itself
    if (object instanceof Bot) {
        setState(object, STATE_DESTROYED);
        setState(STATE_DESTROYED);
    }
}
```

Also, for now, in the GridGameObjectManager, if an object collides with another, its location is restored to its previous location. Later, you'll work to create a more realistic response to an object-to-object collision by sliding to the side of the object.

The Discrete Time Issue

A typical game updates the state of the game in discrete time slices, such as how you update each object based on the amount of time passed since the last update. For example, in Figure 11.6, this bird's-eye view shows an object's discrete time movement. The moving object collides with the larger object in frame 3.

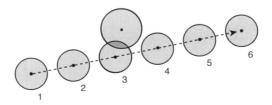

Figure 11.6 Bird's-eye view of an object's discrete time movement.

Unfortunately, this discrete time movement can cause a problem with collision detection. Imagine that the object is moving faster or the frame rate is slower. In this scenario, the moving object could "skip over" the object it collides with. For example, in Figure 11.7 the moving object collides with the larger object between frames 2 and 3.

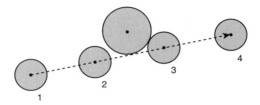

Figure 11.7 The problem with discrete time movement: Objects can "skip over" other objects when a collision should be detected.

A couple solutions to this problem exist. The more accurate but computationally expensive solution is to treat a moving object's bounds as a solid shape from the start location to the end location, as shown in Figure 11.8.

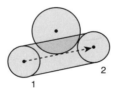

Figure 11.8 A moving object can be treated as a "tube" to alleviate the discrete time problem.

Alternatively, if an object moves a certain distance, you could check various points between the start and end locations for collisions. In Figure 11.7, you could put an extra check halfway between each frame.

Object-to-World Collisions

Object collisions with the world should generally be as accurate as possible. You don't want the player or another object to move through a wall or to jitter when moving along a wall.

In Chapter 5, you implemented object-to-world collisions by moving just one coordinate at a time (first x, then y), which worked great for a simple tile-based world in which the objects don't move more than the length of one tile for each frame.

In the 3D world, you don't have tiles, but you usually have the 3D world described in a structure that can help with collision detection, such as BSP trees. You'll use the 2D BSP tree from the previous chapter to implement collision with floors, ceilings, and walls.

Bounding Boxes for Testing Against Floors

In the 2D game in Chapter 5, you used the bounding rectangles of the sprites for collision detections. In 3D, besides bounding spheres, circles, or cylinders, bounding boxes are another popular type of collision-detection mechanism. Two types of bounding boxes exist: freeform and axis-aligned. Freeform bounding boxes can be turned and rotated any way, while axis-aligned boxes are aligned with the x-, y-, and z-axis. In this chapter, we used cylinders for object-to-object collision and axis-aligned bounding boxes for object-to-world collisions. The first thing to discuss are floors and ceilings. In a world where floors can be of variable height, you'll want objects to stand on the highest floor under its bounding box, as in Figure 11.9. Likewise, you don't want objects to move to areas if the ceiling is too low for the object. Also, you might want objects to be able to cross small steps without stopping. In this figure, the player can make the small step up to the platform.

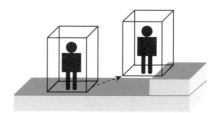

Figure 11.9   Bounding box collision with a floor: The player's bounding box is partially on the stair, so the height of the stair is used as the player's "floor."

In Figure 11.9, the highest floor within the object's bounds is used to determine how high the object stands. When testing an object against the floor and ceilings of the environment, you can check each corner of the box for an intersection with the floor or ceiling. This involves four floor checks, one for each corner of the bounding box.

One thing to note about bounding boxes is that they can also be used for object-to-object collisions. You can even have bounding box trees, like sphere trees.

Finding the BSP Leaf for a Specific Location

With a 2D BSP tree, floor information is stored in the leaves of the tree. You can find the leaf for a specific location pretty easily, similarly to how you traversed the tree in the last chapter. This is shown in Listing 11.3.

Listing 11.3 `getLeaf()` Method of BSPTree.java

```
/**
    Gets the leaf the x,z coordinates are in.
*/
public Leaf getLeaf(float x, float z) {
    return getLeaf(root, x, z);
}


protected Leaf getLeaf(Node node, float x, float z) {
    if (node == null || node instanceof Leaf) {
        return (Leaf)node;
    }
    int side = node.partition.getSideThin(x, z);
    if (side == BSPLine.BACK) {
        return getLeaf(node.back, x, z);
    }
    else {
        return getLeaf(node.front, x, z);
    }
}
```

Of course, this just finds the leaf for one location, while an object's bounding box can potentially span multiple leaves. So, you check the leaf of each corner of the bounding box.

Implementing Floor and Ceiling Height Testing

Testing each corner of the bounding boxes for the floor and ceiling height is summed up in some methods in the `CollisionDetection` class, shown here in Listing 11.4.

Listing 11.4   Checking the Floor and Ceiling (CollisionDetection.java)

```
/**
    Bounding game object corners used to test for
    intersection with the BSP tree. Corners are in either
    clockwise or counter-clockwise order.
*/
private static final Point2D.Float[] CORNERS = {
    new Point2D.Float(-1, -1), new Point2D.Float(-1, 1),
    new Point2D.Float(1, 1), new Point2D.Float(1, -1),
};


...


    getFloorAndCeiling(object);
    checkFloorAndCeiling(object, elapsedTime);


...


/**
    Gets the floor and ceiling values for the specified
    GameObject. Calls object.setFloorHeight() and
    object.setCeilHeight() to set the floor and ceiling
    values.
*/
public void getFloorAndCeiling(GameObject object) {
    float x = object.getX();
    float z = object.getZ();
    float r = object.getBounds().getRadius() - 1;
    float floorHeight = Float.MIN_VALUE;
    float ceilHeight = Float.MAX_VALUE;
    BSPTree.Leaf leaf = bspTree.getLeaf(x, z);
    if (leaf != null) {
        floorHeight = leaf.floorHeight;
```

continues

Listing 11.4   Checking the Floor and Ceiling (CollisionDetection.java)   *continued*

```java
            ceilHeight = leaf.ceilHeight;
        }

        // check surrounding four points
        for (int i=0; i<CORNERS.length; i++) {
            float xOffset = r * CORNERS[i].x;
            float zOffset = r * CORNERS[i].y;
            leaf = bspTree.getLeaf(x + xOffset, z + zOffset);
            if (leaf != null) {
                floorHeight = Math.max(floorHeight,
                    leaf.floorHeight);
                ceilHeight = Math.min(ceilHeight,
                    leaf.ceilHeight);
            }
        }

        object.setFloorHeight(floorHeight);
        object.setCeilHeight(ceilHeight);
}


/**
    Checks for object collisions with the floor and ceiling.
    Uses object.getFloorHeight() and object.getCeilHeight()
    for the floor and ceiling values.
*/
protected void checkFloorAndCeiling(GameObject object,
    long elapsedTime)
{
    boolean collision = false;

    float floorHeight = object.getFloorHeight();
    float ceilHeight = object.getCeilHeight();
    float bottomHeight = object.getBounds().getBottomHeight();
    float topHeight = object.getBounds().getTopHeight();

    if (!object.isFlying()) {
```

```
            object.getLocation().y = floorHeight - bottomHeight;
    }
    // check if below floor
    if (object.getY() + bottomHeight < floorHeight) {
        object.notifyFloorCollision();
        object.getTransform().getVelocity().y = 0;
        object.getLocation().y = floorHeight - bottomHeight;
    }
    // check if hitting ceiling
    else if (object.getY() + topHeight > ceilHeight) {
        object.notifyCeilingCollision();
        object.getTransform().getVelocity().y = 0;
        object.getLocation().y = ceilHeight - topHeight;
    }

}
```

The `getFloorAndCeiling()` method gets the floor and ceiling height for an object by checking the leaves at the object's four corners. Keep in mind that an object could be in multiple BSP tree leaves simultaneously.

Setting the object's y location occurs in the `checkFloorAndCeiling()` method. If the object is not flying, the y value is the floor height. Otherwise, it checks to see if the object hits the floor or ceiling. If so, the object's `notifyFloorCollision()` or `notifyCeilingCollision()` method is called. Just as with `notifyObjectCollision()`, these methods do nothing by default, and subclasses of `GameObject` can override these methods.

The way the floor and ceiling collisions are implemented is primitive at this point; the player just instantly pops to higher or lower floors. Later in this chapter, you'll implement gravity and the capability to scoot smoothly up stairs to make the collision handling seem more realistic.

Bounding Boxes for Testing Against Walls

With floors and ceilings, you were testing only for collisions after an object has already moved and only to determine how high the floor is underneath the player.

However, walls are thin lines, so if you test for a wall collision only after an object has moved, it's possible you could miss walls that the object has already passed right through. To accurately determine whether an object hits any walls, you need to test the entire path the object travels during the update from one frame to the next.

For a 2D BSP tree, because an object's path from one frame to the next is a line segment, you can test this line segment for an intersection with any lines that represent walls. (It's the same concept for a 3D BSP tree, except that the path is tested for an intersection with a plane that represents the walls.)

Of course, the objects are solid shapes, not points. So, if you're using bounding boxes for collision testing, you must test all four corners of the bounding box with the walls in a scene, as in Figure 11.10. In this figure, four paths (for each corner) are tested for an intersection, and three of them intersect a wall.

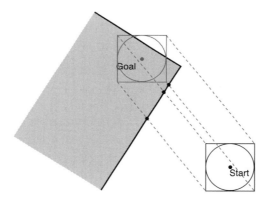

Figure 11.10 Checking the bounding box corners with an intersection with a wall. Each line segment is checked against the BSP tree for a collision.

When more than one intersection is found, as in Figure 11.10, the shortest path from the start location to the intersection is the one to use for the collision, as shown in Figure 11.11. Here, the upper-left corner of the object is the first to collide with the wall (it is the shortest path to a line intersection), so it is used to determine the collision location.

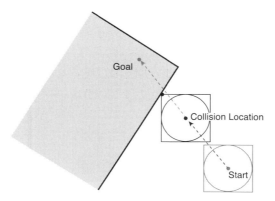

Figure 11.11   The closest intersection from each corner of the bounding box is chosen as the collision location.

Now you need a fast way to determine whether a path intersects with any polygons in the 3D world. In this case, you'll find the first line segment intersection of a BSP tree.

Intersection of a Line Segment with a BSP Tree

Consider a path from (x1,y1) to (x2,y2). The goal is to find the first intersection of this path with a polygon in the BSP tree, if any. The first intersection is the one closest to (x1,y1).

Here is the algorithm for this, starting with the root node of the BSP tree:

1. Check the path against the node's partition. If the path is either in front of or in back of the node's partition, check the front or back nodes, respectively.

2. Otherwise, if the path spans the node's partition, bisect the path into two paths along the partition. One path represents the first part of the path, and the other path represents the second part of the path.

    a. Check the first part of the path for an intersection (see Step 1).

    b. If no intersection is found, check the polygons in this node for an intersection.

    c. If no intersection is found, check the second part of the path for an intersection (see Step 1).

    d. If an intersection is found, return the point of intersection. Otherwise, return null.

This algorithm basically says to look at every partition that the path spans, from the first (closest) partition to the last (farthest) partition, and return the first point of intersection, if any.

Note that just because a path spans a partition doesn't necessarily mean that an intersection occurred. For an intersection, you need to meet three conditions:

➤ For a 2D BSP tree, the line segment representing the polygon spans the path.

➤ The polygon isn't a short polygon that the object can step over, and isn't a polygon too high or too low to be in the object's way.

➤ The path travels from the front of the polygon to the back of the polygon.

The algorithm for finding the intersection (and the conditions for an intersection) is implemented here in Listing 11.5.

Listing 11.5   Intersection with a Line Segment with the BSP Tree (CollisionDetection.java)

```
private BSPTree bspTree;
private BSPLine path = new BSPLine();
private Point2D.Float intersection = new Point2D.Float();


. . .


/**
    Gets the first intersection, if any, of the path (x1,z1)->
    (x2,z2) with the walls of the BSP tree. Returns the
    first BSPPolygon intersection, or null if no intersection
    occurred.
*/
public BSPPolygon getFirstWallIntersection(float x1, float z1,
    float x2, float z2, float yBottom, float yTop)
{
    return getFirstWallIntersection(bspTree.getRoot(),
        x1, z1, x2, z2, yBottom, yTop);
```

```
    }


/**
    Gets the first intersection, if any, of the path (x1,z1)->
    (x2,z2) with the walls of the BSP tree, starting with
    the specified node. Returns the first BSPPolyon
    intersection, or null if no intersection occurred.
*/
protected BSPPolygon getFirstWallIntersection(
    BSPTree.Node node, float x1, float z1, float x2, float z2,
    float yBottom, float yTop)
{
    if (node == null || node instanceof BSPTree.Leaf) {
        return null;
    }

    int start = node.partition.getSideThick(x1, z1);
    int end = node.partition.getSideThick(x2, z2);
    float intersectionX;
    float intersectionZ;

    if (end == BSPLine.COLLINEAR) {
        end = start;
    }

    if (start == BSPLine.COLLINEAR) {
        intersectionX = x1;
        intersectionZ = z1;
    }
    else if (start != end) {
        path.setLine(x1, z1, x2, z2);
        node.partition.getIntersectionPoint(path,intersection);
        intersectionX = intersection.x;
        intersectionZ = intersection.y;
    }
    else {
        intersectionX = x2;
```

continues

Listing 11.5 Intersection with a Line Segment with the BSP Tree *continued*

```
        intersectionZ = z2;
    }

    if (start == BSPLine.COLLINEAR && start == end) {
        return null;
    }

    // check first part of line
    if (start != BSPLine.COLLINEAR) {
        BSPPolygon wall = getFirstWallIntersection(
            (start == BSPLine.FRONT)?node.front:node.back,
            x1, z1, intersectionX, intersectionZ,
            yBottom, yTop);
        if (wall != null) {
            return wall;
        }
    }

    // test this boundary
    if (start != end || start == BSPLine.COLLINEAR) {
        BSPPolygon wall = getWallCollision(node.polygons,
                x1, z1, x2, z2, yBottom, yTop);
        if (wall != null) {
            intersection.setLocation(intersectionX,
                intersectionZ);
            return wall;
        }
    }

    // check second part of line
    if (start != end) {
        BSPPolygon wall = getFirstWallIntersection(
            (end == BSPLine.FRONT)?node.front:node.back,
            intersectionX, intersectionZ, x2, z2,
            yBottom, yTop);
        if (wall != null) {
            return wall;
        }
    }
```

```
    }

    // not found
    return null;
}


/**
    Checks if the specified path collides with any of
    the collinear list of polygons. The path crosses the line
    represented by the polygons, but the polygons may not
    necessarily cross the path.
*/
protected BSPPolygon getWallCollision(List polygons,
    float x1, float z1, float x2, float z2,
    float yBottom, float yTop)
{
    path.setLine(x1, z1, x2, z2);
    for (int i=0; i<polygons.size(); i++) {
        BSPPolygon poly = (BSPPolygon)polygons.get(i);
        BSPLine wall = poly.getLine();

        // check if not wall
        if (wall == null) {
            continue;
        }

        // check if not vertically in the wall (y axis)
        if (wall.top <= yBottom || wall.bottom > yTop) {
            continue;
        }

        // check if moving to back of wall
        if (wall.getSideThin(x2, z2) != BSPLine.BACK) {
            continue;
        }

        // check if path crosses wall
```

continues

Listing 11.5 Intersection with a Line Segment with the BSP Tree   *continued*

```
        int side1 = path.getSideThin(wall.x1, wall.y1);
        int side2 = path.getSideThin(wall.x2, wall.y2);
        if (side1 != side2) {
            return poly;
        }
    }
    return null;
}
```

In this code, `getFirstWallIntersection()` follows the algorithm mentioned before, and the `getWallCollision()` method checks for the conditions of an intersection between a path and a polygon.

As a sidenote, with a 3D BSP tree, you would also use something like this to determine the height of the floor under an object. Just use this algorithm to find the highest polygon underneath the player by checking for the first intersection with a line segment shot straight down from the object.

You've almost got everything to implement a bounding box collision with a BSP tree, but first there's one issue to look into that could cause problems.

The Corner Issue

Alas, all is not well with bounding box collisions! When you're checking each corner of a bounding box with a collision with the world, you run into conditions in which part of the world will collide with the bounding box but not with the corners of the bounding box, as in Figure 11.12.

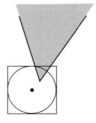

Figure 11.12 An object collision with a corner can be a slight problem.

In this figure, the object collides with a sharp corner that doesn't touch any of the object's bounding box corners.

One way to get around this problem is to treat each edge of the bounding box as a line segment, to test for intersections with the BSP tree. If any of the edges intersect with a polygon in the BSP tree, the object is reverted to its original location. You'll implement this method in the code in this chapter. Alternatively, instead of reverting to its original location, the object could just move back a little bit at a time and test again until no collision is detected. Another solution is to ensure that levels are designed so that this issue never arises. However, this puts a restriction on level design that can make things difficult for the level designer because it's very tempting to make corners, as in the example.

Implementing Object-to-World Collision Detection

That's it for the basic object-to-world collision detection using a BSP tree. The remainder of the code is here in Listing 11.6.

Listing 11.6 Checking Walls (CollisionDetection.java)

```
// check walls if x or z position changed
if (object.getX() != oldLocation.x ||
    object.getZ() != oldLocation.z)
{
    checkWalls(object, oldLocation, elapsedTime);
}

...

/**
    Checks for a game object collision with the walls of the
    BSP tree. Returns the first wall collided with, or null if
    there was no collision.
*/
public BSPPolygon checkWalls(GameObject object,
    Vector3D oldLocation, long elapsedTime)
{
    Vector3D v = object.getTransform().getVelocity();
    PolygonGroupBounds bounds = object.getBounds();
```

continues

Listing 11.6   Checking Walls (CollisionDetection.java)   *continued*

```
float x = object.getX();
float y = object.getY();
float z = object.getZ();
float r = bounds.getRadius();
float stepSize = 0;
if (!object.isFlying()) {
    stepSize = BSPPolygon.PASSABLE_WALL_THRESHOLD;
}
float bottom = object.getY() + bounds.getBottomHeight() +
    stepSize;
float top = object.getY() + bounds.getTopHeight();

// pick closest intersection of 4 corners
BSPPolygon closestWall = null;
float closestDistSq = Float.MAX_VALUE;
for (int i=0; i<CORNERS.length; i++) {
    float xOffset = r * CORNERS[i].x;
    float zOffset = r * CORNERS[i].y;
    BSPPolygon wall = getFirstWallIntersection(
        oldLocation.x+xOffset, oldLocation.z+zOffset,
        x+xOffset, z+zOffset, bottom, top);
    if (wall != null) {
        float x2 = intersection.x-xOffset;
        float z2 = intersection.y-zOffset;
        float dx = (x2-oldLocation.x);
        float dz = (z2-oldLocation.z);
        float distSq = dx*dx + dz*dz;
        // pick the wall with the closest distance, or
        // if the distances are equal, pick the current
        // wall if the offset has the same sign as the
        // velocity.
        if (distSq < closestDistSq ||
            (distSq == closestDistSq &&
            MoreMath.sign(xOffset) == MoreMath.sign(v.x) &&
            MoreMath.sign(zOffset) == MoreMath.sign(v.z)))
        {
            closestWall = wall;
            closestDistSq = distSq;
```

```
                    object.getLocation().setTo(x2, y, z2);
                }
            }
        }

        if (closestWall != null) {
            object.notifyWallCollision();
        }

        // make sure the object bounds is empty
        // (avoid colliding with sharp corners)
        x = object.getX();
        z = object.getZ();
        r-=1;
        for (int i=0; i<CORNERS.length; i++) {
            int next = i+1;
            if (next == CORNERS.length) {
                next = 0;
            }
            // use (r-1) so this doesn't interfere with normal
            // collisions
            float xOffset1 = r * CORNERS[i].x;
            float zOffset1 = r * CORNERS[i].y;
            float xOffset2 = r * CORNERS[next].x;
            float zOffset2 = r * CORNERS[next].y;

            BSPPolygon wall = getFirstWallIntersection(
                x+xOffset1, z+zOffset1, x+xOffset2, z+zOffset2,
                bottom, top);
            if (wall != null) {
                object.notifyWallCollision();
                object.getLocation().setTo(
                    oldLocation.x, object.getY(), oldLocation.z);
                return wall;
            }
        }

        return closestWall;
    }
```

First, this code tests four paths, one for each corner of the bounding box for an intersection. If more than one intersection is found, the closest one is chosen.

If two intersections are found an equal distance away, the intersection is chosen that is closest to the direction of the object's velocity. This helps when you actually implement sliding against the wall later in this chapter.

If an intersection is found, the object's location is set to the collision location, right up next to the wall.

After those tests, the code tests to ensure that the object bounding box is empty (no corners, as in Figure 11.12). If so, the object is reverted to its original location.

That's it—basic collision detection is implemented! Now let's try it out.

Basic Collision-Detection Demo

The `CollisionTest` demo, included with the source code for the book, demonstrates the collision detection so far. It's the same demo as the `BSPMapTest` from the previous chapter, except that it adds collision detection and uses the `GridGameObjectManager`.

In this demo, you are stopped when you run against a wall and you can go up stairs to higher platforms. You are also stopped when you run into an object, such as a robot or a crate. The projectiles you fire destroy the robots, and, just for fun, the projectiles stick to the walls, floors, ceilings, and other objects instead of passing through them.

Collision detection in this demo works great, but it needs some serious help.

➤ You get "stuck" when you collide with a wall. In any 3D first- or third-person game, this can be very distracting to the player who expects to "slide" against a wall, especially when moving tightly around corners.

➤ Movement up and down stairs feels jerky because you are instantly moved up or down instead of scooting smoothly upstairs or allowing gravity to smoothly bring you down.

➤ You can't step over small objects in the way. Try shooting a projectile on the floor and stepping over it—you can't.

➤ You can't jump. Not that it's a part of collision detection—I'm just saying that you can't do it.

But, hey, good collision handling is a goal of this chapter, so let's fix those problems! And even though it's not really a collision-handling issue, this will be a good time to implement jumping as well because you can detect when an object is hitting something, even in midair.

Collision Handling with Sliding

All right, the next step is to provide collision handling that isn't obtrusive—in other words, the collision handling behaves in a way that the user expects.

Instead of collision "sticking," you'll implement collision "sliding." For example, instead of stopping when the player hits an object, the player will slide to the side of it. Likewise, the player will slide against a wall and will be able to step over small objects on the floor.

Also in this section, you'll implement some basic physics to allow objects to smoothly move up stairs, apply gravity, and allow the player to jump.

Object-to-Object Sliding

Previously, if an object-to-object collision occurred, you just resorted to moving the object to its original location. This is what created the effect of the moving object "sticking" to the static object it collided with.

To fix this, you must make sure the moving object slides to the side of the static object. The logical solution is to slide the least amount required to get the two objects out of each other's way. That means the direction to slide is defined by the vector from the static object's center to the moving object's center, as in Figure 11.13. In this figure, when the larger object moves, it collides with the smaller object. The large object then moves away from the smaller object so that, after the slide, the two objects are next to one another but not colliding.

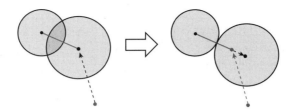

Figure 11.13 Object-to-object sliding: The moving object is pushed away from the static object.

The amount to slide is the difference between the minimum distance and the actual distance:

```
float minDist = objectA.radius + objectB.radius;
float slideDistance = minDist - actualDist;
```

So, because the vector between the two object's centers has the length of `actualDist`, the formula becomes this:

```
float scale = slideDistance / actualDist;
vector.multiply(scale);
```

Or, if you know only the square of the distances, it is this:

```
float scale = (float)Math.sqrt(minDistSq / actualDistSq) - 1;
vector.multiply(scale);
```

Although that square root function is slow, you have to call it only when objects bump into one another, which isn't very often.

A problem with sliding occurs when sliding against an object actually causes the object to slide into a wall or another object. In this case, the moving object can just revert to its previous location so it still appears to "stick"—the player will have to change direction.

Object-to-object sliding is easy enough. All the sliding code is kept in the `CollisionDetectionWithSliding` class, which is a subclass of `CollisionDetection`. The method is shown in Listing 11.7.

Listing 11.7 Object-to-Object Sliding (CollisionDetectionWithSliding.java)

```java
/**
    Handles an object collision. Object A is the moving
    object, and Object B is the object that Object A collided
    with. Object A slides around or steps on top of
    Object B if possible.
*/
protected boolean handleObjectCollision(GameObject objectA,
    GameObject objectB, float distSq, float minDistSq,
    Vector3D oldLocation)
{
    objectA.notifyObjectCollision(objectB);

    if (objectA.isFlying()) {
        return true;
    }

    float stepSize = objectA.getBounds().getTopHeight() / 6;
    Vector3D velocity =
        objectA.getTransform().getVelocity();

    // step up on top of object if possible
    float objectABottom = objectA.getY() +
        objectA.getBounds().getBottomHeight();
    float objectBTop = objectB.getY() +
        objectB.getBounds().getTopHeight();
    if (objectABottom + stepSize > objectBTop &&
        objectBTop +
        objectA.getBounds().getTopHeight() <
        objectA.getCeilHeight())
    {
        objectA.getLocation().y = (objectBTop -
            objectA.getBounds().getBottomHeight());
        if (velocity.y < 0) {
            objectA.setJumping(false);
            // don't let gravity get out of control
            velocity.y = -.01f;
        }
```

continues

Listing 11.7   Object-to-Object Sliding (CollisionDetectionWithSliding.java)   *continued*

```
            return false;
    }

    if (objectA.getX() != oldLocation.x ||
        objectA.getZ() != oldLocation.z)
    {
        // slide to the side
        float slideDistFactor =
            (float)Math.sqrt(minDistSq / distSq) - 1;
        scratch.setTo(objectA.getX(), 0, objectA.getZ());
        scratch.subtract(objectB.getX(), 0, objectB.getZ());
        scratch.multiply(slideDistFactor);
        objectA.getLocation().add(scratch);

        // revert location if passing through a wall
        if (super.checkWalls(objectA, oldLocation, 0) != null) {
            return true;
        }

        return false;
    }

    return true;
}
```

In this code, the `handleObjectCollision()` method is overridden. First, it checks to see whether the moving object can step on top of the static object. If not, it slides the object to the side. If the result of sliding creates a collision with a wall, the object reverts to its original location.

Speaking of colliding with walls, how about implementing some object-to-wall sliding?

Object-to-Wall Sliding

Sliding along the wall might seem like a complicated task, but it really just involves some simple math. If you know the goal location (the location the object would have moved to had there been no wall), you can easily find the slide location, as shown in Figure 11.14.

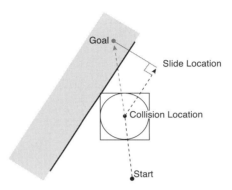

Figure 11.14   Object-to-wall sliding: An object slides against a wall.

In this figure, the gray line points in the direction of the polygon's normal. You can find the slide location if you can find the length of this line. This is a simple right-triangle problem. Consider the vector to the collision location from the goal location:

```
vector.setTo(actualX, 0, actualZ);
vector.subtract(goalX, 0, goalZ);
```

Then the length of the gray line is the dot product between this vector and the polygon's normal:

```
float length = vector.getDotProduct(wall.getNormal());
```

So, the slide location is this:

```
float slideX = goalX + length * wall.getNormal().x;
float slideZ = goalZ + length * wall.getNormal().z;
```

That's the basic idea. Along with some extra checks, the entire code for object-to-wall sliding is in Listing 11.8.

Listing 11.8   Object-to-Wall Sliding (CollisionDetectionWithSliding.java)

```java
private Vector3D scratch = new Vector3D();
private Vector3D originalLocation = new Vector3D();


...


/**
    Checks for a game object collision with the walls of the
    BSP tree. Returns the first wall collided with, or null if
    there was no collision. If there is a collision, the
    object slides along the wall and again checks for a
    collision. If a collision occurs on the slide, the object
    reverts back to its old location.
*/
public BSPPolygon checkWalls(GameObject object,
    Vector3D oldLocation, long elapsedTime)
{
    float goalX = object.getX();
    float goalZ = object.getZ();

    BSPPolygon wall = super.checkWalls(object,
        oldLocation, elapsedTime);
    // if collision found and object didn't stop itself
    if (wall != null && object.getTransform().isMoving()) {
        float actualX = object.getX();
        float actualZ = object.getZ();

        // dot product between wall's normal and line to goal
        scratch.setTo(actualX, 0, actualZ);
        scratch.subtract(goalX, 0, goalZ);
        float length = scratch.getDotProduct(wall.getNormal());

        float slideX = goalX + length * wall.getNormal().x;
        float slideZ = goalZ + length * wall.getNormal().z;
```

```
    object.getLocation().setTo(
        slideX, object.getY(), slideZ);
    originalLocation.setTo(oldLocation);
    oldLocation.setTo(actualX, oldLocation.y, actualZ);

    // use a smaller radius for sliding
    PolygonGroupBounds bounds = object.getBounds();
    float originalRadius = bounds.getRadius();
    bounds.setRadius(originalRadius-1);

    // check for collision with slide position
    BSPPolygon wall2 = super.checkWalls(object,
        oldLocation, elapsedTime);

    // restore changed parameters
    oldLocation.setTo(originalLocation);
    bounds.setRadius(originalRadius);

    if (wall2 != null) {
        object.getLocation().setTo(
            actualX, object.getY(), actualZ);
        return wall2;
    }
    }

    return wall;
}
```

In this code, the checkWalls() method of CollisionDetection is overridden. First the slide is applied; then it checks whether any wall collisions occurred after the slide. If so, the object is moved back to the collision location.

You can always disable object-to-wall sliding. Projectiles, for example, override the notify methods so that projectiles stop when they hit a wall, floor, or ceiling:

```
public void notifyWallCollision() {
    transform.getVelocity().setTo(0,0,0);
}
```

```
public void notifyFloorCollision() {
    transform.getVelocity().setTo(0,0,0);
}


public void notifyCeilingCollision() {
    transform.getVelocity().setTo(0,0,0);
}
```

This creates the effect of a projectile "sticking" to a wall or other object, so you can emulate the previous collision-handling technique.

Now you've got sliding for objects and walls. Next up: sliding up stairs (and a little gravity).

Gravity and Sliding Up Stairs (Object-to-Floor Sliding)

Another common sliding effect is to allow the player and other objects to slide smoothly up stairs. Otherwise, as in the first collision-detection demo, the player seems to jitter when moving up stairs because the y location of the object instantly changes to the higher stairstep.

Also, when you move from a higher platform to a lower one, you instantly drop to the lower level instead of gradually dropping because of gravity.

Gravity will work the same as in Chapter 5, by accelerating the object's downward velocity as time progresses. If the object's y location is higher than the floor's y location, gravity can be applied to the object.

The opposite is true for sliding up stairs: If the object's y location is lower than the floor's y location, a scoot-up acceleration can be applied to the object.

The physics used for the game is summed up in the Physics class in Listing 11.9. This is just a start, and you'll add more to it later.

Listing 11.9 Gravity and Scooting (Physics.java)

```java
/**
    Default gravity in units per millisecond squared
*/
public static final float DEFAULT_GRAVITY_ACCEL = -.002f;


/**
    Default scoot-up (acceleration traveling up stairs)
    in units per millisecond squared.
*/
public static final float DEFAULT_SCOOT_ACCEL = .006f;

private float gravityAccel = DEFAULT_GRAVITY_ACCEL;
private float scootAccel = DEFAULT_SCOOT_ACCEL;
private Vector3D velocity = new Vector3D();

/**
    Applies gravity to the specified GameObject according
    to the amount of time that has passed.
*/
public void applyGravity(GameObject object, long elapsedTime) {
    velocity.setTo(0, gravityAccel * elapsedTime, 0);
    object.getTransform().addVelocity(velocity);
}



/**
    Applies the scoot-up acceleration to the specified
    GameObject according to the amount of time that has passed.
*/
public void scootUp(GameObject object, long elapsedTime) {
    velocity.setTo(0, scootAccel * elapsedTime, 0);
    object.getTransform().addVelocity(velocity);
}
```

The more complicated step is knowing when to apply either gravity or the scoot-up acceleration for various situations. For example, gravity isn't applied to a flying object. Also, you want to stop a scoot-up acceleration if the player is above the ground but not if the object is jumping (we'll get to jumping in a minute).

All the various situations are covered in the code in Listing 11.10.

Listing 11.10   Check Floor and Ceiling (CollisionDetectionWithSliding.java)

```
/**
    Checks for object collisions with the floor and ceiling.
    Uses object.getFloorHeight() and object.getCeilHeight()
    for the floor and ceiling values.
    Applies gravity if the object is above the floor,
    and scoots the object up if the player is below the floor
    (for smooth movement up stairs).
*/
protected void checkFloorAndCeiling(GameObject object,
    long elapsedTime)
{
    float floorHeight = object.getFloorHeight();
    float ceilHeight = object.getCeilHeight();
    float bottomHeight = object.getBounds().getBottomHeight();
    float topHeight = object.getBounds().getTopHeight();
    Vector3D v = object.getTransform().getVelocity();
    Physics physics = Physics.getInstance();

    // check if on floor
    if (object.getY() + bottomHeight == floorHeight) {
        if (v.y < 0) {
            v.y = 0;
        }
    }
    // check if below floor
    else if (object.getY() + bottomHeight < floorHeight) {

        if (!object.isFlying()) {
            // if falling
            if (v.y < 0) {
                object.notifyFloorCollision();
                v.y = 0;
                object.getLocation().y =
                    floorHeight - bottomHeight;
            }
```

```
            else if (!object.isJumping()) {
                physics.scootUp(object, elapsedTime);
            }
        }
        else {
            object.notifyFloorCollision();
            v.y = 0;
            object.getLocation().y =
                floorHeight - bottomHeight;
        }
    }
    // check if hitting ceiling
    else if (object.getY() + topHeight > ceilHeight) {
        object.notifyCeilingCollision();
        if (v.y > 0) {
            v.y = 0;
        }
        object.getLocation().y = ceilHeight - topHeight;
        if (!object.isFlying()) {
            physics.applyGravity(object, elapsedTime);
        }
    }
    // above floor
    else {
        if (!object.isFlying()) {
            // if scooting-up, stop the scoot
            if (v.y > 0 && !object.isJumping()) {
                v.y = 0;
                object.getLocation().y =
                    floorHeight - bottomHeight;
            }
            else {
                physics.applyGravity(object, elapsedTime);
            }
        }
    }
}
```

This code overrides the `checkFloorAndCeiling()` method in the `CollisionDetection` class. The only thing left is to implement jumping— you know, for fun.

Make It Jump

Jumping works pretty much the same as it did in Chapter 5—just apply an upward velocity to an object. The power of this initial velocity diminishes as gravity is applied.

Sometimes, though, you want to guarantee how high an object can jump. Figure 11.15 shows the equation for this.

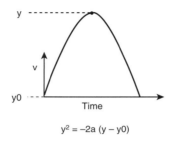

$$y^2 = -2a\,(y - y0)$$

Figure 11.15   Finding the jump velocity to jump at a specific height.

In Figure 11.15, the jump velocity (v) is found based on the height to jump (y–y0) and gravity acceleration (a). This is one of the standard velocity/acceleration formulas found in many physics textbooks.

With this, you can add a few more methods to the `Physics` class to implement jumping, shown here in Listing 11.11.

Listing 11.11   Jumping (Physics.java)

```
/**
    Sets the specified GameObject's vertical velocity to jump
    to the specified height. Calls getJumpVelocity() to
    calculate the velocity, which uses the Math.sqrt()
    function.
*/
public void jumpToHeight(GameObject object, float jumpHeight) {
```

```
        jump(object, getJumpVelocity(jumpHeight));
}


/**
    Sets the specified GameObject's vertical velocity to the
    specified jump velocity.
*/
public void jump(GameObject object, float jumpVelocity) {
    velocity.setTo(0, jumpVelocity, 0);
    object.getTransform().getVelocity().y = 0;
    object.getTransform().addVelocity(velocity);
}


/**
    Returns the vertical velocity needed to jump the specified
    height (based on current gravity). Uses the Math.sqrt()
    function.
*/
public float getJumpVelocity(float jumpHeight) {
    // use velocity/acceleration formal: v*v = -2 * a(y-y0)
    // (v is jump velocity, a is accel, y-y0 is max height)
    return (float)Math.sqrt(-2*gravityAccel*jumpHeight);
}
```

These methods enable you to find the jump velocity needed to jump a certain height (based on the gravity acceleration) and to actually make an object jump.

Collision Detection with Sliding Demo

That's it for collision detection. Included with the source for this chapter is the CollisionTestWithSliding class, which is exactly the same as the previous demo except that it implements sliding. All in all, it demonstrates sliding against a wall, sliding against objects, stepping over objects, getting on top of objects, scooting up stairs, applying gravity, and jumping.

As a side effect to the engine, you can even stand on top of projectiles. Because projectiles stick to walls, you can fire enough projectiles to try to "draw" a ramp of them against the wall. Then you can run up the ramp!

Of course, this is just how we implemented projectiles. Usually, you'll want projectiles to destroy themselves whenever they hit something rather than stick around.

Enhancements

You got some great basic collision detection and handling in this chapter, but there's always room for improvement. Here are a few ideas:

➤ Implement sphere trees for more accurate object-to-object tests.

➤ Perform extra checks for whether an object travels a large enough distance in between frames; a collision could occur between the start and end locations.

➤ Allow the player to crouch or crawl to get in tight places.

➤ Physics-wise, you could implement "head bobbing," which just bounces the camera up and down when the player is moving.

Summary

Ah, collision detection: one of the necessities of almost any game, 2D or 3D.

In this chapter, first we talked about isolating objects on a grid to limit the number of actual collision tests to make. Then we talked about various collision-detection mechanisms, such as bounding spheres, sphere trees, bounding cylinders, and bounding boxes. You implemented collision detection with other objects and with the walls, floors, and ceilings of a BSP tree. You implemented some better collision handling that enables the player (and other objects) to slide against other objects' walls, slide against walls, and scoot up stairs. Finally, you added gravity and jumping for good measure.

You can blast the robots to smithereens, but they aren't much of a challenge, are they? That's what you'll work on next: giving your enemies some artificial intelligence so you can make the games you create more fun and challenging.

Chapter 12

Path Finding

D on't you just hate it when you're just hanging around the city, minding your own business, when all of a sudden a bunch of ninjas jump out and attack you? You knock a few of them out and make a quick getaway, running around buildings and diving in alleys, but next thing you know, a bunch of ninjas jump out at you again. No matter what you do, the ninjas find you. Does this ever happen to you? Anyone?

What you might be wondering is how those ninjas always seem to find you, what they could possibly want, and whether the writer of this book has questionable sanity.

In this chapter, we deal with the first thing you might be wondering: how the ninjas found you. Specifically, we talk about some path-finding algorithms and implement a generic A* search. This search algorithm allows ninjas to find you no matter where you are.

Also, a good path-finding algorithm is essential to artificial intelligence, so we'll use what we create in this chapter when we talk about AI in Chapter 13, "Artificial Intelligence."

Path-Finding Basics

Path finding can be reduced to answering the question, "How do I get from point A to point B?" Generally, the path from a ninja (or, in this case, a bot) to another location could potentially have several different solutions, but ideally, you want a solution that solves these goals:

1. How to get from A to B

2. How to get around obstacles in the way

3. How to find the shortest possible path

4. How to find the path quickly

Some path-finding algorithms solve none of these problems, and some solve all of them. And in some cases, no algorithm could solve any of them—for example, point A could be on an island completely isolated from point B, so no solution would exist.

Some Initial Path-Finding Attempts

If the environment is flat with no obstacles, path finding is no problem: The bot can just move in a straight line to its destination. But when obstacles occur between point A and point B, things get a little hairy. For example, in Figure 12.1, if the bot just moves straight toward the player, it will end up just hitting a wall and getting stuck there.

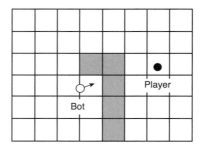

Figure 12.1   Not the best solution: The bot (white circle) just runs straight toward the player (black circle), even if there are obstacles in the way.

This behavior might be fine for some games because it doesn't really matter what the bots do; it matters only what they *appear* to do. In a 3D world from the player's perspective, it might look like the bot is just waiting behind the wall for the player instead of being stuck.

A bird's-eye perspective is a different story. Path finding is virtually required for games with bird's-eye perspectives, such as real-time strategy games or for games like *The Sims*. You wouldn't want to tell a team of fighters to attack something but have the team not be able to do it because the destination was on the other side of the wall! Come on now, use the door.

Also, making a bot smart enough to find a path around an obstacle makes it more interesting for the player and harder to "trick" the bot into doing something or moving a certain way.

Several techniques can be used to get around obstacles. A randomized algorithm finds a solution eventually, if there is one. This technique makes the bot walk around randomly, like in Figure 12.2, until it finds what it is looking for.

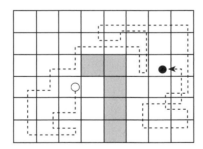

Figure 12.2   The bot (white circle) moves around randomly until the player (black circle) is found.

Of course, the randomized algorithm doesn't give the best-looking results or the shortest path. Who wants to watch a bot move around randomly like it's missing a circuit or two?

This random algorithm could be modified to move randomly only occasionally and at other times move directly toward the player, which would make the bot's movement appear slightly more intelligent.

Another solution can be found when the environment is a simple maze with no loops, like in Figure 12.3. Here, the path-finding algorithm is the "right hand on the wall" algorithm (or the "left hand on the wall" algorithm, if you're into that sort of thing). Just keep your right hand on the wall as you move through the maze, and eventually you'll find the destination.

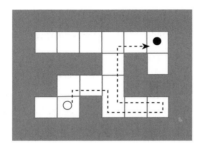

Figure 12.3   The bot (white circle) moves in a maze, keeping its right hand on the wall until it finds the player (black circle).

If a bot follows the "right hand" algorithm literally, it will rarely find the shortest path from A to B. Alternatively, the path could be calculated ahead of time, before the bot makes any moves. Then any backtracking (such as when venturing into the lower-right hall in the figure) could be removed from the path, leaving a shortest-path solution.

However, this algorithm works only for the simple case of a maze with no loops. If a loop was in the path, the bot would veer to the right forever. Also, if rooms had wide spaces, the bot might never find its destination in the middle of a room because the bot is always next to a wall. Ideally, you'll probably want to create more intricate environments than this.

Instead of looking at the environment as a grid, we'll look at it as a graph, like in Figure 12.4. A graph is simply a bunch of nodes grouped by various edges.

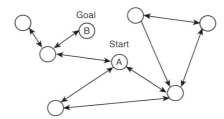

Figure 12.4   A simple graph.

Each node of the graph could be anything. For example, a node could be a cell in a 2D grid. Or, a node could be a "city," with the edges of the graph representing highways. And remember, when finding the path from A to B, any node can be the start or goal node.

A graph is similar to a tree, as discussed in Chapter 10, "3D Scene Management Using BSP Trees," except that, instead of each node having up to two children, each node can have an indefinite number of children, or neighbors. Some graphs are directed, meaning that an edge between two nodes can be traversed in only one direction. Looking at the example in Figure 12.4, all the edges are bidirectional except for one. A unidirectional edge could be useful in such situations as when traveling involves jumping down a cliff that is too high to jump back up.

In this example, you want to find the shortest path from node A to node B, or the fewest number of traversed edges to get to the goal. Looking at the figure, the solution is easy to determine, but how would you find the solution in a computer program? An easy solution is to use a breadth-first search.

Breadth-First Search

Like traversing BSP trees, a *breadth-first search* involves visiting nodes one at a time. A breadth-first search visits nodes in the order of their distance from the start node, where distance is measured as the number of traversed edges. So, with a breadth-first search, first all nodes one edge away from the goal are visited, then those two edges away are visited, and so on until all nodes are visited. This way, you find the path from the start to the goal with the minimum number of traversed edges. Another way to word it is like this: Visit the neighbor nodes, then the neighbor's neighbor nodes, and so on until the goal node is found. An example of a breadth-first search is in Figure 12.5, in which the nodes are numbered in the order they are visited.

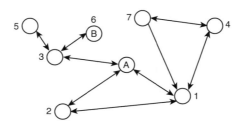

Figure 12.5 An example breadth-first search. The nodes are numbered in the order of the search.

Later in this chapter, you'll use the A* search algorithm, which has several similarities to a breadth-first search. But first, to better understand A*, you'll implement the easy-to-understand breadth-first search algorithm.

First, start with a basic node, which has references to all its neighbors:

```
public class Node {
    List neighbors;
    Node pathParent;
}
```

The neighbors list is simply a list of all the nodes' neighbors.

The pathParent node is used for searching only. Think of the path from the start node to the goal node as a tree, with each node having only one child. The pathParent node is the node's parent in the path tree. When the goal is found, the path can be found by traversing up the path tree from the goal node to the start node, like this:

```
private List constructPath(Node node) {
    LinkedList path = new LinkedList();
    while (node.pathParent != null) {
        path.addFirst(node);
        node = node.pathParent;
    }
    return path;
}
```

Of course, this assumes that the start node has no parent in the path.

Okay! Now you're ready to implement the breadth-first search algorithm. One thing to keep in mind is that you want to be sure to only visit each node once. For example, if A has neighbors B and C, and B has neighbor A, you don't want to visit A again or you'll end up in an infinite loop.

So, you'll keep track of all nodes that have been visited by putting them in a "closed" list. If a node shows up in the search that's already in the closed list, you'll ignore it. Likewise, you'll keep track of all the nodes you want to visit in an "open" list. The open list is a first in, first out list, effectively sorting the list from smallest number of edges from the start goal to the largest. Here's the full code:

```java
public List search(Node startNode, Node goalNode) {
    // list of visited nodes
    LinkedList closedList = new LinkedList();

    // list of nodes to visit (sorted)
    LinkedList openList = new LinkedList();
    openList.add(startNode);
    startNode.pathParent = null;

    while (!openList.isEmpty()) {
        Node node = (Node)openList.removeFirst();
        if (node == goalNode) {
            // path found!
            return constructPath(goalNode);
        }
        else {
            closedList.add(node);

            // add neighbors to the open list
            Iterator i = node.neighbors.iterator();
            while (i.hasNext()) {
                Node neighborNode = (Node)i.next();
                if (!closedList.contains(neighborNode) &&
                    !openList.contains(neighborNode))
                {
                    neighborNode.pathParent = node;
                    openList.add(neighborNode);
```

```
                }
            }
        }
    }

    // no path found
    return null;
}
```

This function returns a list of nodes that represent the path, not including the start node. If a path can't be found, it returns `null`.

That's all there is for breadth-first search. However, taking a step back, it's easy to notice one problem with this search: You found the path with the least number of edges, but edges could have different "costs" associated with them. For example, the cost of one edge could be 10km, while the cost of another could be 100km. Obviously, traversing two 10km edges would be faster than traversing a single 100km edge. Breadth-first search assumes all edges have the same cost, which isn't good enough. This is where the A* algorithm comes in.

Basics of the A* Algorithm

An A*—pronounced "A-star"—search works like a breadth-first search, except with two extra factors:

➤ The edges have different "costs," which is how much it costs to travel from one node to another.

➤ The cost from any node to the goal node can be estimated. This helps refine the search so that you're less likely to go off searching in the wrong direction.

The cost between nodes doesn't have to be distance. The cost could be time, if you wanted to find the path that takes the shortest amount of time to traverse. For example, when you are driving, taking the back roads might be a shorter distance, but taking the freeway usually takes less time (freeways in Los Angeles excluded). Another example is terrain: Traveling through overgrown forests could take longer than traveling through a grassy area.

Or, you could get more creative with the cost. For instance, if you want a bot to sneak up on the player, having the bot appear in front of the player could have a high cost, but appearing from behind could have little or no cost. You could take this idea further and assign a special tactical advantage to certain nodes—such as getting behind a crate—which would have a smaller cost than just appearing in front of the player.

The A* algorithm works the same as breadth-first search, except for a couple of differences:

➤ The nodes in the open list are sorted by the total cost from the start to the goal node. In other words, it's a priority queue. The total cost is the sum of the cost from the start node and the estimated cost to the goal node.

➤ A node in the closed list can be moved back to the open list if a shorter path (less cost) to that node is found.

Because the open list is sorted by the estimated total cost, the algorithm checks nodes that have the smallest estimated cost first, so it searches the nodes that are more likely to be in the direction of the goal. Thus, the better the estimate is, the faster the search is.

Of course, you need to define the cost and the estimated cost. If the cost is distance, this is easy: The cost between nodes is their distance, and the cost from one node to the goal is simply a calculation of the distance from that node to the goal.

Note that this algorithm works only when the estimated cost is never more than the actual cost. If the estimated cost were more, the path found wouldn't necessarily be the shortest.

All right, let's get started on some code. First, you'll create a generic, abstract A* search algorithm that can be used for any type of A* search. The idea is that you'll be able to use this generic abstract class for lots of different situations, and because it's generic, the code will be easier to read. You'll start with an A* node, shown in Listing 12.1.

Listing 12.1   AStarNode.java

```
package com.brackeen.javagamebook.path;

import java.util.List;
```

continues

Listing 12.1 AStarNode.java *continued*

```java
import com.brackeen.javagamebook.util.MoreMath;

/**
    The AStarNode class, along with the AStarSearch class,
    implements a generic A* search algorithm. The AStarNode
    class should be subclassed to provide searching capability.
*/
public abstract class AStarNode implements Comparable {

    AStarNode pathParent;
    float costFromStart;
    float estimatedCostToGoal;


    public float getCost() {
        return costFromStart + estimatedCostToGoal;
    }


    public int compareTo(Object other) {
        float otherValue = ((AStarNode)other).getCost();
        float thisValue = this.getCost();

        return MoreMath.sign(thisValue - otherValue);
    }


    /**
        Gets the cost between this node and the specified
        adjacent (aka "neighbor" or "child") node.
    */
    public abstract float getCost(AStarNode node);


    /**
        Gets the estimated cost between this node and the
        specified node. The estimated cost should never exceed
        the true cost. The better the estimate, the more
```

```
        efficient the search.
    */
    public abstract float getEstimatedCost(AStarNode node);



    /**
        Gets the children (aka "neighbors" or "adjacent nodes")
        of this node.
    */
    public abstract List getNeighbors();
}
```

The `AStarNode` class is an abstract class that needs to be subclassed to provide any search functionality. Like the node used for the breadth-first search, it contains the `pathParent` node used during the search process only. `costFromStart` and `estimatedCostToGoal` are also filled in during the search because these vary depending on where the start and goal nodes are.

The `getCost(node)` abstract method returns the cost between the node and a neighbor node. The `getEstimatedCost(node)` abstract method returns the estimated cost between the node and the specified goal node. Remember, you have to create these functions, depending on what you want the cost to be.

Now you'll implement the A* search, shown here in Listing 12.2.

Listing 12.2   AStarSearch.java

```
package com.brackeen.javagamebook.path;

import java.util.*;

/**
    The AStarSearch class, along with the AStarNode class,
    implements a generic A* search algorithm. The AStarNode
    class should be subclassed to provide searching capability.
*/
public class AStarSearch {
```

continues

Listing 12.2   AStarSearch.java   *continued*

```java
/**
    A simple priority list, also called a priority queue.
    Objects in the list are ordered by their priority,
    determined by the object's Comparable interface.
    The highest priority item is first in the list.
*/
public static class PriorityList extends LinkedList {

    public void add(Comparable object) {
        for (int i=0; i<size(); i++) {
            if (object.compareTo(get(i)) <= 0) {
                add(i, object);
                return;
            }
        }
        addLast(object);
    }
}


/**
    Construct the path, not including the start node.
*/
protected List constructPath(AStarNode node) {
    LinkedList path = new LinkedList();
    while (node.pathParent != null) {
        path.addFirst(node);
        node = node.pathParent;
    }
    return path;
}


/**
    Find the path from the start node to the end node. A list
    of AStarNodes is returned, or null if the path is not
    found.
```

```
    */
    public List findPath(AStarNode startNode, AStarNode goalNode)
{

        PriorityList openList = new PriorityList();
        LinkedList closedList = new LinkedList();

        startNode.costFromStart = 0;
        startNode.estimatedCostToGoal =
            startNode.getEstimatedCost(goalNode);
        startNode.pathParent = null;
        openList.add(startNode);

        while (!openList.isEmpty()) {
            AStarNode node = (AStarNode)openList.removeFirst();
            if (node == goalNode) {
                // construct the path from start to goal
                return constructPath(goalNode);
            }

            List neighbors = node.getNeighbors();
            for (int i=0; i<neighbors.size(); i++) {
                AStarNode neighborNode =
                    (AStarNode)neighbors.get(i);
                boolean isOpen = openList.contains(neighborNode);
                boolean isClosed =
                    closedList.contains(neighborNode);
                float costFromStart = node.costFromStart +
                    node.getCost(neighborNode);

                // check if the neighbor node has not been
                // traversed or if a shorter path to this
                // neighbor node is found.
                if ((!isOpen && !isClosed) ||
                    costFromStart < neighborNode.costFromStart)
                {
                    neighborNode.pathParent = node;
                    neighborNode.costFromStart = costFromStart;
```

continues

Listing 12.2 AStarSearch.java *continued*

```
                        neighborNode.estimatedCostToGoal =
                            neighborNode.getEstimatedCost(goalNode);
                        if (isClosed) {
                            closedList.remove(neighborNode);
                        }
                        if (!isOpen) {
                            openList.add(neighborNode);
                        }
                    }
                }
            }
            closedList.add(node);
        }

        // no path found
        return null;
    }

}
```

The `PriorityList` inner class is a simple `LinkedList` that adds nodes using an insertion sort. In this case, only `AStarNode` instances are added, keeping the list sorted from lowest cost to highest. Nodes are removed only from the front of the list (lowest cost).

The `findPath()` function is very similar to the breadth-first search implementation, except for a couple of changes. The `costFromStart` and `estimatedCostToGoal` fields are calculated as you go along. Also, a node is moved from the closed list to the open list if a shorter path to that node is found. Other than that, they're pretty much the same.

That's it for the basics of the A* algorithm. The next step is to actually apply this algorithm in a game.

Applying the A* Algorithm

To use the A* algorithm in a game, you'll have to interpret the game environment as a graph—or, in other words, decide what the nodes and edges represent.

In a top-down, tiled-based world, this is easy: The nodes represent the tiles, as in Figure 12.6. In this figure, the game environment is laid out on a hexagonal grid, and you can travel from one tile to any of its six neighboring tiles (unless one or more of the neighboring tiles is an obstacle).

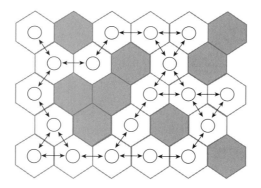

Figure 12.6   A tiled-based game can easily be interpreted as a graph.

In this case, the distance between neighbor nodes is the same, but the cost between neighbor nodes doesn't have to be. As mentioned before, you could make traveling on some tiles, such as muddy sand, take longer than on other tiles, such as sidewalks.

If the tiles were square, traveling diagonally would have a greater cost than traveling straight north, south, east, or west because the diagonal distance between two square tiles is greater.

One benefit of a top-down, tile-based world is that it's easy to dynamically modify the graph. If the player blasts a tile, changing it from an obstacle to a grassy area, the graph can be easily updated.

However, tiled-based worlds aren't the only situation in which you can use the A* algorithm.

Using the A* Algorithm with a BSP Tree

Let's consider a typical floor plan for a 3D world like you used in previous chapters. In this world, what could your nodes be?

First, the nodes could be placed by hand. All you would have to do is make sure the edges between neighbor nodes have a clear path (no obstacles in the way) and that there are enough nodes to cover the entire map.

However, this can be a bit tedious. Who wants to sit around defining where path-finding nodes are on a map? So let's try to come up with an automatic solution for node placement.

Portals

You can take advantage of the fact that your "rooms" in the floor plan are convex. This means a bot traveling from one entryway of the room to another will never hit any walls, as long as the two entryways aren't collinear. If two entryways are collinear (they exist on the same line in space) and a wall was between them (think doorways in a dorm hall), then a bot could collide with the wall between them. So, extra care may be needed to define room boundaries so that collinear entryways in the same room don't occur.

Entryways between convex rooms are often called *portals*. Portals are generally an invisible polygon (or, in a 2D world, an invisible line) that separates two convex areas. See Figure 12.7 for an example: The dotted lines represent the portals.

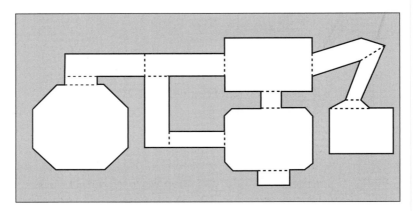

Figure 12.7   Dotted lines represent the portals between convex areas.

Portals can also be used as a rendering technique. With portal rendering, you start by drawing all the polygons in the room that the camera is in. If any portals are in the view, the room on the other side of the portal is drawn, and then so on until the view is filled.

Using portals as nodes means you can easily create a graph for traveling room to room, as in Figure 12.8.

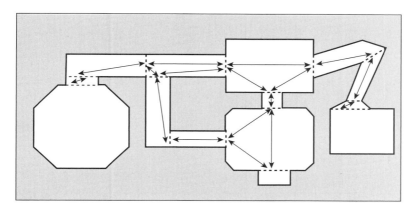

Figure 12.8   The portals can be the nodes in a graph representing the map.

The only issue is that the start and goal locations are within a room, not on a portal. However, because rooms are convex, a bot can move in a straight line from any location in a room to one of the room's portals without running into any walls.

So, when you are doing an A* search, you can make temporary nodes that represent the start and the goal. These node's neighbors are all the portals of the room they are in.

Note that using portals as nodes takes only the world into account—obstacles based on game objects aren't considered. So, if you have a door or other game object in the way, you'll need some extra code to move around those objects or at least consider them in the search.

Implementing Portals

In a BSP tree, portals can be stored in the leaves of the tree because the leaves represent convex areas. This way, you can easily get all the portals for a room. Here you just add a list of portals to the BSP tree leaf you created in Chapter 10:

```
public static class Leaf extends Node {
    public float floorHeight;
    public float ceilHeight;
    public Rectangle bounds;
    public List portals;
}
```

Finding the portals is easy. Because a leaf in a 2D tree represents an area, just check each edge of that area to see if there's a "solid wall" on it. If there is not, you have a portal. The same is true for a 3D BSP tree, except that every face of the leaf volume is checked.

When you have a portal, you need to know what leaf is on either side of it. You can find out by doing a simple tree traversal, shown in Listing 12.3 with the getFrontLeaf() and getBackLeaf() methods of BSPTree.

Listing 12.3   getLeaf() Methods of BSPTree.java

```
/**
    Gets the Leaf in front of the specified partition.
*/
public Leaf getFrontLeaf(BSPLine partition) {
    return getLeaf(root, partition, BSPLine.FRONT);
}



/**
    Gets the Leaf in back of the specified partition.
*/
public Leaf getBackLeaf(BSPLine partition) {
    return getLeaf(root, partition, BSPLine.BACK);
}



protected Leaf getLeaf(Node node, BSPLine partition, int side)
{
    if (node == null || node instanceof Leaf) {
        return (Leaf)node;
```

```
    }
    int segSide = node.partition.getSide(partition);
    if (segSide == BSPLine.COLLINEAR) {
        segSide = side;
    }
    if (segSide == BSPLine.FRONT) {
        return getLeaf(node.front, partition, side);
    }
    else if (segSide == BSPLine.BACK) {
        return getLeaf(node.back, partition, side);
    }
    else { // BSPLine.SPANNING
        // shouldn't happen
        return null;
    }
}
```

These methods assume the partition doesn't span any other partitions because the partition is the edge of a leaf. The correct `Leaf` object is returned depending on whether you want the leaf in front of or in back of the partition.

Finally, you'll make a `Portal` class, as shown in Listing 12.4. This class is a subclass of `AStarNode`.

Listing 12.4   Portal.java

```
package com.brackeen.javagamebook.bsp2D;


import java.util.*;
import com.brackeen.javagamebook.math3D.Vector3D;
import com.brackeen.javagamebook.path.AStarNode;

/**
    A Portal represents a passable divider between two
    leaves in a BSP tree (think: entryway between rooms).
    The Portal class is also an AStarNode, so AI creatures
    can use the A* algorithm to find paths throughout the
    BSP tree.
```

continues

Listing 12.4 Portal.java *continued*

```java
*/
public class Portal extends AStarNode {

    private BSPLine divider;
    private BSPTree.Leaf front;
    private BSPTree.Leaf back;
    private ArrayList neighbors;
    private Vector3D midPoint;

    /**
        Create a new Portal with the specified divider and front/
        back leaves.
    */
    public Portal(BSPLine divider, BSPTree.Leaf front,
        BSPTree.Leaf back)
    {
        this.divider = divider;
        this.front = front;
        this.back = back;
        midPoint = new Vector3D(
            (divider.x1 + divider.x2) / 2,
            Math.max(front.floorHeight, back.floorHeight),
            (divider.y1 + divider.y2) / 2);
    }


    public float getCost(AStarNode node) {
        return getEstimatedCost(node);
    }


    public float getEstimatedCost(AStarNode node) {
        if (node instanceof Portal) {
            Portal other = (Portal)node;
            float dx = midPoint.x - other.midPoint.x;
            float dz = midPoint.z - other.midPoint.z;
            return (float)Math.sqrt(dx * dx + dz * dz);
```

```
        }
        else {
            return node.getEstimatedCost(this);
        }
    }


    public List getNeighbors() {
        if (neighbors == null) {
            neighbors = new ArrayList();
            if (front != null) {
                neighbors.addAll(front.portals);
            }
            if (back != null) {
                neighbors.addAll(back.portals);
            }

            // remove all references to this node
            while (neighbors.remove(this));
        }
        return neighbors;
    }

}
```

The neighbors of a portal are the portals in the front and back leaves. The getNeighbors() method fills the neighbors in a list.

The getEstimatedCost() estimates the cost between portals as the distance between the midpoints of each portal. Note that for two adjacent nodes, getEstimatedCost() is the same as the actual cost.

Finally, you just need one more type of AStarNode that is a location anywhere within a convex area defined by the leaf. These nodes are generally just temporary because they are used only for the start and goal nodes of a specific path search.

Listing 12.5 `LeafNode` Inner Class of `AStarSearchWithBSP`

```java
/**
    The LeafNode class is an AStarNode that represents a
    location in a leaf of a BSP tree. Used for the start
    and goal nodes of a search.
*/
public class LeafNode extends AStarNode {
    BSPTree.Leaf leaf;
    Vector3D location;

    public LeafNode(BSPTree.Leaf leaf, Vector3D location) {
        this.leaf = leaf;
        this.location = location;
    }

    public float getCost(AStarNode node) {
        return getEstimatedCost(node);
    }

    public float getEstimatedCost(AStarNode node) {
        float otherX;
        float otherZ;
        if (node instanceof Portal) {
            Portal other = (Portal)node;
            otherX = other.getMidPoint().x;
            otherZ = other.getMidPoint().z;
        }
        else {
            LeafNode other = (LeafNode)node;
            otherX = other.location.x;
            otherZ = other.location.z;
        }
        float dx = location.x - otherX;
        float dz = location.z - otherZ;
        return (float)Math.sqrt(dx * dx + dz * dz);
    }

    public List getNeighbors() {
```

```
        return leaf.portals;
    }
}
```

The `LeafNode` class is fairly straightforward. The neighbors of a `LeafNode` are all the portals of the BSP tree leaf the node is in. The estimated cost is calculated as the distance between the node location and a portal's midpoint.

Now you have all the little pieces you need to perform an A* search on a BSP tree. Next, you'll put all the little pieces together in a wrapper that implements a generic path-finding interface.

Generic Path Finding

The A* search function you created returns a list of `AStarNodes`, which is great for generic implementation but isn't too friendly when you need something more concrete. Really, you want something like a list of locations, as in the `PathFinder` interface in Listing 12.6.

Listing 12.6   PathFinder.java

```
/**
    The PathFinder interface is a function that finds a path
    (represented by a List of Vector3Ds) from one location to
    another, or from one GameObject to another. Note that the
    find() method can ignore the requested goal, and instead
    give an arbitrary path, like patrolling in a set path or
    running away from the goal.
*/
public interface PathFinder {

    /**
        Finds a path from GameObject A to GameObject B. The path
        is an Iterator of Vector3Ds, not including the start
        location (GameObject A) but including the goal location
        (GameObject B). The Vector3D objects may be used in
        other objects and should not be modified.
```

continues

Listing 12.6   PathFinder.java   *continued*

```
            Returns null if no path found.
    */
    public Iterator find(GameObject a, GameObject b);


    /**
        Finds a path from the start location to the goal
        location. The path is an Iterator of Vector3Ds, not
        including the start location, but including the goal
        location. The Vector3D objects may be used in other
        objects and should not be modified. Returns null if no
        path found.
    */
    public Iterator find(Vector3D start, Vector3D goal);
}
```

In this interface, two methods are provided: one to find a path between two points, and another to find a path between two objects. The specification of the interface says that these functions should return `Iterator` objects that iterate over a list of `Vector3D` locations.

So, if you use `PathFinder`, it doesn't matter what the underlying algorithm is, whether it is A*, random, or some other idea. Also, you can use this interface for other types of paths, such as simple paths that follow the perimeter of a room or a flocking bird pattern as a background effect. You'll use the `PathFinder` interface a lot in the next chapter.

But, hey, we're getting ahead of ourselves here! First, let's create an implementation of the `PathFinder` interface for finding the shortest path between two points in a BSP tree using the A* algorithm. Sound like a mouthful? Well, at least the `AStarSearchWithBSP` class in Listing 12.7 is straightforward.

Listing 12.7   AStarSearchWithBSP.java

```
package com.brackeen.javagamebook.path;

import java.util.*;
```

```
import com.brackeen.javagamebook.game.GameObject;
import com.brackeen.javagamebook.math3D.Vector3D;
import com.brackeen.javagamebook.bsp2D.BSPTree;
import com.brackeen.javagamebook.bsp2D.Portal;

/**
    The AStarSearchWithBSP class is a PathFinder that finds
    a path in a BSP tree using an A* search algorithm.
*/
public class AStarSearchWithBSP extends AStarSearch
    implements PathFinder
{

    private BSPTree bspTree;

    /**
        Creates a new AStarSearchWithBSP for the specified
        BSP tree.
    */
    public AStarSearchWithBSP(BSPTree bspTree) {
        this.bspTree = bspTree;
    }


    public Iterator find(GameObject a, GameObject b) {
        return find(a.getLocation(), b.getLocation());
    }


    public Iterator find(Vector3D start, Vector3D goal) {

        BSPTree.Leaf startLeaf = bspTree.getLeaf(start.x, start.z);
        BSPTree.Leaf goalLeaf = bspTree.getLeaf(goal.x, goal.z);

        // if start and goal are in the same leaf, no need to do
        // A* search
        if (startLeaf == goalLeaf) {
            return Collections.singleton(goal).iterator();
```

continues

Listing 12.7 AStarSearchWithBSP.java *continued*

```
        }

        AStarNode startNode = new LeafNode(startLeaf, start);
        AStarNode goalNode = new LeafNode(goalLeaf, goal);

        // temporarily add the goalNode we just created to
        // the neighbors list
        List goalNeighbors = goalNode.getNeighbors();
        for (int i=0; i<goalNeighbors.size(); i++) {
            Portal portal = (Portal)goalNeighbors.get(i);
            portal.addNeighbor(goalNode);
        }

        // do A* search
        List path = super.findPath(startNode, goalNode);

        // remove the goal node from the neighbors list
        for (int i=0; i<goalNeighbors.size(); i++) {
            Portal portal = (Portal)goalNeighbors.get(i);
            portal.removeNeighbor(goalNode);
        }

        return convertPath(path);
    }


    /**
        Converts path of AStarNodes to a path of Vector3D
        locations.
    */
    protected Iterator convertPath(List path) {
        if (path == null) {
            return null;
        }
        for (int i=0; i<path.size(); i++) {
            Object node = path.get(i);
            if (node instanceof Portal) {
```

```
                path.set(i, ((Portal)node).getMidPoint());
            }
            else {
                path.set(i, ((LeafNode)node).location);
            }
        }
        return Collections.unmodifiableList(path).iterator();
    }

}
```

The actual searching in the find() method is just like we said it would be: First, you create temporary nodes representing the start and goal nodes, add them to the graph, and then perform the search. After the search, you clean up by removing those temporary nodes from the graph. Also, if the start location and the goal location are in the same leaf of the BSP tree, no search needs to be performed, so the method just returns an Iterator over the goal location.

The convertPath() method converts a list of AStarNodes to actual locations. Here, you use the midpoint of each portal as the location to use. Another idea instead of using the midpoint is to use a point within the portal that is closest to the location on either side of it, as long as you leave room for the size of the object. But midpoints work well, so you can stick with that simpler solution.

Making a *PathBot*

Here's something you might have already thought about: Let's say you have a bot that finds a path to the player and starts to follow it, but by the time the bot reaches the goal location, the player is long gone. Kinda pointless, eh?

You could recalculate the path every frame, but what a waste of resources! Performing an A* search makes quite a few temporary objects and takes up a chunk of processor power (including several Math.sqrt() calls), so you don't want a bot to recalculate the path every frame. Also, the player or any other goal location isn't likely to change much from frame to frame, so the path wouldn't need to change much, either.

Instead, you can just keep a calculated path around for a while and recalculate it occasionally, every few seconds or so. This way, the path is fairly up-to-date but doesn't hog the processor or waste memory.

Another thought along those lines is, what if you have several bots calculating their path at the exact same time? You might see little drops in the frame rate of the game as this happens because several bots are hogging the processor at once. To alleviate this, you can just take the easy route and make sure each bot starts calculating a path after a random amount of time. In this case, you'll make sure bots don't calculate the path until 0 to 1000 milliseconds have passed.

Another idea is to cache common A* searches from portal to portal (not including start and goal nodes). This way, two bots in the same room can share a path, and a path that's already been calculated wouldn't need to be calculated again.

All right, let's do it. You'll make that bot here in Listing 12.8. The `PathBot` follows the path given to it from a `PathFinder`. It has a few default attributes, such as its speed, how fast it can turn, and how high above the floor it "flies." The turn speed is purely cosmetic—the bot will turn to face the direction it's facing, but the turn speed doesn't affect how fast a bot travels along a path.

Listing 12.8 PathBot.java

```
package com.brackeen.javagamebook.path;

import java.util.Iterator;
import com.brackeen.javagamebook.path.PathFinder;
import com.brackeen.javagamebook.math3D.*;
import com.brackeen.javagamebook.game.GameObject;

/**
    A PathBot is a GameObject that follows a path from a
    PathFinder.
*/
public class PathBot extends GameObject {

    // default values
    protected PathFinder pathFinder = null;
    protected Vector3D facing = null;
```

```
protected long pathRecalcTime = 4000;
protected float turnSpeed = .005f;
protected float speed = .25f;
protected float flyHeight = 64;

// for path following
protected Iterator currentPath;
protected Vector3D nextPathLocation = new Vector3D();
protected long timeUntilPathRecalc;


public PathBot(PolygonGroup polygonGroup) {
    super(polygonGroup);
    setState(STATE_ACTIVE);
}


public boolean isFlying() {
    return (flyHeight > 0);
}


/**
    Sets the PathFinder class to use to follow the path.
*/
public void setPathFinder(PathFinder pathFinder) {
    if (this.pathFinder != pathFinder) {
        this.pathFinder = pathFinder;
        currentPath = null;

        // random amount of time until calculation, so
        // not all bot calc the path at the same time
        timeUntilPathRecalc = (long)(Math.random() * 1000);
    }
}


/**
```

continues

Listing 12.8 PathBot.java *continued*

```
        Sets the location this object should face as it follows
        the path. This value can change. If null, this object
        faces the direction it is moving.
    */
    public void setFacing(Vector3D facing) {
        this.facing = facing;
    }


    public void update(GameObject player, long elapsedTime) {

        if (pathFinder == null) {
            super.update(player, elapsedTime);
            return;
        }

        timeUntilPathRecalc-=elapsedTime;

        // update the path to the player
        if (timeUntilPathRecalc <= 0) {
            currentPath = pathFinder.find(this, player);
            if (currentPath != null) {
                getTransform().stop();
            }
            timeUntilPathRecalc = pathRecalcTime;
        }

        // follow the path
        if (currentPath != null && currentPath.hasNext() &&
            !getTransform().isMovingIgnoreY())
        {
            nextPathLocation.setTo((Vector3D)currentPath.next());
            nextPathLocation.y+=flyHeight;
            getTransform().moveTo(nextPathLocation, speed);

            // face either the direction we are traveling,
            // or face the specified face location.
```

```
        Vector3D faceLocation = facing;
        if (faceLocation == null) {
            faceLocation = nextPathLocation;
        }
        getTransform().turnYTo(
            faceLocation.x - getX(),
            faceLocation.z - getZ(),
            (float)-Math.PI/2, turnSpeed);

    }

    super.update(player, elapsedTime);
}


/**
    When a collision occurs, back up for 200ms and then
    wait a few seconds before recalculating the path.
*/
protected void backupAndRecomputePath() {
    // back up for 200 ms
    nextPathLocation.setTo(getTransform().getVelocity());
    if (!isFlying()) {
        nextPathLocation.y = 0;
    }
    nextPathLocation.multiply(-1);
    getTransform().setVelocity(nextPathLocation, 200);

    // wait until computing the path again
    currentPath = null;
    timeUntilPathRecalc = (long)(Math.random() * 1000);
}


public void notifyWallCollision() {
    backupAndRecomputePath();
}
```

continues

Listing 12.8   PathBot.java   *continued*

```
    public void notifyObjectCollision(GameObject object) {
        backupAndRecomputePath();
    }

}
```

`PathBot` is fairly uncomplicated. It keeps track of how much time is left until the path is recalculated again, and if that amount of time has passed, the path is recalculated in the update() method. The rest of the update() method simply follows the path in this manner:

1. The bot's transform is set to move to the first location in the path.

2. When the bot has finished moving, the next location in the path is chosen.

3. If there are no more locations in the path, the bot stops until the path is recalculated.

Also note that the bot turns to look at the location specified by the *facing* vector. If this value is null, the bot just looks at the direction it's traveling. You'll use this later when you want a bot to focus its attention on, say, the player.

The last thing that `PathBot` does is handle collisions. If a collision with a wall or an object is detected, the bot backs up, stops, and then waits a few seconds before recalculating the path.

That's it for path finding! The source code with this book also includes the `PathFindingTest` class, which creates a few pyramid-shape `PathBots` in the same 3D map used in the last couple of chapters. The `PathBots` follow the player around, no matter where the player is. No matter where you go, the ninjas will find you!

Enhancing the A* Search

When you run the `PathFindingTest` demo, you might notice some strange behavior in the bots related to the portals. Because the BSP building process splits polygons, sometimes a few portals can exist within a convex room. So, when the bot travels from portal to portal, it occasionally won't travel in a straight line from the bot to the player, even though it looks like it should.

You can fix this in a few ways. One way is to do extra checks at runtime to see if you can skip a portal in the path. For instance, instead of traveling from portal A to B to C, you would just travel from A to C if there was nothing in the way to block you.

Another way is to just define the portals yourself by hand, like we mentioned before. Yuck, right?

A third way to fix this is what we implement in the next chapter. In that chapter, if a bot can "see" the player, it can just head straight toward it. This isn't a perfect solution, considering things such as small holes the bot could see though but not travel though, but combined with other AI abilities, it works well.

Another idea is to enhance a path by smoothing out the corners using a Bézier curve. This way, instead of making sharp turns, the bot gradually turns around a corner, presenting a more natural movement.

Finally, some larger worlds might be so big that doing an A* search between frames could cause a visible slowdown. What you could do is create a low-priority "worker" thread which has the sole job of calculating paths. A bot could make the request to the worker to calculate a path, and later the worker would signal to the bot that the path was found.

Keep in mind that this worker thread would work only if there was just one of them. Only one path should be found at a time because various fields of `AStarNode` are changed during the searching process. Two threads modifying nodes at the same time will destroy the path. So, the worker thread could hold requests in a queue (such as a one-thread `ThreadPool` from Chapter 1, "Java Threads") and perform all path calculations in that thread.

Also, remember that the `PathBot` knows nothing of the A* search—all it does is follow the path given to it by a `PathFinder`. As we mentioned earlier, this means you can modify your underlying search algorithm or give a bot other interesting paths to follow. You'll actually create several different path patterns in the next chapter.

Summary

In this chapter, you started with the basics: ninjas.

Actually, you started with some basic path-finding routines on a tile-based map, such as a randomized search and the popular "right hand on the wall" trick. Then you went to more advanced environments based on graphs and implemented a generic A* algorithm that could be used for graph- or tile-based environments (because tile-based worlds could be interpreted as a graph anyway).

Finally, you merged your A* searching with the BSP tree you've been working with for the past couple of chapters, and you created a generic path bot that follows any type of path, whether it was created by an A* search or not. As usual, you made a demo to show off the stuff from this chapter.

Path finding is one of those required elements of a game, and it's also the building block of a lot of artificial intelligence in games. Currently, your A* path bots are god-like, meaning they always "know" where the player is. In the next chapter, you'll use your path-finding capabilities to dumb down the bots' godlike powers, but you'll also give the bots a little more smarts about making decisions such as attacking, dodging, and chasing the player. In addition, you'll make the bots "strike back" so you can fight against your robots.

Which makes me wonder, is killing robots okay?

Chapter 13

Artificial Intelligence

One of the first games I ever tried to make was a *Pac-Man* clone. It had 16 colors, was written in BASIC, ran on a 486, and flickered—a lot.

But the point is, my first attempt at making the ghosts move was a little bit off the mark. Whenever a ghost would have to decide which way to go, it would always move in the direction of the player. This essentially made "super-ghosts" that were so good at tracking Pac-Man down that he rarely had time to eat a power dot. But if he was lucky enough get to a power dot in time, all the ghosts would be nearby, ready for Pac-Man to chomp them. Advantage: Pac-Man.

The lesson here is that it's easy to make enemies too smart. It's also easy to make them too dumb. The trick is finding the right balance of intelligence that makes the game both enjoyable and challenging. In the Pac-Man clone, I had to "dumb down" the ghosts so that they occasionally made a decision to move in a random direction rather than toward the player. This solution wasn't exactly like the original Pac-Man game, but it made the game playable.

Artificial intelligence is simply mimicked intelligence and behavior. AI is a rather large topic and has countless applications, but in this chapter, we just scratch the surface and focus on game-related AI. In this chapter, we talk about seeing and hearing, state machines, probability, attack-and-dodge patterns, aiming, and even evolution. Plus, we touch on a few topics such as object spawning and graphical overlays to make the demo a little better.

AI Basics

AI in games is really about creating bots that show a certain behavioral appearance, whether it's a rodent scampering along the ground or a human-shape creature making seemingly intelligent decisions. In this chapter, we use the term *bot* to refer to any "intelligent" game object. With convincing bots, AI can help define the feel of a game almost as much as the visual parts of the game.

The appearance of the behavior is the important part.

When designing the AI for a game, you should design from the top down: Think about how you want your bots to *appear*, and then try to implement it. It can be tempting to take AI design from a bottom-up approach by first designing complicated patterns and infrastructures. For example, perhaps you want to design different bots with different search patterns that just wander around a maze looking for the player. But in a 3D world, this might just appear to the player like bots randomly showing up to attack. So, think about how you want your AI creatures to appear to the player before you do anything.

Of course, many AI bots need to start with a good path-finding algorithm so that they know how to travel from any two points in a map. Without path finding, you could end up with annoying or distracting AI that makes bots get stuck next to walls or not be able to turn around a corner. You can use the A* algorithm implemented in the previous chapter.

On that note, one of your overall goals of your AI bots is to not be distracting. Little things such as bots moving around in unnatural patterns can be annoying to the user. Sometimes AI is noticeable only when it's bad.

You also should try to give different characters different behaviors that match their appearance. For example, a human-shape creature would need to appear to make intelligent choices because users would expect a human-shape creature to do so; on the other hand, a spiderlike creature could follow simple patterns and still be believable.

Another idea is to make progressively smarter and more difficult enemies as the game moves along. Stay away from AI that easily becomes predictable so that the game play doesn't become too tedious as the game progresses. Also, always keep in mind the goal of AI in the first place: finding that perfect zone where enemies are not too smart and not too dumb, making the game fun and challenging at the same time. Finding the right balance is up to you.

In this chapter, you'll design an AI system to work with the 3D engine in this book. The bots will exhibit slightly different personalities, and each bot will have different movement and attack patterns to distinguish themselves from the others.

Take Away Those Godlike Powers!

In the previous chapter on path finding, you created a demo in which bots had godlike powers: They always knew the player's location and could find a path to the player every time. This is basically the same problem as the Terminator-like Pac-Man ghosts.

You rarely want to give bots godlike powers like this. Instead, you can force certain situations in which the bot doesn't know where the player is.

One realistic idea that works wonders in a 3D game is to allow a bot to know where a player is only if the player is somewhere in the bot's sight. That is, the bot has artificial vision.

Seeing

Generally, the goal with artificial vision is to perform a check to find out whether a bot can see the player. Obviously, the bot shouldn't see anything that's behind an obstacle, such as something on the other side of a wall or above a ceiling.

What you can do is fire a "vision ray" from the bot to the player to see if that ray hits any obstacles, as in Figure 13.1.

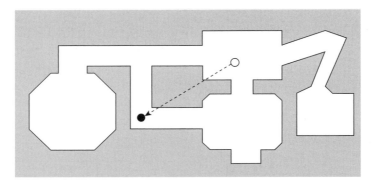

Figure 13.1 A bot (white circle) tries to locate the player (black circle). The bot uses a "vision ray" to determine whether it can "see" the player. In this case, the bot can't see the player.

If the vision ray doesn't hit an obstacle, you can assume the bot "sees" the player and, therefore, knows the player's location. When the location is known, the bot can attack or whatnot. But how do you implement a vision ray?

In a tile-based world, this is a simple problem to solve. Just draw a line using a standard line equation, and find all tiles that intersect that line. Then check each tile to determine whether it is "see-through."

For a BSP tree, you've already implemented something like a vision ray. In Chapter 11, "Collision Detection," your collision-detection code had a method called getFirstWallIntersection() that found the first wall intersection between two points. You can use this function to check whether a line segment intersects any walls in the BSP tree. If no wall intersection is found, this method returns null and you can assume the player is visible. Let's try it. In this chapter, most of the AI-related code goes in the AIBot class, which is a subclass of the PathBot you created in the previous chapter. The first addition to AIBot is the canSee() method in Listing 13.1.

Listing 13.1 AIBot.canSee()

```
/**
    Checks if this object can see the specified object,
    (assuming this object has eyes in the back of its head).
*/
public boolean canSee(GameObject object) {
    // check if a line from this bot to the object
```

```
    // hits any walls
    boolean visible =
        (collisionDetection.getFirstWallIntersection(
        getX(), getZ(), object.getX(), object.getZ(),
        getY(), getY() + 1) == null);

    if (visible) {
        timeSincePlayerLastSeen = 0;
    }
    return visible;
}
```

Notice that you set the field `timeSincePlayerLastSeen` to 0. This variable is incremented in the `update()` method, so you always know the time since the player was last seen. This way, you can perform certain functions if the player is not visible but was visible recently, such as using the A* search if the player was visible just a few seconds ago.

One problem with using `getFirstWallIntersection()` is basically a problem with using a 2D BSP tree: The ray is horizontal, which means the vision ray can't go upstairs. Ergo, bots can't see upstairs. Hopefully, with the combination of other AI capabilities, this won't be an issue.

Another issue is that the bot has eyes in the back of its head. The vision ray is cast out in any direction, no matter which way the bot is facing, so the player can't sneak up behind the bot. To fix this, you could implement a "blind spot" behind the AI creature, like in Figure 13.2.

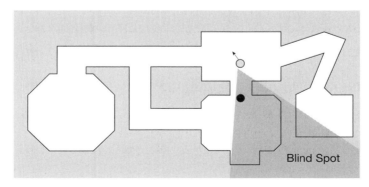

Figure 13.2   You can implement a vision "blind spot" so the player can still sneak up on the bot.

This is fairly easy to do. Just check to make sure the angle between the vision ray and the direction the bot is facing isn't too large. (This is one of those "exercise for the reader" tricks. Enjoy!)

But what if you snuck up behind a bot and just started screaming? Well, the bot couldn't hear, so it wouldn't matter. But what if the bot could hear you, such as when the player jumps, falls, or fires a weapon?

Hearing

In the real world, when you make a sound, the sound waves bounce off walls, run into each other, and travel down the hallway and around corners, and a sound gets quieter with distance until you're so far away from the sound source that you can't hear it at all.

So in a game, you can give bots a "hearing radar" that can hear any noises within a certain distance, whether or not there are walls in the way, as in Figure 13.3.

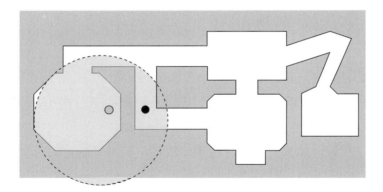

Figure 13.3   A bot (gray circle) tries to locate the player (black circle). The can "hear" any noises within a certain distance.

So, if the player is making a noise, the code to check whether it's within range merely involves checking the distance from the player, as in Listing 13.2.

Listing 13.2   `AIBot.canHear()`

```
float hearDistance;

. . .
```

```
/**
    Checks if this object can hear the specified object. The
    specified object must be making a noise and be within
    hearing range of this object.
*/
public boolean canHear(GameObject object) {

    // check if object is making noise and this bot is not deaf
    if (!object.isMakingNoise() || hearDistance == 0) {
        return false;
    }

    // check if this bot is close enough to hear the noise
    float distSq = getLocation().
        getDistanceSq(object.getLocation());
    float hearDistSq = hearDistance * hearDistance;
    return (distSq <= hearDistSq);
}
```

Here, you're actually using the square of the distances, so you don't have to perform the `Math.sqrt()` operation.

That was easy enough, but how can you tell whether an object makes a noise? When does the `isMakingNoise()` method return `true`?

Usually, a noise isn't just an "instant" event, but it actually lasts for a few seconds or more. So, you can keep track of the remaining time of the last noise made by each object. It's all summed up in a couple extra methods in the base `GameObject` class, in Listing 13.3.

Listing 13.3   Noise Methods of `GameObject`

```
private long noiseDuration;

...

 /**
     Returns true if this object is making a "noise."
 */
 public boolean isMakingNoise() {
```

continues

Listing 13.3   Noise Methods of `GameObject`   *continued*

```
        return (noiseDuration > 0);
    }



    /**
        Signifies that this object is making a "noise" of the
        specified duration. This is useful to determine if
        one object can "hear" another.
    */
    public void makeNoise(long duration) {
        if (noiseDuration < duration) {
            noiseDuration = duration;
        }
    }



    public void update(GameObject player, long elapsedTime) {
        if (isMakingNoise()) {
            noiseDuration-=elapsedTime;
        }
        . . .
    }
```

In the player code, whenever the player fires a shot, you'll call `makeNoise(500)` so the shot is audible to the bots for 500ms. Note that this is completely separate from the `SoundManager` code—a virtual noise is just imaginary and makes no audible sound through the speakers.

In the code, we assume all noises have the same volume. In real life, however, loud noises travel farther than faint noises. You could extend this code to give each noise a volume or distance level that would specify either the volume of the sound or the maximum distance the sound can carry. Again, this is another exercise for the reader!

Before I forget, to help out with some common AI path routines, I added a couple of methods to the `Vector3D` class to get the distance between two locations, as in Listing 13.4.

Listing 13.4 Distance Methods of `Vector3D`

```
/**
    Gets the distance squared between this vector and the
    specified vector.
*/
public float getDistanceSq(Vector3D v) {
    float dx = v.x - x;
    float dy = v.y - y;
    float dz = v.z - z;
    return dx*dx + dy*dy + dz*dz;
}


/**
    Gets the distance between this vector and the
    specified vector.
*/
public float getDistance(Vector3D v) {
    return (float)Math.sqrt(getDistanceSq(v));
}
```

Okay, now the bots can see and hear the player, but they still don't act any differently. Next, you'll work on getting the bots to react to these different situations.

State Machines and Reacting

A bot will react differently for each situation. Depending on what is happening in the environment and whether the player can be seen or heard, a bot could be doing a multitude of things, such as resting, patrolling, attacking, dodging, chasing, running away, powering up, hiding, or whatever else you can think of.

In previous chapters, you've already taken advantage of state machines, in which an object can have different states that cause it to perform different actions. For example, the base game object class had the idle, active, and destroyed states. State machines are also called *finite state machines* because there are a limited number of possible states.

A finite state machine also defines how and when the object's state can change. For example, a bot can go from stopped to walking to running, but it can't go directly from stopped to running. Also, a bot might start walking only if the player is visible.

Additionally, you can create a hierarchy of states. For example, the bots in this chapter will have three states that are considered "battle" states: dodging, attacking, and running away. Furthermore, the attack state could have different kinds of attack patterns. So, the hierarchy is battle as a parent, with three children and possibly a few grandchildren.

Check out Figure 13.4 for a visual look at the state machine you'll use for the AI bots in this chapter. This state machine has two basic parent states: battle and normal. A bot goes into a battle state only if the player is visible, and it returns to the normal state when the player is no longer seen.

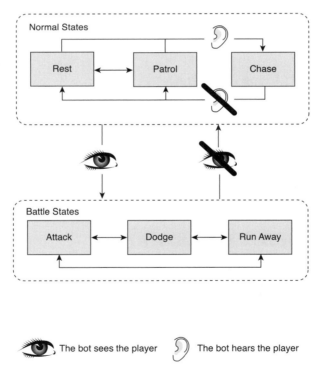

Figure 13.4 A bot state machine.

But just because the states show a hierarchy in theory doesn't mean you have to create any elaborate state code. Here you use plain old integers like you did for the previous state machines:

```
public static final int NORMAL_STATE_IDLE = 0;
public static final int NORMAL_STATE_PATROL = 1;
public static final int NORMAL_STATE_CHASE = 2;
public static final int BATTLE_STATE_ATTACK = 3;
public static final int BATTLE_STATE_DODGE = 4;
public static final int BATTLE_STATE_RUN_AWAY = 5;
```

You'll treat the AI state separately from the game object state so they won't interfere with each other. You'll actually use a few more states than this, but this a good starting point. Setting the correct AI state is straightforward, shown here in Listing 13.5.

Listing 13.5   State Machine Methods of `AIBot`

```
private int aiState;
private long elapsedTimeInState;

...

/**
    Sets the AI state for this bot (different from the
    GameObject state).
*/
protected void setAiState(int aiState, GameObject player) {
    if (this.aiState != aiState) {
        this.aiState = aiState;
        elapsedTimeInState = 0;
    }

    // later, set the appropriate path for this state here.
    ...
}


public void update(GameObject player, long elapsedTime) {
    elapsedTimeInState+=elapsedTime;
    ...
}
```

Besides setting the state, you're keeping track of how long you've been in that particular state. This can be used if, say, you want to stop chasing if you've been chasing for too long.

The `setAiState()` isn't complete: You also need to set the bot's path (using the `PathFinder` interface for the previous chapter) so that it follows the appropriate attack path, chase path, or whatever other path you are going to use. You'll add this a little later.

Probability Machines

As you can tell in Figure 13.4, there isn't really any order to the different battle states. So, what determines whether you're attacking, dodging, or running away?

Sometimes you want the decision between different states to occur purely on deterministic reasoning. For example, you might want to dodge only if you detect projectiles heading your way.

Sometimes, though, you just want to randomly select one of these states, giving preference to one state or the other. Check out Figure 13.5 as an example.

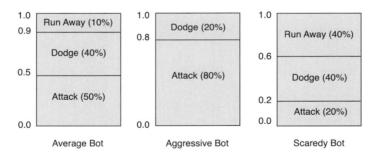

Figure 13.5 Each bot could have a different probability of performing each battle state.

This figure shows three different types of bots, with different probabilities of each state occurring. Note that the sum of the probabilities equals 100%.

You might be used to observing probability as a percentage—for example, when you flip a coin, there's a 50% chance of the coin turning up heads. You also might have thought of probability as a fraction, such as a 1/6 chance of rolling a certain number with a die or a one-in-a-million chance of winning a lottery. In this chapter, we use the decimal representation of probability that's common in statistics textbooks. In this representation, the probability of an event occurring is between 0 and 1. A probability of 1 means the event always occurs, 0 means the event never occurs, and 0.5 means the event has a 50% chance of occurring.

Figure 13.5 could easily have been a described as a pie chart, but laying it out in this way shows how you can determine which state is chosen. For example, a random number generator returns a number between 0 and 1. With an average bot, if the result is between 0 and 0.5, the state could be attack; between 0.5 and 0.9 would be dodge; and between 0.9 and 1.0 would be run away.

You can keep track of these probabilities like this:

```
// probability of each battle state
// (the sum should be 1)
float attackProbability;
float dodgeProbability;
float runAwayProbability;
```

Notice that the sum of these is assumed to be 1.0, just like in Figure 13.5—that way, at least one of these events will always occur. You can randomly choose a state as in Listing 13.6.

Listing 13.6   `AIBot.chooseBattleState()`

```
/**
    Randomly choose one of the three battle states (attack, dodge,
    or run away).
*/
public int chooseBattleState() {
    float p = (float)Math.random();
    if (p <= attackProbability) {
        return BATTLE_STATE_ATTACK;
    }
    else if (p <= attackProbability + dodgeProbability) {
        return BATTLE_STATE_DODGE;
```

continues

Listing 13.6   `AIBot.chooseBattleState()`   *continued*

```
    }
    else {
        return BATTLE_STATE_RUN_AWAY;
    }
}
```

Because you assume the sum of the probabilities is 1.0, you can assume that if attack or dodge isn't chosen, then run away is the resulting state.

Some Useful Random Functions

Using `Math.random()` in the `chooseBattleState()` method was fine because the random function returns a number from 0 to 1, but you're going to be using random numbers a lot on this chapter, and you'll often want more flexibility than just a range from 0 to 1. Now is a good time to introduce some handy random functions. You'll add them to the `MoreMath` class, shown here in Listing 13.7.

Listing 13.7   Random Functions of MoreMath.java

```
/**
    Returns a random integer from 0 to max (inclusive).
*/
public static int random(int max) {
    return (int)Math.round(Math.random() * max);
}



/**
    Returns a random integer from min to max (inclusive).
*/
public static int random(int min, int max) {
    return min + random(max-min);
}



/**
    Returns a random float from 0 to max (inclusive).
```

```
*/
public static float random(float max) {
    return (float)Math.random()*max;
}



/**
    Returns a random float from min to max (inclusive).
*/
public static float random(float min, float max) {
    return min + random(max-min);
}



/**
    Returns a random object from a List.
*/
public static Object random(List list) {
    return list.get(random(list.size() - 1));
}



/**
    Returns true if a random "event" occurs. The specified
    value, p, is the probability (0 to 1) that the random
    "event" occurs.
*/
public static boolean chance(float p) {
    return (Math.random() <= p);
}
```

The first four functions return a random number between certain ranges. The next function returns a random object from a list of objects. Finally, the last function returns true if a random "event" occurs, with the probability of the event occurring between 0 and 1.

Making Decisions

Making decisions is an easy part, but as we've talked about, it's also easy to make creatures too smart. Obviously, you don't want to make a new decision every frame, so your code should provide limits so that decisions are made on a periodic basis—say, every second or so. You can make "dumb" creatures have a longer decision period.

How often the bots make a decision is just one of those things you'll have to tweak until you get the right feel.

Listing 13.8 has some sample code you'll use for decision making in the AIBot. Here, a special state called DECISION_READY is used to signify that a decision needs to be made. The bot makes decisions every few seconds (based on decisionTime) but makes decisions more often if it's idle. In this manner, it can quickly move to other states if it notices the player. Decisions are also made when you're done with the path you're traveling on (from the code in the PathBot class).

Listing 13.8 Decision Making in AIBot

```
// time (milliseconds) between making decisions
long decisionTime;

...

public void update(GameObject player, long elapsedTime) {

    elapsedTimeSinceDecision+=elapsedTime;
    elapsedTimeInState+=elapsedTime;
    timeSincePlayerLastSeen+=elapsedTime;

    // if idle and player visible, make decision every 500 ms
    if ((aiState == NORMAL_STATE_IDLE ||
        aiState == NORMAL_STATE_PATROL) &&
        elapsedTimeInState >= 500)
    {
        aiState = DECESION_READY;
    }
```

```
    // if time's up, make decision
    else if (elapsedTimeSinceDecision >= decisionTime) {
        aiState = DECESION_READY;
    }

    // if done with current path, make decision
    else if (currentPath != null && !currentPath.hasNext() &&
        !getTransform().isMovingIgnoreY())
    {
        aiState = DECESION_READY;
    }

    // make a new decision
    if (aiState == DECESION_READY) {
        elapsedTimeSinceDecision = 0;

        if (canSee(player)) {
            setAiState(chooseBattleState(), player);
        }
        else if (timeSincePlayerLastSeen < 3000 ||
            canHear(player))
        {
            setAiState(NORMAL_STATE_CHASE, player);
        }
        else {
            setAiState(NORMAL_STATE_IDLE, player);
        }
    }
}
```

When making a decision, the bot chooses from a battle state, a chase state, or an idle state. If the player is visible, it picks a battle state. If the player was visible recently (in the last 3 seconds) or if the player is heard, the bot chooses the chase state. If none of those conditions are met, it chooses the idle state.

But what happens when a bot chooses a state? You have to make the bot actually perform an action, with most of the actions being some sort of movement. This is where patterns come in.

Patterns

So far, we've talked about the different states a bot has, such as attacking and dodging. In a game, a creature generally performs different movement patterns when in a particular state. For example, when dodging, a bot might zigzag left and right.

You'll use the `PathFinder` interface from the previous chapter to write some patterns. This interface has methods that return an `Iterator` of locations in a path to follow. You'll actually create an abstract `AIPattern` class, in Listing 13.9, that implements this interface. The `AIPattern` class has a couple of convenience methods to help when making patterns.

Listing 13.9   Convenience Methods in `AIPattern`

```
/**
    Calculates the floor for the location specified. If
    the floor cannot be determined, the specified default
    value is used.
*/
protected void calcFloorHeight(Vector3D v, float defaultY) {
   BSPTree.Leaf leaf = bspTree.getLeaf(v.x, v.z);
   if (leaf == null || leaf.floorHeight == Float.MIN_VALUE) {
       v.y = defaultY;
   }
   else {
       v.y = leaf.floorHeight;
   }
}



/**
    Gets the location between the player and the bot
    that is the specified distance away from the player.
*/
protected Vector3D getLocationFromPlayer(GameObject bot,
    GameObject player, float desiredDistSq)
{
```

```
    // get actual distance (squared)
    float distSq = bot.getLocation().
        getDistanceSq(player.getLocation());

    // if within 5 units, we're close enough
    if (Math.abs(desiredDistSq - distSq) < 25) {
        return new Vector3D(bot.getLocation());
    }

    // calculate vector to player from the bot
    Vector3D goal = new Vector3D(bot.getLocation());
    goal.subtract(player.getLocation());

    // find the goal distance from the player
    goal.multiply((float)Math.sqrt(desiredDistSq / distSq));

    goal.add(player.getLocation());
    calcFloorHeight(goal, bot.getFloorHeight());

    return goal;
}
```

The first convenience method, `calcFloorHeight()`, gets the height of the floor for any location. If the location is out of bounds, the default height is used.

The second convenience method helps make several patterns easier to write. It returns the location between the bot and the player that is a specific distance away from the player. A lot of times, a bot wants to attack or dodge from a certain distance.

Dodging

The first pattern we discuss is dodging. Dodging can be very complicated or very simple, depending on what you want to accomplish. Check out Figure 13.6 for some sample dodge patterns.

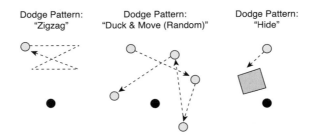

Figure 13.6   Some sample dodge patterns.

The first two dodge patterns, zigzag and random, just move the bot to specific locations relative to the player, which is what most patterns do. The third pattern, hiding, is a bit more complicated. This pattern finds a spot in the environment where the player can't see the bot, so the pattern finding needs to know a bit about the environment for this to work. We leave this one as an exercise for the reader (are you liking these exercises yet?).

Let's create the first two dodge patterns as an example. The zigzag pattern is shown here in Listing 13.10.

Listing 13.10   DodgePatternZigZag.java

```java
public class DodgePatternZigZag extends AIPattern {

    private float dodgeDist;

    public DodgePatternZigZag(BSPTree tree, float dodgeDist) {
        super(tree);
        this.dodgeDist = dodgeDist;
    }

    public Iterator find(GameObject bot, GameObject player) {

        // create the vector to the dodge location
        Vector3D zig = new Vector3D(bot.getLocation());
        zig.subtract(player.getLocation());
        zig.normalize();
        zig.multiply(dodgeDist);
        zig.rotateY((float)Math.PI/2);
```

```
        // 50% chance - dodge one way or the other
        if (MoreMath.chance(.5f)) {
            zig.multiply(-1);
        }

        // convert vector to absolute location
        zig.add(bot.getLocation());
        calcFloorHeight(zig, bot.getFloorHeight());

        Vector3D zag = new Vector3D(bot.getLocation());
        calcFloorHeight(zag, bot.getFloorHeight());

        List path = new ArrayList();
        path.add(zig);
        path.add(zag);
        return path.iterator();
    }
}
```

This zigzag pattern makes a pattern that moves the bot a certain distance (`dodgeDist`) at a tangent to the player and then back to the bot's starting point. There's a random chance the bot moves either left or right.

Easy enough, right? Patterns are pretty simple. The next dodge pattern, random, moves the bot to a random location within a half-circle of the player. By limiting to a half-circle, you can ensure the bot doesn't have to cross the player to get to the dodge location. The code is in Listing 13.11.

Listing 13.11   DodgePatternRandom.java

```
public class DodgePatternRandom extends AIPattern {

    private float radiusSq;

    public DodgePatternRandom(BSPTree tree, float radius) {
        super(tree);
        this.radiusSq = radius * radius;
    }
```

continues

Listing 13.11 DodgePatternRandom.java *continued*

```
    public Iterator find(GameObject bot, GameObject player) {

        Vector3D goal = getLocationFromPlayer(bot, player,
            radiusSq);

        // pick a random location on this half-circle
        // (-90 to 90 degrees from current location)
        float maxAngle = (float)Math.PI/2;
        float angle = MoreMath.random(-maxAngle, maxAngle);
        goal.subtract(player.getLocation());
        goal.rotateY(angle);
        goal.add(player.getLocation());
        calcFloorHeight(goal, bot.getFloorHeight());

        return Collections.singleton(goal).iterator();
    }

}
```

This just involves some more vector math for this pattern.

Note that these patterns don't do any environment-based checks to see whether there is room for a pattern. For example, a bot might be able to zigzag one way but not the other. An ideal pattern might check the environment and adjust its pattern accordingly.

Of course, these dodge patterns implemented here are just a beginning—you can come up with plenty more dodge patterns. Another idea for dodging is to keep track of incoming projectiles and move perpendicular to the projectile's path, or to do other movements such as ducking or jumping.

Attacking

Now you'll implement some attack patterns. Your attack patterns will vary depending on how your bots attack. For example, some might fire projectiles, some might try to ram the player, and others might simply try to make themselves look bigger to scare you away. Figure 13.7 shows some attack patterns you'll implement for the bots in this chapter.

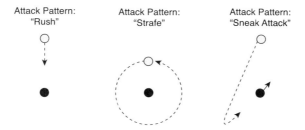

Figure 13.7   Some sample attack patterns.

The rush pattern is probably the easiest pattern we could come up with. Here the bot just moves so that it's within a certain distance of the player. You can just use the getLocationFromPlayer() method you created in AIPattern, as shown in Listing 13.12.

Listing 13.12   AttackPatternRush.java

```java
public class AttackPatternRush extends AIPattern {

    private float desiredDistSq;

    public AttackPatternRush(BSPTree tree, float desiredDist) {
        super(tree);
        this.desiredDistSq = desiredDist * desiredDist;
    }

    public Iterator find(GameObject bot, GameObject player) {
        Vector3D goal = getLocationFromPlayer(bot, player,
            desiredDistSq);
        if (goal.equals(bot.getLocation())) {
            return null;
        }
        else {
            return Collections.singleton(goal).iterator();
        }
    }

}
```

Note that this pattern returns `null` if the bot is already at the rush location.

Strafing around a player might seem difficult at first, but if you can pull it off, it will really help boost the apparent intelligence of your bots. Strafing makes the bot circle around the player. This makes it easy for the bot to fire projectiles but harder for the player to fire at the bot, so it's a great offensive tactic.

Instead of actually moving in a circle, just have the bot move in an octagon around the player. This reduces the path to eight locations. The code is in Listing 13.13.

Listing 13.13   AttackPatternStrafe.java

```java
public class AttackPatternStrafe extends AIPattern {

    private float radiusSq;

    public AttackPatternStrafe(BSPTree tree, float radius) {
        super(tree);
        this.radiusSq = radius * radius;
    }

    public Iterator find(GameObject bot, GameObject player) {

        List path = new ArrayList();

        // find first location within desired radius
        Vector3D firstGoal = getLocationFromPlayer(bot, player,
            radiusSq);
        if (!firstGoal.equals(bot.getLocation())) {
            path.add(firstGoal);
        }

        // make a counter-clockwise circle around the player
        // (it's actually an octagon).
        int numPoints = 8;
        float angle = (float)(2 * Math.PI / numPoints);
        if (MoreMath.chance(0.5f)) {
            angle = -angle;
        }
```

```
        float lastY = bot.getFloorHeight();
        for (int i=1; i<numPoints; i++) {
            Vector3D goal = new Vector3D(firstGoal);
            goal.subtract(player.getLocation());
            goal.rotateY(angle * i);
            goal.add(player.getLocation());
            calcFloorHeight(goal, lastY);
            lastY = goal.y;
            path.add(goal);
        }

        // add last location (back to start)
        path.add(firstGoal);
        return path.iterator();
    }
}
```

In this pattern, with a vector from the player to the desired radius, you can rotate this vector around the y-axis eight times to get the eight different points you want.

Again, you could come up with a million other patterns besides these two. There's the sneak attack as in the previous figure. (Reader exercise? You bet!) There are also other attacks, such as ramming, doing kamikaze attacks, waiting and ambushing, or jumping on the player.

Of course, in a game, a bot doesn't always have to attack. Plenty of baddies, such as spiders or little animals, can be completely ambivalent to the player, just wandering around minding their own business. Games such as Nintendo's Mario series have plenty of creatures like these. Be sure to add some creativity and variety to the different types of patterns.

Running Away

A bot might run away from the player for lots of reasons. Perhaps the player has a really big, scary weapon, or the bot is so low on health that it just wants to get away. A lot of the time, you might want to just make a nervous bot that runs away often, or runs away for short periods as a defensive tactic.

All you need for a run–away pattern is a spot to run to. Listing 13.14 shows a panic pattern that just makes the bot run directly away from the player, even if there is a wall in the way.

Listing 13.14   RunAwayPattern.java

```java
public class RunAwayPattern extends AIPattern {

    public RunAwayPattern(BSPTree tree) {
        super(tree);
    }

    public Iterator find(GameObject bot, GameObject player) {
        // dumb move: run in the *opposite* direction of the
        // player (will cause bots to run into walls!)

        Vector3D goal = new Vector3D(player.getLocation());
        goal.subtract(bot.getLocation());

        // opposite direction
        goal.multiply(-1);

        // far, far away
        goal.multiply(100000);
        calcFloorHeight(goal, bot.getFloorHeight());

        // return an iterator
        return Collections.singleton(goal).iterator();
    }
}
```

Another solution to running away might be to pick a location on the map and do a path-finding search to get a path to that location. The point could be the location where the bot originated, a predetermined "safe" location, or a "meet-up" location for a group of bots.

Or, in a heavily lit game, a bot could try to hide in a shadow. Again, you can come up with lots of different patterns.

Aiming

Although it's not really a movement pattern, often a bot needs to "aim" a weapon at the player, with various degrees of success: You'll probably want to give some bots better aiming than others. Figure 13.8 shows a few aim pattern ideas.

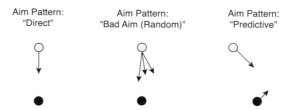

Figure 13.8   Some sample aim patterns.

You'll just implement one aim pattern that can aim with a specified accuracy from 0 to 1 (see Listing 13.15). If the accuracy is 0, the aim can be off up to 10°. If the accuracy is 1, the aim is dead on with the player, not taking the player's velocity into account.

Listing 13.15   AimPattern.java

```java
public class AimPattern extends AIPattern {

    protected float accuracy;

    public AimPattern(BSPTree tree) {
        super(tree);
    }



    /**
        Sets the accuracy of the aim from 0 (worst) to 1 (best).
    */
    public void setAccuracy(float p) {
        this.accuracy = p;
    }



    public Iterator find(GameObject bot, GameObject player) {
```

continues

Listing 13.15 AimPattern.java *continued*

```
        Vector3D goal = new Vector3D(player.getLocation());
        goal.y += player.getBounds().getTopHeight() / 2;
        goal.subtract(bot.getLocation());

        // Rotate up to 10 degrees off y-axis
        // (This could use an up/down random offset as well.)
        if (accuracy < 1) {
            float maxAngle = 10 * (1-accuracy);
            float angle = MoreMath.random(-maxAngle, maxAngle);
            goal.rotateY((float)Math.toRadians(angle));
        }
        goal.normalize();

        // return an iterator
        return Collections.singleton(goal).iterator();
    }
}
```

Note that this aim pattern returns a normalized vector direction rather than an absolute location because you're aiming in a direction.

That's it for patterns—these are all the patterns you'll use in this chapter. Patterns are simple to write, so be sure to try out some of your own. Now, though, let's talk about actually firing a projectile after you're done aiming.

Firing

When aiming, another thing to consider is the amount of time it requires a bot to aim. You don't want a bot to simply fire its weapon for every frame; instead, you want it to wait for a bit, as if it's actually aiming, so that shots are fired only after the bot has spent time aiming the shot.

In the code, we make the amount of time spent aiming proportional to the accuracy of the shot. Spending two seconds or more gives perfect aim, and anything less results in a slightly inaccurate aim. You add the code in the AIBot class in Listing 13.16.

Listing 13.16   Aiming and Firing in `AIBot`

```
AimPattern aimPathFinder;
long aimTime;

public void update(GameObject player, long elapsedTime) {

    ...

    if (aiState == BATTLE_STATE_ATTACK &&
        elapsedTimeInState >= aimTime &&
        aimPathFinder != null)
    {
        elapsedTimeInState-=aimTime;

        // longer aim time == more accuracy
        float p = Math.min(1, aimTime / 2000f);
        aimPathFinder.setAccuracy(p);
        Vector3D direction = (Vector3D)
            aimPathFinder.find(this, player).next();
        fireProjectile(direction);
    }
}


/**
    Fires a projectile in the specified direction. The
    direction vector should be normalized.
*/
public void fireProjectile(Vector3D direction) {

    Projectile blast = new Projectile(
        (PolygonGroup)blastModel.clone(),
        direction, this, 3, 6);
    float dist = 2 * (getBounds().getRadius() +
        blast.getBounds().getRadius());
    blast.getLocation().setTo(
        getX() + direction.x*dist,
        getY() + getBounds().getTopHeight()/2,
```

continues

Listing 13.16 Aiming and Firing in `AIBot`   *continued*

```
            getZ() + direction.z*dist);

    // "spawns" the new game object
    addSpawn(blast);

}
```

One thing you're doing in the `fireProjectile()` method is creating a brand-new game object that represents the projectile. But what do you do with the object? You don't want it; the game object manager does. So, mark the object as a spawn and allow the game object manager to pick it up. Let's talk about object spawning next.

Object Spawning

As in the projectile example, sometimes an object needs to spawn another object. For example, an object could explode into several pieces, resulting in several spawns traveling in different directions; a bot could drop its weapon; or "sparks" could fly off a bot when it gets hit.

It's probably a good idea to let any game object spawn another, so you'll add code in the `GameObject` class to add and retrieve spawns, shown here in Listing 13.17.

Listing 13.17 Spawning in `GameObject`

```
private List spawns;

...

/**
    Spawns an object, so that the GameManager can
    retrieve later using getSpawns().
*/
protected void addSpawn(GameObject object) {
    if (spawns == null) {
        spawns = new ArrayList();
    }
```

```
        spawns.add(object);
}


/**
    Returns a list of "spawned" objects (projectiles,
    exploding parts, etc) or null if no objects
    were spawned.
*/
public List getSpawns() {
    List returnList = spawns;
    spawns = null;
    return returnList;
}
```

After an update, the game object manager should call getSpawns() and add any spawns to the list of objects it manages.

Putting It All Together

Besides making a bot "explode" when it gets hit, you need to do a few other things to create a working demo using the AI bots:

> ➤ You might want to show different object animations for each state. For example, the bot could have different animations for walking, running, strafing, aiming, or firing.

> ➤ The bot should give some visual feedback when it gets wounded so the player knows it is damaging the bot.

> ➤ Now that the bots can attack the player, you also need some visual feedback on the player's state. For instance, you could use a health bar and a damage indicator.

In this chapter, you're using the same simple pyramid-shape bots from the previous chapter, keeping the object animations to a minimum. You'll also create a simple overlay framework to draw a health bar. First, though, let's sum up all the different AI bot attributes you'll use.

Brains!

You'll store all the movement patterns and other attributes of the bots in a simple Brain class, shown in Listing 13.18. Every AIBot will have an instance of the Brain class.

Listing 13.18 Brain.java

```
public class Brain {

    public PathFinder attackPathFinder;
    public PathFinder dodgePathFinder;
    public PathFinder aimPathFinder;
    public PathFinder idlePathFinder;
    public PathFinder chasePathFinder;
    public PathFinder runAwayPathFinder;

    // probability of each battle state
    // (the sum should be 1)
    public float attackProbability;
    public float dodgeProbability;
    public float runAwayProbability;

    public long decisionTime;
    public long aimTime;
    public float hearDistance;

    public void fixProbabilites() {
        // make the sums of the odds == 1.
        float sum = attackProbability + dodgeProbability +
            runAwayProbability;
        if (sum > 0) {
            attackProbability /= sum;
            dodgeProbability /= sum;
            runAwayProbability /= sum;
        }
    }
}
```

This is a bare class that just includes fields for each brain attribute. The only function here is one to fix the probabilities so their sum is 1.

You can add a lot to the brain class. We could extend the class to include other AI attributes, such as speed and maximum amount of health. You could also make the system more intricate, allowing bots with certain brains to be resistant to specific weapons.

Health and Dying

Of course, now that you've got bots that can move around an attack, you need to make it so bots can be destroyed.

In previous chapter demos, we had the "one strike and you're out" rule, where a projectile hitting a bot destroyed it, making it immediately disappear. In a game, you'll want to make it a bit more realistic than that. Here are some examples:

➤ Make some bots take more hits to destroy them than others.

➤ Make some bots more vulnerable to certain weapons. For example, a bot might be able to shield laser blasts but might be completely defenseless against missiles.

➤ When hit, make a bot move to a wounded state that causes the bot to stop for a moment. Also, make the bot invulnerable to any more damage for the short period of time it's in the wounded state.

➤ Make different decisions depending on the health of a bot. A bot with full health might be brave, while a bot with critically low health might just run away from the player.

➤ After a bot is destroyed, don't make it immediately disappear. Have it lie there for a short amount of time, and remove it a few seconds later. Some games just let dead bots lie there throughout the entire game. Another idea is to make the robot explode into oblivion (making blast marks on the floors) or disappear in a puff of smoke.

➤ A destroyed bot could drop certain items, such as ammo or energy, that the player can pick up.

➤ Be sure to find the right balance between the player and bad guys in your game, and make enemies progressively more difficult as the game moves forward.

➤ As always, be creative!

In this chapter, you'll create fairly simple health and dying routines. Each bot will start with 100 health points, and the player's weapon will cause a random amount of damage between 40 and 60 health points. Remember, the player fires projectiles that are game objects, so you can use our collision code to check whether a projectile hits anything.

First, you'll add a couple more states to the bot, to signify when the bot has been hit and when it is dead:

```
public static final int WOUNDED_STATE_HURT = 6;
public static final int WOUNDED_STATE_DEAD = 7;
```

Keep a bot in the hurt state for a few seconds after it gets hit. Likewise, if the bot's AI state is dead, keep it in that state for a few seconds and then remove it from the game object manager.

First, add some health functions to the `AIBot` class, shown here in Listing 13.19.

Listing 13.19   Health Methods in `AIBot`

```
private static final float DEFAULT_MAX_HEALTH = 100;
private static final float CRITICAL_HEALTH_PERCENT = 5;

private float maxHealth;
private float health;

...

protected void setHealth(float health) {
    this.health = health;
}

/**
    Adds the specified amount to this bot's health. If the
    amount is less than zero, the bot's state is set to
```

```
       WOUNDED_STATE_HURT.
*/
public void addHealth(float amount) {
    if (amount < 0) {
        if (health <= 0 || aiState == WOUNDED_STATE_HURT) {
            return;
        }
        setAiState(WOUNDED_STATE_HURT, null);
    }
    setHealth(health + amount);
}



/**
    Returns true if the health is critically low (less than
    CRITICAL_HEALTH_PERCENT).
*/
public boolean isCriticalHealth() {
    return (health / maxHealth < CRITICAL_HEALTH_PERCENT / 100);
}
```

The addHealth() method is where all the action happens. Note that this method decreases the health and puts the bot in the hurt state only if it's not currently hurt.

The isCriticalHealth() method returns true if the bot's health is critically low; if so, you can make it run away.

Next you must make some decisions based on the bot's health and wounded state. You need to make sure a bot stays in the hurt state for a short period of time, and you need to destroy a bot if it has been dead for a while. The code to do all this is here in Listing 13.20.

Listing 13.20 Wounded and Dying Methods in AIBot

```
public void update(GameObject player, long elapsedTime) {

    elapsedTimeInState+=elapsedTime;


    . . .
```

continues

Listing 13.20   Wounded and Dying Methods in `AIBot`   *continued*

```
    if (aiState == WOUNDED_STATE_DEAD) {
        // destroy bot after five seconds
        if (elapsedTimeInState >= 5000) {
            setState(STATE_DESTROYED);
        }
        return;
    }
    else if (aiState == WOUNDED_STATE_HURT) {
        // after 500ms switch to either the idle or dead state.
        if (elapsedTimeInState >= 500) {
            if (health <= 0) {
                setAiState(WOUNDED_STATE_DEAD, player);
                return;
            }
            else {
                aiState = NORMAL_STATE_IDLE;
            }
        }
        else {
            return;
        }
    }

    // run away if health critical
    if (isCriticalHealth() && brain.runAwayPathFinder != null) {
        setAiState(BATTLE_STATE_RUN_AWAY, player);
        return;
    }

    . . .

}
```

The code shows some decision-making routines in the `update()` method of `AIBot`.
After a bot is hurt, 500ms later it either moves to the idle state or, if the bot's health is
0, moves to the dead state. When in the dead state, it destroys itself after five seconds.
Finally, if the health of the bot is critically low, the bot runs away from the player.

Note that here you just make the bot disappear after five seconds, no matter what. It might seem kind of clunky to the user to watch a bot suddenly vanish. Another idea is to make the bot disappear only when it's offscreen so the player doesn't notice it vanish. Alternatively, many games show some sort of explosion effect when a bot disappears. Earlier, we talked about how you need to set the appropriate `PathFinder` whenever you set the AI state. You also need to change the object's animation at this time. Listing 13.21 shows the extended `setAIState()` method in `AIBot`. In this code, when a bot is hurt, it stops moving and spins around a little bit, as if getting hit made it dizzy.

Listing 13.21   Extended `setAIState()` Method of `AIBot`

```
protected void setAiState(int aiState, GameObject player) {

    if (this.aiState == aiState) {
        return;
    }

    this.aiState = aiState;

    elapsedTimeInState = 0;
    Vector3D playerLocation = null;
    if (player != null) {
        playerLocation = player.getLocation();
    }

    // update path
    switch (aiState) {
        case BATTLE_STATE_ATTACK:
            setPathFinder(brain.attackPathFinder);
            setFacing(playerLocation);
            break;
        case BATTLE_STATE_DODGE:
            setPathFinder(brain.dodgePathFinder);
            setFacing(null);
            break;

        . . .
```

continues

Listing 13.21   Extended `setAIState()` **Method of** `AIBot`   *continued*

```
        case WOUNDED_STATE_HURT:
            setPathFinder(null);
            setFacing(null);
            getTransform().stop();
            getTransform().setAngleVelocityY(
                MoreMath.random(0.001f, 0.05f),
                MoreMath.random(100, 500));
            break;
    }

}
```

Okay! Now you've got everything you need to demo the AI bots. Now you need to show the health of the player because the AI bots can attack, thus depleting the player's health. You'll accomplish this by adding a heads-up display.

Adding a Heads-Up Display

As far as I can tell, the term *heads-up display*, or HUD, originated from certain car instrument panels. On common cars, the driver has to look down to see the speed, fuel meter, odometer, flux capacitor, and whatever other gauges are on the instrument panel. But with cars that have a heads-up display, the instrument panel is projected onto the windshield or is displayed in a racing driver's helmet so drivers can keep their heads up while driving.

The primary purpose of heads-up displays is to provide information on the state of the game that can't be displayed in the game itself. Some types of information that are common in heads-up displays are listed here:

➤ Amount of health, ammo, remaining lives, and so on

➤ In-game messages (which could include displaying icons when you pick up an item)

➤ Any currently active power-ups (such as super health or quad damage)

➤ Time left to play

Heads-up displays in games are normally drawn as an overlay on top of the view window. Also, they are often resolution independent, meaning they stay the same size onscreen no matter what the resolution of the screen is. Conversely, a resolution-dependent HUD, such as one designed for a 640×480 screen, would look smaller on a higher-resolution screen such as 1,024×768.

This implementation will be resolution independent. Start your implementation by creating a simple `Overlay` interface in Listing 13.22.

Listing 13.22   Overlay.java

```java
public interface Overlay {

    /**
        Updates this overlay with the specified amount of
        elapsed time since the last update.
    */
    public void update(long elapsedTime);

    /**
        Draws an overlay onto a frame. The ViewWindow specifies
        the bounds of the view window (usually, the entire
        screen). The screen bounds can be retrieved by calling
        g.getDeviceConfiguration().getBounds();
    */
    public void draw(Graphics2D g, ViewWindow viewWindow);



    /**
        Returns true if this overlay is enabled (should be drawn).
    */
    public boolean isEnabled();
}
```

Overlays are updated just like game objects and are drawn after each frame is drawn so they appear on top.

As an example, you'll create a simple heads-up display that shows the health of the player, both as a number and as a bar. The HeadsUpDisplay class, in Listing 13.23, is a resolution-independent display of the player's health. Also, it's animated: The displayed health slightly lags behind the actual health of the player.

Listing 13.23   HeadsUpDisplay.java

```java
public class HeadsUpDisplay implements Overlay {

    // increase health display by 20 points per second
    private static final float DISPLAY_INC_RATE = 0.04f;

    private Player player;
    private float displayedHealth;
    private Font font;

    public HeadsUpDisplay(Player player) {
        this.player = player;
        displayedHealth = 0;
    }

    public void update(long elapsedTime) {
        // increase or decrease displayedHealth a small amount
        // at a time, instead of just setting it to the player's
        // health.
        float actualHealth = player.getHealth();
        if (actualHealth > displayedHealth) {
            displayedHealth = Math.min(actualHealth,
                displayedHealth + elapsedTime * DISPLAY_INC_RATE);
        }
        else if (actualHealth < displayedHealth) {
            displayedHealth = Math.max(actualHealth,
                displayedHealth - elapsedTime * DISPLAY_INC_RATE);
        }
    }

    public void draw(Graphics2D g, ViewWindow window) {
```

```
        // set the font (scaled for this view window)
        int fontHeight = Math.max(9, window.getHeight() / 20);
        int spacing = fontHeight / 5;
        if (font == null || fontHeight != font.getSize()) {
            font = new Font("Dialog", Font.PLAIN, fontHeight);
        }
        g.setFont(font);
        g.translate(window.getLeftOffset(), window.getTopOffset());

        // draw health value (number)
        String str = Integer.toString(Math.round(displayedHealth));
        Rectangle2D strBounds = font.getStringBounds(str,
            g.getFontRenderContext());
        g.setColor(Color.WHITE);
        g.drawString(str, spacing, (int)strBounds.getHeight());

        // draw health bar
        Rectangle bar = new Rectangle(
            (int)strBounds.getWidth() + spacing * 2,
            (int)strBounds.getHeight() / 2,
            window.getWidth() / 4,
            window.getHeight() / 60);
        g.setColor(Color.GRAY);
        g.fill(bar);

        // draw highlighted part of health bar
        bar.width = Math.round(bar.width *
            displayedHealth / player.getMaxHealth());
        g.setColor(Color.WHITE);
        g.fill(bar);
    }


    public boolean isEnabled() {
        return (player != null &&
            (player.isAlive() || displayedHealth > 0));
    }
}
```

The font size and the health bar size are determined by the size of the view window. Other than that, there's really nothing special about this heads-up display. A text string and a couple of rectangles are drawn, and that's it. The health bar makes a great animated effect, though.

This chapter's demo (called `AIBotTest`) includes one more overlay that acts as a message queue. In this case, the message queue displays the various changes in the AI bots' state in the upper-right corner of the screen. This helps debug the AI bots' behavior and gives developers a clue to what the bots are thinking, including whether a bot really can see or hear the player. Check out Figure 13.9 for a screenshot.

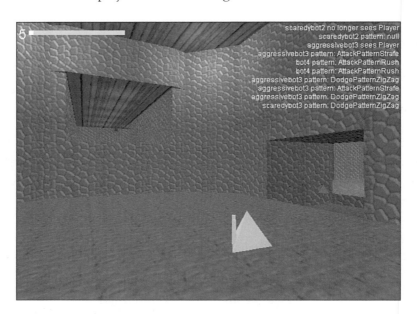

Figure 13.9 An example with a heads-up display: a health meter (upper left) and a message queue (upper right). The message queue shows debug messages for the AI bots.

Note that you should include a heads-up display only when it's necessary. If you can show the health of the player in the game itself, do so. For example, in the original Mario games, Mario's health was directly related to his size: A big Mario could get hit twice before dying, but a small Mario could get hit only once. The game didn't need the words *big* or *small* in the heads-up display because it was already visually apparent.

And you don't have to limit the health display to a bar, either. Some games use pie charts or heart icons. Feel free to be creative with how you display the health because a bar can be considered passé. For example, the game *Doom* shows a graphic of your face—the more damage you take, the bloodier your face becomes.

Finally, keep in mind that the heads-up display doesn't have to be onscreen at all times. Parts of it could appear only when a significant change occurs, such as when the player gets more points or acquires a new power-up. In this case, the heads-up display could scroll on and off the screen as needed.

Evolution

The last topic on our list of game AI concepts is evolution. Evolving AI bots gradually change their behavior over time, ideally becoming more adept at offensive and defensive tactics against the player.

The advantage of adding evolution in a game is that the bots can become more challenging to an individual user's playing style. The idea is that each user will play a game using different tactics, and evolving bots will be able to adjust accordingly and gradually become more difficult for the player.

You can implement evolution in a game in several ways. It can be done on the fly or with a bot occasionally modifying its own attributes to become better at attacking the player. Here are a few examples:

➤ The bot could change attack and aim patterns until it finds one that hits the player more often.

➤ The bot could fire several simultaneous "virtual" projectiles using different aim patterns to see which one is more likely to hit the player. Using virtual projectiles that the bot keeps track of instead of real projectiles means the bot can test several different aim patterns at once, instead of waiting to aim before firing a real projectile one at a time.

➤ The bot could tweak other attributes on the fly as well, such as speed, decision time, hearing distance, and amount of time between making decisions.

Another way to implement evolution is the old-fashioned way: through reproduction and genetic mutation. No, you won't actually make bots mate and have children—sorry to disappoint. But you can implement the idea of reproduction and mutation. Here it goes:

> ➤ Only the "best" bots reproduce.

> ➤ An offspring is a slightly mutated version of its parent—or, in other words, is the same as its parent, but with a few altered attributes.

The idea behind mutation is that if a "bad" brain is created, it will be at the low end of the gene pool and won't be able to reproduce. But "good" brains will be at the high end of the gene pool and can reproduce. So, over time, the high end of the gene pool will get better and result in better bots. Here's how you'll implement evolution in this chapter:

> ➤ When a bot is destroyed, it records how well it performed, which is the same as the amount of damage it caused to the player. The bot's brain is kept in a "gene pool."

> ➤ Next, the bot is regenerated with a new brain, which is either one of the best-performing brains from the gene pool or a mutated offspring of one of the best-performing brains.

Before we get to implementing evolution, though, we need to fill in one concept: bot regeneration.

Regeneration

Regeneration is a technique common in many games. This technique allows bots to "regenerate" after they die, restoring themselves to their starting location and state. This can be useful if you want to create a never-ending supply of baddies.

You implement regeneration in the AIBot class in Listing 13.24. Instead of destroying the bot when it dies, it has the option to regenerate itself by completely restoring its state.

Listing 13.24   Regeneration Code of `AIBot`

```
/**
    Returns true if this bot regenerates after it dies.
*/
public boolean isRegenerating() {
    return isRegenerating;
}



/**
    Sets whether this bot regenerates after it dies.
*/
public void setRegenerating(boolean isRegenerating) {
    this.isRegenerating = isRegenerating;
}



/**
    Causes this bot to regenerate, restoring its location
    to its start location.
*/
protected void regenerate() {
    setHealth(maxHealth);
    setState(STATE_ACTIVE);
    setAiState(DECESION_READY, null);
    getLocation().setTo(startLocation);
    getTransform().stop();
    setJumping(false);
    setPathFinder(null);
    setFacing(null);
    // let the game object manager know this object regenerated
    // (so collision detection from old location to new
    // location won't be performed)
    addSpawn(this);
}
public void update(GameObject player, long elapsedTime) {

    . . .
```

continues

Listing 13.24 Regeneration Code of `AIBot` *continued*

```
elapsedTimeInState+=elapsedTime;

// record first location
if (startLocation == null) {
    startLocation = new Vector3D(getLocation());
}

// regenerate if dead for 5 seconds
if (aiState == WOUNDED_STATE_DEAD) {
    if (elapsedTimeInState >= 5000) {
        if (isRegenerating()) {
            regenerate();
        }
        else {
            setState(STATE_DESTROYED);
        }
    }
    return;
}

...

}
```

The update() method is modified so that the regenerate() method is called if the bot has been dead for a few seconds and the bot has regeneration capabilities (isRegenerating()). The regenerate() method resets the bot and, in this case, sets its location to the place where it originated (startLocation).

Also in the regenerate() method, you call the addSpawn() method to mark itself as a spawn. This is like sending a note to the game object manager that says, "Hey, I'm regenerating. Please don't perform collision detection on me this time." If collision detection were performed, the engine could think the bot virtually moved from the place where it died to the place where it regenerated instead of just reappearing there, and the bot could get stuck on a wall or against another object between those two locations. Not performing collision detection means the bot can correctly reappear at the location where it originated.

Evolving Bots

To allow only the best brains to reproduce, you need a way to track which brains are, in fact, the best. You can include many different factors in determining what makes one brain better than another, but in this case, you'll just look at the average amount of damage a bot caused with that brain.

It's summed up in the `BrainStat` class in Listing 13.25, which is a subclass of the `Brain` class. It keeps track of the damage caused and the generation of the brain.

Listing 13.25   `BrainStat` Inner Class of `EvolutionGenePool`

```
private class BrainStat extends Brain implements Comparable {
    long totalDamageCaused;
    int numBots;
    int generation;

    /**
        Gets the average damage this brain causes.
    */
    public float getAverageDamageCaused() {
        return (float)totalDamageCaused / numBots;
    }


    /**
        Reports damaged caused by a bot with this brain
        after the bot was destroyed.
    */
    public void report(long damageCaused) {
        totalDamageCaused+=damageCaused;
        numBots++;
    }


    /**
        Mutates this brain. The specified mutationProbability
        is the probability that each brain attribute
        becomes a different value, or "mutates."
```

continues

Listing 13.25   `BrainStat` Inner Class of `EvolutionGenePool`   *continued*

```
    */
    public void mutate(float probability) {
        ...
    }


    /**
        Returns a smaller number if this brain caused more
        damage that the specified object, which should
        also be a brain.
    */
    public int compareTo(Object obj) {
        BrainStat other = (BrainStat)obj;
        if (this.numBots == 0 || other.numBots == 0) {
            return (other.numBots - this.numBots);
        }
        else {
            return (int)MoreMath.sign(
                other.getAverageDamageCaused() -
                this.getAverageDamageCaused());
        }
    }
}
```

The `BrainStat` class implements the `Comparable` interface so that a list of brains can easily be sorted from best to worst. You could use lots of other criteria to decide which brains are better, but using the amount of damage works well in this case.

When a bot's projectile hits the player, the projectile needs to report back to the bot to tell it how much damaged was caused. You'll accomplish this when you implement the `EvolutionBot` in a little bit.

The `mutate()` method isn't shown here, but it simply mutates each brain attribute if a certain random chance occurs. For example, if `mutationProbability` is `0.10`, each attribute has a 10% chance of mutating. The code for mutating the aim time would look like this:

```
if (MoreMath.chance(mutationProbability)) {
    aimTime = MoreMath.random(300, 2000);
}
```

When a brain is mutated, its generation count is incremented.

Also, we're not showing the `clone()` method because it's a trivial method.

Next, you must come up with a storage mechanism for all these brains in the `EvolutionGenePool` class in Listing 13.26.

Listing 13.26   EvolutionGenePool.java

```
public class EvolutionGenePool {

    private static final int NUM_TOP_BRAINS = 5;
    private static final int NUM_TOTAL_BRAINS = 10;

    private List brains;

    ...

    /**
        Gets a new brain from the gene pool. The brain will either
        be a "top" brain or a new, mutated "top" brain.
    */
    public Brain getNewBrain() {

        // 50% chance of creating a new, mutated brain
        if (MoreMath.chance(.5f)) {
            BrainStat brain =
                (BrainStat)getRandomTopBrain().clone();

            // 10% to 25% chance of changing each attribute
            float p = MoreMath.random(0.10f, 0.25f);
            brain.mutate(p);
            return brain;
        }
        else {
```

continues

Listing 13.26   EvolutionGenePool.java   *continued*

```java
                return getRandomTopBrain();
        }
    }


    /**
        Gets a random top-performing brain.
    */
    public Brain getRandomTopBrain() {
        int index = MoreMath.random(NUM_TOP_BRAINS-1);
        return (Brain)brains.get(index);
    }


    /**
        Notify that a creature with the specified brain has
        been destroyed. The brain's stats are recorded. If the
        brain's stats are within the top total brains
        then we keep the brain around.
    */
    public void notifyDead(Brain brain, long damageCaused) {
        // update statistics for this brain
        if (brain instanceof BrainStat) {
            BrainStat stat = (BrainStat)brain;

            // report the damage
            stat.report(damageCaused);

            // sort and trim the list
            if (!brains.contains(stat)) {
                brains.add(stat);
            }
            Collections.sort(brains);
            while (brains.size() > NUM_TOTAL_BRAINS) {
                brains.remove(NUM_TOTAL_BRAINS);
            }
        }
```

```
        }
}
```

This class keeps track of 10 brains total, and only the top 5 brains are allowed to have offspring.

When a bot dies, it calls the `notfyDead()` method to let the gene pool know how much damage it caused using the specified brain. When a new bot is created or regenerated, it calls the `getNewBrain()` method to get a brain. This method has a 50% chance of creating a mutated offspring and a 50% chance of just returning one of the top brains.

Finally, create the `EvolutionBot` class in Listing 13.27. This bot is a subclass of `AIBot` and performs all the necessary functions to regenerate and report how much damage it caused to the gene pool.

Listing 13.27   EvolutionBot.java

```java
public class EvolutionBot extends AIBot {

    private EvolutionGenePool genePool;
    private long damagedCaused;

    public EvolutionBot(PolygonGroup polygonGroup,
        CollisionDetection collisionDetection,
        EvolutionGenePool genePool, PolygonGroup blastModel)
    {
        super(polygonGroup, collisionDetection,
            genePool.getNewBrain(), blastModel);
        this.genePool = genePool;
        setRegenerating(true);
    }

    public void regenerate() {
        genePool.notifyDead(brain, damagedCaused);
        brain = genePool.getNewBrain();
        damagedCaused = 0;
        super.regenerate();
```

continues

Listing 13.27 EvolutionBot.java *continued*

```
    }

    public void notifyHitPlayer(long damage) {
        damagedCaused+=damage;
    }
}
```

The `regenerate()` method just overrides `AIBot`'s method to perform the extra functionality you need.

Well, that's all you need for evolution bots involving reproduction and mutation. The `EvolutionBotDemo` demos the code, starting with giving each bot a random brain from the gene pool and regenerating bots after they die. Bots regenerate indefinitely in this demo.

Furthermore, when the game exits, it prints the attributes of the top five brains to the console so you can get an idea of what the best brains were. The longer you play, the more likely it is that this list will contain really valuable brains.

Note that the player has one of the biggest effects on evolution. The player might have a preference to kill certain types of bots first. For example, bots that perform the strafe attack pattern might be so dangerous that the player tries to kill them first, allowing others to get in more damage, thus affecting evolution. Also, some bots might have a worse tactical advantage at their starting location than others, and a player could just hover around the regeneration location to pick off bots quickly, even if they would have been really smart.

As we mentioned earlier, the amount of damage a bot causes isn't the only way to choose which brains are the best. Some other ideas include long life, the percentage of shots that hit the target, and the number of bullets dodged. Ideally, the best bots would have a combination of these positive characteristics.

Demo Enhancements

As usual, lots of features can be added to make the demo better. The game demo could use refinements such as health and ammo power-ups, different weapons, and "lock-on" targeting so the player can more easily attack the bots.

The bots could use more patterns in general, including a better run away pattern, and the patterns could be smart enough to check the environment to decide on the best possible pattern (for example, a pattern could attempt to avoid a wall collision).

Finally, the player could lose all of its health, but it never dies. You could use some sort of death sequence here. Also, a damage indicator on the heads-up display would help show when the player gets hit. This could be as easy as flashing the screen red for a few milliseconds.

Other Game AI Ideas

You can implement a lot more game AI techniques. Most of it depends on the type of game you are creating.

If you're making a 2D platform game, the AI will probably be minimal, with creatures following simple patterns most of the time. Be sure to give the creatures varying level of intelligence, though. For example, some creatures could detect the edge of a platform and avoid them, while others would just fall right off.

For a first-person shooter, the bots could spend some time trying to predict the movement of the player and adjust patterns accordingly. A bot could fire its weapon in the direction the player is predicted to be rather than where the player is when the shot was fired. Also, bots could try to "learn" a player's common patterns.

Besides hearing and seeing, some bots could have other senses. For example, a bot could "smell" to pick up on the player's trail. Or, some bots could have special heat-sensing or x-ray vision to help them track down the player.

You could extend evolution in a game by running the reproduction and mutation simulation over a long period, and then including only the smartest bots in the final game.

Team AI

In a strategy game, it can often be advantageous for AI bots to be arranged in a hierarchy of leadership. The team leaders would send commands to troops, trying to create a tactical advantage for the group as a whole rather than each troop trying to make decisions individually. This can make a game more challenging for the user. If the team leader is killed, either the troops become disorganized or one of the troops is promoted to team leader.

There could also be team-based patterns, such as flocking to one point or completely surrounding a player on all sides.

Flocking can show some cool AI behavior and is also common with AI for groups of fish or birds. Flocking algorithms involve keeping each bot near the group, keeping each bot a certain distance away from each other (having a "personal space"), and steering each bot in the average direction of the group. The group can be defined explicitly or can be just the bot's nearest neighbors.

Also, troops could call for backup. Note that if you do something like this, make it visually apparent that a troop is calling for backup, or it could just look like more troops showing up randomly.

Or, instead of a hierarchy, nearby troops could simply "communicate" with each other and negotiate the best possible strategy among them.

Summary

In this chapter, we covered a lot of useful game AI, such as seeing and hearing, state machines, probability, and evolution. In the process, you made a demo with bots that can attack the player, and you added some basic game elements to accommodate this demo, such as bot health and dying, regeneration, and a simple overlay framework showing a heads-up display.

As mentioned before, how you implement AI is really up to the needs of your game. A lot of the work will just be in finding a good balance that makes the game both challenging and fun. And sometimes you just have to find that balance by trial and error. So experiment, make the bad guys smart, and make some games with some cool AI.

Chapter 14

Game Scripting

You walk into a dark room and flip a switch. A second later, a door opens across the way and light comes pouring in. But you don't get a chance to walk through the door—a couple of seconds later, the door slams shut and the room grows dark again. The trick? The door is only open for a few seconds, so you've got to flip the switch and run to get through the door.

How would you implement something like this in a game? That's what you'll solve in this chapter.

Every level in a typical game has a certain amount of unique code for environment interaction, and those unique bits are what add a lot of value to a game, making it more fun, interesting, and exciting.

But programmers aren't the only ones who will be creating these unique environment interactions—in a lot of cases, level designers will do most of it. So in this chapter, we go over how to connect your game objects to external scripts that are easy to write. This way, level designers won't need to know how to implement an interface or compile—all they'll need to know is how to write simple functions.

Also, allowing anyone to create levels and write scripts opens up room for users to create their own content or even make their own mods for a game. A *mod* is simply a modification of an existing game—for example, *Counter-Strike* is a *Half-Life* mod.

Besides scripting, this chapter covers triggers (something that causes an event to occur) and delayed events (performing tasks after a certain delay).

Scripting Cookbook: What You Need

You'll need to create a few things for your game-scripting system, at minimum: unique object names, event listeners, an embedded scripting language interpreter, and delayed events. Here's what you need in detail:

➤ It helps if every game object is derived from the same ancestor class. This makes it easier for objects to interact with each other because they share a common set of methods. We already have a common ancestor class in this book with the GameObject class.

➤ You need to be able to reference each object by a unique ID—preferably, a human-readable name. That way, you can give commands such as, "When the player touches blueSwitch, open doorToGrandHall." You already have unique names with GameObject's getName() method, and you can define object names in your map files.

➤ You need to be able to listen for certain events and perform actions based on those events. That way, the listener can be notified when the player touches blueSwitch and can perform the necessary actions. You already have a simple notification architecture with the GameObject methods such as notifyObjectCollision(), but you'll need to expand on this a bit.

➤ You need touch and release notifications for when the player (or another object) first touches and finally releases (stops touching) another object. Currently, you have only collision notifications.

➤ Likewise, you need to be able to perform delayed actions, such as closing a door after a certain time period.

➤ Finally, you'll want to design the system to allow level designers to code easily and to be as creative and flexible as possible. In this chapter, you'll hook up your game to a scripting language. This solution will be simple and flexible and will allow for rapid development.

First, you'll upgrade the event notifications. Then you'll move on to scripting and delayed events.

Implementing Touch and Release Notifications

In a game, you often want to perform some action when the player or another object touches another object. For example, a door might open when the player touches a switch, and close when the player touches the switch again.

So far in this book's game engine, an object receives all collision events whenever it collides with another object. This means that in this example, as long as the player is touching the switch, the door would just open and close continuously until the player lets go. This isn't the effect you want!

In this situation, you're interested only in the first collision event: when the player first touches the switch. In other cases, besides the "touch" notification, you might want the "release" notification, to notify when the player stopped touching an object.

See Figure 14.1 for an example of when the different events occur. In this figure, the player collides with the box on frame 2, sending a touch and collision notification. The player is still moving toward the box in frames 3 and 4, so collision notifications are still sent. In frame 5, the player stops, and no notifications are sent. Finally, in frame 6, the player moves away from the box, so a release notification is sent.

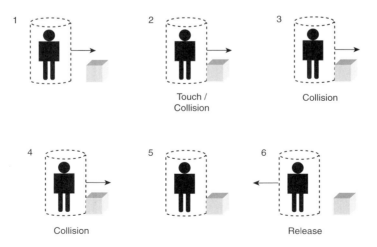

Figure 14.1   In this example, the player sends a touch notification on frame 2 and a release notification on frame 6. Collision notifications are sent on frames 2, 3, and 4.

Keep in mind that there might also be situations where an object could be touching several other objects simultaneously.

Okay, now let's get to implementing touch and release notifications in code. Each game object keeps a list of objects that it is touching. When a new object is added to this list, you send a touch notification; when one is removed, you send a release notification. The code for this is in Listing 14.1.

Listing 14.1   Touch and Release Code in GameObject.java

```java
private List touching = new ArrayList();
private List touchingThisFrame = new ArrayList();

...

public void notifyObjectCollision(GameObject otherObject) {
    touchingThisFrame.add(otherObject);
}


/**
    After this object has moved and collisions have been checked,
    this method is called to send any touch/release notifications.
*/
public void sendTouchNotifications() {
    // send release notifications
    Iterator i = touching.iterator();
    while (i.hasNext()) {
        GameObject obj = (GameObject)i.next();
        if (!touchingThisFrame.contains(obj)) {
            notifyObjectRelease(this, obj);
            i.remove();
        }
    }

    // send touch notifications
    i = touchingThisFrame.iterator();
    while (i.hasNext()) {
```

```
        GameObject obj = (GameObject)i.next();
        if (!touching.contains(obj)) {
            notifyObjectTouch(this, obj);
            touching.add(obj);
        }
    }

    // clean up
    touchingThisFrame.clear();
}
```

In this code, the additional list called `touchingThisFrame` is a list of objects that the game object was touching in the last frame. After the objects move and all collisions are detected, the game object manager calls `sendTouchNotifications()`. This method compares the `touchingThisFrame` list to the `touching` list. If an object is in the `touching` list but not in the `touchingThisFrame` list, a release notification for that object is sent. Likewise, if an object is in the `touchingThisFrame` list but not in the `touching` list, a touch notification for that object is sent, and the object is added to the `touching` list.

Note that `sendTouchNotifications()` is called only if the object moves. So, only moving objects keep track of what they are touching—the box in Figure 14.1 doesn't know what it's touching. Likewise, an object that normally moves but isn't moving for a particular frame doesn't send any notifications for that frame, as in frame 5 in Figure 14.1.

Triggers

Besides touching and releasing certain objects, sometimes you want certain areas of the map to trigger events. For example, in Figure 14.2, an invisible trigger area is used to open and close a door. When the player steps within the trigger area (touches it), the door opens; when the player steps outside it (releases it), the door closes.

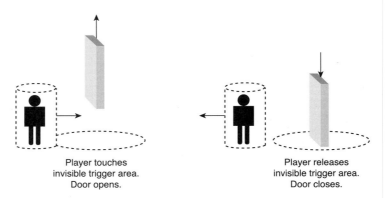

Player touches
invisible trigger area.
Door opens.

Player releases
invisible trigger area.
Door closes.

Figure 14.2   In this example, the player interacts with an
invisible trigger area to open and close a door.

Because you're using cylinders for collision detection here, you can define triggers in map files just like objects, only with a specified radius:

```
v 512 32 1150
trigger doorTrigger -1 256
```

This command in the map file creates the game object called `doorTrigger` at location (512,32,1150) and with a radius of 256.

You have to treat triggers as special game objects in only one case: collision detection. You want the player and other objects to walk through triggers, not slide around them as implemented in Chapter 11, "Collision Detection." Listing 14.2 shows how to avoid sliding for trigger objects but still send the collision notification.

Listing 14.2   Trigger Case in CollisionDetectionWithSliding.java

```java
protected boolean handleObjectCollision(GameObject objectA,
    GameObject objectB, float distSq, float minDistSq,
    Vector3D oldLocation)
{
    objectA.notifyObjectCollision(objectB);

    // if objectB has no polygons, it's a trigger area
    if (objectB.getPolygonGroup().isEmpty()) {
        return false;
```

```
    }

    ...

    // (perform sliding)
}
```

Here, if the object is a trigger area, it has no polygons and you notify the object collision and return from the method as if no collision occurred, without performing any sliding.

That's it for triggers. At the moment, however, all these notifications don't do anything; you would have to subclass every object that you want special actions for. Next, you'll create game object listeners that can "listen in" on notifications for certain objects and perform actions based on those notifications.

Game Object Listeners

You're already familiar with event/listener architectures—an example is AWT's `MouseListener` interface for receiving mouse events. Because it's an interface, any object can listen in on mouse events.

You'll make a similar architecture for game object notifications. First, create the `GameObjectEventListener` interface, shown here in Listing 14.3.

Listing 14.3   GameObjectEventListener.java

```
package com.brackeen.javagamebook.scripting;

import com.brackeen.javagamebook.game.GameObject;

/**
    Interface to receive GameObject notification events.
    See GameObject.addListener().
*/
public interface GameObjectEventListener {
```

continues

Listing 14.3   GameObjectEventListener.java   *continued*

```
    public void notifyVisible(GameObject object, boolean visible);

    public void notifyObjectCollision(GameObject object,
        GameObject otherObject);

    public void notifyObjectTouch(GameObject object,
        GameObject otherObject);

    public void notifyObjectRelease(GameObject object,
        GameObject otherObject);

    public void notifyFloorCollision(GameObject object);

    public void notifyCeilingCollision(GameObject object);

    public void notifyWallCollision(GameObject object);

}
```

This interface has methods for every type of notification:

➤ Object, floor, ceiling, and wall collisions

➤ Object touch and release notifications

➤ Visible notifications (when an object appears or disappears in the view)

You don't have to limit yourself to these seven notifications, of course. You can always add more later, such as `notifyMoving()`, `notifyStopped()`, or `notifyDestroyed()`, just to give you an idea.

Before you adapt your new listeners to the game objects, you should create an easy way for a game object to have multiple listeners. You might need multiple listeners when a game object has regular actions for its class and special unique actions for that game object. You'll make a class that acts as a listener that simply dispatches events to other listeners. This is similar to the `AWTEventMulticaster` class and is shown in Listing 14.4.

Listing 14.4   GameObjectEventMulticaster.java

```java
package com.brackeen.javagamebook.scripting;

import java.util.*;
import com.brackeen.javagamebook.game.GameObject;

/**
    Adapter to multicast GameObject notifications to multiple
    listeners.
*/
public class GameObjectEventMulticaster
    implements GameObjectEventListener
{

    private List listeners;

    public GameObjectEventMulticaster(GameObjectEventListener l1,
        GameObjectEventListener l2)
    {
        listeners = new LinkedList();
        addListener(l1);
        addListener(l2);
    }


    public void addListener(GameObjectEventListener l) {
        if (l != null) {
            listeners.add(l);
        }
    }


    public void removeListener(GameObjectEventListener l) {
        if (l != null) {
            listeners.remove(l);
        }
    }
```

continues

Listing 14.4 GameObjectEventMulticaster.java *continued*

```
    public void notifyObjectCollision(GameObject object,
        GameObject otherObject)
    {
        Iterator i = listeners.iterator();
        while (i.hasNext()) {
            GameObjectEventListener l =
                (GameObjectEventListener)i.next();
            l.notifyObjectCollision(object, otherObject);
        }
    }

    . . .

}
```

This `GameObjectEventMulticaster` class is itself a `GameObjectEventListener`, but it just dispatches event notifications to other listeners. Here, only the `notifyObjectCollision()` method is shown, but you get the idea—it's the same for all other notification methods. Here, the constructor takes two listeners as its parameters because you'll want to multicast to at least two listeners in your code.

Okay, the next thing to do is adapt these listeners to work with your existing game objects. First, add get, add, and remove methods to the `GameObject` class in Listing 14.5.

Listing 14.5 Listener Get/Add/Remove Methods of GameObject.java

```
private GameObjectEventListener listener;

. . .

/**
    Gets the GameObjectEventListener for this object.
*/
public GameObjectEventListener getListener() {
    return listener;
}
```

```
/**
    Adds a GameObjectEventListener to this object.
*/
public void addListener(GameObjectEventListener l) {
    if (l == null) {
        return;
    }
    else if (listener == null) {
        listener = l;
    }
    else if (listener instanceof GameObjectEventMulticaster) {
        ((GameObjectEventMulticaster)listener).addListener(l);
    }
    else {
        listener = new GameObjectEventMulticaster(listener, l);
    }
}


/**
    Removes a GameObjectEventListener from this object.
*/
public void removeListener(GameObjectEventListener l) {
    if (l == null) {
        return;
    }
    else if (listener == l) {
        listener = null;
    }
    else if (listener instanceof GameObjectEventMulticaster) {
        ((GameObjectEventMulticaster)listener).removeListener(l);
    }
}
```

This code keeps track of one listener, which can be a multicast listener if more than one listener is registered.

With these listeners, the collision-detection and -handling code needs to be changed. The previous way to notify an object was like this:

```
object.notifyWallCollision();
```

But using listeners, you use this code:

```
object.getListener().notifyWallCollision(object);
```

With that final change, that's all for your new listener architecture. One more thing to do, however, is adapt your existing game objects to easily use the new listener architecture, shown in Listing 14.6.

Listing 14.6   Adapting the New Listener Architecture in GameObject.java

```java
// adapt the listener to older design
listener = new GameObjectEventListener() {

    public void notifyVisible(GameObject object,
        boolean visible)
    {
        object.notifyVisible(visible);
    }

    public void notifyObjectCollision(GameObject object,
        GameObject otherObject)
    {
        object.notifyObjectCollision(otherObject);
    }

    public void notifyObjectTouch(GameObject object,
        GameObject otherObject)
    {
        object.notifyObjectTouch(otherObject);
    }

    public void notifyObjectRelease(GameObject object,
        GameObject otherObject)
    {
```

```
        object.notifyObjectRelease(otherObject);
    }

    public void notifyFloorCollision(GameObject object) {
        object.notifyFloorCollision();
    }

    public void notifyCeilingCollision(GameObject object) {
        object.notifyCeilingCollision();
    }

    public void notifyWallCollision(GameObject object) {
        object.notifyWallCollision();
    }
};
```

This code simply forwards the notification to the existing game object methods. This way, subclasses of `GameObject` (such as `Player` and `PathBot`) will still work without any changes.

Now you have a listener architecture and triggers. Next, we discuss different ways of scripting actions.

Scripting

You implement game scripting in a few different ways, depending on what goals you're trying to achieve. Here are some options, along with pros and cons:

➤ **Compiled Java**. Using compiled classes has a speed advantage and is easily embedded, but the level designer must download the Java SDK and know how to create classes, set the classpath, and compile. Also, sometimes creating entire classes just to call `door1.open()` is overkill.

➤ **Your own command interpreter**. Writing simple commands such as `door1.open` is easy, but this solution isn't very flexible because it limits what you can do. Plus, you have to write code to interpret the different commands.

➤ **Use a scripting language**. Using a scripting language is easy for casual users and gives them the flexibility they need. The right scripting language can even access live Java objects directly. The drawback is that scripts are slower than compiled code and you need a separate interpreter.

In this chapter, we use a scripting language. Besides the stated advantages, scripting is great for rapid development when compared to compiled classes because you can just edit a file and run, skipping the compile stage. Also, you can add a command to dynamically update scripts at runtime, which is great for in-game level designing and debugging.

The drawback is that scripted code won't run as fast as Java code because it's interpreted at runtime. However, usually scripts call only a few methods here and there, and the computationally expensive tasks are kept in the Java code. For complete mods, you might need both compiled and scripted code.

Many scripting language interpreters are available for Java. For example, BeanShell interprets Java-like code. Other interpreters include Rhino (JavaScript) and Jython (Python). There are also interpreters for other languages, such as Tcl, Scheme, Smalltalk, and Visual Basic.

When you're choosing a scripting language, be sure to pick one that can directly access live Java objects from scripts. Connecting with live Java objects is key to game scripting—with this functionality, scripts can call the methods of any live object, so you don't have to provide any sort of communication layer between scripts and actual code.

Scripts can directly access live Java objects through the use of the Java Reflection API. Reflection allows you to invoke a method of an object just by knowing the name of the method.

Embedding a scripting language interpreter is fairly easy and generally requires only a few method calls. In this chapter, you'll embed BeanShell, which is a free Java interpreter that can easily connect with live Java objects. BeanShell code is similar to Java code but is more flexible. BeanShell is loosely typed, so coders don't have to do any casting or declare the type of any variables. Plus, it's fairly small, running at about 125KB for the core interpreter. More information on BeanShell can be found at `www.beanshell.org`.

You need to perform two steps to implement scripting:

➤ Design how the scripts are called. What does the level designer need to write?

➤ Embed the interpreter. How do you call scripting functions?

In other words, look at this from the point of view of what you want to accomplish, and then implement it.

First things first, right? Let's start on designing the scripts.

Designing the Script

First, you want to avoid requiring level designers to create classes and interfaces. Simple functions will do just fine.

Second, you don't want to make it cumbersome to get access to game objects. You want to avoid writing code like this:

```
openDoor(gameObjectManager.getObject("door1"));
```

This code retrieves the game object named `door1` from the game object manager. Instead, it would be nice if you could refer to game objects as if they were variables, like this:

```
openDoor(door1);
```

Here's a look at what you might do in Listing 14.7. Note that BeanShell files end in .bsh.

Listing 14.7   level1.bsh

```
/**
    Functions to open and close the door.
*/

player_doorTriggerTouch() {
    // move the door up
    moveDoor(180);
}
```

continues

Listing 14.7   level1.bsh   *continued*

```
player_doorTriggerRelease() {
    // move the door down
    moveDoor(0);
}

moveDoor(int y) {
    // move all seven pieces of the door
    speed = 0.5f;
    moveYTo(door1a, y, speed);
    moveYTo(door1b, y, speed);
    moveYTo(door1c, y, speed);
    moveYTo(door1d, y, speed);
    moveYTo(door1e, y, speed);
    moveYTo(door1f, y, speed);
    moveYTo(door1g, y, speed);
}
```

In the map for this script are seven objects that represent the door. These objects look like tall poles, so the door resembles a gate. Also, there is an invisible trigger area called `doorTrigger`.

This script provides two functions: `player_doorTriggerTouch()`, which opens the door, and `player_doorTriggerRelease()`, which closes it. The variables named `door1a`, `door1b`, and so on refer to game objects defined in the map file.

This is pretty simple: There are only a couple of functions, and it doesn't need functions for notifications that aren't used in this case, such as wall collisions.

You'll follow this naming convention for the function names in your scripts. Each function starts with the name of the object that receives the notification. For example, the methods for collision notifications for the `player` object are listed here:

```
playerFloorCollision()
playerWallCollision()
playerCeilingCollision()
```

Likewise, if the `player` object collides with the `box` object, these methods are called:

```
player_boxCollision()
player_boxTouch()
player_boxRelease()
```

Of course, these functions don't have to be defined in the script.

One problem arises when implementing doors this way: AI bots currently check only the BSP tree for vision tests, not game objects. This means that bots can "see" right through doors, finding players on the other side of the door or not considering a door during path finding. Bots would probably attempt to move through or shoot through doors to get to the player. You could fix this by having the door covered by a fake, invisible polygon that acts as a vision barrier to the robots.

Note that the moveYTo() method in level1.bsh isn't defined yet. You can create a BeanShell file called main.bsh that defines common functions that will be helpful in scripts for each level. This script is in Listing 14.8. At the moment, only the moveYTo() method is defined.

Listing 14.8   main.bsh

```
// useful imports
import com.brackeen.javagamebook.game.*;
import com.brackeen.javagamebook.math3D.*;
import com.brackeen.javagamebook.util.*;
import com.brackeen.javagamebook.path.*;

moveYTo(GameObject object, int y, float speed) {
    object.setFlying(true);
    loc = new Vector3D(object.getLocation());
    loc.y = y;
    object.getTransform().moveTo(loc, speed);
}
```

BeanShell imports packages just like Java, so a few packages have been imported here to make it easy. You can use main.bsh as a place to put many methods to make the BeanShell scripts for the game easier to write.

Now you've designed how your scripts are written and even have a sample script. Next, you'll embed the BeanShell interpreter into your code.

Embedding BeanShell

Embedding BeanShell or any other interpreter generally will not take a lot of work.

For BeanShell, first create a BeanShell `Interpreter` object, which is in the .bsh package:

```
Interpreter bsh = new Interpreter();
```

You can use the `eval()` method of the interpreter to evaluate any Java expression, like this:

```
bsh.eval("System.out.println(5+3)");
```

Also, you can set variables with the `set()` method:

```
bsh.set("a", myObject);
```

Finally, you can load entire BeanShell scripts with the `source()` method:

```
bsh.source("level1.bsh");
```

This is all you really need, but be sure to check out the complete API documentation for BeanShell at www.beanshell.org.

We sum up all the BeanShell methods in the `ScriptManager` class here in Listing 14.9.

Listing 14.9   ScriptManager.java

```
package com.brackeen.javagamebook.scripting;

import java.io.IOException;
import java.util.*;
import com.brackeen.javagamebook.game.*;
import bsh.*;

public class ScriptManager {

    private static final Class[] NO_ARGS = new Class[0];
```

```java
private Interpreter bsh;
private GameObjectEventListener scriptedListener;

public ScriptManager() {
    scriptedListener = new ScriptedListener();
}

/**
    Sets up the ScriptManager for a level. The list of
    script files are executed, and every object in the
    GameObjectManager that has a name is added as a named
    variable for the scripts.
    Also, the scripted method initLevel() is called if
    it exists.
*/
public void setupLevel(GameObjectManager gameObjectManager,
    GameTaskManager gameTaskManager, String[] scriptFiles)
{
    bsh = new Interpreter();
    try {
        // execute source files (and load methods).
        for (int i=0; i<scriptFiles.length; i++) {
            bsh.source(scriptFiles[i]);
        }

        bsh.set("gameTaskManager", gameTaskManager);

        // Treat all named objects as named variables in
        // beanshell.
        // NOTE: this keeps all objects in memory (live) until
        // the next level, even if they are destroyed during the
        // level gameplay.
        Iterator i = gameObjectManager.iterator();
        while (i.hasNext()) {
            GameObject object = (GameObject)i.next();
            if (object.getName() != null) {
                bsh.set(object.getName(), object);
```

continues

Listing 14.9   ScriptManager.java   *continued*

```java
                    // add scripted listener to object
                    if (hasScripts(object)) {
                        object.addListener(scriptedListener);
                    }
                }
            }

            // init level code - call initLevel()
            invoke("initLevel");
        }
        catch (IOException ex) {
            ex.printStackTrace();
        }
        catch (EvalError ex) {
            ex.printStackTrace();
        }

    }


    /**
        Checks to see if the specified game object has any
        scripts (check to see if any scripted method starts with
        the object's name).
    */
    public boolean hasScripts(GameObject object) {
        if (object.getName() != null) {
            String[] names = bsh.getNameSpace().getMethodNames();
            for (int i=0; i<names.length; i++) {
                if (names[i].startsWith(object.getName())) {
                    return true;
                }
            }
        }

        // none found
        return false;
```

```
    }


    /**
        Returns true if the specified method name is an existing
        scripted method.
    */
    public boolean isMethod(String methodName) {
        return (bsh.getNameSpace().
            getMethod(methodName, NO_ARGS) != null);
    }



    /**
        Invokes the specified scripted method.
    */
    public void invoke(String methodName) {
        if (isMethod(methodName)) {
            try {
                bsh.eval(methodName + "()");
            }
            catch (EvalError e) {
                e.printStackTrace();
            }
        }

    }
}
```

In this code, the setUpLevel() method loads the source BeanShell files (you'll want to load main.bsh and level1.bsh) and sets the gameTaskManager (which we talk about in the next section). Also, it uses the set() method to set variables for each game object, so you can easily refer to each game object by name (as in door1). Next, it checks to see if a particular object has any scripts; if so, it adds the ScriptedListener to it (we talk about that next). A game object has scripts if any functions exist that start with the name of the game object. Finally, it calls the initLevel() script function to perform any code necessary to initiate the level.

A call to `isMethod()` returns `true` if the specified name is a no-argument method in the script.

Note that evaluating an expression in BeanShell or loading a BeanShell script can cause an `EvalError` to be thrown. This can happen if there is a problem with the BeanShell script and the error message will help with debugging. In this code, we just print the error to the console.

The `ScriptedListner` class is, of course, a game object event listener that calls BeanShell scripts based on your function-naming convention. It's added as a listener only to game objects that have scripts. The code is listed here in Listing 14.10.

Listing 14.10 `ScriptedListener` **Inner Class of ScriptManager.java**

```java
/**
    A GameObjectEventListener that delegates calls to scripted
    methods. A ScriptedListener is added to every GameObject
    that has at least one scripted method.
*/
public class ScriptedListener implements GameObjectEventListener {

    public void notifyVisible(GameObject object,
        boolean visible)
    {
        invoke(object.getName() +
            (visible?"Visible":"NotVisible"));
    }

    public void notifyObjectCollision(GameObject object,
        GameObject otherObject)
    {
        if (otherObject.getName() != null) {
            invoke(object.getName() + "_" +
                otherObject.getName() + "Collision");
        }

    }
```

```java
    public void notifyObjectTouch(GameObject object,
        GameObject otherObject)
    {
        if (otherObject.getName() != null) {
            invoke(object.getName() + "_" +
                otherObject.getName() + "Touch");
        }

    }

    public void notifyObjectRelease(GameObject object,
        GameObject otherObject)
    {
        if (otherObject.getName() != null) {
            invoke(object.getName() + "_" +
                otherObject.getName() + "Release");
        }

    }

    public void notifyFloorCollision(GameObject object) {
        invoke(object.getName() + "FloorCollision");
    }

    public void notifyCeilingCollision(GameObject object) {
        invoke(object.getName() +"CeilingCollision");
    }

    public void notifyWallCollision(GameObject object) {
        invoke(object.getName() + "WallCollision");
    }
}
```

This class is an inner class of ScriptManager and calls the invoke() method of ScriptManager to invoke the script functions.

That's all you need for scripting. Here's an example of how it breaks down, if you're a little fuzzy:

1. The player touches `switch1`.

2. Collision-detection code gets the player's listener and dispatches the touch event.

3. One of the listeners is a `ScriptListener`, which calls the appropriate touch function in the script.

One final note, however, is that you should be wary of the problems from obfuscating code. Obfuscation, which we talk about in Chapter 18, "Game Design and the Last 10%," mangles class, method, and field names so that they are harder to read when decompiled. This causes problems with scripts that are trying to call certain methods because the name of the method is different in obfuscated code. So, if you obfuscate your code, be sure to leave public APIs alone (keep public method names) and obfuscate only internal, private code. This way, the scripts will still work.

Delayed Events

One more thing you need to implement is the capability to easily create delayed events. An example of the type of delayed events you might want to create is in Figure 14.3.

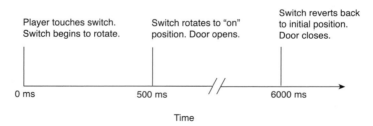

Figure 14.3 When the player touches a switch, several delayed events are set up.

In this figure, a few delayed events are set up when the player touches the switch: The door is opened, and seconds later, it closes again.

Your first crack at creating a system to handle delayed events might be to simply use the `Timer` utility class. The `Timer` class can easily execute tasks after a specific delay. However, the `Timer` class won't work in a typical game, for a couple reasons. First, the `Timer` class keeps track of tasks by system time, not game time. The system clock keeps on ticking even if the game is paused, so events could be fired up at the wrong time when the game is paused. Secondly, the Timer class executes code in a separate thread, which could lead to synchronization problems in your game.

So, you need to create an alternative system to do two things: manage the delayed tasks in the main thread, and keep track of them using game time, not system time.

Start with the basic GameTask class shown here in Listing 14.11. This class takes a Runnable and a delay as a parameter, with the idea that the Runnable is executed after the specified delay.

Listing 14.11   GameTask.java

```
package com.brackeen.javagamebook.scripting;

/**
    A game task that can be scheduled for one-time execution.
*/
public class GameTask implements Runnable {

    private long remainingTime;
    private Runnable runnable;
    private boolean done;

    /**
        Creates a new GameTask that will execute the specified
        Runnable after a delay.
    */
    public GameTask(long delay, Runnable runnable) {
        this.remainingTime = delay;
        this.runnable = runnable;
    }



    /**
        Cancels this task.
    */
    public void cancel() {
        done = true;
```

continues

Listing 14.11 GameTask.java *continued*

```java
    }


    /**
        Runs this task.
    */
    public void run() {
        if (runnable != null) {
            runnable.run();
        }
    }



    /**
        Checks to see if this GameTask is ready to execute; if
        so, it is executed. Returns true if the task is done
        (either it executed or it previously canceled).
    */
    public boolean check(long elapsedTime) {
        if (!done) {
            remainingTime-=elapsedTime;
            if (remainingTime <= 0) {
                done = true;
                try {
                    run();
                }
                catch (Exception ex) {
                    ex.printStackTrace();
                }
            }
        }

        return done;
    }

}
```

This class is designed so that its check() method is called on every frame. The remaining time the task has left until execution is kept track of, and this value is decremented in the check() method. When it reaches 0, the task is executed.

Next, you create the GameTaskManager, in Listing 14.12, which keeps track of all the pending game events.

Listing 14.12   GameTaskManager.java

```java
package com.brackeen.javagamebook.scripting;

import java.util.*;

/**
    Manages a queue of GameTask objects.
*/
public class GameTaskManager {

    private List tasks;


    /**
        Creates a new GameTaskManager with an empty task queue.
    */
    public GameTaskManager() {
        tasks = new ArrayList();
    }


    /**
        Adds a task to the queue that executed the specified
        runnable after a delay.
    */
    public void addTask(long delay, Runnable runnable) {
        addTask(new GameTask(delay, runnable));
    }


    /**
```

continues

Listing 14.12 GameTaskManager.java *continued*

```
        Adds a task to the queue.
    */
    public void addTask(GameTask task) {
        tasks.add(task);
    }


    /**
        Clears the task queue.
    */
    public void clear() {
        tasks.clear();
    }


    /**
        Updates this manager, executing any ready tasks.
    */
    public void update(long elapsedTime) {

        List removeList = null;
        int size = tasks.size();

        // note that executing a task can potentially add more
        // tasks onto the queue.
        for (int i=0; i<size; i++) {
            GameTask task = (GameTask)tasks.get(i);
            if (task.check(elapsedTime)) {
                // add object to list of objects to remove later
                if (removeList == null) {
                    removeList = new ArrayList();
                }
                removeList.add(task);
            }
        }

        // clear tasks that executed
```

```
            if  (removeList  !=  null)  {
                tasks.removeAll(removeList);
            }
        }
    }
}
```

The `GameTaskManager` has an `update()` method just like `GameObject` and many other classes in this book. It calls the `check()` method of every `GameTask`. All you have to do is make sure the `update()` method is called every frame and you have implemented delayed tasks.

In this code, we consider the fact that executing a game task can potentially add more tasks onto the queue. The code is careful about removing executed game tasks in the list, removing tasks from the list only after it has exited the loop.

Creating Delayed Events in BeanShell

BeanShell has the capability to create arbitrary interfaces, so creating delayed events is easy in your scripts. You can do something like this:

```
gameTaskManager.addTask(delay, new Runnable() {
    run() {
        doSomething();
    }
});
```

Of course, this conflicts with the goal of not requiring scripts to have classes or interfaces. We make this a bit easier with the `delay()` function in main.bsh, shown in Listing 14.13.

Listing 14.13   Delayed Tasks in main.bsh

```
/**
    Convenience method for executing a statement after a specified
    delay using the game task manager.
*/
delay(long delay, String statement) {
    gameTaskManager.addTask(delay, new Runnable() {
        run() {
```

continues

Listing 14.13   Delayed Tasks in main.bsh   *continued*

```
            this.interpreter.eval(statement);
        }
    });
}
```

This function executes a statement after the specified delay. For example, if you wanted to call the `closeDoor()` method after six seconds, you would write this:

```
delay(6000, "closeDoor()");
```

Notice that the function is in quotes. This is because the statement is a string, which
is, in turn, interpreted by BeanShell.

Okay, your delayed event system sounds great. Now let's try it out.

Putting It All Together

A BeanShell script to demonstrate delayed tasks is in Listing 14.14. In this script, when
the player touches the `stairTrigger`, the switch begins to move; the stairs begin to
move up after 750ms. After five seconds, the `closeStairs()` method is called to
bring the stairway down to the floor.

Listing 14.14   Moving Stairs in level1.bsh

```
/**
    Functions to open and close a stairway.
*/
global.stairsOn = false;
player_stairTriggerTouch() {
    if (global.stairsOn) {
        return;
    }
    openStairs();
}

openStairs() {
    // swing the switch ("turret") to the "on" position
```

```
    group = stairTrigger.getPolygonGroup().getGroup("turret");
    group.getTransform().turnYTo(3.14159f, 0.005f);
    // move the stairs up after 750 ms
    delay(750, "toggleStairs(true)");
    delay(5000, "closeStairs()");
    global.stairsOn = true;
}

closeStairs() {
    // swing the switch ("turret") to the "off" position
    group = stairTrigger.getPolygonGroup().getGroup("turret");
    group.getTransform().turnYTo(0, 0.005f);
    // move the stairs down
    toggleStairs(false);
    delay(750, "global.stairsOn = false;");
}

toggleStairs(boolean raise) {
    moveYTo(stair1, raise?192:0, .1f);
    moveYTo(stair2, raise?192:0, .1f);
    moveYTo(stair3, raise?192:0, .1f);
    moveYTo(stair4, raise?192:0, .1f);
    moveYTo(stair5, raise?192:0, .1f);
    moveYTo(stair6, raise?128:0, .1f);
    moveYTo(stair7, raise?64:0, .1f);
}
```

As a demonstration, the code for this chapter in the book includes the EventTest class, which uses the 3D engine in this book and combines it with scripting and delayed tasks. The only update this class needs over previous chapters is setting up the script manager and updating the game task manager every frame.

To run this test, you need to include the BeanShell library in your classpath. You can use the run task in the Ant build file included with the source, or you can run the test from the command line from the build folder, like this:

```
java -cp ..\lib\bsh-core-1.2b7.jar;. EventTest
```

A screenshot of the demo is in Figure 14.4.

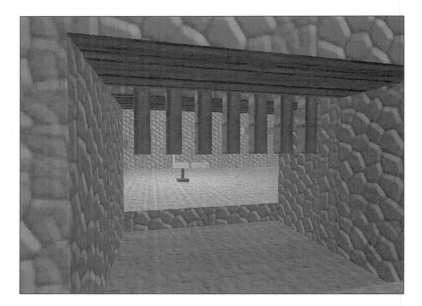

Figure 14.4   This screenshot of this chapter's demo shows a door opening (the bars) and a switch in the background. The switch activates a staircase.

Remember, part of the fun of making environment interaction like this is letting the player discover what happens. Be sure to occasionally make your environment interaction unique and not obvious. Occasionally let the players explore around a little and find things on their own.

Enhancements

You can do an endless number of things with game scripting like this. Here are just a few ideas for some additional environment interaction:

➤ Pull three levers (perhaps in a certain order) to open a door.

➤ Pull a lever to partially fill the room with water, which allows you to walk on the (now floating) platforms up to higher locations.

➤ Cut the suspending rope of a bridge to cause the bridge to fall, where you can find a secret room below.

➤ Set fire to a wall to burn it down so you can get to the other side.

➤ Push a block onto a button to keep a door open.

➤ Touch a button to turn on a hologram that gives you information about the map.

Also, the code in this chapter can be extended and enhanced in many ways. Here are some ideas for extending functionality:

➤ Make lots of commonly used scripted objects, such as doors and switches, so they don't have to be written repeatedly.

➤ Show a different polygon group, depending on an object's state. For example, a red button could glow green when touched.

➤ Perform actions when the user presses an "action key," such as the right-mouse click or the Enter key.

➤ The player can stand on platforms that move up and down, but also let the player stand on platforms that move side to side.

➤ Allow creation of scripted heads-up displays.

➤ Script all objects of the same type instead of just unique objects (for example, add scripted methods to all `Projectile` objects).

➤ Add other types of notifications (destroyed, moving, stopped moving, and so on).

➤ Perform certain actions when the player has specific items or when the player tries to give an item to another character.

➤ Create UI notifications, such as activating in-game help screens when the player touches a never-before-seen object.

➤ Add a hot key that reloads scripts on the fly so that the level designer can easily tweak scripts in-game.

➤ Allow scripts to be compressed and stored in a file in such a way that would make it difficult or impossible for players to edit the scripts (no cheating!).

Summary

In this chapter, we covered game scripting, one of the things that can make a game really fun and exciting. We demonstrated opening doors and a staircase that appears for a short time and then disappears. We talked about delayed events, scripting, touch and release events, and a new listener architecture.

Really, this chapter was just about the technical side of scripting—the biggest part is the creativity, which is up to you. So get out there and create some games with intense environment interactions!

Chapter 15

Persistence—Saving the Game

By Laurence Vanhelsuwé

KEY TOPICS

- Game-Saving Basics
- Using Java's Serialization API for Game State Persistence
- Creating Game Screen Snapshots
- Saving Games to the Right Destination
- Summary

Half-Life 2, *Doom III*, the latest *Tomb Raider* sequel, *The Sims*—all these games offer a game world so realistic and addictive that players will want to continue the experience from where they left off, time after time. You, the developer, would be taking your life in your own hands by not including a game-save feature in your next killer game.

Players quite understandably (even fanatically) expect to be able to continue playing at exactly where they last submerged themselves in their favorite fantasy world. Accumulated game progress, whether in the form of puzzles solved, areas discovered, armies defeated, objects collected, or simply points scored, is too valuable to your players to simply disappear when quitting the game.

Game-Saving Basics

From a game programming point of view, saving means that your game needs to be able to save its *state* to a persistent storage device (hard disk or network) and subsequently also be able to reload such a saved state at any point during game play.

A simple approach in a game with multiple levels is to save only the level the player was currently on. This has the advantage of being easy to implement: All you have to do is write a number (level=5) or code word (level=forestWorld9) to a file. The code word could also be secret so that players can't cheat by guessing the name of an upcoming level and modifying the save-game file themselves.

The disadvantage of this idea is that when players load a game, they must restart the level from the beginning, even if they saved the game seconds from the end of the level. Also, the player's capabilities aren't saved, so the player can't evolve over the course of the game (for example, by getting new items or abilities).

Most modern games provide more advanced save-game functionality: Saving "freezes" the game state at any point in the game, and loading returns to that exact point. The entire state of the game is saved—the player returns to the same location, enemies continue to run from where they were, and a bomb about to explode underneath the player still explodes.

A from-scratch approach to game saving typically relies on saving the core collection of program variables that make up the game's current *player-dependent* state to a flat, binary file. The file format normally is a custom proprietary format tailored to the game.

This saved-game state includes any information that *cannot* be recalculated from a freshly installed copy of the game:

> ➤ The player(s)'s progress (position in game world, accumulated score, damage, and objects such as weapons, spells, ammunition, and special items)

> ➤ The current state of all moveable game objects (location, orientation, animation cycle, velocity, artificial intelligence state, and so on), including the player and his foes or fellow players

> ➤ Pending events and any variables defined in game scripts (an event to close a door, an event to activate a staircase after five seconds, and so on)

> ➤ All global game-configuration data, as configured by the player (keyboard mappings, game difficulty setting, rendering quality, sound/music settings, and so on)

There's nothing inherently difficult in saving all this data manually, but this approach could be time-consuming to implement and would ignore the siren call of reuse potential offered by Java's Serialization API. This standard API can be leveraged to do much of the hard work for you, so the bulk of this chapter shows you how to safely exploit the Serialization API's features to implement game snapshot saves and reloads.

Unfortunately, Java's Serialization API addresses only part of the overall problem of game snapshots. When letting your users save a game, you normally let the user associate a name with this snapshot so that later, when the user wants to revert to a saved game, a list of named snapshots can be browsed and picked from. In the ever-escalating game features stakes, modern games also typically show a thumbnail-size screenshot for each saved game. This way, your player needs to simply visually browse the thumbnails and must refer to the snapshot label only if there's any ambiguity in the list of screenshots. Toward the end of this chapter, we show you how to implement such a feature, necessitating some help from AWT's automation butler, Mr. Robot.

Using Java's Serialization API for Game State Persistence

As a games developer, if you plan to rely on the Serialization API, you have no choice but to learn how most of the framework works in detail. Unlike some APIs, in which you can restrict yourself to learning how to exploit just the tip of the API iceberg, the Serialization API doesn't lend itself to such a short-cut approach. The next few sections give you an in-depth look at serialization techniques and pitfalls.

Introduction to Serialization

The core function of Java's Serialization API is to transform objects into byte streams, and vice versa. The terms used are *serialization* and *deserialization*, respectively.

The Serialization API was added to the Java Platform back in the Stone Age days of the switch from Java 1.0 to Java 1.1 (around the end of 1996). The API's main *raison d'être* at the time was as an enabling technology to support Remote Method Invocation (RMI—that is, distributed objects) and Java's reusable component architecture, JavaBeans. You'll use the API for a far more exciting goal: game state persistence.

For any object to *persist*—that is, be saved from the inevitable death of the JVM it lives in—all that needs to happen is for that object to be transformed into an output byte stream and for this byte stream to be transmitted to some external storage entity that is independent from the current JVM, such as a file or a network socket. (The remainder of the chapter assumes you are familiar with Java's basic I/O stream APIs.) The net effect is object persistence.

Serialization: The Basics

The Serialization API lives in the java.io package; at the heart of the API are the Serializable interface and two special stream classes capable of serializing and deserializing objects that implement the Serializable interface: ObjectOutputStream and ObjectInputStream.

If you are familiar with java.io's venerable DataOutputStream and DataInputStream classes, you can think of ObjectOutputStream and ObjectInputStream as enhanced versions of these classes that can also read/write objects, in addition to reading/writing primitive data values and Strings.

Before exploiting these stream classes, though, let's see what behavior the Serializable interface expects from any objects that want to take part in any serialization/deserialization round-trip:

```
public interface Serializable {
    // empty !
}
```

The Serializable interface specifies no behavior whatsoever. Unlike the vast majority of interfaces, Serializable requires no methods to be implemented. It also does not define any constants. The interface exists purely to *tag* classes as being serializable.

But what exactly does this mean? Can you just load up all your Java source files and sprinkle implements Serializable willy nilly over all your classes? Most definitely not. The reasons why this is not possible are uncovered in increasing levels of detail as you progress through the remainder of this chapter.

> **NOTE**
> The Serializable interface has a closely associated subinterface called Externalizable. You can find out more about it in the Java Object Serialization Specification, available online on Sun's Java website, java.sun.com.

A Simple Serialization Example

Let's just see how simple the Serialization API can be at its simplest (be warned, it can get pretty hairy at its most complex). Listing 15.1 shows how an example program serializes an everyday StringBuffer object and writes it out to a file.

Listing 15.1   SaveStringBuffer.java

```java
import java.io.*;

class SaveStringBuffer {

public static void main (String[] args) {

    StringBuffer sb = new StringBuffer("Beam me up!");

    try {
        FileOutputStream fos = new FileOutputStream("sb.ser");
        ObjectOutputStream oos = new ObjectOutputStream(fos);

        oos.writeObject(sb);
        oos.close();

    } catch (IOException ioException) {
        System.out.println(ioException);
    }
}

}
```

The sharp end of this example is the `writeObject()` call on an `ObjectOutputStream` object. The stream object does all the hard work of serializing the argument object: It analyzes, via core reflection, the list of instance fields making up the `StringBuffer` and converts the values of these fields into a byte stream. If you have a quick peek at the source code for `StringBuffer`, you'll find that every `StringBuffer` consists of a `char[]`, an `int`, and a `boolean`; these fields are read out of the object and streamed to an `OutputStream`. In this example, you send the resulting byte stream to hard disk via a terminus `FileOutputStream`.

If you run this program, you'll find a new file called sb.ser in the current directory, which contains the serialized `StringBuffer`.

To prove this claim, you can run the following complementary program to reload, deserialize, and print your `StringBuffer` (see Listing 15.2).

Listing 15.2   LoadStringBuffer.java

```java
import java.io.*;

class LoadStringBuffer {

public static void main (String[] args) {

    StringBuffer sb = null;

    try {
        FileInputStream fis = new FileInputStream("sb.ser");
        ObjectInputStream ois = new ObjectInputStream(fis);

        sb = (StringBuffer) ois.readObject();

        ois.close();

    } catch (IOException ioException) {
        System.out.println(ioException);
    } catch (ClassNotFoundException classNotFoundException ) {
        System.out.println(classNotFoundException );
    }

    System.out.println("Welcome back aboard, Sir! : " + sb);
}

}
```

Running this program produces the following output on the console, confirming that sb.ser contains a persistent StringBuffer object:

```
Welcome back aboard, Sir!  : Beam me up!
```

Although it is marginally more complex than its saving counterpart, the heart of this LoadStringBuffer example is the readObject() call on an ObjectInputStream object. readObject() simply does the reverse of writeObject(): It deserializes a byte stream into a *copy* of the original object that was serialized. Because readObject() is declared as returning an Object, you will always need to cast the return value to some more specific subtype—in this example's case: StringBuffer.

Serialization: The Rules

For any class to be `Serializable`, it should be possible for its objects' states to be extracted as a sequence of bytes—that is, a byte stream. Object state means the collection of values of an object's nontransient instance fields (by definition, transient fields are ignored by the serialization engine).

Any primitive fields (boolean, char, byte, short, int, long, float, and double) can always be transformed into bytes without any problems, but reference fields that are not null at runtime can be serialized only if the objects referred to by the references also implement the `Serializable` interface. This latter rule is applied recursively, so any objects referred to, either directly or indirectly, by some root object to be serialized need to be serializable, in turn.

In practice, this means that you can declare, or tag, as being serializable any of your classes that declare only primitive fields, without having to worry about the truth of such a declaration. The resulting class will always be serializable.

On the other hand, any classes that declare references to other objects require very careful analysis to determine whether such classes can be declared serializable.

When a class declares any reference fields, you need to check one by one whether the types of the objects referred to are serializable. If any type referred to is not serializable, your class cannot normally be declared serializable (but you'll see later how to possibly get around this problem via customization of the serialization process). Only if all references refer to serializables can the declaring class also be declared serializable.

Later in this chapter, we return to this fundamental nature of serializability.

Core Classes Support for Serialization

Given that most nontrivial classes do declare references, and given that these references often refer to core library types such as `String`, `Point`, `Color`, and so on, you need to be aware of the serializability landscape of the core library's classes. In particular, it is handy to know which classes in the java.lang and java.util packages are serializable. Tables 15.1 and 15.2 contain this information for the 1.4 release of the Java 2 platform.

Table 15.1 JDK 1.4 java.lang Classes and Their Serializable Status

Class Name	Serializable?	Class Name	Serializable?
java.lang.Boolean	✔	java.lang.Process	
java.lang.Byte	✔	java.lang.Runtime	
java.lang.Character	✔	java.lang.RuntimePermission	✔
java.lang.Class	✔	java.lang.SecurityManager	
java.lang.ClassLoader		java.lang.Short	✔
java.lang.Compiler		java.lang.StackTraceElement	✔
java.lang.Double	✔	java.lang.StrictMath	
java.lang.Float	✔	java.lang.String	✔
java.lang.InheritableThreadLocal		java.lang.StringBuffer	✔
java.lang.Integer	✔	java.lang.System	
java.lang.Long	✔	java.lang.Thread	
java.lang.Math		java.lang.ThreadGroup	
java.lang.Number	✔	java.lang.ThreadLocal	
java.lang.Object		java.lang.Throwable	✔
java.lang.Package			

Table 15.2 JDK 1.4 java.util Classes and Their Serializable Status

Class Name	Serializable?	Class Name	Serializable?
java.util.AbstractCollection		java.util.Collections	
java.util.AbstractList		java.util.Currency	✔
java.util.AbstractMap		java.util.Date	✔
java.util.AbstractSequentialList		java.util.Dictionary	
java.util.AbstractSet		java.util.EventListenerProxy	
java.util.ArrayList	✔	java.util.EventObject	✔
java.util.Arrays		java.util.GregorianCalendar	✔
java.util.BitSet	✔	java.util.HashMap	✔
java.util.Calendar	✔	java.util.HashSet	✔

Class Name	Serializable?	Class Name	Serializable?
java.util.Hashtable	✔	java.util.PropertyResourceBundle	
java.util.IdentityHashMap	✔	java.util.Random	✔
java.util.LinkedHashMap	✔	java.util.ResourceBundle	
java.util.LinkedHashSet	✔	java.util.SimpleTimeZone	✔
java.util.LinkedList	✔	java.util.Stack	✔
java.util.ListResourceBundle		java.util.StringTokenizer	
java.util.Locale	✔	java.util.Timer	
java.util.Observable		java.util.TimerTask	
java.util.Properties	✔	java.util.TimeZone	✔
java.util.PropertyPermission	✔	java.util.TreeMap	✔
		java.util.TreeSet	✔
		java.util.Vector	✔
		java.util.WeakHashMap	

As you can see from Tables 15.1 and 15.2, not all standard java.lang and java.util classes are serializable. This probably comes as a bit of a surprise, but there are valid reasons for this patchy support which we touch upon in a minute.

Crucially, Object itself does not implement the Serializable interface. This implies that any direct subclasses of Object are not serializable unless explicitly tagged (and, hence, designed) as such.

If you modify the earlier SaveStringBuffer example to attempt saving a plain Object:

```
oos.writeObject( new Object() );
```

then running this modified version would produce the following runtime exception:

```
java.io.NotSerializableException: java.lang.Object
```

NotSerializableException often competes with NullPointerException for your gray hairs when you're trying to debug nontrivial serialization aspects of any Java application.

Looking at other classes in the java.lang package, you can see that most bread-and-butter classes are serializable: All wrapper classes are—String, StringBuffer, and even Throwable. Because the Throwable class is serializable, all exceptions, regardless of which package they are declared in, and whether checked or not, are also serializable.

In the java.util package, you can see that most classes are serializable, except the abstract skeleton implementations of the Collection and Map interfaces. Note that both interfaces Collection and Map could theoretically have extended Serializable (remember, in Java, multiple inheritance can be achieved only via interfaces), thus forcing all collection classes to be serializable; however, Sun apparently decided against this possibly too restrictive approach.

Classes that do not declare themselves as serializable normally have a perfectly valid reason for doing so, typically because serialization simply does not make sense for the class. Classes consisting only of static methods (Math and Collections, for example) never produce any objects, while other classes with very intricate dependencies on underlying JVMs (Thread and System, for example) do not support serialization for complex technical and class-specific reasons.

> **NOTE**
>
> The companion website includes a console utility called IsSerializable that you can use to interactively determine the serializability of any fully qualified class. If no command-line argument is passed to this utility, it lists the serializability of all classes in the 1.4 java.lang package.

Serialization: The Pitfalls

Java's built-in support for object serialization can be a great help when it is working transparently for you. Unfortunately, more than a few pitfalls are waiting to shatter that transparency if you don't arm yourself with an understanding of the trickier sides of serialization.

No Deserialization of Unknown Objects

If you imagine for a second that you just left your desk for a coffee break between running your earlier SaveStringBuffer example and running LoadStringBuffer, and if you also imagine that some joker substituted behind your back your sb.ser for another sb.ser containing a serialized ButYouDontHaveSuchAClassAnywhere-OnYourClassPath object, you can see why ObjectInputStream.readObject()

also forces you to deal with a possible `ClassNotFoundException`. Not surprisingly, the deserialization engine hiding behind `readObject()` needs to have access to the classes of any objects it is asked to reconstitute. If these classes are not already present in the JVM or are not loadable via the current `ClassLoader`, deserialization fails.

`ClassNotFoundExceptions` are not uncommon when working on RMI applications, but they should not be a problem in standalone games that rely on conventional (that is, default) `ClassLoader` behavior. After all, serialized objects normally are deserialized by exactly the same game program that serialized them in the first place.

Nonserializable Object Graphs

If you modify the `SaveStringBuffer` example to save a `HashSet` object containing the following mixed bag of elements:

```
Set bag = new HashSet();
bag.add("Hello");
bag.add(new Object());
bag.add(new Integer(2003));

oos.writeObject(bag);
```

then running this new version again produces that all-too-common runtime exception when dealing with serialization:

```
java.io.NotSerializableException: java.lang.Object
```

Although `HashSet` implements the `Serializable` interface and, therefore, should be serializable at face value, a `HashSet`'s runtime content might not be. In this case, the `Object` included in the bag isn't serializable.

When you ask an `ObjectOutputStream` to serialize a single object and that object refers to other objects, and those other objects, in turn, refer to more objects, and so on, then all of those objects (that is, the *entire object graph*) are serialized. If any object in this graph is not itself serializable, the entire operation fails with a `NotSerializableException`. Figure 15.1 illustrates this very common serialization pitfall.

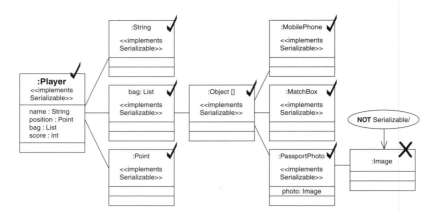

Figure 15.1 The *entire* object graph must consist of `Serializable` objects. For example, any image that is part of an object graph to be serialized will cause serialization of the entire graph to fail.

The `HashSet` containing a plain `Object` is a good example of the more common scenario of wanting to serialize a container object that is polluted, as far as serialization is concerned, by one or more elements that are not serializable.

Serializing Arrays

Let's check the precise method signatures for `ObjectOutputStream.writeObject()` and `ObjectInputStream.readObject()`:

```
public final void writeObject(Object obj)
        throws IOExceptionpublic final Object readObject()
        throws ClassNotFoundException, IOException
```

You should see what, at first sight, might look like sloppy parameter and return value typing: You probably wonder why these methods use a `Serializable` instead of an `Object`, as follows

```
public final void writeObject(Serializable aSerializable)
        throws IOException
public final Serializable readObject()
        throws ClassNotFoundException, IOException
```

After all, only `Serializable` objects are accepted, respectively produced, by these methods. The existing method signatures can be explained by the quasi-exception to the rule: arrays.

Arrays are full-fledged objects in Java; given that any `<array> instanceof Serializable` test always returns `true`, passing arrays to the serialization engine poses no problems as long as every array element is serializable, too. This caveat is essentially the same as the one that applies to serializing container objects.

Class Evolution and Versioning

Another serialization pitfall lies in attempting to use serialization for *long-term persistence* of objects. By "long-term," we mean any stretch of time long enough to accommodate changes to the classes that spawned the serialized objects.

Let's say you wrote a chess game that allows any game in progress to be saved. The following classes would be at the heart of your implementation:

```
public class ChessGameState implements Serializable {

private ChessBoard theBoard;
private ChessPlayer white;
private ChessPlayer black;

}

class ChessPlayer implements Serializable {
private String name;
}

class ChessBoard implements Serializable {
private ChessPiece[][] squares;
}
```

Saving the game in this chess scenario boils down to serializing the singleton `ChessGameState` object and storing this serialized object to hard disk.

Now imagine your v1.0 chess game has become a popular success (maybe because you're using the classic Internet marketing tactic of giving your product away for free in the hope of building critical mass market share). The success of MyChess v1.0 enables you to attract venture capital to fund the development of an improved v2.0 version for which you intend to charge hard cash.

On the to-do list for v2.0 is fixing one v1.0 bug: In v1.0, you forgot to implement the 50 moves rule when one player is left with nothing but his king. Fixing this should be trivial. To address this rather embarrassing bug, you add an int field and associated logic to ChessGameState:

```
public class ChessGameState implements Serializable {

private ChessBoard theBoard;
private ChessPlayer white;
private ChessPlayer black;
private int fiftyMovesCounter;

}
```

But now, regression testing of MyChess v2.0 unearths a problem. Restoring a saved v1.0 game crashes with the following runtime exception:

```
java.io.InvalidClassException: ChessGameState; local class
incompatible: stream classdesc serialVersionUID =
8698504323191665099,
local class serialVersionUID = 3813626932283615031
```

The deserialization engine detected that the v2.0 ChessGameState class present in the JVM is not the same v1.0 ChessGameState class from which the object was serialized in the past. In other words, the deserialization engine noticed and objected to the fact that the fiftyMovesCounter field was added.

To avoid this type of *class evolution* problem, you need to ensure that your evolving classes remain serialization version–compatible.

What does this mean? Serialization version–compatible classes are classes that, as far as serialization is concerned, are identical. This equality is evaluated via the intermediary of 64-bit class signature numbers called serialVersionUIDs. For output (that is, serialization), these class signatures either are calculated on the fly by the serializing engine or can be explicitly declared in a serializable class by the programmer:

```
private static final long serialVersionUID = 3786198910865385080L;
```

Upon input (that is, deserialization), the `serialVersionUID` embedded in the serialized object stream is compared with the `serialVersionUID` of the class of the object. If the two differ, deserialization fails.

The `serialVersionUID` for a class is calculated by essentially taking the fully qualified class name and all the declared nontransient instance fields for the class and forming a value similar to an object's runtime hash code. So adding, removing, or changing an instance field alters the value of a computed `serialVersionUID` and leads the deserializer to throw an `InvalidClassException`.

To get around this problem, you can explicitly tag a class with a static serial VersionUID field that stays constant across class changes. That way, any changes that would otherwise change a computed `serialVersionUID` will *not* result in an `InvalidClassException` during deserialization. As long as any changes to the class are compatible as far as serialization goes, long-term persistence of objects of evolving classes can be made to work.

Serialization-incompatible class changes include these:

➤ Deleting or changing the type of instance fields

➤ Changing the name of an instance field (watch out when using obfuscation)

➤ Changing the position of the class in the inheritance tree

➤ Making incompatible changes to the logic of any private `writeObject()` or `readObject()` methods

Serialization-compatible class changes include these:

➤ Adding instance fields

➤ Changing the access scope of any field

This list of changes consists of only the most common changes. The full list is beyond the scope of this book but can be analyzed in the Java Object Serialization Specification.

Overriding Default Serialization Engine Behavior

ObjectOutputStream serializes object graphs into a byte stream formatted according to a serialization stream protocol. The default protocol is essentially little more than a binary representation of object field values and a clever way of dealing with object types and references.

From a game programmer's point of view, this format might be problematic in that the protocol's simplicity also results in data transparency. Serialized objects can easily be hacked by cheating players blessed with some Java knowledge. For example, typical saved games record the player's current score, how many lives a player has left, and what kinds of objects or powers the player has so far accumulated. These attributes form juicy hacking targets (to a cheat, that is). To foil hackers and cheats, persistent objects need be made as opaque as possible.

To this end, the serialization API allows its default behavior to be overridden. This is not done by extending the ObjectOutputStream and ObjectInputStream classes and overriding their public writeObject() and readObject() methods, as you might expect (as you saw earlier, the methods cannot be overridden because they are final). Instead, the API employs nongeneric techniques that we will now explore.

Adding Private *writeObject()* or *readObject()* Methods

Let's say you have writeObject() and the following game state classes:

```
class GameState implements Serializable {

private Player player;

}

class Player implements Serializable {

private short livesLeft;

}
```

Saving your game's singleton `GameState` object using default serialization would leave your game open to fairly trivial hacking of a player's lives left status. What you need is extra data armor to protect the serialized `livesLeft` fields from being trivially altered with a file editor (typically a hex editor).

One approach supported directly by the serialization engine is to implement in your vulnerable `Serializable` class private methods that write and read the fields of your class manually, without the help of the serialization engine. This then opens the door to writing field values in an obfuscated, or even strongly encrypted, format.

These complementary private methods must be declared using the following signatures:

```
private void writeObject(ObjectOutputStream s) throws IOException
private void readObject(ObjectInputStream s) throws IOException
```

Listing 15.3 shows how you would `writeObject()` and enhance the `Player` class to exploit this technique.

Listing 15.3 GameState.java

```
import java.io.*;

public class GameState implements Serializable {

private Player player = new Player(3);

public static void main (String[] args) {

    try {
        FileOutputStream fos = new FileOutputStream("game.ser");
        ObjectOutputStream oos = new ObjectOutputStream(fos);

        oos.writeObject( new GameState() );
        oos.close();

        FileInputStream fis = new FileInputStream("game.ser");
        ObjectInputStream ois = new ObjectInputStream(fis);

        System.out.println( ois.readObject() );
```

continues

Listing 15.3 GameState.java *continued*

```java
            ois.close();

        } catch (Exception exception) {
            System.out.println(exception);
        }
    }

    public String toString() {

        return "GameState[ " + player.toString() + " ]";
    }
}

class Player implements Serializable {

private short livesLeft;

/*package*/ Player(int lives) {
    livesLeft = (short) lives;
}

private void writeObject(ObjectOutputStream s) throws IOException
{
    System.out.println("Encrypting lives left...");
    s.writeByte(- livesLeft);
}

private void readObject(ObjectInputStream s) throws IOException {
    System.out.println("Decrypting lives left...");
    livesLeft = (short) - s.readByte();
}

public String toString() {

    return "Player[" + livesLeft + "]";
}
}
```

When running GameState's main(), you can see from the console output that the additional writeObject() and readObject() methods were called not by our own code, but by the serialization engine. The serialized GameState object (containing one serialized Player object) now has the player's livesLeft variable stored, not in what cryptologists call *plain text*, but in an encrypted form. To keep this example as short as possible, the "encryption" used here is nothing more than some bits-massaging negation of the value (using the unary minus operator). In a real-life game, you might want to give your game's hackers some tougher encryption to chew on.

Explicitly Specifying Which Fields Should be Serialized

Adding private writeObject() and readObject() methods takes you a big step away from the default serialization engine's behavior because the methods essentially take over total responsibility for the serializing and deserializing of your particular class's objects.

For classes that contain lots of fields, most of which do not require encryption or obfuscation, this all-or-nothing approach undermines some of the benefits of using the serialization API in the first place. You need a way to use the default mechanism for most of your fields, but deal with the minority of likely hacking targets in a customized way.

Java's Serialization framework lets you deal with this problem by explicitly specifying which fields should be handled via the default mechanism. Reminiscent of the serialVersionUID field approach, this is done by defining in your Serializable class another magic private final static field, called serialPersistentFields, as follows:

```
class Player implements Serializable {
private String playerName;
private short livesLeft;

private static final ObjectStreamField[] serialPersistentFields = {
new ObjectStreamField("playerName", String.class)
};

    // .. Player methods here.
}
```

As you can see, this serialPersistentFields field must be typed as a one-dimensional array of ObjectStreamField objects. This array defines which *instance* fields, present and declared in the current class, should be subjected to the default serialization mechanism. Each ObjectStreamField array element object defines a field by way of its declared name and type; field scope and any other field attributes are unnecessary and are therefore writeObject() and objectignored.

When you include the serialPersistentFields field in a Serializable class, you also need to alter the way your writeObject() and readObject() methods are implemented by invoking ObjectOutputStream.defaultWriteObject() and ObjectInputStream.defaultReadObject(), respectively:

```
private void writeObject(ObjectOutputStream s) throws IOException
{
    s.defaultWriteObject();
    System.out.println("Encrypting lives left...");
    s.writeByte(- livesLeft);
}

private void readObject(ObjectInputStream s) throws IOException {
    s.defaultReadObject();
    System.out.println("Decrypting lives left...");
    livesLeft = (short) - s.readByte();
}
```

To summarize, by mixing the following two techniques:

➤ Adding a private writeObject() or readObject() duo to your Serializable class

➤ Explicitly specifying which fields need to be serialized using the default mechanism

You can tune the way your objects are serialized on a field-by-field basis instead of on the often too coarse level of entire classes. This flexibility enables you to encrypt any sensitive fields that form part of your game's persistent state.

Creating Game Screen Snapshots

If the visible screen was accessible as some kind of system Java object (`System`, `Runtime`) and such a hypothetical class implemented the `Serializable` interface, then taking screen snapshots could be handled in exactly the same way as taking snapshots of any other Java objects: via serialization. Unfortunately, Java does not map the screen to a convenient object, so serialization can't help with your screen snapshots requirement.

With 1.3.0 came a new class in the AWT package, `Robot`. This, at first sight, oddly named class contains the solution to your screenshot requirement:

```
public BufferedImage createScreenCapture(Rectangle screenRect)
```

This method isn't static, as you might expect, so you need to first instantiate a `Robot` using one of the two available `Robot` constructors:

```
public Robot() throws AWTException
```

```
public Robot(GraphicsDevice screen) throws AWTException
```

The possibly thrown `AWTExceptions` neatly help explain why `Robot` is called "Robot": This class was designed to help automated testing of GUIs. If you consult `Robot`'s complete API (via the online Java API documentation), you'll see that the API allows a program to trigger GUI input (key and mouse events) as if they were generated by a human interacting with a physical keyboard and mouse (you used the `Robot` class to implement mouselook in Chapter 3, "Interactivity and User Interfaces"). The `createScreenCapture()` method was never designed to support games development, but it was included to allow an automated GUI testing framework to visually check that programmed user interface inputs produce the required graphical response from the GUI. So, `Robot` is supposed to represent a GUI-testing robot (presumably little more than a mechanical arm, in this case) that can hit keys, move the mouse about, and view the results of these actions. So, what about those `AWTExceptions` in `Robot`'s constructor signatures? Well, unfortunately, not all host platforms support the direct injection of fake input events into their GUI event subsystem. On these systems, attempting to instantiate a `Robot` will fail with an `AWTException`.

Now that we've explained the purpose of and legitimacy behind the Robot name, let's call createScreenCapture() to satisfy ourselves that it does what it says on the label.

The GrabScreen example shown in Listing 15.4 contains the following grabScreen() method.

Listing 15.4 grabScreen() Method

```
/******************************************************************
 * Grab the visible screen
 *
 * @return a BufferedImage containing the specified screen sub-rectangle

 ******************************************************************/
private BufferedImage grabScreen(Rectangle screenRect) {

    Robot robot = null;
    try {
        robot = new Robot();
    } catch (AWTException awtException) {
        System.out.println(awtException);
        return null;
    }

    BufferedImage screenImage = robot.createScreenCapture(screenRect);

    return screenImage;
}
```

If you run the demo, you'll see your screen being overlayed with a darkening filter effect. This illusion is achieved by making a copy of the original screen, via the previous grabScreen() method, and then overwriting the visible screen with pixels that have had their intensity halved (red, green, and blue components divided by two; see Listing 15.5).

Listing 15.5   Halving the Intensity of RGB

```
screenImage = grabScreen(screenRect);
darkenImage(screenImage);


...


/***********************************************************************
 * Overridden Component.paint()
 *
 * @param g the Graphics context to paint to.

 ***********************************************************************/
public void paint(Graphics g) {

    if ( screenImage != null ) {
        g.drawImage(screenImage, 0,0, null);
    }

}


/***********************************************************************
 * Darkens a BufferedImage

 ***********************************************************************/
public void darkenImage(BufferedImage image) {
    int width = image.getWidth();
    int height = image.getHeight();

    for (int y=0; y < height; y++) {
        for (int x=0; x < width; x++) {
            int color = image.getRGB(x,y);
            color = color >> 1;
            color = color & 0x7F7F7F;
            image.setRGB(x,y, color);
        }
```

continues

Listing 15.5   Halving the Intensity of RGB   *continued*

```
        }

    }

}
```

Clearly, making copies of the screen is a no-brainer on any Java platform that supports a full `Robot` implementation.

The next goal is to transform this screen snapshot into a thumbnail image.

Creating Screen Thumbnail Images

Given a `BufferedImage` holding a full-screen snapshot of the current game screen, the next goal is to transform this image into a thumbnail image file. This comprises two subtasks: resizing the original image and saving the resulting thumbnail as either a GIF, a PNG, or a JPEG file.

To resize an image, you can draw a scaled version of the image onto a new thumbnail-size image, like this:

```
BufferedImage screenThumbnail = new BufferedImage(width, height,
    BufferedImage.TYPE_INT_RGB);

Graphics2D g = screenThumbnail.createGraphics();
g.drawImage(screenImage, 0, 0, width, height, null);
g.dispose();
```

Here, `width` and `height` define the size of the thumbnail.

Scaling from a large image to a small one could look rather pixelated using the default rendering hints, however. You can use bilinear interpolation, described in Chapter 8, "Texture Mapping and Lighting," to help smooth out the resulting thumbnail so it doesn't look so pixilated. Just set the interpolation rendering hint for the `Graphics2D` object before you scale the image:

```
g.setRenderingHint(RenderingHints.KEY_INTERPOLATION,
    RenderingHints.VALUE_INTERPOLATION_BILINEAR);
```

Now that you have a thumbnail, you need a way to save it to disk.

Saving an Image

To save an image to disk, you can use the Image I/O framework. The nontrivial architecture of this framework consists of a highly pluggable system of image readers and writers (encoders and decoders), associated listeners, and "service providers." Luckily for your immediate needs, you do not need to learn the inner workings of this framework to save a few JPEGs.

The javax.imageio root package of the Image I/O API contains a utility class called `ImageIO` that features some high-level static convenience methods to save images to various destinations, in easily selectable image formats:

```
public static boolean write(RenderedImage im, String formatName,
File output)
public static boolean write(RenderedImage im, String formatName,
OutputStream output)
public static boolean write(RenderedImage im, String formatName,
ImageOutputStream output)
```

All three methods return a boolean indicating whether the image-write operation succeeded; they can also throw an `IOException` if any operation failure is due to an I/O problem.

These methods' `RenderedImage` argument is not the same as the `Image` type, but it's close: `BufferedImage` implements the `RenderedImage` interface, and your thumbnail is a `BufferedImage`, so you have what you need to save the image thumbnail.

The `formatName` argument needs to be a simple `String` such as jpeg, png, or gif.

With the help of the previous `write()` methods, saving a single thumbnail becomes the following piece of code:

```
File snapshotFile = new File( .. );
try {
```

```
    ImageIO.write(thumbnailImage, "jpeg", snapshotFile);
} catch (Exception exception) {
    // appropriate exception handling here
}
```

By default, this saves the image as a medium-quality JPEG file.

Putting all the previous pieces together, you obtain the following refreshingly high-level saveScreenSnapshotAsThumbnail() routine to save game screen snapshots as JPEG thumbnail image files (see Listing 15.6).

Listing 15.6 saveScreenSnapshotAsThumbnail() Method

```
/*************************************************************************
 * Grab the visible screen, turn into thumbnail, and save as JPEG.
 *
 * @param screenRect the Rectangle defining the screen
 * @param thumbnailDimension the desired thumbnail Dimension
 * @param thumbnailFilename the generated JPEG filename
 *

 *************************************************************************/
private void saveScreenSnapshotAsThumbnail( Rectangle screenRect,
                       Dimension thumbnailDimension,
                       String thumbnailFilename) {

    BufferedImage screenImage = grabScreen(screenRect);

        BufferedImage screenThumbnail = new BufferedImage(
            thumbnailDimension.width,
            thumbnailDimension.height,
            BufferedImage.TYPE_INT_RGB);

        // scale the image
        Graphics2D g = screenThumbnail.createGraphics();
        g.setRenderingHint(RenderingHints.KEY_INTERPOLATION,
            RenderingHints.VALUE_INTERPOLATION_BILINEAR);
        g.drawImage(screenImage, 0, 0,
            thumbnailDimension.width,
            thumbnailDimension.height, null);
```

```
        g.dispose();
    try {
        ImageIO.write(screenThumbnail, "jpeg", new File(thumbnailFilename));
    } catch (Exception ignored) {
        System.out.println("OOPS " + ignored);
    }
}
```

Saving Games to the Right Destination

So far, your serialized objects and JPEG thumbnails have simply been "dumped" in the current directory. For a quality game, this approach is often not acceptable. Your game's players will appreciate any files generated by the program ending up in neatly organized folders, stored under one root directory that holds all game files. The logical question then becomes, "Where should this root directory be created?"

Every Java runtime environment defines a set of system properties that can be accessed via the static System.getProperty() routine:

```
String getProperty(String propertyName)
```

The complete list of properties can be obtained by calling the associated getProperties() method (note plural), but for your immediate game-saving needs, all you need to know is that there's one system property called user.home. This String property holds the filing system path for the current user's home directory. On Linux and Mac OS X, this directory will be something like /home/smith. On multiuser Windows systems such as Windows XP or Windows 2000, the directory is something like C:\Documents and Settings\smith, and on older, single-user Windows systems such as Windows 98, the directory is usually C:\WINDOWS. Via user.home, you can create a root game directory to hold all files that the game creates from time to time. Creating directories is achieved with a little help from File.mkdir().

Listing 15.7 shows how to implement this approach.

Listing 15.7   SaveGameState.java

```java
import java.io.*;

class SaveGameState {

private final static String GAME_ROOT          = "MyGame";
private final static String SAVED_GAMES     = "saved";

private void saveGame() {

    File gameDirectory = createGameDirectory();

    saveGameStateTo(gameDirectory);
}

private File createGameDirectory() {

    String userHome = System.getProperty("user.home");

    File dir = new File(userHome);

    dir = new File(dir, GAME_ROOT);
    if ( ! dir.exists() ) {
        dir.mkdir();
    }

    dir = new File(dir, SAVED_GAMES);
    if ( ! dir.exists() ) {
        dir.mkdir();
    }

    return dir;
}

private void saveGameStateTo(File gameDirectory) {
    // serialize and store all game state objects to specified dir.
}
```

```
public static void main (String[] args) {
    new SaveGameState().saveGame();
}

}
```

The guts of this example is the `createGameDirectory()` method. You start by finding out where the user's home directory is. From that point in the filing system, you add a new branch and subbranch to the hierarchy, one branch at a time. The end result is a `File` object pointing at the directory where you can safely and unobtrusively store the game's state.

Summary

Including a feature to save and reload the game isn't a luxury in today's competitive games market. Java's Serialization API provides a powerful standard mechanism to enable you to persist most of your game's internal state to disk, or any other destination external to the currently executing JVM.

Unfortunately, the Serialization API comes with a price tag: a learning curve, a degree of complexity, and more than a few potential pitfalls. This chapter showed you how to exploit the API while staying clear of the most common problems.

One final aspect of game saving required two additional APIs unrelated to serialization: Java's screenshot-grabbing `Robot` and the high-level JPEG-saving functionality of the Image I/O framework.

Part III

Tuning and Finishing Your Game

Chapter 16

Optimization Techniques

Back in the 19th century, an Italian economist named Vilfredo Pareto noticed something about the distribution of wealth in many countries: About 80% of the wealth was controlled by about 20% of the people.

Pareto's principle came to be known as the 80:20 rule, and since then, the basic idea has been applied to all sorts of other fields, including business sales, project management, and computer science.

What's that? Computer science, you say? Yup. The computer science version of this rule (or one of them, anyway) says that 80% of your program's time is spent in 20% of your code.

The good news here is the HotSpot VM: It finds that 20% (the "hot" code) and compiles it into optimized machine code.

However, HotSpot doesn't do everything. It doesn't perform every possible optimization, and it won't rewrite your code to use more efficient algorithms.

In this chapter, we talk about how to find that 20%, what optimizations HotSpot does and doesn't do, and memory usage and the garbage collector.

What's not in this chapter is size optimization (making classes as small as possible). Obfuscators take care of code size (which we talk about in Chapter 18, "Game Design and the Last 10%"), but for larger games, the bulk is really in resources such as maps, images, and 3D models, not in the code.

Optimization Rules

First off: a warning. Optimized methods can sometimes be much less readable than their unoptimized counterparts. Take, for example, the texture mapping code from Chapter 8, "Texture Mapping and Lighting." The simple, unoptimized code was just a few lines long, but the final optimized version grew to a few pages. Although the code is fast, unfortunately it's also less readable and more difficult to maintain. In past instances, I've optimized a method so much that I've forgotten how it works!

Also, hand-optimizing your code can introduce errors, such as rare bugs or different behavior in different situations. In short, optimized code can often become quite a mess.

So, when optimizing, consider these ideas:

➤ Don't optimize! First, attempt to create code that is easier to read, maintain, and modify.

➤ Optimize only methods that absolutely need it—the 20%.

➤ When you do optimize a method, it's a good idea to keep the original, unoptimized version in case you need to refer to it later.

➤ Make test cases to ensure the optimized method behaves the same as the unoptimized method.

➤ Don't bother optimizing in ways that HotSpot already does for you.

➤ If you try to optimize something and get zero benefit, undo the optimization.

With this in mind, let's get started on finding that 20%.

Profiling

Whether it's blitting sprites to the display or rendering 3D texture-mapped polygons, your game will spend most of its time in small areas of the code.

Although many times you can guess where the bulk of the code execution is, there almost always are surprises. Methods you think will be slow might turn out not to be slow at all, and methods you might have glanced over might be more computationally expensive than you thought.

Benchmarking

Benchmarking methods on your own can be wildly inaccurate. You can try to benchmark a method to see how long it takes by doing something like this:

```
int count = 1000000;
long startTime = System.currentTimeMillis();
for (int i=0; i<count; i++) {
    myCoolMethod();
}
long totalTime = System.currentTimeMillis() - startTime;
System.out.println("total time: " + totalTime);
```

This code calls a method a million times to see how long it takes.

What's happening here is that you're writing a micro-benchmark. Lots of things can have an effect on the results of this benchmark, such as current memory conditions and the granularity of your system timer (which we talk about later in this chapter). Furthermore, a method could perform well by itself but poorly in other situations, such as in the final game. Also, HotSpot could be performing optimizations that would work for the benchmark but not for the actual game. In short, it's best to profile your entire application rather than try to benchmark a method.

Using the HotSpot Profiler

Luckily, HotSpot has a thorough profiler that allows you to easily check where all that time is spent, whether it's in your code or in the Java APIs. Run your game with the -Xprof flag:

```
java -Xprof MyCoolGameClass
```

When the game exits, the profiler spits out profiling information to the console. These real-world results are more detailed, more useable, and easier to measure than trying to benchmark your game by hand.

The profiling data is broken down for each thread. Each thread has information for the interpreted, (HotSpot) compiled, and native methods that were called in that thread.

Compiled methods are the ones that HotSpot compiles into optimized code; the interpreted methods are the method that aren't compiled or optimized by HotSpot. The native methods are the methods in native code, most often operating system–specific code that HotSpot doesn't touch, of course.

Take a look at the example in Listing 16.1. This is a profiler output for the main thread of 3D engine from Chapter 11, "Collision Detection."

Listing 16.1 Profiled Main Thread

```
Flat profile of 179.23 secs (16583 total ticks): main

   Interpreted +   native     Method
   2.3%       0  +    379      sun.java2d.loops.Blit.Blit
   0.2%       2  +     32      sun.awt.windows.Win32SurfaceData.flip
   0.1%       0  +     21      com.brackeen.javagamebook.graphics.
                                    ScreenManager.setFullScreen
   0.1%      17  +      0      com.brackeen.javagamebook.test.
                                    GameCore.gameLoop
   0.1%       0  +     10      sun.java2d.loops.MaskFill.MaskFill
   0.0%       6  +      0      sun.awt.windows.WComponentPeer.flip
   0.0%       0  +      5      sun.java2d.loops.DrawGlyphList.
                                    DrawGlyphList
   0.0%       0  +      5      java.io.WinNTFileSystem.getLength
   0.0%       1  +      3      java.lang.System.currentTimeMillis
   0.0%       0  +      4      java.lang.Thread.sleep
   3.5%      76  +    509      Total interpreted (including elided)

     Compiled + native     Method
  59.9%    9933  +      0      com.brackeen.javagamebook.graphics3D.
```

				FastTexturedPolygonRenderer$ ShadedSurfaceRenderer.render
8.1%	1346	+	0	com.brackeen.javagamebook.bsp2D. BSPRenderer.setScanDepth
2.6%	435	+	0	com.brackeen.javagamebook.bsp2D. BSPRenderer.drawCurrentPolygon
2.3%	384	+	0	com.brackeen.javagamebook.graphics3D. ScanConverter.convert
1.7%	289	+	0	com.brackeen.javagamebook.graphics3D. SortedScanConverter$SortedScanList.add
1.7%	278	+	0	com.brackeen.javagamebook.graphics3D. SortedScanConverter.isFilled
1.3%	218	+	0	com.brackeen.javagamebook.graphics3D. SortedScanConverter$SortedScanList.add
1.0%	164	+	0	com.brackeen.javagamebook.graphics3D. SortedScanConverter.convert
0.7%	111	+	0	com.brackeen.javagamebook.graphics3D. SortedScanConverter$ SortedScanList.insert
0.5%	87	+	0	com.brackeen.javagamebook.math3D. Vector3D.rotateY
0.5%	80	+	0	com.brackeen.javagamebook.math3D. Vector3D.rotateZ
0.5%	78	+	0	com.brackeen.javagamebook.math3D. Vector3D.rotateX
0.4%	70	+	0	com.brackeen.javagamebook.graphics3D. ScanConverter.clearCurrentScan
0.4%	60	+	0	com.brackeen.javagamebook.math3D. ViewWindow.project
0.4%	60	+	0	com.brackeen.javagamebook.math3D. Polygon3D.isFacing
0.3%	54	+	0	com.brackeen.javagamebook.math3D. Polygon3D.clip
87.2%	14449	+	6	Total compiled (including elided)

	Stub	+	native	Method
8.1%	2	+	1343	sun.java2d.loops.Blit.Blit
0.5%	0	+	87	sun.awt.windows.Win32SurfaceData.flip

continues

Listing 16.1   Profiled Main Thread   *continued*

0.1%	1	+	12	java.lang.Float.floatToIntBits
0.0%	1	+	6	sun.awt.image.BufImgSurfaceData.
				getSurfaceData
0.0%	0	+	6	java.lang.StrictMath.pow
0.0%	2	+	3	java.lang.StrictMath.floor
0.0%	1	+	3	java.lang.Runtime.totalMemory
0.0%	0	+	3	java.lang.StrictMath.atan2
0.0%	0	+	2	java.lang.Runtime.freeMemory
0.0%	0	+	1	sun.java2d.loops.MaskFill.MaskFill
8.9%	8	+	1467	Total stub

Runtime	stub	+	native	Method
0.1%	18	+	0	interpreter_entries Runtime1 stub
0.0%	6	+	0	alignment_frame_return Runtime1 stub
0.1%	24	+	0	Total runtime stubs

Thread-local ticks:

0.0%	8	Blocked (of total)
0.1%	12	Class loader
0.1%	17	Interpreter
0.0%	7	Compilation

The amount of time the thread ran (179.23 seconds) is displayed at the top.

Most of this listing shows the amount of time spent in each method, in a percentage of the total time. It shows the "ticks" for interpreted, compiled, and native methods. The ticks are a measurement of time spent in each method.

At the bottom, you see 0.0% for "Blocked (of total)" This is the percentage of time this thread was blocked from executing. A thread can be blocked for several reasons, such as if it is sleeping or waiting for I/O, or if another thread is running. Because the amount of time this thread was blocked is very low, the nonblocked amount of time was very high, so you can tell this thread is taking up most of the processor for the game.

If you optimized this code based on the profiler output in Listing 16.1, obviously the texture mapping would be a first choice because it's hogging up 59.9%. Also note that the entire scan-conversion process involves several methods that total about 9.1%. This makes all the scan-conversion methods take more time than the single setScanDepth() method, which takes 8.1%. In short, scan conversion is taking more time than setting the Z-buffer.

Note that the compiled methods are the ones that HotSpot determines are "hot." For a long-running game, you probably won't see a lot of time spent in an interpreted method.

Profiling lists information for all the threads, not just the ones you create. You'll see AWT-EventQueue-0 and AWT-Shutdown, among others. These threads will be blocked most of the time.

One other thread I want to show is AWT-Windows, here in Listing 16.2.

Listing 16.2   Profiled AWT-Windows Thread

```
Flat profile of 181.55 secs (16723 total ticks): AWT-Windows
   Interpreted +   native     Method
  99.9%       0  +   16699      sun.awt.windows.WToolkit.eventLoop
   0.0%       1  +       1      java.util.EventObject.<init>
   0.0%       0  +       2      sun.awt.PostEventQueue.postEvent
   0.0%       1  +       0      java.awt.event.ComponentEvent.<init>
   0.0%       0  +       1      sun.awt.SunToolkit.wakeupEventQueue
   0.0%       0  +       1      java.awt.EventQueue.wakeup
   0.0%       1  +       0      java.awt.AWTEvent.<init>
   0.0%       1  +       0
java.util.WeakHashMap.expungeStaleEntries
  99.9%       4  +   16704      Total interpreted

      Compiled +   native     Method
   0.0%       0  +       2      sun.awt.AWTAutoShutdown.setToolkitBusy
   0.0%       1  +       0      java.awt.event.InputEvent.getModifiers
   0.0%       1  +       0      java.awt.GraphicsEnvironment.
                                  getHeadlessProperty
   0.0%       0  +       1      java.awt.EventQueue.wakeup
```

continues

Listing 16.2   Profiled `AWT-Windows` **Thread**   *continued*

```
0.0%       2  +      3        Total compiled


         Stub +    native   Method
0.0%       0  +      1        sun.awt.SunToolkit.wakeupEventQueue
0.0%       0  +      1        Total stub


Runtime stub +    native   Method
0.0%       1  +      0        monitorexit Runtime1 stub
0.0%       1  +      0        Total runtime stubs


Thread-local ticks:
0.0%       2                 Blocked (of total)
0.0%       6                 Compilation
```

As you can see, this thread also shows that it's blocked 0.0% of the time. Does this mean the `AWT-Windows` thread is hogging the processor, with the `eventLoop()` native method taking 99.9% of the time?

Luckily, no, it's not. Whew! The profiler isn't foolproof. In this case, the `eventLoop()` method is blocked most of the time, waiting for events, but it's blocked in native code (all of its 16,699 ticks are shown in the native column). The profiler can't detect that a thread is blocked if it's blocked in native code. Therefore, you can't estimate time spent in native code in cases like this.

Finally, at the end of the profiler output you get a summary:

```
Global summary of 181.75 seconds:
100.0% 16830              Received ticks
  0.1%    13              Received GC ticks
  0.1%    25              Compilation
  0.4%    75              Other VM operations
  0.1%    13              Class loader
  0.1%    18              Interpreter
  0.0%     8              Unknown code
```

The summary in this case is great news because so little time is spent in garbage collection, compilation, and all the other things the VM does.

Another method to profile your code is with the -Xrunhprof flag. This has more detailed information and can also monitor the heap, but it is in a format that is less easy to read. For all the options for this flag, run this command:

```
java -Xrunhprof:help
```

HotSpot

As you know, instead of compiling to native machine code, Java source is compiled to bytecodes in the form of class files.

In the beginning, Java VMs were interpreters, deciphering one byte code at a time in a loop.

Faster JIT (Just In Time) compilers appeared later, which compiled byte code to native code. A JIT compiler is basically a fast compiler that compiles at runtime. When a Java class is loaded, it is quickly compiled, even if methods in the class are used only once.

Today you have HotSpot, a dynamic optimizing compiler. With HotSpot, methods are interpreted at first. When a method is called enough times—in other words, it's "hot"—HotSpot compiles and optimizes it. Also, HotSpot can use global analysis to better optimize, tuning those optimizations as the program runs, and to perform aggressive inlining. Inlining reduces the overhead of calling an often-used method.

Two HotSpot VMs exist: client and server. The server has a few more optimizations than the client does. However, whereas the SDK includes both the client and server VMs, the JRE includes only the client VM.

In addition to a few Java-specific optimizations, HotSpot implements many of the standard optimizations found in common C/C++ compilers, such as dead code elimination, loop invariant hoisting, common subexpression elimination, constant propagation, method inlining, and loop unrolling. We'll go over each of these optimizations so you'll know you don't have to perform these optimizations yourself.

Java-Specific Optimizations

These are some of the Java-specific optimizations HotSpot performs:

➤ **Fast synchronization.** If two threads aren't trying to run the same method ("contention"), the method call is comparable in speed to a normal, unsynchronized method call. However, synchronized methods cannot be inlined.

➤ **Null check elimination.** If HotSpot can prove that a field will never be null, it can remove the null check in the optimized code.

➤ **Range check elimination.** Likewise, if HotSpot can prove that an array access will never be out or range, it can remove the range check in the optimized code.

In the next few sections, we show the performance optimizations that HotSpot performs on example code. Of course, HotSpot works with bytecode and machine code, not source code. But we'll show the equivalent source code version of what HotSpot is doing.

Dead Code Elimination

Dead code elimination is a technique to remove code that has no effect on the execution of the code. Take this function, for example:

```java
public int function(int x) {
    int i = 100*x*x;
    return x;
}
```

Here, the i variable is set, but it's never used. So, HotSpot would eliminate the dead code:

```java
public int function(int x) {
```

```
        return x;
}
```

Loop Invariant Hoisting

An *invariant* is something that doesn't change, such as a constant. Loop invariant hoisting (also called loop invariant code motion) is essentially moving invariants out of loops so they don't have to be recomputed over and over again. Take this loop, for example:

```
for (int i=0; i<array.length; i++) {
    int y = 4*x*x + 2*x;
    array[i] = y + i;
}
```

Here, the value y is the invariant because its value never changes while inside the loop. Its computation can be moved out of the loop:

```
int y = 4*x*x + 2*x;
for (int i=0; i<array.length; i++) {
    array[i] = y + i;
}
```

Common Subexpression Elimination

Subexpressions that are common (in other words, those that are seen more than once) can be eliminated by HotSpot. Consider this example:

```
int a = 4*x*x + 2*x + 3;
int b = 4*x*x + 2*x + 5;
```

You can precompute most of those two equations:

```
int temp = 4*x*x + 2*x;
int a = temp + 3;
int b = temp + 5;
```

Performing common subexpression elimination often makes code easier to read and can make code more maintainable if you have to modify the subexpression. So there's no harm in performing this optimization trick yourself.

Constant Propagation

A constant multiplied by a constant is still a constant. That's the basic idea with constant propagation, in which expressions involving constants (and no variables) are calculated only once, instead of over and over again. For example, this code:

```
int x = 10; // constant
int a = 5*x;  // therefore, also constant
```

would be compiled to:

```
int a = 50;
```

Loop Unrolling (Server VM Only)

Take a look at a typical loop:

```
for (int i=0; i<array.length; i++) {
    array[i] *= y;
}
```

The loop can be "unrolled" so that each statement is executed several times:

```
// (4 is a factor of array.length)
for (int i=0; i<array.length; i+=4) {
    array[i] *= y;
    array[i+1] *= y;
    array[i+2] *= y;
    array[i+3] *= y;
}
```

This speeds things up a bit by reducing the overhead of the loop itself: In the example, the check for the end of the loop and the counter increment occur four times less.

However, this feature is in the HotSpot server VM only.

Method Inlining

One of HotSpot's strengths is its aggressive inlining capabilities. *Inlining code* reduces the overhead of calling a method. Take a glance at this example:

```
for (int i=0; i<array.length; i++) {
    array[i] = mathObject.calc(i);
}

...

public class MathClass {
    public void calc(int x) {
        return x * 5;
    }
}
```

The inlined code would look like this:

```
for (int i=0; i<array.length; i++) {
    array[i] = x * 5;
}
```

Aggressive method inlining is one of HotSpot's strengths. In languages such as C++, all methods are nonvirtual by default, meaning subclasses cannot override them. But in Java, the opposite is true: All methods are virtual by default, and methods are declared final to signify that they are nonvirtual. The good news is that HotSpot can analyze classes at runtime to determine whether a method is overridden by another class (thus, it is truly virtual). If not, the method can be inlined, even if it's not declared final.

The example back in Chapter 8 is a good example for tuning the code to make HotSpot perform inlining. In that example, you had an abstract Texture class and two subclasses, PowerOf2Texture and ShadedTexture. Unfortunately, when the reference was a Texture instead of one of its subclasses, HotSpot could not inline the virtual getColor() method. However, the getColor() methods of PowerOf2Texture and ShadedTexture were not virtual, so referencing these subclasses explicitly meant that HotSpot could perform inlining. In other words, instead of this:

```
Texture texture; // has virtual methods
```

you did this:

```
PowerOf2Texture texture; // has no virtual methods
```

HotSpot then could inline the `getColor()` method.

HotSpot cannot inline a couple other types of methods as well. In short, HotSpot cannot inline methods that do the following:

➤ Explicitly throw exceptions (unchecked methods, such as `NullPointerException`, are okay)

➤ Are synchronized

➤ Are overridden by another class (truly virtual)

Optimization Tricks

In this section, we go over some optimization tricks that HotSpot doesn't automatically do for you. Many of these are strength-reduction optimizations, which is simply a way to calculate a function more efficiently. We also talk about lookup tables and fixed-point math.

Algorithms

First, though, let's talk about algorithms. Choosing a better algorithm will give you better performance than applying other optimization tricks. An example is using a BSP tree instead of sorting polygons by z-depth or arranging objects so that fewer collision tests need to be made. Use your head and think creatively: Whenever you're using a "brute force" algorithm, try to come up with something better.

Here are a few examples of using the right algorithms in the Java collection classes:

➤ Use a fast sort algorithm, such as QuickSort instead of Bubble Sort.

`Arrays.sort()` and `Collections.sort()` use a tuned QuickSort algorithm.

➤ Use a `HashMap` for quick searches. Using a `HashMap` is faster than iterating through a `List`.

➤ Choose the right list: `LinkedList` has faster insertion and removal, but `ArrayList` has faster random access. The `Vector` class is like `ArrayList`, but with synchronized methods.

Also with lists, think about how you traverse them. Because an `ArrayList` has random access, you can use something like this:

```
// works fine for ArrayList, slower for LinkedList
for (int i=0; i<list.size(); i++) {
    System.out.println(list.get(i));
}
```

But this wouldn't work as well for a `LinkedList` because the `get()` method searches through the list to find the index you're looking for. Instead, use an `Iterator` to traverse the items in a `LinkedList`:

```
// works better for LinkedList
Iterator i = list.iterator();
while (i.hasNext()) {
    System.out.println(i.next());
}
```

Besides these basic examples, a great way to find some more ideas is to just pick up an algorithm textbook. (Well, you might have to read it, too.)

Strength Reduction: Bit Shifting

Remember that internally to the computer, numbers are stored as binary values, as in 1001011. With binary math, you can perform all sorts of neat operations, such as ultra-fast bit shifting.

If you shift bits to the left, you have the same effect as multiplying by 2. In Java, shifting to the left looks like this:

```
(x << 1)
```

This statement shifts the bits to the left by 1, resulting in a multiplication of 2. Likewise, shifting over 2 bits is the same as multiplying by 4, and by 3 bits is the same as multiplying by 8.

In short, multiplications of a power of 2 can be reduced using bit shifting. Instead of this:

```
int a = x * 32;
```

the bit-shifting version would be this:

```
int a = x << 5;
```

Likewise, the same works for division, only to the right. This division:

```
int a = x / 32;
```

becomes this:

```
int a = x >> 5;
```

This optimization varies in usefulness depending on the processor. Some processors show no speed increase because integer multiplication and division is pretty fast anyway, but other processors show a modest improvement.

Strength Reduction: Modulus

If you're performing a modulus operation on a power of 2, such as this:

```
int a = x % 32;
```

you can use the super-fast & operator instead. This involves using a bitmask, where the bitmask is the modulus number minus 1. For example, the binary value of 32 is 100000, and the bitmask is 011111 (or 31 in decimal form). So, using the & operator and the bitmask, you get this:

```
int a = x & 31;
```

Note that this works only for powers of 2.

Strength Reduction: Multiplication

Sometimes you want to calculate an entire series of multiplications, like this:

```
for (int i=0; i<array.length; i++) {
    array[i] = x*i;
}
```

In this example, if x was 5, the result would be 0, 5, 10, 15, 20, and so on. See the pattern? Instead of multiplying in each iteration of the loop, you can use addition, which is faster than multiplication. Here, you start with a value of 0 and add x to this value every iteration of the loop:

```
value = 0;
for (int i=0; i<array.length; i++) {
    array[i] = value;
    value+=x;
}
```

Strength Reduction: Exponentiation

Similarly to how you reduced multiplication to addition, you can reduce exponentiation to multiplication. Here's an example:

```
for (int i=0; i<array.length; i++) {
    array[i] = (int)Math.pow(x,i);
}
```

So, if x was 5, the result would be 1, 5, 25, 125, 625, and so on. Here, each number is simply the previous number times 5. Instead of calculating using the expensive pow() function, you can use a series of multiplications:

```
value = 1;
for (int i=0; i<array.length; i++) {
    array[i] = value;
```

```
    value*=x;
}
```

Both the multiplication and exponentiation examples show how to recognize patterns in a series of numbers and to base a calculation off the previous result rather than from scratch. Be sure to use this idea for other number patterns as well.

More Loop Invariant Hoisting

It's generally a good idea to move as much code out of a loop as possible so that those statements aren't executed repeatedly within the loop. HotSpot cannot do every loop invariant optimization itself. Here are a couple more examples.

In this first example, the `if` statement is executed for every iteration of the loop, even though the result of the statement will never change while in the loop:

```
for (int i=0; i < 1000; i++) {
    if (bool) {
        doSomething();
    }
}
```

So, move the `if` statement out of the loop:

```
if (bool) {
    for (int i=0; i < 1000; i++) {
        doSomething();
    }
}
```

In this next example, the exact same `Color` objects are created every time a line is drawn:

```
for (int i=0; i < 100; i++) {
    g.setColor(new Color(0xff3366));
    g.drawLine(i*10, 0, i*10+100, 100);
    g.setColor(new Color(0xff3366));
```

```
    g.drawLine(i*10+1, 0, i*10+101, 100);
}
```

So, you can move the object creation out of the loop:

```
Color red = new Color(0xff3366);
Color blue = new Color(0x6633ff);
for (int i=0; i < 100; i++) {
    g.setColor(red);
    g.drawLine(i*10, 0, i*10+100, 100);
    g.setColor(blue);
    g.drawLine(i*10+1, 0, i*10+101, 100);
}
```

Lookup Tables

Another age-old optimization trick is to use lookup tables for computationally expensive functions. Lookup tables work by calculating many values of an expensive function and storing the results in a table. Later, the game can just look up a value from the table instead of computing it every time. This takes up a small amount of memory but makes things run faster.

For example, instead of computing an equation:

```
y = computeFunction(x);
```

you can get the value from a table, where x is the index in the table:

```
y = table[x];
```

The drawback to lookup tables is that you have to limit the number of values that you precompute. However, in many cases you won't need every possible value anyway.

For an example, you'll create a sine and cosine lookup table. For these trig functions, you usually want to compute the radian values from 0 to 2π. However, you can't use the values from 0 to 2π as indices in an array. There are only six integer values between those numbers, and you want way more than six precomputed values.

In this case, use your own system instead of radians. In this system, you can create

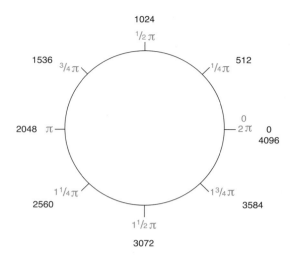

4,096 precomputed values, from 0 to 4095. The value 2048 would be the same as π, and 4096 would be the same as 2π. To get a visual picture, take a look at Figure 16.1.

Figure 16.1   The conversion from radians (0 to 2π) to your own system (0 to 4096).

I pretty much picked 4096 arbitrarily. A value as low as 256, for instance, wouldn't be enough granularity, but 4096 gives pretty good results.

Also, by using 4,096 values, which is a power of 2, you can easily keep values within a valid range. If you want the cosine of –200 or the sine of 5,000, you can translate the value using the & operator with the bitmask:

```
x = x & 4095
```

Also, you can take advantage of one little trick with this equation:

```
cos(x)  =  sin(π/2-x)
```

Using this equation, you can get the cosine of a value from the sine lookup table. So, for both cosine and sine, you only need one table, not two.

Now you'll implement a lookup table. The complete code is in Listing 16.3 and is part of the MoreMath class.

Listing 16.3   Trig Table Functions in MoreMath.java

```java
package com.brackeen.javagamebook.util;

/**
    The MoreMath class provides functions not contained in the
    java.lang.Math or java.lang.StrictMath classes.
*/
public class MoreMath {

    // a trig table with 4096 entries
    private static final int TABLE_SIZE_BITS = 12;
    private static final int TABLE_SIZE = 1 << TABLE_SIZE_BITS;
    private static final int TABLE_SIZE_MASK = TABLE_SIZE - 1;
    private static final int HALF_PI = TABLE_SIZE / 4;
    private static final float CONVERSION_FACTOR =
        (float)(TABLE_SIZE / (2 * Math.PI));

    private static float[] sinTable;

    // init trig table when this class is loaded
    static {
        init();
    }

    private static void init() {
        sinTable = new float[TABLE_SIZE];
        for (int i=0; i<TABLE_SIZE; i++) {
            sinTable[i] = (float)Math.sin(i / CONVERSION_FACTOR);
        }
    }


    /**
        Cosine function, where angle is from 0 to 4096 instead of
        0 to 2pi.
    */
    public static float cos(int angle) {
        return sinTable[(HALF_PI-angle) & TABLE_SIZE_MASK];
```

continues

Listing 16.3   Trig Table Functions in MoreMath.java   *continued*

```java
    }


    /**
        Sine function, where angle is from 0 to 4096 instead of
        0 to 2pi.
    */
    public static float sin(int angle) {
        return sinTable[angle & TABLE_SIZE_MASK];
    }


    /**
        Converts an angle in radians to the system used by this
        class (0 to 2pi becomes 0 to 4096)
    */
    public static int angleConvert(float angleInRadians) {
        return  (int)(angleInRadians * CONVERSION_FACTOR);
    }
}
```

When this class loads, the static init() method is called, which initiates the lookup table for sine. Also included is a function to convert radians to the system this class uses, in the angleConvert() method.

The sin() and cos() functions return the floating-point value for the specified angle.

Of course, lookup tables don't have to be limited to trig functions. They can be used for more complicated formulas. You could also use them on the server side, to cache expensive lookups from the database. Use tables wherever they will help speed things up.

Fixed-Point Math

We covered fixed-point math in Chapter 7, "3D Graphics," so I won't repeat it here. Just keep in mind that floating-point arithmetic can sometimes be too slow, especially for operations such as converting a float to an int. Fixed-point math can help speed it up, but it also has a couple drawbacks: less accuracy and overflow issues when multiplying two fixed-point values.

Exceptions

Using exceptions can hurt HotSpot compilation and also limit what HotSpot can inline.

First, don't catch exceptions if you don't need to. For example:

```
try {
    return array[index];
}
catch (ArrayIndexOutOfBoundsException ex) {
    // do nothing
}
```

Instead, just perform the bounds check yourself:

```
if (index > 0 && index < array.length)
    return array[index];
}
```

Of course, exceptions are commonly used in object-oriented systems, and many times throwing an exception won't noticeably hurt performance. Take this example:

```
public void takeItem(Item item) throws InventoryFullException;
```

In a game, a player might not pick up an item very often, so something like this would not hurt performance.

Input/Output

I/O can be one of the bottlenecks of a game, mainly because you have to wait for something slow to occur, such as accessing the hard drive or getting bytes from a painstakingly slow modem. Here are a few tips on making I/O a little easier to deal with:

> ➤ Use `BufferedInputStream` (for binary files) and `BufferedReader` (for text files). These classes read chunks of data at a time instead of 1 byte at a time. This will help no matter what you're reading from, either a file or a stream from the server.

➤ Perform I/O in a separate thread from your main loop. Reading and writing to a file or communicating with a server takes some time, so there's no reason to cause the game to appear to "freeze" when you're performing I/O.

➤ Consider combining several little files into one big file so that fewer files have to be opened.

➤ For large files (several megabytes), consider using memory-mapped files.

What? Memory-mapped files, what's that all about? Hey, I'm glad you asked.

Memory-Mapped Files

Memory-mapped files are files on, say, a hard drive, that are mapped to a region of memory. Programs can read from memory-mapped files just like reading from memory. Sections of the file are copied and removed from memory as needed.

To memory-map a file for reading, just open the file as usual and use the `FileChannel` class to map it to a buffer:

```
File file = new File(filename);
FileInputStream stream = new FileInputStream(file);
MappedByteBuffer buffer = stream.getChannel().map(
    FileChannel.MapMode.READ_ONLY, 0, file.length());
stream.close();
```

The `map()` method allows you to map any part of the file you want. Here, you're mapping the entire file. The method returns a `MappedByteBuffer`.

After the file is mapped, you can close the original stream (`stream.close()`).

The operating system handles the memory management of the file. Typically, none of the files is loaded into memory until you start reading from it.

You can read from the file using any of `MappedByteBuffer`'s `get()` methods. Here's an example to copy a portion of the file to a 1KB array:

```
byte[] array = new byte[1024];
buffer.get(array);
```

A memory-mapped file is unmapped after it is garbage-collected. So, when you're done with the file, you can just clear the reference so that the garbage collector can do its work:

```
buffer = null;
```

Memory-mapped files don't always give a performance increase. With smaller files, memory-mapped files will probably be slower, and you won't see much of a difference if you're reading a file sequentially. But memory-mapped files are great for large files that need random access, such as databases or large map files with embedded textures.

Memory Usage and the Garbage Collector

When working with memory and garbage collection, keep a couple goals in mind:

➤ Don't use too much memory for the target system you're writing the game for, whether it's 64MB or 256MB.

➤ Try to limit garbage-collection pauses as much as possible.

Pauses due to the garbage collector can make your game seem jerky. However, if you limit the number of objects you create per frame and tweak the Java heap settings, you can get around many garbage-collection pauses. In this section, we go over some techniques to monitor memory usage and tune heap settings to get things to run a bit more smoothly.

The Java Heap and Garbage Collection

Java memory is stored in a *heap*—a large chunk of memory—that is managed by the VM. This has a few advantages over letting the operating system manage memory because HotSpot can optimize memory management for typical Java apps.

By default, HotSpot starts with a small heap, such as one a couple megabytes. As more objects are created, the heap grows as needed.

When no more references to an object exist, HotSpot can clear the object from the heap. This is called garbage collection.

Note that some memory exists outside the heap, such as NIO buffers, memory-mapped files, or images in video memory.

The heap is partitioned into two sections: young and tenured. Objects are first created in the young section. Object creation in this section is fast, often involving just a pointer increment. If an object is around long enough, it is moved to the tenured section.

The idea here is that most objects are around for only a short amount of time. For example, an `Iterator` object created to traverse the items in a list usually is in use for a short time. HotSpot can clear the unreferenced objects in the young section fairly quickly, so creating a few short-lived objects won't have much of an impact on performance.

Clearing unreferenced objects in the tenured section is a bit slower, however, because this section is larger and involves many long-lived objects. This is where you might see a noticeable pause from the garbage collection. Ideally, you want to limit tenured garbage collections as much as possible.

To do this, though, you need to take a look at how much memory the game is using and when the garbage collections occur.

Monitoring Garbage Collection

Garbage collection can impact game performance, but luckily there are some ways to make it a less significant issue. You can't get rid of garbage collection completely, but you can make its effects almost negligible. First, though, it's a good idea to monitor garbage collection to get a good idea of how your game is handled by the garbage collector.

You can get on information whenever garbage collection occurs by using the `-verbose:gc` flag:

```
java -verbose:gc MyCoolGameClass
[GC 16373K->16311K(17760K), 0.0028920 secs]
[GC 17316K->17311K(18568K), 0.0028735 secs]
[Full GC 17311K->6412K(18568K), 0.0587969 secs]
```

Each line shows a particular garbage collection. Garbage collections that involve just the young section are marked as GC, and garbage collections that involve the tenured section are marked as Full GC.

The first numbers (17311K->6412K) show the amount of memory used before and after the garbage collection. The number in parenthesis (18568K) is the total heap space (not including some of the heap used by HotSpot itself).

Finally, the amount of time taken to perform the collection is shown. As you can see, the young garbage collections took only about 3ms each, which doesn't have a significant effect on performance. However, the tenured garbage collection (Full GC) took almost 60ms, which results in a few dropped frames. For example, if it takes 20ms to draw a frame (50 frames per second), the garbage collection took the time to draw about 3 frames.

You can get more details from the garbage collections by using the -XX:+PrintGCDetails flag:

```
java -verbose:gc -XX:+PrintGCDetails MyCoolGameClass
[GC [DefNew: 1123K->0K(1152K), 0.0027800 secs]
     14013K->14012K(16292K), 0.0028174 secs]
[GC [DefNew: 376K->1K(1152K), 0.0013854 secs]
     14388K->14388K(16292K), 0.0014222 secs]
[GC [DefNew: 1014K->1K(1152K), 0.0026643 secs]
     [Tenured: 15396K->12400K(16152K), 0.0415779 secs]
     15401K->12400K(17304K), 0.0443534 secs]
```

Here, the garbage collections are broken down into the young section (DefNew) and the tenured section. The size of each section is shown, along with the total size. Here, the young section is 1152K, and the tenured section is 16,152K. Again, the young garbage collections took about 2–3ms, but the tenured collections took a total of about 45ms.

Luckily, a few dropped frames are not noticeable, so the garbage collector isn't having much of an impact in this case.

You can get still more garbage collection information by using the -XX:+PrintGCTimeStamps flag. This flag prints the time stamps of each garage collection, so you can get a good look at how often the collections occur. By adding a time stamp to your own logging, you can also easily match up when garbage collection is occurring relative to important sections of your own code.

Monitoring Memory Usage

If you're creating 20KB of garbage every time you draw a frame, at 60 frames per second, that comes out to about 1.2MBps, or nearly 12MB every 10 seconds. That's a lot of junk, a lot more work for the garbage collector to do. So, it's important to monitor the rate at which memory is allocated in your game, to get an idea of how you can tune the heap to better suit your needs.

You can get information on the memory that each object uses by using the -Xaprof flag:

```
java -Xaprof MyCoolGameClass
Allocation profile (sizes in bytes, cutoff = 0 bytes):
____Size__Instances__Average__Class_____
39954200        590      67719  [S
 2949360      10406        283  [B
 2838936     118289         24  com.brackeen...Vector3D
 1036904       9062        114  [C
  718848       3744        192  sun.java2d.SunGraphics2D
  475008      29688         16  sun.awt.MostRecentKeyValue
  421400       7525         56  java.awt.event.MouseEvent
  298464      18654         16  java.awt.Point
  273960      11415         24  java.lang.ref.WeakReference
  245936       3942         62  [Ljava.lang.Object;
  239680       3745         64  java.awt.geom.AffineTransform
  212736       8864         24  java.awt.EventQueueItem
  203760       8490         24  java.lang.String
  161504       5047         32  java.util.LinkedList$ListItr
  149760       3744         40  sun.java2d.loops.FontInfo
  141632       8852         16  sun.awt.EventQueueItem
  130560       8160         16  com.brackeen...ScanConverter$Scan
```

```
129600          5400          24    java.util.HashMap$Entry
119840          3745          32    sun.java2d.pipe.Region
114864          4786          24    java.util.LinkedList$Entry
```

In this list, `[S` is a short array, `[B` is a byte array, `[C` is a char array (often used in the `String` class), and `[Ljava.lang.Object` is an array of objects (often used for `ArrayList`).

This gives a look of every object that lived at one point or another, not necessarily the memory usage at any particular time. Keep this in mind when interpreting results. For example, a new `sun.java2d.SunGraphics2D` object was created for every frame drawn, and the total size of all those objects was about 700KB, even though probably only one of those objects was referenced at any given time.

Obviously, a lot of these objects, such as the `WeakReference` and `MouseEvent` objects, are created by the Java API itself.

In this example, the short arrays, used for polygon surfaces and usually created only once, take up the most amount of space. Using MIP mapping (as discussed in Chapter 8) to create smaller surfaces for distance polygons would help reduce this usage.

The `Vector3D` objects are using a large amount of space as well. This can be helped in a couple ways: First, `Vector3D` objects can be shared more often (in the current state, some abutting polygons have equal vertices but use different `Vector3D` instances). Second, there is a large overhead per object. You need only 12 bytes of data (4 bytes each for x, y, and z), but with object overhead and rounding to the 8-byte boundary, it comes out to 24 bytes per object. One idea to fix this is to create a `Vector3DList` object that would hold a list of vectors in an array like this:

```
float[] x, y, z;
```

This would reduce object overhead but would give array-access overhead instead.

Because using `-Xaprof` gives a look at only memory used by the instances of each class, you need another way to monitor memory during the game.

The Runtime class has a few methods to monitor the heap usage, notably totalMemory() and freeMemory(), which return the heap size and the amount of free heap space, respectively.

You can use these methods to monitor the memory usage from frame to frame so you can see how much memory you're allocating (or garbage you're creating) every time you render a frame. To get the amount of memory allocated, just use totalMemory()-freeMemory(). This is summed up in the MemMonitor class in Listing 16.4.

Listing 16.4   MemMonitor.java

```
package com.brackeen.javagamebook.util;

/**
    Monitors heap size, allocation size, change in allocation,
    change in heap size, and detects garbage collection (when the
    allocation size decreases). Call takeSample() to take a
    "sample" of the current memory state.
*/
public class MemMonitor {

    /**
        The Data class contains info on a series of float values.
        The min, max, sum, and count of the data can be retrieved.
    */
    public static class Data {

        float lastValue = 0;
        float min = Float.MAX_VALUE;
        float max = Float.MIN_VALUE;
        float sum = 0;
        int count = 0;

        public void addValue(float value) {
            lastValue = value;
            sum+=value;
            count++;
            min = Math.min(min, value);
```

```
            max = Math.max(max, value);
        }


    public String toString() {
        return "Min: " + toByteFormat(min) + "   " +
               "Max: " + toByteFormat(max) + "   " +
               "Avg: " + toByteFormat(sum / count);
    }
}

private Data heapSize = new Data();
private Data allocSize = new Data();
private Data allocIncPerUpdate = new Data();
private int numHeapIncs = 0;
private long startTime = System.currentTimeMillis();


/**
    Takes a sample of the current memory state.
*/
public void takeSample() {
    Runtime runtime = Runtime.getRuntime();
    long currHeapSize = runtime.totalMemory();
    long currAllocSize = currHeapSize - runtime.freeMemory();

    if (currHeapSize > heapSize.lastValue) {
        numHeapIncs++;
    }
    if (currAllocSize >= allocSize.lastValue) {
        allocIncPerUpdate.addValue(
            (currAllocSize - allocSize.lastValue));
    }

    heapSize.addValue(currHeapSize);
    allocSize.addValue(currAllocSize);
}
```

continues

Listing 16.4 MemMonitor.java *continued*

```java
/**
    Convert number of bytes to string representing bytes,
    kilobytes, megabytes, etc.
*/
public static String toByteFormat(float numBytes) {
    String[] labels = {" bytes", " KB", " MB", " GB"};
    int labelIndex = 0;

    // decide most appropriate label
    while (labelIndex < labels.length - 1 && numBytes > 1024) {
        numBytes/=1024;
        labelIndex++;
    }
    return (Math.round(numBytes*10)/10f) + labels[labelIndex];
}


public String toString() {
    long time = System.currentTimeMillis() - startTime;
    float timeSecs = (float)time / 1000;
    return "Total Time: " + timeSecs + "s\n" +
        "Heap: " + heapSize + "\n" +
        "Allocation: " + allocSize + "\n" +
        "Allocation inc/update: " + allocIncPerUpdate + "\n" +
        "Num Heap Incs: " + numHeapIncs;
}
}
```

In this code, the takeSample() method records the current state of the heap usage. In a game, you call this method after drawing every frame.

The toString() method returns a string presenting statistics of the samples taken.

I ran the test using the 3D engine from Chapter 11 using the flags -verbose:gc and -XX:+PrintGCDetails and got these results:

```
Total Time: 241.859s
Heap: Min: 10.7 MB   Max: 63.6 MB   Avg: 51.8 MB
Allocation: Min: 5.5 MB   Max: 43.3 MB   Avg: 34.1 MB
Allocation inc/update: Min: 384.0 bytes   Max: 8.5 MB   Avg: 6.1 KB
Num Heap Incs: 5
```

Also, it reported 73 young garbage collections and 15 tenured garbage collections. That's one garbage collection about every 2.75 seconds!

With this information, you can get an idea about how much memory the game allocates at a maximum (about 44MB). A lot of the garbage collections occur because you start with a small heap that grows in size. When the heap is small, the VM might work harder on garbage collections to try to keep everything in memory.

If the memory monitor is accurate, it appears as if drawing a frame requires a minimum of 384 bytes, but on average, you're creating 6.1KB per frame. In this example, a lot of the allocation is caused by created polygon surfaces, which are generally permanent, but things such as new objects for projectiles are also created.

Using this information, let's try to tune the heap a little to give fewer garbage collections.

Tuning the Heap

Let's make a goal with the game: Make one garbage collection every 10 seconds, and make the time required to perform a garbage collection short enough that only a frame or so is dropped each time.

First pick a heap size. Note that the bigger the heap is, the longer a garbage collection will take. You don't want to just create an arbitrarily large heap.

From the previous test, you know the game uses about 44MB and that the max heap size is about 64MB. So, just start with a 64MB heap. You can specify the starting heap size by using the -Xms flag, like this:

```
java -Xms64m MyCoolGameClass
```

Next, you know you are creating about 6.1KB per frame. This is just an estimate, and probably an inaccurate one, but it gives you an idea. If you want to collect the garbage once every 10 seconds and you want garbage-collection times to be short, make sure all the memory you create over 10 seconds fits in the young section of the heap. At 60 frames per second, that's 3660KB every 10 seconds. Make sure the young section starts off with about 4MB. You can specify the starting young size with the -Xmn flag, like this:

```
java -Xmn4m MyCoolGameClass
```

Okay, let's try it out! I ran the test again with these flags:

```
-Xms64m -Xmn4m -verbose:gc -XX:+PrintGCDetails
```

I got these results:

```
Total Time: 248.094s
Heap: Min: 63.6 MB   Max: 63.6 MB   Avg: 63.6 MB
Allocation: Min: 10.1 MB   Max: 42.7 MB   Avg: 38.8 MB
Allocation inc/update: Min: 384.0 bytes   Max: 10.1 MB   Avg: 3.1 KB
Num Heap Incs: 1
```

Also, it reported 19 young garbage collections, each between 2ms and 16ms, and no tenured garbage collections. At 248 seconds, that's about one minor garbage collection every 13 seconds, and at 60 frames per second, a 16ms garbage collection results in only one dropped frame. Not bad!

You met your goal, but this time you also got a lowered average allocation per frame, at 3.1KB. This could be due to many factors, but my guess is that polygon surfaces are kept in memory the entire time because there is enough heap space. With a smaller heap, polygon surfaces might have been flushed out and then re-created later.

Notice that these tests were very simple because you ran the demos for only about four minutes. You should gather more data, such as what happens with longer play (20 minutes or more) and with more runs of the game, before making any final decisions on heap tuning.

Also, the MemMonitor class could easily be extended to show a visual representation of memory usage within the game. Or, when the game exits, the class could spit out a graph of memory usage from the start of the game until the end. This could help recognize the rate of memory creation for typical scenes and what scenarios cause memory usage to jump.

Tuning the Garbage Collector

Within a program, you can always force a garbage collection yourself by calling this:

```
System.gc();
```

For most applications, Sun recommends you don't call this method. However, for games, it might be a good idea to perform a garbage collection in certain situations, such as right before starting a new level or after the startup sequence, if you know you're creating a lot of garbage during those times. This way, you get off to a clean start.

Besides the default garbage collector, HotSpot has a few more collectors that might work better in different situations. Here's a quick overview of the available collectors:

➤ **Incremental garbage collector** (-Xingc). Also called the train garbage collector. This garbage collector spreads larger garbage collections over time instead of having longer pauses due to major garbage collections. Unfortunately, this garbage collector uses a lot of processor power, so I don't recommend using it for action games that hog the processor.

➤ **Parallel garbage collector** (-XX:+UseParallelGC). Also called the throughput garbage collector. This performs young garbage collection in a separate thread and works best with multiprocessor machines.

➤ **Concurrent garbage collector** (-XX:+UseConcMarkSweepGC). This performs tenured garbage collection with lower pauses and also works best with multi-processor machines. The idea is that it can perform garbage collections concurrently while the program runs, instead of stopping the program. You can use a parallel young garbage collector by using (-XX:+UseParNewGC).

Most home users won't have multiprocessor machines, so the default garbage collector will be fine. But as always, experiment with these different collectors to see what kind of results you can get for your game.

Reducing Object Creation

You tuned the heap to make the garbage-collection times almost negligible by keeping the temporary objects you create in the young section of the heap. However, it's still important to create as few objects as possible so that garbage collection can occur less often.

Note that you won't be able to avoid all object creation completely. A lot of object creation takes place in the Java API. If you're ever curious about whether a certain class or method creates any objects, look at the Java API source included with the SDK to get an idea of what kinds of objects are created and when.

For example, getting an `Iterator` from a list creates a new `Iterator` object. Adding an object to a `LinkedList` creates a new object to store it in the list. And concatenating `String` objects creates a new object.

A few ways to avoid those issues are to use `ArrayLists` instead of `LinkedLists`, traverse `ArrayLists` without using an `Iterator`, and use a `StringBuffer` instead of `Strings` when possible.

Object Reuse

Ideally, you want to try for object reuse as much as possible. In the code of this book, we used plenty of scratch objects used for computations of, for example, polygon transforms. That way, we didn't create a new `Vector3D` object for every vertex of every polygon we transformed.

If you can use one object from frame to frame instead of re-creating it every frame, do it.

Sometimes you want to keep an object around only if there's enough memory for it. For example, with polygon surfaces, we didn't need a surface when it went off the screen, but we wanted to keep a copy of it in case we needed it again soon, if there was enough memory for it.

In that case, we used soft references. If an object's only reference to it is a soft reference, the garbage collector doesn't collect the object unless there is not enough memory to keep the object around. Objects with no references are collected first.

When the heap is full with no other objects to collect, the softly reachable objects are collected. This way, soft references can be used as a sort of object cache.

Forgotten how to use soft references already? Well, then, check out Chapter 8 for an overview.

Object Pools

An *object pool* is a collection of objects that can be reused during the execution of an app. Objects are removed from the pool when they are needed and are added to the pool when they are no longer needed. The idea is that using an object pool saves the overhead of continuously allocating and deallocating memory for those objects.

Sun actually recommends against using object pools in modern VMs such as HotSpot. Object creation is much faster than it used to be, and if you're creating many short-lived objects, the young section of the heap will do a better job.

Think of the young section of the heap as an object pool, and try to keep temporary objects in that section. If the young section starts to overflow with objects, the objects will move to the tenured section, which is slower to garbage-collect. So, if this happens, increase the size of the young section so it doesn't overflow.

Probably the worst-case scenario is when you are creating large, temporary objects that live long enough to be copied to the tenured section of the heap and have to be garbage-collected from there. If increasing the young section of the heap doesn't fix this problem, using an object pool might help.

Another scenario arises when it is computationally expensive to create an object. For example, building a polygon surface in the 3D engine is computationally expensive (this isn't a great example for an object pool, though, because each polygon surface is different). Most objects won't be computationally expensive to create, however.

A third scenario is when you have some large tenured objects that you're finished with, but you don't want the garbage collector to remove them until, say, after a level is finished. If you know you have enough memory, you can put those objects in a pool and then clear the pool at a better time.

There's really nothing special about object pools. Basically, you can implement an object pool by keeping a list of objects:

```
ArrayList objectPool = new ArrayList();
```

The pool can be filled with objects, and new objects can be removed from the end (removing from the end ensures the array elements don't have to shifted over, unlike if you removed from, say, the beginning). When you are finished with an object, you simply put it back in the list.

Optionally, you can extend the idea of object pools using soft references. If each object in the pool is a soft reference, it will be cleared only if the heap runs out of memory. So, HotSpot would garbage-collect items in the soft object pool only if absolutely necessary. The pool would stick around, but the objects in the pool would get collected as needed.

Perceived Performance

Sometimes performance has little to do with raw numbers or benchmarks, but instead with what the user perceives. Does it look like it's running smoothly?

One idea is to make sure the game doesn't look like it's "frozen" when it's really just communicating with a server or loading a lot of files. Put long-running tasks such as these in a separate thread.

Also give the user visual notification if something is happening in the background, by using progress bars or wait cursors. For example, give the user something to do while the game is loading, such as an interesting animation, or even let the user play a simple pong game.

Timer Resolution

One of the biggest factors in perceived performance is the granularity of the system timer. Unfortunately on Windows machines, timer resolution isn't very accurate. Here are the different timer granularities of `System.currentTimeMillis()` for different operating systems:

Windows 95/98/Me: 55ms

Windows NT/2000/XP: 10–15ms

Mac OS X: 1ms

Linux: 1ms

With a 55ms timer resolution, that means about 18 updates per second, even if the game is capable of drawing 60 frames per seconds. To get an idea of what this is like, take a look at Figure 16.2. In this figure, the gray ball represents the poor timer resolution, and the white ball represents a high-resolution timer.

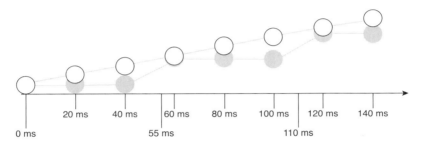

Figure 16.2   A poor timer resolution (gray ball) gives bumpy visual
updates, unlike a high-resolution timer (white ball).

If you're curious what the timer resolution of your system is, run the test in Listing 16.5.

Listing 16.5   GranularityTest.java

```java
/**
    Measures the granularity of System.currentTimeMillis().
*/
public class GranularityTest {

    public static final int NUM_SAMPLES = 100;

    public static void main(String[] args) {
        long sum = 0;
        int count = 0;

        long lastTime = System.currentTimeMillis();
```

continues

Listing 16.5 GranularityTest.java *continued*

```
        while (count < NUM_SAMPLES) {
            long currTime = System.currentTimeMillis();

            // if the time changed, record the difference
            if (currTime > lastTime) {
                long granularity = currTime - lastTime;
                // keep a running sum of the granularity
                sum+=granularity;
                count++;
                lastTime = currTime;
            }
        }

        // display results
        System.out.println("Average granularity of " +
            "System.currentTimeMillis(): " + ((float)sum / count));
    }
}
```

One solution to this problem is to use JNI, or the Java Native Interface, to call some native code that uses a more accurate timer. This problem manifests itself only on Windows, so you'd need a JNI call only for Windows machines and would continue to use System.currentTimeMillis() on other machines. Windows has a multimedia timer that is more accurate. You can learn more about JNI in the Java documentation.

However, if you're not interested in working with native code, there are a few other solutions. One is to just use the refresh rate of the display as a timer. However, this works only if you know your game can run at that refresh rate. For most games, the frame rate varies.

Another idea is to make timer estimates based on previous time samples. You can do this by averaging the last few timer values. As an example, consider this hypothetical situation, in which the times represent the amount of time passed for each frame:

Actual Time	Timer Value	Average Time
Frame 1: 28ms	Frame 1: 0ms	Frame 1: 0ms
Frame 2: 28ms	Frame 2: 55ms	Frame 2: 28ms
Frame 3: 28ms	Frame 3: 0ms	Frame 3: 18ms
Frame 4: 28ms	Frame 4: 55ms	Frame 4: 28ms
Frame 5: 28ms	Frame 5: 0ms	Frame 5: 22ms
Frame 6: 28ms	Frame 6: 55ms	Frame 6: 28ms

Here, the timer has a 55ms granularity. The game runs at about 35 frames per second, or 28ms per frame. Averaging the timer values is not perfect but gives better results than the actual timer value. Because there are more timer samples, the estimate becomes more accurate.

You'll actually implement this technique now. The TimeSmoothie class, in Listing 16.6, keeps track of the last few time samples and averages them to get the current time value. It also has functions to calculate the frame rate.

Listing 16.6   TimeSmoothie.java

```
package com.brackeen.javagamebook.util;

/**
    Smoothes out the jumps in time due to poor timer accuracy.
    This is a simple algorithm that is slightly inaccurate (the
    smoothed time may be slightly ahead of real time) but gives
    better-looking results.
*/
public class TimeSmoothie {

    /**
        How often to recalc the frame rate
    */
    protected static final long FRAME_RATE_RECALC_PERIOD = 500;

    /**
        Don't allow the elapsed time between frames to be more than 100 ms
```

continues

Listing 16.6   TimeSmoothie.java   *continued*

```java
*/
    protected static final long MAX_ELAPSED_TIME = 100;

    /**
        Take the average of the last few samples during the last 100ms
    */
    protected static final long AVERAGE_PERIOD = 100;

    protected static final int NUM_SAMPLES_BITS = 6; // 64 samples
    protected static final int NUM_SAMPLES = 1 << NUM_SAMPLES_BITS;
    protected static final int NUM_SAMPLES_MASK = NUM_SAMPLES - 1;

    protected long[] samples;
    protected int numSamples = 0;
    protected int firstIndex = 0;

    // for calculating frame rate
    protected int numFrames = 0;
    protected long startTime;
    protected float frameRate;

    public TimeSmoothie() {
        samples = new long[NUM_SAMPLES];
    }


    /**
        Adds the specified time sample and returns the average
        of all the recorded time samples.
    */
    public long getTime(long elapsedTime) {
        addSample(elapsedTime);
        return getAverage();
    }


    /**
```

```
        Adds a time sample.
*/
public void addSample(long elapsedTime) {
    numFrames++;

    // cap the time
    elapsedTime = Math.min(elapsedTime, MAX_ELAPSED_TIME);

    // add the sample to the list
    samples[(firstIndex + numSamples) & NUM_SAMPLES_MASK] =
        elapsedTime;
    if (numSamples == samples.length) {
        firstIndex = (firstIndex + 1) & NUM_SAMPLES_MASK;
    }
    else {
        numSamples++;
    }
}


/**
    Gets the average of the recorded time samples.
*/
public long getAverage() {
    long sum = 0;
    for (int i=numSamples-1; i>=0; i--) {
        sum+=samples[(firstIndex + i) & NUM_SAMPLES_MASK];

        // if the average period is already reached, go ahead and return
        // the average.
        if (sum >= AVERAGE_PERIOD) {
            Math.round((double)sum / (numSamples-i));
        }
    }
    return Math.round((double)sum / numSamples);
}
```

continues

Listing 16.6   TimeSmoothie.java   *continued*

```
    /**
        Gets the frame rate (number of calls to getTime() or
        addSample() in real time). The frame rate is recalculated
        every 500ms.
    */
    public float getFrameRate() {
        long currTime = System.currentTimeMillis();

        // calculate the frame rate every 500 milliseconds
        if (currTime > startTime + FRAME_RATE_RECALC_PERIOD) {
            frameRate = (float)numFrames * 1000 /
                (currTime - startTime);
            startTime = currTime;
            numFrames = 0;
        }

        return frameRate;
    }
}
```

To use this class, you simply have to add one line of code in the main game loop to
return an estimated elapsed time based on the elapsed time reported by the clock:

```
public void update(long elapsedTime) {
    ...
    // smooth out the elapsed time
    elapsedTime = timeSmoothie.getTime(elapsedTime);

    // update the world based on the elapsed time
    // from the time smoothie.
    updateWorld(elapsedTime);
}
```

This code works best when the frame rate is fairly consistent. Change can be okay,
but if the frame rate tends to vary wildly, TimeSmoothie won't give as accurate results.
In that case, a JNI function might be more appropriate.

Summary

This chapter quickly went over a lot of optimization topics and ideas. You used a profiler to find the 20% of code that needs to be optimized, and then you learned about the optimizations that HotSpot performs so you don't have to. Of course, HotSpot doesn't do everything, so you learned about optimizations that HotSpot doesn't perform.

Finally, you explored memory usage and the garbage collector, and you even tuned the heap so that the impact of garbage collection was almost negligible, taking only about 10ms every 10 seconds.

Of course, the biggest boost from optimization you'll get is not from a computer but from your brain. More efficient algorithms, such as those using BSP trees, allow you to do some amazing tricks, but you'll need to spend time trying new ideas to get things to work. So be creative and come up with some fantastic, efficient code!

Chapter 17

Creating Game Art and Sounds

So, you've got your great game idea and you've started coding, but—uh, oh—there's no art or sounds!

Maybe you'll get lucky and find an artist or sound engineer to work with who's willing to devote free time to the project. However, a lot of the time, this isn't going to be the case.

This chapter is oriented toward creating "programmer art," the type of game art that might not be the best looking but that is good enough for a demo.

When making any type of media for a game, keep these rules in mind:

1. Half of what you make is crap.

That's it.

Personally, I've spent hours creating that perfect texture, only to realize later it's just not working and throw it away. That's the important part: Throw it away! Maybe not literally—you could save unused art to refer to later—but don't include it in the game if it doesn't work.

And don't let it bother you if you create some game art or sound that doesn't work. It just means you're one step closer to creating media that *does* work. Consider the crap you create a badge of honor, not a drawback. If half of what you make is crap, then the more crap you create, the more usable stuff you create. So let's get started on making some crap.

Choosing a Look and Feel

First, you'll want to decide on an overall look and feel for your game. For example, do you want a dark, gritty look, or a smooth, flat-shaded look? Realistic or surreal? Or, you could get more creative and do a sketchy look or something that looks like a 1950s black-and-white detective film.

A lot of this depends on the target audience. An adult might enjoy a darker game with dramatic lighting and shadows, but a younger kid might prefer a bright, colorful game.

Looking for Inspiration

Sometimes inspiration for your game's look and feel can be the hardest. Think about what games you like to play and also movies and TV shows you like to watch. Sci-fi films generally pull off some great stunts and effects that are inspiring, but also think about other genres, such as westerns, mysteries, or even sports.

Take a look at the world around you for inspiration. Would it be fun to create a tag game in an environment based off your apartment building? Or an adventure game in a setting like the woods and creek near your house?

Finally, don't forget about the more classical forms of inspiration you'll find at an art museum. Imagine playing a game that looks like Van Gogh's *Starry Night* or one of Magritte's strange worlds. And Salvador Dali's melting clocks are always a popular surreal favorite.

While you're busy being inspired by the world around you, keep in mind that there's a fine line between finding inspiration and ripping off something. It's okay to be inspired by the latest blockbuster game or movie, as long as you're not creating a game that looks a little bit too much like it.

Staying Consistent

Do you want some textures in your game to look like a cartoon while others look dark and realistic? Probably not. Likewise, you wouldn't want a weapon-toting demon fighter to make cheesy "boing" sounds when jumping.

It's generally a good idea to make sure your game art, interface art, and sounds mesh together well. For example, try to keep textures for a 3D game at similar brightness levels (because lighting is done in-game).

Also, the user interface should have some sort of consistency with the overall look of the game. For example, a cartoon-like game might have colorful buttons that are big and shiny, while a first-person shooter might have dark buttons with eerie shadows.

Getting Royalty-Free Game Media

You can find CDs full of royalty-free art and sounds either at a store or over the Internet. "Royalty-free" basically means you don't have to pay royalties to use the art (but be sure to read over any license the art comes with, to make sure).

Many types of art collections are more suited for desktop publishing, with simple line-art drawings of computers, businessmen shaking hands, and whatnot. However, you can also find many collections geared more toward graphics designers, such as texture collections or photographs. Many are available; your best bet is to search the Internet for royalty-free graphic packages that suit your needs.

Photographs can be a great start for creating background images and textures. Consider Figure 17.1, for example. In this example photograph, the top part can be used for a scrolling background (the large rectangle), and other parts of the photo can be used for interesting textures (the small square).

Figure 17.1   A photograph is used for a background (the large rectangle) and a texture (the small square).

Other royalty-free media to consider looking into are icons and fonts. Icons can be very useful for user interface elements, like those you had in Chapter 4, "Sound Effects and Music." These icons came from a paint program (Paint Shop Pro) and were modified slightly by giving them a drop shadow.

Working with Artists and Sound Effect Engineers

If you're lucky enough to have another person to create game art or sound effects, that means you also have the task of working with artists. Here are a few ideas to keep in mind:

➤ Make sure creating media is fun for the artists and not just work. Give them flexibility to create their own style, and don't try to control every little detail.

➤ Be specific about what the game needs. For example, you might need 3D models (different monsters, power-ups, and so on) and different types of sounds (jumping, firing a weapon, and so on).

➤ Likewise, be as specific as possible about the technical requirements of the game media. For example, specify the dimensions of textures (do the textures have to be powers of 2?), whether or not textures have to be seamless, file formats, number of colors, polygon count limits, and so on.

➤ Set up a schedule that works best for both of you. Ask about how long it will take to make some media, and work from there.

➤ If some game art or sound is not working in the game or just doesn't look right, be sure to mention it. Both of you will need to decide whether to include that particular medium or to rework it.

In summary, keep the communication lines open and keep the process fun!

Tools

What good is making programmer art without tools, right? Right. First, learn your tools as best you can, and don't be afraid to experiment. If you're worried you'll ruin some art or a sound, make a backup copy first.

Sound tools allow you to record, edit, and add effects to sound waves. Some inexpensive sound tools include Pro Tools FREE, Cool Edit, GoldWave, GLAME, GSMP, and LAoE for Java.

Graphics tools allow you to create and edit textures and sprites. Some inexpensive graphics tools include Photoshop Elements (`www.adobe.com`), Paint Shop Pro (`www.jasc.com`), and the GIMP (`www.gimp.org`).

3D tools allow you to create and render 3D graphics. Some free 3D tools include Blender and POV-Ray. Blender is a polygon modeler, while POV-Ray is a ray-tracing renderer. Although ray-tracing doesn't really help you, POV-Ray has some interesting texture-generation capabilities that you can take advantage of. If you have the money, some professional 3D tools include 3ds max and Maya.

Creating Sounds

Most sound effects start with a natural recorded sound and then are edited to add effects. For example, in the original *Star Wars* movie, the engine sound of one of the starships was the sound of a lion roar played backward.

Start with an organic sound of things around you, such as a car starting, a door shutting, someone sneezing, or a bathtub draining.

When recording, be sure not to record at too high of a level, or the sound will clip and sound distorted. Try to record at a good midrange level—not too loud and not too quiet.

Also, make use of a noise-reduction filter using your sound tool. This will help eliminate background noises and make up for cheap, lo-fi microphones.

When you've got your recorded sound, apply filters and effects to make the sound interesting, or try combining two or more separate organic sounds. You'll probably want to avoid "fake" sounds, such as a sound effect that is obviously a person trying to imitate a gunfire noise.

Remember, in many sound tools, filters are "destructive," meaning the audio samples themselves are modified. Keep a copy of the original sound, in case you've applied so many filters that you need to revert back to it.

Of course, sound effects don't have to originate from an organic, recorded sound. You can also use waveform generation in many sound tools to create artificial sounds.

Finally, make sure your sounds start and end with zero amplitude to eliminate popping, as in Figure 17.2. Don't add too much of a delay at the beginning, though, or there will be a longer delay before your sound is heard.

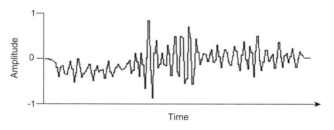

Figure 17.2 Make sure the sounds start and end with zero amplitude.

Here are a few examples of how sounds were created for this book:

➤ In Chapter 4, the "boop" sound was a recording of me opening a mailing tube.

➤ Also in Chapter 4, the "fly buzz" sound was me imitating a fly, with the pitch turned up a little.

➤ In Chapter 5, "Creating a 2D Platform Game," the "prize" sound was completely generated in software using waveforms and effects.

Another good example of creating sound effects is from one of the first Java games I created, a 3D first-person shooter called *Scared*. This was a standard first-person shooter in which the player runs around a maze, opening doors, finding keys, and advancing to the next level. Here are a few examples from that game:

➤ The door closing is a recording of my old door closing with extra bass.

➤ The laser guns are a recording of me imitating a laser gun, but with the pitch and everything else messed with.

➤ The player "grunt" and "die" sounds are recordings of me grunting and (dramatically) dying.

➤ The "growl" of the power generator is a recording of my old window air-conditioning unit with extra bass.

➤ The "swoosh" sound of an opening door is a recording of me opening a 20 oz bottle of Dr Pepper.

➤ The "shh-click" sound when the player picks up a key is a recording of me opening a 12 oz can of Dr Pepper played backward.

➤ The "crunch" sound played when an enemy is destroyed is a recording of me crunching a 12 oz can of Dr Pepper in a can cruncher.

Come to think about it, most of the sounds for that game were inspired by Dr Pepper.

Sound File Formats

We discussed sound file formats back in Chapter 5, but we rehash this topic a bit here.

Basically, the Java Sound API can read three formats: AIFF, AU, and WAV. Additionally, you can install other format readers from third parties, such as an OGG decoder. For the book, we used 16-bit, mono, 44,100Hz WAV files, which is CD quality, but mono instead of stereo.

Creating Textures and Sprites

When you're creating textures and sprites, it's a good idea to define the scale of the pixel or texel size in terms of real-world dimensions. For example, in a 3D game, you could say that 100 texels is 1m, or 1 texel per centimeter. This way, you can determine what size to make a light switch or door handle, and the size will be logical relative to everything else in the world. For sprites, it's sometimes easier to work with basic graphics primitives such as ovals, lines, and other simple shapes rather than drawing by hand. You'll notice the sprites used in the platform game in Chapter 5 are all made up of simple shapes, such as circles, stars, and even hearts. Most graphics programs can create shapes like these easily.

For those of you who can draw on paper better than you can by using a graphics program, here's another idea: You can always scan in drawings and then use a graphics program to clean up the lines and fill in some color.

When you're creating textures, consider how textures are usually tiled across a polygon. If the texture has, for example, a noticeable blotch of color, then when the texture is tiled, it will end up looking like a polka-dot pattern of blotches. Instead, keep textures fairly subtle.

One idea for creating a texture is to start the texture as a solid color and work your way from there. Add noise and subtle texture effects to make it look more realistic. Many graphics programs have effects to make an image look like an asphalt, metal, or wooden texture, for example.

Also, bad art sometimes looks better when it's scaled down to a smaller size. If you want 64×64 textures for your game, initially create 128×128 or 256×256 textures and then later scale them down.

Don't be afraid to experiment! Work with color adjustments such as gamma and brightness and contrast. Apply shadow effects, such as a drop shadow, to give a texture more depth. But remember, these are textures: For a 3D engine, you don't want to draw too much depth onto a texture, or it will look incorrect when you're not looking straight at the polygon.

Graphics File Formats

We talked about graphics file formats back in Chapter 2, "2D Graphics and Animation," but here's a quick overview.

For photographic work, the JPEG format is a good choice because it offers high compression and high quality, even though it's a lossy format.

Textures and sprites are better off saved as PNGs, though, because this is a lossless format.

One note about PNGs: If you're looking to make a PNG image use bitmask transparency (as opposed to alpha translucency), you'll need to convert the PNGs to 8-bit, 256 color using index transparency. If you save it using more than 8-bit color, it will be a translucent image that isn't hardware accelerated (as of J2SDK 1.4.1).

Sometimes you want to decrease the file size of an image—for example, to decrease the overall size of the game media. The best way to decrease the file size of a PNG image is to reduce the number of colors in the image. Also, make sure the image isn't dithered, which tends to look bad in most game situations anyway.

Creating Seamless Textures

Speaking of tiling textures, when the textures are tiled across the polygon, you'll want to make sure the edges of the texture aren't noticeable—you want the texture to look seamless when it's tiled. Figure 17.3 shows a texture that looks cool but doesn't tile well. Luckily, many graphics programs offer this functionally built in. Try to make it difficult to tell where the seam is, as in Figure 17.4.

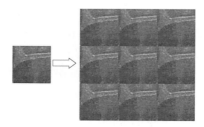

Figure 17.3 A texture might look nice by itself, but seams are apparent when it's tiled.

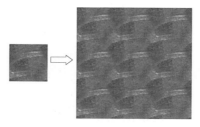

Figure 17.4 Many graphics programs can modify a texture so that it is seamless when tiled, as in this example.

One idea to create a seamless texture is to use a repeating pattern, such as a square grid (or even a hexagon grid). Some more seamless tile examples are in Figure 17.5.

Figure 17.5 Some more seamless tiles.

In this figure, the first texture is a 3×3 grid, so the seams of the texture aren't noticeably different from the lines of the grid.

The second texture is solid gray except for a pattern of ridges, some black lines, and a rusty spot in the center. With the ridge pattern repeating four times in the texture and the black line breaking once, it will be difficult to tell where the seam is when the texture is tiled horizontally. When it is tiled vertically, it will be very noticeable.

Finally, the third texture is an all-around seamless tile. It's a wood-like texture that was made seamless by using Paint Shop Pro. It can be tiled on all sides without much of a seam, but it does have a noticeable pattern.

Creating "Alternate" Textures

Sometimes a tiled texture can get very monotonous to look at. Lighting in a 3D engine helps this a lot, but another way to break up the monotony is to use an alternate texture that is slightly different from a tiled texture.

For example, check out the alternate texture in Figure 17.6.

Figure 17.6   An example of an alternate tile.

Using this texture helps break up the monotony of a tiled texture, as shown in Figure 17.7.

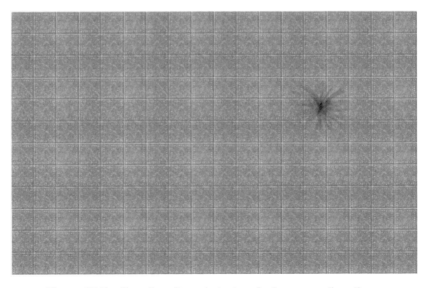

Figure 17.7   How the alternate texture looks among the others.

Figure 17.8 shows more alternate textures, using a texture with fake lighting and a texture with an interesting object.

Figure 17.8   Another example of using alternate tiles.

Creating Transition Textures

In top-down games, you often have all sorts of different textures to define the terrain, such as water textures and grass textures. Unfortunately, you come up with an ugly situation when different textures are next to one another, as with the grass and water tiles in Figure 17.9.

Figure 17.9   Two different tiles, grass (left) and water (right) butt up against one another.

To fix this, you can use a "transition" texture that gives a better-looking boundary between grass and water. In Figure 17.10, a transition texture is inserted to represent the beach between the grass and the water.

Figure 17.10   Using a transition tile to smooth the boundary between the two tiles.

Of course, the solution in Figure 17.10 fixes the problem only when a grass tile is on the left of a water tile. In a game, there will be many different situations, such as when grass is to the right of water, or when grass surrounds water on two sides.

First, you'll create three different transitions, as shown in Figure 17.11. This allows water to be on one side, two sides, or a corner of the transitions texture. Optionally, you could make more transitions to allow water to be on three and four sides, but this will work for many situations.

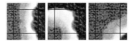

Figure 17.11 Three different transition tiles.

An asymmetrical tic-tac-toe pattern is drawn over the transitions tiles in Figure 17.11 to show the edges of the different parts of a transition. The outside border of the texture should be the same for every texture: either completely water, completely grass, or the gradient from water to grass.

Luckily, these three transitions are all you need. At runtime, you can rotate each transition texture three different ways (90°, 180°, 270°) to get the transition textures shown in Figure 17.12.

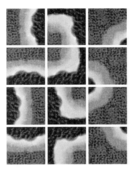

Figure 17.12 The three different transition tiles can be rotated to create a total of 12 transition tiles.

Using these 12 transition textures, you can create all sorts of nice-looking types of terrains, such as islands, lakes, and rivers, and you won't have any ugly situations when different textures are next to each other.

Of course, this is just the tip of the iceberg with transition textures. You can also create transitions when three different textures run into each other. Also, some games use two or more textures for the same transition, so there is a bit of variation in the look of the transitions.

Creating Multi-Layer Textures

Another neat trick is layering textures on top of one another. This works by having one "background" texture and a "foreground" texture that is partially see-though. Take Figure 17.13, for example. This shows two separate layers: the terrain layer and the road layer. Each is composed of the same size textures. The two layers are combined in Figure 17.14.

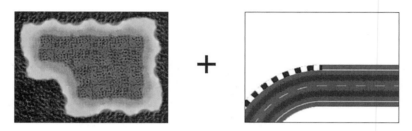

Figure 17.13   Two layers exist: the ground (left) and the road (right).

Figure 17.14   The road layer is layered on top of the ground layer within the game.

This way, roads have the flexibility to go over any type of terrain, whether it be grass, sand, beach, or whatever.

Of course, you don't have to stop with just two layers. For example, in addition to the background and road layers, there could be a "path" layer that shows a dirt path on top of the grass terrain.

Creating Splash Screens and HUD Graphics

Splash screens are usually pretty simple. For an introduction screen, all you need is an image with a cool logo. Graphics programs have plenty of tools to create text-based logos.

Also, you might need splash screens for different states of the game, such as when a level is loading, after a level is finished, and when the game is over. Again, this can be pretty simple, and all you might need is a logo.

The *heads-up display*, or the *HUD*, is often another place that needs some graphics. It might need something minimal, such as icons to signify health and ammo, or it might need an entire interface with lots of buttons, as in common strategy or simulation games.

Creating UI Graphics

Finally, don't forget about UI graphics! Mostly, you'll probably just need things such as image buttons, to give your game a particular look and feel.

When designing UI graphics keep in mind the meanings that different colors imply. For example, think of the stoplight: Red means stop, green means go, yellow means caution. Try to pick colors that signify the meaning you're trying to convey.

Also, use simple yet descriptive UI graphics that quickly allow the user to find out what to click on. In the example in Chapter 3, "Interactivity and User Interfaces," you used icons for buttons.

Customizing Swing

If you're using Swing for any part of your UI, such as text boxes for username input, you might want to change the default Swing look to suit your own needs. The most flexible way to do this is to create your own *look and feel*, but this can be a difficult process.

Another solution is to simply change the colors of the default Java look and feel to match those of your UI. The good news is it's easy to change the color of a Swing component. All you have to do is store a value in the UI defaults table, like this:

```
ColorUIResource myColor = new ColorUIResource(0xf9f9f9);
UIManager.put("Button.background", myColor);
```

A `ColorUIResource` object is a subclass of the `Color` object that implements the `UIResource` interface, which Swing uses internally. Here, we set the background color of all buttons to our own color.

The bad news is that there are hundreds of different color properties in Swing, including `Button.shadow`, `Button.highlight`, and several others.

If you're curious what all those properties are, you can use the code in Listing 17.1 to display them all, along with their default values.

Listing 17.1   SwingDefaults.java

```
import java.awt.Color;
import java.util.*;
import javax.swing.UIManager;
import javax.swing.UIDefaults;

/**
    Prints a list of all the Swing defaults for the default
    look and feel.
*/
public class SwingDefaults {

    public static void main(String[] args) throws Exception {

        List allValues = new ArrayList();

        // store all the values in a list
        UIDefaults defaults = UIManager.getDefaults();
        Enumeration e = defaults.keys();
        while (e.hasMoreElements()) {
            Object key = e.nextElement();
```

```
            Object value = defaults.get(key);
            if (value instanceof Color) {
                allValues.add(key + " = " + value);
            }
        }

        // sort and print the values
        Collections.sort(allValues);
        for (int i=0; i<allValues.size(); i++) {
            System.out.println(allValues.get(i));
        }

    }
}
```

Note that this code displays the color properties; you can also modify things such as borders.

Creating Your Own Fonts

You can do a lot with Java2D and fonts, but creating the more interesting font designs can be difficult. For example, drawing text with an outline and a gradient fill isn't the easiest thing to code in Java2D.

A lot of games use their own image-based fonts. An image-based font is a font in which each character is an image. This way, the artist has more flexibility in designing the look of a font, and drawing text with image-based fonts is fast because you can take advantage of hardware acceleration.

In this section, you'll implement a class to draw text from image-based fonts. One goal of this implementation is to allow variable-width characters, as in Figure 17.15. The figure shows how the m is wider than the i character.

Figure 17.15   Fonts can be variable width—the *m* is wider than the *i*.

An easy way to implement image-based fonts with variable-width characters is to just include a separate image for every single character. You'll do this in the ImageFont class, shown here in Listing 17.2.

Listing 17.2   ImageFont.java

```java
package com.brackeen.javagamebook.graphics;

import java.awt.*;
import java.awt.image.BufferedImage;
import java.io.*;
import javax.swing.ImageIcon;

/**
    The ImageFont class allows loading and drawing of text
    using images for the characters.

    Reads all the png images in a directory in the form
    "charXX.png" where "XX" is a decimal unicode value.

    Characters can have different widths and heights.
*/
public class ImageFont {

    public static final int HCENTER = 1;
    public static final int VCENTER = 2;
    public static final int LEFT = 4;
    public static final int RIGHT = 8;
    public static final int TOP = 16;
    public static final int BOTTOM = 32;

    private char firstChar;
    private Image[] characters;
    private Image invalidCharacter;


    /**
        Creates a new ImageFont with no characters.
    */
```

```
public ImageFont() {
    this(null);
    firstChar = 0;
    characters = new Image[0];
}



/**
    Creates a new ImageFont and loads character images from
    the specified path.
*/
public ImageFont(String path) {
    if (path != null) {
        load(path);
    }

    // make the character used for invalid characters
    invalidCharacter =
        new BufferedImage(10, 10, BufferedImage.TYPE_INT_RGB);
    Graphics g = invalidCharacter.getGraphics();
    g.setColor(Color.RED);
    g.fillRect(0,0,10,10);
    g.dispose();
}



/**
    Loads the image files for each character from the
    specified path. For example, if "../fonts/large"
    is the path, this method searches for all the images
    names "charXX.png" in that path, where "XX" is a
    decimal unicode value. Not every character image needs
    to exist; you can only do numbers or uppercase letters,
    for example.
*/
public void load(String path) throws NumberFormatException {
    // in this directory:
    // load every png file that starts with 'char'
    File dir = new File(path);
```

continues

Listing 17.2 ImageFont.java *continued*

```java
        File[] files = dir.listFiles();

        // find min and max chars
        char minChar = Character.MAX_VALUE;
        char maxChar = Character.MIN_VALUE;
        for (int i=0; i<files.length; i++) {
            int unicodeValue = getUnicodeValue(files[i]);
            if (unicodeValue != -1) {
                minChar = (char)Math.min(minChar, unicodeValue);
                maxChar = (char)Math.max(maxChar, unicodeValue);
            }
        }

        // load the images
        if (minChar < maxChar) {
            firstChar = minChar;
            characters = new Image[maxChar - minChar + 1];
            for (int i=0; i<files.length; i++) {
                int unicodeValue = getUnicodeValue(files[i]);
                if (unicodeValue != -1) {
                    int index = unicodeValue - firstChar;
                    characters[index] = new ImageIcon(
                        files[i].getAbsolutePath()).getImage();
                }
            }

        }

    }


    private int getUnicodeValue(File file)
        throws NumberFormatException
    {
        String name = file.getName().toLowerCase();
        if (name.startsWith("char") && name.endsWith(".png")) {
            String unicodeString =
                name.substring(4, name.length() - 4);
```

```
            return Integer.parseInt(unicodeString);
    }
    return -1;
}



/**
    Gets the image for a specific character. If no image for
    the character exists, a special "invalid" character image
    is returned.
*/
public Image getImage(char ch) {
    int index = ch - firstChar;
    if (index < 0 || index >= characters.length ||
        characters[index] == null)
    {
        return invalidCharacter;
    }
    else {
        return characters[index];
    }
}



/**
    Gets the string width, in pixels, for the specified string.
*/
public int stringWidth(String s) {
    int width = 0;
    for (int i=0; i<s.length(); i++) {
        width += charWidth(s.charAt(i));
    }
    return width;
}



/**
```

continues

Listing 17.2 ImageFont.java *continued*

```
        Gets the char width, in pixels, for the specified char.
    */
    public int charWidth(char ch) {
        return getImage(ch).getWidth(null);
    }


    /**
        Gets the char height, in pixels, for the specified char.
    */
    public int charHeight(char ch) {
        return getImage(ch).getHeight(null);
    }


    /**
        Draws the specified string at the (x, y) location.
    */
    public void drawString(Graphics g, String s, int x, int y) {
        drawString(g, s, x, y, LEFT | BOTTOM);
    }


    /**
        Draws the specified string at the (x, y) location.
    */
    public void drawString(Graphics g, String s, int x, int y,
        int anchor)
    {
        if ((anchor & HCENTER) != 0) {
            x-=stringWidth(s) / 2;
        }
        else if ((anchor & RIGHT) != 0) {
            x-=stringWidth(s);
        }
        // clear horizontal flags for char drawing
        anchor &= ~HCENTER;
        anchor &= ~RIGHT;
```

```
        // draw the characters
        for (int i=0; i<s.length(); i++) {
            drawChar(g, s.charAt(i), x, y, anchor);
            x+=charWidth(s.charAt(i));
        }
    }



    /**
        Draws the specified character at the (x, y) location.
    */
    public void drawChar(Graphics g, char ch, int x, int y) {
        drawChar(g, ch, x, y, LEFT | BOTTOM);
    }



    /**
        Draws the specified character at the (x, y) location.
    */
    public void drawChar(Graphics g, char ch, int x, int y,
        int anchor)
    {
        if ((anchor & HCENTER) != 0) {
            x-=charWidth(ch) / 2;
        }
        else if ((anchor & RIGHT) != 0) {
            x-=charWidth(ch);
        }

        if ((anchor & VCENTER) != 0) {
            y-=charHeight(ch) / 2;
        }
        else if ((anchor & BOTTOM) != 0) {
            y-=charHeight(ch);
        }
        g.drawImage(getImage(ch), x, y, null);
    }
}
```

In the `ImageFont` constructor, you can specify the path where the font images are located, like this:

```
ImageFont medFont = new ImageFont("../fonts/medium");
```

This path is a directory that contains an image for every character. The code is smart enough to search the directory for every available character rather than attempting to load every possible Unicode value. This means you could make a font with only numerical characters if you wanted.

The filenames of the character images are in the form char*XX*.png, where *XX* is the Unicode value of the font. For example, char65.png is the image for the letter *A*.

The text-drawing methods in this class are flexible enough to handle alignment for you. For example, you can use flags to automatically center or right-justify a text string. Here's an example using an upper-left anchor so that the text appears at the top of the screen:

```
medFont.drawString(g, "Hi", 0, 0, ImageFont.LEFT | ImageFont.TOP);
```

Of course, the drawback to using image fonts is that they don't scale to different sizes very well. If you're looking for multisize fonts, you might want to stick with the plain Java2D font rendering or create multiple sizes of your image fonts.

That's about it for image fonts. A demo showing the use of image fonts is included in the source distribution for this book. The demo shows left-justified, centered, and right-justified text, and even some simple text animation, similar to how you moved sprites on the screen in Chapter 2.

Summary

Well, that's it for programmer art. Even if you're not interested in making game art, this chapter showed you how to make a cool, reusable `ImageFont` class to use images for text. We also talked about making sounds and shared some tips and tricks for making textures. Hopefully, this chapter will help you make some usable stuff—after you've made some "crap," of course!

Chapter 18

Game Design and the Last 10%

"I've made my game, now what?"

Okay, so you've made a game. It's fun and challenging, and has fantastic graphics and sound. But what happens next?

What you do next with your game depends on what you want to accomplish. You might want to share it with a few friends or use it as a demo to help get yourself a job. Or, you might want to release it on CD-ROM or over to the web and try to make money off of it.

If you decide to release it, you're going to want to refine the game as much as possible. The refining might be the last 10% of the game, but be warned: Sometimes it takes 50% of development time to finish the last 10% of the game.

This chapter discusses what to add to your game to polish it up a bit. This chapter also includes some implementations of techniques such as creating a game state machine and distributing your game using Java Web Start.

The Last 10%

You'll need to do lots of things to polish a game or even a demo to make it more professional-looking. This includes adding things such as extra special effects, loading screens, menus, and intro sequences.

One of the most important things is to keep your game as robust and well–behaved as possible. Make sure the game feels "solid" and doesn't have any quirky behavior. Eliminate all the bugs you can. If the user minimizes the app or switches to another application, you'll want to pause your game. Also, when the user clicks Exit, the game should actually exit, not just hide the game window and continue to hog the processor or network connection in the background. Try to leave the user's computer in the state it was in when the game started.

Effects

Don't forget about adding plenty of sound effects. Sound effects are one of those game elements that are sometimes noticeable only when they are missing. Here are some ideas on when to add sounds need for something like an adventure game:

➤ When the player is hurt or dies

➤ When the player jumps and falls

➤ When a bot is hit or destroyed

➤ When a lever is pulled or a door opens

➤ When an item is picked up

➤ When a background generator is on or another piece of machinery is buzzing or humming

➤ For background environment noises, such as a brook gurgling, flames crackling, wind rustling through trees, birds chirping, ocean waves crashing, or rain drops spilling

➤ For user interface sounds, such as when the user clicks a button, changes to the map view, or selects a different weapon, or when the UI is waiting for input

➤ For "hint" sounds, such as when a bad guy is about to fire a weapon or the player is near a hidden cave

➤ For negative feedback sounds, such as when the player tries to select a weapon that isn't available

Of course, these are ideas. You can come up with your own checklist of sounds you'd like in your game.

Besides sound effects, visual effects really help refine a game and can also add a bit of the "wow" factor. Some visual effects you might want to add are listed here:

➤ Particle explosions

➤ Flames

➤ Heat warping effects

➤ Lightning

➤ Dramatic flickering lights

➤ Environment effects, such as rain, snow, and moving clouds

➤ Object animations, such as running creatures and growing vines

It might sound crazy, but be sure not to add too many special effects. Effects should be fun and cool, but they shouldn't get in the way of game play. For example, you don't want so many simultaneous sounds that they are difficult to distinguish. You'll also want to avoid graphical effects that cover the entire screen, confusing or disorienting the user for no reason (unless that's the point of the effect!).

The Game State Machine

In most of the demos in the book, the games started directly in the "game" mode and stayed there until they exited. There were no loading screens, intro sequences, menus, or help screens, all of which are be essential in making a mature game.

When you want to add these different screens, you can treat the entire game as a state machine, as in Figure 18.1.

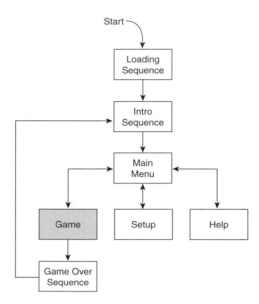

Figure 18.1 A game state machine.

In this simple state machine example, the game starts with a loading screen and moves to an intro sequence (which could be a splash screen, an animation, or a demo of the game). Typically, you want to allow users to escape from any intro sequences like this so they don't have to sit through them every time they start the game.

The next state is the main menu, and from there, the user can move to many of the other games states, such as help screens or setup.

This is just a simple design. For your own game, you'll probably want something more detailed. For example, the main game state shown here could even be broken down into several different states: The game state could go from a level loading sequence to a level intro, to the game, and then to the level end sequence.

Implementing state machines is easy enough, and you can do it similar to how you wrote other state machines in this book. For example, you could do something like this when you handle input for a game:

```
if (state == STATE_INTRO) {
    // handle intro input
}
```

```
else if (state == STATE_GAME) {
    // handle game input
}
else {
    ...
}
```

Furthermore, you need these if/then statements when you update and draw each frame.

As you can imagine, this code can quickly become tedious and confusing as more states are added to the game.

Instead, you can just give each state its own object that handles things such as input, updates, and drawing, avoiding long if/then chunks of code. Start by making the GameState interface, shown here in Listing 18.1.

Listing 18.1   GameState.java

```
public interface GameState {


    /**
        Gets the name of this state. Used for
        the checkForStateChange() method.
    */
    public String getName();



    /**
        Returns the name of a state to change to if this state
is
        ready to change to another state, or null otherwise.
    */
    public String checkForStateChange();


    /**
```

continues

Listing 18.1 GameState.java *continued*

```
        Loads any resources for this state. This method is called
        in a background thread before any GameStates are set.
    */
    public void loadResources(ResourceManager resourceManager);


    /**
        Initializes this state and sets up the input manager
    */
    public void start(InputManager inputManager);



    /**
        Performs any actions needed to stop this state.
    */
    public void stop();



    /**
        Updates world, handles input.
    */
    public void update(long elapsedTime);



    /**
        Draws to the screen.
    */
    public void draw(Graphics2D g);
}
```

This is a fairly simple interface. The start() method should map any key and mouse
bindings for this game state. The stop() method performs any cleanup when a state
is done, such as pausing sounds or freeing resources. The update() and draw()
methods update and draw each frame. checkForStateChange() returns the name
of a state to change to, or null if it's not ready for a state change. For example, this
method could return the string Main after the intro sequence is finished.

One thing to note is that the `loadResources()` method is designed to be called in a separate thread outside the main thread. This way, resources can be loaded separately from the update/draw process. This also means a "loading" screen can easily be shown while all the resources are loading in the background. Ideally, you'll probably want this method to throw an exception if there is an error loading a resource so that the game engine can respond accordingly. The entire life cycle of a `GameState` is shown visually in Figure 18.2.

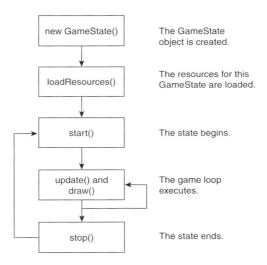

Figure 18.2   The flow of a GameState object.

As an example, you'll create a `GameStateManager` class that manages the change from state to state and keeps track of the current state. Check it out in Listing 18.2.

Listing 18.2   Relevant Methods of GameStateManager.java

```
/**
    Sets the current state (by name).
*/
public void setState(String name) {
    // clean up old state
    if (currentState != null) {
        currentState.stop();
    }
    inputManager.clearAllMaps();
```

continues

Listing 18.2   Relevant Methods of GameStateManager.java   *continued*

```java
    // set new state
    currentState = (GameState)gameStates.get(name);
    if (currentState != null) {
        currentState.start(inputManager);
    }
}


/**
    Updates world, handles input.
*/
public void update(long elapsedTime) {
    // if no state, pause a short time
    if (currentState == null) {
        try {
            Thread.sleep(100);
        }
        catch (InterruptedException ex) { }
    }
    else {
        String nextState = currentState.checkForStateChange();
        if (nextState != null) {
            setState(nextState);
        }
        else {
            currentState.update(elapsedTime);
        }
    }
}


/**
    Draws to the screen.
*/
public void draw(Graphics2D g) {
    if (currentState != null) {
        currentState.draw(g);
```

```
    }
    else {
        // if no state, draw the default image to the screen
        g.drawImage(defaultImage, 0, 0, null);
    }
}
```

In this code, the `draw()` method delegates the work to the current state; if the state is
`null`, a default image is drawn. You could make the default image be a splash image
that says the game is loading.

Besides updating the state, the `update()` method checks to see whether the current
state signals that it is time to change to another state. Finally, the `setState()` method
actually switches the states. Notice that all the key and mouse maps are cleared from
the input manager when changing to a different state.

As an example, you'll create a simple splash screen game state, shown here in Listing
18.3. This `GameState` just keeps a splash image on the screen either for three seconds
or until the user presses the spacebar, whichever comes first.

Listing 18.3   SplashGameState.java

```
public class SplashGameState implements GameState {

    private String splashFilename;
    private Image splash;
    private GameAction exitSplash;
    private long totalElapsedTime;
    private boolean done;

    public SplashGameState(String splashFilename) {
        exitSplash = new GameAction("exitSplash",
            GameAction.DETECT_INITAL_PRESS_ONLY);
        this.splashFilename = splashFilename;
    }

    public String getName() {
        return "Splash";
    }
```

continues

Listing 18.3 SplashGameState.java *continued*

```java
public void loadResources(ResourceManager resourceManager) {
    splash = resourceManager.loadImage(splashFilename);
}


public String checkForStateChange() {
    return done?"Main":null;
}


public void start(InputManager inputManager) {
    inputManager.mapToKey(exitSplash, KeyEvent.VK_SPACE);
    inputManager.mapToMouse(exitSplash,
        InputManager.MOUSE_BUTTON_1);

    totalElapsedTime = 0;
    done = false;
}

public void stop() {
    // do nothing
}

public void update(long elapsedTime) {
    totalElapsedTime+=elapsedTime;
    if (totalElapsedTime > 3000 || exitSplash.isPressed()) {
        done = true;
    }
}

public void draw(Graphics2D g) {
    g.drawImage(splash, 0, 0, null);
}
}
```

When this game state starts, it maps the spacebar and main mouse button to the `exitSplash` game action. The state signals to change to the main state after it is done.

Now it will be a lot easier to create different game states. Be sure to create everything you need, including setup and help screens.

Elements of Game Design

Remember, the goal of any game is to be entertaining.

First, the game needs to be easily accessible so people can be entertained in the first place. Make the game straightforward to learn how to play, not to mention easy to download and install.

As for the game itself, having great game play, exciting environments, and an attention-grabbing story can keep people entertained. In this section, we go over some of the details to help refine these elements in your game.

Also, to get even more game design concepts, the best idea is to try out lots of existing games (which you probably already do) and pay attention to even the most minute detail of those games. There are lots of game design concepts out there that you can emulate or improve upon. Just don't rip anything off, of course!

Environments

Variety is the spice of life. Variety also helps add interest to a game and can keep the player motivated to see what is coming up next.

One of the best ways to add variety to a game is to provide different environments. The entire game doesn't have to be set in a dilapidated research compound overrun by hostile aliens. You can set different levels of a game in other environments, such as forests, sewers, deserts, caves, starships, creeks, and anything else you can come up with. Furthermore, the enemies can vary from environment to environment, such as robots in a spaceship or giant insects in a forest.

Also, dynamic weather can really add to the "wow" factor of a game. You could make it start raining in the middle of a level, or the player could return to an earlier level that was previously grassland but that is now covered in snow and blanketed by dark clouds.

Adding unique textures and objects to each level helps as well. Repeating textures from an earlier level can create a sense of nostalgia for the player, but it can be a drag if some textures are used too much.

The environment should also allow a certain amount of interaction with it. This could be as simple as blasting rocks to find a hidden door, moving statues to block the enemy's path, or incorporating effects such as leaving blast marks on concrete or tearing up the grass.

Be sure not to "tease" the player with the environment, though. If a box of radioactive material looks like it could be blown up, let the player blow it up, even if it serves no useful purpose. Useless interaction can add a sense of realism to a game. A great example is the *Zelda* series, in which the player can tear up grass, cut down trees, and pick up chickens.

Hidden treasures also add a bit of fun to an adventure game. Be sure to add plenty of secret areas and concealed items that might not be necessary to complete the game but that can help the player and make the game more entertaining.

Story Elements

Speaking of entertaining, what about the story behind the game? Is there a reason why the player is blasting all these robots?

An interesting story can inspire the player to reach various goals in the game and can just make the whole game more entertaining as a whole. How in-depth your story is depends on your target audience. Kids might be okay with having virtually no story, but a game for adults might be better with a more involved plot.

At a minimum, you could provide a background story at the beginning of the game and an end game sequence in which the player defeats the game. A more intricate story could involve showing cut scenes between levels or developing the plot within the game itself.

Cut scenes don't have to be fancy videos. They could be created using the game engine itself, overlaid with speech bubbles as the players communicate, as in an animated comic book. At a minimum, a cut scene could be as simple as displaying a short story on a splash screen.

The story could also progress within the game itself by making some characters talk to the player. They don't necessarily have to actually produce speech—voiceovers take an extraordinarily large amount of work—but you could use speech bubbles here as well.

As for the story itself, try to not to use a plot that is overused and mundane. Saving the princess and defeating a super villain bent on your destruction has been worked over a million times before.

The final goal of the game doesn't have to be immediately apparent to the player. Part of the game could be a mystery ("Why is the space station overrun by robots?") that inspires the player to find the answers.

Mysteries typically give the audience more questions whenever one is answered. For example, you could find out why the space station was overrun by robots: The space station team wasn't killed by the robots, but instead they departed before the robots arrived. Why did they abandon the space station? Try giving the player more questions to answer as the plot moves forward.

Additionally, plot twists can really add interest to a story. For example, players could find they weren't hired by the police as originally thought, but instead were hired by a bounty hunter.

The end of the story doesn't have to mean all questions have been answered, either. Cliffhangers always make room for sequels!

Speaking of which, having a cliffhanger at the end of a shareware demo can especially lure the user to pay for the full game, if only to find out what happens next.

Finally, the game doesn't have to end the same way every time. The plot could change based on decisions the player makes, allowing for multiple endings. This can add re-playability to the game. Check out Figure 18.3 for an example. This figure shows a plot tree with different outcomes and the game levels associated with each part of the story.

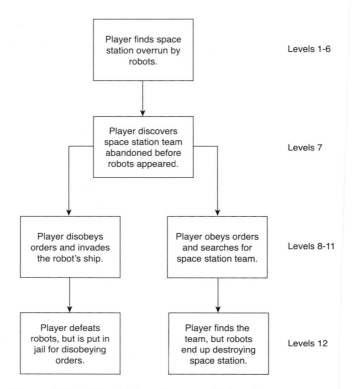

Figure 18.3 This plot tree shows multiple outcomes—a game doesn't have to end the same way every time.

Game Play

Besides being challenging and fun, game play can be broken down into two topics: goals and rewards.

Goals can be either presented by the game itself or determined by the player. For example, in an adventure game, the final goal presented to the player might be to find the ultimate treasure. But in a more open-ended game such as *SimCity*, the players might decide on their own goals, such as whether to build a large metropolis or a crime-free, environmentally sound suburb.

Besides the final goal of the game, there might be other goals, which can be divided into long-term and short-term goals. A long-term goal might be to advance to the next level, acquire new weapons and abilities, or expand the player's territory. A short-term goal might be to solve a puzzle, find some supplies, or climb over a cliff.

A player could lose interest without goals. This doesn't mean the game play has to be linear, but in general, you should try to make sure the player always has some sort of goal.

Also, during the course of a game, the goals should get harder to solve, gradually making the game more difficult. Ramping up the difficulty keeps the game continually challenging, which, in turn, keeps the game fun. On that note, you could also make your game have different levels of difficulty to appeal to a wider audience. Upping the difficulty might mean more enemies, harder challenges, or fewer supplies to work with.

But what is the player's motivation? Why does the player want to accomplish these goals, anyway?

The answer is: rewards. Rewards keep the user interested in playing the game by rewarding the player for solving goals or performing certain actions.

Rewards don't necessarily have to be for the player, such as points or prizes—they could also be for the user, such as special visual effects or a gratifying music sequence. Here are a few example rewards you can put in a game:

➤ Getting bonus points for picking up coins.

➤ Seeing a cool special effect or hearing a positive sound.

➤ Finding a hidden area in the game (make the user feel smart!) or discovering a shortcut between two places.

➤ Advancing to the next level or to an area of the game that has never been seen before.

➤ Seeing a satisfying "crush" or explosion when a bot is destroyed.

➤ Defeating a powerful enemy. You might want to include occasional "boss" enemies to spice things up.

➤ Acquiring a new weapon, item, or ability.

Keep the rewards unpredictable. It can become tedious if the only reward is finding coins. Also, consider how often the player receives a reward—you might want to ensure the player gets several rewards per minute. Too much time between awards can bore the player.

Teaching Users How to Play

Teaching a user how to play your game involves two different areas: the game input and the game play. Obviously, you're going to want players to know how to play the game, or they won't play it. So, it's up to you to teach them.

Input using the keyboard and mouse should be as easy to understand as possible. You don't want to confuse the player with too many buttons to press or require certain arcane keyboard combinations. Also, be sure to use keyboard and mouse controls that are common in other games because this is what players are familiar with. For example, first-person shooter games commonly use the WASD keyboard configuration, where W moves forward, A strafes left, S moves backward, and D strafes right.

The game play itself should be taught gradually. You don't want to overwhelm the player with every possible thing you can do in a game, such as 10 different weapons and half a dozen ways to jump, or how to use every game object. Instead, teach the basics at first and steadily add more bits to their wealth of knowledge. This might involve either implementing a tutorial or designing the game so that the player starts with just a few abilities and adds other powers and abilities over time. Also, the game could start with just a few different game objects to use, and the player could learn how to use more objects over time.

Users don't have to feel like they are learning, however. Some games make learning tightly integrated with the game so that it's part of the game play rather than being interrupted by a "tutorial" dialog box or an obnoxious character.

However, if the learning experience is too slow for experienced players, you might want to consider allowing the user to skip through parts of the teaching process or start the game at an advanced level.

That's it for game design. But remember, as you're tweaking the design of your game, paying attention to the details, the goal is to make the game entertaining. Do whatever it takes to make it fun.

Creating a Map Editor

The design of a level is really what makes the game fun, and a level designer typically edits and tweaks any particular level an immeasurable number of times. When you're making a game with different levels, you're going to want the map-creation process to be as easy as possible.

It can quickly become tedious to edit maps by hand in a text file. Plus, if you have someone acting as a level designer for your game, you want the map-creation process to be as streamlined as possible so you don't have to spend a lot of time on support and training.

You should try to let level designers use the tools they want to use. If they want to use tool X, this might mean you'll just have to write a parser to read files created by tool X, or you'll have to write a converter to convert tool X files to the file format used by the game.

However, if the level designer wants to use the latest ultraexpensive, do-everything cool 3D tool, hobbyists who can't afford the tool will be left out.

So, you might want to consider creating a free, easy-to-use map editor so that anyone who wants to can create and edit maps for your game. A free map editor would be specific to your game and allow someone to easily edit and create maps, including placing objects and possibly editing simple scripts. You don't need to provide an editor for things such as 3D objects or textures—those can be created in external programs.

Creating a free map editor has several advantages:

> ➤ It's easy to create levels and thus easy to extend your game.

> ➤ It's easy for other people to create levels. You don't have to spend lots of time on support or training.

> ➤ Releasing an editor helps build a user community around your game.

> ➤ User-created content adds variety and re-playability to your game.

If you decide to create a map editor, you'll want to make it as easy to use as possible while providing every possible option in the game. You might want to provide the following in the map editor:

➤ Provide an easy way to design the environment, whether it's 2D or 3D. Think about how easy it is to build roads in *SimCity* or houses in *The Sims*.

➤ Provide an import function to import 3D graphics formats.

➤ Provide a media library to store textures and sounds. Media could easily be added with drag and drop, and level designers could use drag and drop to place textures into the environment (walls, terrain, and so on).

➤ Provide a "common structure" library to store commonly used environment structures. Level designers could store things such as a common "elevator room" or winding hallway.

➤ Provide drag-and-drop placement of environment effects, such as lighting.

➤ Provide drag-and-drop placement of game objects.

➤ Provide a method to easily tweak game object properties.

➤ Provide an easy interface to add scripting to any object.

➤ Provide a preview button that shows what the map looks like in the game.

➤ Provide a launch button that automatically launches the game with the map the user is working on.

➤ Provide an automatic deployment button that puts all the necessary files for a game in one place.

For a Java game, you'll probably want to implement a map editor using the Swing UI toolkit so the editor will be flexible and cross-platform. While you're making an editor, don't forget about common application commands such as cut, copy, paste, undo, and redo.

NOTE
Sometimes editors are so fun to make that you spend more time creating editors than creating the game itself. Be sure to budget your time wisely.

Debugging

With any project, there will be bugs and—this is the surprising part—you're going to have to debug them. Types of bugs can range anywhere from slight display problems, crashes due to exceptions, or the game simply not working as it was intended.

You can put bugs into three different categories:

➤ **Bugs due to design**. For example, collision-detection code might not be designed to handle certain situations that weren't originally considered in the design. Because these bugs involve redesigning part of your game, they can be difficult to fix.

➤ **Bugs due to human error**. This could be just something missing in the code or a simple typo. These bugs are often easy to fix but can occasionally be difficult to track down.

➤ **Bugs due to machine differences**. What works on one machine (or virtual machine) might not work on another. These can be difficult to fix if you don't have access to the machine that exhibits the bug.

It might sound ridiculous, but the best way to debug is to not write bugs in the first place. Being careful with your code and design can take less time than trying to track down a strange bug or having to redesign huge sections of code later. Also, bugs due to machine differences can often be avoided by just paying close attention to potential exceptions and return values of methods in the API.

These bug-prevention techniques will help limit the number of bugs in the first place:

➤ Don't "compile, run, and pray." Whenever you write a piece of code, look over it once to check for anything you missed. Look over it twice if you don't feel sure it will work. Try to do what it takes to be confident that your code will work before you run it.

➤ Pay attention to the API documentation. Make sure you understand the specification of a method, catch exceptions, check return values, and pass in legal parameters.

➤ Document your code. It's harder to debug something later if you can't tell what's going on. Documentation really helps clear it up. (I'm still not the best at this one.)

➤ Likewise, make the code as readable as possible. Use meaningful, descriptive variable names such as `numberOfItems` instead of short, ambiguous names such as `num`.

➤ Write unit tests, and run the game often. Unit tests are simple instructions that test one of your method's various ways to make sure it follows its specifications. You can then run these unit tests when you change a method, to make sure everything is still working properly. But you don't have to unit-test everything. Don't be tempted to spend most of your time writing tests—there's a game to create!

➤ Log errors, warnings, and information. This can help you track down bugs if any occur, and you can always turn off logging by default in the final release.

➤ Eventually, you'll get a sort of "Spidey-sense," knowing something is wrong just at first glance!

In my own experience, a lot of hard-to-find bugs commonly occur after writing or rewriting a lot of code at once (thousands of lines) without doing any runtime tests. If you can, write or rewrite only small portions at a time so you can test major code additions and changes incrementally.

Of course, no matter what you do, bugs will creep in. When you get bugs, here are some tips on fixing them:

➤ If you're getting an exception, make sure you compile the code in debug mode and run the game from the console. This way, you'll get a stack trace so you can get the exact line number of the method that throws the exception. Because it's so easy to find the source of exceptions, this is one of the easiest problems to fix in Java.

➤ Use a debugger to step though the code, line by line.

➤ Write extra log statements to help narrow down the source of the bug.

➤ If you suspect thread deadlock, run the game from the console, wait for the deadlock to occur, and then return to the console and enter Ctrl+break on Windows (or Ctrl+\ on Mac OS X and UNIX). This shows the state of the threads, any locks acquired, and any deadlock detected.

Using `println debugging` is a quick-and-dirty way to narrow down a bug. For example, let's say you have a bug somewhere dealing with a couple of `Point` instances. You could print the values of each of the points to the console:

```
Point p1 = new Point(x1, x2);
Point p2 = new Point(y1, y2);
System.out.println("Two points: " + p1 + " and " + p2);
```

In this case, you use `println debugging` to make sure the point values are correct right after you create them. In this trivial example, the points are created incorrectly, and the code should instead look like this:

```
Point p1 = new Point(x1, y1);
Point p2 = new Point(x2, y2);
```

This debugging technique can be useful for exceptions. Here, you print the stack trace for a thrown exception:

```
try {
    ...
}
catch (Exception ex) {
    // print stack trace and continue
    ex.printStackTrace();
}
```

Or, you can print a stack trace without throwing or catching anything:

```
new Throwable().printStackTrace();
```

Or, you can just print the first line (last method called) of a stack trace:

```
System.out.println(new Throwable().getStackTrace()[0]);
```

Here, the `getStackTrace()` method returns an array of `StackTraceElements`, and you print the first one.

Of course, not all bugs lead to disastrous results or incorrect behavior. Some of them cause problems only in rare cases. For example, memory leaks could be one of those problems.

Memory leaks are common in languages that require you to deallocate memory, but you shouldn't have that problem in Java because of the garbage collector, right? Well, that's not the only cause of memory leaks. Remember, the garbage collector collects only objects that no longer have references to them. So, another reason why you might get leaks is because the application is keeping objects around that are no longer needed, and that collection of unneeded objects grows over time. For example, you could put objects in a `HashMap` that stays alive during the course of the game. If new objects are continually added but unneeded objects are never removed, the memory used by the `HashMap` will grow, resulting in a leak. This is something to keep in mind.

If you're trying to detect a leak and suspect it's because of something like this, you could periodically check the size of the `HashMap` (or other `Collection` class) to see how it changes during the course of a game. If its size grows in a way that it shouldn't, it could be a leak.

Debugging Java2D Issues

If you suspect your game has bugs related to graphics issues on Windows machines, first make sure the machine has the latest video drivers. If the problem persists, try disabling various Java2D enhancements using these command-line flags:

```
-Dsun.java2d.d3d=false
```

```
-Dsun.java2d.ddoffscreen=false
```

```
-Dsun.java2d.noddraw=true
```

You can find out more of what Java2D is doing by logging everything that is drawn, from lines to rectangles to images. This can help you both debug and track down performance problems. Use this command-line flag:

```
-Dsun.java2d.trace=<options>
```

Here, `<options>` is a comma-separated list of these options:

➤ `log` logs each Java2D draw operation when it is invoked.

➤ `timestamp` adds a timestamp (in milliseconds) of the time of each operation.

➤ `count` displays a count of each invoked operation when the app exits.

➤ `out:<filename>` sends output to the specified file rather than the console.

➤ `help` displays the usage of this flag.

➤ `verbose` displays a summary of the options used.

For example, you could use this flag to log the count of each operation to the file log.txt:

```
-Dsun.java2d.trace=count,out:log.txt
```

This would give a general idea about the Java2D operations used in a game. Here's an example output from the tile-based game in Chapter 5, "Creating a 2D Platform Game":

```
85339 calls to sun.awt.windows.Win32BlitLoops::
    Blit("Short 565 RGB DirectDraw with 1 bit transp",
    SrcOverNoEa, "Short 565 RGB DirectDraw")
31698 calls to sun.awt.windows.Win32BlitLoops::
    Blit("Short 565 RGB DirectDraw",
    SrcNoEa, "Short 565 RGB DirectDraw")
...
118723 total calls to 18 different primitives
```

Only the two highest-used primitives are produced here—18 primitives are shown altogether. For these two blit operations, the first parameter is the type of the source image, the second parameter is the composite type, and the third parameter is the type of the destination image. The composite type is like the types in the `AlphaComposite` class, except with `NoEa` as a suffix to specify that the image has "no extra alpha" information.

Logging

As mentioned here and in Chapter 6, "Multi-Player Games," logging can help diagnose problems and provide warnings and information about how a game executes. And, of course, if you log to a file, you can study the log later.

Using a logger also allows you to easily control the granularity of the log information so you can see only warnings and severe messages instead of seeing all information. Also, you can redirect the log output in various ways, such as to the console, to a file, or to a network stream.

Logs don't necessarily have to be simple text sentences. They can also be data that is later externally parsed into another format. For example, if you are trying to debug the creation of an internal 2D geometric map, you could log the structure of the map as SVG data and then use a SVG viewer to get a visualization of the data.

Apache log4j was used in Chapter 6, and in Chapter 13, "Artificial Intelligence," you rolled your own logger using an in-game message queue to log the decisions bots make. Besides using these methods and println logging, the java.util.logging package is included with J2SE 1.4; we'll give a quick overview of that next.

First, you need your own `Logger` object:

```
static final Logger log =
Logger.getLogger("com.brackeen.javagamebook.tilegame");
```

This statement gets the `Logger` named `com.brackeen.javagamebook.tilegame`, or creates a new one if it doesn't exist. You can use this statement in every class in your code, and it will return the same `Logger` object. You can log statements at various levels, like this:

```
log.info("Loading resources");
log.warning("No MIDI soundbank available.");
log.severe("Dude, we can't find that file!");
```

Logging at different levels means you can get an idea of the severity of each log statement, and you can also choose to output information at only the level you want to see. For example, if you want to see only severe log information, use this code:

```
log.setLevel(Level.SEVERE);
```

The logger itself uses two objects to log your information: a `Handler`, which handles log statements, sending this to, say, a file or the console; and a `Formatter`, which formats the look of your log statements, optionally adorning it with things such as time stamps and class/method information. By default, a `Logger` uses its parent handler, which uses the `ConsoleHandler` and the `SimpleFormatter`. Here's an example of using your own handler and formatter:

```
// log to the console
ConsoleHandler myHandler = new ConsoleHandler();

// use a minimal formatter
myHandler.setFormatter(new Formatter() {
    public String format(LogRecord record) {
        return record.getLevel() + ": " +
            record.getMessage() + "\n";
    }
});

// only use our own handler
log.setUseParentHandlers(false);
log.addHandler(myHandler);
```

Here, you use a `ConsoleHandler`, make your own `Formatter`, and turn off use of the parent formatter.

Of course, there are lots of possibilities for different handlers. For example, you might want to create a handler that sends severe log statements to an external server. This way, you can find out severe problems that other people have when they play your game.

If you do something like this, however, be sure to pop up a dialog box, tell the user what data you want to send, and ask the user if it is okay to send this data to your server. Otherwise, people could get upset about their computers sending data, even if the data does not personally identify them or their computer.

In a final game, you might want to just turn off all logging, like this:

```
log.setLevel(Level.OFF);
```

Notice that even if logging is turned off, objects created for the log record are still created, and any calculations for the log statement are still performed. For example, in this log statement, the distance is still calculated and converted to a string, which is then appended to the existing string:

```
log.info("Dude, the distance is: " + point.distance(x, y));
```

Obviously, if you were calculating the distance between two points several times a frame, it could impact performance. If you want to avoid things such as this, you can use a search-and-replace function to comment out every log statement in your Java files.

Protecting Code

As you probably already know, Java class files aren't very well protected from being decompiled. Plenty of free Java class file decompilers (such as Jode and Jad) can decompile your class files into Java files, and even show the original method and field names, all with the click of a button.

If your game is open source, this isn't an issue. But there are a few reasons why you might want to protect your code, such as to prevent cheating in multiplayer games or to protect your work from being copied and used by others.

One way to protect code is to create your own class-encryption mechanism. However, you still need to create a "bootloader" class to actually decrypt everything. This bootloader class could be decompiled, which is a problem: If the decryption methods can be decompiled, the class files can be decrypted and decompiled outside the game. Although it's not a secure solution, it would make it harder for the game to be decompiled.

An imperfect but very useful way to protect code is to use an obfuscator. An obfuscator mangles class names, method names, and field names, with the idea that the resulting class file, if decompiled, would be extremely difficult to read and comprehend (though not impossible). For example, an obfuscator would take some code that looks like this:

```
public int getSecretValue(int code) {
    return translator[code];
}
```

and mangle it into something like this:

```
public int a(int a) {
    return b[a];
}
```

Of course, obfuscators mangle these names in ways that still produce valid Java code—the VM won't think the class file is broken.

A couple issues arise with obfuscation, however. For example, using `Class.forName()` to get a class by its name won't work anymore. Also, you should be careful not to obfuscate public APIs that plug-ins or scripts use.

Another advantage of obfuscators is that they can dramatically shrink class size, making them smaller for distribution.

Some useful obfuscators include ProGuard (free) and DashO (commercial).

Game Deployment

When you're ready to deploy your game over the web, you should make it as easy as possible for people to download and install, with the goal that everyone who wants to play the game has an opportunity to do so.

In other words, you want to avoid something like this scenario:

1. The user clicks a link to download a zip file and waits for it to download.

2. The user unzips the file and sees some jar files, some class files, some images, and a readme file. (This assumes the user knows how to unzip a file, which isn't always the case.)

3. A user familiar with jar files might double-click the jar file, expecting it to run, but nothing happens. At this point, the way to run the game isn't immediately apparent, and many users will just give up.

4. Some users will actually open the readme file, which says to type in this code to run the game:

```
java -cp game.jar coolgame.MainClass
```

However, many people will not even know what a command line is. Again, at this point, you've just lost more users.

5. The user opens a command window but doesn't know to navigate to the folder where the zip file was expanded, so the command doesn't work.

This can be a frustrating nightmare—nobody wants to spend time downloading a game only to be unable to run it. And even the extra steps involved can be annoying for tech-savvy people.

So, be sure to use a game-deployment technique that the most computer-illiterate people you know can handle and that requires the least amount of steps to perform. The more steps that are involved, the more problems people will have.

Here are a few other ways to deploy a game:

➤ Applets are incredibly easy because running an applet involves only navigating to a web page. However, this means the applet must be downloaded every time the person visits the page, and applets have many restrictions. Also, most browsers support only Java 1.1 applets.

➤ Executable jar files save a lot of time, but sometimes it's not obvious that a jar file is executable.

➤ Create your own installer, either as an executable jar file or a native executable.

➤ Use an existing installation product such as InstallAnywhere (both free and commercial editions available).

Another thought to consider is that many people won't have the latest Java runtime on their machines, and they'll have to download it separately. Some installation products can optionally bundle a Java runtime with the installer, however.

When considering installers, something to think about is that some people don't realize that they actually have to run an installer after they've downloaded it—they think whatever they downloaded is automatically installed and they don't have to do anything else. Or, they forget to run the installer.

Wouldn't it be great if the download, installation, and execution were all automatic? In other words, the only steps involved would be something like this:

1. The user clicks a link to download a file and waits for it to download.

2. The game automatically installs and runs.

Well, good news—that's exactly what Java Web Start does.

Game Deployment with Java Web Start

Java Web Start is a deployment technology that can automatically download and install your games. All the users have to do is click a link on a web page, and the rest is automatic. It's one of the easiest methods of game deployment.

You'll need a few tricks to set up your game to use Java Web Start. Here's an overview:

➤ Put all game resources (images, sounds, and maps) in a jar file.

➤ Sign the jar files.

➤ Create a JNLP file, which descries the game and its resources.

➤ Set up your web server to correctly serve JNLP files.

Retrieving Resources from .jar Files

First, you need to make sure all the game resources are stored in jar files. These can be separate jars, if you like—for example, you could have one jar for code, another for sounds, another for images, and so on.

In the game itself, you can retrieve a file from a jar (as long as it's in the classpath) by using the `getResource()` method of `ClassLoader`, like this:

```
String filename = "path/image.png";
ClassLoader classLoader = this.getClass().getClassLoader();
URL url = classLoader.getResource(filename);
```

This returns the URL to a resource. You can also directly get the `InputStream` to a resource:

```
InputStream is = classLoader.getResourceAsStream(filename);
```

Signing .jar Files

Next, you need to sign the jar files (all of them, even if they don't contain any code). Signing the jar files is required for Java Web Start to assign the correct security permissions to your game. For example, you need security permissions to switch to full-screen exclusive mode.

Signing the jar is like signing a contract—you sign it with your name to ensure that you wrote it and that the program will do no harm to the user's machine. First, you need to generate a key by using the keytool command-line tool included with the J2SDK:

```
keytool -genkey -keystore samplekeystore -alias Nobody
```

This creates a new key for the alias Nobody stored in the file samplekeystore. This command-line tool prompts you to enter a password and other information about you, including your name, organization, city, state, and country.

To sign a jar, you can use the `<signjar>` task in your Ant build file, like this:

```
<signjar jar="${basedir}/tilegame.jar"
    storepass="secret"
    alias="Nobody"
    keystore="${basedir}/samplekeystore"/>
```

Here, you specify the alias Nobody, the password, the keystore, and, of course, the jar to sign. Remember, you've got to sign all jars for your game.

Creating a JNLP File

Next, you need to create a JNLP file. A JNLP file, short for Java Network Launching Protocol, describes the game and what security permissions and resources (jar files) it needs.

JNLP files are XML files. You can see an example in Listing 18.4.

Listing 18.4   tilegame.jnlp

```
<?xml version="1.0" encoding="utf-8"?>
<jnlp spec="1.0+"
  codebase="http://www.brackeen.com/javagamebook"
  href="tilegame.jnlp">
  <information>
    <title>Tile-based game</title>
    <vendor>David Brackeen</vendor>
    <homepage href="."/>
    <description>Tile-based game</description>
    <description kind="short">A demo from chapter 5.</description>
    <icon href="icon.gif"/>
    <icon kind="splash" href="splash.gif"/>
    <offline-allowed/>
  </information>
  <security>
    <!-- get all permissions so we can access
    fullscreen exclusive mode -->
    <all-permissions/>
  </security>
  <resources>
    <j2se version="1.4+" initial-heap-size="32m"/>
    <jar href="tilegame.jar"/>
    <jar href="tilegameres.jar"/>
  </resources>
  <application-desc
    main-class="com.brackeen.javagamebook.tilegame.GameManager"/>
</jnlp>
```

Here you set the codebase for the game (www.brackeen.com/javagamebook) and the reference to the JNLP file (tilegame.jnlp) relative to the codebase.

In the information section, there are references to two images: the icon and the splash image. The icon is used with the Java Web Start Application Manager, as in Figure 18.4.

Figure 18.4 The Java Web Start Application Manager shows an icon for every application, along with the name, home page, and description.

This shows a 32×32 version of the icon. A 64×64 version of the icon is used when downloading the app (see Figure 18.5); Java Web Start will resize the icon for any size needed. The icon can be in either the GIF or the JPEG format. Here, we use GIF to take advantage of transparency.

Figure 18.5 The Java Web Start Application Manager uses a 64×64 icon when downloading the application.

Icons are used with the operating system's window manager as well—for example, if the user puts a link to the application in the Start menu in Windows.

The splash screen is displayed when the app is loading. Java Web Start opens a new instance of the Java VM to run your app, and the splash screen is displayed during this time. If there is no splash screen, it uses the icon and displays something like the download dialog box in Figure 18.5.

Permissions are set in the `<security>` tag, which you need for full-screen mode. The only choice is All Permissions, so you also can do other things such as save games to the user's computer or access a remote server.

The rest of the JNLP file specifies the jar files you need (relative to the codebase) and the main class to start. Note that Java Web Start apps ignore the jar's manifest files: You still need to specify the main class in the JNLP file.

Setting Up a Web Server

There's really only one thing to do to set up a web server for JNLP files, and that's to associate the JNLP files with the correct MIME type: `application/x-java-jnlp-file`. This is required so that Java Web Start clients can load the file instead of web browsers.

If you have your own Apache web server, you'll need to edit the mime.types file (often located at /etc/mime.types). Just add this line to the file:

```
application/x-java-jnlp-file      JNLP
```

Then restart the server:

```
/etc/rc.d/init.d/httpd restart
```

If you're running on a shared web server or otherwise don't have root access, ask your webmaster to make the change. If your webmaster can't or won't, there's one other possible solution: Place a file named .htaccess in the top directory of your website that contains only one line:

```
AddType application/x-java-jnlp-file      .jnlp
```

Note, however, that this works only on an Apache web server if it is set up to read the `AddType` command of .htaccess files. Ask your webmaster if you are unsure.

It can be confusing to tell whether what you've changed actually works. If you've previously opened the JNLP file in your browser, you might have to restart your browser or even clear your browser's cache. If it is still difficult to tell what is going on, use the code in Listing 18.5 to get the returned MIME type of a remote file.

Listing 18.5   GetContentType.java

```java
public class GetContentType {

    public static void main(String[] args) throws IOException {
        if (args.length != 1) {
            System.out.println("Shows the value of the " +
                "\"content-type\" header field of a remote file.");
            System.out.println("Usage: GetContentType (url)");
            System.out.println(
                "Example: GetContentType http://www.yahoo.com");
        }
        else {
            URL url = new URL(args[0]);
            URLConnection connection = url.openConnection();
            System.out.println(connection.getContentType());
        }
    }
}
```

You can use this simple program like this:

```
java GetContentType http://server/path/mygame.jnlp
```

If you set up your web server correctly, the program prints `application/x-java-jnlp-file` to the console. If not, it prints `text/plain` or something similar.

That's it for Java Web Start. Another useful feature is some JavaScript and VBScript code to detect whether Java Web Start is installed and even to offer a one-click install of the Java runtime on Windows machines. You can download the JavaScript code at `java.sun.com/products/javawebstart/1.2/docs/developersguide.html`.

Game Deployment with Native Compilation

A drawback to using Java Web Start is that the size of the Java runtime is rather large (10MB or more), and a user who doesn't already have it will have to spend some time downloading it, which can be a while for people on modems.

One solution that still allows you to distribute your game over the web is to use native compilation to compile Java classes to native code. The idea is to compile to native code so the Java runtime isn't needed; unfortunately, this idea doesn't work.

Two products that natively compile Java classes are GCJ and Excelsior JET. Unfortunately, GCJ currently doesn't support AWT or Swing. Excelsior JET does support AWT and Swing, but it actually requires the Java runtime for it to work. In short, for graphical applications, users need the Java runtime installed on their system anyway, so native compilation doesn't really help.

Updates and Patches

A good thing about Java Web Start is that it automatically downloads the latest jars for your game, so you don't have to provide extra support for updates and patches. Java Web Start downloads only the jars that have changed, so it downloads only the code jar or the media jar instead of everything at once.

If you're not using Java Web Start, at a minimum you'll want to provide a way to check in-game if there are updates available. If there are, either download the updates in-game or provide a link to the website so users can download them.

Checking for the latest version is fairly simple. All you have to do is keep a file on a web server somewhere that contains the latest version number, like this:

```
latest-version: 5.0.6
```

The updater checks this file to see if its version is lower than the version of the file. If so, there's a new update available, and the game can act accordingly.

Bandwidth Issues

If you make a game only for a demo to hand out to friends or add to your private port-folio, you won't have to host your game on a website. But if you want as many people to play your game as possible and you host your game on a site, you could quickly run into bandwidth issues. Don't be caught by surprise!

Even if your game is under the radar, it doesn't mean it won't become popular. If your site is popular, or if a site that gets a lot of traffic links to yours, several hundreds or even thousands of people could be downloading your game every day. Sounds great, doesn't it?

However, keep in mind the amount of bandwidth this is going to use. There is no such thing as "unlimited bandwidth"—read the fine print. Every web-hosting company will limit how much bandwidth your web site can use, usually around 10GB per month for cheap accounts or even as low as 1GB per month. If you have your own dedicated server, this will be higher, usually from 25GB per month to even 400GB per month or more.

Let's say your game is distributed in a 1MB bundle. If your host limits your bandwidth to 10GB per month, not counting things such as HTML pages and images, that limits you to 10,000 downloads per month, or 333 downloads every day. Furthermore, your hosting company will either charge you mad amounts of money or simply pull the plug on your site.

This means that not everyone who wants to download your game will have an oppor-tunity to do so, which is a problem you'll want to solve.

The easiest way to fix this problem is to not host the game, and instead to provide the download only on sites such as download.com. Or, if you're actually making money from your game, be sure to look at different hosting companies and their bandwidth options, try to estimate how much bandwidth you could possibly use, and pick a host-ing company that will allow you to easily expand as needed.

Getting Feedback and Beta Testing

Generally, you want to test your game on as many different machines as possible to see how it runs on different operating systems and hardware. Even though Java is cross-platform, your game might have slight differences in the way it behaves on different operating systems; this can depend on the processor, processor speed, memory, video card, and every other piece of hardware a computer has.

If you don't have access to different computers, generally you'll find enough people on the web to test the game. All you have to do is provide an easy way to download the game, such as by using Java Web Start, as mentioned earlier.

During testing, before the final game is released (often called beta testing), you'll want to provide a bug-reporting e-mail address, a web form, or even a form within the game itself so that users can easily provide feedback. Providing an in-game bug-reporting tool makes it easer for the users to report bugs, and the tool can provide information about the user's environment, such as the operating system or Java version. You can get this information by using the `getProperty()` method of the `System` class.

When your game is "out there," you'll be getting a lot of feedback from different people, and not just on machine-specific issues or bugs. This feedback can be one of the best methods to find ways to tune and polish your game. You'll want to get feedback on these aspects of your game:

➤ **Game play.** Is the game challenging and well-balanced?

➤ **Graphics and sound.** How does it compare to other games?

➤ **Performance.** Did it run smoothly?

➤ **Ease of use.** Were the controls intuitive? Did the game teach the player how to play at a satisfactory rate?

➤ **Fun and re-playability.** Is it genuinely entertaining? Can you play it over and over and still have fun?

➤ **Installation process.** Was it trivial to install and run the game?

Be sure to provide an easily accessible e-mail address, feedback form, or discussion board so people can voice their opinions and give feedback on your game.

Also be aware that many people on the Internet are incapable of providing constructive criticism. Don't be offended by questionable or offensive comments. Instead, turn on your translator to interpret those comments into something meaningful! For example:

> **User comment:** "d00d, ur keyboard controls suck! u suck!"

> **Translation:** "I found the keyboard controls of your game to be something different from what I am used to and/or difficult to control, and suggest you modify that behavior. I do not hold this against you personally."

> **User comment:** "this game is dumb it don't work"

> **Translation:** "Either the download and installation process was too difficult, or the game does not run on my system. You might want to ask me more questions to help find the problem. I also have issues with spelling and grammar."

> **User comment:** "this is stoopid, the game _____ is much better"

> **Translation:** "I found another game to be more entertaining than yours, but I didn't tell you why, so my comment isn't very useful in helping you make your game better."

Many times, though, you'll get lots of ideas from people on how to make your game better or more intuitive to play. Be sure to listen to what they have to say, and try to implement the best ideas. But keep in mind that you don't have to implement every requested feature. If you did, the game could end up with so many features that it would be a burden to play or would just not be as fun anymore. Know when to listen to and when to ignore feedback—you've got to say "no" sometimes.

Making Money

So, you're looking to put some bread on the table with your Java game, eh?

Making money with a game is one of the most difficult things to accomplish, and how you attempt to make money depends on the audience you are aiming for, what type of game you make, and how polished your game is. But it can be done, and it has been done with many different Java games before.

One way to indirectly make money with your game is to just make a demo that can help you get a higher-paying job.

If you want your game to end up in retail stores, you're going to need to find a publisher, which is one of the hardest and potentially costliest things to do. Alternatively, here are a few other ideas for making money:

➤ License the game engine to third parties. If your engine is unique, flexible, and well documented, other development companies might be interested in licensing it for their own products.

➤ Create branded applet games for commercial web sites. For example, a soda company might want you to create "Fizzy Drink Racer" for its web site.

➤ Show advertisements next to or within the game.

➤ Make the game shareware, giving away the first few levels for free and charging for the full version of the game. You can charge for your game with the help of online payment systems such as PayPal, Kagi, or BMT Micro.

➤ Charge a monthly fee to play a massively multi-player online game.

For some examples of Java games, the Race3D engine (by yours truly) has been licensed and customized for more than half a dozen companies, including Snapple and Subaru. *RuneScape* by Jagex is a massively multi-player online game that charges a monthly fee. Yahoo! games show advertisements next to the game. There are a whole slew of J2ME pay-to-play games on cell phones. Also, the commercial CD-ROM games *You Don't Know Jack* and *Who Wants to Be a Millionaire?* are partially written in Java.

Putting It All Together

As an example of some of the ideas from this chapter, the source for this chapter includes a variant of the tile-based game from Chapter 5 that shows different game states (including a loading screen), logging using the java.util.logging package, and JNLP capability. You could still add plenty to this game, but I'll leave that part up to you!

Summary

This chapter has covered a wide range of topics to help complete the last 10% of your game. We talked about the game as a state machine, game design and storytelling, game play, debugging, logging, game deployment, Java Web Start, and how to make money with your game.

Finishing a game can be hard. It can take up a lot of your time and sometimes seems pointless. But the end result is worth it, so get working on finishing your game!

Chapter 19

The Future

KEY TOPICS

- How Java Evolves
- The Future: Java 1.5 "Tiger"
- What the Java Platform Needs
- New Devices and the Java Games Profile (JSR 134)
- Summary

Writing about "the future" in a printed text is a bit silly. The future is rarely what someone predicts it to be: Some predictions will come to pass, others won't, and some things will happen that no one can expect. By the time some people read this, the so-called "future" will have already passed by and the world will be radically different.

But this chapter isn't only about the future at the time of writing; it's also about what you can do to help shape the future of the Java platform.

This chapter covers three aspects of the future: how Java evolves, what's going to happen to Java, and what changes Java needs to make developing games in Java better.

How Java Evolves

Although Sun ultimately gets to decide the direction Java takes, many features are made at the request of users like you and me. So, it's important to voice your opinion on how you want Java to evolve, and it's just as important to voice those opinions in the right channels so that Sun can hear you. The two main channels are the Java Community Process and the Bug Parade.

Java Community Process

The Java technology specifications and implementations evolve through the Java Community Process (located at www.jcp.org). Any member of the JCP can submit a Java Specification Request, or JSR, which either defines a new Java specification or updates an existing one.

Although most developers aren't interested in taking the time to submit a JSR, the JCP website allows you to review and comment on existing JSRs. Also, the site is a great way to look at what's coming in the Java platform.

In this chapter, we mention a few JSRs that are relevant to programming or technology and APIs that will be useful for Java games.

Bug Parade

The Bug Parade, (located at developer.java.sun.com/developer/bugParade) is the central location to submit bug reports and Requests for Enhancements (RFEs), and to check the status of existing bugs and RFEs. Bug reports and RFEs are for any Java technology, whether it's part of J2SE, another Java API led by Sun, or a VM.

Of course, if you ever have a bug to report or want to request a feature, do a thorough search of the Bug Parade first. Someone might have already reported the bug or made the request; if so, you could vote for the bug or add it to your watch list.

In this chapter, we mention a few features that will make Java games better, along with the Bug IDs that are associated with them.

The Future: Java 1.5 "Tiger"

A lot of potential technology is coming in Java 1.5, code-named "Tiger." However, we won't know what's actually included until it appears. At the moment, it's targeted to ship in the first half of 2004.

In this section, we cover some of the new bits of technology planned for Tiger and also how to use some of the new Java language additions.

Generics (JSR 14)

Unlike some languages, in Java, every object is a subclass of the `Object` class. Because of this, the collection classes (`List`, `Set`, `Map`, and so on) were designed to contain `Objects` so that any object could be contained in a collection.

However, working with collections in this manner has its problems. Consider this example:

```
// this list can hold any Object
List stringList = new ArrayList();
stringList.add("Hello");
stringList.add("World");

// this will cause a ClassCastException later
stringList.add(new Integer(13));

for (int i=0; i<stringList.size(); i++) {
    String s = (String)stringList.get(i);
    System.out.println(s);
}
```

In this code, the string list can hold any type of object, not just instances of the `String` object. If a different class, such as an `Integer`, is added to the list, during runtime the VM would throw `ClassCastException` when you try to cast that object to a `String`.

Of course, this problem can be solved with more attentive programming, but no one is perfect, right?

Generics, also called *parameterized types* or *templates*, offers to solve this problem. Generics is an upcoming addition to the Java language that will enable you to create a group of classes that have the same behavior but work with different types. As an example, the `List` collection class has similar behavior for whatever objects it contains, but you could define a specific `List` to work with different types such as `Strings` or `Integers`. This moves the type-checking to compile time rather than runtime.

In code, you would create a List<String> or a List<Integer> instead of a List. Consider the same example as before, but with generics:

```
// this list can only hold Strings
List<String> stringList = new ArrayList<String>();
stringList.add("Hello");
stringList.add("World");

// this would cause a compile-time error
//stringList.add(new Integer(13));

for (int i=0; i<stringList.size(); i++) {
    String s = stringList.get(i);
    System.out.println(s);
}
```

In this example, the string list can contain only String objects. If an Integer is added to the list, the source code wouldn't compile.

Also, the get() method of a List<String> returns a String, so you don't have to cast to a String in the source code.

Altogether, using generics gives these advantages:

➤ Safety (stricter compile-time checks).

➤ Code that is easier to read. (You know what types of elements a collection should contain.)

➤ Less casting.

NOTE
Using generics doesn't require any special bytecodes. The Java compiler will generate code that is backward-compatible with older VMs. So, the casting is still there in the compiled class.

The drawback to how generics are implemented is that they do not work with primitive types such as ints and floats. So, you'll either have to wrap primitive types in wrapper classes (Integer or Float) or implement your own collections for working with primitive types.

Enumerations (JSR 201)

In a lot of code in this book, we use integers to define enumerations, like this:

```
public static final int STATE_IDLE = 0;
public static final int STATE_ACTIVE = 1;
public static final int STATE_DESTROYED = 2;
```

This works but has its problems. Take a look at the basic `set` method:

```
public void setState(int state) {
    // doesn't check for illegal values!
    this.state = state;
}
```

First, in this case, illegal values aren't checked. Some rogue code could set the state as `42`. Optionally, you could check whether the value sent to this method is legal, as long as you maintained this code if the enumerations changed.

Also, for documentation purposes, you must explicitly state the valid values for this method.

Type-safe enumerations will fix this issue. Enumerations in Java will be defined similarly to how they are in C:

```
public enum State { IDLE, ACTIVE, DESTROYED }
```

In Java, however, enumerations are objects. The `setState()` method could be rewritten as follows:

```
public void setState(State state) {
    // null is only illegal value
    if (state == null) {
        throw new NullPointerException("Null State");
    }
    this.state = state;
}
```

Each value is its own instance, so you can still use the `==` operator:

```
if (state == State.IDLE) {
    state = State.ACTIVE;
}
```

To sum it up, enumerations give you similar productivity advantages as generics do:

> ➤ Safety (no illegal enumerations).

> ➤ Code that is easier to read. (Defining enumerations takes less code, and you do not need to document "legal" values.)

> ➤ Code that is easier to maintain. If additional values are added to the enumeration, no changes need to be made for illegal values.

Static Import (JSR 201)

Consider invoking a couple static methods like this:

```
System.out.println(Math.abs(-1));
```

The basic idea with static import is to provide easier-to-read code. With the upcoming static import language addition, you could import the static classes:

```
import static System.*;
import static Math.*;
```

Then you use their fields and methods directly, as if they were members of the class you are writing:

```
out.println(abs(-1));
```

This helps with readability. However, static import could confuse others in some cases as well. For example, another programmer might have trouble finding which class a particular method or field comes from. Be sure to use this feature when you're certain it actually helps readability, not when it could be confusing.

Enhanced *for* Loop (JSR 201)

Also part of JSR 201 is a language enhancement of the `for` loop when iterating over collections and arrays. This enhancement makes code easier to write, cleaner, and more readable.

Currently, iterating a list involves something like this (with generics):

```
for (Iterator<String> i = stringList.iterator(); i.hasNext();) {
    String s = i.next();
    System.out.println(s);
}
```

But with the enhanced `for` loop, the loop can be written like this:

```
for (String s : stringList) {
    System.out.println(s);
}
```

Similarly, for an array (in this example, an `int` array), it can be written like this:

```
int sum = 0;
for (int value : intArray) {
    sum += value;
}
```

Compiler API (JSR 199)

The new compiler API is designed to make compiling source code within Java applications easier.

Instead of using the command line to call the compiler and then parsing the results, the compiler API will allow Java applications to interact with the Java compiler directly and then retrieve the compilation results as structured data.

This will help if you want to do runtime compilation of game scripts. For example, you could compile Java source for a particular map directly within a map editor.

Network Transfer Format (JSR 200)

Currently, Java apps are typically compressed and distributed in JAR files.

JAR files are basically ZIP files. ZIP files contain files that are individually compressed and then combined into one file. The compression used in ZIP files is a dictionary-based compression technique in which common symbols found in the file are encoded to smaller, variable-length bit strings and the symbols are stored in a table.

JAR files are typically composed of dozens, hundreds, or even thousands of class files. Unfortunately, compressing each class file individually doesn't get as high compression rates as if the class files were compressed as a whole.

For example, consider the uncompressed rt.jar file included with J2SE 1.4.1. This file is about 22.4MB in size, but if it were a compressed JAR, it would be about 11.6MB. However, using tar and bzip2 (common UNIX tools) to combine and compress the class files contained in rt.jar results in a file about 6.2MB in size.

The network transfer format is designed to overcome the compression shortcomings of JAR files. It uses a few tricks that are purposely designed to compress class files. Users will be able to download smaller files that can be converted to standard JAR files on the local machine.

Shared VM (JSR 121)

Highly anticipated in Tiger is the shared virtual machine. A shared VM means one VM runs all Java applications, instead of starting a new VM for every application. This will save memory because only one heap is used, and Java applications will have a faster startup time if the VM is already running.

JSR 121 helps define how to isolate Java applications within this shared VM so that they cannot interfere with one another.

What the Java Platform Needs

The Java platform has made great strides for gaming, especially with version 1.4. However, there's still some technology and APIs that would make games written for the Java platform even better. In this section, we cover some.

Luckily, almost everything mentioned here either has a Bug Parade ID or is known to be considered for a future release. So, it won't be long until you see some of these features.

Needed: More Options for Mouse and Keyboard Input

For full-screen games, the AWT event architecture is a bit of overkill, and it doesn't give the kind of mouse and key input a typical game needs. You don't need a separate event thread to create a `MouseEvent` and a `KeyEvent` every time the user presses a key or moves the mouse. Also, the event architecture can create a delay from the time the user presses a key to the point that the game actually receives it.

Instead, it would be great to poll the keys pressed on the keyboard and the state of the mouse. That is, you would directly sniff out the state of the keyboard and mouse in the main game loop and react accordingly. This would also minimize the delay from the time the user presses a key to the time the game reacts to it.

Also, in this book we provided a way to implement mouselook-style movement because the current API gives only an absolute mouse location. Instead, it would be very useful to provide relative mouse movement to make mouselook-style movement more robust.

Also, some mouse devices are employing force-feedback capabilities, which would be great to control from a Java game. Force feedback is the name given to vibrating joysticks, mouse devices, or other devices to give the player feedback on what is happening within a game. For example, the mouse could vibrate when the player gets attacked by a monster or falls to the ground. Also, some force feedback mouse devices and joysticks add resistance so that as the player throttles a plane in a flight simulator, for example, the joystick becomes harder to press forward.

Finally, the mouse cursor can be made invisible by sending a custom mouse image, but it's not perfect on all platforms. For example, moving the mouse on some machines causes strange repaint behavior to occur, even when the mouse is invisible. It would be nice to switch off the cursor completely.

```
Input polling Bug ID: 4083501
```

```
Mouse cursor invisibility Bug ID: 4526950
```

Needed: Joystick Input

The mouse and keyboard are fine for many gamers, but a lot of people like to use joysticks, game pads, and steering wheels with all the buttons. You need a way to poll the joystick for input similarly to how you want to poll the mouse and keyboard. And don't forget about force-feedback capabilities!

```
Input polling Bug ID: 4083501
```

Needed: Hardware-Accelerated Translucent Images

Although having translucent graphics isn't that important in 2D games, anti-aliased graphics are almost expected, and you need fast translucency for anti-aliased graphics.

Currently, drawing a translucent image requires a read-and-set for every pixel in the image, which, of course, is rather slow. Video cards can do this quickly in hardware, so Java should provide a way to draw translucent images in hardware. Most of this will happen without any programmer intervention, but you also need updated APIs to support translucency in a `VolatileImage`.

Luckily, hardware-accelerated translucent image support is coming soon. Chances are, it will be available in J2SE 1.5.

Needed: Higher Resolution Timer

As mentioned before, the timer that Java uses doesn't have the best resolution. Calling `System.currentTimeMillis()` has a resolution of 55ms on Windows 95/98/Me and 10–15ms on NT/2000/XP, which isn't granular enough for many games. 55ms means that the timer changes only 18.2 times per second, but you're trying to create games that run at 30 frames per second or higher.

However, Linux and Mac OS X have 1ms granularity.

Either the `System.currentTimeMillis()` method needs to guarantee 1ms resolution on all platforms or there needs to be a high-resolution timer API with 1ms or even microsecond resolution.

Bug ID: 4478186

Needed: Hardware-Accelerated Graphics and Full-Screen on Linux

Even though Linux isn't the most popular OS for the home market, you still need hardware-accelerated graphics on Linux, including the capability to change the display mode on the fly and make full-screen games. Without it, Java games on Linux are inferior to those on other operating systems.

Also, hardware-acceleration will greatly speed up Swing performance on Linux.

Rumor has it that this feature is coming in J2SE 1.5.

Bug ID: 4498974

Needed: Hardware-Accelerated 3D Included with the Runtime

Java3D is currently not included with the Java runtime and isn't available on all platforms—most notably, Mac OS X. First, for game developers to create cross-platform Java games, Java3D should work on all platforms that Java runs on.

Second, the Java3D API should be included with the runtime. If that is not possible, there could be a "lite" version of Java3D included with the runtime because the Java3D API provides some functionality that not all developers need. Or, instead of a "lite" Java3D, a simple OpenGL-binding (such as GL4Java) could be included with the runtime.

Needed: HotSpot SIMD Optimizations

SIMD, or *Single Instruction Multiple Data*, is a processor instruction set that performs the same task on a set of data at the same time. For example, in one instruction, instead of telling the processor to add two numbers, you can tell the processor to add one array of numbers to another array of numbers, as in Figure 19.1.

Single Instruction, Single Data   Single Instruction, Multiple Data

Figure 19.1 A SIMD instruction can do the same amount of work with multiple data that a SISD instruction does for single data.

SIMD is great for things such as MP3 decoding, sound processing, image processing, software texture mapping, and speech processing, to name a few applications.

The good news is almost all processors sold today have some sort of SIMD instructions capability:

➤ AMD's Athlon has 3DNow!

➤ Intel's Pentium 4 has MMX, SSE, and SSE2.

➤ Motorola's PowerPC G4 has AltiVec.

➤ Sun's UltraSparc has VIS.

At first, developers had to write in Assembly language to take advantage of these hardware instructions. Now, this isn't the case. Some modern C/C++ compilers can automatically make SIMD optimizations without any input from the programmer.

The downfall is that if you compile your C/C++ code for a certain platform, such as the Pentium 4, it'll only run on a Pentium 4 or better. For a Pentium 3 or an Athlon, you'll need a separate executable.

But Java is meant to be portable. When Java byte-code is compiled to native code with HotSpot, HotSpot is really competing with C/C++ compilers. So, HotSpot should include automatic SIMD optimizations.

Of course, if implemented, HotSpot would have a few advantages over automatic SIMD optimization in C/C++ compilers:

➤ HotSpot could check which SIMD instructions the processor supports, if any, and automatically generate SIMD code for that processor.

➤ No need would exist for Java apps to create different executables or code paths for each processor.

➤ Older Java applications could take advantage of the SIMD HotSpot upgrade without being recompiled.

Desired: More Font-Smoothing Options

Even though the Java platform has the capability to draw anti-aliased fonts, there are a few problems:

➤ Swing components (buttons, menus, lists, and so on) aren't anti-aliased.

➤ The anti-aliasing default is off, even if the operating system has anti-aliasing on.

➤ No support exists for sub-pixel font rendering.

Although Swing is usually used for applications, in Chapter 3, "Interactivity and User Interfaces," we showed how Swing can be used for the user interface in full-screen games. Unfortunately, text in Swing components does not have any font smoothing, even if the operating system has font smoothing on by default. So, Swing components don't look as nice as they could.

As far as font-smoothing techniques go, another technique besides anti-aliasing is called sub-pixel rendering. This is also called ClearType by Microsoft.

Sub-pixel rendering takes advantage of the pixel layout of LCD displays. LCDs actually show three tall, thin sub-pixels for each pixel onscreen: one each for red, green, and blue. An example of this is in Figure 19.2 (in glorious black and white!). This figure shows how a single white pixel is composed of a red, green, and blue sub-pixel. Your eyes blend the sub-pixels so that the pixel appears white.

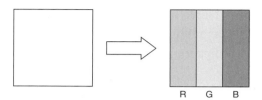

Figure 19.2 A single pixel on an LCD display is actually composed of three vertically oriented pixels: one each for red, green, and blue.

So, a completely white display would have a sub-pixel layout like the one shown in Figure 19.3.

Figure 19.3 A completely white display is composed of alternating red, green, and blue pixels.

In a typical text representation, fonts are drawn with black text on a white background. With no font smoothing, every pixel is either completely white or completely black. For anti-aliasing, pixels on the edge of the fonts can be various shades of gray to help smooth the edges of the text.

Sub-pixel rendering takes font smoothing a step further by taking advantage of the sub-pixel layout. Instead of turning each pixel either completely on or off, it turns each sub-pixel completely on or off, like in Figure 19.4.

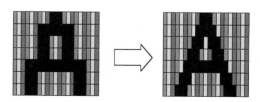

Figure 19.4 The difference between a font rendered without any anti-aliasing and a font rendered with sub-pixel rendering.

If you wanted to draw only the red and green sub-pixels, for example, you would draw a yellow pixel (red+green=yellow). The eye still blends everything to see black text on a white background.

This is just the basic theory of sub-pixel rendering. It can also be combined with anti-aliasing for even better results.

Of course, sub-pixel rendering isn't perfect for all situations. It really works best for black and white images on LCD displays (even though it helps on many CRT displays as well). Also, it works well for fonts because there are lots of high slopes in the letter shapes, but it won't help as much for shapes with low slopes.

```
Sub-pixel Bug ID: 4726365

Anti-aliasing for Swing components Bug ID: 4808567
```

Other Possibilities

Here are a few more ideas that could make the Java platform better for games:

➤ The Java Sound API could be updated with OGG support, possibly NIO buffers, and hardware-accelerated 3D sound.

➤ Optionally, vertical retrace synchronization could be turned off after a buffer flip. As discussed in Chapter 2, "2D Graphics and Animation," buffer flipping synchronizes with the vertical retrace to eliminate tearing. However, games on some systems might run at a faster frame rate if no synchronization were involved, which would create a better experience for the user. Many current games give the user the option of playing with it on or off.

➤ Class file obfuscation is coming in javac (Bug ID: 4809554), but additional protection is needed to keep people from decompiling and editing the Java class files. If people can edit the code, they will, which could result in people cheating at multi-player games. Cheaters in multi-players games spoil the game for the others. Some sort of secure class or secure JAR file support might be needed.

New Devices and the Java Games Profile (JSR 134)

Although J2SE 1.4 isn't included with Windows, computer manufactures are starting to include it on machines they sell. This will help bring the Java platform into new homes.

Another exciting development is the new devices that the Java platform is showing up on. Java is already popular on cell phones. The Java 2 MicroEdition (J2ME) MIDP 1.0 API is widespread among cell phones, and MIDP 2.0 phones are starting to appear. There's even technology available to bring MIDP 1.0/2.0 to the Game Boy Advance (the JAM interactive device, www.jamid.com). It would also be interesting to see the Java platform available on a console game system such as Sony's PlayStation 2 or Nintendo's GameCube. The PlayStation 2 market, for example, is a huge market, with more than 55 million units sold worldwide.

The upcoming Java Games Profile (JSR 134) is a J2ME profile designed for game consoles (and PCs as well). Some of the cutting-edge Java technologies included in the scope of this ambitious profile are 2D and 3D rendering, streaming media, physics modeling, character animation, game networking, and support for game controllers. This profile is still in its early stages, however. See JSR 134 for more information.

Summary

This chapter has gone over the basics of what's coming in the future for the Java platform, what needs to happen to make Java games better, and what you can do to help shape the future of Java.

Of course, the future really relies on you. Amazing things can be done with Java, and I hope the future involves people like you getting out there and showing off your mad game-programming skills.

The information and technology in this book is enough to make some amazing games. But there's always more to learn. You'll learn a lot more just by going out there and doing it—the best way to learn game programming is to make some games. Be creative, be smart, use your brainpower and imagination, and build some fun and remarkable games.

And remember, you can contact me and download the all source code and demos for this book at this site: www.brackeen.com/javagamebook.

Goodbye and good luck with your games!

Index

Q-R

W

X-Z

www.informit.com

YOUR GUIDE TO IT REFERENCE

New Riders has partnered with **InformIT.com** to bring technical information to your desktop. Drawing from New Riders authors and reviewers to provide additional information on topics of interest to you, **InformIT.com** provides free, in-depth information you won't find anywhere else.

Articles

Keep your edge with thousands of free articles, in-depth features, interviews, and IT reference recommendations— all written by experts you know and trust.

Online Books

Answers in an instant from **InformIT Online Books'** 600+ fully searchable online books.

POWERED BY
Safari

Catalog

Review online sample chapters, author biographies, and customer rankings and choose exactly the right book from a selection of over 5,000 titles.

New Riders

www.newriders.com

VOICES THAT MATTER

HOW TO CONTACT US

VISIT OUR WEB SITE

WWW.NEWRIDERS.COM

On our web site, you'll find information about our other books, authors, tables of contents, and book errata. You will also find information about book registration and how to purchase our books, both domestically and internationally.

EMAIL US

Contact us at: **nrfeedback@newriders.com**

- If you have comments or questions about this book
- To report errors that you have found in this book
- If you have a book proposal to submit or are interested in writing for New Riders
- If you are an expert in a computer topic or technology and are interested in being a technical editor who reviews manuscripts for technical accuracy

Contact us at: **nreducation@newriders.com**

- If you are an instructor from an educational institution who wants to preview New Riders books for classroom use. Email should include your name, title, school, department, address, phone number, office days/hours, text in use, and enrollment, along with your request for desk/examination copies and/or additional information.

Contact us at: **nrmedia@newriders.com**

- If you are a member of the media who is interested in reviewing copies of New Riders books. Send your name, mailing address, and email address, along with the name of the publication or web site you work for.

BULK PURCHASES/CORPORATE SALES

The publisher offers discounts on this book when ordered in quantity for bulk purchases and special sales. For sales within the U.S., please contact: Corporate and Government Sales (800) 382-3419 or **corpsales@pearsontechgroup.com**. Outside of the U.S., please contact: International Sales (317) 581-3793 or **international@pearsontechgroup.com**.

WRITE TO US

New Riders Publishing
201 W. 103rd St.
Indianapolis, IN 46290-1097

CALL/FAX US

Toll-free (800) 571-5840
If outside U.S. (317) 581-3500
Ask for New Riders
FAX: (317) 581-4663

New Riders

WWW.NEWRIDERS.COM